THE CYCLE OF THE YEAR
AS A PATH OF INITIATION

winter pull inward
inbreath

Summer outbreath

Epiphany → Easter → Pentecost → Ats of Michaelmas
from of Flesh? to the
uw +
nectar
Christmas

Michael - autumnal equinox
impulse - cleaning
opens path to Christmas
ie conquers the dragon
over winter

Christmas advent
deepest inbreath - the last week of
trial of solitude
13 nights from Christmas to 14th nt
advent

By the same author:

The East in the Light of the West, Part 1: Agni Yoga
Eternal Individuality, Towards a Karmic Biography of Novalis
The Occult Significance of Forgiveness
Prophecy of the Russian Epic
Rudolf Steiner and the Founding of the New Mysteries
Rudolf Steiner's Research Into Karma and the Mission of the
    Anthroposophical Society
The Spiritual Origins of Eastern Europe and the Future Mysteries of the
    Holy Grail
The Twelve Holy Nights and the Spiritual Hierarchies

The Council of the Holy Archangel Michael
(An eighteenth-century Russian icon)

The Cycle of the Year as a Path of Initiation Leading to an Experience of the Christ-Being

An Esoteric Study of the Festivals

Sergei O. Prokofieff

TEMPLE LODGE
London

Translated from the Russian by Simon Blaxland de Lange

Temple Lodge Publishing
51 Queen Caroline Street
London W6 9QL

First English 1991
Second edition 1995

Originally published in German under the title *Der Jahreskreislauf als Einweihungsweg zum Erleben der Christus-Wesenheit, Eine esoterische Betrachtung der Jahresfeste* by Verlag Freies Geistesleben, Stuttgart, in 1986

A catalogue record for this book is available from the British Library

ISBN 0 904693 70 8

Typeset by DP Photosetting, Aylesbury, Bucks

Printed and bound in Great Britain by Cromwell Press Limited, Broughton Gifford, Wiltshire

*Anthroposophy is in all its aspects
an endeavour that the world be
permeated by Christ.*

Rudolf Steiner, 11 June 1922

Contents

Foreword 1
Introduction: The Living Being of the Year and its
Principal Festivals 4

I   THE FESTIVAL OF MICHAEL AS A GATE OF
    MODERN INITIATION

    1. The Time of Preparation 11
    2. Michaelmas—the Festival of Enlightenment 17
    3. From Michaelmas to Christmas
       (Michael and the Nathan Soul) 27

II THE MYSTERY OF ADVENT AS THE MYSTERY
    OF THE NATHAN SOUL

    1. The Three Supersensible Deeds of the Nathan Soul . . . 39
    2. Of Michael's Participation in the Supersensible Deeds
       of the Nathan Soul 45
    3. The Fourth Deed of the Nathan Soul.
       The Transformation of Michael's Mission at the
       Time of the Mystery of Golgotha 48
    4. The Fourth Deed of the Nathan Soul and the Human
       Faculty of Memory 55
    5. The Time of Advent and the Four Mystery Virtues of
       Antiquity 59
    6. The Trial by Solitude 69
    7. The First Three Weeks of Advent as Three Stages of
       'Occult Trials' 73
    8. 'Occult Trials' and the Threefold Temptation of Christ
       in the Wilderness 77
    9. The Final Week of Advent. The Temple of Higher
       Knowledge 83

III THE MYSTERY OF CHRISTMAS

    1. The Christmas Imagination of Anthropos-Sophia 89
    2. From Christmas to Epiphany 91

3. The Thirteen Holy Nights as the Revelation of the
   Mystery of Memory 96
4. The Uniting of the World Impulses of Wisdom and
   Love in the Experience of Christ 103
5. The Thirteen Holy Nights and Their Connection with
   the Macrocosm 107

IV   FROM EPIPHANY TO EASTER

1. The Path of the Christ-impulse through the Sheaths
   and its Reflection in the Gospels 115
2. The Threefold Revelation of Christ and the Three New
   Mystery Virtues 120
3. The Virtue of Faith and the Fifth post-Atlantean
   Epoch 123
4. The Virtue of Love and the Sixth post-Atlantean
   Epoch 139
5. The Virtue of Hope and the Seventh post-Atlantean
   Epoch 143
6. The Spiritual-scientific Idea of God-manhood and its
   Reflection in the Apocalypse and in the Gospel of
   St John 149
7. From Epiphany to Easter. The Experience of the
   Holy Trinity 159

V   THE PATH FROM ADVENT TO EASTER THROUGH
     THE SEVEN MYSTERY VIRTUES

1. The Old and the New Mysteries 167
2. The Working of the Nathan Soul in the Old and the
   New Mysteries. Christ-bearer and Christ-receiver 172

VI   THE MYSTERY OF EASTER

1. The Forty-day Conversations of the Risen One and
   their Rebirth in Modern Spiritual Science 181
2. The Mission of the Master Jesus in the Cycle
   of the Year 189
3. The Significance of the Mystery of Golgotha for
   the World of the Gods 197
4. The Significance of the Mystery of Golgotha for
   the World of Men 203

VII   THE MYSTERY OF ASCENSION

    1. The Ascension as an Indication of Christ's Participation
      in the Life of the Human Soul after Death 209

VIII THE MYSTERY OF PENTECOST

    1. The Transition from the Old to the New Initiation ... 221
    2. The Modern Experience of the Holy Spirit 229

IX   EASTER, ASCENSION AND WHITSUN

    1. The Three Stages of Christ's Union with the Sphere
      of the Earth and their Reflection in the Festivals of
      Easter, Ascension and Whitsun 235
    2. The Exoteric and Esoteric Working of the Etheric Bodies
      of the Great Initiates in the Twentieth Century 241
    3. Easter, Ascension, Whitsun and the Essential Nature
      of the Foundation Stone of the Christmas Conference
      of 1923/1924 245

X   ST JOHN'S-TIDE

    1. St John's-tide: a Festival of the Future 257
    2. The Modern Path of Initiation and its Reflection in
      the Seven Principal Christian Festivals 260

XI   THE PATH OF CHRIST AND THE PATH OF
    MICHAEL IN THE CYCLE OF THE YEAR

    1. The New Path of the Shepherds and the New Path of
      the Magi 273
    2. The Working of the Forces of Lucifer and Ahriman
      in the Cycle of the Year 277
    3. The Quest for Isis-Sophia and the Quest for Christ ... 280
    4. The Cycle of the Year as a Path Leading to a New
      Experience of the Christ Being 284
    5. The Cycle of the Year as a Social Reality that Unites
      Human Beings. The Working of the Christ Being in
      Social Life 293

XII THE MODERN MYSTERIES OF THE
     ETHERIC CHRIST

1. The Vidar Mystery 301
2. The New Appearance of Christ in the Etheric
   Realm 324
3. The Imagination of the Etheric Christ 353

Conclusion: The Spiritual Experience of the Cycle of the
Year Viewed as the Beginning of a Cosmic Cultus
Appropriate to the Needs of Present-day Humanity 359

Appendices 365

1. Christmas and Epiphany (one aspect) 367
2. The Mystery Temple of the Year 371
3. Concerning a Representation of Vidar 374
4. When Should the Festivals be Celebrated in the
   Southern Hemisphere? 381
5. Some Words about the Icon *The Council of the Holy
   Archangel Michael* 387
6. Foundation Stone Meditation 390
   Grundstein-Meditation 393

Notes and Additions 397

Foreword

Knowledge of the spiritual foundations of the world, which could be acquired through inwardly accompanying the cycle of the year, was the natural property of all human beings in ancient times. Subsequently this knowledge had to be lost in the name of individual freedom. In our time, this knowledge must be found anew through the free, light-filled consciousness of the fully developed human personality.

Conscious union with the spiritual essence of the cycle of the year enables us to approach Christ, the central Being of our cosmos. Since the Mystery of Golgotha, He has become the Representative of the spiritual world-foundations in their fullness, and in our time reveals Himself in the etheric realm that surrounds the Earth.

In this connection the following question was once put to Rudolf Steiner: how may a soul prepare itself most effectively for an experience of the Etheric Christ? He answered: 'Through meditatively living with the cycle of the year, through a meditative participation in its rhythms. For the mysteries of the year are nature's gift to the meditator who is seeking access to the sphere of the Christ.'[1]

In the following words, Rudolf Steiner refers to a union with the Christ or the Son in the rhythm of the yearly cycle: '... in the course of a year man participates in a rhythm which is in accordance with the rhythm of the year and in which he experiences a union with the world of the Son.' And somewhat later in the same lecture: 'And so we shall find that, closely connected with what lives in the rhythm of the year, in the same way that breathing indwells the human individual, there lives a spiritual essence which is part of the human soul, which is the human soul itself; we find that to the yearly cycle and all its secrets there belongs the Christ Being who has passed through the Mystery of Golgotha.'[2]

From these words it is clear to what extent the theme of the cycle of the year is of truly fundamental significance for the spiritual-scientific research of Rudolf Steiner, who turned again and again to it—and to the examination of the inner nature of the principal festivals—in the course of his anthroposophical activity. It is also possible to say that this theme is the most important single element in anthroposophical Christology, which in its turn permeates, and unites into a whole, all the other areas of anthroposophical research: cosmology, the picture of the world and of man, spiritual-scientific historical research and the modern path of initiation.

1

Within Anthroposophy, however, the theme of the spiritual life of the yearly cycle is least of all the object of a 'theoretical' exposition of definite spiritual-scientific facts but is, in contrast, in its whole character more of a *practical path* leading to the very centre of the spiritual-scientific world, into the holiest of holies of that physically imperceptible temple of the new life of spirit, where for Rudolf Steiner all his supersensible investigations bore the character of a religious rite. For as he was a Christian initiate, everything which he said, accomplished and investigated in the spiritual-scientific realm was carried out by him in the light of and in an awareness of the constant presence of the Christ Being.[3]

In this sense the inner experience of the cycle of the year may become for us a living key to Rudolf Steiner's Christology and to Anthroposophy in its entirety; it can also enable us to transform Anthroposophy into what it is in its deepest nature—a real *spiritual deed*. To show this and at the same time to outline the first steps towards a conscious union with the spiritual essence of the cycle of the year as a modern path of initiation leading to a new experience of the Christ Being is the principal task and the central aim of the present work.

The book is constructed in such a way that, apart from serving as a general introduction to the esoteric nature of the cycle of the year, it may also become a *guide* for the reader through the principal annual festivals. To this end, this book may be read in the sections corresponding to one or another of the yearly festivals, and may thus serve as a foundation for deeper penetration into their spiritual essence.

The only part of the book that to some extent represents an exception to this compositional plan is the extensive chapter on Vidar (The Vidar Mystery) which is necessary for a true understanding of the nature of the Second Coming. This theme of the Second Coming is the most important fruit and indeed the aim of living spiritually with the course of the year.

It should also be said that the present work and Rudolf Steiner's *Calendar of the Soul* mutually complement each other, but exemplify two different ways of looking at the cycle of the year. The *Calendar of the Soul* is not spoken of directly here, but could be said to express the soul to spirit approach, while this present work comes out of the spirit to soul approach.

The present work is not intended for a beginner in Anthroposophy, in that it presupposes a basic acquaintance with the various aspects of Rudolf Steiner's spiritual science. As to its inner nature, it represents a continuation and further development of a work by the present author which appeared in 1982 [and in English translation in 1986]—*Rudolf Steiner and the Founding of the New Mysteries*.[4] Hence an acquaintance with that volume could be of real help for a right understanding of the contents of this book, although it has been written in such a way that it can be read completely independently.

Sergei O. Prokofieff
Stuttgart, Michaelmas Day 1985

Introduction:
The Living Being of the Year and its Principal Festivals

Just as the life-cycle of a human organism begins with an inhalation followed by an exhalation, so does the life-cycle of the Earth, like a living being, begin with a great macrocosmic in-breathing which lasts for fully half the year, from the summer solstice to the winter, followed by an out-breathing of similar duration which occupies the other half of the year.[1] This parallel between microcosm and macrocosm, between man and the Earth, is not confined solely to the sphere of life but extends to the more inward sphere of consciousness.

The principal poles of human existence are, on the one hand, the waking consciousness of day which is associated with the presence of the ego and astral body within the etheric and physical bodies and, on the other hand, 'sleep-consciousness', when ego and astral body work upon the physical and etheric bodies from outside, from the macrocosm. In the second case (during sleep), only man's physical and etheric bodies remain as a microcosm on Earth, so that for clairvoyant vision man leads at such times a purely vegetative existence. Thus Rudolf Steiner observes that, for the clairvoyant, a sleeping person yields an impression similar to that of a flowery meadow in summer.

A comparable situation pertains in the macrocosm. The Earth, too, passes in the course of the year through these two states of consciousness. Thus winter is the time of the greatest wakefulness, the strongest vigilance of the Earth, while summer is the Earth's sleep, its blissful surrender to the cosmic distances, the departure of the soul and spirit of the Earth from its physical and etheric bodies out into the macrocosm, into the sphere of the starry worlds. We find a description in poetic form of this process in the following words of Rudolf Steiner:[2]

> Asleep is the soul of Earth
> In Summer's heat,
> While the Sun's outward glory
> Rays through the realms of space.
>
> Awake is the soul of Earth
> In Winter's cold,
> While the Sun's inmost being
> Lightens in spirit.

Summer's day of joy
For Earth is sleep;
Winter's holy night
For Earth is day.

(translation by George and Mary Adams)

The fundamental precondition for man's waking consciousness is the faculty of thinking. Rudolf Steiner frequently speaks of how it is only in thinking that man experiences himself as a fully awake being. In his feeling-life he lives in a world of dreams, while in his will he is deeply asleep even during the day. In this sense, thinking is that 'mediator' with whose help the human ego attains that self-consciousness through which alone a person becomes, in the fullest sense of the world, human. 'I am'—this experience is possible only through thinking. Without this capacity the ego exists only as spiritual substance, and it is only through uniting with thinking that there arises that *ego-consciousness* whereby man experiences himself as a self-contained individual being.

However, not only man, the microcosm, but also the great macrocosmic organism of our Earth has supersensible members—not only an etheric, but also an astral body and an ego. Thus for the Earth, too, the time of winter wakefulness is the time of the greatest intensification of its ego-consciousness—which is, as has been observed, made possible only through thinking. Hence we may say: just as a person's field of consciousness is filled by day with the thoughts through which he becomes aware of himself as an ego-being, so is the Earth filled in autumn and winter with the thoughts, the great world thoughts, which are brought to it from the macrocosm, from the distant worlds of the stars. So it is that in winter the Earth reflects upon its summer experiences in the far reaches of the universe and attains in this pondering its planetary ego-consciousness.

From this we may see that what occurs for man, as microcosm, within the rhythm of the twenty-four hours of the day, takes place for the Earth, as macrocosm, within the rhythm of the year, in the course of twelve months as the Sun passes through the twelve principal regions of the starry world. In both cases the visible movement of the Sun plays an essential part, for it connects the one rhythm with the other. As microcosm, man is connected through his ego-consciousness principally with the microcosmic rhythm of the day. He is no less deeply connected with the macrocosmic yearly rhythm, though in a far less conscious way.

Anthroposophy wishes to lead mankind in our time to a *conscious* union with the macrocosm. For it is '. . . a path of knowledge which would lead the spiritual in man to the spiritual in the universe.'[3] And the most harmonious and most natural way for this to happen is through rightly living

5

with the macrocosmic rhythm of the Earth, which has its outer reflection in the cycle of the year. This may also be expressed as follows. A person who experiences the spiritual in himself lives in the rhythm of the day (a twenty-four hour period), while anyone who wishes to experience 'the spiritual in the universe' must learn to live *consciously* in the rhythm of the year. For such a person, life in connection with the macrocosmic rhythm of the Earth is not at all unlike the conscious pursuing of the modern path of initiation; while the principal yearly festivals become for him the great lamps that illuminate his path into the macrocosm.

In ancient times this living with the rhythm of the year as a connecting link between man and the macrocosm was a life-necessity for humanity, even though in those times it still proceeded to a certain extent in unconsciousness and had therefore to be directed from the Mystery Centres. The four annual festivals formed the spiritual high-points in the life of the Earth, which is expressed outwardly in the changing seasons. In these celebrations, guided by the ancient Mysteries, man connected himself with the Sun-sphere and, through this, with the world of the stars, that is, with the macrocosm.

When the Sun Spirit Himself, the Christ, descended at the Turning Point of Time to the Earth and united with it through the Mystery of Golgotha, He became the new Spirit of the Earth. He endowed the four principal yearly festivals, the great cross of the autumn and spring equinoxes and the summer and winter solstices, with new meaning. For what gave meaning and significance to these festivals before the Mystery of Golgotha was to be found not on the Earth but outside it on the Sun. Hence the festivals of that time bore more the character of a presentiment of what was to be fulfilled only in the future. 'Before the Mystery of Golgotha the meaning of the Earth was on the Sun. Since the Mystery of Golgotha the meaning of the Earth lies in the Earth itself. It is this that Anthroposophy would ... bring to mankind.'[4] These words can also be related in full measure to the meaning of the festivals, which since the time of the Mystery of Golgotha are an expression of the great cosmic-earthly Mystery of Christ Jesus and of the spirits connected with Him.

Christ came to the Earth from the sphere of the Sun, from the great realm of time, and at the Turning Point of Time entered its spatial sphere of being.[5] He thereby bore the impulse of time into the world of space: the principle of sevenfoldness into that of twelvefoldness. In so doing He did not only transform the four ancient festivals, which in the light of the Christ-impulse attain their ultimate fulfilment as the festivals of Michaelmas, Christmas, Easter and St John's-tide, but He added the three new festivals of Epiphany, Ascension and Whitsun, so that this Holy Sevenhood, like the seven stars in the right-hand of God,[6] might shine in the darkness of earthly being and so shed its light upon the twelvefold space of the cycle of the year.[7]

Through a right understanding of this Sun-borne revelation of sevenfoldness within twelvefoldness these festivals can become true landmarks on the great path that leads man in the cycle of the year to a new free and conscious union with the macrocosm; thus they can become steps towards a true Christian initiation that reveals to man the central Mystery of the Earth and leads him to a direct experience of the living Christ.

I

THE FESTIVAL OF MICHAEL AS A GATE OF MODERN INITIATION

1. The Time of Preparation

In ordinary conditions of life we experience the spiritual aspect of the cycle of the year only very dimly. Spring, summer, autumn, winter—these four principal seasons reveal themselves to us directly for the most part only in an outward way. It is a different matter with the more inward processes which concern the spiritual life of the Earth itself; these are at first completely hidden from outward view and can be discovered only indirectly through their influence upon our inner being.

The focus of our inner life is our faculty of self-knowledge which, as we have seen, is made accessible to us through our activity of thinking. A more careful and exact effort of self-observation will, however, reveal the influence of the spiritual aspect of the course of the year, the influence of the Earth's living rhythm. Indeed, with a certain sensitivity, it is not difficult to observe that, beginning in the spring and ever more towards summer, our faculties of thinking become weaker and to a certain extent our faculty of self-knowledge as a whole is likewise enfeebled. As summer approaches, we become far less self-contained and set in opposition against the world. We seem to be, to some extent, going beyond ourselves and uniting with the natural world around us. Our sense of self-knowledge becomes imbued with a yearning to become, rather, a nature-consciousness. This process in us is somewhat akin to falling asleep. There is, however, an essential difference. In this case, we do not become completely unconscious; it is simply that the focus of our consciousness shifts to some extent from the sphere of thinking to that of willing. This is outwardly expressed in that our powers of thinking grow weaker, while on the other hand our faculties of perception become stronger and more active and the wish to be active and industrious becomes intensified. In summer, we live with our whole being in the world of perceptions which are moulded by our will; while our thinking, together with the faculty of self-knowledge that is based upon it, is at this time of year somewhat diminished and limited in its activity.

During the other half of the year, from the summer solstice through to autumn and winter, we find a quite different picture. The strength of our perceptions begins to wane, as does the power of will that is founded upon nature-consciousness. In contrast, our power of thinking begins ever more to strengthen; thoughts flow easily and form logical connections almost by themselves. Our faculty of self-knowledge also becomes stronger, as does

11

our sense of self-containment, of detachment from the surrounding world. Our inner life is enriched and stimulated because of the lessening of interest in all that is going on in the world without; we are more strongly inclined to the outwardly more passive, contemplative life. The centre of gravity of our human nature moves perceptibly from the without to the within as autumn approaches. Thus in the cycle of the year there is expressed a harmonious interplay between what in the Middle Ages was called *vita activa* and *vita contemplativa.*

All these processes, the traces of which everyone can discern within himself with more careful self-observation, are the microcosmic reflection in our inner being of the great macrocosmic processes that underlie the yearly rhythm of our Earth. This rhythm consists in that, in spring, the soul and spirit of the Earth—one could also say its astral body and ego— gradually leave its physical and etheric bodies and unite with the far distances of space, drawing in their wake countless numbers of elemental beings, which are for the Earth what the thought-beings that work at the foundation of our thoughts are for man. As they leave the planetary body of the Earth in spring, these elemental beings, these living thoughts of the Earth, also take hold to a certain extent of our thoughts which at this time of year slip away from our direct authority and lead their own independent life, more akin to the natural processes in the surrounding elemental world.

After the middle of summer and ever more towards autumn there begins the process of the gradual reunion of the Soul and Spirit of the Earth with its planetary body.

Countless numbers of elemental beings, the living thoughts of the Earth, descend again into its bosom, though now fructified with the great wisdom of the cosmos, the World Thoughts of the Hierarchies. The thoughts of human beings to some extent follow this general cosmic-earthly tendency that manifests itself during the autumn in the Earth's surroundings. For, having been drawn away by nature spirits in the course of their ascent from the Earth, these human thought-beings now again return to their human origin. But they return fructified by the world thoughts of the cosmos, enlivened by the spirit of the universe, as fresh and clear as the thoughts of someone who has just been awakened from sleep. One could also say that our human thoughts, which by the end of winter have become increasingly dead, immobile and devoid of all spirituality, are in the spring gradually borne away in order that, after being cleansed and enlivened in the far distances of space, they may again return to us inwardly permeated by the wisdom and the life of the cosmos, by the World Thoughts of the spirit. These thoughts that are most richly filled with spirituality may be apprehended at that time of year when summer passes over into winter, which is when the most favourable conditions arise for the fructifying of human thoughts with cosmic thoughts.

Since ancient times that being whom we in our time, in accordance with Judaeo-Christian terminology, call by the name of Michael, 'he who stands before the Countenance of God', has been the ruler of the World Thoughts of the Gods, of the cosmic Intelligence, in the macrocosm. Michael is that spirit who, in the autumn of the year, endows human thoughts with the strength which enables them to approach the World Thoughts of the cosmos. For just as showers of meteors fall to the Earth in August so does Michael send the World Thoughts of the Gods down to the earthly thoughts of men. These meteors of late summer and early autumn are none other than a vast image of how human thoughts return fructified by the thoughts of the cosmos.

The organ for perceiving earthly human thoughts is man's head, in particular the brain. The organ for perceiving the World Thoughts, the living thoughts of the cosmos, is the human heart. Michael is that spirit who, in the present epoch of his rulership amongst humanity, '... frees thoughts from the region of the head ...' and 'makes the path to the heart accessible to them'. For now 'the epoch of Michael has come. Hearts begin to have thoughts ... Thoughts which strive to grasp the spiritual in our time must proceed from hearts which beat for Michael as the fiery Prince of the World Thoughts'.[1] Thus the fiery shafts of light of the meteor showers, which irradiate man's head, his world of thoughts, with the wisdom of the cosmos, must now—on the path designated by Michael—find their way from the head to the heart and awaken within man a true inner life, so that in his heart they may become that fiery sword of the spirit, the relentless sword of Michael which is able to overcome the thought-annihilating power of the ahrimanic dragon.

From all that has been said it becomes clear that the period from the summer solstice to the festival of Michaelmas in the autumn is the most propitious time for finding the path from human thoughts to cosmic thoughts, from head-thinking to 'heart-thinking', in so far as this now lies within the intentions of the Leading Spirit of our time. But what can best help us to fulfil these intentions? Where shall we find on Earth the path from the thoughts of human beings to the World Thoughts of the spirit? The answer to this question has been given to all mankind over half a century ago in the form of anthroposophically orientated spiritual science. Therein we find, clothed in human thoughts, the World Thoughts of the Gods, these thoughts which the soul and spirit of the Earth bear with them every year from out of the cosmos: the great stages of world evolution, the creation of the world and of man, the mysteries of the Hierarchies.

Our modern civilization is wholly founded upon human thoughts that

13

have been slain by the dragon, upon the activity of the human head alone, whereas in spiritual science World Thoughts approach us clothed in human, conceptual form. This conceptual *form* must at first also be perceived by our head, but the World Thoughts that lie *behind them* must find their way to our heart 'as a new organ of cognition', where they can be enlivened and inspired by our feeling and permeated by our will. This is the beginning of the new Michael epoch: 'The process of forming thoughts has for a time been lost in cosmic matter. It must find itself anew in the cosmic spirit. Into the cold, abstract world of thoughts, both warmth and a life-imbued spirit-presence may enter. This marks the beginning of the Michael epoch.'[2]

Thus modern spiritual science is addressed not only to man's head but, above all, to his heart—not in a sentimental but in a deeply occult sense. Rudolf Steiner frequently refers to this particular quality—as, for instance, in the following words: 'In our time it is necessary for man to perceive the *World Thoughts* in full, clear waking consciousness in such a way as they are presented in the anthroposophically orientated spiritual science which we profess.' And then he describes in detail *how* these World Thoughts of Anthroposophy must be grasped in order that they may work directly upon the moral sphere of the soul that is associated with the human heart: 'Try, in the sense intended here, to grasp in a living way the spirit thoughts of the world rulership rightly, and in a manner appropriate for today; try to grasp them not merely as a teaching, not merely as a theory, but rather in order that they may—as deeply and as inwardly as possible—move, warm, illumine and permeate your soul, in order that you may bear them in a living way. Try to feel those thoughts with such strength that they become for you something which enters the soul through the body and so transforms it. Try to do away with everything that is abstract or theoretical in these thoughts. Try to bring these thoughts to the point where they become real food for the soul, so that through them it is not mere thoughts that are entering the soul but rather that the spiritual life which proceeds from the spiritual world enters our souls through these thoughts.'[3]

Only through such a *real* study of spiritual science, where not mere thoughts alone but the 'spiritual life which proceeds from the spiritual world' permeates the soul, may it become what it is in its deepest essential being: the New Revelation of Christ in the twentieth century, which enters our souls in our present epoch under the rulership of the Sun Archangel Michael.

Herein also lies the reason why the *study* of what has been given through spiritual science is the first step along the path of modern spirit-pupilship. For if what it has to communicate is grasped not only with the head but also with the heart; if, once having penetrated behind the veil of its conceptual form, a man is able to commune with the World Thoughts of the cosmos and to fill his human thoughts with World Thoughts, Michael himself enters into earthly being and works within it: 'And this Michael, this St George, who comes from without and who has the power to conquer the dragon, is none other than real spiritual knowledge ... Man can, if he wishes, have spiritual science—which is to say: Michael is then truly penetrating our earthly realm from the realms of spirit ...'[4]

If at this point we also recall that man's head is a microcosmic reflection of the starry cosmos, that is, of the highest spiritual realms, while the heart is the only organ that fully lives *on the Earth*,[5] we may say: this descent of Michael from the cosmos to the Earth[6] is connected in a very direct way with the penetration of the human intelligence from the region of the head to that of the heart.

The path towards the attainment of this goal lies through rightly attaining the first stage of pupilship, which Rudolf Steiner formulates in the fifth chapter of *Occult Science*: 'The study of spiritual science, where one initially avails oneself of the power of judgement which one has achieved in the sense-perceptible world.'[7] This stage forms the necessary condition for embarking upon the path of modern Christian-Rosicrucian initiation and at the same time serves as real *preparation* for it. The most favourable period for accomplishing this is the most 'Michaelic' time of year: from the first shooting stars of summer to the autumnal festival of Michael. For since the ending in 1899 of the dark time of Kali-Yuga and the beginning in 1879 of his new period of rulership amongst human beings, Michael has become the inspirer of the modern path of initiation. He also becomes the ruler of human souls wishing to hear his 'morning call', through whose autumnal shooting stars he expresses the extent to which the forces of morning correspond in the yearly rhythm of the Earth to those of autumn:

> We men of present time
> Need to give ear to the Spirit's call—
> The call of Michael.
> Spiritual Knowledge seeks
> To open in the soul of man
> True hearing of this morning call.
> (translated by George and Mary Adams)[8]

This morning call is none other than Michael's call to human souls to embark upon the newly unveiled path of initiation, at whose wide open gates Michael now appears 'like the Cherubim with the flaming sword', admonishing and beckoning.

Thus every true modern Christian initiation stands under the sign of Michael. The beginning of this path lies within the rhythm of the year at autumn, the spiritual morning in the life of the Earth, and is marked by the autumnal festival of Michael, the festival of the dawn of the spirit. For at the time when the forces of the outer Sun are gradually dying, the festival of Michael signifies the beginning of the rising of the Spiritual Sun within man, the beginning of the *Enlightenment* of the human soul.

outer dying, inner enlivening

2.   Michaelmas—the Festival of Enlightenment

It follows directly from the character of the spirit of our time that the first stage of modern initiation must needs incorporate a thorough inner acquaintance with what has been imparted through spiritual science. In our present cycle of evolution this is the only right way in which the world thoughts, which stand behind the veil of the conceptual (human earthly) form in which spiritual science is now presented to mankind, may find in man the path from head to heart and thus enable Michael himself to enter the earthly domain. 'Michael,' says Rudolf Steiner, 'is not that Spirit who nurtures intellectuality but everything that he gives by way of spirituality yearns to become manifest amongst humanity in the form of ideas, in the form of thoughts—though in the form of ideas and thoughts that can grasp the spiritual. It is Michael's wish that man becomes a free being who, in his concepts and ideas, also gains an understanding of what approaches him as revelation from the spiritual world ... Michael inspires men with the expression of his own spiritual being, so that on the Earth a spirituality may appear that is accessible to their own human intelligence, so that it is possible to think and at the same time be truly spiritual; *for this alone is a sign of Michael's rulership.*'[9]

This possibility 'to think and at the same time be truly spiritual' has come into our world through anthroposophically orientated spiritual science, for it has for the first time brought to people 'a spirituality accessible to their own human intelligence' and may therefore be regarded—in so far as it is received into human souls—as the beginning of Michael's rulership on Earth. This study, given through modern spiritual science, is the first stage in the process of re-spiritualizing the Divine Intelligence of Michael, which in former times descended into human heads. That Intelligence has, since ancient times, belonged to his cosmic sphere and from our time onwards is to enter upon the path of its re-spiritualization through the inner activity of human beings. As Rudolf Steiner observes: 'This is what stands before us as a demand of Michael, that we become active even in our thoughts, so that we form our conception of the world for ourselves as human beings through our own inner activity.'[10]

Thus in our epoch we have this twofold movement: from above downwards and from below upwards. From above comes Michael himself, who '. . . in the last third of the nineteenth century, in descending from the Sun to the Earth, wishes to take hold of the earthly intelligence of human

17

beings...'[11] and on the other hand, from the human side, there takes place the gradual spiritualization of this human intelligence, the enlivening of human thinking. This last is accomplished to the extent that individual human beings make modern spiritual science their own, not merely theoretically but in such a way that it becomes living food for the soul, an air, an atmosphere, in which the soul cannot but live and breathe.

Allusions to this twofold movement, which determines the entire character of the modern epoch, are also to be found expressed with full clarity in the third, 'Michaelic', part of the Foundation Stone Meditation.[12] There we have on the one hand the picture of the new Michael revelation, which since the last third of the nineteenth century has been raying 'from above downwards' upon humanity:

> Where the eternal aims of Gods
> World Being's Light
> On thine own I
> Bestow
> For thy free Willing.

While on the other hand there arises from this revelation the urgent call which is addressed to the whole of present-day humanity: to begin the task of spiritualizing what has now become the earthly intelligence, which, buried in the darkness of human existence, 'beseeching Light', craves for the new union with the cosmic sphere of Michael:

> For the Spirit's Universal Thoughts hold sway
> In the Being of all Worlds, beseeching Light ...[12]

Thus in the new epoch of Michael's rulership a bridge must be built between the world of the Gods and mankind through the combined efforts of Gods and men. Rudolf Steiner speaks about this in the following words: 'A science such as anthroposophical spiritual science, which seeks to spiritualize anew spatial judgement (that is, a faculty of discernment which is dead and bound up with matter) and makes it again supersensible, works from below upwards—in order to grasp the hands of Michael reaching down from above. It is here that the bridge between man and the Gods can be built.'[13]

In modern spirit-pupilship, entering in full consciousness upon that path which leads from below upwards to meet Michael 'descending' from the Sun, corresponds to what Rudolf Steiner refers to as 'Preparation' in his book *Knowledge of the Higher Worlds: How is it Achieved?* Preparation—this is the start of the building of that bridge which, in time, will again unite the human soul with the world of the Gods. But what is this bridge-building process? As in the previous chapter, we may answer that spiritual knowledge must be grasped with such intensity by the human soul that the World Thoughts it contains, which are first apprehended by the human head, may then find their way to the human heart where they may becomes *living* thoughts. These living thoughts would then represent the spiritual substance which—once he had received it into himself—Michael would be able to proclaim to the highest Gods: 'In the course of my epoch human beings have raised to the supersensible what they have achieved from a position of distance from the divine-spiritual world by way of forms of judgement gained purely in the world of space; and we can again receive them in that they have united their thoughts, their imaginations, with ours.'[14] Thus we see that the first condition for 'the uniting of the thoughts of human beings with the thoughts of the Gods' is that these divine thoughts so permeate human hearts that 'hearts begin to have thoughts'—and this 'marks the beginning of the Michael epoch' (see p.14).

'Heart-thinking', in contrast to normal head-thinking, is that faculty of knowledge with whose help the communications of spiritual science have also come into our world. As Rudolf Steiner observes: 'True descriptions of the higher worlds proceed from such a *heart-thinking*, even though they appear outwardly as logical statements. In descriptions that are indeed brought down from the higher worlds, there is nothing that would not have been *conceived by the heart*. Whatever is expressed from the standpoint of spiritual science has been experienced by the heart. But anyone whose task it is to give outward expression to what he is experiencing through the heart must, of course, cast it in such thought-forms as to render it comprehensible to others.'[15] In another lecture this thought is developed further: 'If the spirit-pupil wishes to explore the higher worlds, his head-logic passes over into heart-logic . . .[16] From this it becomes clear that the path of initiation which we are entering upon here, and whose leader is Michael, is also that path whereby Rudolf Steiner himself attained such knowledge of the higher worlds as he then gave to the world in the form of anthroposophically orientated spiritual science. This path—in a form in which other people, too, might adopt it—was described by him in detail in the book *Knowledge of the Higher Worlds: How is it Achieved?* and in the fifth chapter of *Occult Science*.

Let us now turn to a further examination of this path. If the pupil who is embarking upon it is able to live in that part of the yearly rhythm that corresponds to the period of preparation (from the end of summer to the beginning of autumn) as intimately as possible with the thoughts that he has gleaned from modern spiritual science, so that they become completely alive within him, that they are grasped not with his head alone but with his *whole* being, then, as we have seen, the path to the human heart will become accessible to these thoughts—the path, that is, to that spiritual organ where the first stage in the spiritualization of that Michaelic Intelligence which has descended to the Earth may be attained. As a result of this first stage of its spiritualization, however, a quite special spiritual event takes place. If we are to characterize this event it will be enough to cite *fully* those words of Rudolf Steiner which we quoted in part in the previous chapter: 'He [Michael] frees thoughts from the region of the head; he awakens a spiritual fire within the soul in such a way that *a man can surrender his whole soul to what he is able to experience in the light of thought.* The epoch of Michael has come. Hearts begin to have thoughts ... inspiration no longer streams from a mystic twilight but from a thought-illumined clarity of soul. To understand this is to receive Michael into one's soul-life. Thoughts which strive to grasp the spiritual in our time must proceed from hearts that beat for Michael as the fiery Prince of the World Thoughts.'[17] In these words Rudolf Steiner sums up the whole essence of this process. If the thoughts of spiritual science are allowed to take hold of one and thereby extend their transforming influence to one's heart, what enters into one 'as thoughts' is then changed into the substance of light, into the purest *light of thought.* And in the living enthusiasm of the heart, in thus surrendering one's soul, this light of thought then rays from one's heart out into the macrocosm as the light of the purest redeemed Intelligence of Michael, as enlivened human thoughts which are able again to unite with the World Thoughts of the Gods. These are the radiant hands of light which, as they stretch upwards from below, are able to take hold of the hands of Michael reaching down from above. For everything which thus lives in the heart's light of thought is visible to Michael and can again be received by him into his realm.

The inner light that is enkindled shines as the light of the impending resurrection in human being's thoughts, as a real witness of the immediate presence of the power of Michael in the centre of the human heart, within the human soul. The lines of the fourth part of the Foundation Stone Meditation,[18] which refer to the working of Michael, also testify to this:

> Darkness of Night
> Had held its sway;
> Day-radiant Light
> Poured into the souls of men ...

This experience corresponds[19] to the very essence of the festival of Michael as the true festival of *Enlightenment.*

In his lectures and cycles of the years 1923–24 Rudolf Steiner frequently, and from very different points of view, characterizes the spiritual meaning of the new Michael festival. But it is in the last of his letters on this theme, in January 1925, that he perhaps touches most deeply upon its inmost essence. The following words, written by Rudolf Steiner two and a half months before his departure from earthly life and referring to the fundamental leitmotif of this festival as one of *Enlightenment*, are like the final testament of Michael's greatest earthly ambassador to the hearts and souls of all true Michaelites: 'When man again becomes capable of inwardly experiencing ideas, even at such a time when he is no longer dependent for his ideas upon the sense-world, a shining splendour will stream towards him as he gazes out into the cosmos. This is what it means to acknowledge Michael in his realm. And if there comes a time when the autumnal Michael festival becomes true and heartfelt, then in the experience of those who are celebrating this festival with innermost integrity this leitmotif will emerge and live in full consciousness: A *soul that is filled with ideas experiences the light of spirit when what appears to the senses echoes on within one only as a memory.*'[20] While in the next 'Leading Thought' Rudolf Steiner formulates this idea in the following way: 'Man must find the strength to fill his world of ideas with light and to experience it as light-filled, even when he no longer depends in this respect upon the numbing effect of the sense-world. In such an experience of a world of ideas that is self-sustaining and permeated—in independence—with light, there awakens a feeling of belonging to the extra-terrestrial cosmos. From this will arise the foundation for the festival of Michael.'[21]

For the spirit-pupil, such an experience of the Michael festival as a festival of Enlightenment is the beginning of his spiritual path, the threshold of the next stage which is that of initiation itself, the kindling of the inner Spiritual Sun within the human soul, the arising of the Sun forces of man's higher self in the darkness of winter's night.

More will be said in the later pages of this book about how the Mystery of initiation, the process of the birth of the second, higher self in the human soul, is connected in the yearly rhythm with the inner experience of the Mystery of Christmas. For the time being we must confine ourselves to the Michaelic aspect of this Mystery, for Michael is that cosmic Spirit who stands as the Guardian of the whole period stretching from his own festival until the festival of Christmas, from the festival of the kindling of the first morning rays of 'Spirit-light' within the soul to the rising of the 'Spiritual Sun' itself at the moment of initiation.

In the words that follow, Rudolf Steiner indicates how it is Michael who is today that great being who leads man to a real experience of the Mystery of Christmas: 'Then it may be understood by present-day humanity that, just as the festival of Christmas at one time followed the Michael festival in the autumn, so after the revelation of Michael which began—in the season of autumn—in the last third of the nineteenth century there must follow *a holy festival*, a Christmas festival, through which people may come to an understanding of the *spirit-birth* that is necessary for their future earthly path, so that this once inspirited Earth may gradually find its way to the forms and conditions of the future. We now live at a time when not only does the yearly festival of Christmas follow the yearly festival of Michael, but when we must also understand the revelation of Michael—which began in the last third of the nineteenth century—in the depths of our souls, out of the very essence of our human nature, and then seek the path leading to the true Christmas festival, when, as our knowledge of the spirit grows, we *become permeated with that same spirit* . . . Now is the time when we must find the path from the festival of Michael to the festival of the winter solstice, which must, however, incorporate *a dawn of the spirit.*'[22]

We should now compare these words with the following lines written by Rudolf Steiner in the autumn of 1924, if we are to experience with all intensity the fact of Michael's position in our time as the leader on the modern path of initiation: 'Michael, who in former times spoke "from above", can now be heard "from within", which is where he wishes to establish his new habitation. Or, to put it more imaginatively, the Sun-nature, which man has in the course of long ages received into himself only from the cosmos, will begin to shine within his soul. Man learns to speak of an "inner Sun". He will in the life between birth and death feel himself to no less a degree an earthly being but he will recognize that this being of his that roams the face of the Earth is *led by the Sun*. He will learn to experience as truth that there is a Being who places him inwardly in a light which, indeed, shines in Earth's darkness but which is not kindled there.'[23]

Here we have an indication of the third phase of Michael's work in the earthly domain. All these three phases, however, correspond in their entirety to that part of the cycle of the year lasting from the end of summer to the beginning of winter. We shall now briefly examine these.

In the first place there is Michael's fructifying of earthly thoughts with World Thoughts. In the macrocosm this is expressed in the streams of shooting stars, in the meteorite showers of August and September. In the microcosm there is a correspondence with World Thoughts clad in *human form*, as is the case in what is imparted through spiritual science. These thoughts, which have their source in the extra-terrestrial cosmos and have through their form become wholly human, must now be taken up on Earth by the heads of as many people as possible, grasped by the purely human intellect, in order that this human intellect may, through them, gradually find its way to the spirit. On the path of initiation this process corresponds to the stage of *Preparation*, and it can take place only if the spiritual-scientific thoughts that have been taken in by the head are deepened to the point of being experienced in the sphere of the heart. For the spiritualization of the human intellect takes place not in the head but in the heart. Rudolf Steiner says: 'What will be decisive is what human *hearts* do about this matter of Michael in the world in the course of the twentieth century' (that is, in the first instance, what they do with the spiritual-scientific knowledge that has been received into their souls).[24] (Compare with Rudolf Steiner's words quoted on pp. 20).

If man is able to grow so familiar with spiritual-scientific ideas that they become alive in him and penetrate to his very heart, then thoughts that have hitherto been dry and perhaps even abstract will become transformed into light, into a living *light of thought*, flowing from his heart into the world. And this experience of *Enlightenment* in the human soul is the true festival of Michael, the beginning of his real presence in man!

The spirit-pupil may, however, go still further. He can strengthen the presence of Michael in his own soul, filling himself with this 'Michael thought'—which he has initially grasped with his head through spiritual science—not merely in his heart, where it is transformed into light, the dawning glow of morning, but, still more deeply, in the realm of his *will*, where it may become a *Sun*. In terms of spiritual development such a deepening would correspond to the beginning of the path leading gradually from *Enlightenment* to *Initiation*, or—in the yearly rhythm—from the autumn festival of Michael to the winter festival of Christmas. Then, as Christmas gradually approaches, man would increasingly come to feel himself guided through the darkness of winter's night by the inner Sun of the Spirit which alone is capable of overcoming the ahrimanic death-forces surrounding him everywhere at this time of year in nature.

And so, while the principal leitmotif of the Michael festival (as outlined on p.21) is a direct indication of its essential substance, the following words of Rudolf Steiner relate more to that stage of inner development that has to be attained by the soul at the darkest time of the year through a rightly celebrated Michael festival: 'Take up into yourself the Michael thought that can conquer the ahrimanic forces, that thought which gives you the power to acquire spirit-knowledge here on Earth in order that you can overcome the forces of death ... Thus does this thought [of Michael] relate to the *will*-forces: to take hold of Michael's power is to take hold of the power of spiritual knowledge with the *forces of one's will*.'[25]

Thus we have a threefold penetration of the Michael-impulse into man. It is first prepared in the extra-terrestrial cosmos, in the showers of meteorites falling to the Earth; then the Michael-impulse enters directly into man in the form of the thoughts of modern spiritual science and gradually permeates the *whole* of his being, beginning with his head, then his heart, and finally his will, where it opens the gate to the Spiritual Sun and becomes the source of the resurrection-forces which enable the human intelligence to unite again with the cosmic Intelligence in the sphere of Michael.

We may see that this process of development leads us gradually from the extra-terrestrial spaces ever more inwards, to the depths of man's being. And this progression from without inwards through the stages of the spiritual path is an exact repetition on the microcosmic plane of those processes which take place out in the macrocosm with the Earth itself at the transition from summer through autumn to winter. The Earth, too, passes at this time through a process of 'inner deepening'. It passes through a gradual experience of 'awakening' with the return from the widths of space of its soul and spirit, which are absorbed ever more deeply into its planetary body so as to penetrate right to its very centre at Christmas-time.[26] Thus if we examine from this particular standpoint the whole 'descending' half of the year, from the summer solstice to Christmas, we may have the feeling that this time of the year is particularly favourable for embarking upon the path which leads to a truly modern form of initiation.

Three stages of spiritual training are described in anthroposophically orientated spiritual science: 1) *Preparation* (this develops the spiritual senses); 2) *Enlightenment* (this kindles the spiritual light); 3) *Initiation* (this establishes intercourse with the higher beings of the spiritual world).[27] We have already considered in detail the connection of these stages with the cycle of the year and also with the modern Mystery of Michael. In conclusion there remains only to observe that the path of the spiritual exercises suggested to the pupil at each of the above stages does itself lead gradually from the outer world that surrounds him to an ever greater immersion in his inner being.

To the first stage of *Preparation* belong such well-known exercises from spiritual-scientific literature as meditating upon the growth and dying of plants, upon sounds emanating from living and lifeless things—exercises which gradually lead the pupil to a new way of perceiving the surrounding natural world. If one is familiar with the chapter in *Knowledge of the Higher Worlds: How is it Achieved?* that is devoted to a description of this stage, one may feel how at first the whole of the pupil's attention is directed towards the outer world, towards a contemplation of the natural world, and that on the path of meditation he is enjoined gradually to make the transition from outer perception to inner experience, to an experience of the hidden side of nature, of the spiritual speech with which it is imbued. If, guided by an inner feeling, we now seek that part of the yearly cycle which corresponds most fully to these experiences, we find it in the period that directly follows St John's Day and lasts until the festival of Michael in the autumn. As was already mentioned, there begins at this time for the macrocosmic life of the Earth a gradual transition from full out-breathing to an ever-growing in-breathing. This means that the whole Earth now enters upon a path which leads from outer to inner experience—with the result that this time is especially suitable for passing through the first stage of the modern path of spirit-pupilship, that of *Preparation*.

The next stage is that of *Enlightenment*. Here the pupil again begins from a meditative study of the elements of the outer world: the exercises with crystal, plant and animal, the exercise with the seed of a plant. However, the transition from outer to inner experience now takes place in a much more intensive way. While at the previous stage there arose the necessity of developing within oneself a more delicate and intimate relationship to the outer world, the principal focus now shifts to the pupil's inner being and the elements of the outer world play no more than a subsidiary and supportive part in the exercises. For in *Enlightenment* the aim is to attain an experience of *inner light*. So not only the spiritual counterparts of outer objects but also higher beings who do not incarnate physically can reveal themselves to the pupil at this stage. Thus it is that at this point a further inner step is taken where particular attention is devoted to the development of man's inner, moral qualities. Herein lies the reason why, in *Knowledge of the Higher Worlds: How is it Achieved?*, between the chapter on *Enlightenment* and that on *Initiation*, a chapter is inserted under the title 'Control of Thoughts and Feelings'. It is there that we find a reference to the golden rule of genuine occult science: '... For every *one* step forward that you take in seeking knowledge of occult truths, take *three* steps forward in the improvement of your own character.'[28] And then immediately afterwards there follows the description of an exercise whereby one calls to mind a person who desires something and then someone whose wish has been satisfied. A comparison of these exercises with the analogous exercise from the chapter about *Preparation* is enough in order to see the significant progression in the direction of inner deepening. Later in the same chapter, in connection with the necessity of developing control of thoughts and feelings and with the achievement of a heightened endurance and persistence in carrying out the exercises, two qualities are especially singled out: 'courage and self-confidence'. These are 'two beacons,' writes Rudolf Steiner, 'which must never be extinguished on the path to occult vision.'[29] At the end of this chapter Rudolf Steiner mentions these two qualities for a second time, in order that through mentioning them again their importance with regard to the stage of *Enlightenment* may be underlined: 'What the would-be initiate must bring with him is a certain mature *courage* and *fearlessness*. He must go out of his way to find opportunities through which these qualities are developed ... The pupil must be prepared to look danger calmly in the face and be resolute to overcome difficulties unswervingly ... He must reach the point where, in circumstances when he would formerly have been fearful, "to be frightened", "to lack courage", are out of the question for him.' For '... as a being of soul he needs the force which is developed only in courageous, fearless natures.'[30] These words, together with the ensuing description of the need for the pupil to develop 'a strong trust in the beneficent powers of existence, and also endurance and steadfastness in the unremitting yearning 'for the spiritual power which uplifts and carries him ...'[31] (that is, the need to be in the highest sense *true* to his chosen spiritual path), are an indication of the two fundamental *Michaelic* virtues of courage and faithfulness of which Rudolf Steiner repeatedly speaks in his lectures. For in our time Michael *is* in need of people who are courageous and faithful to him if his mission among humanity is to be fulfilled.

So the description of the stage of *Enlightenment* in *Knowledge of the Higher Worlds: How is it Achieved?* offers an indication of the time in the yearly cycle that is most suited to crossing this threshold. This is the time starting from the autumnal festival of Michael, the festival of courageous and faithful souls.

Regarding the need for *courage* in taking up the Michael-impulse, the Michael-thought, for the overcoming of the ahrimanic dragon[32] to which our modern civilization is gradually submitting, and also for *faithfulness* in the sphere of Michael, faithfulness to his new revelation which has been streaming into humanity since the last third of the nineteenth century, the concluding words of Rudolf Steiner's final lecture—given on Michaelmas Eve 1924—perhaps speak to us in the most meaningful way of all: 'This is what would be addressed to your soul through the words spoken today: that you receive this Michael-thought as it can be felt by *a heart that is true to Michael* when, *clothed in the radiant light of the Sun*, Michael appears and indicates what must take place if this Michael garment, this garment of light, is to become the words of worlds ...'[33] In these 'world-words' there is also an allusion to the essential reality of the Michael festival as the festival which opens up the path to Christmas, the path to initiation in our time: 'First the awakening of the soul, then death, so that in death the resurrection, which man himself celebrates within his own being, may be accomplished'[34]—that is true initiation.

We shall speak in more detail in the subsequent chapters of this book of how, with initiation, there takes place within man a further deepening following on from the stages of *Preparation* and *Enlightenment*—and also of initiation itself and its relationship in the cycle of the year to the Mystery of Christmas.

26

3. From Michaelmas to Christmas (Michael and the Nathan Soul)

At the time of his festival in the autumn, Michael's image appears to us as sternly warning, calling for inner wakefulness and responsibility. Bearing aloft the flaming sword of world thinking forged of cosmic iron, he points upwards to man's higher self,[35] as if to remind him of the higher aim of his existence—which must be striven towards with particular intensity in the time that directly follows *after* the festival of Michael.

This is indeed a time of trials, but it is also a time filled with the inner activity of expectation. For in autumn the forces of the Sun become ever weaker and the forces of darkness, of twilight, of the approaching cosmic night, grow ever stronger. Every year at this time, when the Sun is entering the sign of the Scorpion, all the spiritual forces seeking to hinder true evolution again receive the hope that they may prevent the rising of the Spiritual Sun in the darkness of Earth's night and thus win authority over human evolution and make use of it for their own ends. The time that follows the festival of Michael leads man 'from knowledge of [outer] nature to a contemplation of evil.'[36] You must receive *into* yourself the inner power of resurrection, the power of the Spiritual Sun, before the death-forces that rule over this time in nature seize hold of you—such is the underlying devotional mood of this time of year.

'Temptation by the forces of evil'[37]—thus does Rudolf Steiner characterize this period. And from the furthermost reaches of the cosmos, whither the powers of light gradually recede from man's outward gaze, a last warning is sounded to the spirit-pupil: 'Guard yourself against evil!'[38] Be inwardly awake! For at this time of year, every time again, forces of opposition approach the human soul with particular strength, as though seeking to repeat on a microcosmic scale in the yearly cycle what once occurred 'macrocosmically' in human evolution in the form of the 'temptation in Paradise'.

However, this time is not only one of temptation and trial; it is also a time filled with inner *expectation* and also preparation⋆ for the celebration

---

⋆ The word 'preparation' is used here in a more general sense than in the chapter, 'The Time of Preparation', where it refers to the initial stage of modern initation. In this case the word denotes preparation for a definite annual festival, in the sense that the time preceding *each* of the principal yearly festivals is always connected with an inner preparation for it.

27

of the birth on Earth of a quite special being. Both these moods, of *trial and preparation* (expectation), attain a quite particular strength and concentration in the period of Advent, during the four weeks that precede Christmas.

For whose birth is humanity preparing itself at this time? Only modern spiritual science can give a comprehensive answer. For it is necessary to turn to earlier times in the Earth's development, to that prehistoric epoch when man became man, that is, a being possessed of his own individual ego. This is the epoch of ancient Lemuria, when there occurred the great crisis in human evolution referred to in the Bible as 'the Fall'.

We know through spiritual science that at this time, which was after the Sun's separation from the Earth but before the departure of the Moon, luciferic forces approached humanity—which had just been endowed with individual egohood as an outpouring of the substance of the Spirits of Form—with temptation. This penetration of luciferic forces into the human astral body is the occult fact that stands behind the description of the Fall in the Bible. However, it was not only the astral body that was touched by the influence of these forces, for the danger proceeded to spread to man's etheric body. This danger was all the more significant in that if the etheric body were also to succumb to the forces of Lucifer mankind would at that time have been threatened with the complete impossibility of continuing its evolution on Earth at the time of the so-called 'lunar crisis' (that is, before the departure of the Moon). For according to the true path of evolution, the forces of opposition should not have been able to approach the etheric body with temptation in the Lemurian epoch but only in the epoch of Atlantis, when the ego-substance would have incarnated not only into the astral but also into the etheric sheath of man's being. Thus in order to avert the danger of the etheric body prematurely succumbing to the opposing forces, even before the Fall a part of its purer and more refined forces, corresponding to the chemical and life ethers, was removed from the general evolution of humanity and preserved in the spiritual world under the protection of the great Mother Lodge of the rulership of humanity.★

This important event, which had significance for the whole further evolution of the Earth, was subsequently reflected in the biblical imagination of the Tree of Knowledge and the Tree of Life. In these images the Tree of Knowledge represents the forces of man's astral body and the Tree of Life the forces of his etheric or life-body. And the bearer of these human

---

★ We learn through spiritual science that this great Mother Lodge has its focus in the high Sun-sphere, while the central Sun-oracle was its representative on Earth in the Atlantean epoch and, in post-Atlantean times, 'a certain Mystery-centre in Asia Minor.'[39]

life-forces which had not been affected by the Fall became that being who is known to us through spiritual-scientific literature as the soul of the Nathan Jesus-child or simply as the Nathan Soul.

Rudolf Steiner defines this whole process in the following words: 'The luciferic influence came and extended its effects into the astral body of this ancestral couple and as a result of this it became impossible for the full forces of "Adam and Eve" to be transmitted to their descendants, through the blood of these descendants. It was necessary for the physical body to be reproduced through all the generations; but the powers guiding humanity held something back from the *etheric body*. This was expressed in the words: "Men have eaten of the Tree of Knowledge of Good and Evil"—that is, of what had come under the influence of Lucifer. But it was also said: "Now we must take from them all possibility of tasting of the Tree of Life!" This means that *a certain portion of the forces of the etheric body was held back, and these forces were not handed down to the descendants*. Thus in Adam a certain portion of the forces had been removed before the Fall. This "still innocent" part of Adam was preserved in the Mother Lodge of humanity, where it was lovingly protected and nurtured. This was, so to speak, the Adam soul that was as yet untouched by human guilt, that was not as yet entangled in what had led man to the Fall. These pristine forces of the Adam-individuality were preserved.'[40]

From this it follows that the origin of the Nathan Soul goes back to the most distant past of earthly evolution. In order to understand it better, it is therefore necessary for us to go still further back, to the moment when the ego-substance of the Spirits of Form first flowed into man's being. 'And the Lord God formed man of the dust of the ground, and breathed into his nostrils the breath of life; and man became *a living soul*'[41]—thus it is described in the Bible. Only with the breath, which is connected with the working of man's astral body, did the ego-principle enter in and man became 'a *living* soul.'

Since that time, the Nathan Soul has also appeared in the cosmos as such a 'living soul', for the rest of humanity has—through the temptation by Lucifer—ceased to be a *living* soul and has plunged ever deeper into matter, into the realm of spiritual darkness and death.

In the course of many thousands of years the Nathan Soul remained in the spiritual worlds, holding itself back from any direct contact with the earthly sphere; and only at the Turning Point of Time, as preparation for the descent to the Earth of the Sun Spirit, the Christ, did it incarnate in Palestine as the Jesus-child of the Nathan House of David. This erstwhile appearance of the Nathan Soul on Earth has ever since been celebrated amongst human beings every year at Christmas. The time leading up to Christmas, beginning with Michaelmas though especially during the four weeks of Advent, is one of inner preparation for understanding and rightly experiencing this event.

As we saw, however, the period in the cycle of the year from Michaelmas to Christmas falls under the particular guardianship of the Archangel Michael. Hence, such a juxtaposition of spiritual and temporal affairs necessarily places before us the question: what is the nature of the Archangel Michael's connection to the Nathan Soul? In order to answer this it is necessary that we recall that, according to modern spiritual science, Michael, while indeed being a Sun Archangel, nevertheless worked *before* the Mystery of Golgotha also as the servant of the Moon-Elohim, Yahveh, that is, of that spiritual Being of the rank of the Spirits of Form who is called in the Bible 'the Lord God' and who took the principal part in endowing man with the ego-principle. Rudolf Steiner speaks about this relationship of Michael to Yahveh and to Christ in ancient times in the particularly important words of the lecture given on 2 May 1913 in London: 'Even in the New Testament you find—and I have often referred to this in my books—that Christ revealed Himself through Yahveh, in so far as this was possible before the Mystery of Golgotha.'[42] And later he continues '... thus we may say that *Christ-Yahveh* is that *Being* who has accompanied man throughout his evolution. But in the course of successive epochs, Christ-Yahveh always reveals Himself through various beings of the same rank as Michael.'[43] Thus Michael has from ancient times been the foremost Servant of *Christ-Jahve* among the Archangels, and has therefore in a certain sense participated in 'the creation of man.'[44] This quite special relationship in 'pre-Christian' times to Yahveh and to all mankind, and later to the Hebrew people, is also an indication to us of his deep inner connection with the being of the Nathan Soul that was preserved in the spiritual world.

Through the working of Yahveh, Adam—and in his person the whole of mankind—in former times received his individual ego from the six Sun-Elohim. Hence the genealogy of the Luke Gospel goes back to the Elohim-Yahveh, and thus contains not only the whole history of the Jewish people, in which the Nathan Soul was to incarnate, but also the whole history of mankind even to its ancestors, Adam and God—while giving expression to those *earthly* destinies from which the Nathan Soul was once kept at a distance in the spiritual world. However, Michael, as the Countenance of Yahveh,* 'must have guided humanity through these earthly destinies since ancient times. For as a *Sun Archangel* he has from the beginning of earthly times also been a mediator between the Sun Logos of Christ and the Moon Logos of Yahveh, a mediator between the heavenly

---

* See lecture of 22 November 1919 (GA 174a).

and earthly destinies of humanity, which became separated in the Lemurian epoch and united again only through the events of Palestine. Thus we may say: the principal service afforded by Michael to *Christ-Yahveh* before the Mystery of Golgotha was essentially encompassed in this mediatory activity.

And now it is necessary to try to deepen still further the connection that we have observed between the Archangel Michael and the Nathan Soul. For this we must again turn to the scene of the Fall and examine it from a somewhat different point of view.

Earlier in this chapter it was described how at a certain point in world evolution one part of the etheric forces of humanity, of the Adam-being, was separated out and was preserved in a high spiritual sphere away from the forces of matter and death, while the other part was directed downwards to the path of earthly incarnations. But the question now arises as to which cosmic sphere was the focus of this separation. In other words: where should we seek this heavenly being of the Nathan Soul, this sister-soul of Adam, which as we have seen was preserved in the heavenly heights from the effects of the Fall? In order to answer this question we need to turn to an examination of one very important aspect of the general process of man's descent to the Earth. This macrocosmic process, which the individual human soul repeats on a microcosmic scale every time that he descends from the spiritual worlds for a new incarnation, has amounted to a gradual journey through the spheres of the various Hierarchies.[45] One could say that at such a time the Hierarchies themselves lovingly accompany human beings on their path of descent to the Earth.

First of all mankind dwelt in the sphere of the Archai, or Spirits of Time. This period lasted approximately until the middle of the Hyperborean epoch, until the Sun's departure from the Earth. Then this germ of future humanity passed over into the sphere of the Archangels, those exalted Spirits who were to become the leaders of the various peoples on Earth. This youthful humankind remained in their sphere until the departure of the Moon and even somewhat longer, until finally it entered the sphere of the Angels, the guides of the individual egos of every single human being. There humanity remained until the middle of the Atlantean epoch, and only in the second half of the Atlantean epoch did human beings finally descend to the Earth. Somewhat earlier, at the end of the Lemurian epoch, at the time of transition from the sphere of the Archangels to that of the Angels, there occurred the event which is usually referred to as 'the Fall', preceded as it was by the withholding of a part of Adam's etheric body in the higher spiritual spheres.

Thus the Fall took place while humanity resided in the sphere of the Angels. At this time—at the end of the Lemurian epoch—human beings, physically speaking, inhabited the etheric-airy-watery surroundings of the Earth, and their consciousness still belonged to the paradisaically innocent sphere of the Angels. It was in this sphere that temptation approached mankind. This proceeded from those angelic beings who had not fully completed their evolution on Old Moon and who now approached the astral bodies of human beings gradually drawing nearer to the Earth as retarded Moon Angels who had taken on a luciferic nature. If this temptation had not occurred, man would have been able to dwell still longer in the surroundings of the Earth, without either touching its surface or having outer sense-perceptions. Because of the Fall, however, man began to tread 'the solid Earth' and to perceive the outer world of the senses much earlier than was fore-ordained by the ruling powers of the world.

Hence the Fall—that is, the premature penetration of the physical world—became a possibility only after man made the transition from the sphere of the Archangels to that of the Angels, from the realm of influence of the solar and planetary forces to the realm of the lunar forces. At this turning point there also took place that separation which was called forth through the fact that, on entering the sphere of the Angels in the course of his descent to the Earth, man inevitably encountered not only Angels who had undergone a right spiritual evolution and had thus made themselves ready to become the Guardian Angels of individual people but also the luciferic Angels who had fallen from the path of general world evolution. The Nathan Soul was, however, held back from this transition and was preserved in the Sun-sphere of the Archangels in that sphere whence in future times there would proceed rulership over the various peoples of the Earth. Likewise, it maintained its connection with that part of the Angelic sphere which had not been touched by the luciferic temptation. This explains why Rudolf Steiner sometimes characterizes it as an *Archangel-like* being and sometimes as *Angel-like*.[46] However, these designations have a still deeper foundation.

For what does it mean when we speak of a human etheric and astral body that are untouched by temptation? It is none other than an indication of etheric and astral substances of the purest kind, still permeated with a plenitude of cosmic forces and having a deep inner kinship with the inclinations towards the Life Spirit and Spirit Self reposing in man. These higher members reside as the highest outpouring from the cosmic spheres of Cherubim and Seraphim[47] in the ground of existence of paradisaical humanity and are directly connected with the etheric and astral sheaths of individual people; for the unfallen etheric body is by its very nature connected with the Life Spirit, and the unfallen astral body with the Spirit Self. And as these higher members are fully and consciously developed only by the Archangels and Angels, the words used by Rudolf Steiner regarding the Archangel- and Angel-*like* being of the Nathan Soul are profoundly in accordance with the spiritual reality.

In this sense it is also possible to speak of the 'ego' of the Nathan Soul, though with the reservation that it bears more strongly the nature of the Spirit Self than would a normal earthly human ego. The Nathan Soul was able to preserve an 'ego' which was thus fully permeated by the Spirit Self through the fact that it was, as has been described, held back on the border of the archangelic and angelic spheres from entering into earthly incarnations.

Rudolf Steiner speaks about this 'ego' of the Nathan Soul in the following words: '... that which streamed forth from the Spirits of Form continues to flow on further. But it was as though there was something ego-like which was not permitted to enter into fleshly incarnation: an ego which preserved that form, that substantiality, which man possessed before he embarked upon his first incarnation ... an ego which was still in the same situation as—in biblical terms—the ego of 'Adam' *before* his first earthly, fleshly, incarnation. Such an ego always existed ... This ego was endowed with quite special qualities; it had the peculiarity of not being touched by anything that the human ego could have assimilated on the Earth. It was also untouched by any luciferic or ahrimanic influence ...'[48] 'And so the impression was created that this Nathan Jesus-child, who is depicted in the Luke Gospel, did not have a human ego at all ...'[49]

Through the picture that we have built up there also emerges a deeper understanding of the biblical words that relate how all the people and nations of the Earth proceeded from Adam. For if we consider that the heavenly soul of Adam was held back in the spiritual heights, these words are an indication to us of how it was precisely from the sphere wherein this soul was withheld that Guardian Angels descended to guide individual men and Archangels to rule over the nations.

That Archangel who, being a Sun Archangel, kept a particularly close connection with the Sun-sphere where the Nathan Soul dwelt,[50] and who could also be called the Sun Guardian or guide of the paradisaical soul of humanity which had been preserved from the Fall, became known in later times under the name of *Michael*, 'he who stands before the Countenance of God'. For it follows from what has been said that the Nathan Soul was kept back in that spiritual sphere whence the Archangels subsequently descended to guide the individual nations and to which Michael himself, as the leading Sun Archangel, initially belonged.

However, the Nathan Soul was not 'inactive' during the subsequent evolution of the Earth, as it abided in the Mother Lodge of humanity under the guidance of the Archangel Michael. Spiritual science tells us of

33

the three supersensible deeds accomplished by the Nathan Soul in the extra-terrestrial cosmos—wherein, as we shall come to see, its *Archangel-like* nature came to expression. Its mirror-like appearance in Krishna was a reflection of its *Angel-like* nature, of its kinship with man's Higher Self, his Spirit Self; and it could thereby, in the aspect of Krishna, give a powerful impulse to the generation of individual ego-thinking amongst earthly humanity.[51] Rudolf Steiner speaks in this connection in the lecture-cycle *The Bhagavad Gita and the Epistles of Paul*: 'In so far as it [the being of Krishna] alone is concerned, it is not a question of the physical body of flesh, nor of the finer body of the elements, nor of the forces relating to the sense-organs, and not of Ahamkara and Manas, but of what in *Buddhi and Manas* is directly connected with the great all-embracing world substances, with the divine power that lives and weaves through the world . . . Thus, in beholding Krishna, man is at the same time beholding his own Higher Self [that is, the principle of Spirit Self].'[52]

In conclusion, we should examine one further aspect of the events here described which relates to the deep connection that has existed since the beginning of time in the spiritual world between the Archangel Michael and the Nathan Soul. This aspect is revealed to us through the description of the Fall of man given by Rudolf Steiner in the lecture-cycle *The Mission of the Archangel Michael: The Revelation of Essential Secrets of Human Nature*. In the lecture of 22 November 1919 he says the following: 'After human evolution had passed through the Saturn, Sun and Moon stages and the Earth evolution had begun, that same spiritual power which we know as the power of Michael incorporated the being of Lucifer in the forming of the human head. "And he cast the spirits that opposed him down to the earth", which is to say that, through this overthrowing of the luciferic spirits who opposed Michael, man was endowed with reason, with that which arises from his head. Thus *it is Michael who sent his opponents to man in order that, through taking into himself this luciferic element of opposition, man might acquire his power of reason and all that corresponds to the human head.*'[53] (It is for this reason that in artistic portrayals of the temptation scene in Paradise, Lucifer always appears—if the imagination is rightly conveyed—as a serpent with a human head.)[54] From these words we see that Michael, as 'the Countenance of Yahveh', not only participated in the creation of man as a 'living soul', that is, in the creation of the Nathan Soul, but that he also took part in the Fall of man that followed. And if the Nathan Soul had to be withheld by the wisdom of world rulership from the common fate of humanity and had to remain in the Sun-sphere, this circumstance is due in the first place to the direct mediation of the Archangel Michael, who did not allow the luciferic spirits to penetrate it but drew them down into the heads of men. Thus Michael is, from this standpoint too, that spirit who has been directly associated with the heavenly destiny of the Nathan Soul, and hence also with the destiny of all earthly humanity.

Herein we find a further reason why the festival of Christmas, the festival of the birth on Earth of the Nathan Soul, directly follows the festival of Michael in the cycle of the year.

II

THE MYSTERY OF ADVENT AS THE MYSTERY OF THE NATHAN SOUL

1. The Three Supersensible Deeds of the Nathan Soul

The four weeks of Advent form a period of concentrated preparation for Christmas. Just as at Christmas we turn in memory to the birth of the Nathan Soul on Earth, so in the four preceding weeks must we penetrate into the essential nature of its heavenly destiny, of those deeds in the spiritual worlds of which we know through modern spiritual science. In their sequence these deeds anticipate the appearance of the Nathan Soul on Earth and also form the period of its cosmic preparation for physical incarnation. Hence we have full reason to connect them with the spiritual content of the season of Advent. However, before embarking upon a study of Advent as such, it is necessary first to turn to these supersensible deeds of the Nathan Soul, for there we shall find a real key to a proper understanding of this particular season.

According to modern spiritual science, the first of these supersensible deeds of the Nathan Soul occurred in the last third of ancient Lemurian evolution. At this time, which was after the descent of humanity into the earthly sphere, after the departure of the Moon and man's subsequent attaining of uprightness, spiritual forces hostile to the true path of evolution were threatening with degeneration the most ancient and most perfect part of man's physical body—that part which is associated with his twelve sense-organs. In former times, in the period of Old Saturn, these sense-organs were established as the first traces of the physical body, as the reflection of the twelve cosmic streams proceeding from the lofty spiritual beings of the First Hierarchy and which have their outer expression in the twelvefold circle of the zodiac.

This state of affairs, in Rudolf Steiner's words, '... brought about the danger that the twelve cosmic forces, which bring their influence to bear upon man, might fall into disarray through the work of demonic beings.'[1] If this had happened, 'Saturn man would have fallen prey to a terrible egoism. This would have come directly to expression in the sense-organs, in that, for example, the eyes would not have transmitted to the soul an objective impression of whatever object they were beholding but merely their own egoistic sense of pain or bliss in being in contact with it. The consequence of this would have been that the whole of human evolution might have been brought into disorder. Lucifer and Ahriman would have been able to bring all human evolution into disorder through the fact that man has, as a result of his upright bearing, been torn away from the spiritual forces of the Earth ...'[2] In these words there is contained the essential Mystery of the events of that time. Although the foundations of man's sense-organs were laid on Ancient Saturn,[3] they were able to acquire their full significance and final form only through man's *upright posture*, which became a reality in the last third of Lemurian evolution as a result of the outpouring of ego-substance into man through the Spirits of Form and in the first instance through the Moon-Elohim, Jahve. Only through man's uprightness was it possible for his twelve senses to again be brought into harmony with the cosmic forces that engendered them, forces that streamed from the twelve regions of the zodiacal circle. It was this evolutionary course that first the luciferic and then the ahrimanic powers[4] tried to oppose at that time, for they were trying to wrest man away from the Earth and thus make him into an 'underdeveloped angel', a being who would never in the future be able to acquire a free, individual ego. For although man was, through his uprightness, brought anew into a connection with all the forces of the cosmos that surround the Earth, he was by this on no account to be drawn away from earthly evolution. Hence as a counterweight to the efforts of the luciferic and ahrimanic forces directed upwards from below, it was necessary that something enter in from above downwards from out of the cosmos, from the world of the Hierarchies. And this 'something' was none other than the ideal 'etheric image of man' inscribed in the spiritual world, an image that represented a perfect combination of the ego's forces of uprightness directed upwards from below and, from above downwards, the twelve streams that reflect the harmonious interplay of the twelve sense-organs and that also rightly impart to them a direction towards the Earth, towards the objective perception of earthly objects and conditions. This 'etheric image of man'* imprinted in the spiritual world was subsequently to work as that heavenly archetype whose forces streamed out to save the whole of humanity gradually from the temptation referred to above.

But in what way could this truly cosmic deed be accomplished? It happened as follows. The soul of the future Nathan Jesus, which then abided in the Sun-sphere, had to ascend to the highest regions of Sun-existence, to those regions where the Sun itself appears as a fixed star amongst fixed stars. From there it was then possible to enter into a direct connection with the original sources of the spiritual streams issuing from the twelve cosmic spheres of the zodiac. And then, having permeated its being with all twelve zodiacal forces, which together form not only man's twelve senses but his entire physical aspect,[5] the Nathan Soul was—in this sublime region of Sun-existence—able to sacrifice its own etheric sub-

---

* See note 6

40

stance to the Sun Spirit, the Christ, whereby there arose in the lower regions of the spiritual world that 'etheric image of man' which was referred to above.

Rudolf Steiner describes this process in the following words: 'With this, something new has entered into the cosmos which now rays out upon both Earth and man, upon the physical earthly human form into which there streamed the power of the etheric, super-earthly Being of Christ, thus making it possible for it to be protected from that force of destruction which would have had to enter in if the formative power which makes of man an upright and well-ordered being had not been able to stream in from the cosmos and penetrate man in such a way that it lives in him.'[6] And this occurred '... because he who, as the Nathan Jesus, was permeated with the Christ had, as a being of spiritual-etheric aspect, in Lemurian times received human-etheric form through being permeated with the Christ.'[7]

At that time the twelve cosmic forces that are active in the upright physical human body and form the foundation of the right evolution of his individual ego-consciousness were thus again brought into harmony and his twelve sense-organs thenceforth acquired such a degree of selflessness that they could indeed say: 'Not we, but Christ in us.'

The second danger to which humanity came to be exposed in the course of his further evolution arose at the beginning of the Atlantean epoch. At that time man's etheric body, his life-forces and above all the seven principal life-organs[8] which are their outward expression in the human organism were subjected to the assault of luciferic and ahrimanic powers. On this occasion the danger was that man's boundless egoism had led him to become exposed to the risk of becoming simply the obedient instrument of the experiences of his own inner organs. This would have come to expression outwardly in that, for example, his lungs would have been filled with feelings of desire or aversion quite irrespective of whether he had arrived at a place where the air was good or bad.

Another consequence of this egoistic 'drawing together' or 'gathering up' of the etheric body would have been the perversion of human language. In such an evolutionary context human language would never have been able to become what the divine world-rulership intended. There is a prophetic indication of this higher purpose of language in the Bible, when Adam is allowed to give names to all the beings of the three lower kingdoms of nature.[9] If the opposing forces had prevailed, language would have preserved no more than expressions of inner, subjective human experiences and would have consisted solely of individual sounds and interjections. Thus the capacity to work creatively through the word

41

upon the objective world that surrounds him would have been taken away from man for ever if further help had not come to him from the spiritual world.

However, this help could only be given to man in two stages. He was first endowed with the capacity of objectively expressing his own inner experiences with the help of the Word and then with the higher capacity of naming—again with the help of the Word—all other processes and beings. One could also say that at the first stage the faculty of speaking was transformed in its relationship to man's inner world and at the second to the outer world. And so the first stage was attained through the second cosmic event, which brought about the transformation of language as regards man's inner world.[9a]

This second cosmic event was brought into being through the resolve of the Nathan Soul again to sacrifice itself. But this time the healing deed proceeded not from the highest regions of Sun-existence but from those realms where the Sun appears as the focus of the planetary system: from the spheres of the seven planets which represent the macrocosmic archetype of man's etheric body. The Nathan Soul was to receive the forces of all seven planets into itself, in order that it might for the second time sacrifice its being to the high Sun Spirit of Christ and for the second time become the great bearer of Christ in the cosmos, the divine Christophorus. Because of this, it became possible for Christ so to transform the individual planetary forces gathered together by the Nathan Soul that they could work in a harmonizing and moderating way upon man's etheric body and, through this, bring healing to the seven principal life-organs which—like the organs of sense at the previous stage—were able to say to themselves: 'Not we, but Christ in us'. In addition, this high level of selflessness of the life-organs associated with the etheric body was able to serve as a foundation for the first stage of the healing of human speech, the human word.★

Finally, there arose a third danger in earthly evolution, which threatened man's astral body and above all his three principal soul-forces of thinking, feeling and willing. That splintering of the personality which in our time comes about only at a definite stage of spirit-pupilship,[10] when thinking, feeling and willing separate out from one another and are ruled by man's strengthened ego, was led through the working of luciferic and ahrimanic powers into the situation at the end of the Atlantean epoch of giving rise first to the suppressing and then to the complete extinguishing of the

---

★ The other qualities of the human etheric body—qualities about which Rudolf Steiner later spoke in the lecture of 21 April 1924, *The Easter Festival considered in Relation to the Mysteries*, GA 233— were rescued at that time.

human ego. As a consequence of such a distortion of the true path of evolution, humanity would have again gradually reverted to its animal state, separating itself out in the process into three kinds of animal nature: people with a one-sided development of thought, of feeling or of will, who would have gradually taken on the outward appearance respectively of eagle-like, lion-like and bull-like beings, while in an inner sense they would have borne a dragon-like astral nature.[11] The principal danger in this case lay in the threat to the thinking, for the ahrimanic powers working on the will and the luciferic powers working on the feeling strove together to gain mastery over this sphere with the object of preventing man from attaining full ego-consciousness—which is possible only with the help of the instrument of thinking.

Once again the Soul of the Nathan Jesus appeared in the Sun-sphere to counter this new danger at the end of the Atlantean epoch, this time penetrating into the nether regions of the Sun-sphere which extend to the sphere of the Moon. There, receiving into itself Sun-forces from above, Moon-forces from the surroundings and Earth-forces from below in all their harmonious interplay (the macrocosmic expression of the ideal relationship of the forces of thinking, feeling and willing), the Nathan Soul was again able to sacrifice its etheric being to the Sun Spirit of the Christ and so became for the third time the bearer of His forces in the cosmos. Through this supersensible union with the Christ, the Sun-, Moon- and Earth-forces gathered by the Nathan Soul were transformed and strengthened in such a way that they were then able to become a means for healing and harmonizing the ever more disorientated spiritual soul-forces of people on Earth. Consequently, the soul-forces of man could—like the sense-organs and the life-organs at the previous stages—also say to themselves: 'Not we, but Christ in us.'

As a result of this the second stage of the transformation of human language was also attained, now as regards the outer world.[11a] This time the faculty of speaking was finally healed and at the same time the predisposition was implanted in man for his speech to become in time the true bearer of the Divine Logos.

Thus in the three supersensible deeds of the Nathan Soul described above we have three stages of the penetration of the cosmic forces of the Christ into the three human sheaths and the resultant healing of the three systems of the human organism. And as we ascend in our description from the physical to the etheric and astral bodies, we gradually approach the very centre of man's being, his ego, whose healing is bound up with the *fourth* deed of the Nathan Soul, which took place on the Earth itself. Hence the appearance of this Soul at the Turning Point of Time is the direct karmic

43

consequence of the supersensible evolution that has been described, and it is the remembrance of this event which is celebrated every year at Christmas time.

2. Of Michael's Participation in the Supersensible Deeds of the Nathan Soul

In the whole series of lectures devoted to a description of the supersensible deeds of the Nathan Soul and especially in the lecture of 30 December 1913, Rudolf Steiner also traces their early reflection in the evolutionary process of the various human cultures. Thus we find a reflection of the first deed in the ancient Sun wisdom of Zoroaster, of the second in the astrological knowledge of the Egyptians and the archetypes of the Greek gods, and, finally, of the third deed in the countenance of Apollo, who brings man's soul-forces into harmony by his playing on the lyre. There is an imagination in Greek mythology connected with this image of Apollo playing on the lyre which in the present context has a quite special significance. Apollo is depicted therein as the conqueror of the python-dragon, which, creeping out like a dense cloud of smoke from the earthly depths, from the cleft beside the Castalian spring, rises into the air and there, in the sphere of activity of the Moon-forces encircling the Earth, is vanquished by the streaming Sun-arrows of Apollo. In this imagination there arises before us the victory of the purified forces of thinking over the dark instincts of human nature which rise up from the subconscious realm of the will and become egoistic passions in the realm of feeling. This—in Rudolf Steiner's words—is the true picture of the victory of Michael (and of St George) over the dragon. And this oft-repeated indication regarding the connection of the third sacrifice of the Nathan Soul with the deed of Michael in the astral sphere of the Earth allows us a glimpse into a profound Mystery.

But in order to approach it, we must examine one further aspect of these events which Rudolf Steiner touches upon with the greatest precision in his lecture on the theme of *The Four Sacrifices of Christ* given in Basel on 1 June 1914. In this lecture, Rudolf Steiner speaks in detail of how Christ, in the course of His descent to the Earth, through the spheres of the various Hierarchies, on three occasions 'ensouled' in the spiritual world a being from the Hierarchy of the Archangels, and then, *bypassing the stage of the Angels*, incarnated directly on the Earth in the sheaths of Jesus of Nazareth. Thus it was revealed through spiritual-scientific research '... that Christ employed the form of an Archangel—the Angel form was omitted—and then a human form.'[12] 'And then came the fourth, earthly Mystery, that of Golgotha. That same Christ Being who thrice ensouled an archangelic

45

form, that same Christ-figure now incarnated—through the event that we call the Baptism in the Jordan—into the body of Jesus of Nazareth.'[13]

Thus looked at spiritually, the following constellation can be seen. In the ancient Lemurian epoch, in the period directly following the Fall of man, the being of the Nathan Soul is held back at the border of the archangelic sphere from further descent to the Earth and is then preserved in the Sun-sphere, where it becomes the bearer of the forces of the etheric body of Adam which were untouched by the luciferic temptation, forces which in their essential purity were akin to the principle of the Life Spirit. Only the Archangels bear this principle in its cosmic fullness. Hence there naturally arises a deep kinship and strength of attraction between the Nathan Soul and the beings of the Second Hierarchy and above all with its most exalted member, the Archangel now known as Michael, who is *pre-eminently* a Sun Archangel. He is the regent of that sphere in which the Nathan Soul has abided since Lemurian times.

This spiritual-cosmic constellation permits us to suggest that that being from the Hierarchy of the Archangels who participated in the three pre-Christian sacrifices of Christ through the mediation of the Nathan Soul was *Michael* himself! Rudolf Steiner indicates this in a particularly direct way in his description of the third sacrifice of the Nathan Soul. In the series of lectures on this theme we find references to the fact that the great imagination of Michael's or St George's battle with the dragon is a reflection of the third preparatory stage of the Mystery of Golgotha. Moreover it is emphasized that *two* beings participated in this event: the Archangel Michael and St George, that is, a being of hierarchic nature and a being of human nature.[14]

There follow some remarks of Rudolf Steiner on this question: 'This is the pictorial representation of the third Christ event: the Archangel Michael or St George, the future Nathan Jesus-child permeated by the Christ Being. Hence the archangelic form indeed exists in the spiritual worlds.'[15] 'Humanity has preserved a wonderful imagination of this third Christ Event in the picture of St George conquering the dragon.'[16] 'All who look upon the image of St George and the dragon or Michael and the dragon or other similar events are really speaking of the third Christ Event.'[17]

It is, however, in the lecture of 30 December 1913 that Rudolf Steiner describes this age-old battle of Michael with the dragon in a particularly meaningful way: 'The memory of this holds sway in all the pictures through which the image of St George conquering the dragon has been made known among mankind. St George and the dragon is a reflection of that supersensible event whereby Christ ensouled Jesus and made him capable of banishing the dragon from the soul-nature of man. This was a significant deed which was made possible only through Christ's presence in Jesus who was *at that time an Angel-like being.* For this Angel-like being had indeed to unite himself with the dragon-nature. He had—so to speak—to take on the form of the dragon in order to restrain it from entering the human soul; he had to work within the dragon in such a way that the dragon was ennobled, that the dragon was brought out of chaos into a kind of harmony. *The educating, the taming, of the dragon—therein lies the further task of this being.*'[18]

In all these words and images it is thus possible to see evidence of the direct participation of the Michael-impulse in the evolution and development of mankind.[19] And although the imagination of Michael and the dragon was given by Rudolf Steiner only in connection with the third deed of the Nathan Soul, it nonetheless also has a relationship with the other two deeds in so far as they have to do with temptations and dangers threatening the various members of man's being from the side of the opposing forces, which for higher knowledge always appear in the spiritual world in the form of the dragon—while the force that overcomes them is represented by the figure of Michael.

The fact that Rudolf Steiner does not refer to this imagination in the course of describing the first two deeds of the Nathan Soul may be explained if we bear in mind that they have their source not in the supersensible world closest to the Earth (the Moon-region) but in the Sun-sphere and the realm of the stars, and these are accessible not to imaginative but only to inspirative and intuitive faculties of knowledge.[20]

3. The Fourth Deed of the Nathan Soul.
The Transformation of Michael's Mission at the Time of the Mystery of Golgotha

Having described the three supersensible deeds of the Nathan Soul and also the Archangel Michael's participation in them, we may now pass on to a consideration of the fourth and most significant of the deeds of this Soul, which was called forth through its direct incarnation on the Earth in the person of the Luke Jesus-child, whom Rudolf Steiner in certain lectures calls 'the child of humanity, the child of man.'[21] For now, at the time of the Mystery of Golgotha, the human ego itself was exposed to danger. And this human ego could be saved only through the appearance on Earth of the great Sun Being of the Christ. Only through the uniting of the destinies of earthly and supersensible man—the old and the new Adam—in the Christ event could a real healing and strengthening be brought to the human ego and a firm foundation be laid for human freedom and also for the whole further development of humanity on Earth. The essential purpose of the fourth and most sublime sacrifice of the Nathan Soul was to bring to every human ego the possibility of receiving the strength of Christ directly into itself, of translating the words of the Apostle Paul—'Not I, but Christ in me'[22]—into an inner reality in the deepest sense, that is, to bring this ego into a true equilibrium between the ahrimanic and luciferic forces approaching it from without and within respectively. It was to receive the Christ Being no longer in the cosmos alone but on the Earth, and thus enable the Christ-impulse to gain access to every human ego.

With this redemption of the human ego by means of this fourth and most important deed of the Christ through the Nathan Jesus (in the Mystery of Golgotha) is also associated the rescuing of human thinking, by virtue of which man is alone enabled to attain his full ego-consciousness on Earth. However, in this case what is meant is the inner thinking associated with the ego and not that primordial faculty referred to in connection with the third sacrifice of the Christ through the Nathan Soul, which at the end of the Atlantean era was wholly clairvoyant thinking, where thoughts came to man from without on a more spiritual plane—in a manner similar to the way that the impressions of our external sense-organs come to us today.

The last echoes of this primordial clairvoyant thinking lived on until the time of the philosophers of ancient Greece. And although their thinking had to a large extent already lost its clairvoyant character, it nevertheless remained for them an inner perception streaming to them from without as opposed to being engendered by their own ego—as gradually came to be the case with thinking in the following centuries, after the Mystery of Golgotha.[22a]

It was, on the other hand, the thinking that arises out of the depths of man's being as his own individual creation which was to be rescued by means of the fourth deed of the Christ through the Nathan Soul. In other words, by virtue of this fourth deed (the Mystery of Golgotha) the new faculty of uniting thinking with the ego—thus leading gradually to the attainment of full self-consciousness—was to be implanted in man's being on the Earth. Rudolf Steiner spoke of this as follows: 'Thus the development of this capacity for the thinking of thoughts [i.e. inner thinking, in contrast to the thinking that is received from without] consists in that our ego is taken hold of by this power. The fourth Christ event—the Mystery of Golgotha—came about in order that thinking, too, might be united with the Christ-impulse, that thinking as such might not fall into disorder *in its activity on the ego.*'[22b] For 'the fourth danger was to man's thinking, *the inner representation of his ideas.* Man is saved from this danger through his being filled with thoughts ... [in] such forms as flowed out into the spiritual sphere of the Earth through the Mystery of Golgotha.'

From these words it follows with full clarity that what we are concerned with here is a thinking consisting of an inner experience of thoughts and—hence—associated with man's ego and exerting an influence on the awakening of his individual self-consciousness, a thinking that entered fully into human evolution from the present fifth post-Atlantean epoch onwards (the so-called modern age).

In the fourth and final sacrifice, however, Michael was no longer able to accompany the Nathan Soul, for there was no being from the world of the higher Hierarchies other than the great Sun Spirit who was at that time able to incarnate directly on the Earth. So Michael remained behind in his native Sun-sphere where, according to Rudolf Steiner, he was at the time of the Mystery of Golgotha, at the moment of the Christ Being's final union with Earth-existence, contemplating this event from the Sun.[23] During this period of the Nathan Soul's preparation for incarnation in a physical body, its guidance passed to the Moon-Archangel Gabriel, who also bore the tidings of its birth to the Mary of the Luke Gospel.

The prospect from the Sun of the Mystery of Golgotha—the central event of the whole of earthly and cosmic evolution—taking place on the Earth called forth in the Sun-will of Michael the readiness to sacrifice to earthly humanity, with which the Christ had henceforth united Himself, the heavenly Intelligence, the actual substance of cosmic thinking, over which he himself had ruled in the cosmos since the beginning of time.[23a] As a result of this, the sacrifice of Michael entered as a further element into the rescuing of the human faculty of individual ego-thinking through the Mystery of Golgotha. And these two events together laid the foundation for modern man's experience of the *impulse of freedom*. It could be said that the first and most important event—the Mystery of Golgotha—laid the foundation for the faculty as such whereby man is able to engender thoughts out of himself, whereas the second event gave the instrument, or to be more precise the substance, through which this faculty could be made a reality, a spiritual substance out of which he could inwardly learn to form his thoughts for himself. In the same way that the hand of the experienced sculptor is related to the clay out of which he fashions his artistic forms, so is the sublime gift implanted into man through the Mystery of Golgotha related to the second gift which Michael gave to human beings in the centuries that followed.

However, this sacrifice of Michael's for humanity was only possible for him through the mighty change that was wrought in his own evolution as a consequence of the fact that Christ had descended to the Earth and had passed through the Mystery of Golgotha.

Michael has since ancient times, from an age extending back beyond both Earth- and Moon-evolution to the epoch of Old Sun, been that cosmic being who, serving the higher Hierarchies, has been especially deeply connected with the Sun Spirit of the Christ.[24] It was this ancient connection which enabled this pre-eminent Sun Archangel to participate directly in the three 'pre-Christian' deeds of Christ through the Nathan Soul. Because of this, Michael was fully prepared when that moment came for the Mystery of Golgotha to take place on Earth and for Christ finally to unite Himself with the earthly sphere, to become a true 'substitute' of the great Sun Spirit—the 'Countenance of Christ'—in the Sun-sphere whence the Christ had now departed, and thus to embark upon the path of ascent from the rank of a leader of nations to that of Time Spirit—a leader of all mankind, giving light and warmth to all people just as the Sun shines upon all the nations of the Earth. Thus from then onwards there worked in the cosmos: Christ, as the new Spirit of the Earth and at the same time as the Higher Ego of all mankind,[25] and Michael, as the 'substitute' of Christ on the Sun, as the true 'Sun-countenance of Christ'. Rudolf Steiner expressed this new position of Michael in the cosmos (which began for him at the time of the Mystery of Golgotha) in these words: 'Michael will change from a night-spirit into a spirit of day. The Mystery of Golgotha signifies for him the transformation from a night-spirit into a day-spirit.'[26]

Since the events of Palestine, Christ can be found in full freedom only within man, in the holiest part of the human soul; while Michael, the leading Spirit of humanity's onward march, the cosmic Servant of Christ, can be found in the full glory of the macrocosmic Christ forces only in the highest sphere of the Sun. And although this collaboration between Christ and Michael had been established in the macrocosm from the time of the Mystery of Golgotha, nevertheless it can be grasped by our clear, waking consciousness only since the inception amongst humanity of the new epoch of Michael's rulership—through the anthroposophically orientated spiritual science which he inspires. It is because of this that, from our time onwards, the possibility opens up for the first time of following in full consciousness that 'cosmic path' which represents the direct result of this collaboration between Christ and Michael. Rudolf Steiner gives us an indication of this collaboration and its consequences for the evolution of humanity on Earth in the following words: 'In those regions where man feels that in contemplating the outer world he is looking upon Michael and in contemplating the inner soul-world he is looking upon Christ, there blossoms soul and spiritual confidence whereby he is enabled to take that cosmic path on which, without losing the sense of his origins, he will find his true fulfilment.'[27]

In the cycle of the year this new collaboration between Michael and Christ is also reflected in the particular relationship of the Michael festival to the festival of Easter. Rudolf Steiner refers on several occasions in his descriptions of the spiritual essence of the festive periods of the year to the inner difference, and at the same time to the complementary natures, of these two festivals. Thus the essence of the autumnal festival of Michael is defined by him as follows: first resurrection, then immersion in the realm of death; while at Easter there works the opposite impulse, first death and then its vanquishing through the Resurrection.[28]

These two esoteric formulations, which bring to expression the super-sensible nature of the working of the impulses of Michael and Christ in our time, are also reflected in man's inner being, where they represent the preliminary conditions for the modern Christian path of initiation—for whose initial stages the present period in the yearly rhythm (from the end of summer until Christmas) is the most favourable.

It follows from the above description of the new cosmic relationship of the forces of Michael and Christ since the Mystery of Golgotha that Michael works upon man to a large extent directly out of the macrocosm, from the Sun. His forces enter into man through that *macrocosmic stream* which Rudolf Steiner, in his lecture *The Etherization of the Blood*, characterizes as the 'morally aesthetic.'[29] By means of this stream (which pours forth *from above to below* out of the macrocosm into the human head), that heavenly Intelligence which Michael had once ruled in the cosmos came down and became in this same head the property of man. (In its original form in the sphere of Michael, the Intelligence bore a purely moral character.) On this path from without to within, from macrocosm to microcosm, the substance of the heavenly Intelligence endured something which was for it equivalent to the transition from the sphere of resurrection to that of death; for the human head is none other than a great graveyard of cosmic thoughts.

The stream which proceeds from the macrocosm exerts its influence upon most people largely by night, in sleep, that is, unconsciously. However, through the strength of the consciously apprehended macrocosmic Michael-impulse, we can with the help of intensive inner meditation and other soul-exercises encompassed by modern spiritual science attempt—even though only in part—to raise this stream to full consciousness. In other words: we can try to strengthen this in ourselves to such an extent that it penetrates not only the head but extends even to the heart. Only by means of such a strengthening of this stream by the Michael-impulse can the Intelligence which formerly belonged to Michael and now resides in the human head reach the region of the heart, there to become a radiant light of thought (compare Rudolf Steiner's words quoted on pp.19–20). This new experiencing by man in his heart (as an organ of cognition) of the heavenly Intelligence which has become established in his head represents a more inward aspect of the festival of Michael.

And so we may see how the Intelligence, which originally abided in the cosmic sphere of resurrection, learnt to know death in the human head in order that it might attain to new life in the heart.

The festival of Easter is altogether different and yet nonetheless spiritually complementary in relation to the festival of Michael. It represents an eternally alive memory of the Mystery of Golgotha which took place *once* on the Earth. We learn from spiritual science that after the Mystery of Golgotha it was no longer possible to find Christ in the macrocosm, on the Sun, but only in the microcosm, that is, in the human soul. There He works, not through the macrocosmic stream proceeding from without and from above to below but through the stream ascending *upwards from below* from microcosm to macrocosm, having as it does its outward reflection in the blood which etherizes in the human heart and which—according to what Rudolf Steiner imparts in the lecture *The Etherization of the Blood*—moves in the opposite direction, from the heart to the head. And since the Mystery of Golgotha the etherized substance of the blood of Christ Himself has also ascended with this stream—from the human heart to the human head and from thence back into the macrocosm.

Although both these streams work constantly within man throughout

52

the yearly cycle, nevertheless with more exact observation it is possible to observe that during the descending half of the year the forces of the macrocosmic stream prevail within man, while during the ascending half the forces of the second, microcosmic, or—as Rudolf Steiner also terms it—'intellectual' stream hold sway, forces which have their origin in the heart. Thus Michael and Christ work together in the cycle of the year. Michael leads man to the point where the world thoughts that have been sent down by him in the autumn from the macrocosm become human thoughts in man's head, so that as they stream back from his heart during spring they may embark as earthly intelligence upon the path of redemption, that is, upon the path of transforming human thoughts back into cosmic thoughts.

If man is able to unite in his heart the Intelligence, which has therein become the light of thought, with the stream of the etherized blood of Christ; if, in other words, man becomes conscious of the immediate presence of the Christ within himself, then through his experience he can make in full consciousness the transition from the realm of death (with which he is, as an earthly being, ever connected), to the universal life of the macrocosm, and raise himself up to the realm of universal resurrection. In so doing, he returns to Michael the Intelligence which he had in former times lost but which has now been purified and restored to life in the Christ-impulse. This is the deeper Michaelic aspect of the festival of Easter, which consists in the transition from death to resurrection in the domain of macrocosmic life.

On this path, however, everything is determined by man's absolute freedom. Thus, only through his free resolve can he receive into himself the new knowledge of Christ imparted to mankind through spiritual science, and so enable the thought-light of Intelligence proceeding from his heart to unite with the forces of the Living Christ, so that it (the Intelligence) may together with these forces find the path from the realm of death to the realm of eternal life—into the macrocosmic sphere of Michael. In this way the one path which can now lead man in full consciousness from human existence to cosmic existence is opened up to him. It was precisely for this, for the purpose of indicating this path (the path of modern Christian initiation) to all human beings that Anthroposophy came into the world. For 'Anthroposophy is a path of knowledge which would lead the spiritual in man to the spiritual in the universe. It enters man's being as a need of his *heart*, of his soul.'[30]

In all this we may see that from the time of the Mystery of Golgotha, for whose fulfilment the birth on Earth of the Nathan Soul was a necessary condition, Michael's mission in the cosmos changed in an essential way. From this time he occupies a quite special position in the cosmos, which not only enables him to begin his ascent to the rank of the Archai but also, from the beginning of the epoch of his new rulership amongst human beings (that is, from the last third of the nineteenth century), to become the guardian of the whole 'descending' half of the year, from the appearance of the first shooting stars in August to Christmas.[31] In spiritual-scientific terms this means that since 1879 Michael, who belongs to the great Sun-sphere, also becomes the guardian of the new Christian path of initiation, the true guide of humanity towards the inner experience of Christmas—the guide through the darkness of winter's night to the birth of the Spirit Sun in the human soul.[32]

4. The Fourth Deed of the Nathan Soul and the Human Faculty of Memory

If we sum up the results of our brief study of the four deeds fulfilled by Christ through the Nathan Soul in the supersensible and the earthly realms, three aspects of these events in particular call for our attention. The first is cosmological and concerns the gradual approach of the Spiritual Sun to the Earth. In the first sacrifice its forces work from the sphere of the fixed stars, in the second from the sphere of the seven planets, and in the third from the sphere of the Moon—from the spiritual environment closest to the Earth. In the language of a more traditional description of the supersensible worlds, this movement of the Spiritual Sun, which is fulfilled at the fourth stage by His direct incarnation in the sphere of the Earth, corresponds to the passage through the regions of higher and lower Devachan and through the astral (elemental) world. Rudolf Steiner speaks of this in the following words: 'Thus Christ gradually approached the Earth. The first and second deeds took place in the world of Devachan, the third in the astral world, and the Event of Golgotha on the physical plane.'[33] The second aspect of these events concerns the successive redemption of the four members of man's being: respectively the physical, etheric and astral bodies, and the ego. And finally, as a third aspect, there is the consolidation in every individual of those basic capacities which he has ever since unconsciously employed during the first three years of his life, prior to awakening of real ego-consciousness, and which he needs in order to be able to walk, speak and think. Thus when we observe the gradual development of these three capacities in a child, we may—in Rudolf Steiner's words—see even today on the earthly plane a direct reflection of the three 'pre-Christian' deeds of Christ accomplished through the mediation of the Nathan Soul.[34]

As has already been indicated, the second and third cosmic events—which laid the foundation for the development of human language in its two aspects, on the one hand for the soul's *inner* experience and on the other for its relationship to the *outer* world—are associated with the child's faculty of speaking. Similarly, the child's faculty of thinking is connected with the third and fourth events. The first of these led in former times to the harmonizing of the primordial thinking in its clairvoyant-like effects, which works—as yet unconsciously for the child—in earliest childhood *from without* on the forming of its bodily organs and is then gradually transformed into an inner, conscious thinking, a faculty for which the foundation was laid on Earth through the Mystery of Golgotha, simultaneously with the rescuing of the ego.

However, there is still a mystery associated with all this. For between the two epochs in child development, on the one hand the time when the child is acquiring the capacities of uprightness, speaking and (as yet unconsciously perceived) thinking and on the other the moment when it for the first time becomes conscious of its ego (approximately from the third year onwards), a further faculty awakens, that of *remembrance* or *memory*. For as a rule a person remembers nothing about the unfolding of the three former faculties, which are associated with the first three cosmic events. He does not remember how he learnt in childhood to walk, speak and think. On the other hand he can, generally speaking, recall very well the first awakening of his ego to conscious life, which is associated with the beginning of the work of *inner* thinking—that is, with the two faculties engendered by the central, fourth event (the Mystery of Golgotha). (In his book *Theosophy*, Rudolf Steiner cites in this connection an experience of this kind on the part of Jean Paul.)[34a]

In other words, between the three cosmic events or 'preparatory stages' of the Mystery of Golgotha and the Mystery of Golgotha itself there lie two further *earthly* events which are associated with the awakening of the individual *memory* and man's *inner thinking*—a thinking that arises through the 'outer' thinking coming directly from the spiritual (astral) world (and therefore in the little child still having the character of forces that work in an unconscious way), at a particular moment diving down into the individual and then becoming manifest as an inner activity which issues from him and which he himself carries out.

The first of these two earthly events is the incarnation, as celebrated at Christmas, of the Nathan Soul on the Earth in the person of the Jesus child described in the Gospel of St Luke. The second event is the mystery of the Baptism of Jesus in the Jordan, Epiphany, when the cosmic Being of Christ united with him. Of course, Christ was already connected with Jesus before this moment, that is, during the time between his birth and the Baptism, though He worked upon him more from without.[34b] After the Baptism in the Jordan, however, He unites Himself completely with him and begins to work *from within,* as a result of which He accomplishes macrocosmically that process which on a microcosmic scale the faculty of thinking brings about in the growing child when at a certain moment it shifts its earthly focus from without to within.

Thus in addition to the three human faculties—associated with the three *cosmic* events—of uprightness (walking), speaking (in its inner and outer aspects) and primordial (outwardly absorbed) thinking, the emergence of which we do not usually remember, there are three further faculties which are connected with earthly or cosmic-earthly events and whose awakening within us we subsequently recall very well. These are the faculties of self-remembering, of conscious (inner) thinking and finally the awakening of ego-consciousness, with their macrocosmic correspondences at the Turning Point of Time to the events of Christmas, Epiphany and the Mystery of Golgotha.

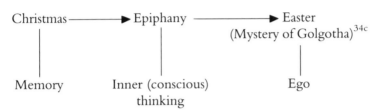

The fact that we remember (our first memory of outer events, our first memory of what we have thought, our memory of the awakening of ego-consciousness) is due to the archetypal pictures of these faculties being already *earthly* or cosmic-earthly events, whereas the archetypal pictures of the three other faculties, whose awakening we do not remember in later life, are purely *cosmic* events, that is, they are such that their reality can either be experienced in the spiritual world before birth or as a result of modern initiation.

In the chapter on the Mystery of Christmas it is therefore necessary that we concern ourselves at some length with the first, the Mystery of Memory.

Rudolf Steiner repeatedly speaks in his lectures about the significance of the deep connection which exists between human memory and the forces of the individual ego.[35] And this could not be otherwise. For the ordinary human memory is only an outward and thoroughly imperfect reflection of that mighty and all embracing 'inner memory' which every human ego secretly bears within itself from one incarnation to the next. From this is gradually fashioned that mature fruit of past Earth-lives which in each sojourn in the spiritual world between death and a new birth becomes the foundation of our future karma, thus forming that individual and unbroken thread which binds together all one's separate incarnations as the single ego-principle that permeates them all.

This hidden 'memory', this faculty of an individualized 'cosmic memory' which forms the foundation of our self-conscious ego and represents that substance in which the macrocosmic Ego of the Christ may dwell, was brought to all humanity and to each individual human being by the Nathan Soul through its birth on the Earth; it brought this gift to human beings at that very time when they were about to lose their 'hidden memory', to forget about their original connection with the spiritual worlds, with their true home.

It brought as a Christmas gift to the Earth, to all 'men of good will', a living memory of the paradisaical origin of mankind, the first tidings of the original immortality of the individual human ego. For to be 'immortal' means 'to have the power to be able to preserve in one's memory that part of existence which has passed away'.[35a]

In so far as the yearly rhythm is concerned, this fourth deed of the Nathan Soul corresponds—as we have already observed—to Christmas,[36] which may most appropriately be called the festival of *Memory*. For the Nathan Soul, who was once born at this season, is the bearer of the only—still wholly paradisaical—etheric body that was untouched by the Fall, and is the guardian of the *cosmic memory of all mankind*.[37] From the beginning of time it preserved in the high Sun-sphere the purest *memory* (untouched by temptation) of mankind's distant origin in the divine-spiritual worlds, and it is in itself the direct, living embodiment of those esoteric words which became known to the world through the occult traditions of Rosicrucianism: '*Ex Deo nascimur.* From God, mankind has being.' These words bear within them the whole inner content of the festival of Christmas.

5. The Time of Advent and the Four Mystery Virtues of Antiquity

If we contemplate the whole history of the evolution of ego-humanity on Earth from the ancient Lemurian epoch until the Mystery of Golgotha, we may see that it was rescued during this time from four great dangers through the cosmic and earthly deeds of the Sun Being of Christ and also of that being who we know as the Nathan Soul, thanks to whose four sacrifices this rescuing of humanity became at all possible.

Every year on 25 December we call to mind the birth on Earth of the Nathan Soul, this pure archetypal soul of Adam, while on the previous day, 24 December, we celebrate the day of Adam and Eve, thus bringing together the beginning and the end of the heavenly and earthly history of the Nathan Soul.

As we have already observed, the time from the autumnal Michael festival (29 September) until Christmas is a period of deep inner trial. In the cycle of the year this period corresponds to the cosmic prehistory of mankind, in the course of which the three preparatory stages of the Mystery of Golgotha took place. The radiant light of the Sun is waning at this time, and the growing intensity of the night is an indication of that condition which humanity increasingly entered at the time of the events of Palestine. Rudolf Steiner characterizes this period of the year as that of 'the temptation by evil'. For at this time the opposing luciferic and ahrimanic powers approach man again and again with particular strength, even though in different forms from those of earlier epochs of his evolution when they were repulsed by the deeds of Christ wrought through the Nathan Soul.

However, that which in ancient times bore a more outward character—a temptation which proceeded from without and a redemptive deed similarly proceeding from without, from the expanses of the heavenly world— becomes after the Mystery of Golgotha, and especially from the beginning of the consciousness-soul epoch, a purely *inward* process. Forces of temptation now approach man from within, from the most hidden grounds of his being, and it is only in freedom, through his own individual efforts, that he can accomplish inwardly what the Nathan Soul formerly accomplished for all mankind from out of the cosmos. The human soul has the task at this time of year of achieving an inner repetition of the cosmic deeds of the Nathan Soul through the strengthening of its own moral-spiritual forces.

59

Those words from the ancient Mysteries, 'Guard against evil' ('*Hüte dich vor dem Bösen*'),[38] which relate to the autumnal time of Michael, are an indication of the preparation required for the impending trials. One may feel how the voice of Michael himself, summoning us to wakefulness and responsibility at the dawning of this season, can be heard in them. However, the forces which we need for withstanding these inner trials are accessible to us only through rightly experiencing the Michael festival, the essential mood of which Rudolf Steiner describes in words that we have already quoted in part: 'In the festival of Michael one should feel with the fullest intensity in one's soul: if I do not want to sleep like someone who is half dead—so that my consciousness of self between death and a new birth is dulled—but instead wish to pass in full clarity through the portal of death, I must, in order to do this, awaken my soul through inner energy before death. First the awakening of the soul, then death, in order that, in death, that resurrection may be celebrated which man himself celebrates within.'[39]

Thus a true enlivening of our soul through the 'Michael thought' can impart to us that inner power of resurrection which in the ensuing period of the dying of our environment of earthly nature will enable us to *keep fully awake* and so find the inner forces to accomplish those deeds which the Nathan Soul accomplished in former times out in the cosmos. *Thus at the time of his autumnal festival, Michael summons us to set forth upon the path of inner imitation of the Nathan Soul.* What was then achieved without man's participation and only through the help of the higher worlds is now to be accomplished through his own inner *moral development.*

Only through the soul's moral development can evil be truly vanquished. Thus the task in this time is that of developing quite definite *soul qualities.* And in so far as this particular time of year still in a certain sense reflects the 'pre-Christian' evolution of humanity,[40] so must we seek the necessary qualities in the sanctuaries of the ancient Mysteries. These are the qualities which later become known as the four 'Platonic virtues' of justice, temperance (prudence), courage (presence of mind) and wisdom. With the help of these four soul qualities and a right conception of the festival of Michael, man has now to forge for himself an inner weapon against those forces of temptation which at this particular season he stands to encounter in his own sheaths, into which they seemingly penetrate from without. In this sense the process referred to is essentially one of *self-knowledge*, of a gradual approach to a conscious meeting *with the Lesser Guardian of the Threshold.*

Four kinds of temptation approach the human soul in the period from the festival of Michael until Christmas, though their influence upon man becomes particularly strong at the time of Advent, when in outer nature

60

the preponderance of the forces of darkness over those of light attains its peak.

Thus, in the first week of Advent the seductive forces of Lucifer and Ahriman approach, in particular, man's physical body. They strive to draw a veil of illusion over his outer and inner perceptions with the help of 'irrefutable' proofs of the triumph of death and mineralization in nature, and hence to destroy the right relationship between man and the world. If man succumbs to this temptation, he is threatened with the danger of losing his inner sense of independence, of being deprived of his 'uprightness' and this would inevitably plunge him into the depths of *despair*, into a real inner death. Thus in order to counteract this first temptation, man needs to develop to a high degree the virtue of *justice* within his soul: a sensitive inner receptivity to the just cosmic forces which rule everywhere in nature and in man and which have their ultimate source in the twelve spheres of the zodiacal circle, in the twelve cosmic initiates, the great guardians in our world of the cosmic justice reflected in the world karma lived out in nature and in man.[41]

It is not for nothing that this purely spiritual perception of world justice, which works everywhere as the revelation of universal karma and finds its microcosmic reflection in the human soul as the karma of the individual, is connected with the inner process which corresponds to man's attaining of uprightness, for in deep antiquity individual karma entered into human evolution simultaneously with this uprightness. 'Only now is karma beginning,' observes Rudolf Steiner. 'Human karma only became possible when man began to employ his hands for his work. Until then there was no such thing as individual karma. It was an important step in human evolution when man was changed from a horizontal into a vertical being and liberated his hands.'[42]

In the second week of Advent the opposing powers approach more the etheric body, where they attempt to awaken all inclinations leading to an egoistic and immoderate growth of desires, to a luxuriant proliferation of the life-forces. What at the beginning of the Atlantean epoch had, rather, to do with the physiological processes of our body now extends into a more inward and etheric soul-experience. At this time, inner instincts seek to rule man in a quite particular way. Everything which as unbridled egoism, as every kind of self-love, continues to nestle in the hidden depths of our character, all the one-sided aspects of our temperament, these now stir within us like a boundlessly expanding sea of poisonous plants. However, the forces of opposition lay particular emphasis upon approaching our faculty of speech, in that they try to make it in a spiritual sense their weapon or, pictorially speaking, they attempt to turn our tongue into a malicious serpent's sting rather than a fiery, twin-bladed sword of truth. Such an onslaught on the part of the opposing forces in our etheric body can only be resisted by the virtues of *temperance* and *prudence*, consciously developed with all the strength of our soul. These mobile, inner virtues are particularly capable of keeping our life-organism in a state of equilibrium, just as the seven planets of our solar system support one another through the unity and interdependence of their movements, thus attaining the highest degree of harmony with the greatest moderation in the use of their forces. Thus until it became possible through the Mystery of Golgotha for every human ego to gain access to the cosmic substance of love, the virtues of temperance and prudence were—in the 'pre-Christian' Mystery-centres of ancient times—the only means whereby the soul could strive to overcome the egoism which was the source of the wishes and desires that were constantly overpowering man's being. On the other hand the development of these two virtues also helped the pupil of the Mysteries to penetrate the profound secrets associated with the forming of speech in the human organism.

Rudolf Steiner describes the process of the fashioning of human speech in connection with his studies of the ancient Mysteries of Ephesus: 'And so the pupil of Ephesus was made aware of the fact that when he speaks a wave pours from his lips—fire, water—fire, water. However, this is none other than the reaching of the word up to the thought, and the flowing of the word down to the feeling. Thus do both thought and feeling weave in speech, in that, in the living wave-movement of speech, air is refined into fire, condensed into water and so forth.' (In this same lecture, Rudolf Steiner goes on to indicate that this 'watery element' of speech is 'like the secretions of a gland' in the human organism.)[43] It is evident from this description that in order that the word—which is diffused through the element of air—might be fully freed from egoism and thus become, as human Logos, a true expression of the world Logos, it was necessary to overcome both the luciferic forces, which penetrate that element of speech that unites with thought, and the ahrimanic forces, which work in that element of speech which flows, droplike, down into feeling. In order to purify the 'ascending' element of speech the pupil had to develop the virtue of prudence, while for the 'descending' element he needed the virtue of temperance. For only through a proper balance between prudence and temperance can human speech gradually approach its great macrocosmic archetype.

In the third week of Advent, luciferic and ahrimanic forces approach the third member of man's being, his astral body. Here they try to awaken all manner of passions, fears and anxieties. Man is filled with paralysing terror before the approaching threshold of the spiritual world, engendered by forebodings of its Guardian, and also with fear of the impending division of his inner being into thinking, feeling and willing. He fears not only the loss of inner equilibrium but also his own self, in that he is aware of a tendency in his three soul-forces to turn into wild, ungovernable animals—the rapacious eagle, the roaring lion, the angry bull—which would assault and devour him. However, if man does not have the inner strength consciously to meet these three monsters which lie in wait for him, an all-absorbing fear will then pass into the subconscious depths of his being, while his consciousness will be given over to self-illusion. In daily life this is expressed as a heightened form of *deceitfulness*. For all lies spring ultimately from a subconscious fear, while the utterance of even the smallest truth demands a significant degree of courage. Furthermore, all intolerance towards the thoughts and opinions of others derives from the same subconscious cowardliness. In all this there is an indication of the decisive importance of working upon that virtue of fortitude, *bravery* or—in a more general sense—of a constant *presence of mind*, the capacity never to lose hold of oneself in any situation, which from an esoteric point of view corresponds to the ability to maintain the three fundamental soul-forces of thinking, feeling and willing in harmonious interaction and perfect balance.

For the spirit-pupil, however, there is a further point. For the virtue of fortitude is necessary not merely in order that the division of the personality at the threshold of the spiritual world may be endured but also for a true orientation in this same world. Hence a right mode of *thinking* is for him of particular significance even here in the physical world of the senses. For only a strict schooling in thinking in the sense of Rudolf Steiner's *Philosophy of Freedom* (*Philosophy of Spiritual Activity*) can gradually develop in the soul of the pupil the capacity to distinguish between truth and falsehood also in the world of spirit.[44]

The modern form of initiation, which is clearly manifested in the life of Rudolf Steiner and described in his books *Knowledge of the Higher Worlds* and *Occult Science*, can be attained in our time only through the fact that the spiritual experiences derived through *consciously immersing oneself* in the spheres of feeling and will, which in their hidden nature already inhabit a purely spiritual world, are constantly controlled and permeated by the light of a higher 'sense-free thinking'. The acquisition of a sense-free thinking which is capable of approaching the facts and events of the spiritual world is therefore the foundation stone of modern initiation.[45] Rudolf Steiner emphasizes its particular significance for the path of modern spirit-pupilship in the following words: 'Inner firmness at the stage of imaginative knowledge will be attained if the soul's contemplations [meditations] which have been described are supported by what is generally called "sense-free thinking" ... The surest and most accessible path for the spirit-pupil to come to such sense-free thinking can be that of making the facts communicated to him by spiritual science the property of his thinking.'[46] And further: 'The path that leads through the communications of spiritual science to sense-free thinking is certainly a sure one. There is another path, which is more sure and above all more exact, but also for many people more difficult; it is set forth in my books, *The Theory of Knowledge Implicit in Goethe's World-Conception* and *The Philosophy of Freedom*. These writings speak of what human thought can achieve when thinking is given over not to impressions of the physical world of the senses but *to itself alone*. Then pure thinking works ... as a being which is inwardly alive ... These writings occupy a very important intermediate stage between knowledge of the sense-world and of the spiritual world ... Anyone who feels himself to be able to experience the effect of this intermediate stage is following a sure, pure path.'[47]

The development of thinking for the new path of initiation is a fundamental necessity in the present cycle of world-evolution, for only in his thinking does the individual of today attain true freedom on the Earth. And from this freedom he must then forge for himself the Michaelic sword of 'sense-free thinking' so as to ward off the luciferic and ahrimanic powers, which approach him from the depths of his own soul and lie in wait for him in the underlying spiritual regions of feeling and will. The *courage to have thoughts*, courage in the realization and experience of one's own freedom—this is the virtue that most fully corresponds to the inner experience of the third sacrifice of the Nathan Soul, which is associated with the great imagination of the Archangel Michael (or St George) conquering the dragon.

Finally, in the concluding fourth week of Advent the opposing forces approach what is at once the highest and also the most inward of the principles that are developed in man today—his ego. This period immediately before Christmas, when—in contrast to summer—man is most fully abandoned by the highest cosmic rulership and, hence, most fully left to himself, is that short interval when there opens up for every individual, on the one hand, the opportunity for the deepest self-knowledge and, on the other, the greatest danger of falling prey to all manner of illusions in this regard.

Already in ancient times, the period immediately before the winter solstice was revered as the season of the greatest mystery, in the course of which man inwardly approached the threshold of the spiritual world and—though imperceptibly for ordinary consciousness—is confronted by the

64

Lesser Guardian of the Threshold. The principal efforts of the luciferic and ahrimanic forces are directed at this time to ensuring that people do not pass *consciously* through this experience or, in other words, to denying them real self-knowledge. To this end, Lucifer strives to dissolve man's self-knowledge in clouds of mysticism, in dreams and fancies about himself; while Ahriman seeks to bind him with a net of hard, dry thoughts and concepts which are incapable of approaching his inner being. Thus the opposing forces strive to hide from man's view those distortions which they themselves have—in the course of his previous earthly lives—contributed to the evolution of his ego, and which with right spiritual training should at this stage come before man in objective form, in the aspect of the Lesser Guardian of the Threshold. One could also say that, at this time, when the gates leading to the higher worlds would, in the course of the yearly cycle, open up for every individual, Ahriman tries in every possible way to ensure that man does not notice this, while Lucifer allows him into the spiritual world by *circumnavigating* the Guardian of the Threshold. Rudolf Steiner says of this latter situation: 'If man were to enter the spirit-soul world without meeting the Guardian of the Threshold, he would fall into one error after another.'[48]

This twofold temptation can also come to expression in the form of a particular inner condition related to that of *losing one's memory* inasmuch as the Guardian of the Threshold wishes initially to reveal to the human soul the objective results of its past activity, the objectivized *essential memories* of the individual karma associated with a human ego. For just as the Akashic Chronicle is the bearer of the world-memory of our whole cosmos, so the Guardian of the Threshold is the bearer of the world memory of each individual human.

In contradistinction to this world memory, however, there is the ordinary faculty of memory of the person concerned. (Not for nothing does Rudolf Steiner speak of its steady deterioration in the course of rightfully pursued spirit-pupilship.) This 'lower memory', which serves as the foundation for an individual's experience of his lower self, must be fully overcome in the process of spiritual development,[49] and this is achieved through the gradual ascendancy of the world memory associated with the higher, immortal ego.

Thus the whole of a person's past karma, which forms an essential part of the inner content of his ego, is a matter of deep recollection, of profound memory, and it is the task of a true self-knowledge to gain mastery over it. Hence to stand before the Lesser Guardian of the Threshold demands from the pupil who passes through such an experience consciously a significant degree of bravery and courage—which, however, he must have already acquired at the previous stage through overcoming the fear induced by the division of his personality. This division is by then already complete, as the appearance of the Guardian of the Threshold bears witness: 'It is through this meeting that the pupil first becomes aware of the fact that his thinking, feeling and willing have freed themselves from the connections that have been implanted in them.[50] From this it becomes clear that the *presence of mind* that has been achieved at the previous stage is essentially the beginning of sensing the invisible presence and rulership of man's higher ego, which alone is capable of again bringing his scattered soul-forces into harmony with one another. But this stage demands not only courage of soul and the strength objectively to recollect the experiences and events of the past year but, in a wider sense, an objective remembering of one's whole past life. To this belongs one further special quality; this is the so-called fourth Platonic virtue, that of *wisdom*.

It has already been observed that man is most fully abandoned by the cosmic rulership—represented in outer nature principally by the forces of the Sun, which are now at the minimum extent of their influence upon man—in the days immediately before Christmas. As never before he is now left to himself. One could say that he is invited at this time of year to take his inner development fully into his own hands for a short while, for the world-wisdom seems to withdraw from him. He is alone and must go on through life drawing strength from those inner forces which his ego has already won for itself as its own forces of wisdom, which, in other words, he has been able to raise from his ordinary lower self to his higher immortal self. And so this is, in a particular way, a touchstone for all that an individual has achieved in his spiritual development. For the question now follows: is it possible for him from now on to take upon himself full responsibility for his own spiritual development, can he go on alone without the support of either inner or outer help?

In this regard, enshrouded in the darkness of winter's night, the Guardian of the Threshold speaks to every individual at the approach of Christmas, although most people are not aware of it: 'Step not across my threshold before you realize that you must yourself illumine the darkness ahead of you; take not a single step forward until you are certain that you have enough oil in your own lamp.'[51] While to the spirit-pupil, who experiences this meeting consciously, the Guardian speaks these words: 'I am that very being who has formed a body out of your noble and ignoble doings. My spectral form is woven out of the entries in the ledger of your life. Until now you have borne me invisibly within yourself. But it was well for you that this should be; for the *wisdom* of your destiny, though hidden from you, has thus also worked within you to eliminate the hidden flaws in my form. Now that I have come out of you, *that hidden wisdom too has departed from you*; henceforth it will pay no further heed to you—it will leave the work in your hands alone. I must become a perfect and splendid being in myself if I am not to fall prey to corruption—and if that were to happen I should drag you too down with me into a dark, corrupted world. If you would avoid this, then your *own wisdom* must become great enough to take over the task of that other, hidden wisdom which has departed from you.'[52]

From these words, it is absolutely clear why a heightened development of 'one's own wisdom', as the highest inner virtue, is appropriate at precisely this time of year. The bearer of wisdom in man is the higher self; and so the pupil must now, from out of his own forces, embark upon the task of purifying his negative karma, which comes objectively before him in the image of the Lesser Guardian of the Threshold. For this being, the Guardian of the Threshold, 'places a particular task' before the pupil. He must, with the help of his newborn [higher] self, lead and guide what he is in his ordinary self and what appears to him in the image ... One should observe what appears as the double, as the "Guardian of the Threshold", and compare it with the "higher self" so as to be able to see the discrepancy between what one is and what one is to become. In the course of such observations, however, the "Guardian of the Threshold" begins to take on a quite different form. It comes to represent an image of all the *obstacles* that stand in the way of the development of the "higher self".' One begins to realize what a burden one drags about in one's ordinary self.'[53] And the 'burden', these obstacles, which we bear within us on the path to our higher self, is the result of the real presence within us of the forces of Lucifer and Ahriman, and it is this that is revealed to the pupil at this stage. Only through the encounter with the Guardian of the Threshold can the pupil meet these opposing powers face to face. The pupil perceives them not as vague forces, rising up out of the depths to tempt his soul, but as real beings of the spiritual world endowed with will and consciousness.

Rudolf Steiner describes this experience in the fifth chapter of *Occult Science* as follows: 'In this double there could be perceived all those qualities which man's ordinary self possesses as a result of the influence of the Lucifer-forces. But there is a further power which, through the influence of Lucifer, has entered man's soul in the course of human evolution. It is that which is known as the power of Ahriman ... What the human soul has become under the influence of this force, that is what is indicated by the form which arises in the experience that has been characterized.'[54]

Thus the Guardian of the Threshold at this stage reveals to the pupil's spiritual sight the true form of both Lucifer and Ahriman, showing him the nature of their influence upon the human ego and also indicating those paths whereby they seek to draw this fourth and most inward member of man's being into temptation.

However, the experiences of this stage of the spiritual path are not confined merely to knowledge of the activity of the forces of opposition in the sheaths of human beings. No one would be able to bear this difficult ordeal in the right way if something else did not approach him from the other side. This is an altogether new sensation, and is connected with the first stirrings in the pupil of his higher self. Rudolf Steiner describes this experience in the following words: 'His [the pupil's] *lower* self is before him as a mirror image only; but within this image there appears the true reality of the *higher* self. The form of the spiritual ego becomes visible out of the picture of the lower personality.'[55] One now begins to understand why there is such a need to develop a right thinking at the previous stage, for '... it is at this [new] stage of development especially that training in sound judgement and clear, logical thinking proves its value ... No one can give birth to a healthy higher self who does not live and think in a healthy way in the physical world. A natural and rational way of living is the basis of all true spiritual development ... Indeed, one *must* live in this way if the higher self is to come into the world as a fully developed being,'[56] writes Rudolf Steiner. And in his other work on this theme, he continues his thought thus: 'It is of the greatest significance that the spirit-pupil has attained a quite definite condition of soul when he becomes conscious for the first time of a newly born ego. For it is through his ego that man is the ruler of his sensations, feelings and ideas, his inclinations, desires and passions. Perceptions and ideas cannot be left wholly to the soul. They must be governed by the laws of thinking. And it is the ego which, ruled by these laws of thinking, with their help brings order into the life of thoughts and ideas. The same is true with desires, inclinations, dispositions and passions. Ethical laws become the rulers of these soul-forces.'[57] Through these words we may feel how very important it is to work before the birth of the higher self upon developing the inner virtues of justice, temperance, prudence and courage in sense-free thinking, continual presence of mind, and wisdom; for these lead the pupil directly into the supersensible world. Truly, it is impossible *rightly to attain the birth of the higher self* in the human soul without developing these virtues.

6.   The Trial by Solitude

From all that has been said we may see that the four holy weeks of Advent offer the most favourable opportunity in the yearly rhythm for true *self-knowledge*. For as at this time the Earth, with respect to the macrocosm, is, in the period of its greatest in-breathing, living its own secluded life quite separate from the rest of the cosmos, so is man at this time most predisposed to self-contemplation and self-knowledge, to becoming truly aware of the activity of the forces of opposition in the four members of his being. But this is not all. The human individual is passing, together with the Earth, through the period when he is most fully abandoned by the spiritual world, that is, through the period of his greatest freedom in the course of the year. This time, which ends just before Christmas with the meeting—for the most part unconscious—with the Guardian of the Threshold, witnesses the gradual weakening of the hold which the spirits of the higher Hierarchies have upon him.

Thus in the first week of Advent the influence of the Archai withdraws to some extent from the individual, in order that, through his own power of justice, he might aspire to interests that are common to all mankind. In the second week the Folk Spirit, an Archangel, withdraws to a certain degree, thus placing before him the task of rediscovering in full freedom a connection with this Folk Spirit through imbuing his speech with true idealism. Finally, in the third week the influence of a person's Guardian Angel withdraws from the deepest layers of his astral body, with the result that the connection of the three soul-forces of thinking, feeling and willing with the people in his immediate environment—which would otherwise be left to the working of his destiny—must become, to a significantly greater extent than before, the consequence of his own conscious work. And all this is necessary in order that in the course of the last weeks before Christmas one may be able to endure the inner trial of *total solitude*, which for the spirit-pupil is associated with the further broadening of his experiences at the threshold of the spiritual world. Rudolf Steiner describes those experiences thus: 'What actually happens is that the pupil adds a new body to his finer soul-body. He puts on another garment. Hitherto he has made his way through the world with the sheaths enveloping his personality and what he had to accomplish for his community, his people, his race and so on was looked after by higher Spirits who made use of his personality [that is, mainly Angels, Archangels and Archai]. A further revelation now made to the pupil by the Guardian of the Threshold is that henceforth these Spirits will withdraw their guiding hands from him. He must step right out of his community. And as an isolated individual he would become rigidly hardened within himself, he would head for destruction, if he did not himself acquire the powers that are inherent in the Folk and Race Spirits.'[58] 'The Guardian of the Threshold now draws aside a veil which hitherto had concealed deep mysteries of life. The Family, Folk and Race spirits are revealed in their full reality, so that the pupil sees clearly how he has been led up to now, and no less clearly that he will henceforth no longer have this guidance.'[59]

Thus the 'trial by solitude' at this stage becomes the deepest and most difficult experience for the pupil. No one who wishes to follow the modern path of initiation *in the right way* is able to avoid it. Rudolf Steiner describes this 'cosmic feeling of solitude' in one of his lectures as follows: 'On the one hand one experiences the grandeur of the world of ideas which embraces all things; on the other hand one experiences with the deepest bitterness that one must separate oneself from space and time if one wishes to remain with one's ideas and concepts. Isolation! One experiences an icy coldness. And then it is revealed to one that the world of ideas has drawn together as though into a point, into the point of isolation. One experiences: now you are alone in your isolation. It is necessary that one is able to experience this. One then experiences the disturbing loss of trust in this world of ideas, an experience which is profoundly upsetting to the soul. One then experiences oneself saying: perhaps all this is only you yourself, perhaps all that is true in these laws is what lives in the point of your own isolation. Then one experiences, infinitely enlarged, every doubt regarding existence.'[60] With these words, we have a description from a more 'inward' aspect of certain feelings that arise when the individual experiences for the first time being fully left to his own resources and having to pass through the tormenting process of 'doubting existence'. Can his own wisdom now become his soul guide, his inner light, leading him on through the darkness of winter's night to the new birth of the Sun Spirit? This question, which in itself is a most profound human experience, stands with full force before the pupil *at the threshold* of the higher worlds. In order to answer it in a positive way, and thus find at this fourth stage the path from solitude and doubt in existence to the temple of higher knowledge, it is necessary in the course of the three previous weeks of Advent to endure three 'occult trials'.

However, before we proceed to characterizing these trials more fully in connection with the seasonal round, a further positive aspect of this solitude needs to be considered. For in reality it is none other than a reaction of the spiritual world to the egoism that every individual brings with him in his astral body on the path to its threshold, which is why solitude constantly increases as one approaches it: 'One has a sense of increasing solitude, of icy solitude. This icy solitude is also part of what one experienced in this inner psychic tumult, and it is this same quality which cures one from allowing egotism to run riot.'[60a] Thus only one thing can help a person if he is, in spite of everything, to reach the threshold and to cross it without losing himself in cosmic solitude—he must make the most intense efforts to expand his own egoistic interests: '... [he must] make the interests common to mankind and the world more and more his own'. In the inner development of a person who has followed the path of modern spirit-pupilship, this can lead to what in western Christendom is in the cycle of the year commemorated on Christmas Eve, 24 December, the day of Adam and Eve, the day that is dedicated to the memory of the primordial, paradisaical condition of mankind, the representative of which is the Nathan Soul born on Earth on 25 December.

For this reason this time of year would appear to be especially suitable for approaching on the path of modern spirit-pupilship that inner experience which Rudolf Steiner describes as follows: 'When these two elements—the egoism which expands to world interests and the frosty solitude—join forces, one draws ever nearer to the Paradise imagination. And when this imagination has been engendered in the living way that is appropriate to it, the time will have come when the meeting with the Guardian of the Threshold is experienced in the right way.' (See Appendix 1.)

This does not in any sense mean a return to the original paradisaical condition of mankind, for evolution must continue and not go backwards. Nevertheless, the *picture* or *imagination* of Paradise must appear before the soul of the pupil at the threshold, since he can only enter once again into the higher world—though now in full consciousness—where he formerly left it in the course of his descent to the Earth. Thus the imagination of Paradise appears here as a living testimony that he will enter the spiritual world in the right way. He should then unite himself with this imagination of Paradise and receive it into himself as a guide on his further path. Rudolf Steiner then continues: 'Only when a person has progressed sufficiently, when the icy solitude has become his teacher to the extent that he is able to make the interests of the world his own, does he pass the Guardian of the Threshold. He can then feel what may be called the union with the Paradise imagination; he becomes one with it. He feels himself to be within it.' This wholly occult experience, which—as said—is accessible only on the path of modern spirit-pupilship, corresponds esoterically to what Christian humanity experiences exoterically when it turns with its best thoughts and feelings to the Holy Child lying in the manger, who restored to mankind the paradisaical forces by making the imagination of Paradise manifest to it through his being.

7. The First Three Weeks of Advent as Three Stages of 'Occult Trials'

The chapter in the book *Knowledge of Higher Worlds: How is it Achieved?* that is expressly devoted to the process of initiation begins with a description of the three 'trials' that serve to develop certain soul-qualities within the pupil which are absolutely necessary if initiation is to be passed through in the right way. It is, moreover, not difficult to feel that the most suitable period in the cycle of the year for these inner trials is the time after the festival of Michael and, in particular, the *first three weeks of Advent.*

The first 'trial' which is spoken of in *Knowledge of the Higher Worlds: How is it Achieved?* is called 'the trial by fire'. Through this the true spiritual foundations of all earthly things are revealed to the pupil: first '... lifeless things, then of plants, animals and human beings.'[61] It is as though a shroud falls away from all the objects and beings of the world around him and 'they then lie disclosed—naked—before the beholder ... [and this] is connected with a process known as "spiritual burning-away".'[62]

The moral qualities that are being spoken of here are frequently developed by those who have passed through a stern school of life. 'Such people,' writes Rudolf Steiner, 'have passed through manifold experiences of such a kind that their self-confidence, courage and fortitude have been enhanced in a healthy way, and they learn to bear sorrow, disappointment and failure in undertakings with greatness of soul, and above all with equanimity and unbroken strength.'[63] These words summon before one's inner eye the image of a person who is able in all life's storms and tribulations to remain *inwardly upright,* who does not bend beneath the pressure of life but preserves an unshakeable inner trust in the power of the higher justice that invisibly rules the world and sends him 'sorrows, disappointments and failures' as trials.

If the pupil manages to endure this trial, there will—in Rudolf Steiner's words—be revealed to his soul 'the signs of the occult script', which are none other than 'the happenings and beings of the spiritual world'.[64] And he adds: 'The language of things is learnt through these signs.'[65] Through this language, each thing and every being reveals to the pupil the secret name of its origin, that part of the archetypal cosmic Word that once created our world which rests upon its particular foundation. Hence this experience gradually becomes for the pupil the beginning of a penetration into the mystery of the cosmic Word, the divine Logos, and this, in turn, leads him gradually to the next 'trial'. For now the pupil learns to be ruled in his actions not by his own egoistic wishes but by world-justice, by the divine purposes of the cosmos which he has been able to recognize through the secret Word that has been revealed to him. This first trial corresponds in its inner character to the spiritual content of the first week of Advent.

The second trial bears the name of 'trial by water'[66] and is a direct continuation of the first. 'This is to prove whether he can move with freedom and certainty in the higher worlds.' The pupil must now carry out a certain action, the substance of which he can come to know only through the inner language which he has learnt, in what he has gleaned at the previous stage, of the 'secret script'. Rudolf Steiner describes the essence of this trial as follows: 'Should he, in the course of his action, introduce any element of his own wishes, opinions, and so forth, or should he for one moment evade the laws he has recognized to be right in order to indulge his own arbitrary will, the result would be altogether different from what should properly come about.'[67] According to Rudolf Steiner, this is largely a matter of developing the quality of *self-control*. But this will be achieved to the highest degree by someone who in everyday life '... has acquired the faculty of following high principles and ideals while setting aside personal predilections, who is capable of always performing his duty when inclinations and sympathies are only too ready to divert him from it ...'[68] Of particular importance at this stage, adds Rudolf Steiner, is the mastery of one further quality, '... an absolutely *healthy and reliable faculty of judgement*.'[69]

It is not difficult to see that these two basic requirements have a close correspondence with the inner qualities associated with the second week of Advent: temperance and prudence. Thus the development of the first of these is made possible through overcoming personal wishes and opinions, whims and egoistic arbitrariness in the fulfilment of higher duties, while the development of the second quality of prudence is dependent on a reliable faculty of judgement. Both of these together enable the pupil to endure this second trial.

If he succeeds in this, the third 'trial' awaits him. Here he has no feeling of a goal. Everything is left in his own hands. He finds himself in a situation where nothing prompts him to act. He must find his way quite alone, from out of himself.[70] 'All that is necessary is that the pupil should quickly be able to come to terms with his own nature, for here he must find his "higher self" in the truest sense of the word. He must instantly decide to listen in all things to the inspiration of the spirit. There is no time for doubt or hesitation ... Whatever keeps him from listening to the voice of the spirit must be boldly overcome. It is essential in this situation to have presence of mind, and the training at this stage is concerned with the full development of this quality.'[71] Here again, ordinary earthly life can be a good occult schooling: 'Individuals who have reached the point of being able to come to a swift decision, without hesitation or much deliberation, when faced with tasks suddenly devolving upon them—for such individuals life itself is a training in this sense.'[72]

If we now recall that just at this time the pupil begins to experience the first consequences of the splitting apart of thinking, feeling and willing, we will understand the deeper meanings of the words, 'developing presence of mind'. This is none other than the constant and fully conscious guidance of the three divided soul-forces by the higher self; while the inner virtue, without which this guidance would not exist (thus making it impossible to pass rightly through this particular trial), is that of *courage*, of *fearlessness*. Only an individual who has developed this virtue to a high degree within himself can, 'without losing himself',[73] accomplish the task which he has set himself. For in the third trial '... he can find the single firm point to which he can hold only within his own being.'[74] To endure such an ever-growing isolation and not to lose, in so doing, the capacity for action, for inner activity—this indeed requires fortitude, the development of which is greatly furthered by a conscious experience of the spiritual content of the third week of Advent, the essence of which is distilled in the words: 'Whatever keeps [the pupil] from listening to the voice of the spirit must be boldly overcome.' In accordance with the terminology of *The Philosophy of Freedom*, we could also say that in this trial one is to accomplish a deed out of the purest impulses of moral imagination.

It is not difficult to see the connection of these trials with all that was said in the chapter 'The Trial by Solitude' about the gradual withdrawal from the individual of the ruling wisdom of the Archai, Archangeloi and Angeloi. For his partial separation from the hierarchic beings who are closest to him is the esoteric reality that stands behind the corresponding trials. Thus the beings of the Hierarchy of the Archai, who passed through their human stage on Old Saturn in bodies of fire and have on Earth risen to the stage of Spirit Man, that of the transformed physical body, gradually withdraw from the rulership of someone who has successfully borne the 'trial by fire'. Similarly, the beings of the Hierarchy of the Archangels, who bear within themselves the fully evolved Life Spirit—the transformed etheric body, whose physical reflection on Earth is the element of *water*—withdraw from the individual who has passed successfully through the 'trial by water'. And finally, the beings of the Hierarchy of the Angels, who have an evolved Spirit Self—that is, a transformed astral body whose physical reflection on Earth is the element of *air*—withdraw their guidance when the 'trial by air' has been successfully withstood.

Thus as he stands, in the final experience of total solitude, at the threshold of the spiritual world, man shows himself as what he has become through the personal efforts which he has directed towards his individual development. For only as he is *in reality* can he enter the temple of higher knowledge.

8. 'Occult Trials' and the Threefold Temptation of Christ in the Wilderness

In considering the esoteric nature of Advent we have been able to see how the three heavenly deeds of the Nathan Soul have come to be inwardly reflected in the form of certain virtues of soul which the individual is to make his own at this time. Furthermore, we were able to examine the extent to which a more intensified and conscious work in this direction leads him to certain purely occult trials which, if successfully withstood, result in a fully conscious, *occult* experience of Christmas as a true festival of initiation, of the birth in his soul of his higher ego. At this point there is, however, one further highly significant question: in what way was this transition from the cosmic to the earthly, from the three heavenly deeds of the Nathan Soul to the three trials of the path of modern Christian initiation, enabled to take place? Through what means did it become possible for the human soul *to make* what the Nathan Soul accomplished in former times in the macrocosm an *inner reality*?

We know from the various descriptions given by Rudolf Steiner that a strict spiritual rule prevails in this realm which ordains that cosmic impulses can be brought into the human sphere only through a quite specific individuality who is incarnate in a human body.[75] Only when the new possibilities or capacities have *once* been realized in all their fullness by this one individuality can they become thereafter the common property of all mankind, that is, able to be developed by *every* human soul. And as we know from all that has been said, the direct karmic consequence of the three heavenly deeds of the Nathan Soul was its incarnation on the Earth and subsequent union with Christ at the Baptism in the Jordan. It is clear that the three trials—in the form in which they are described in Rudolf Steiner's book *Knowledge of the Higher Worlds: How is it Achieved?*—could have entered human evolution only as a result of the events of Palestine. For even the possibility of *enduring* these trials came into the world only through the fact that Christ's first deed on the Earth was an 'earthly' repetition of what had on three occasions been accomplished by Him from the heights of the Sun through the Nathan Soul. And just as in ancient times, in the Lemurian and Atlantean epochs, the three sheaths of man's being were saved through cosmic influences, so an analogous deed was now necessary on *the Earth itself*, the luciferic and ahrimanic forces of temptation, which approach every individual from out of his own sheaths, now had to be resisted. This was the event of the temptation of Christ Jesus in the wilderness, which immediately followed the Baptism in the Jordan. If this event had not occurred, if Christ had not overcome for all mankind the seductive forces of evil working in the three sheaths of Jesus, no one would ever have been able to aspire to withstanding the aforementioned three occult trials through his own forces. As in ancient times, one would have needed abundant help from higher worlds; for one could not have vanquished the forces of temptation out of one's own independent efforts while on the Earth. However, in order that this might happen and that in the course of further evolution the possibility of a new, conscious and free path of initiation might be brought before man, it was necessary to accomplish this deed once *historically* on the physical plane so that its fruits might enter the whole future evolution of mankind as a spiritual ferment.

The first temptation, as it is described in the fourth chapter of St Matthew's Gospel, concerns man's physical body. The tempter in this case approaches Christ with the following words: 'If you are the Son of God, let these stones become bread *through the power of your Word*.'[76] In an occult sense this is possible only through a misuse of those occult forces which are revealed to the pupil when he has entered the sphere of the first temptation. These are the forces that lie at the foundation of the visible world and that ceaselessly create the physical world out of the world of the spirit. In order to master them, the pupil must learn to read the true names of things, the 'occult script', for these forces proceed from the substance of the cosmic Word which lies at the foundation of all things. Hence the tempter, in turning to Christ, says: '. . . let these stones become bread *through the power of your Word*.' And Christ answers: 'Man shall not live by bread alone, but by every Word that proceeds from the mouth of God.'[77] Christ therefore refuses to misuse the spiritual Word, to misuse that authority which is revealed to Him at this stage behind the beings and appearances of the physical world. Thus in His answer there is a real power which works henceforth as a kind of spiritual substance in man's physical body. It enables the pupil on the modern path of initiation to avoid falling into the temptation of using the now emerging spiritual forces in a magical or egoistic way or for the purpose of extending his authority over nature and his fellow humans, but to employ them instead for man's gradual development and for his inner moral perfection. Without this deed of Christ such a misuse of spiritual powers must inevitably have occurred, and on each occasion man would have become *possessed* by these forces as they appeared at this stage. Now, in contrast, he commits himself to living the rest of his life in accordance with 'the Word that proceeds from the mouth of God' and which he can learn to know through study of the 'occult language'. Rudolf Steiner writes of this as follows: 'Through this language the pupil becomes acquainted also with certain rules of conduct, and with certain duties of which he had known nothing. Having come to know these rules he can perform actions endowed with a significance such as the actions of one who is not initiated can never possess. He acts from out of higher worlds. Indications for such actions can be understood only in terms of the occult script.'[78] Thus this first trial is followed directly by a second, which is intended to show whether the pupil is able to fulfil the obligations he has undertaken not only in the earthly world but also—and this is far more difficult—in the spiritual world. The possibility of also living through this new trial in the right way was brought into the world through Christ's overcoming of the second temptation in the wilderness.

In the case of this second temptation the opposing forces approached Christ with the egoistic enticement of wilfully misusing those occult powers which were revealed to Him as He penetrated the etheric body of Jesus of Nazareth and which He recognized through reading the 'secret script'. The words from Psalm 91 which the tempter cites: 'He will give his Angels charge of you, and they will bear you up with their own hands lest you strike your foot against a stone,'[79] were inscribed in the spiritual world in the 'occult language' from the earliest times. The Christ Being was now being invited to use this power not for sacrificial service to the world, but as a proof of His higher magical authority over the Earth's etheric forces. He was to throw Himself down from the heights of the temple in order to accomplish something whereby He would, like someone swimming in water, have no outer support except the indications of the 'secret script'. This deed was to be accomplished not in the name of service to mankind but wholly out of an impulse of pure egoism, for the self-glorification that would accrue through the manifestation of magical capacities. The Christ, however, spurned this temptation, thus introducing into the spiritual evolution of humanity the possibility of using the indications of the 'occult language' *only* for serving divine forces and the higher aims of humanity and the world. He replies: 'You shall serve the divine power *which guides you* and not your own whims.'[80] In other words: you must place yourself in the service of that divine Word which is proclaimed to you in the 'occult language' and follow your higher calling, and not your own egoistic wishes and aspirations. Rudolf Steiner has this to add about this second temptation: 'This [trial] is to prove whether he [the pupil] can move with freedom and certainty in the higher worlds.'[81] '... And he must recognize what he has to do through the understanding he has acquired of the secret script.'[82] But '... should he, in the course of his action, introduce any element of his own wishes, opinions, and so forth, or should he for one moment evade the laws he has recognized to be right in order to indulge his own arbitrary will, the result would be altogether different from what should properly come about.'[83] If Christ had succumbed to the temptation in the wilderness, He would—and this can be said with absolute certainty—have been dashed to pieces on the stones. But as He overcame the second temptation, something was introduced into the etheric bodies of all human beings that works there as a living substance enabling the pupil of the New Mysteries in modern times to place all that he accomplishes in the spiritual world at the sole service of 'the divine Power which guides him'.

The third temptation relates to the astral body. It concerns the possibility of exercising magical powers over all visible and invisible worlds,[84] but in a purely egoistic manner. It is, however, the case that an authority which is in this particular way directed towards the world is completely illusory, in that there stands behind it the need for total submission to the opposing forces (even though in this case it is altogether unnoticed). Christ overcomes this temptation also, and expresses His victory in the words: 'You shall worship the divine Power that guides you, and Him only shall you serve.'[85] In these words we have an example of the highest *fortitude* and the greatest *presence of mind,* which man is able to manifest on Earth only through acknowledging the divine Power of the Father which guides him. And as a result of this third deed of Christ something akin to a light-bearing substance was now instilled into people's astral bodies, through which the modern pupil of spiritual science receives the strength for withstanding the third temptation. Compelled by nothing and no one, out of absolute freedom and total solitude—for at this stage not only the Archai and Archangeloi but also the Angeloi who guide individual human beings have abandoned him—the spirit-pupil accomplishes out of himself a pure sacrificial deed, which he dedicates to that 'divine Power' which he is called to serve: the archetype of this higher obedience is given by Christ Jesus in the answer quoted above. Let us recall what Rudolf Steiner writes about this third temptation: 'All that is necessary is that the pupil shall be able quickly to come to terms with his own nature, for here he must find his "higher self" in the truest sense of the word. He must instantly decide to listen in all things to the inspiration of the spirit. There is no time for doubt or hesitation. Every minute of delay would prove only that he is still unfit. Whatever keeps him from listening to the voice of the spirit must be boldly overcome. It is essential in this situation to have *presence of mind.*'[86]

Let us now try to enter more deeply into the nature of this trial, irradiating it with the light of Christ's third victory over the forces of opposition. According to the Gospel, this third temptation takes place on a high mountain. (Here one may recall the mountain of purgatory described in Dante's *Divine Comedy.*) This mountain, surrounded on all sides by the element of air, is none other than an imagination of the path that leads the pupil of the Mysteries into the astral sphere of the cosmos. Here, in these heights inaccessible to ordinary consciousness, he encounters an ever-growing solitude. 'Nobody who reads this without further acquaintance with these matters,' writes Rudolf Steiner in this connection, 'should feel antipathy at this idea of being thrown back on oneself.'[87] The reasons for this are connected with the pupil's new experiences in his astral body. For only at this stage does he experience the dismembering of his personality, the complete separation of his basic soul-forces. However, this arises in such a way that his thinking extends upwards as though to the fixed stars, his feeling opens out to the spheres of the planets, and his will enters into the very depths of the Earth. Through such a split in his soul-life, the pupil experiences himself as being completely hollow, and this feeling becomes the source of his profound sense of solitude. The pupil now seems to be hanging in the air over an abyss, and he can be overwhelmed by a sense of terror that cannot be compared with anything else... When he is in this condition, the tempter approaches his soul. Instead of showing him the thinking, feeling and willing which a person can in general call his own and which must at this stage be brought again into harmony and unity through the power of the 'higher self' gradually awakening within the pupil, he [the tempter] holds up a luciferic mirror to his soul, as if his thinking would already comprehend the starry spheres, his feeling would govern the movement of the planets and his will would have penetrated the depths of the Earth. It is indeed so that in this condition a person can feel himself to be the owner of all the riches in the world, and the tempter speaks to him about this: 'I want to give you power over all that you see, in the earthly and the super-earthly realms.'[84] This is, however, merely the whole domain of luciferic illusion, which appears as a consequence of a premature division of the personality, before the forces of the 'higher self' have been sufficiently awakened. In such a case, the individual concerned risks entering the spiritual world in an unprepared way, bypassing the Guardian of the Threshold and thus arriving not in the divine but in the luciferic realm, where he will gradually lose his individual human ego altogether. For this reason Rudolf Steiner makes a particular emphasis in his description of this third trial: 'In order not to remain inactive he must not lose himself, for only within his own being can he find the single firm point to which he can hold.'[88]

In the sixth chapter of *Occult Science*, Rudolf Steiner refers from a somewhat different point of view, though one which corresponds precisely to the stage of spirit-pupilship that has been described here, to this danger of the pupil becoming imprisoned in Lucifer's realm. For if the pupil does not have sufficient *presence of mind* for a fully conscious meeting with the Guardian of the Threshold, whom he approaches at this stage, the Guardian of the Threshold can, through the lack of fortitude displayed by the pupil in his quest for self-knowledge, take on an illusory luciferic form. 'Then,' writes Rudolf Steiner, 'one [the pupil] is immersed in the soul–spiritual world but refuses to work further upon oneself. One becomes a prisoner of that form which now stands before one's soul through the Guardian of the Threshold. What is significant is that one does not in this experience have the feeling of being a prisoner. On the contrary, one thinks that one is experiencing something quite different. The form called forth by the Guardian of the Threshold can be such that it evokes in the soul of the observer the impression that this being has, in the images that appear at this stage of evolution, the whole world in all its fullness before him; it is as if one were at the summit of knowledge and had no need to go any further. Far from feeling like a prisoner, one senses oneself to be the immeasurably rich possessor of all the world's secrets.'[89] In these words there is an indication of that danger which threatens the pupil through the working of the opposing forces, which are present in the astral body of every human being. If he is to be able to overcome them, the spirit-pupil needs above all that substance of light which he can find within himself as a latent inner legacy of the victory of Christ Jesus in the third temptation. Through becoming aware of this substance, he has also gained a real strength which enables him to endure the third, and last, trial in the best possible way.[90]

The nature of these three trials, in so far as they are connected with the three temptations of Christ in the wilderness, can also be expressed from a more inward aspect as follows. To the extent that the *outer* guidance of Archai, Archangeloi and Angeloi withdraws from man as he passes through these trials, so—in a right path of development—do there increasingly begin to work *within* him those forces which came to permeate human evolution through Christ Jesus withstanding the temptations in the wilderness. For through the fact that Christ Jesus, in these three victories over the tempters, refused to misuse His cosmic powers which originate in the sphere of the Archai, Archangeloi and Angeloi, He was able to instil them, in a unique way, into human evolution so that they work imperceptibly for all future ages in the depths of human souls, thus enabling those people who strive towards initiation to withstand these trials.

9. The Final Week of Advent.
The Temple of Higher Knowledge

'When this [third] trial has been successfully endured, the pupil may enter the "Temple of Higher Wisdom".'[91] With these words Rudolf Steiner begins the description of the stage of initiation in his book *Knowledge of the Higher Worlds: How is it Achieved?*

When the pupil has, in the course of the first three weeks of Advent, passed through the physical, etheric and astral sheaths and has overcome the forces of temptation that lie therein, he stands before the gates of the spiritual temple which in a sense is none other than an imagination of his own higher ego. The principal virtue which man has to have mastered to a significant degree at this stage of his development and which is also the principal virtue of the fourth, and last, week of Advent (see p.66) is that of wisdom. This is the inner quality which needs most especially to be broadened and deepened at this stage. In this connection, the would-be initiate is bound by that 'oath' which Rudolf Steiner describes as one of the first experiences of the pupil in 'the temple of higher knowledge', that is, in the temple of divine Wisdom.

From this time the vast treasures of world wisdom are directly revealed to the would-be initiate: 'The pupil learns how to apply the occult teaching, how to place it in the service of humanity. He begins really to understand the world.'[92] From now onwards '... everything is left to his own responsibility. He learns that in every situation he has to discover entirely through himself what he has to do. And the "oath" means simply that he is fit to bear this responsibility.'[93]

We have already spoken above (p.65) of how in addition to his ordinary everyday memory, which is the foundation of his ordinary mortal ego, a human being bears within himself an individual world memory which threads like a single stream through all his separate incarnations on the Earth and is connected with his higher, immortal ego. For just as our mortal ego is clothed in the garment of our earthly memory, so is our higher, immortal ego clothed in the garment of world memory, which is at the same time our own karma.

The fact that a person's consciousness is firmly tied to his lower ego forms a considerable obstacle to receiving his higher self. As we have already seen, it is therefore impossible to penetrate the sphere of world memory without overcoming one's ordinary earthly faculty of memory.

Hence it becomes understandable that when the pupil receives the 'draught of forgetfulness' for the lower memory and then the 'draught of remembrance' for the higher, this is none other than a pictorial description of the conscious transition from the lower self to the higher. Such a transition is the most important experience in the 'temple of higher knowledge' and it is also the aim of the whole process of initiation.

The next scene in the Gospel after the temptation in the wilderness, where water is turned into wine at the wedding feast at Cana of Galilee, is an allusion to this inner transformation of memory, which corresponds to the transition from the lower to the higher ego. This is the *first* miracle accomplished by the Christ on Earth. In this scene the water is an imaginative picture of ordinary earthly human memory, which is rooted in man's etheric body, while the wine—a transformed water that arises in the plant through the forces of the Sun's light and warmth—is living. It bears within itself the forces of cosmic life, and is the picture of a memory that is permeated with the cosmic forces of the Sun. And it is with this experience of a living, or as one might say, a *Sun*-memory, that man's first perception of the higher ego is connected. In truth, this is in the deepest sense a marriage ceremony which takes place at the threshold of the profound mystery of the birth of a *new being* in the human soul.

In *Occult Science* Rudolf Steiner refers to this significant experience in the following words: 'At this moment the soul feels as though it has given birth to a new being within itself as its essential soul-kernel. And this being is endowed with qualities that are altogether different from those which were in the soul before.'[94] Of such a nature is one experience of the spirit-pupil. It corresponds to the aforementioned 'bearing of an oath' in 'the temple of higher knowledge'. For 'there is no question of an "oath" in the ordinary sense of the word, but far rather of something learnt by *experience* at this stage of development.'[95] And that is the experience of the higher self. In *Occult Science*, Rudolf Steiner describes as follows two other experiences issuing from this first experience, which concern the relationship of the newborn ego to the lower ego and to the spiritual world without: 'At times we feel ourselves to be outside of that which we generally call our own being, *our* ego. It is as though we were now living, with full awareness, in two egos. One of these is the one we have always known. The other stands over it like a being that is newly born. And we can sense how the first acquires a certain independence with regard to the second.'[96] This experience corresponds to receiving into oneself 'the draught of forgetfulness' in the 'temple of higher knowledge'. Later on we read: 'The second—the newborn—ego can now be led to perception in the spiritual world. What has significance for this spiritual world can be developed therein, just as the sense organs serve as a vessel for the physical world of the

84

senses. When this development attains the appropriate stage, the individual will not feel himself to be simply a newborn ego but he will henceforth perceive around himself spiritual facts and spiritual beings, in the same way that he apprehends the physical world by means of his physical senses. And this is a *third* significant experience.'[97] This corresponds to drinking the 'draught of remembrance' in the 'temple of higher knowledge'. Only through receiving this 'draught' does the pupil become a fully-fledged servant of the temple, a true representative in the world of its esoteric impulses.

And just as, in the cycle of the year, the difficult period of Advent concludes with the birth of the new Sun in the darkness of winter's night, so does this process of initiation end with the birth within the pupil of his higher ego, his inner Spiritual Sun. At this moment the macrocosmic and the microcosmic Christmas are for him united in a single, all-embracing experience.

III

THE MYSTERY OF CHRISTMAS

1. The Christmas Imagination of Anthropos-Sophia

All the experiences described here are (as has been said several times already) the result of consciously treading the modern path of initiation. In the present cycle of evolution this path is not directly associated with the rhythm of the year, though it is nevertheless true that the most suitable time for arriving at these experiences is that of the four weeks of Advent. For at this time before Christmas every man passes unconsciously through his sheaths to his higher ego. And if he, as a pupil of anthroposophically orientated spiritual science, is able to bring to this a corresponding inner development and, above all, the unfolding of certain virtues—justice during the first week of Advent, temperance and prudence during the second, fortitude and presence of mind during the third, and finally wisdom during the fourth—it is then possible for him to attain at Christmas *conscious* experience of the birth of the higher self in his own soul. Then the festival of Christmas becomes for him not merely a festival that is associated with more or less externally understood traditions but with a real inner experience: *the birth of the higher ego out of the mother substance of wisdom* that has been acquired by the soul on the path of inner development. This is, for the soul of the pupil, the fulfilment of the words of Angelus Silesius:

> Christ could in Bethlehem a thousand times be born
> But if not in your soul were you eternally forlorn.[1]

This experience, the result and completion of the path of knowledge, can at Christmas come in a wholly real way before the soul in the form of the following imagination. Beneath the vault of a sublime temple there appears the form of the Virgin Mother, filled with the deepest wisdom, heavenly purity and mildness, with the Child, radiant with spirit-knowledge, in her arms. This image of Mary, which is also described in the Luke Gospel, is according to spiritual science none other than the earthly reflection of the heavenly, divine being of Isis-Sophia, while the Child in her arms—the Jesus of the Nathan house of David—is the Nathan Soul, the heavenly archetype of man, true Anthropos in his paradisaical, unfallen state, now descending to Earth and incarnating in a physical body.

Anthropos—the living soul from the world's beginning—in the arms of mother Sophia is the great Christmas imagination of *Anthropos-Sophia*. It is the picture of the new being born from the substance of Wisdom, that is, of the heavenly Sophia. He is the true Anthropos who is destined to receive into himself the Spirit Sun of Christ. And so *Christmas* is the true festival of Anthroposophy. It is that time of year when on Earth, in the heart of Europe on 25 December 1923, the Foundation Stone of the new Christian Mysteries was laid which stand under the direct guidance of Michael-Christ.[2] And if the evergreen crown of the sublime Christmas tree of the New Mysteries points towards the future and its mighty trunk is an indication of the immediate influence of these Mysteries in the present, so do its roots extend into the distant past to the time when that imagination, which we are now able to experience at Christmas in a purely inward way as the imagination of Anthropos-Sophia, became manifest on the physical plane as a real historical event. For just as the final goal of the Anthroposophy of today is to lead us to a true 'Spirit-vision' through the strict school of ceaseless 'Spirit-mindfulness' (that is, in the first instance through the study of modern spiritual science), so does it also stir in us 'Spirit-recollection', which as a *Christmas act of recollection or remembering* refers us back to the birth in the darkness of winter's night of that Anthropos who has lived since the beginning of time, the Nathan Soul.

Rudolf Steiner speaks about this remembering of the first Christmas night in the following mighty words on the second day of the Christmas Conference: 'We plant this [the soul-light impulse of the Foundation Stone], my dear friends, at the moment when a *human recollection* which really understands the World looks back to that point in human evolution at the Turning Point of Time when amidst the darkness of night and *the darkness of people's moral feeling*, like a shaft of heavenly light, that divine Being was born who then became the Christ, when that Spirit Being came down among humanity ... And so may the feeling of our hearts be turned to the first Christmas night in Palestine ...'[3]

'Practise *Spirit recollection*/In depths of soul ...' these words from the first part of the Foundation Stone Meditation★ may be related in the fullest sense to the festival of Christmas, for at this festival our *remembering* is directed towards an experience of the original 'Ex Deo nascimur', towards the birth in the earthly world of the Nathan Soul, the heavenly archetypal image of man, the true Anthropos. And just as in the experience of the first three weeks of Advent there lives a memory of the three pre-earthly sacrifices of the Nathan Soul, so is the last week of Advent, and in particular its culmination in the festival of Christmas, a memory of the fourth and greatest sacrifice of the Nathan Soul—its incarnation on Earth in order subsequently to receive into itself the Sun of Christ.

★ See Appendix 6 at the end of the book.

2. From Christmas to Epiphany

In the following lines of the Foundation Stone Meditation we have an exact characterization of the condition of the Nathan Soul before its appearance on the Earth, when the particular divine-human ego of this being still dwelt fully in the 'Divine Ego' of the higher Hierarchies of the Sun:

> Soul of Man! . . .
> Practise *Spirit-recollection*
> In depths of soul,
> Where in the wielding
> World-Creator-Life
> Thine own I
> Comes to being
> Within the I of God.

A dim feeling for this ancient condition, which lies hidden in the form of the higher memory in the 'depths of soul' of *every* human soul, can be awakened at Christmas, in so far as this time is particularly favourable for the awakening of the deepest—or highest—memories within man, for a true enlivening of his faculty of memory.

> Practise *Spirit-recollection* . . .
> Then in the All-World-Being of Man
> Thou wilt truly *live*.

The italicized words in the lines that have been quoted from the first part of the meditation, 'Spirit-recollection' and 'live', point towards such an enlivening of the faculty of memory. For only *a remembering that is filled with life* can serve as a thread that is able to lead us in the right way through the thirteen Holy Nights★ which lie between the festival of the birth of Jesus and the festival of the birth of Christ through the Baptism in the Jordan, Epiphany.

In former times, until AD 354, Christmas was still celebrated by the early Christians on 6 January, the festival of Christ's birth in the earthly sphere. In the world of today, however, the central event of this time of year has become the birth of Jesus, which is celebrated on 25 December. This shifting

---

★ Occultly the new calendar day does not begin at midnight but at 6 p.m. the previous evening. Hence The Thirteen Holy Nights are from Christmas Eve through Epiphany Eve.

of the festival was the result of the fact that people had ceased altogether to have any understanding of the *divine* being of Christ, in contrast to the *human* being Jesus of Nazareth. Only on the ground of anthroposophically orientated spiritual science can humanity again acquire a real understanding not merely of the man, Jesus, but also of the cosmic being of the Christ who descended into him at the time of the Baptism in the Jordan. 'Hence in our time,' says Rudolf Steiner, 'an understanding of the Christ-impulse must come to the fore: the path of Christ must be wedded to the path of Jesus.'[4] Through such an understanding, the thirteen Holy Nights again acquire for the anthroposophist their deeply esoteric significance as a real inner path leading from the experience of the earthly mystery of Jesus (25 December) to the experience of the cosmic mystery of Christ (6 January).

'*From Jesus to Christ*'—these words are an indication of the esoteric nature of the thirteen Holy Nights; while the thread that can serve as a guide along the path which leads from 'thine own I' to 'God's I', to living in 'the All World-Being of Man', is the memory of the fourth sacrifice of the Nathan Soul, the birth on Earth of the Luke Jesus-child. And if this memory passes through an inner process of *enlivening*, Christ Himself can enter into this *enlivened and life-filled* memory. In our own soul-being we should at this time come, through the inner enlivening of the faculty of memory, in some way to resemble the Nathan Soul, in order that we may also—though not now in an outward way, as at the Baptism in the Jordan, but purely inwardly—receive the Christ into our own ego.

Thus the thirteen Holy Nights become for us a path towards a profoundly real experience of the words of Paul the Apostle: 'Not I, but Christ in me.'[5] A star that can guide us in this endeavour is the following meditation of Rudolf Steiner, where the words that stand at the beginning of the Gospel of St John have taken on a form that expresses the hidden nature of the mystery of human memory:

> In the beginning is memory,
> And memory lives on,
> And divine is memory.
> And memory is life
> And this life is the human ego
> Which streams within man.
> Not he alone, the Christ in him.
> When he recalls the life divine,
> Christ is in his remembering,
> And as the radiant life of memory
> Will Christ shine
> In all immediately present darkness.[6]

In these twelve lines we are given a truly esoteric indication of the path that leads to the enlivening of our inner faculty of memory in the course of the thirteen Holy Nights. The recollection of the birth of the Nathan Soul forms the point of departure, but our striving must be to enliven our memory so that the Christ Being may gradually enter and work in it. This is a profoundly intimate soul process which reaches its culmination in the fulfilment of the words 'Not I, but Christ in me', words which represent the high point and the goal of the thirteenfold ascent 'from Jesus to Christ'. For these deep Mystery-words of the Apostle Paul contain a real and full *understanding* of the all-embracing Mystery of *Christ-Jesus*, of Christ and the Nathan Soul. To understand the 'Christ-impulse', says Rudolf Steiner in this connection, 'means not only to strive towards perfection but to receive into oneself what comes to expression in the words of the Apostle Paul, "Not I, but Christ in me." "I" is the word of Krishna [that is, of the Nathan Soul]; "Not I, but Christ in me" are the words of the Christ-impulse.'[7]

If we employ the terminology used by Rudolf Steiner in his book *The Threshold of the Spiritual World*, we could say: the four weeks of Advent lead us from an experience of the ordinary, everyday ego to the 'other' or 'higher self', while the esoteric path through the thirteen Holy Nights leads from this to the '*true ego*' of man, to the awareness of the macrocosmic ego of Christ in us.[8]

This thought can also be expressed from the standpoint of the modern path of initiation. Then we would say: just as the development that takes place in Advent is a gradual penetration by the pupil into his inner being prior to his encounter at the threshold of Christmas with the Lesser Guardian of the Threshold, who holds the keys of true self-knowledge, so does a conscious experience of Epiphany lead the pupil into the great world of the macrocosm at whose gates the Greater Guardian of the Threshold comes to meet him.

In this way the path from Jesus to Christ becomes for the spirit-pupil a path that leads him from the experience of the Lesser Guardian of the Threshold to the meeting with the Greater Guardian. Thus it is that both at Christmas and Epiphany it is a matter of crossing the threshold of the spiritual world, albeit respectively in its microcosmic and macrocosmic aspects. Hence in the first case the concern is more with the Lesser Guardian of the Threshold, who guards the entrance to the microcosm; the second has to do with the Greater Guardian of the Threshold, who guards the entrance to the macrocosm. Rudolf Steiner refers to this as follows: 'Anyone who on waking enters consciously into his sheaths learns to know this Lesser Guardian of the Threshold ... The mystical life leads, therefore, through this gate past the Lesser Guardian of the Threshold into man's own inner being.'[9] And regarding the second Guardian: '... At the gate through which we must pass when we go to sleep, there also stands a Guardian of the Threshold. This is the Greater Guardian of the Threshold, who does not admit us into the spiritual world as long as we are still unready, who does not admit us because if we have not first strengthened and affirmed ourselves inwardly we would be exposed to certain dangers if we wished to pour out our ego over the spiritual world into which we enter upon going to sleep.'[10]

In modern initiation the pupil must necessarily pass through a personal experience of *both* Guardians, for only in their togetherness do they give him a perspective of the past and future of the world without which he cannot orientate himself aright in the higher worlds. Rudolf Steiner writes about this in the following words from the concluding chapter of his book *Knowledge of the Higher Worlds: How is it Achieved?*: 'When the pupil enters the supersensible world, life acquires an entirely new meaning for him; he discerns in the physical world the seed-bed of a higher world. And in a certain sense this "higher" world will appear defective without the "lower". Two vistas open out before him: one into the past, the other into the future. He looks into a past when this physical world did not yet exist ... He knows that the supersensible world existed first, and that everything physical evolved out of it.'[11] And then he turns towards what is arising out of the future: 'And here a view into the future opens out. It points towards a higher stage of the supersensible world—a stage that will be enriched with fruits brought to maturity in the sense-world. The sense-world as such will be overcome, but its results will be incorporated into a higher world.'[12]

That spiritual being who opens up to the pupil 'the vista into the past' is the Lesser Guardian of the Threshold, for 'in that Guardian of the Threshold, as described above, the product *of the past alone* is made manifest, containing only such seeds of the future as were woven into it in past times. But the individual must take with him into the *future* supersensible world everything he can draw from the world of the senses. If he were to bring with him only what has been woven into his counterpart out of the past, his earthly task would have been only partly accomplished. For this reason the Lesser Guardian of the Threshold is joined, *after some time*,[13] by the Greater Guardian.'[14] This Greater Guardian of the Threshold unfolds before the pupil the vista into the future.

Thus if we examine these initiation experiences of the pupil from the standpoint of the cycle of the year, we may say, to summarize: at Christmas, as he attains true *self-knowledge*, man approaches the Lesser Guardian of the Threshold—who can then open up to him the vista into the past, which principally extends over the half-year that has just run its course; while at Epiphany, which stands at the threshold of true *world-knowledge*, man

94

approaches the Greater Guardian of the Threshold—who is then able to unveil to him the vista into the future and, in the first instance, into the next (ensuing) half-year. This corresponds fully with the observation of Rudolf Steiner cited above concerning how the Lesser Guardian of the Threshold appears to man as he consciously *awakens*, while the Greater Guardian of the Threshold appears as he consciously *goes to sleep*. For the half-year prior to Christmas corresponds to the Earth's awakening, and the equivalent period after Epiphany to its gradual falling asleep (see p.4). The thirteen Holy Nights, that 'unified time' which separates these two experiences in the course of the yearly rhythm, represent a key to experiencing the Mysteries of the whole yearly cycle.*

---

* See Appendix 1 at the end of the book.

3. The Thirteen Holy Nights as the Revelation of the Mystery of Memory

As we have seen already, the inner experience of the thirteen Holy Nights is directly associated with a process that leads gradually to the enlivening of the human faculty of memory, for this time corresponds in the yearly rhythm to the period of the Earth Soul's most intensive *memory* of the experiences it has gathered in the cosmic expanses in summer. Thus in the ensuing study of the esoteric nature of the thirteen Holy Nights we shall follow this path of the inner enlivening of memory as indicated by the meditation of Rudolf Steiner that was quoted in the previous chapter.

> In the beginning is memory,
> And memory lives on,
> And divine is memory.
> And memory is life
> And this life is the human ego
> Which streams within man.
> Not he alone, the Christ in him.
> When he recalls the life divine,
> Christ is in his remembering,
> And as the radiant life of memory
> Will Christ shine
> In all immediately present darkness.

It is apparent from the most cursory acquaintance with its content and composition that it divides symmetrically into two parts with six lines in each, the principal difference being the threefold reference to the name of Christ in the second of these. Thus the first line runs:

> In the beginning is memory

These words at once direct our memory to the very beginning of human existence, to the epoch of ancient Lemuria, when all people on Earth received in the person of the ancestor of mankind, Adam, the predisposition towards the development of individual ego-consciousness. For just as an adult who returns in memory to his childhood can only remember back as far as the time when the first sparks of ego-consciousness ignited within him (which usually takes place at the age of around three years), so does the memory of all humanity, which slumbers latently in each human individual and becomes conscious through what is communicated by spiritual science, extend until the moment of the first stirrings of ego-consciousness within humanity—that is, until the last third of the Lemurian epoch.[15]

Human life passes through a continual alternation between wakefulness and sleep, yet merges in the flow of memories into a single, whole and uninterrupted stream. Likewise in such a single, uninterrupted stream, the memory of all humanity which is set forth in the genealogy in the Gospel according to Luke, extending as far as our ancestor Adam and even to God, comes together.[16]

Modern man, without the help of spiritual science, can no longer penetrate to the 'memory which is in the beginning', that is, to the Fall, for the consequences of that other memory—of what he has acquired in the course of his incarnations on the Earth and which separates him from the 'memory of the beginning'—have grown too strongly within him. However, the wisdom of world-rulership has taken care that this memory, which was in the beginning of time, has not been lost for mankind. This was done by withholding one (human) being from the general stream of evolution and making him the heavenly bearer of the 'memory which is in the beginning'. This being is the Nathan Soul, the representative of the paradisaical, pure condition of humanity which existed before the Fall.

And the memory lives on

These words are an indication to us of how the heavenly memory of the paradisaical condition of humanity preserved by the Nathan Soul from the beginning of time continues to live on. It is carefully guarded by the Nathan Soul in the Sun-filled heights for the good of the whole future evolution of humanity. In a certain sense it is also possible to say that this memory—which is not the abstract, shadowy memory that people ordinarily possess but a *living*, real memory—is indeed the Nathan Soul. For just as in ordinary life man's earthly memory forms the principal content of his ego, so the 'memory which is in the beginning' is connected in a substantial way with the 'ego' of the Nathan Soul.[17]

And divine is memory

From what has been said above, this third line also becomes comprehensible. 'The memory which is in the beginning', that is, which extends back to the epoch before the Fall, is of divine nature. For only because of the Fall did man leave the divine-spiritual world. Until then he abided in the bosom of divine beings of higher worlds (Archai and Archangels), and was an inseparable part of their existence. The lines from the first part of the

Foundation Stone Meditation that have already been quoted also have to do with this ancient human condition:

> Where in the wielding
> World-Creator-Life
> Thine own I
> Comes to being
> Within the I of God.

In this 'coming into being' or 'abiding' of the 'own I' of the Nathan Soul in the 'divine I' of the beings of the higher Hierarchies may also be found the reason why in his lectures Rudolf Steiner sometimes calls it a human, and on other occasions a superhuman, divine being. For example, in the lecture of 30 December 1913 in Leipzig: 'Thus what we have to do with here is not a human but *a superhuman being* . . . who lived in the spiritual world';[18] and at the end of the lecture: 'this kind of working together, of according the Christ Being with the *human nature* of the Nathan Jesus . . .'[19] Or in the lecture of 10 February 1914: 'Regarding this Nathan Jesus-child, we must be clear that he is not a human being like other human beings, that he has not . . . had many lives behind him . . . but has spent his former existence fully in the spiritual worlds.'[20] While in the lecture of 5 March 1914 we read: 'This *part of the divine being of man* which has remained in the spiritual worlds, this spiritual being descended for the first time into a physical body as the Nathan Jesus-child . . .'[21]

> And memory is life

Life is the basic quality of the Nathan Soul. For it (the Nathan Soul) is the guardian of the unfallen etheric body of Adam, which appears in the Bible in the imagination of the 'Tree of Life'. It is also truly a 'living soul', for 'the memory which is in the beginning' (that is guarded by it) is a *living* memory, bearing within itself the whole fullness of those creative powers which in the rest of humanity were to become almost completely exhausted as a result of man's immersion in the realm of matter. Rudolf Steiner speaks of this as follows: 'This sister soul, to a certain extent withheld from being plunged into earthly evolution, continued to be permeated by *man-creating forces.*'[22]

> And this life is the human ego

This line indicates to us how in the spiritual worlds the Nathan Soul is also the bearer of man's higher ego, of that ego the consciousness of which has been extinguished amongst the rest of mankind as a result of the Fall, and has been gradually replaced by the consciousness of the ordinary human ego—which, by virtue of its independence from the world of the Gods, is the gift of Lucifer. However, in order that the influence of Lucifer might not gain too great a power over humanity, the Nathan Soul appeared in a 'reflected incarnation' in the third millennium, that is, just before the beginning of the Kali-Yuga, in the figure of Krishna. Krishna emerges at this time as the awakener of the principle of the higher ego which has been preserved in the soul of every man, albeit in a darkened state. Rudolf Steiner speaks about this in these words: 'And so as he gazes at Krishna, a person is at the same time regarding his own higher self—but at the same time also another [being], who is able to stand before him like another man and in whom he can, as in another [being], revere at once what he is himself according to his own disposition and what makes him a different [being], who relates to him as God relates to man.'[23] In this sense the Nathan Soul (Krishna) is also the principal opponent of Lucifer,[24] in that in the Lemurian epoch it was, with Michael's help, able to ward off the temptation in Paradise and to remain thereafter completely free from his influence. Hence it embodies '... that most inward part of man, his real self, which we have seen addressed as Krishna, whose radiance we have seen in the impulse of Krishna ...'[25] For with Krishna it is a matter of what in Buddhi and Manas is directly connected with the great all-embracing world-substance, with the Divine Power, that lives and weaves in the world.[26] 'As macrocosm to microcosm, man as such [the higher self] to the lesser man of everyday [the ordinary ego]—so stands Krishna with regard to the human individual.'[27]

Which streams within man

The higher ego continues nonetheless to stream unconsciously within man. And it will be so until that time when he is able to experience this streaming of the higher ego within himself in a conscious way. This epoch dawned among humanity in 1899 with the end of the Kali-Yuga. Since then a new, light-filled age has begun which enables the individual *consciously to experience* for the first time what entered as a completely new impulse into human evolution at the Mystery of Golgotha, and which since then lives and works invisibly within his ego.

Not he alone, the Christ in him

This *seventh* line is central to the whole meditation. It is an indication of how, in rightly traversing the esoteric path which is given in the thirteen stages of the Holy Nights, in becoming truly immersed in the secrets of the Christmas Mystery, an individual who strives towards a conscious experience of this time may come to feel that he does not travel this path alone. From a certain moment *Someone* walks beside him. And if this meditative deepening in the essence of the Christmas memory is sufficiently intensive, so that this memory can really lead to '... this first Christmas night, which took place two thousand years ago, *coming to life* in our hearts, in our feeling, in our will ...'[28], so that this memory may become completely *alive* within us as a Being who is close to us, then there may be revealed to us the mystery of Him Who henceforth accompanies us on our lonely path. From now on the individual is no longer alone but becomes inwardly conscious of the divine presence: Christ Himself is present within him!

> When he recalls the life divine

That is, he enters with all his inner strength into the essence of the Christmas Mystery, into the essence of the Mystery of the Nathan Soul, the bearer of that 'divine life' which man possessed until his fall and which he will again attain at a higher level when the old Adam in him will have been fully transformed into the new Adam through the power issuing from the Mystery of Golgotha.

However, it is possible to initiate this process of inner transformation even now if, through pondering the primeval 'divine life' which in past times he had to abandon, man becomes able to summon forth, as though from a source which reveals itself in his soul, the forces capable of enlivening his memory. If this happens, the great secret of his own being—which is contained in the next line of the meditation—will be revealed to him:

> Christ is in his remembering

Since the time of the Mystery of Golgotha, Christ has been present in man's ego, in the depths of his memory. He has so united Himself with man's soul that He can be consciously experienced. Something occurs that is similar to what formerly took place at the Baptism in the Jordan. Now, after the Mystery of Golgotha, this arises not as an outer spiritual process associated at that time with the ego's departure from the three sheaths (as did the ego of Zarathustra), but in an inward spiritual manner in the sphere of *enlivened memory* (which is the foundation of the human ego), through which the human individual comes inwardly to resemble the Nathan Soul. This is possible only through awakening within him the deep powers of memory, which in the period *before* the awakening of his ordinary earthly memory, that is until approximately his third year,[29] work subconsciously within his being. In this time the child learns to stand upright and to walk, speak and think. Rudolf Steiner describes these three faculties as a microcosmic repetition of the three cosmic sacrifices of Christ through the Nathan Soul.[30]

Thus as every child masters the capacities of walking, speaking and thinking in early childhood he is repeating the three 'preparatory stages of the Mystery of Golgotha', and he receives the impulses for this from the 'deep memory' which, with the subsequent awakening of the individual ego, withdraws fully into the subconscious regions of his soul. Rudolf Steiner describes this process in the following words: 'Only what is childlike in the individual of today still preserves a last trace of that nature which was his before he succumbed to the influence of luciferic beings (that is, before the Fall). Hence the human being that stands before us now is such that he has a childlike part [corresponding to the 'deep memory'] and an adult part [corresponding to the ordinary memory] ... The luciferic forces permeate even the child in such a way that what entered into man before the luciferic influence cannot manifest itself in ordinary life. This childlike part must be reawakened by the Christ-power. The Christ-power must unite with what are the best forces of the child-nature in man. It cannot link itself to capacities that have been spoilt by man, capacities that stem from a being that is born of the intellect alone; rather it connects itself with that best part in man which has been preserved in his child-nature from ancient times (that is, with what in every individual is still related to the Nathan Soul). This must be reinvigorated and must thereafter fructify the rest ... Everyone has the childlike nature within him, and if this is *filled with life* it will become receptive to union with the Christ-principle.[31]

From these words we may see that the process of becoming inwardly akin to the Nathan Soul is none other than the awakening within man of his 'childlikeness', his 'essentially alive memory', that memory in which the Christ can be truly present.

> And as the radiant life of memory

This means not shadowy, as is one's ordinary memory, and not merely enlivened, but living *and* radiant, that is to say, permeated by the light of the Christ Sun.

> Will Christ shine

There now rays forth not only the memory that is permeated by life and light, but Christ Himself shines from out of the true ego and drives away all darkness from the sheaths of man. Christ shines

> In all immediately present darkness.

The imaginative picture that corresponds to the last two lines may also be found in the Gospel of St John in the deeply significant scene of the 'Cleansing of the Temple'* when Christ drives from the sphere of His

---

* Gospel of St John, 2:14–21.

immediate presence (the Temple is, here, an image of the sheaths which surround the human ego) the opposing forces of Lucifer and Ahriman; those of the former appear in this scene as the animal dealers (animals are the astral counter-images of human passions), while those of the latter are represented by the money-changers. Christ thereby clears the way for His light to shine, without hindrance, from the human ego through the purified sheaths out into the world.

Thus the path through the thirteen Holy Nights, the beginning of which was an immersion of the human memory into the Mystery of Jesus, ends with a direct experience of the Being of Christ.

'From Jesus to Christ'—in these brief words is contained the essential esoteric content of the Holy Nights. The birth of Christ in the holy of holies of the human ego is the ultimate goal towards which the soul can strive and which it may reach, through a real enlivening of its faculty of memory, on the thirteenth day, at Epiphany, the festival of the entry of the Sun Spirit of Christ 'into the stream of earthly being' through the Baptism in the Jordan.

4. The Uniting of the World Impulses of Wisdom and Love in the Experience of Christ

In a lecture of 20 February 1917, in Berlin, Rudolf Steiner spoke in a particularly impressive way about the three meetings of the human soul with the three basic creative principles of our cosmos—the principles of the Father, the Son (Christ) and the Holy Spirit—through the mediation of the beings of the Third Hierarchy, Archai, Archangels and Angels. Accordingly every human soul encounters the Father-principle in the rhythm of human life, although this remains for the most part a deeply unconscious experience. This meeting takes place in the period from 28 to 42 years of age. The principle of the Spirit, on the other hand, is encountered every night as the soul enters into the spiritual worlds between going to sleep and waking. And, finally, the meeting with the Son-principle (Christ), which is of particular interest to us in our present studies, comes about *in the rhythm of the year*, and especially in the period from Christmas until Easter. In the lecture mentioned above Rudolf Steiner speaks of this as follows: 'For the time of Easter is that period in the actual course of the year when every-thing that has been called forth in us *through the encounter with the Christ in the Christmas season* becomes again united in a real way with our earthly, physical humanity.'[32] This is why, as we have already seen, the festival of Epiphany is a particularly suitable moment for this encounter 'in the Christmas season'.

A further indication of the quite special significance of 6 January in the yearly rhythm as the day which brings the period of the Holy Nights to an end is the Dream Song of Olaf Åsteson, the Norwegian initiate of the eleventh century, concerning whose experiences Rudolf Steiner says the following: 'So the human soul, the soul of the seer, lives from the festival of the birth of Jesus until the festival of Christ's appearance in such a way that the Mystery of the Christ is disclosed to it, and it can come at this time to recognize in a most profound way what is meant by the Baptism by John in the Jordan.'[33] The visionary soul of Olaf Åsteson attains to this profound knowledge at the end of the thirteen Holy Nights in such a way that '... the visions of the seer in the thirteen Holy Nights are seemingly crowned on 6 January by the Imagination of Christ.'[34] And Olaf Åsteson beholds, '... as he approaches the time of 6 January, the Christ Spirit entering into humanity *preceded by* the spirit of Michael.'[35]

The significance of this latter indication also becomes clear from the

103

lecture of 31 March 1923 where it is said that during the season of autumn and until Christmas Michael *precedes* Christ, the new Spirit of the Earth, thus preparing in the yearly cycle His subsequent union with the Earth in the course of the thirteen Holy Nights. While, in contrast, during the second half of the year, beginning from the period after Epiphany, Michael follows *behind* Christ out into the macrocosm, whither the soul and spirit of the Earth ascend at this time in the course of their outbreathing.

We can recognize in the cycle of the year the relationship between Michael and Christ as a constant interworking of the impulses of *wisdom* and *love*, especially when we recall that, since ancient times in the spiritual world, Michael has been the ruler of the heavenly Intelligence—that is, the cosmic thoughts as the entire *wisdom* of the hierarchic cosmos which is connected with the Sun, while Christ is the representative of the cosmic principle of *love*.

The Nathan Soul is connected quite directly with the first impulse, with the impulse of wisdom proceeding from Michael. For it is the guardian in the spiritual world of that 'etheric human archetype' that was spoken of in the description of its first sacrificial deed in the Lemurian epoch (see pp.40–41). This archetype, the quintessence of all the work of the higher Hierarchies from Old Saturn until the Earth-epoch, is also the focus of all the wisdom implanted by the divine-spiritual worlds in the human form throughout the whole course of evolution until this time. In the Christmas Imagination this came especially to expression in that the heavenly Isis-Sophia, the all-encompassing wisdom of the spiritual cosmos, found her earthly reflection in the mother of the Nathan Jesus.

Summing up we may say that the thirteen Holy Nights, which represent the Mystery-journey from Christmas to Epiphany, from the festival of the Nathan Soul's birth on Earth until the festival of the birth of Christ at the Baptism in the Jordan, form that period of the year when, in everyone who experiences this time consciously, the impulse of wisdom (Christmas) and the impulse of love (Epiphany) may unite in his newly born higher ego.[36] And so the following words of Rudolf Steiner, with which he concluded his book *Occult Science*, can be related in the yearly rhythm directly to the Mystery of the thirteen Holy Nights. 'Through the co-operation of the Spirits of Will, Wisdom and Movement there arises what reveals itself as wisdom. Earthly beings and processes can collaborate in wise harmony with the other beings of their world because of the work of these three ranks of spirits. Through the Spirits of Form man receives his independent ego. This ego will in the future enter into harmony with the beings of Earth, Jupiter, Venus and Vulcan through the power which is added to wisdom in the course of Earth-evolution. This is the power of *love*. This power of love must have its beginning in earthly humanity. And the "cosmos of wisdom" develops into a "*cosmos of love*". *Love* should arise out of everything which can unfold the ego within itself. The exalted Sun Being to which it was possible to refer in the description of the evolution of the Christ-impulse may be seen in His revelation of the all-embracing archetype of love. The seed of love has thus been implanted in the inmost core of man's being. And from thence it shall stream out into the whole of evolution. Just as the wisdom that has been previously developed manifests itself in the forces of the outer sense-world of the Earth, in the "natural forces" of the present, so in future will love be manifest in all appearances as a new force of nature. The secret of all future evolution lies in this: knowledge and everything which man achieves by way of a true understanding of evolution is the sowing of a seed which will ripen as *love*. And as much as is born of the power of love, so much is forged of creative power for the future. In what will arise from love, great forces will be harnessed which lead to the end-result of spiritualization as described above . . . What has been prepared during Saturn, Sun and Moon evolutions as wisdom works in the physical, etheric and astral body of man. There it shows itself as "world-wisdom"; in the ego, however, it becomes "inner wisdom". *From Earth-evolution onwards, the "wisdom of the outer world" becomes inner wisdom in man. And having become internalized, it becomes the seed of love. Wisdom is the pre-condition of love. Love is the fruit of wisdom reborn in the ego.*'[37]

If these concluding lines are taken as a meditative or mantric text, their complete correspondence to the esoteric cycle of the year becomes clear. For the words 'from Earth-evolution onwards, the "wisdom of the outer world" becomes inner wisdom in man' express with precision the whole character of one half of the year (from the summer solstice until Christmas). And then the words 'and having become thus internalized, it becomes the seed of love' reflect especially the essential nature of the last week of Advent and Christmas itself. The words 'wisdom is the pre-condition of love' (meaning the birth of the Nathan Soul on Earth is the pre-condition for the subsequent birth of the Christ Being) relate to the thirteen Holy Nights. And finally, the words 'love is the fruit of wisdom reborn in the ego' refer to the second half of the year, *after* Epiphany, when man's higher ego—which has been born of wisdom at Christmas and has then consciously taken this wisdom into itself during the thirteen Holy Nights— begins to manifest wisdom to the world as *love*, just as Christ manifested Himself after the Baptism in the Jordan to the world and to humanity as its higher Cosmic Archetype.

Thus the architectonic structure of the cycle of the year is revealed to us in the form of a building with two cupolas which harmoniously unites in itself the two principles of wisdom and love, beneath whose vaults the gates may be called the gate of the Moon (Christmas) and the gate of the Sun

(Epiphany). Of these, one leads into the sphere of world karma and the beings of the higher Hierarchies who rule therein, while the other leads into the sphere of a future humanity working creatively in the world out of the forces of freedom and love.[38]

5. The Thirteen Holy Nights and their Connection with the Macrocosm

A particularly significant aspect of the Holy Nights is their connection with the cycle of the year and, therefore, with the macrocosm. Twelve,★ the number of space—which separates the day of the appearance of Jesus from the day of the appearance of Christ—is a direct indication of the connection of this time with the archetype of twelvefoldness in our cosmos, the twelve heavenly spheres or powers of the zodiac. The following words of Rudolf Steiner express this with a particular clarity: 'It is as though humanity, if it uses this opportunity to take these temporal landmarks as material for meditation, can become really aware of its pristine origin in the cosmic forces of the universe. Only when lifting his gaze to the cosmic forces of the universe and penetrating a little, through Theosophia, through a truly spiritual wisdom, into the secrets of the universe, can man become once again mature enough to know that the festival of the birth of Christ, which should be celebrated on 6 January as the festival of the birth of Christ in the body of Jesus of Nazareth, is—as the Gnostics understood—a higher stage of the festival of the birth of Jesus. And as though in order that man might be able to immerse himself in the twelve universal forces of the cosmos, these twelve Holy Nights stand between the Christmas festival, the birth of Jesus, and the festival which should be celebrated on 6 January—this being now the festival of the Three Kings (Magi)—and which is actually the festival characterized above.

'Again, without this being so far recognized by scholars, these twelve Holy Nights stand there, as though established out of the wise, hidden depths of the human soul, as if to say: experience the Christmas festival in all its profundity, but then plunge during the twelve Holy Nights into the holiest Mysteries of the cosmos! This means, *into the realm of the universe whence Christ descended to the Earth.* For only if mankind has the will to allow itself to be inspired by thoughts of the Holy Child, of man's divine origin, to be *inspired* by that wisdom which permeates the twelve forces, the twelve holy forces of the universe, symbolically represented as they are by the twelve signs of the zodiac (which, however, can be represented in their true reality only with the help of spiritual wisdom)—only if man immerses himself in true spiritual wisdom and learns to recognize the course of time

---

★ The significance of the thirteenth night will be considered later.

107

in the widths of the universe and in the human individual, only then will a humanity that is fructified by spiritual science *find that inspiration* for its own future well-being which can spring from the festival of the birth of Jesus in order that it may penetrate to the most confident and hopeful thoughts of the future.'[39]

These words speak above all of the real possibility of entering in the course of the thirteen Holy Nights not merely into the Mysteries of the human soul, of the microcosm, but also into the profound Mysteries of the universe which surrounds us, of the macrocosm. These latter Mysteries cannot at this time of year be known directly through entering into extra-terrestrial spheres but only through their *reflection* within the Earth, for, in Rudolf Steiner's words, it is at Christmas-tide that the Earth *recollects* the Mysteries of the cosmos. Furthermore, it not only 'remembers' them but has borne them within itself since the Mystery of Golgotha when Christ Himself, the 'Representative of all cosmic forces on Earth', became the Spirit of the Earth.

But how at this time does the transition from the microcosm—into which man enters with the greatest intensity at Christmas-tide—back into the macrocosm take place? How does he find the path from his own 'deep memory', which is revealed to him through his meeting with the Lesser Guardian of the Threshold, to the 'deep memory' of the Earth, which embraces all the Mysteries of the macrocosm, the keys of which are held by the Greater Guardian?

In order to answer this question we must take into consideration one further aspect of the process of the birth in man of his higher ego at Christmas-tide. Rudolf Steiner touches upon this in the cycle *Macrocosm and Microcosm*, in the lecture of 29 March 1910. There he speaks in particular of how at the crossing of the threshold of the spiritual world in initiation—if the pupil enters it with imaginative consciousness—one of the first of his experiences is the complete objectivization of his ego. His own ego comes before him in an objectivized form, not in an individualized but in a *twelvefold* form. Hence, each of the twelve images of his ego at the same time reveals to him his connections with one of the forces of the universe, his relationship with one of the spheres of the zodiacal circle. This is one of the pupil's first experiences and comes as a direct consequence of the birth in him of his higher ego. Rudolf Steiner describes this process as follows: '. . . And it is so, that at the moment when, through the training that we have described, we enter the imaginative world and see an image of our ego, we must be fully aware of the fact that *twelve different images of our ego* can be seen. There are twelve different images of any particular ego; and indeed, only when we have looked back upon ourselves from twelve different viewpoints *outside our physical ego* have we understood our ego in its totality. This way of viewing the ego from without corresponds exactly with what is reflected in the relationship of the twelve constellations [of the zodiac] to the Sun. Just as the Sun passes through the twelve constellations and has a different power in each, just as it appears in spring in a certain constellation and then moves on in the course of the year and, even, in the course of the day through the constellations and illumines our Earth from twelve different viewpoints, so too does the human ego illuminate itself from twelve different viewpoints, irradiate itself from twelve different viewpoints, when it looks back upon itself from the higher world.'[40]

It is clear from this that as the pupil ascends to his higher ego he at the same time, in a certain sense, ceases to experience himself as a microcosm and feels within himself the working of the twelve forces of the macrocosm, with which he now experiences a direct connection. Now his task becomes that of reviewing the twelve images of his ego, in the same way that the Sun encircles all twelve constellations of the zodiac, so as to unite them in a new synthesis, to bring twelvefoldness again into a unity, though now on a higher plane. This is, however, possibly only if in the course of the twelve Holy Nights the pupil finds the path from his higher ego, which reveals to him the twelve forces of the universe lying at the foundation of his individual ego, to his *true ego*, that is, to the Christ-impulse within him. Expressing this more cosmologically, one could say: during the twelve Holy Nights the pupil must pass through all twelve spheres of the zodiacal circle in order that he may in the thirteenth night step into *the sphere beyond the zodiac*, into that world whence the Christ Being, the Ego of our cosmos and at the same time the 'true ego' of every man on Earth, Himself proceeds.

Thus we have found that the thirteen Holy Nights may become a thread that can lead us through the twelve heavenly spheres of the zodiacal circle, from the experience of the human initiation of Jesus (the higher self) to the all-encompassing macrocosmic initiation of Christ (the true ego). The initiation of Jesus of Nazareth (the Nathan Soul) stands under the sign of the Fishes, the sign which is associated with man's origin in the Lemurian epoch. The initiation of the Apostles, who were all 'fishermen', stands under the same sign. In later times, this tradition is continued in the Grail-stream, where the initiate who guards the Holy Chalice is called the 'Fisher King'.

Rudolf Steiner refers in the following words to the particular nature of the initiation of Jesus of Nazareth, comparing it with the initiation of John the Baptist: 'Therefore John the Baptist said to his intimate pupils: "Through the Waterman initiation I can place at the disposal of my Angel only those forces with whose help he can proclaim that the Lord Κυριος is coming. But one is coming who has the powers which are symbolized in the initiation of the constellation of the Fishes. And he will receive the Christ into himself. In this way did John the Baptist refer to Jesus of Nazareth.'[41] And then Rudolf Steiner continues: '. . . As there is coming into the world one possessed of the initiation of the Fishes, one who is able to receive those spiritual impulses whose instrument is the Fish-initiation, the possibility arises not only for that baptism by which John baptized but for a higher baptism which John calls the Baptism by the Holy Spirit.'[42]

And so the spiritual path through the macrocosm begins with the sign of the Fishes, the symbol of the initiation of Jesus of Nazareth (that is, the initiation of the Nathan Soul, as an image of true *man*, Anthropos). This path of ascent should, in the course of the twelve Holy Nights, embrace all twelve regions of the zodiacal circle so as to reach its culmination in the 'Initiation' of Christ, which stands under the sign of the Ram and encompasses the whole circle of the zodiac.[43] Rudolf Steiner speaks of this all-embracing 'Initiation' of Christ in the following way in the lecture of 27 January 1908 in Berlin: 'That is why this Being [Christ] is designated as the sacrificial "Mystic Lamb", for the lamb is the same as the Ram, hence the designation of Christ as the sacrificial lamb or ram. Christ has now been characterized for you as belonging to the whole cosmos. His Ego reaches as far as the Ram; and when an ego streams upwards to the Ram, He Himself becomes the "Great Sacrifice". He relates thus to the whole of mankind, and in a certain way those beings and forces that exist on the Earth are His creations.'[44]

Rudolf Steiner refers to this from another viewpoint in the last chapter of his book *The Spiritual Guidance of Man and Humanity*, where he speaks of how, while every man in the course of his life is able to experience the predominant influence of *one* sign of the zodiac, Christ, during His sojourn on the Earth, was under the influence of the whole macrocosm, that is, the whole twelvefoldness of the zodiacal circle: 'Christ always stood under the influence of the *whole* cosmos. He took no step without the cosmic forces being active within Him. What was making itself felt here in Jesus of Nazareth [after His Baptism in the Jordan] was a perpetual realization of the horoscope; for at every moment there occurred what otherwise happens only when a human being is born. This could take place only because the whole body of the Nathan Jesus had remained susceptible to the influence of *the totality of the forces of the cosmic-spiritual Hierarchies guiding our Earth . . . the whole spirit of the cosmos was working within Christ Jesus.*'[45]

These last (italicized) words point to a further aspect of the esoteric significance of the thirteen Holy Nights—for the supersensible path through the twelve signs of the zodiac which they encompass is at the same time a path which leads man through the ascending ranks of the Hierarchies to the divine-spiritual origin (primal causes) of the world. Thus, while the essentially *human* initiation, the initiation of Anthropos, comes to manifestation in the sign of the Fishes, we enter in the sign of the Waterman into the world of the Angels (hence the initiation of John the Baptist was a Waterman initiation, that is, one that worked through his Angel).[46] We then ascend in the sign of the Goat into the world of the Archangels and into the world of the Archai in the sign of the Archer. Similarly, the Exusiai, who once endowed man with the ego-principle, come to manifestation in the sign of the Scorpion, the Dynamis, the Spirits of Movement, in the sign of the Scales, and the Kyriotetes, the Spirits of Wisdom, in the sign of the Virgin, the divine Isis-Sophia. Finally, the Thrones, or the Spirits of Will, come to manifestation in the sign of the Lion, the Cherubim in the sign of the Crab, and the Seraphim in the sign of the Twins; and there then follows the revelation of the sphere of the Holy Spirit in the sign of the Bull, and of the sphere of the Son, the 'Mystic Lamb',[47] Christ, in the sign of the Ram.★

This great twelvefold path, which is revealed to the soul only in the time of the Holy Nights, has its sublime culmination in the thirteenth night, when the soul—having, through inner union with the deep memory of the Earth, embraced the forces of all the twelve signs of the zodiac—can be touched by the influence of the highest cosmic sphere, that sphere beyond the zodiac whence in former times the Christ,[48] the bearer of the universal Ego-principle, descended to the Earth. The words that sounded from out of the macrocosm at the moment of the Baptism in the Jordan 'This is My beloved Son, this day have I begotten Him', and the words of Christ, 'I and the Father are one', point to this connection of Christ with the highest sphere of cosmic being.

All this can be read by the soul at Christmas-tide in the Earth's living memory. And if the soul can thus experience the forces of the sphere beyond the zodiac as the primordial home of Christ, with which it comes in contact in the deepest layers of the Earth's memory, it can also approach the bearer of this memory, the Ego of the Earth, which since the Mystery of Golgotha—when He became the new Spirit of the Earth—has been the Ego of Christ Himself.

With this knowledge of the highest and the deepest, of the true heights and depths of the world, united as they are into a single whole in the all-embracing experience of the Christ Being, the path 'from Jesus to Christ' comes to an end on 6 January. This path begins with an inner deepening of the human soul and then leads to a direct experience of Christ as the new

★ See further about this in the book *The Twelve Holy Nights and the Spiritual Hierarchies* (Temple Lodge 1993).

Spirit of the Earth, who bears within Himself all the mysteries of the macrocosm. Henceforth Christ works within the human ego as its highest aspect, as the 'true ego', and His divine presence can become for man a conscious experience:

> And as the radiant life of memory
> Will Christ shine
> In all immediately present darkness.

The divine Light of Christ must now find its way from the human soul, from the deepest grounds of man's being, from his true ego, out into the world, and for this purpose all the 'immediately present darkness' in human sheaths must first be overcome. For these sheaths represent the chief hindrance in Christ's endeavour to gradually spiritualize our whole cosmos, a process which must necessarily precede the Earth's transition to its next planetary incarnation, that of Jupiter.

The words of Rudolf Steiner quoted earlier (see p.103), where he speaks of how the consequences of the direct encounter with Christ in the period of Christmas *become united at the time of Easter with man's physical body*, are an indication of this endeavour of the Christ-impulse proceeding from man's true ego gradually to permeate his sheaths: the astral body, the etheric body, and, finally, the physical body itself.

IV

FROM EPIPHANY TO EASTER

1.   The Path of the Christ-impulse through the Sheaths and its Reflection in the Gospels

The most suitable period in the yearly cycle for penetrating one's own sheaths—one's astral, etheric and physical bodies—with the Christ-impulse working within man's ego, is the time from Epiphany to Easter, which is a reflection of the three years lived by the Christ Being in the three sheaths of Jesus of Nazareth from the Baptism in the Jordan until the Mystery of Golgotha. For what is the essential nature of this three-year sojourn of the Christ Being on the Earth, which ended with His death on the Cross and His subsequent Resurrection? It could in its essence be described as God becoming man through a gradual deed of sacrifice, the Son of God becoming the Son of man: *Ecce homo.* In an occult sense, it is the union of the divine macrocosmic Ego of Christ with the dark, mortal sheaths of man. In uniting with them, Christ changes them—through this union with the immortal forces of His Ego—into something higher. He combines the deepest past with the most distant future and manifests, in the course of the three years of His life on Earth, the meaning and purpose of world evo- lution. Thus in the first year Christ's Ego unites with the astral body of the man, Jesus, which has its origin in the Old Moon incarnation of our planet, and transforms it into the radiant Spirit Self, the final goal of Jupiter evolution. In the second year Christ's Ego unites with the etheric body of Jesus, the gift of the Old Sun condition of our Earth, and transforms it into the Life-Spirit, filled with cosmic love—the goal of Venus evolution. Finally, in the third year, Christ's Ego unites with the physical body of Jesus of Nazareth, the legacy of Old Saturn, and transforms it into the Spirit Man, filled with the forces of cosmic sacrifice, into the imperishable Resurrection-body—the goal of the whole of world-evolution, which will be reached by man only in the very distant future, on Vulcan. Thus the three years of Christ's earthly life encompass *the whole* of world-evolution *from Saturn to Vulcan*, from the emergence of the first rudiments of man's physical body to the independent cosmic creativity of the Spirit Man.

With his microcosmic ego, man can now re-enact this grand path of the macrocosmic ego in a microcosmic way in the period from Epiphany until Easter—though not *in actuality*, as formerly accomplished by Christ, but *through the metamorphosis of his consciousness*. For, in penetrating human sheaths from out of the ego, the Christ-impulse is capable of raising the consciousness of such a man to those cosmic regions whence these sheaths are created by the higher spirits every time before he incarnates on the Earth. In other words, when a man immerses himself within the Christ-impulse in his sheaths, he gradually penetrates to their sources of origin, which are the various spheres of the great world or macrocosm. Rudolf Steiner gives the following description in this regard: 'And as human beings pass from incarnation to incarnation in the course of the rest of earthly evolution, those who wish to permeate their souls with the power of that Personality who once lived on Earth [that is, with the power of Christ] can ascend to ever loftier heights [of the spiritual world] ... Being permeated with the power of Christ *at first inwardly, then ever more and more in one's outer being*—this will become possible for all who wish it. The future will not merely understand Christ but will be permeated by Him.'[1]

Thus the spiritual path of the cycle of the year leads us from self-knowledge (in the period from the summer solstice to Christmas) to world-knowledge (in the period from Epiphany until the height of summer). As an archetype of this 'microcosmic' path into the macrocosm upon which we embark at this time with our consciousness, there stands before us the experiences of the Apostles of Christ Jesus, of whose conscious ascent into ever higher regions of the spiritual world we find indications in the tenth and eleventh lectures of Rudolf Steiner's cycle devoted to the Gospel according to St Matthew. He describes its more general character in the following way: 'As you know, one aspect of initiation consists in going out into the macrocosm. And as Christ bears the impulse for such an initiation, so does He direct his disciples—in so far as He leads them—out into the cosmos. Just as the individual pupil who pursues this path of initiation *grows consciously into the macrocosm, which he learns to know sphere by sphere*, so does Christ, so to speak, encircle the whole macrocosm, everywhere manifesting the forces working within it and transmitting them to His disciples.'[2]

Here, however, the question arises: what is meant by 'growing consciously into the macrocosm, which he learns to know sphere by sphere'? We may find an answer to this in these same lectures of the cycle devoted to the Gospel of St Matthew,[3] where there is a detailed description of the individual stages through which the Apostles pass in their consciousness on their spiritual path out into the sphere of the macrocosm.

The first stage in the Apostles' penetration in consciousness into the spiritual world is the imaginative picture of the feeding of the five thousand, which took place in the evening, and the walking on the sea that followed that same night. We are concerned here with the elemental world, the so-called Moon-sphere or the soul-world. The *vesperal* and *nocturnal* character of both these events, their connection with the Moon, the mistress of the night—that world through which man's soul passes between falling asleep and waking—is similarly an indication of this sphere. In this spiritual world closest to the Earth, the Apostles have to accomplish deeds which relate to the next phase of human evolution and which only begin to bear fruit in our time. They bestow the gifts of cosmic wisdom received from Christ to those souls who dwell in the Moon-sphere and whose task it is to incarnate and work on the Earth in our fifth post-Atlantean epoch.*[3] In the scene of the walking on the waters, the disciples are borne fully into the elemental, astral world which comes before them in the picture of the watery element (of which Old Moon, where man acquired his astral body, consisted in former times). This is where the Apostles—led by Christ—arrive through the awakening of their consciousness in the astral body. This first 'awakening' is the result of the union of the macrocosmic Ego of Christ with the astral body of Jesus of Nazareth. They have to withstand two principal temptations at this stage: fear and the resultant tendency to illusion, to self-deception, to inner untruthfulness.[4]

At the second stage the consciousness of the Apostles ascends directly to the spiritual world itself, to lower Devachan. This stage in the inner development of the Apostles comes before us in the scene of the Transfiguration on Mount Tabor. However, of the twelve Apostles only three of them, John, James and Peter, are able to rise as far as this. In this new supersensible experience, the Apostles immerse themselves first in the world of the six planets—which is why it is said that this event takes place 'after six days'[5]—in order then spiritually to approach the heart of the whole planetary system, the Sun itself, and to experience Christ as the most exalted Sun Being. 'And His face shone like the Sun,'[6] the Gospel tells us. Inwardly supported by Christ, the Apostles, their consciousness having awakened in the etheric body, now reach the sphere of the Sun or the region of lower Devachan—an attainment which is the consequence of the union of Christ's Ego with the etheric sheath of Jesus of Nazareth. The principal temptation encountered in consciously penetrating one's etheric body is that of egoism. In the scene as it is described, the overcoming of egoism is expressed in the words which characterize the behaviour of Peter and the two other Apostles: 'But he did not know what to say, for they were *drawn out of themselves* through their exceeding fear'[7]—that is, out of that part of man's being where the self-love and egoism that are associated with the activity of the lower ego are rooted.

The third stage[8] forms the ascent to higher Devachan—to the point of its boundary with the Buddhi plane, with the world of Providence. This is reached in the scene of the prayer about the cup in the Garden of Gethsemane. It is there that Christ calls the Apostles to rise to a yet higher stage

---

* More will be said later about the nature of these gifts of wisdom.

in their ascent into the macrocosm. But they are not able to do this, they are not able to follow Christ any further with their consciousness, they leave Him alone, they go to sleep ... Then, when Christ Jesus has been taken prisoner, despair overwhelms their hearts and an impenetrable darkness clouds their minds. Only one disciple, 'the disciple whom the Lord loved', is in a position to raise his consciousness to this particular spiritual sphere and, hence, to follow Christ to the point of standing consciously beneath the Cross of Golgotha. This sole disciple is the Apostle John, who thenceforth embodies the deepest Mystery of human evolution, the inner meaning of which Rudolf Steiner, on the basis of words from the Gospel of St John, describes as follows: 'The scriptural words can, therefore, be interpreted: But standing by the cross of Jesus was His mother, "Sophia". To His mother He says: "Woman, behold your son". He entrusted the Sophia which was in Him to John. He made him the son of the Sophia, saying: "Behold your mother ... You must henceforth acknowledge the divine wisdom as your mother and dedicate yourself to her alone."'[9] In other words, John, who through the union of the Christ-Ego with the physical body of Jesus of Nazareth had also supersensibly awakened in the forces of his physical body, was there on Golgotha able to receive Christ's Sophia, that is, the Holy Spirit who proceeded from Him.[10] Through this third 'awakening', the whole sphere of the macrocosm, whence man's physical body has its spiritual foundations, was revealed to John's clairvoyant gaze. The secrets of all the starry spheres of the zodiac became accessible to his spiritual perception, and also that which is hidden, as the most sublime mystery of the world, *beyond the zodiac*, in the sphere of Providence: the great starry colleagueship of the twelve Bodhisattvas, immersed in ceaseless contemplation of the archetypal source of divine Light, Love and Life. From Christ, who, in Rudolf Steiner's words, can be found at this 'dizzy height wholly divested of all that He has become on Earth and in its surroundings,'[11], there proceeds, streams, as a light-bearing substance of purest world-wisdom, the substance of the Holy Spirit. This substance is bestowed upon the Apostle John as he stands beneath the Cross, his clairvoyant gaze beholding at that moment the highest aspect of Christ's Sun Being, while he is receiving the Sophia of Christ (the Christosophia).[12]

Thus in this threefold ascent of the Apostles into the macrocosm we may find expressed the gradual process of the awakening of their consciousness in the respective sheaths. This process, as a purely inward soul experience, can become accessible to the human soul in the cycle of the year in the period from Epiphany until Easter. It corresponds to the gradual penetration of the Christ-impulse, first kindled in the human ego, into the darkness of man's outer sheaths, through which means man is able to contemplate those spheres of the macrocosm which reveal themselves to the spirit-pupil who has reached the corresponding stages of imaginative, inspirative and intuitive knowledge.

However, what is represented in human experience as the microcosmic path of the Christ-impulse from man's ego through the three sheaths out into the outer world is for the Christ Being Himself the macrocosmic path of His ascent back into the cosmos, though now together with all humanity which belongs to Him. For in working within the human ego, Christ wins back the earthly sphere. In entering man's astral body, He wins the Moon-sphere. In penetrating the etheric body, He regains possession of the planetary spheres, even the Sun itself. And finally, entering the physical body, He bestows upon mankind the whole world of the fixed stars and so gains access for all mankind to that great colleagueship in the world of Providence of which we spoke earlier.

2. The Threefold Revelation of Christ and the Three New Mystery Virtues

What has been described in the previous chapter as the new ascent of Christ into the macrocosm, which corresponds to the awakening in the sheaths of human beings of that consciousness which is able to penetrate into ever wider regions of the macrocosm, will be accompanied for humanity by a deepening and a widening of the knowledge of Christ Himself. This will come to expression in that Christ will, in the measure of the development within humanity, send ever higher revelations of His own being down from the supersensible worlds. These two processes, which are beginning already in our own time, will in future gradually run parallel to one another. On the one hand, the gradual awakening of man's ego-consciousness in his sheaths will generate an influx of spiritual forces from the corresponding regions of the spiritual cosmos which Rudolf Steiner describes in the following words: 'In our time the forces of the astral world enter the human soul; in the sixth cultural epoch the forces of lower Devachan will to a greater extent enter the human soul; and in the seventh cultural epoch it will be especially the forces of higher Devachan that will work within humanity.'[13] While on the other hand, as though parallel to this process, ever higher revelations of Christ Himself will pour into mankind as a direct consequence of His influence working within human being's sheaths. Rudolf Steiner refers to this second process as follows: 'That individuality which was the Christ-individuality, who was on Earth for only three years in the body of Jesus of Nazareth, will never return again in a physical body but only in an etheric body in the fifth cultural epoch, in an astral body in the sixth cultural epoch, and, in the seventh cultural epoch, in a great cosmic Ego, which will be like a great Group-soul of humanity.'[14] In other words: this threefold revelation of Christ to humanity will correspond precisely to the gradual awakening within man of higher faculties: of imaginative faculties in the astral body, beginning from our own time; inspirative faculties in the etheric body, in the Slavonic epoch; and intuitive faculties in the physical body, in the seventh, American epoch, the last before the great catastrophe.*

Let us turn at this point once more to words of Rudolf Steiner, where he characterizes the three stages of this ascending path of human development.

---

* See *Rudolf Steiner and The Founding of the New Mysteries* by S.O. Prokofieff, p. 7.

We shall direct particular attention to certain deeper characteristics in the quotations that follow, inasmuch as they can offer us considerable help in what we have to say later. Thus in the lecture of 4 November 1911 in Leipzig, Rudolf Steiner says: 'Whereas at an earlier time, when Christ came down to Earth in a physical body, people would not have been able to perceive Him otherwise than in a physical body, in our age forces are actually awakening through which we will see Christ not in a physical body but in an etheric form which will exist on the astral plane. Thus already in our century, beginning from the thirties and increasingly towards the middle of the century, a large number of people will behold Christ etherically. This will constitute a great advance beyond those earlier times when people were not yet sufficiently mature to behold Him in this way. This is also what is meant by the saying that Christ will appear in the clouds [that is, in the spiritual environment of the Earth], for this means that He will appear as an etheric form on the astral plane ... Then will come a time when even greater powers will awaken within man. This will be a time when Christ will manifest Himself in a still loftier manner; in an astral form in the world of lower Devachan.'[15]

Rudolf Steiner describes this second revelation of Christ in another lecture: 'Christ will appear to a certain number of people in the world of lower Devachan *in a form of light, as a sounding Word,* proclaiming to the receptive minds of human beings, *from out of His astral Body of Light, that Word which was active in astral form at the beginning of time, as John sets forth in the first words of his Gospel.*'[16] Finally, regarding the seventh epoch: 'The age of morality will, through a certain number of people, perceive Christ as He reveals Himself from higher Devachan in His true Ego, which immeasurably surpasses the ordinary human ego and in which there shines forth all that can endow man with the highest possible moral impulses.'[17] And in another lecture: '... The final epoch, that of moral impulses [the seventh], will be the time when human beings who have passed through the other stages *will behold the Christ in His glory, as the form of the greatest Ego, as the spiritualized Ego-Self, as the great Teacher of human evolution in higher Devachan.*'[18]

This new threefold revelation of Christ in future epochs, which corresponds to the natural awakening of higher faculties within humanity, can also become accessible—although in a somewhat different form—to every individual in the yearly rhythm between Epiphany and Easter. It is nevertheless so that anyone who wishes to approach a real experience of these revelations, that is, who wishes to experience the Christ Being in his three sheaths, must embark at this time upon a path of inner spiritual and moral development, which is, in turn, directly associated with the acquisition of certain moral virtues.

Just as the virtues of justice, temperance and prudence, fortitude and wisdom have come to us from the 'pre-Christian' Mysteries of antiquity, so from out of the Christian Mysteries of today do there appear before us three new virtues which are, in a sense, the daughters of the all-embracing wisdom, the cosmic Sophia. These are the virtues of faith, love and hope.[19]

The experiences of Advent, the culmination of which is the birth of our higher ego from out of the mother-substance of wisdom at Christmas, lead us in the yearly rhythm through the four ancient virtues. During the thirteen Holy Nights that follow, this higher ego is to rise gradually to a conscious experience of the Christ Being. If such an experience is attained by Epiphany, this Christ-force which has entered into the human ego will be able to penetrate the three sheaths of man's being and ultimately encompass the *whole* of his nature, that is, to the point of penetrating the physical body at Easter. However, the magic keys which open the gates to the respective human sheaths for the Christ-impulse are the new Mystery-virtues: faith opens up the way for the Christ-impulse into man's astral body, love into the etheric body, and hope into the physical body. Hence they are the themes of the three stages of inner development which in the cycle of the year unite the festival of Epiphany with the festival of Easter; for, as stages of metamorphosis in the human soul, they are a microcosmic expression of the great macrocosmic path uniting the Christ Being with the three sheaths of Jesus of Nazareth during the time from the Baptism in the Jordan until the Mystery of Golgotha.

Finally, there is one very important area which is illumined through a more detailed study of these virtues—that of the historical evolution of mankind. For in the general course of human evolution, the entry of the Christ-impulse into the sheaths of earthly human beings will, as we have seen, take place during, respectively, the fifth, sixth and seventh cultural epochs. And so the chapters that follow will also help us to penetrate more deeply into the nature of the underlying historical forces and spiritual impulses working within these three epochs.

3. The Virtue of Faith and the Fifth post-Atlantean Epoch

The first of the three new Mystery-virtues is that of faith. Through this virtue man can experience the immediate presence of the Christ-impulse in his astral body. One could also say that true faith is born of a 'super-abundance' in the human ego of the Christ-impulse, which is at the same time and above all an impulse of universal cosmic love.[20] This universal cosmic love which fills the human ego to abundance begins to flow out from it into man's astral body where it appears in the form of faith. Rudolf Steiner refers to this deeper origin of faith in man as follows: 'Faith is the capacity of going beyond oneself, of flowing out beyond what I can do for my own self-perfection'.[21] ('Flowing out beyond the ego' initially means here the penetration of the Christ-impulse from the ego into the astral body.) Somewhat earlier in the same lecture we read: 'That person has faith who receives Christ into himself in such a way that his ego is not merely an empty vessel but is filled to overflowing with content. And this content which fills him to overflowing is none other than the content of love.'[22] It is clear from these words of Rudolf Steiner that, esoterically speaking, faith is a particular form of the all-embracing cosmic substance of love, as it appears in man's *astral* body; it is that inner power through which the Christ-impulse can penetrate the human soul in our time.

In two lectures which he gave in December 1911 in Nürnberg under the title, *Faith, Hope, Love—Three Stages in the Life of Humanity*, Rudolf Steiner speaks of how the whole character of the modern epoch is delineated by the development of the power of faith in man's astral body. One can detect the working of this power in even the most fully materialistic manifestations of modern civilization, although often in an almost unrecognizably distorted form. In Rudolf Steiner's words: 'Thus it is essentially the power of faith of the astral body which shines into the soul and gives our age its particular character. Some people might say: "It is rather strange that you are telling us now that the power of faith is the most important power of our time. Yes, perhaps we can acknowledge this with respect to those people who have kept alive the old faith, but now there are so many who, because they have abandoned it, look upon faith as a childish stage of human evolution." Of course, those people who call themselves monists may be allowed to believe that they do not believe, but nevertheless they are believers just as much as those others who call themselves believers. And everything which comes to light in the various forms of monism is nothing but blind faith, even though people are not aware of this: they believe it to be knowledge.'[23] This is a power which in our time aspires to have a determining influence on the inner development of mankind. However, in speaking about faith in this way we touch upon only one aspect of our fifth post-Atlantean epoch.

In order to characterize the other aspect as well, we need to turn to what, in no less a degree than the power of faith, defines its distinctive character. This second essential quality is the force of 'intellectuality'. Rudolf Steiner speaks of this in the following words: 'Thus intellectuality forms the general spiritual character of our epoch, but there is a difference between the way it is manifested in the materialistic thinking of today and in spiritual science. Man is connected by means of his intellectuality with the astral plane, but he is able to become conscious of this—and only then can he make proper use of it—if he develops to the point of clairvoyance. During the twentieth century this will begin to happen with an ever-growing number of people. Progress now depends on human beings developing a revitalized intellectuality not only for themselves but bearing it up into the astral world. Those who have advanced to intellectual clairvoyance in this sense will in the course of the next three thousand years be able to approach the etherically visible Christ with an ever greater clarity.'[24] Later on in the same lecture: 'In the excesses of its growth in the outer world the intellectual element has a strong tendency towards dogmatism, but in spirit-knowledge the intellect has to become spiritualized in order that it may understand the higher results of occult research.'[25] Thus when Rudolf Steiner speaks repeatedly in his lectures of how Anthroposophy should not be brought as a dry, abstract theory but that anthroposophical truths should be inwardly enlivened and warmed by feeling and so be led to a truly inner sense of sympathy, he is referring above all to the need for *a true faith* in the human heart, for that faith which the Apostle Paul speaks of as an unshakeable inner *certainty*[26] and which can, indeed, never be in contradiction with genuine knowledge.

This thought is expressed, entirely in the spirit of the Apostle Paul, by Rudolf Steiner in words which everyone who, in our intellectual and natural-scientific epoch, wishes to come nearer to an experience of true faith really ought to say to himself: 'I only believe what I know for certain. Knowledge is the only foundation of faith. We ought to know so that we may rise ever more to the powers which exist in the human soul as powers of faith. *We must have that in our soul which is able to behold a supersensible world, which is capable of directing all our thoughts and conceptions towards a supersensible world.* And if we do not have this power, which is expressed in the word "faith", a sense of desolation enters into us, we become parched and dried up, like an autumn leaf.'[27]

Thus the power of faith in its true spiritual aspect is that power which, unfolding and working in man's astral body, is capable of taking hold of intellectuality and drawing it forth on the path leading to the spiritual world.[28] For only if it is transformed by the power of faith can intellectuality rise to a true state of spiritualization and, thereby, to a new clairvoyance which can enable modern man to behold the Etheric Christ.

In modern civilization the powers of faith and intellectuality work in divergent ways. It is even so that the rift between them grows wider as the age of materialism sinks into the abyss. This gulf can be bridged only through modern spiritual science with the help of the Michael-Christ impulse, through the spiritualization of the intellectual foundations of external human culture. And this can come about only as a result of a true development of the power of faith in the human soul (in the astral body). If this does not happen, if modern spiritual science is not perceived to a sufficient extent by humanity to be a living source of nourishment for man's astral body, '... the astral body will become ill and, through it, also man's physical organism.'[29] The various sicknesses of the soul which are spreading over the whole world today are the dire symptoms of this. It is not sickness alone which threatens mankind but also what is spreading like a devastating epidemic over the world: an all-consuming fear and, proceeding from it, an inner deceitfulness, a tendency to self-deception and various forms of illusion. Even if these are not always experienced consciously, it is nevertheless so that fear and uncertainty about the future—qualities which are taking on an increasingly animal-like character—are dominating human thoughts, feelings and actions to a significantly greater degree than is generally supposed. Thus the stern words of the spiritual researcher stand as a warning against this danger: 'And if people were really to lose faith, they would come to see, even in the next century, what this would mean for evolution. For if the power of faith were lost, people would have to move around the world in such a way that no one would know any longer what to do with himself in order to cope with life, that no one would be able to stand in the world because he has *fear, care and anxiety* about this or that.'[30]

In the scenes in the Gospels of the feeding of the five thousand and the walking on the waters, in which, as already observed, the consciousness of the Apostles is awakened on the astral plane, we have a prophetic indication of all these grave dangers of our time and also of the path of overcoming them through the development of the *power of faith* in man's astral body.

Rudolf Steiner, in the lecture-cycle of 1912 on the Gospel of St Matthew, reveals the esoteric significance of the figure of 5000—in connection with the occult symbolism of numbers in ancient Jewish mystery-wisdom—as an indication of our fifth post-Atlantean epoch.[31] Thus everything that happens in this scene, as in the scene of the walking on the waters that follows it, takes the form of prophetic events experienced by the Apostles in the spiritual world nearest to the Earth, through the opening up within them of an imaginative consciousness, as a direct supersensible indication of the epoch which is in our time only gradually beginning and will last for a further fifteen hundred years or so.*

The Gospel of St Matthew tells us before the story of the feeding of the five thousand that 'it was evening' and 'the day is now over'.[32] This evening and nocturnal character of these events is an indication to us of that world where they actually take place. They take place in the world where the souls of all human beings dwell at night, that is, on the astral plane, in the soul-world. The disciples have five loaves and two fishes. These number relationships correspond, according to the most ancient esoteric tradition, to the Mysteries of certain signs of the circle of the zodiac. In the final lecture of the cycle *The East in the Light of the West. The Children of Lucifer and the Brothers of Christ*, Rudolf Steiner says: 'Remember that I have directed your attention to how, if one enters *the region of the astral*, one has to do with a world of transformation, where what works from one point of view as good can from another viewpoint work as something evil. These differences between good and evil have their significance in the realm of becoming, and the number seven serves as a guide in this realm; while the Gods, who are represented symbolically in the twelve points of space, in the twelve constant points, are exalted above good and evil.'[33]

Evil arises, as Rudolf Steiner says in this same lecture, when the higher archetype of twelvefoldness which abides in Devachan enters into the time-bound astral region of the cosmos and at once separates into two spheres, into good and evil, light and darkness.[34] To the first belong the signs from the Bull to the Virgin; to the second those from the Scorpion to the Fishes. According to a profound esoteric law the two signs of the Ram and the Scales which stand on the watershed of the two spheres also belong to the realm of light. Then Rudolf Steiner continues: 'As soon as that which in Devachan has an element of duration and has nothing to do with time, as soon as this enters into time, it immediately divides into good and evil. Of the twelve constant points, five remain in the sphere of the good which, with the two points at the extremities, makes seven altogether. Hence we speak of the seven which remain over from the twelve ... Hence, too, there arises the imagination whereby seven signs of the zodiac belong to the world of light, the upper world, and the five lower signs, beginning with the Scorpion, belong to the world of twilight.'[35] From

---

* Until, that is, the beginning of the sixth post-Atlantean epoch.

these words we may gain an understanding of the significance of the five loaves, corresponding to the five light constellations, and the two fishes, lying at the boundary between the spheres of light and darkness, which in nature live at the border of the two elements of air and water. This initial number of the loaves and fishes, namely seven, acquires, however, a further significance if it is compared with the conclusion of the 'meal', with the *twelve* full baskets of scraps (from the loaves *and* the fishes). The world-Mysteries such as are hidden in this scene are truly inexhaustible. For this reason they should be examined again and again from many different aspects so as to obtain the fullest possible picture. And so in this scene we have to do with a definite process of transition from the number seven (5 + 2) to the number twelve. What is the initial number of this transition? In world evolution the number seven is the numerical foundation of the stream of time. 'Thus everything which leads us into time also brings us to the number seven,'[36] as Rudolf Steiner says. In this sense, the law of seven is, on the one hand, the law of our inner world, of our soul-life (astral body)[37] and, on the other, it works everywhere in what is transmitted through the blood from parents to children, from ancestors to descendants; for in what lives in time one thing always follows another. In this is also expressed the luciferic character of the law of seven as it appears on the astral plane.[38] 'We recognize what evolves in time when we pass from the later to the earlier, as from child to father. When we enter the world of time which is ruled by the number seven, we speak of children and their origin, of the children of spiritual beings, of the children of Lucifer.'[39] The law of twelve, which is connected with the reverse transition from time to space, stands over and against this luciferic aspect of the sevenfold law: 'When we translate time into space, we are speaking of those beings who stand next to one another, for whom it is significant that they stand beside one another and that *soul impulses* pour forth from one to the other in space. Where the number seven is, through the flowing of time into space, transformed into twelve, the concept of "children" ceases to have its former meaning; instead there appears the concept of "brotherhood"; for those who live beside one another are brothers.'[40]

Thus, this scene in the Gospel is an indication that the Apostles, as a result of their past lives, bear in their astral bodies the profound Mystery of the seven light signs of the zodiac. (To Christ's question, they answer that they have only five loaves and two fishes). But in the course of time, as the epoch of the events of Palestine drew nearer, this ancient wisdom acquired an increasingly luciferic character, so that humanity began to be threatened by the danger of succumbing completely to the forces of Lucifer and of remaining in his realm in a state of eternal childhood, altogether deprived of the possibility of attaining true freedom, that is, a genuine morality and a true capacity for love. To become eternally 'children of Lucifer'—such was the first danger which threatened mankind. Christ set against this principle of 'Lucifer sonship' a 'brotherhood' founded upon freedom which became possible only because Christ Himself became the brother of human beings, the elder brother of the Apostles. 'They need not go away; you give them something to eat,'[41] He says to them, as free co-workers in His labours, who carry out their deeds not on the basis of blood or sonship but out of spiritual, brotherly love. In this sense the 'transition' from the seven-principle to the twelve-principle described in the Gospels at the feeding of the five thousand is none other than—in Rudolf Steiner's expression—'... the transition from the sons or children of Lucifer's realm [and of his being] to the brothers of Christ.'[42] In this scene in the Gospels there is, therefore, an indication of the possibility of fully overcoming the luciferic forces in man's astral body with the help of the Christ-impulse.

In the Gospel of St Mark, on the other hand, the connection of the ahrimanic forces with this scene is particularly referred to. Here the disciples answer Christ's words 'you give them something to eat'[43] by saying: 'Shall we go and buy *200 denarii worth* of bread and give it to them to eat?'[44] This reference to the '200 denarii' which the Apostles still possess conceals a Mystery of some significance. It is known that in the Mystery-wisdom of the Jews the number of 200 corresponded to the letter *Resh* in the Hebrew alphabet and signified the lower forces of man's astral body,[45] that is, the dark signs of the zodiac. In so far as it is 200 *denarii*, that is, the sum of money that this answer refers to, it is clear that this has to do with the forces of the astral body that are under the power of Ahriman, forces which in present-day humanity belong to the Beast of the Apocalypse and are preparing to place themselves at the service of the future Antichrist. That this 'money-principle' should in the course of the fifth cultural epoch enter into the purely supersensible process of the spiritual nourishment of mankind must be seen in connection with the fact that immediately *after* this scene Christ suddenly abandons the disciples, having first induced them to set forth on a dangerous night voyage. Now the disciples are alone, and in this solitude they have to struggle with the opposing forces of Lucifer (wind) and Ahriman (waves). At first Christ does not help them but nevertheless remains connected with them and, according to the Gospel of St Mark, before coming to their aid, He *sees them* clairvoyantly: 'And when evening came, the boat was out on the sea and He was alone on the land. *And He saw that they were distressed in rowing*, for the wind was against them...'[46]

In St Matthew's Gospel the continuation of this scene is depicted in these words: 'And in the fourth watch of the night He came to them, walking on the sea. But when the disciples saw Him walking on the sea, they were terrified, saying, "It is a ghost!" And they cried out for fear.'[47] Of course, the fear and terror of the disciples were not in this case called forth merely by a 'ghost'. On the contrary. The long night voyage on the stormy 'astral sea' would in itself have already aroused considerable shock and terror in the Apostles. For this reason their astral vision was temporarily darkened and they *did not recognize* Christ Jesus coming towards them to their aid. Furthermore, not only did they not recognize Him but took Him for an entirely different being, for a ghost—and this was why their terror grew to such a boundless extent that they even 'cried out' for fear. 'But immediately He spoke to them, saying, "Take heart, it is I; have no fear."'[48] Through His *word* Christ led the Apostles out of the condition of spiritual darkness which had been called forth by fear, restored to them a true spiritual vision and consequently helped them to overcome fear and inner illusion. But when Peter, who had elected to go and meet Him on the sea, again 'was afraid' and began 'to sink', 'Jesus immediately reached out His hand and caught him, saying to him, '*O man of little faith*, why did you doubt?'[49] For the essential reason why Peter did not stand the test which he had taken upon himself lay in *his lack of faith*, that is, in the weakness of the spiritual consciousness in his astral body.

Mark the Evangelist refers in a striking way to this weakness of the spiritual consciousness of all the Apostles in connection with the previous scene of the feeding of the five thousand: 'for they did not understand about the loaves, because *their hearts were hardened*.'[50] In reading these words it is impossible to view them otherwise than as inwardly connected in the scene of the 'feeding', as described by Mark, with the presence of the ahrimanic forces which appear in the picture of the 200 denarii with which the Apostles suggested that bread be bought for the people. It is not difficult to feel in this suggestion of the Apostles a distant echo of Christ's first temptation in the wilderness, when the tempter suggested that He turn stones into bread.

Now we may once more recall that both these scenes reflect in a prophetic way the inner character of the new age and, in particular, that quite special epoch which began in the early years of our own twentieth century. From this point of view the events that have been described can come to have an additional, highly important significance and can serve as a key to an understanding of the immediate present. Let us return to the first scene of the 'feeding with the loaves and fishes' and examine it once again in this context. There we learn that it is precisely in our time when Christ will gradually become visible to an increasing number of people as an 'etheric form on the astral plane', that the final transition from 'the children of Lucifer' to 'the brothers of Christ' will be made. For in the twentieth century Christ will appear to people not only as the great teacher and shepherd of souls but as a 'loving friend', as a brother seeking His brothers amongst human beings. Rudolf Steiner speaks of this, in words which are striking in their depth and warmth of feeling, in a lecture of 6 February 1917 in Berlin: 'And if only this would be sought, it would now be wholly possible to be near Christ, to find Christ in an altogether different way from how He was found in former times ... He will appear at the indicated time in the twentieth century in a new form, in a form particularly accessible to the human soul ... For as Christ approaches, the time will come when people will learn to ask Christ not only about their own souls but also about how they will, with help, establish their immortal part here on the Earth. Christ is not only the Lord of man but the *Brother of man*, who wants to be asked, particularly in the future, about all life's details ... In our time events appear to occur where people seem to stand at the greatest possible distance from asking this of Christ ... But all the same the time must come, it is already near, when the human soul in its immortal aspect will ask Christ about what it wishes to undertake: should this happen or should it not? Then the human soul will see Christ *beside it* in certain situations of life as *a loving friend*, receiving from the Christ Being not only comfort and strength but also an indication of what is to come. The Kingdom of Christ Jesus is not of this world but it must work in this world, and human souls must become the instruments of this kingdom which is not of this world ... But humanity must learn to consult Christ. How shall this happen? It can happen only if we learn His language. Anyone with insight into the deeper meaning of what our spiritual science would achieve sees in it not merely theoretical knowledge ... but seeks in it an altogether special language which is capable of expressing spiritual things ... And if we learn rightly to speak this language of spiritual life, then, my dear friends, Christ will stand beside us and give us an answer ... And if anyone tries to learn to think about the world in accordance with the strivings of spiritual science ... the form of Christ Jesus will approach him out of the dim, dark depths of world-mysteries, and will be for him a strong force in which he will live, *supported in a brotherly way* by the One who stands *beside* him, so that he might be strong in heart and soul, so that he might become mature for the tasks of future human evolution.'[51]

The luciferic and ahrimanic powers are, from our time onwards, making every possible effort to prevent this new appearance of Christ in the realm of the etheric. In the present age, however, when everything is resolved through the free will and free decisions of the human individual, the forces of opposition have to work in the world principally through human beings, and they employ the most refined spiritual devices to allure as many people as possible. Their chief instruments in this battle against the new Advent are the various secret societies of both East and West which, albeit in a variety of ways, nonetheless serve one and the same purpose: that of preventing mankind from attaining a new experience of Christ.

The eastern brotherhoods are inspired in this sense principally by luciferic powers. Through the artificial regeneration of the old luciferic wisdom of the East and its diffusion in the West, they attempt in many ways to prevent mankind from making the transition from the old principle of the seven to the new Christian principle of the twelve. These secret societies of the East strive to deny humanity the experience of the new 'brotherly' relationship to the Christ, and in the circles of their initiates they have firmly resolved to turn all human beings into 'children of Lucifer', who are nourished only by the old luciferic wisdom—which would finally prevent any real knowledge of the Christ-impulse. Because of their influence, western man would gradually lose the free, individual ego that he has won in the course of Christian evolution and would plunge into an eternal state of childhood filled with mere misty dreams of the spiritual world and, instead of the *new* clairvoyance which is capable of perceiving the Etheric Christ, he would receive as a gift the old atavistic clairvoyance which has subsisted until now in the East and is based upon a weakly developed individual ego. In this event the whole West would in a spiritual sense come fully under the influence of the East and would altogether renounce its own Christian mission.[52] Such are the goals pursued by these societies with regard to the West. In the East these secret societies—according to Rudolf Steiner—use in particular the discarded etheric bodies of dead ancestors, of a race or a community—that is, they develop occult powers and influences with respect to *blood-connections* from father to children and so forth. This is done so that, with the help of special magical procedures, these forces might be given over to luciferic demons, which then appear to people in the form of their dead relative or ancestor in order to lead them astray in the sense of the goals described above.[53]

The western secret societies actively resisting the new Advent of Christ are inspired by ahrimanic powers. In their occult practices they do not, according to Rudolf Steiner, reject the new Advent of Christ, as happens in the East, but they try occultly to falsify it so that, instead of Christ, they advance the cause of a purely ahrimanic supersensible being who inspires them and whom they serve.[54] The 200 denarii, with which the Apostles, in the scene of the feeding of the five thousand, wanted to buy bread for the people, represent a deeply prophetic indication of the basic character of the activity of these western secret 'brotherhoods'. They strive through the power of money and political intrigue to achieve the gradual formation of a secret government that is above the state, which would have control over all social and economic relationships between people (these intentions of the western 'brotherhoods' were memorably described in artistic form in

131

Dostoyevsky's *Legend of the Grand Inquisitor*) in order that, having thus attained the greatest possible influence in this realm, they might secure for the ahrimanic being who inspires them, and who through them is gradually preparing an ahrimanic incarnation in a physical body, boundless power and universal recognition.[54a] Through their full control of the material side of life and their gradual attainment of economic dominion in the world, these secret western 'brotherhoods' strive to eradicate completely the free, spiritual life amongst mankind, replacing it with a purely ahrimanic 'wisdom'—the 'loaves bought with money' and the 'stones turned into bread' of the Gospel—and gradually transforming man into a reasoning beast who has been deprived of free will and individuality, who increasingly associates himself exclusively with the world of matter, and who in all his outer and inner actions is subjected solely to the orders of the invisible 'Grand Inquisitor'. In this sense the most effective means for the attainment of this goal would appear to be the gradual diffusion amongst mankind, on the one hand, of mass materialism and unbelief founded upon the achievements of a purely intellectual culture, and, on the other hand—in more confined circles—of various forms of *occult materialism*, which indeed acknowledges occult phenomena but tries to use them only for the satisfaction of lower animal desires, group egoism and purely material needs. In their occult practices these secret 'brotherhoods' of the West employ their own dead members, who, through special occult machinations brought forth in the lodges, continue to be of service to the particular lodge even after death, as invisibly present 'brothers' who are even now preparing the 'ahrimanic subhumanity' of the future.[55]

The principal result of these endeavours is the falsifying of the new purely spiritual principle of brotherhood which the Etheric Christ would bring to birth amongst humanity. But these 'brotherhoods' go still further in this direction.

In the scene in the Gospel where Christ is depicted as walking on the waters, we have none other than a prophetic indication of the Etheric Christ Who is to come in the fifth post-Atlantean cultural epoch. Through the raging airy element (air is an image of the astral world), Christ walks on the waters (water is an image of the etheric), that is, in the etheric body. However, the souls of the Apostles, paralysed by fear because the forces of the 200 denarii are working in their astral bodies, do not recognize Christ. Furthermore, they consider Him to be an altogether different being, they consider Him to be a *ghost*. In this mistake of the Apostles there is a stern, earnest warning for our time, an indication of the terrible danger that now stands before mankind: failure to recognize the Etheric Christ in His new Advent and to recognize instead of Him that ahrimanic individuality whose appearance is presently being prepared with great energy by the occult western 'brotherhoods'. 'People of the fifth post-Atlantean cultural epoch should be wary that they do not receive an ahrimanic spectre instead of Christ!'—this is what this Gospel scene would tell us.[56]

What, then, can we do to counteract this great seduction of humanity by the 'ahrimanic spectre'? The answer to this question is given in the above-quoted words from the Berlin lecture of 1919 regarding the necessity of receiving modern spiritual science into ourselves, receiving it not as a theory but as a spiritual language, in which we may turn directly to the Etheric Christ and put to Him the questions that are most needful for our time. 'Let us try,' continues Rudolf Steiner in this lecture, 'to make spiritual science our own, not merely as a teaching, but as a language, and then await the moment when we shall find those questions which we may address to Christ. And He will answer. Yes, *He will answer!* And he who out of the twilight depths of the spirit in which human evolution rests in our time *hears the advice of Christ, which He wants to give in the immediate future to him who seeks it,* will be endowed as a result with a wealth of soul forces, soul-strength and soul impulses.'[57]

Immediately after the description in the Gospel of the Apostles' experience of fright we read: 'But immediately He spoke to them saying, "Take heart, it is I; have no fear."'[58] These words are an indication of how Christ will, from our time onwards, help each soul that turns to Him, in the language through which He can converse, to overcome the seductive powers of the 'ahrimanic spectre', to overcome the fear and illusion which come to expression in the form of inner deceitfulness. For *fear*, which is engendered by a dread of developing the powers of faith that lead to the supersensible, and *falsehood*, which arises from an intellectualism that strives to resist spiritualization, are the two chief portents in our time of the manifestation of the 'ahrimanic spectre', those forces which may best facilitate his attempt to appear amongst mankind in place of the Etheric Christ.

And then in the Gospel we read: 'And Peter answered Him, "Lord, if it is you, bid me come to you on the water." He said, "Come." So Peter got out of the boat and walked on the water and came to Jesus.'[59] In these words of Peter we have an archetypal picture of those questions which we can *even today* ask of Christ in the language of modern spiritual science. And we may be assured that '... He answers. Yes, *He will answer!*',[60] just as He once answered Peter by saying, 'Come'. Only at this moment we ought not to be *of little faith.* In our time we should be so permeated by the strength of the new revelation of Christ that we may indeed set forth upon the waters of the astral sea to meet the Etheric Christ without having to hear His reproachful words, '... O man of little faith, why did you doubt?'[61]

A strong *faith*, which is at the same time an *unshakeable sense of certainty*, is what we must now cultivate in our soul. This real faith, this confidence in the reality of the spirit, which are the result of a strong soul, of a powerful and healthy astral body, spiritual science alone can give; for '... knowledge is food, food for the soul. The soul feeds upon what we apprehend as concepts through spiritual science.[62] It feeds upon that in which it believes, and it has healthy nourishment only in what spiritual science offers it.'[63] Thus in our time faith becomes that fundamental virtue which we must cultivate in our astral body so as to be able to advance with all inner confidence towards the Etheric Christ who now approaches us. It is precisely for this reason that, immediately after the scene of the walking on the waters (as described in the Gospel of St John), Christ answers the question of the people 'What must we do to be doing the works of God?' by saying: 'This is the work of God, that you *believe* in Him whom He has sent.'[64]

The scene of the walking on the waters conveys to us some remarkable subtleties in the new experience of Christ. In the Gospel of St Mark it is said that Christ '... saw that they were distressed in rowing',[65] that is, that they needed help, comfort. How profoundly these words accord with those in which Rudolf Steiner describes the new appearance of Christ in the etheric. 'A man—and it could be anyone—is going hither and thither, he is experiencing this or that. Only if he has really sharpened his vision through his studies of Anthroposophy may he notice that Someone has suddenly come near him, in order to *help* him, to turn his attention to this or that: that the Christ has come to him ... Many a person will even experience, when sitting quietly in his room, with heavy heart, oppressed with sorrow and not knowing which way to turn, that the door opens: the Etheric Christ appears and speaks to him words of consolation. Christ will become for people a living bearer of comfort!'[66] This element is also present in the scene of the feeding of the five thousand. In the Gospel of St Mark it is expressed as follows: 'As He landed He saw a great throng, and He had *compassion* on them, because they were like sheep without a shepherd: and He began to teach them many things.'[67] While in the Gospel of St Matthew it says at this point: 'As He went ashore He saw a great throng; and He had *compassion* on them, and *healed* their sick.'[68] Thus Christ works in our time as a teacher (bestowing help through the Word), as a comforter (in grief and suffering), and as a healer (bringing health to our astral body).[69]

The conversation of Christ with the Jews on the day after the feeding of the five thousand, which is to be found in the sixth chapter of St John's Gospel, also belongs to the whole esoteric content of these scenes. In the other Gospels this scene is missing—an indication that the Apostle John passed through this initiatory stage in a particularly complete way. In the

Gospels of Mark and Matthew there is at the corresponding points—that is directly after the scene of the walking on the waters—only a reference to the numerous acts of healing performed by Christ Jesus, the necessary condition of which was in each case a *faith* in His divine origin. It is true that the power of faith still works in a hidden way here, as though from the very depths of man's being, as a transforming force within the astral body, so that it ceases to give rise to destructive influences in the etheric body—which has, as a result, the possibility of bringing healing to the physical body. At the corresponding point of the Luke Gospel we do not even find references to this healing activity of Christ Jesus, and this would appear to be the result of Luke's omission of the entire scene of the walking on the waters. In this respect the Gospels of Luke and John form a polarity, while the Gospels of Mark and Matthew hold a middle position between them.[70]

The essential content of the conversation of Christ Jesus with the Jews, which is reported in the sixth chapter of St John's Gospel, is the need for *faith* as a necessary pre-condition for the penetration of the Christ-impulse into man's astral body: 'Then they said to Him, "What must we do, to be doing the works of God?" Jesus answered them, "This is the work of God—that you *believe* in Him whom He [the Father] has sent."'[71] This penetration of the Christ-forces into man's astral body in the form of faith leads, as we have seen, gradually to the unfolding of astral organs of perception and to an imaginative contemplation of the astral plane or the soul-world. This spiritual sphere is also where the man of our time may meet the Etheric Christ, who works there in all the fullness of the forces of His etheric body as the true 'bread of life'. (Both these words refer to the *etheric* nature of Christ. Bread is connected with the plant-world and has since ancient times been experienced as 'Sun-nourishment',[72] while life is the basic quality of the etheric body and was bestowed upon man on the Old Sun by the Spirits of Wisdom.)

Before the words quoted above, Christ speaks of the need not merely of perishable—that is, physical—food for human life but above all of the spiritual food 'which endures to eternal life.'[73] And they are followed by a detailed exposition of the teaching of 'the heavenly bread', which represents those etheric forces in whose garment Christ will, in times to come, spiritually enter into human existence. Here mention is also made of Moses, who had received into himself the etheric body of Zarathustra and had thereby been granted a vision of the forces of the macrocosmic etheric body of Christ in the burning bush on Mount Sinai, forces which Christ sacrificed in the course of His incarnation on Earth.[74]

Let us now give our attention to this great pronouncement regarding the 'bread of life' which has its fulfilment from our time onwards through the new appearance of Christ in an etheric body, and the conscious development of forces of faith in man's astral body.[75] Christ says: 'For the bread of God is that which comes down from heaven, and gives *life* to the world' (verse 33). 'I am *the bread of life*; he who comes to Me shall not hunger, and he who *believes*[76] in Me shall never thirst' (verse 35). 'For this is the will of My Father, that everyone who *sees* the Son and *believes*[77] in Him should have eternal life; and I will raise him up at the last day'[78] (verse 40). 'I am *the bread of life*' (verse 48). '... the *words* that I have spoken to you are *spirit* and *life*' (verse 63). For, in transforming the astral body, they lead to a direct clairvoyant experience of the Ego of Christ (the Spirit) in the etheric sheath (life). At the end of the conversation there is a reference to *unbelief* as the principal force which prevents Christ's penetration into man's astral body and which has been effective within it ever since: '... many of His disciples drew back and no longer went about with Him' (verse 66).

We may see from this that Christ's conversation with the Jews in the sixth chapter of St John's Gospel refers precisely to our time, to the time of the appearance of Christ in the etheric as the true 'bread of life', and that it also refers to *faith* as that soul-power which can now enable each to behold Him directly.

In all these scenes from the Gospels which, according to spiritual science, relate to the fifth post-Atlantean epoch, we find how the opposition of the two impulses of the Etheric Christ and the 'ahrimanic spectre', of the true 'bread of life' and the forces which lead to 'the hardening of hearts', comes ever more into the forefront. But the spiritual battle between these two impulses as the determining factor in the evolution of present-day humanity takes place not only in the hearts and souls of human beings but also—and with particular intensity—in the *social sphere*, where it manifests itself as the struggle between the social and anti-social tendencies of our time.

How does the particular character of these two impulses come to expression in our time? In what manifestations of modern civilization are they most in evidence? In order to answer this question we need to examine one further aspect of the working in the world of the Etheric Christ and of the opposing ahrimanic spirit who appears in the form of the 'spectre'.

According to the indications of spiritual science the word 'spectre'—as distinct from words such as 'demon', 'phantom' and so forth—is a technical occult term for ahrimanic elemental beings which arise in man's *etheric body* as a result of bad social relationships between people on Earth. Rudolf Steiner characterizes this emergence of 'spectres' in the following words: 'The sort of things which have a bad effect on the etheric body are, for instance, bad laws or bad social relationships in one or another human community. Everything which, for example, leads to unrest, which makes itself felt in bad relationships from man to man, works through the mood which is generated by this kind of social life in such a way that the effects reach the etheric body. And whatever gathers in the etheric body through the working of these soul-attributes leads, in turn, to the separation from the etheric body of certain spiritually active beings who then come to be found in our surroundings. These are called "spectres" or "ghosts".[79]

The strengthening of these processes through introducing into humanity social conditions that are as unhealthy as possible and favourably disposed to the authority of the 'ahrimanic spectre' is the essential task of the secret western 'brotherhoods' mentioned above. For this reason, these 'brotherhoods' inspire a very active enmity and resistance to the development of a 'threefold social organism'. For what these 'brotherhoods' have as their goal, in the organization of their social life, is directly opposed to the ideas of social threefoldness. The fulfilment of this goal leads to the appearance in the astral world of as large a number as possible of 'little ahrimanic spectres' which, in their turn, inspire human beings to wars[80] and to other destructive social processes that are gradually preparing the future War of All against All.

Against all these antisocial influences in our time must be set the *social* impulses proceeding from the Etheric Christ. There is a suggestion of this in the picture of the feeding of the five thousand, that is, of a large social community of people. Rudolf Steiner, out of his modern spiritual experience, also refers to the *social* nature of the working of the Etheric Christ from our time onwards: 'However extraordinary it may seem as yet, it is nevertheless true that many a time when people are sitting together not knowing which way to turn, if even a large number of people are sitting together, waiting—they will see the Etheric Christ! He Himself will be there. He will give advice, He will cast His word into such gatherings. We are now approaching these times.'[81]

Thus we may see how, on the one hand, certain occult circles battle as intensively as possible against the new appearance of Christ in the realm of the etheric through spreading bad social influences among mankind, with the object of ensuring that a humanity that has fallen prey to ahrimanic illusions meets not Christ but the 'ahrimanic spectre' in the spirit-land bordering upon the Earth and so falls finally under its influence. On the other hand, it is possible, through the diffusion of spiritual science, gradually to forge within humanity the right conditions for the social influences of the Etheric Christ, who is then able to help mankind to overcome the power of the 'ahrimanic spectre'. This will, however, be possible only through the development of that power of *faith* which, now slumbering in the depths of every human soul, can, through being united with the *spiritual intelligence* of our age, become a firm foundation for the new supersensible vision which is capable of leading to a direct experience of Christ.

Anthroposophists, in particular, are now increasingly called to participate *consciously* in this spiritual struggle which is being waged behind the scenes of contemporary events and which is expressed in the great imagination of the battle of Michael, the Countenance of Christ, with the dragon; for upon the outcome of this struggle at the end of our century depends the entire future of European culture. In this sense a great—one could even say, a cosmic—*responsibility* has been placed on the shoulders of those who, through their karma, have now found access to the new revelation of Michael-Christ, which works in the world in the form of modern anthroposophically orientated spiritual science.

Regarding this responsibility, and also the tasks which the spiritual world has set before people of today, the spiritual researcher addresses these stern words to the anthroposophists of the end of the century: 'Mankind stands today before a great potential crisis, before the possibility of either seeing all that pertains to civilization falling down into the abyss or of uplifting it through spiritualization and leading it onwards in the sense of what *is comprised in the impulse of Michael, of him who stands before the Christ-impulse.*'[82] 'It will indeed be decisive what human hearts do with this Michael-impulse in the world in the course of the twentieth century. In the course of the twentieth century, when the first century after Kali-Yuga has elapsed, humanity will either stand at the grave of all civilization or at the beginning of the epoch when Michael's battle on behalf of his impulse will be fought out in the souls of those people who in their hearts have united reason with spirituality.'[83]

4. The Virtue of Love and the Sixth post-Atlantean Epoch

The next stage in the penetration of the Christ-impulse into human sheaths is His descent into the etheric body. This union of Christ with the etheric body brings about an awakening of man's consciousness in lower Devachan, the planetary spheres (the macrocosmic reflection of the etheric body), and in particular in the Sun-sphere, that is, the world of Inspiration. Here, too, we have a picture of such an ascent of consciousness to lower Devachan in the second stage of the supersensible experiences of the Apostles, which is recorded in the Gospels in the scene of the Transfiguration on Mount Tabor.[84] That certain chosen Apostles could have such high spiritual experiences not as a result of an initiation in the Mysteries—which was all that was possible in olden times—but through their inner connection with the Christ, such an altogether new possibility opened up before them, and with them before all mankind, because of the union of the Christ Being with the etheric body of Jesus of Nazareth.

In the scene of the Transfiguration, Christ reveals Himself to John, Peter and James as the Spiritual Sun of the world between Elijah and Moses—the first of whom represents the forces of the upper planets, Mars, Jupiter and Saturn, while the second represents those of the lower planets, Venus, Mercury and the Moon. Thus the spiritual forces of the whole planetary system are revealed to the Apostles 'conversing with one another' in the great harmony of the spheres through the universal music. The images of Elijah and Moses are here also representative of the two principal 'pre-Christian' streams of the old Mysteries, the northern and the southern, which sought access to world mysteries through an ecstatic ascent into the macrocosm (with the help of the forces of the upper planets), or through a mystical immersion in man's inner being (with the help of the forces of the lower planets). Hence the initiation of Elijah, which is associated more with the astral body and ego, ends with his fiery ascent into Heaven, that is, into the macrocosm; while Moses, who received his first initiation—which was associated with insight into the mysteries of the physical and etheric bodies—in the Egyptian Mysteries, was able to describe the story of the creation of the world in six days, a story which was revealed to him through his connection with the etheric body of Zarathustra. In ancient times both Mystery-streams led in the end to one and the same goal, although along different paths: to an experience of the Midnight Sun of all existence and of Christ as the great Sun-Spirit who abides on the Sun. In the scene of the Transfiguration, Christ, appearing to the disciples between Elijah and Moses, like the Sun between the planets, is thus pointing prophetically to the future union of the two streams in the united all-embracing Mysteries of the Risen Christ. 'And behold, two men talked with Him, Moses and Elijah, who appeared in supersensible light and spoke of His departure, which He was to accomplish at Jerusalem.'[85] They were speaking of that central event which would forever unite the two streams: the Mystery of Golgotha.

In an esoteric sense this scene, like that of the feeding of the five thousand and the walking on the waters, is also a prophetic indication—in this case of Christ's future revelation to humanity in His *astral body* in the Sun-sphere or lower Devachan. This second revelation, which will become accessible in a natural way to humanity in the sixth cultural epoch, will enable man to experience at a new stage what Zarathustra in former times beheld as the great astral Sun-aura, as Ahura-Mazdao, just as the newly awakening, imaginative vision of the Etheric Christ, who now appears as the Lord of the Elements, is in its turn a rebirth at a new stage of what Moses once beheld in the burning bush on Sinai, as *'ehjeh, asher ehjeh'* ('I am the I AM').

Rudolf Steiner, in the passage quoted above (see p.121) characterizes this future manifestation of Christ as Spirit-Sun in lower Devachan, in the world of Inspiration, with the words: 'form of light', 'sounding Word', 'body of light', 'the Word which was active in astral form at the beginning of time (as at the beginning of St John's Gospel)'. All these experiences correspond precisely with the description in the Gospel of the scene of the Transfiguration. There too, 'light' and 'Word' are of paramount importance: 'And His face *shone* like the Sun, and His garments became white as *light*.'[86] 'He [Peter] was still speaking, when lo, a *bright* cloud overshadowed them, and *a voice from the cloud said*, "This is My beloved Son, with whom I am well pleased. In Him have I revealed Myself. *Hear His Word.*"'[87]

And if in the sixth cultural epoch people really 'hear' Christ, and allow Him to flow into their etheric bodies, they will create for Him the possibility of entering anew into the rulership of the Sun-realm, which has been His from eternity, whence He will from then on shine out before humanity as the great *Sun of love* which bestows life and warmth upon the whole world. Thus Christ's words which, in St Matthew's Gospel, immediately precede the Transfiguration scene, tell of how it will be granted to the disciples to behold Him in His own high Sun-kingdom: 'Truly, I say to you, there are some standing here who will not taste death before they see the Son of man *coming in His Kingdom.*'[88]

As we have already seen, this second future revelation of Christ can to some extent become accessible to man in the cycle of the year in the period from Epiphany until Easter. This is possible through an intensive inner development of that virtue which can, even in our time, open the gates of man's etheric body to the Christ-impulse. For just as faith enables Christ to be experienced in the astral body, so does *love* enable His presence to be experienced in the etheric body. In other words: through inwardly developing an all-embracing love, man can even today experience Christ in his etheric body. 'For the forces which have always worked, from the depths of our being, upon us from our etheric body are those forces which are expressed in man's capacity to love, to love at all stages of his existence.'[89] With these words the modern spiritual researcher tells us of the great potential which, since the Mystery of Golgotha, has been incorporated in our etheric body 'to love at all stages of our existence'—which is none other than a direct witness of the presence in our etheric body of the power of the living Christ. His presence must, however, become fully *conscious* within us. The scene of the Transfiguration on Mount Tabor is for us a prophetic indication of this *becoming conscious*.

Let us turn again briefly to the description of this event. We have already observed that words such as 'Sun', 'light', 'shining' have a special place in it. Why? Because all these words characterize with particular precision that fundamental principle which comes outwardly to expression here as light. Rudolf Steiner speaks about this deeply hidden mystery of light, and its connection with the essence and the origin of man's etheric body, as follows: 'Let us recall that man received the predisposition for the etheric body on Old Sun, that this fiery light-filled radiance of the Sun was the predisposition for the etheric body. Herein is expressed another aspect of love, love as it is manifested in the Spirit (i.e. in Devachan). *Light is love.* And so love, and love's yearning, is given to us in the etheric body, and we may with full justice call the etheric body the body of love; light and love.'[90]

The opposite of light is darkness, and that which is opposed to love we call *egoism*. In modern times even the most powerful egoism cannot altogether eradicate love from the soul. In future, however, from the sixth cultural epoch onwards, this will become possible through those black-magical occult methods which will then be widespread. These will give rise to a quite particular illness, a sort of spiritual leprosy, which will lead not merely to physical death but also to the *death of the soul*. That division of humanity into two races, the good and the evil, which is only gradually becoming perceptible in our time, will in the sixth epoch attain its full development. The conversation of Christ with the disciples which immediately precedes the Transfiguration scene also points to this future division. In the first place there is the twofold characterization of Peter:

141

'Blessed are you, Simon, Bar-Jona!'[91] and, 'Get behind Me, power of Satan!,'[92] this being an indication of the future division of humanity into two parts, one of which will be inspired by God and the other by Satan, that is, Ahriman. What will be of decisive weight in this process of division will be the inner, personal relationship of each individual person to Christ, as expressed in the testimony of Peter, 'you are the Christ, the Son of the living God,'[93] and a true understanding of the Mystery of Golgotha: 'From that time Jesus began to show His disciples that He must go to Jerusalem and suffer many things from the elders and chief priests and scribes, and be killed, and on the third day be raised.'[94] For at the beginning of the sixth cultural epoch there will not be a single person, either in the East or in the West, who has never encountered the Christ-impulse on the Earth and would not in one form or another have been confronted *consciously* with the question: do you want—on a basis of freedom—to act out of 'human' thoughts or 'divine' thoughts? In the latter case one path alone is open to him, one which is also open today, but which in the sixth epoch will be the only path of redemption: 'Then Jesus told His disciples, "If any man would come after Me, let him deny himself [that is, overcome his egoism] and take up his cross. Only in this way can he follow Me." '[95] Regarding the opposite path, which leads to the death of the soul, that is, which brings irredeemable harm to bear upon the human soul, Christ speaks the following words: 'For whoever would save his soul [that is, would make it an instrument of egoism] will lose it, and whoever loses his soul for My sake [that is, opens it up to the love of Christ] will find it. For what will it profit a man if he gains the whole world and forfeits his soul? Or what shall man give in return for his soul?'[96] Thus in the sixth epoch Christ will appear as the true *Saviour* of the human soul.

5. The Virtue of Hope and the Seventh post-Atlantean Epoch

The final stage in the descent of the Christ-impulse into human sheaths is His union with man's physical body, His penetration of the hardest parts of man's organism, even the bone system itself. Through this means human consciousness can awaken in the sphere of higher Devachan, in the world of Intuition, and it can also enter into a still higher sphere, that of Providence or Buddhi. The archetype for such an ascent of consciousness is, for all times, the individuality of the Apostle John, 'the disciple whom the Lord loved'. He alone could raise his consciousness up to the sphere beyond the zodiac, in order to receive there the Holy Spirit, who enabled him *consciously to experience the Mystery of Golgotha*, to experience the most sublime revelation of Christ as the great macrocosmic Ego of the world, of which the holy Rishis once told in dim foreboding when they said: Vishvakarman still abides *beyond the confines* of our sphere. This experience now comes before John in a new, one could say renewed, form. But Vishvakarman now dwells, not in the sphere beyond the zodiac but on the Earth, and through His union with the physical body of Jesus of Nazareth He unites the world of human beings for all future ages with the most sublime cosmic sphere, with the ultimate source of the Holy Spirit. The other Apostles could not at that time attain such a high degree of consciousness. Hence they sink into a state of sleep which, according to the Fifth Gospel, was to last until the coming of Pentecost.[97]

But why did the disciples go to sleep? Why were they not able to receive the impulse of the Holy Spirit consciously into their souls? Luke the Evangelist speaks of this as follows: 'And when He rose from prayer, He [Christ Jesus] came to the disciples and found that they had fallen asleep from *sorrow*.'[98] Then when Jesus had been seized by the high priests in the Garden of Gethsemane, this 'sorrow' grows into *despair*. 'And they all forsook Him and fled.'[99] This *inner despair*, a force which prevents the Christ-impulse from penetrating man's physical body, fully overwhelms the souls of the Apostles after their flight and reaches a kind of culmination in the three denials of Peter.

Thus in these Gospel scenes there stands before us, on the one hand, the sublime picture of the Apostle John and, on the other, the picture of all those hindrances which lie in the path of a humanity that seeks to experience the Christ-impulse in the innermost regions of the physical

143

body. The picture of these hindrances should not discourage us or lead us to doubt our own powers, for although in these events one is speaking of the most exalted individualities, such as the Apostles, it has to be remembered that all these events relate to the time *before* the Mystery of Golgotha. In our time, however, almost two thousand years after the Mystery of Golgotha, and with the passing of the Kali-Yuga in 1899, it is possible to strive also towards a conscious experience of Christ in the physical body. For the experience of the final stage in the penetration of the Christ-impulse into human sheaths, is—in so far as the yearly rhythm is concerned—especially possible during the seven weeks of Lent and the Easter season.

Just as at the previous stages, here too there is a need for the development of a certain virtue which in our time can alone enable man to experience the Christ-impulse in the physical body itself. For the substance of cosmic love experienced by man at Epiphany as a consequence of the real presence of Christ within the ego, 'overflowing' its bounds in the process (of this we have already spoken in our earlier considerations), penetrates the sheaths and enters into the astral body as the power of faith, into the etheric body as the power of love and, finally, into the physical body as the power of *hope*.[100] The power of hope in us is essentially that power which builds up and sustains our physical body from within, making us people who are 'upright' also in a physical sense. Rudolf Steiner speaks of this in the following way: 'It is precisely for physical life that we need hope, for hope keeps the whole of physical life in a state of unity and *uprightness*. Nothing can happen on the physical plane without hope. Hence the forces of hope are connected with the final sheath of our human organism, with our physical body. What the forces of faith are for the astral body and the forces of love for the etheric body, the forces of hope are for the physical body,' for 'hope *builds up* our physical body'.[101]

How, then, in an age which appears increasingly to be without hope, are we to find ourselves a hope which is able to work right into the physical body? In our time such a possibility is opened up before humanity *only* through anthroposophically orientated spiritual science. 'What does spiritual science give us?' asks Rudolf Steiner; and he answers: 'Through making us familiar with the all-embracing *law of karma*, together with *the law of repeated Earth-lives*, it gives us something which in a spiritual sense is permeated with hope, just as our awareness that the Sun will rise again in the morning and that plants will grow out of seeds fills us with hope on the physical plane.' Spiritual science tells us how '. . . if we understand karma, this physical body *will be built up again in a new life* by those forces which permeate us as forces of hope.'[102] Thus through modern spiritual science the forces of hope become real *resurrection-forces*.

144

Only these spiritual resurrection-forces, which work in our physical body as a result of the presence there of the Christ-impulse (through the inner development of the virtue of hope), are able to overcome in us those forces of *despair* which even the Apostles (other than John) could not master—for Christ had not yet arisen from the dead. From our time onwards, and especially during the sixth and *seventh* cultural epochs, these forces of *despair* will appear in man not only as forces which extinguish consciousness, as was the case at the time of the events in Palestine, but will gradually envelop him with '*spiritual* death' which would lead to immediate and irreversible changes in his physical body: 'Thus a man who is unable to hope, who is always *despondent* about what he must arrange for the future, goes through the world in such a way that it becomes clearly discernible in his physical body,' says Rudolf Steiner.[103] In the future— which already begins in our own time—one thing only will be able to counteract this gradual dying of the physical body, and that is if all people embrace the teaching of karma and reincarnation, which is the teaching of world-*justice* and world-*hope* in the new, *truly Christian form*, as given in Rudolf Steiner's Anthroposophy.

But why did this teaching, of which Rudolf Steiner once said that its diffusion is the principal task of Anthroposophy in the modern world, enter the world precisely today? Rudolf Steiner unfolds this supremely important mystery of modern times in the following words: 'With this we have pointed to what is so important and so essential for our age, to the new appearance of Christ in the etheric body; for any connection of this new manifestation of Christ with the physical body is ruled out by the whole character of our times. Hence we have indicated that Christ is now appearing on Earth—in a manner quite unlike the suffering Christ of Golgotha—in the role of a judge, as Christ triumphant, as the *Lord of Karma*, whose coming has been foreshadowed by those who portrayed Christ in the scenes of the Last Judgment ... In truth, this is something *which begins in the twentieth century and will last until the end of the Earth. The judgment, that is to say the ordering of karma, begins in our twentieth century.*'[104] These words are above all an indication of the fact that Christ enters, in our time, upon the path which leads from the human ego into human sheaths, a path which will end in the seventh cultural epoch with His entry into people's physical bodies; this in turn will enable Him to win for mankind the whole sphere of the zodiac, so that all people might come to be able consciously to enter the realm of world-karma. Thus Rudolf Steiner says: 'So we see how Christ, as He descends to the Earth, gradually—from out of a physical, earthly human being—develops as an etheric-, an astral-, and finally as an ego-Christ, in order as an ego-Christ to become the Spirit of the Earth, who then *rises with all human beings up to higher stages.*'[105] 'And just as man's individual ego is the bearer of his own individual karma, which passes as an unbroken stream through all his separate incarnations, so does the macrocosmic Ego of Christ gradually become the bearer of world-karma, of the karma of all mankind. This comes esoterically to expression in that His three new revelations, which are prophetically reflected in the Gospels in the scenes of the feeding of the five thousand, the Transfiguration on Mount Tabor and the prayer about the cup in the Garden of Gethsemane, together with the Mystery of Golgotha, are also indications of the Christ Being's rulership over all the consequences of former conditions of the Earth, as inscribed in the Akashic Chronicle.'[106]

Thus the first supersensible revelation of Christ in our time is connected with the process of Christ's rulership over the karmic forces that are the consequence of the Old Moon condition of the Earth; the second, in the sixth epoch, is connected with His rulership over the karmic forces that have arisen as a result of the Old Sun condition and, finally, the third revelation, in the seventh epoch, with the forces of karma that emerged from the metamorphosed forces of Old Saturn.[107] For the ascent, up to that time, of the Christ Being 'together with all human beings' into the sphere of the zodiac and also His union with the sphere of the world-karma of the Earth's past, extending even to Old Saturn, is that spiritual reality which stands behind the words that, beginning from the twentieth century and until the end of Earth-evolution, Christ will increasingly take it upon Himself to work as the Lord of Karma. In this sense the following words of Rudolf Steiner may acquire for us a quite particular significance: 'Thus if we seek what still exists of the forces which were, should I say, the nature-forces of Old Sun evolution, we must turn to the laws of our personal karma ... And if we try to bring personal karma into a connection with those constellations which relate to the circle of the zodiac, we are then living approximately in the sphere of the world-view which would have to be associated with the laws of the epoch of Ancient Saturn.'[108] These nature-forces of Old Saturn, which have their ultimate source in the realm of the zodiac, were also the true creators of the twelvefold human physical body, and are in their inner essence none other than the cosmic forces of hope: 'The germ of man's physical body was laid on Old Saturn. How did this come about? Spiritually it was laid in what is to continue, in hope. Thus the physical body can with full justice be called the *body of hope.*'[109]

In these two observations of Rudolf Steiner, we have a direct indication of the connection that exists, on the one hand, between the ancient laws of Saturn and the karma of the world (for in the sphere of the zodiac the karma of each individual human being cannot be separated from world-karma) and, on the other, between this human karma and the forces of hope, the principal moving force of the seventh epoch. From all this we may sense how in the seventh epoch, when Christ will have fulfilled the process of taking upon Himself the karma of the world, karmic laws will work in quite another way within humanity in that, in a spiritual respect, humanity will have then become something altogether different.

In order to form for oneself an (albeit approximate) impression of this possibility of working consciously with karma, which will in that distant epoch open up before mankind, we shall turn to a phenomenon that, from the present age of Michael onwards, will become increasingly accessible to those people who in the course of their earthly life are able in the fullest measure to permeate their astral body with the light of Michael's wisdom and their etheric body with the love of Christ. Rudolf Steiner describes in the following words what such people will experience in the spiritual world directly before their birth on Earth: 'We are always in danger of harming others through what we accomplish. The judgement regarding what we have done to another person will shine especially clearly before us at that moment when we are still in the etheric body, but have not yet clad ourselves in the physical body; it is here that the light of Michael and the love of Christ will work in the future. We will then find ourselves in the position of bringing about a change in our resolve: to hand over that [physical] body which we have prepared for ourselves and to take upon ourselves that body which was prepared for him to whom we caused this grave injury. This is the mighty transition which, from our time on into the future, will take place with respect to the spiritual life of human beings. We will be in the position of clothing ourselves in a body which will have been prepared by another person, by him to whom we have caused the grave injury; and the other person will be in the position of entering into the body which has been prepared by us. And because of this, what we are able to accomplish on Earth can be balanced out karmically in a completely different way than it would have been. In a sense we will come to be able to exchange our physical bodies. The Earth could never attain its goal if this were not to come about; humanity would otherwise never be able to become one. And this must happen! ... This is magic of a truly ideal kind. It is what in former times was called true white magic.'[110]

If we recall the path that we have traced in the last few chapters, we will see what a truly immeasurable significance accrues from the fact that it is precisely in the present epoch, which particularly suffers from *unbelief* and materialism, that into people's astral bodies there can stream the light of spiritual science, the light of the new revelation of Michael-Christ, in order to awaken in them the power of true *faith* which is capable of embracing the human being in his entirety and of bringing intellectuality itself into a state of spiritualization. For only such a full penetration of the whole of man's being by the light of the new revelation can, from our time onwards, enable human individuals to attain the possibility of working upon their karma in the manner described.

In the sixth epoch this phenomenon will be far more widespread, whereby the white magic of love—as a consequence of the entering of the Christ-forces into people's etheric bodies—will arise among mankind. It will then unfold in the struggle with the black magic of egoism which will also emerge on the Earth at that time. Finally, in the seventh epoch, those people who have been permeated with the power of Christ as far as the physical body will be granted the possibility of sacrificial service to humanity and conscious work with karma, not only in the spiritual world before birth but while in incarnation on the Earth itself, of sacrificing their physical body to another person, of transferring in full consciousness from one body to another as a part of the good common evolution of mankind.[111] In these processes the individuality of Zarathustra[112] (the Master Jesus) will be for all mankind the chief archetype of such a working upon karma as extends even to physical inter-relationships, and also the great teacher on the path of this sacrificial service. For Zarathustra had, in preparation of the events of Palestine, to sacrifice his physical body on *two* occasions: by withdrawing first from the Solomon Jesus-child and then from the Nathan Jesus.* He accomplished both these 'transitions' out of the purest forces of divine *hope*, out of the hope that through this, the great Sun Being of the Christ would be able to enter 'the stream of Earth-existence'. Hence we may say: only such a possibility of working with the forces of karma right into the physical body will be able to stir into life those higher forces of hope which mankind will come to need by that time, by the end of the seventh cultural epoch. For 'the Earth could never attain its goal if this were not to come about; *humanity would never be able to become one. And this must happen!*'[113]

---

* One could say that on the first occasion Zarathustra sacrificed his physical body to 'Jesus' and on the second occasion he sacrificed it to 'Christ'.

6. The Spiritual-scientific Idea of God-manhood and its Reflection in the Apocalypse and in the Gospel of St John

The words of Rudolf Steiner, with which the preceding chapter was concluded, regarding the need for humanity's ultimate attainment of oneness leads us to a fundamental mystery of post-Atlantean evolution. We find a more concrete expression of this in a brief reference of Rudolf Steiner's concerning how in the seventh cultural epoch Christ will appear '... in the great cosmic Ego which is *like a great group-soul of humanity*.'[114] For what is meant by the words '... like a great group-soul of humanity'? In order to answer this question it is necessary to turn to the lecture that Rudolf Steiner gave on 30 May 1912 in Norrköping. There he speaks in detail of how the future evolution of the Christ-impulse within humanity is dependent upon people's free decision gradually to form among themselves sheaths for the Christ. This will become possible only through a definite moral development, through the development among mankind of certain inner qualities, certain virtues. Rudolf Steiner proceeds to characterize these virtues in the following way: 'We form the astral body for the Christ-impulse through all moral acts of wonder, trust, reverence, *faith*—in short, through everything which *paves the way to supersensible knowledge* ... We form the etheric body for Christ through deeds of *love*; and through what arises in the world because of the impulses of *conscience*, we form for the Christ-impulse that which corresponds to man's physical body. When the Earth has finally reached its goal, when human beings have come to understand the true moral impulses upon which all that is good depends, then will deliverance come to what has flowed, in the form of the Christ-impulse, through the Mystery of Golgotha into human evolution as an ego. It will then be clothed with an astral body which has been formed by *faith* and by all deeds of human wonder and amazement. It will be clothed with something similar to an etheric body which is formed out of deeds of *love*, with something surrounding it which is similar to a physical body, formed out of deeds of *conscience*. Thus the future evolution of humanity will be fulfilled through the combined work of the moral impulses of human beings and of the Christ-impulse. We can see this future humanity in perspective before us as a great living 'orchestra'. When people learn to include their acts and their impulses in this great organism, and to form

149

through their own deeds a kind of sheath around it, they will create through earthly evolution *the foundation for the great community which is penetrated through and through by the Christ-impulse, by Christ Himself.*[115] For '... those who arrange their lives in this kind of way will surround this Christ-impulse like limbs in such a way that something is formed around Him which will be like a sheath around the essence, around the seed.'[116]

In these words we have an indication of the further evolution of the Christ-impulse within man, of the fashioning of the three sheaths into which the Christ Himself will then enter as the true Ego which enlivens and permeates them. Rudolf Steiner characterizes what then arises with an expression taken from Goethe, the 'great immortal individuality', that is, the new sensible-supersensible being who, with an actual existence in the world and united by a single karma, will then be fully borne by the macrocosmic Ego of Christ.

Of course, it must be observed that this 'great immortal individuality' will be *fully* completed only at the end of the *whole* of earthly evolution. It must, however, be fashioned *to a certain extent* by the end of the seventh cultural epoch, if humanity is to survive that stupendous catastrophe which will break out at the end of the post-Atlantean cycle of evolution and will change the entire outer aspect of the Earth.

All these future events are referred to in a remarkably exact way in the Revelation of St John. In the second and third chapters the ambassadors to the seven churches express the nature and fundamental character of the seven post-Atlantean epochs[117]—the message to the church in Laodicea relates to the seventh of these. At the *conclusion* of this message come the words of Christ from the vision of John which relate particularly to the end of post-Atlantean evolution: ' "Behold, I stand at the door and knock; if anyone hears My voice and opens the door, I will come in to him and eat with him and he with Me. He who conquers, I will grant him to sit with Me on My throne, as I Myself conquered and sat down with My Father on His throne" ... After this I (John) looked, and lo, in heaven an open door! And the first voice, which I had heard speaking to me like a trumpet, said, "Come up hither and I will show what must take place after this." At once I was in the spirit and lo, a throne stood in heaven, with one seated on the throne.'[118] And then we find a description of the rainbow, the four and twenty elders, the seven torches of fire, 'which are the seven divine creator-spirits'[114] and the four living creatures.[119] Then there comes the book with the seven seals and the Lamb on the throne, who is the only one in the whole world who can open them.[120]

Thus at the end of the seventh epoch Christ will stand at the gate of the 'immortal individuality' in expectation as to whether this 'individuality' will by that time have been sufficiently matured—through deeds of faith, love and conscience—that the voice of Christ, which addresses mankind from the World of Providence,[121] will be heard; for if so, He, as the higher Ego of all mankind, will be able to enter into the sheaths that have been prepared for Him. For by that time Christ will, through penetrating people's physical bodies, be able to win for humanity the whole sphere of the zodiac, and from there to reveal Himself to them, in His most exalted aspect, as the great Representative of the macrocosmic Ego-principle ('... as *I* myself won the victory of the spirit and sat down with My Father on His throne').[122] This central image gives us a key to understanding the images that follow. For just as it is possible to say that, for imaginative consciousness, the higher ego of every man is enthroned amidst its three outer sheaths of the astral, etheric and physical bodies, so will the macrocosmic Ego of Christ, as the higher Ego of the 'immortal individuality', become in time enthroned amidst His three new sheaths which have been formed for Him by people out of deeds of faith, love and conscience. Furthermore, anyone who at the end of the seventh cultural epoch is unable to rise to this experience of 'sitting on the throne' will not be able to 'enter' the 'immortal individuality' (the New Covenant) and will therefore have no *hope* of surviving the great catastrophe. In this sense, too, the picture of the Apostle John is prophetic. He *beholds* in Imagination 'an open door in heaven'[123] and *hears* (in Inspiration) 'the first voice ... *like the sound of a trumpet*',[124] that is, the voice of Christ, who turns to him from the sphere beyond the zodiac and says: 'Come up hither [into the sphere of Intuition], and I will show what must take place after this [which is to say, after the great catastrophe].'[125] John 'comes up' to this sphere and is 'at once in the realm of Spirit',[126] that is, in that cosmic sphere whence the Holy Spirit descends, in the Buddhi-sphere, where he experiences in Intuition 'a throne ... with One seated on the throne.'[127] In other words: John enters the 'immortal individuality' and beholds His Ego as the 'Christ-Lamb' seated on the throne.[128]

The further images of this chapter, which are referred to in the three kinds of beings surrounding the throne, reveal to us the mystery of the corresponding sheaths of the 'immortal individuality': His physical body—formed by deeds of conscience—which is represented by the twenty-four elders (a picture of the twenty-four epochs in the course of which man's physical body was formed out of the forces of the double crown of the zodiac, from the beginning of Old Saturn until the present); His etheric body—formed by deeds of love—which is represented by the seven spirits of God (a picture of the seven spirits of the planets, which are the original sources of etheric forces); and His astral body—formed by deeds of faith, wonder and reverence—is represented by the four living creatures (the macrocosmic picture of man's soul—astral-forces). All these beings bow down before Him who 'is seated on the throne.'[129] This picture of the relationship between the new sheaths—fashioned in man through sacrificial deeds of conscience, love and faith, and the Christ who dwells within them—bears a similarity to the way in which the physical, etheric and astral bodies of each human individual, as microcosm, 'bow down before' their sovereign lord, the higher ego.*

Rudolf Steiner indicates that it is an especially important task of anthroposophically orientated spiritual science *consciously to develop* within people the three virtues of 'faith, love and conscience' which gradually lead, even in our time, to the fashioning of the great 'immortal individuality' among mankind. 'These three powers will be the guiding stars of the moral forces which will enter human souls in particular through the anthroposophical[130] world-view.'[131] Here the question may well arise as to the incomplete correspondence of these words with the above description of the development, in the course of the year, of the three fundamental Christian virtues, faith, love and *hope*; for in the one case it speaks of 'hope' and in the other of 'conscience'. This inconsistency does, however, become clarified if we take into consideration that conscience, which—in its present form—entered into human evolution only with the Christ-impulse,[132] is none other than the voice of human karma, the voice of world justice, which—working from the very foundation of man's being—expresses during physical life, in what one could describe as the form of a reflection, the judgement of the spiritual cosmos of our deeds, thoughts and feelings.[133]

On the other hand, hope is connected with the experience of individual karma which is the reflection of the world justice that works in the cosmos. It, too, entered the world with the coming of the Christ Being to the Earth. For without His union with Jesus of Nazareth and without the Mystery of Golgotha, the whole of earthly evolution would have been *hopelessly* condemned to gradual destruction. The only difference is that in esoteric work with the forces of hope one has to do not with an indeterminate voice rising from the dim depths of the soul but with a conscious ascent to that sphere whence the impulses of conscience proceed. In this sense the development of the forces of hope within man may in time lead him to a *conscious* experience of that sphere whence human conscience now speaks from its dim depths, to a direct beholding of the all-embracing cosmic sphere of karma, the sphere of world justice.

As we have already seen, such a development of the forces of hope to the

---

* The images of the Apocalypse are extraordinarily complex. The meaning which is selected here from the many possible interpretations of the passage under consideration is that which is directly connected with our theme.

point of a direct intuitive comprehension of karma in the sphere of the zodiac[134] will be attainable by man only in the seventh post-Atlantean epoch. It will also make clear to humanity the deeper meaning of the great necessities of world-becoming, which often come to expression in global catastrophes. Of such a kind will be the catastrophe which will bring post-Atlantean evolution to an end. Only forces of hope, which have been occultly developed, can help mankind rightly to relate to, and to survive, such an event. 'And then will come the last great epoch [the seventh] in which what we call hope will be reflected in the human soul. But at that time people will be strengthened through the power which proceeds from the Mystery of Golgotha and from the moral epoch [the sixth], strengthened so as to be able to receive into themselves forces of hope. And this is the most important aspect of what they will need in order to pass through the catastrophe and to begin a new life in a similar way beyond it, just as the post-Atlantean age once brought a new life into being.'[135]

However, the forces that are necessary for such a purely occult development of hope can *only* be acquired by humanity in the course of fashioning the 'immortal individuality', the true spiritual-scientific archetype of God-manhood which the Russian religious philosopher Vladimir Soloviev beheld as a prophetic premonition. For in this archetype, Christ reveals Himself to human beings as the macrocosmic Ego of the world, as the great bearer of the karma of our cosmos, as the bringer of world hope. This will be the time when for those people who have participated, in freedom, in the fashioning of the 'great, immortal individuality' and have penetrated the realm of intuition, of world-karma, which stretches to the sphere of Providence, the sphere of origin of the Holy Spirit, there will open up the possibility of *consciously* working with the great Company of Bodhisattvas surrounding the Christ Being, the Ego of our cosmos, in the region beyond the zodiac. 'A being such as Christ is surrounded by twelve Bodhisattvas. We cannot speak of more than twelve, for when the mission of the twelve Bodhisattvas has been accomplished earthly existence will come to an end ... Before us are the twelve and in their midst the thirteenth. We have ascended to the sphere of the Bodhisattvas, we have entered a circle of twelve stars—and in their midst is the Sun, illuminating and warming them, giving them that spring of life which they will then bring down to the Earth.'[136] And as this great company of Bodhisattvas in its totality forms—in Rudolf Steiner's words—the heavenly vessel for the Holy Spirit,[137] who proceeds from the Christ Being and is like the illuminating and warming light of the Sun, we may rightly say that in the seventh cultural period the Holy Spirit Himself will work *directly* within humanity, and that only those people who receive Him *consciously* into themselves will be able to withstand those immense forces of evil which will appear at that time and lead to the 'War of All Against All', the cause of the final catastrophe at the end of the post-Atlantean age.

The archetype for all times of this conscious work on the Earth in partnership with the Holy Spirit is John, the Apostle and Evangelist, who received the *impulse of the Holy Spirit,* the impulse of the cosmic Sophia, from Christ Himself on Golgotha (see p.118). Hence the Gospel that he went on to write is a direct embodiment of the impulse of the Holy Spirit, of the Divine Sophia within mankind: 'What John has written was this divine Wisdom, the Sophia, who herself incarnated in the Gospel of John. He received his knowledge directly from Jesus and was authorized by Christ to bring this wisdom to the Earth.'[138] These words of Rudolf Steiner fully correspond with another of his observations which may be found in the eighth lecture of the cycle *The Background to the Gospel of St Mark* where he speaks of how, of the four Gospels, it is the Gospel of St John which is the 'inspired book' for the *seventh* and last epoch of post-Atlantean evolution. And so the great truths which are now revealed to all humanity in modern spiritual science occur with and complement one another in a striking way.★

In conclusion, let us turn to the Gospel of St John itself, in order to see how all the great truths of man's future evolution described above find their reflection therein. If from this point of view we first examine this Gospel as a whole, we discover three essential elements which we do not in any way encounter in the synoptic Gospels. These are the prologue of the Gospel according to John, the scene of the raising of Lazarus and the farewell discourses of Christ Jesus with His disciples, which occupy four whole chapters (14–17). The raising of Lazarus, as we know, concerns the spiritual biography of John the Evangelist himself.[140] As regards the other two elements, they relate respectively to the world-past and the world-future in human evolution. The prologue refers to the whole pre-history of earthly evolution extending to the Mystery of Golgotha, the farewell discourses to the future path of earthly evolution from the Mystery of Golgotha onwards. In this sense we can also consider the farewell discourses of Christ Jesus as a concrete description of the path leading to the fashioning of the 'great immortal individuality', the future God-manhood, whose *initial* completion will, as we have seen, come at the end of the seventh cultural epoch.[141]

Let us now try to immerse ourselves in some small way in the content of the four chapters of St John's Gospel referred to above in the quest of the

---

★ To this one could add that the 'Apocalypse' of John, which concludes with the vision of the New Jerusalem and the complete victory of the Christ-forces of light, is also the great book of promise and hope for all mankind.[139]

correlations that we have observed. In the first of the chapters of the farewell discourses (the fourteenth) we can distinguish three principal themes. Firstly, there is the threefold summons to the power of *faith* in man's being, the first of which begins the whole chapter (verses 1, 11, 12),[142] then the theme of *love* (verses 15, 21, 23, 24, 28) and finally that of *hope*, which comes in the (albeit still veiled) allusions to the future overcoming of death through the Resurrection: 'And when I go and prepare a place for you, I will come again ...'; 'Yet a little while and the world will see me no more, but you will see me'; 'I go away, and I will come to you' (verse 28).

The composition of the first chapter is built round three questions that three disciples in turn put to Christ Jesus. It is not difficult to see these three disciples as representatives of the three basic forces of man's astral body— thinking, feeling and willing—directed towards the higher ego. Thus Thomas, in putting the question of *knowledge* 'We do not know where you are going', and 'How can we know the way?', represents the impulse of *thinking*. Judas (not Iscariot), in answer to whose question Christ unfolds the theme of love as the fundamental Christian virtue (23, 24), represents the impulse of *feeling*. While Philip, who wishes to be 'shown' the sphere of the Father, that is, the sphere of the cosmic will (8–10), represents the impulse of *will* in the human soul. Hence we may understand why all three themes of faith, love and hope are present in this first chapter; for here the concern is with the inner world of man's *astral body* and its principal forces, of which only thinking, the foundation of man's clear, waking consciousness, belongs fully to the astral body. Feeling is associated with the processes of the etheric body, while the will, as the most unconscious member of the life of soul, works right into the physical body itself.★

In the second (fifteenth) chapter, we enter already (from the first lines) into the world of the life-forces which form man's *etheric body*. The frequent references to the vine, its branches and fruits (1–8), serve as an indication of this. Then the central theme of the whole chapter enters with full force: the necessity of developing *love*, the basic Christian virtue (9–17). This theme is then intersected by the opposite theme of hatred, with which the world will confront the true servants of Christ (18–25). In this antithesis of love and hatred we also have an indication of the contrast between the good and evil races which will be manifested from the sixth cultural epoch onward. In the light of what we have said about the sixth epoch, the following verses are of particular importance: 'You are already made clean by the word which I have spoken to you. Abide in Me and I in you' (3, 4).

★ Thus the words about the inner overcoming of weaknesses and about *fearlessness* (verse 27) may be related to the forces of thinking which penetrate to the heart.

In the third (sixteenth) chapter the principal theme is that of hope (although this word is not actually used). This comes to expression in Christ's frequent—though veiled and hidden—references to His future victory over death and His reunion with the Kingdom of the Father in Resurrection. The beginning of the chapter, with its chronicling of the dangers which threaten the human ego, and which will await even the chosen few (1), together with the particularly cruel persecutions of bearers of the Christ-impulse on the part of those who 'kill the body' in the period leading up to the 'War of All Against All' (2–4), is already an indication to us of the seventh cultural epoch. Then as the basic theme of the chapter we have the motif of Christ's going away, together with the *sadness and suffering* of the Apostles (6, 22). This theme is translated into the—as yet still hidden—motif of Resurrection, which is inseparably connected with the penetration of the forces of the Christ into the physical body for its subsequent spiritualization:[143] 'A little while, and you will see Me no more; again a little while, and you will see Me' (16, 17, 19). These words can also be brought into a connection with the coming catastrophe at the end of the seventh period and with the beginning of the new life that will follow it.

Nearer to the end of the chapter we have the indication that at a certain time mankind will no longer be spoken to in parables, but will be told directly about the Kingdom of the Father: 'I have said this to you in parables; but the hour is coming when I shall no longer speak to you in parables but shall tell you plainly of the Father' (25). This means that in the seventh epoch the Kingdom of the Father will become directly accessible to humanity through the faculties of intuitive understanding which will quite naturally awaken within man at that time. (Here it should also be recalled that in the synoptic Gospels, which relate to the fourth, fifth and sixth cultural epochs, Christ speaks throughout in parables which He only sometimes explains to the disciples; while in St John's Gospel, which relates to the seventh epoch,[144] Christ hardly ever uses parables.) The chapter ends with the Apostles, who in the given situation represent earthly humanity, fully acknowledging and confessing Christ's divine origin, and this is followed by the words: 'I have said this to you, that in Me you may have peace. In the world you have tribulation; but be of good cheer, I have overcome the world' (33). Here is revealed to all mankind the highest assurance of *hope* that those people who have received the Christ-impulse into their physical body will be able to pass through all future trials and to attain the final victory of the spirit over the whole of material existence in the epoch that will come *after* the great catastrophe.[145]

These are the three main stages in the fashioning of the sheaths of the 'great immortal individuality' as they are contained in the farewell discourses of Christ Jesus with the Apostles. As for the fourth (seventeenth) chapter, we have there the most sublime completion of the whole path: the union of the macrocosmic Ego of Christ Jesus with this 'great immortal individuality', a union that comes about as a result of His third revelation from the highest sphere beyond the zodiac, where Christ dwells 'in the light with which He was illumined through the Father before the beginning of the world' (5). Then will all people who have by that time risen to an intuitive experience of Christ be able, out of their own understanding, to develop the conviction that 'Christ truly came from the sphere of the Father ... and that the Father sent Him' (8). Christ then speaks of how He does not pray for all people but only for those who have by that time entered into the 'immortal individuality': 'I am praying for them; I am not praying for the world but for those whom thou hast given me, for they are Thine' (9). And finally, at the end of the whole chapter, we are given a most sublime picture of future God-manhood as the great oneness of human beings with Christ in the 'immortal individuality': '. . . that they may all be one; even as Thou, Father, art in me, and I in thee, that they also may be in us, so that the world may *believe* that Thou hast sent me. The glory which Thou hast given me I have given to them, that they may be one even as we are one, I in them and Thou in me, that they may become perfectly one, so that the world may know that Thou hast sent me and hast *loved* them even as Thou hast *loved* me' (21–23).

Only in this oneness is the highest, intuitive understanding of Christ also revealed: 'Father, I desire that they also, whom Thou hast given me, may be with me where I am, to behold my glory which Thou hast given me in Thy love for me before the foundation of the world. O righteous Father, the world has not known Thee, but I have known Thee; *and these know that Thou hast sent me.* I made known to them Thy Name, and I will[146] make it known, that the love with which Thou hast loved me may be in them, *so that* my "I" may be revealed in their "I" (24–25).'

To this one further point should be added.[147] Such a lofty ideal of cognition will only be realized in the future if the Holy Spirit, who proceeds from the macrocosmic Ego of Christ in the sphere of Providence, is then able to work directly within humanity, gradually penetrating the astral, etheric and physical sheaths of the 'immortal individuality' which are gradually being fashioned therein. John, the greatest pupil of Jesus Christ, also reveals to us this profound secret of all future evolution, in that he received from Him the impulse of the Holy Spirit on Golgotha. The Holy Spirit is mentioned eight times in the farewell discourses of Christ Jesus as communicated by John the Evangelist, of which five are references to the Comforter (Paraclete), that is, the 'Spirit of hope':[148] twice in the fourteenth chapter, then once in the fifteenth and twice in the sixteenth,[149] and these are direct indications of His working within the three sheaths referred to above.

In that future epoch of severe trials, the good aspect of humanity will be able to derive the profoundest support and comfort from the farewell discourses contained in the Gospel of St John, which will then become *a reality directly accessible to experience*, and also from the descriptions (contained in all four Gospels) of the Last Supper, the solitude of Gethsemane, the Mystery of Golgotha—the results of the union of the Christ Being with the physical body of Jesus of Nazareth—and the *Resurrection*. Two sayings from the Gospels will come to have a particular significance in the time immediately prior to the great catastrophe. If both utterances are taken as a whole, their significance is also considerable in our own, truly apocalyptic, age. These sayings are as follows: 'Then Jesus said to them: "... remain here, and *watch with me* ... Watch and pray that you may not fall into temptation; *man's spirit indeed is willing*, but his *physical body* is weak",'[150] and ' "Father, if thou art *willing* remove this cup from me; nevertheless not my *will*, but Thine, be done." '[151]

For just as our epoch must, with the help of the power of faith, transform human intellectuality, human *thinking*, into the faculty of imaginative cognition, and the sixth epoch must, with the help of love, transform human *feeling* into forces of Inspiration, whence a higher morality can enter into humanity, so the seventh epoch must, with the help of conscious experience of the sphere of cosmic hope, fill human earthly *willing* with the cosmic will, which—in full spirit-wakefulness—will then open the gates to the realm of Intuition, to the conscious apprehending of world-karma as the impulse of cosmic justice, as the will of Christ Himself:

> For the Christ-Will in the encircling Round holds sway
> In the Rhythms of Worlds, blessing the Soul.[152]

7. From Epiphany to Easter.
The Experience of the Holy Trinity

In our studies of the esoteric nature of the cycle of the year, we approach, with the development of the virtue of hope, the festival of Easter, which is connected with the central event of world history, the death on the Cross of Christ Jesus and his subsequent Resurrection from the dead. In several of his lectures Rudolf Steiner also calls the festival of Easter the 'festival of hope for the future' (*Zukunftshoffnungsfest*) and he indicates that 'Easter Sunday is the day of remembrance and the *day of hope*, the day which symbolically expresses the Mystery of Golgotha.'[153]

If in the period of Christmas we were more connected with the depths of the Earth, and were in the course of the thirteen Holy Nights able to experience, in the form of a reflection, the memories of the Earth and of the cosmic expanses of the world of the fixed stars—which comes about through the fact that the days from Christmas until Epiphany are firmly bound up with the conditions of earthly time—in Easter, the moving festival, we have a reflection of purely cosmic relationships.

According to esoteric Christian tradition, the true day of the Easter festival is always the first Sunday after the first Full Moon after the day of the spring equinox. In this way of establishing the festival of Easter we have, therefore, three kinds of cosmic law. One of these relates to the phases of the Moon, that is, it is connected with the lunar sphere or the elemental world, in which there works principally the Third Hierarchy or the Spirits of Soul. Another concerns the weekly rhythm that is connected with the spheres of the planets and in the first instance with the Sun, in whose realm there weaves the Second Hierarchy or the Spirits of Light. And finally, the third law is connected with the point of the spring equinox and points us towards the world of the fixed stars, to the region of the zodiac where dwells the First Hierarchy or the Spirits of Strength. The Easter festival itself must, properly speaking, direct our consciousness to a still higher sphere beyond the zodiac, to the sphere of the macrocosmic Ego of our world. Thus we may say that *all nine* of the divine-spiritual Hierarchies participate in the annual cosmic constellation of Easter, as though indicating at this time the union with the Earth of Him who brought to mankind an impulse which has its sources in the regions beyond the Hierarchies.

At the time of the Mystery of Golgotha, when the blood of Christ Jesus flowed from His wounds to the Earth, His macrocosmic Ego penetrated with His blood right to the centre of the Earth and from that time united the sphere of the Earth with the highest sphere beyond the zodiac, thus forming the foundation for its future transformation into a new Sun, that is, into a fixed star. At that moment when Christ fully united with the physical body of Jesus, even with the structure of His bones—whereby the forces of mineralization and death were overcome—He laid the foundation of the future spiritualization of humanity, and gave to the whole of earthly evolution a new ascending impulse for that power which will still be required for aeons of world evolution so as to lead it to full manifestation and realization.

Through the Mystery of Golgotha, a *divine being* entered directly into the evolution of humanity on Earth for the first time in the history of the world and became connected with it for all future ages. 'And lo, I am with you always, until the end of the world'[154]—these words of Christ represent the greatest *hope* and promise of humanity for all future ages. From now on, Christ will gradually ascend with the Earth, and the humanity which it bears, into the macrocosm. Just as through His sole and unrepeatable revelation *on the physical plane* at the time of the Mystery of Golgotha, Christ will in the future—which in this sense already begins in our time—send new revelations to mankind, though now from the spiritual worlds. We are all going towards this time. Modern anthroposophically orientated spiritual science is none other than a real testimony of the first supersensible revelation of Christ which is now beginning. In our epoch this revelation proceeds from the spiritual world that immediately borders upon the Earth, from the sphere of the Third Hierarchy, the sphere which represents the principle of the Holy Spirit[155] in our cosmos and reaches its culmination in the new appearance of Christ in the etheric.

It is as though every word which Rudolf Steiner spoke about this new appearance of Christ was surrounded by the most refined golden aura: Christ as the teacher and guide of souls, giving answers to the most difficult life-questions; Christ as man's comforter in all the sufferings and misfortunes of life, his divine *Brother*, who accompanies man on all the paths of his destiny. His voice can be heard in a humble room amidst quiet contemplation just as amidst noisy and multitudinous gatherings. The whole of nature becomes His garment, for He is also the *Lord of the Elements*. Every stone, every plant, every cloud and brook bears within itself the imprint of His invisible touch. Thus in our time the book of nature is, in the deepest sense, a Christian book,[156] which everywhere reveals to us Christ's invisible presence.

Thus the esoteric development of the power of faith in our time can lead to the enlightenment of man's astral body and, through this, to a real experience of Christ in the etheric. For 'what has legitimately existed in the world until now as faith will be succeeded by what one may call the "contemplation of Christ",' says Rudolf Steiner,[157] and he at the same time points to the path which leads to the experience of the first super-sensible revelation of Christ. In the second revelation which follows it, Christ reveals Himself to human beings as the *Sun of heavenly love*, warming and giving life to all that exists. The fullness of universal love—the foundation of all that is and becomes—which gives itself to the world in inexpressible grace, then finds its reflection in human love that is impregnated with universal love. For 'the Mystery of Golgotha is a free cosmic deed springing from world love and it can be grasped only by human love.'[158] Thus will Christ appear to human beings in His second revelation which will proceed from the high Sun-sphere of the Second Hierarchy, the representative in our world of the Sun-kingdom of the Son, as One who *saves* through love, who endows man with the capacity of, and awakens him to, truly moral deeds.

Finally, in His third and highest revelation, Christ will appear to mankind as the archetype of the great sacrifice, the cosmic sacrifice, which connects the heights and depths of the world, encompassing and uplifting the whole universe. For only the very greatest sacrifice, as deep as all worlds and as boundless as the whole cosmos, is capable of transforming the force of necessity which pervades the created world into the power of grace, and punitive justice into blessing. Thus the Sun becomes love, Christ in His third revelation becomes the *Lord of Karma*, now working from the highest sphere of the First Hierarchy, the representative in our world of the forces of the divine Father.[159]

Rudolf Steiner refers in the most majestic words to this relationship of Christ to karma in lectures which he gave in 1906: 'Karma and Christ supplement one another as the means to salvation and the Saviour. Through karma the deed of Christ becomes cosmic law, while through the Christ-principle, the revealed Logos, karma attains its goal, which is the freeing of souls for self-consciousness and for an experience of their likeness to God.'[160] 'Christ is the living consciousness of the Akashic Chronicle of the Earth, whereupon the Father endows Him with the power of judgement; He has the power to forgive sins and to take them upon Himself... In Christ there lives the whole earthly karma of human beings; He is the living incarnation of earthly karma.'[161] These words of the Christian initiate of the twentieth century are a true continuation—arising out of the Time Spirit of the present age—of the words of Christ from the Gospel of St John: 'For as the Father raises the dead and gives them life, so also the Son gives life to whom He will. The Father judges no one, but has given all judgement to the Son, that all may honour the Son, even as they honour

161

the Father. He who does not honour the Son does not honour the Father who sent Him. Truly, truly, I say to you, he who hears my word and believes Him who sent me has eternal life; he does not come into judgement, *but has passed from death to life.*'[162]

It is precisely this transition 'from death to life' which is given to us, as the most sublime archetype of the final goal of human evolution, in the Mystery of Golgotha. Thus in contemplating the Mystery of Golgotha, we are at the same time beholding the completion of the path from Epiphany to Easter, which is made possible for modern humanity only through the development of the virtues of faith, love and hope. For that which occurred between these two fundamental events (Epiphany and Easter) in the earthly life of Christ, namely, His gradual union with the three bodies of Jesus of Nazareth, brought for every man in the world the possibility to develop these same virtues. For this reason, faith, love and hope form in the cycle of the year those three stages which inwardly unite the festival of Epiphany with the festival of Easter.

As a culmination of this ascent, however, there sounds through all the centuries from the heights of the hill of Golgotha, directed to all people of the Earth, the Sun-prophecy of the threefold promise to humanity, springing from the very greatest sacrifice and leading through faith to love, and from love to the highest hope, the prophecy of which the modern spiritual researcher speaks in the following words: 'When a man's whole being is pervaded with the love that streamed from the Cross of Golgotha, he can turn his eyes to the future and say: evolution on the Earth must gradually bring it about that the spirit living within me *transforms the whole of physical Earth-existence.* What was there before the luciferic influence, the Father-principle, the Spirit whom we have received, we shall in time give back to the Father-principle, but we shall let our whole spirit be permeated by the Christ-principle and our hands will bring to expression what is living in our souls as a clear, faithful picture of that principle. Just as our hands were not created by us but by the Father-principle, so the Christ-principle will stream through them. As people pass through incarnation after incarnation, the spiritual power flowing from the Mystery of Golgotha will stream into what they accomplish in their physical bodies—right into the Father-principle—so that even the outer world will eventually be imbued with the Christ-principle. People will experience that calm confidence which resounded from the Cross on Golgotha and leads to the highest hope for the future, to the ideal which can be expressed by saying: *I let faith germinate within me, I let love germinate within me; then will faith and love dwell in me, and I know that when they grow strong enough they will permeate all external life. I know too that they will permeate everything within me that is the creation of the Father-principle. Thus hope for humanity's future will be added to faith and love, and people will understand that in regard to the future they must acquire the calm confidence: if only I have faith, if only I have love, then I may also entertain the hope that what has come into me from Christ Jesus will gradually find its way into the outer world.* And then the words resounding from the Cross as a sublime ideal will be understood:[163] "Father, into Thy hands I commend my spirit!"'[164]

Thus the human spirit ascends, during the time from Epiphany until Easter, through an inner development of faith, love and hope to an experience of the Holy Trinity on the hill of Golgotha: to an experience of the Holy Spirit, which is revealed to true faith; of the Son, to spirit-filled love; of the Father, to the highest form of hope. Then will the words of the spiritual researcher of our time become an immediate inner reality: 'Whoever contemplates the Cross on Golgotha must at the same time contemplate the Holy Trinity, for in His becoming one with the earthly evolution of mankind Christ manifests the Holy Trinity.'[165]

V

THE PATH FROM ADVENT TO EASTER
THROUGH THE SEVEN MYSTERY VIRTUES

1. The Old and the New Mysteries

Now that we have examined the inner path of development which the soul can undergo in connection with the spiritual rhythm of the year during the time from the festival of Michaelmas until the festival of Easter, through the fashioning of certain soul-spiritual virtues, we shall briefly summarize what has been said so far. There are seven qualities, seven distinct virtues, which a person who is striving to participate in this part of the year esoterically needs gradually to develop within himself. These seven virtues are: justice, temperance or prudence, fortitude or presence of mind, wisdom, faith, love and hope. The first three of these, which constitute the so-called 'Platonic' virtues, are wholly connected with the traditions of the old 'pre-Christian' Mysteries; the last three are associated with the new Christian Mysteries; while the fourth virtue, *wisdom* or the Sophia, forms the transition, just as the Holy Spirit who proceeds from the Father *and* the Son, encompasses in the realm of eternity the whole past and future of world evolution.

This Sophia-principle, which has always manifested itself in the Mysteries of esoteric Christianity as the purified and enlightened human astral body,[1] appears in our present fifth post-Atlantean epoch in the fully developed consciousness soul which, like a delicately formed chalice, is preparing to receive into itself the higher principle of the Spirit Self. 'We should not conceive of the transition from the astral body to the Spirit Self in so simple a way. The ego slowly and gradually transforms the astral body into sentient soul, intellectual soul and consciousness soul. Then the ego works on and only when it has led the astral body to the consciousness soul is it in a position to purify it in such a way that the Spirit Self can arise within it.'[2] Rudolf Steiner goes on to characterize this birth of the Spirit Self within the consciousness soul in the following way: 'Those who inwardly gave birth to the Spirit Self were called "God's children"; in them "the light shone in the darkness" and "they received the light". Outwardly they were people of flesh and blood, but they bore within themselves a *higher man*. Within them the Spirit Self was born out of the consciousness soul. The "mother" of such a spiritualized human being is not a corporeal mother; his true mother dwells within him as his purified and spiritualized consciousness soul. *This is that principle from which the higher man is born.* This spiritual birth, a birth in the highest sense,' is described in the Gospel of St John. Into the purified consciousness soul there descends the Spirit Self or *Holy Spirit*. To this also relate the words, "I saw the Spirit descend as a dove from heaven, and it

167

remained on Him."[3] And as the consciousness soul is that principle in which the Spirit Self unfolds, it is called the "Mother of Christ" or, in the Mystery-schools, the "Virgin Sophia". It was through the fructifying of the Virgin Sophia that Christ could be born in Jesus of Nazareth."[4]

This birth of the higher being in the human soul is also engraved in the composition of the words 'Anthropos-Sophia', words which have a highly significant meditative content. For through becoming more deeply immersed in them one may come to feel that, just as in Imagination we experienced the Christmas image of Mary-Sophia holding the Nathan Soul, the true Anthropos, in her arms, so—in deepening these words through the forces of *Inspiration*—do we find their connection with Epiphany, with the mystery of the descent of the Sun Spirit of Christ into Jesus of Nazareth, into the Nathan Soul (Anthropos), through the mediation of the Divine Sophia. In the sense of our present considerations, it is also possible to conceive of this as a process whereby the three 'pre-Christian' virtues (whose bearer is Jesus of Nazareth, that is, the Nathan Soul, still fortified by the eighteen-year presence of the ego of Zarathustra)[5] are augmented by the three new virtues which the Christ Being has brought into the evolution of humanity, and which are united with the 'old' virtues through the mediation of the central virtue of wisdom or the Sophia.

Thus we have the following picture. Supported by the past, by the development of the virtues of justice, temperance (prudence) and fortitude (presence of mind), we come to the present, to wisdom, to the Sophia, which is then seen as a connecting link between past and future, between pre-Christian and Christian evolution—the latter being represented by the virtues of faith, love and hope. In our studies we have seen that the first four, or 'old', virtues relate respectively to the human sheaths—to the physical, etheric and astral bodies and to the ego.[6] How is it then with the three new virtues, whose source is the Christ-impulse working in the human ego, filling it and flowing forth into the sheaths—as faith in the astral body, as love in the etheric body, and as hope in the physical body? In order to answer this question we must recall that these three fundamental virtues of the new Christian Mysteries, which manifest themselves in our time as purely inward forces fashioning and transforming the human sheaths, must—according to Rudolf Steiner—continually receive the nourishment and forces that they need for their development. Only through receiving a certain nourishment can they accomplish what they should in man's being. This nourishment lies principally in the truths of modern spiritual science, Anthroposophy, which in our time is alone able to awaken within humanity the forces of faith, love and hope which proceed from wisdom, from the Sophia.[7] For in its essence modern anthroposophically orientated spiritual science is not merely a theoretical doctrine, but is intended to become a real food for man's soul, a bread of life that is able so to transform and strengthen his sheaths that Christ may dwell within them. In this sense the following words of Rudolf Steiner open up for us vast horizons of world-evolution: 'If we but receive the truths which Anthroposophy[8] communicates to us, and if we give them as nourishment for the forces of faith within our soul, then will Manas (the Spirit Self) arise in us out of itself; the transformation of the astral body into Manas will come about by itself. While if we receive these truths and give them as food to our love, then will Buddhi (the Life Spirit) arise out of itself. And if we receive anthroposophical truths and give them as nourishment to hope, then will Spirit Man, Atma, arise in us of itself.'[9] From these words we may see that the seven virtues which we have considered encompass the *whole* of man's being and so form a sure foundation for the Christian Mysteries of today, the aim of which is to awaken in every human individual his primordial divine archetype which is none other than the Cosmic Christ who united with the true Anthropos—the Nathan Soul.

If we now recall that the Mysteries of modern times do not annul the Mysteries of the past but receive and transform them and lift them to a higher plane,[10] then all that has just been said can be summarized in the following way:

| Virtues | Human Sheaths (the members of man's being) |

	Virtues	Human Sheaths (the members of man's being)
Past (Old Mysteries)	1. Justice 2. Temperance (prudence) 3. Fortitude (presence of mind)	Physical body Etheric body Astral body
Present (Anthroposophy)	4. Wisdom—Sophia	Ego
Future (New Mysteries)	5. Faith 6. Love 7. Hope	Spirit Self (Manas) Life Spirit (Buddhi) Spirit Man (Atma)

With more exact observation it is not difficult to see that this is merely a kind of metamorphosis of the words which are engraved in invisible letters beneath the image of the *new* Isis, the Divine Sophia.★ These words run: 'I am man. I am the past, the present and the future. Every mortal shall lift my

---

★ This is a reference to the sculptural Group in Dornach, which depicts the Representative of Man between Lucifer and Ahriman. In the lecture of 6 January 1918 (GA 180), Rudolf Steiner also connects the esoteric significance of the Group with the mystery of the new Isis.

veil.'[11] In the sense of the above this signifies sevenfold man, who encompasses the past, present and future of world evolution and from whose esoteric being *every* human soul that embarks upon the path of the new Mysteries, through the inner development of the seven virtues, can lift the veil.

The modern Christian initiate, who has developed within himself the virtues of faith, love and hope to the degree that they have become in him organs of imaginative, inspirative and intuitive knowledge, can as a result of this carry out research in the Akashic Chronicle regarding the cosmic and earthly destiny of the Christ Being. According to what Rudolf Steiner says in the lecture of 18 December 1913,[12] in order to research into the deeds of Christ in world-evolution from Saturn to Vulcan it is necessary for the spiritual researcher to experience the thinking of an Angel, that is, to attain a conscious experience of the supersensible activity of the Angel in his astral body. In order, however, that he may be able to recognize the deeds of Christ in the successive cultural epochs, he needs to sacrifice his own life-forces to the being of an Archangel, that is, consciously to experience this presence in his own etheric body. Finally, in order to read in the Akashic Chronicle about the actual events of the *earthly* life of Christ Jesus, he needs to feel himself to be the 'spiritual nourishment of the Archai', consciously to experience the work of the Archai, extending as it does even to man's physical body. These processes are essentially none other than powers of faith, love and hope that have become essentially real; for the first of these opens the gates into the realm of the Angels, the second to the realm of the Archangels, and the third to the realm of the Archai. (The metamorphosis of thinking, feeling and will corresponds to a preliminary stage of this process.)

In the course of the general evolution of humanity, these stages come to expression in that ever higher categories of hierarchic beings will, from our time onwards and into the future, become bearers of the new supersensible knowledge of Christ *to all 'men of good will'*—which is to say, they will lead them directly to Him. Rudolf Steiner writes about this in his book *The Spiritual Guidance of Man* in the following way: 'As in our fifth post-Atlantean epoch, it is the Angels who are the beings that bear the Christ into our spiritual evolution, so the sixth cultural period will be guided by those beings of the rank of the Archangels who were the leaders of the Ancient Persian cultural period. The Spirits of the primal beginnings, the Archai, who led humanity during the Ancient Indian period, will lead humanity under the guidance of Christ in the seventh cultural epoch . . . In this way will mankind be led up from one stage to another into the spiritual world.'[13]

If we now turn again to man's inner development, associated as it is with the mastering of certain spiritual moral qualities (virtues) in the yearly rhythm, we may say: the influence of the Archai, Archangels and Angels—from which man is gradually liberating himself as their activity within him is replaced by the virtues of justice, temperance and fortitude in order that he may come in full freedom and solitude to an experience of Christ in his own ego, who is born within him out of the mother substance of wisdom, or the Sophia—will now be restored in full consciousness and in full freedom as man inwardly develops the powers of faith, love and hope into faculties of imaginative, inspirative and intuitive knowledge.[14] Thus, having in this way previously separated himself from the hierarchic macrocosm, man now begins once more to grow into it through the Christ-impulse which he has consciously received.[15]

2. The Working of the Nathan Soul in the Old and the New Mysteries. Christ-bearer and Christ-receiver

The transition from the epoch of the old to the epoch of the new Mysteries, which was fulfilled by the deeds of Christ Jesus at the Turning Point of Time, is marked by the most momentous event in the entire spiritual evolution of mankind. Thenceforth the life of the Mysteries, as it existed until this point, acquired a different direction. If, until the Mystery of Golgotha, the task of all the ancient Mysteries was not only that of maintaining man's connection with the higher worlds but also—and this was no less important—of effecting his *right* descent into the earthly sphere so as to achieve individual freedom and a fully developed ego-consciousness, then the task of the new Mysteries which arose on the foundation of the Mystery of Golgotha is the gradual preparation of human beings for a new, altogether free and conscious ascent into the spiritual worlds.

However, that which was cultivated in antiquity in Mystery-temples, which were deeply hidden from the outer world, did not completely disappear from human evolution in the new age but went through a spiritual metamorphosis and became internalized—passing from the secret sanctuaries of olden times into human souls as their inner power. The 'Platonic virtues' that we have described at various points are a particularly important element of this 'heritage' of the old Mysteries. Hence we shall now turn to them once more, dwelling in particular upon one aspect which will enable us to approach the principal theme of the present chapter.

As we have seen, the most important aspect of these virtues—we shall to begin with consider the first three, justice, temperance (prudence) and fortitude (presence of mind)—consists in this: their right development by man in the period of Advent represents, in a certain way, the inner, soul-moral repetition of the three sacrificial deeds of the Nathan Soul accomplished in the higher worlds in the Lemurian and Atlantean epochs. In these far-off times the Nathan Soul was on three occasions able to sacrifice its own being to the Sun-Spirit of Christ, that is—in the sense of the ancient Mystery-traditions—it was able thrice to become in the spiritual world a *Christophoros*, a heavenly Christ-bearer. Through this it appeared for all future times as the great archetype of all pre-Christian Mysteries, both in their northern and southern aspects, for in both these Mystery-streams, although in different ways, the pupils aspired to one and the same goal: of becoming a Christophoros which, in those ancient times, was attainable only through a direct experience of the Christ *beyond* the Earth, in the high Sun-sphere.

Rudolf Steiner refers to this unceasing participation of the Nathan Soul in the Mysteries of antiquity in the following words: 'This [Nathan] Soul is, therefore, one which it was impossible to meet outwardly as a human being and which could be perceived only by the seers of old. And was indeed perceived by them; it . . . frequented the Mysteries.'[16] 'It . . . was, so to say, fostered and nurtured in the Mysteries, and was sent forth to wherever something important for mankind was to take place, but it could only be present in such cases in an *etheric body*, and hence it could strictly speaking be perceived only while the old clairvoyance continued to exist.'[17] 'Thus everywhere . . . where such Schools [Mysteries] appear in history one may observe that they have perceived this Soul which has *accompanied mankind*.'[18]

Thus the Nathan Soul has participated in the spiritual evolution of humanity since ancient times and represents the heavenly *archetype* of the highest aims of all pre-Christian Mysteries. This fundamental significance which it had for the Mystery life of mankind in the past places before us— on the basis of what we have considered hitherto—a question of the greatest importance: what is its role with regard to the new, modern Mysteries? In other words: how does the Nathan Soul work amongst mankind *after* its fourth sacrifice, which we can approach in a soul-moral way through the development of a real understanding of the Mystery of Golgotha, on the foundation of the new Christian wisdom, the new Isis-Sophia? And what is its relationship to the virtues of faith, love and hope, those three pillars on which the temple of the new Mysteries is founded?

In order to answer these questions we must recall at this point the essential difference which exists between the first three sacrifices of the Nathan Soul and its fourth sacrifice. In the first three sacrifices it entered into human evolution as the great heavenly Christophoros who thrice became the Bearer of the Christ Being in the cosmos. In the fourth sacrifice, when it incarnated on Earth as the Jesus of the Luke Gospel, it was, until the thirtieth year of Jesus's life, no longer the 'outward' *bearer* of Christ in the macrocosm but the foremost human being, the one who *received* Christ into himself even to his innermost core, so that Christ could unite in the course of the Baptism in the Jordan with his most hidden essence and then, during the three subsequent years, penetrate his astral, etheric and physical bodies. Thus through this fourth sacrifice the Nathan

Soul entered the world as a being who appears not as a Christ-*bearer* but as a Christ-*receiver*. And this was an entirely new stage in the evolution of humanity which was never attained in the old 'pre-Christian' Mysteries and which revealed to people an altogether new possibility of uniting with Christ, and through Him—as we have seen—with the whole macrocosm.[19]

This new union with Christ that arose, not through an ascent into the high sphere of the Sun but through receiving the Christ-impulse here on Earth into the human ego, the holiest part of man's being, subsequently became the ultimate goal of all truly Christian Mysteries which had their source in the central event of world-evolution, the Mystery of Golgotha. The following words of Rudolf Steiner speak with particular clarity about this principal difference between the old and the new Mysteries and the unattainability of the highest aims of the new Mysteries in 'pre-Christian' times: 'And this was in effect the level of initiation [in the old Mysteries] at which man became a Christ-bearer, which is to say, a bearer of the Sun Being, not one who receives the Sun Being into himself but a bearer of the Sun Being. As the Moon is, during Full Moon, a bearer of the Sun's light, so did man become a bearer of the Christ, a Christophoros. This initiation whereby man became a Christophoros was, therefore, a wholly real experience.[20]

But the essential nature of the fourth sacrifice of the Nathan Soul was that, *for the first time* in the history of the Mystery-life of humanity, it became not a Christ-bearer but a *Christ-receiver* and thereby appeared for all future ages as an *archetype* of the final goal and the highest aspirations of all truly Christian Mysteries and, above all, of the new Mysteries of Michael-Christ which came to mankind through anthroposophically orientated spiritual science, and were founded upon the Christmas Foundation Meeting of 1923. For, as Zeylmans van Emmichoven has observed, the first of the two key lines of the fourth part of the Foundation Stone Meditation

O Light Divine,
O Sun of Christ

relate to the Nathan Soul.[21] Hence these lines in their totality are at once an indication of the highest ideal of the new Mysteries, and an indication of the primordial *human* being who *received into himself* the Sun of Christ in such fullness that it became possible for him fully to permeate his sheaths with the substance of 'Light Divine', the substance of the Holy Spirit proceeding from the Christ, and through this to enter upon the path leading to the attainment of the goal of the Earth-aeon in its entirety.[22] Thus since the events of Palestine, the Nathan Soul has worked in the world as *the archetypal image of man wholly permeated by Christ* and at the same time as the archetype of the future evolution of mankind, of which we have already spoken in connection with the description of the three revelations of Christ in successive cultural epochs (see p.120).

This altogether new relationship of the Nathan Soul to Christ and all humanity after the Mystery of Golgotha served as a foundation whereby the Apostle Paul, who outside Damascus prophetically experienced a manifestation of Christ—in the form in which, from the twentieth century onwards, He will appear to man—could behold Him surrounded by a radiant aura of light, which was the Nathan Soul itself, who thenceforth accompanied Christ like a garment of light. Rudolf Steiner describes this manifestation in these words: 'But what was necessary in order that the Risen One might appear in as condensed a soul-form as He appeared to Paul? What, shall we say, was that *light-filled radiance* in which Christ appeared to Paul before Damascus? What was this? Whence did it come?'[23] Then, in answer to this question, Rudolf Steiner continues: 'When Paul had his vision before Damascus, what appeared to him was the Christ. But the *light-filled radiance*, in which Christ was arrayed, was Krishna. And just because Christ took Krishna as his own *soul-sheath through which He might work further*, everything which was once the content of the sublime Gita was included in what now radiated from Christ.'[24] From these words we may see that the '*light-filled radiance* in which Christ was arrayed', that '*soul-sheath through which He might work further*'—until our time and from today on into the future—was the Nathan Soul, weaving a radiant garment for the etheric Sun of Christ in the astral world out of streams of divine (astral) light ('O Light Divine, O Sun of Christ!').

Thus it is that this reference of Rudolf Steiner to the Nathan Soul at the event of Damascus speaks to us of the Nathan Soul as the great archetype of man, who has fully embodied in itself the first supersensible revelation of Christ, has become a Christ-receiver in its astral body and has therein fashioned for Him a garment woven of the purest, radiant astral light.* This is only the beginning, for this working together in humanity of the Christ Being and the Nathan Soul will continue on into the future. Thus in the sixth cultural epoch, when Christ will reveal Himself to mankind in His astral body in lower Devachan, the Nathan Soul will appear as the archetype of the man who has become a Christ-receiver in his *etheric body*,[25] which has been woven by Christ as a new garment out of all the planetary and solar forces of lower Devachan, where the formative forces of the etheric sheaths of man have their abode. Finally, in the seventh epoch,

---

* More will be said about this process in the chapter 'The New Revelation of Christ in the Etheric'.

175

when Christ will reveal Himself to humanity in His macrocosmic ego in higher Devachan, the Nathan Soul will also go with Him as the archetype of a man who has become a Christ-receiver even in the supersensible forces of his physical body, forces which have their source in higher Devachan, in the world of the fixed stars, out of whose forces the Nathan Soul then weaves for Christ a heavenly, starry garment.

Such is the picture of these events from the cosmic point of view. But from the human standpoint, too, they appear as something of the greatest significance. We have already seen how in its three 'pre-Christian' sacrifices the Nathan Soul was able, in still working wholly from the extra-terrestrial cosmos, to bring the Christ-impulse to bear upon man's being, upon the various systems of the human organism, while through its fourth sacrifice it enabled him also to gain access to the human ego and there become the source of his intellectual and moral forces. Rudolf Steiner sums up this combined working of the Christ Being and the Nathan Soul in relation to the various elements of the human organization in the following way: 'Yes, spiritual science will show us ever more deeply how this human ego may come to a true unselfishness as a result of the fourth Christ-event [through the Nathan Soul], as a result of the Mystery of Golgotha. The senses have said: "Not I, but Christ in us" [the first sacrifice]. The life-organs have said: "Not I, but Christ in us" [the second sacrifice]. The soul-organs have said: "Not I, but Christ in us" [the third sacrifice].[26] Man's moral and intellectual life [in so far as it is the result of the free development of his ego] must now learn to say: "Not I, but Christ in me".'[27] This latter experience was, however, made accessible for man through the Baptism in the Jordan (Epiphany) and the ensuing Mystery of Golgotha (the fourth sacrifice of the Nathan Soul), the consequence of which was Paul's experience outside Damascus and the words spoken by him, which since then have been the foundation and the goal of all true Christian Mysteries.

However, this development must now be taken further. For in our time the Nathan Soul, who has accompanied the Christ on the path of His ever higher revelations, is to enable—through the manifestation of its archetype—a development to take place within humanity whereby man's astral body may even in our time, through the unfolding of the power of faith, come to say: 'Not I, but Christ in me.' In the sixth epoch the etheric body may come to say the same through the unfolding of the power of love and, finally, in the seventh epoch, through the development of the power of hope, to some extent also the physical body.[28] Only when this occurs—through the working of the Nathan Soul in the new Christian Mysteries, the foundation of which was openly laid among mankind at the Christmas Foundation Meeting of 1923—is man able to approach his ideal, his archetype. Only then will he be able to become a *conscious Christ-receiver*.[29]

The final lines of the fourth part of the Foundation Stone Meditation refer to this same sublime goal; for there it speaks of the Christ Sun which now works in the Nathan Soul's sheath of light which shall warm human hearts (feelings), enlighten human heads (thoughts) and then flow forth into man's whole being, even to the impulses of his will, so that human beings who, in the new Mysteries are striving consciously to receive Christ into themselves,[30] might then be able, through His strength, to bring true *goodness* into the outer world:[31]

That good may become	[hope]
What from our Hearts we would found	[love]
And from our Heads direct	[faith/knowledge]
With single purpose.	

From all that has been said in this chapter regarding the significance of the Nathan Soul for the old and the new Mysteries, and also its path with Christ in ancient times from Heaven to Earth and now from the Earth ever higher into the starry worlds, one may come to sense its profoundly intimate connection with the three Rosicrucian dicta which contain the very essence of the esoteric path of the modern Christian Mysteries: *Ex Deo nascimur, In Christo morimur, Per Spiritum Sanctum reviviscimus.* Furthermore, the cosmic-earthly destiny of the Nathan Soul, its indissoluble, direct connection with the Christ Being since ancient Lemurian times through to our own age and from now on into the future—all this speaks to us of how it is itself the *human vessel* of these three dicta, just as Christ is their cosmic vessel.[32] Indeed, who other than the Nathan Soul may truly be called *born of God*, at the time when the first man was created by the Elohim, and also the preserver of these primordial divine forces in all their purity, so that it came to sacrifice itself three times to Christ in the spiritual worlds and once on the Earth, at the Baptism in the Jordan? Furthermore, of whom other than this Soul, the only human being who received Christ into himself on Earth and *passed with Him through the Mystery of Golgotha,* can it be said that it 'died' in Christ, 'died' *with* Christ? Finally, of whom else can it be said that it *resurrected* in the Holy Spirit who came forth from Christ, when it appeared to Paul at Damascus as the 'sheath of light' of the Risen One?

Thus it can truly be said that the Nathan Soul is not only the archetype of the highest goal of the new Mysteries but also the direct guide to their fulfilment: through the *recollection* of its three heavenly sacrifices, through the *mindfulness* of its sublime fourth sacrifice which it made at the Turning Point of Time, and through the *vision* of its three future supersensible sacrifices, the first of which is, from the twentieth century onwards, now being accomplished. For it is the most important task of the Christian Mysteries of today to open the gates whereby this may be *seen* in the light of the new Spirit of the Age.

VI

THE MYSTERY OF EASTER

1. The Forty-day Conversations of the Risen One and their Rebirth in Modern Spiritual Science

'For forty days He presented Himself to their beholding souls and spoke to them of the Mysteries of the Kingdom of God'

Acts of the Apostles 1:3
(following the Emil Bock translation)

'But whoever is approaching Anthroposophy can gradually come to a living contemplation of the Mystery of Golgotha and gain an idea of what the Christ taught His initiated pupils after His Resurrection. And as people familiarize themselves with this, the spiritual world around them will also become more and more comprehensible to them.'

Rudolf Steiner,
lecture of 11 June 1922

In our study of the cycle of the year we now stand directly before the festival of Easter, that festival which is *central* to the year's course and leads us to the greatest event in the whole of earthly evolution, the Mystery of Golgotha. This event also represents the culmination of the process whereby God becomes man, a process which comes to fulfilment through the final union of the Sun Being of Christ with the *physical body* of Jesus of Nazareth. And if the previous stages of the union of the Christ Being with the astral and etheric bodies of Jesus of Nazareth, accessible as they are to imaginative and inspirative knowledge, have revealed the deep secrets of the lunar and solar (planetary) spheres, so in the Mystery of Golgotha itself does the mystery of man's physical body appear before us, a Mystery which embraces the whole sphere of the fixed stars and is accessible only to the highest *intuitive* knowledge. This is what is uniquely distinctive about the Mystery of Golgotha, that although it takes place on the *physical plane*, nevertheless it cannot be apprehended by ordinary human understanding but only by the highest supersensible knowledge. In the final chapter ('On Initiation') of his book *Occult Science*, Rudolf Steiner writes of this as follows: 'The spirit-pupil is thereby *initiated* into that great mystery which is associated with the name of Christ. Christ stands before him as the great earthly Archetype of man. When a man has come thus to know Christ in the spiritual world, he begins to understand what has taken place on Earth as a historical event in the fourth post-Atlantean period of earthly evolution [this refers to the Mystery of Golgotha]. How the high Sun Being, the

181

Being of Christ, has in this period entered into Earth-evolution and how this Being continues to work in this same Earth-evolution, becomes for the spirit-pupil knowledge that is personally experienced. Hence the meaning and significance of Earth-evolution is revealed to the spirit-pupil through Intuition.'*

In a number of lectures Rudolf Steiner speaks again and again of how the Mystery of Golgotha is the connecting link between the heights and the depths of the world: between the great macrocosmic man, Adam Cadmon, who was formed out of the activity of all the nine Hierarchies, and his microcosmic reflection, the human physical body, which in its forms and structure represents the essential revelation of the individual ego-principle. The following words in particular express this all-embracing significance of the Mystery of Golgotha: 'And so that figure which has passed through the Mystery of Golgotha can come before the human soul only if, from out of human organology, there first arises the possibility of beholding Cosmic Man. For *Christ came from the Sun as Cosmic Man*. Until then He had not been an earthly man. He came down as Cosmic Man.'[1]

Rudolf Steiner spoke in a lecture given on 25 May 1924 in Paris about this 'Cosmic Man' whose forces were brought in all their fullness into earthly evolution through the Mystery of Golgotha and were manifested in the imperishable Resurrection-body. We find there a detailed description of how in the 'head organization' of the Cosmic Man, which corresponds to the sphere of the outer planets, there works the First Hierarchy; in the 'rhythmic system', which corresponds to the Sun, the Second Hierarchy; while in the 'limb-system', which is connected with the inner planets, there works the Third Hierarchy.[2] If we now add to this the further fact that the original sphere of activity of the First Hierarchy is the world of the fixed stars extending to the sphere of the outer planets, that of the Second Hierarchy the Sun, and of the Third in particular the Moon-sphere,[3] while also recalling our earlier description of the participation of all nine Hierarchies in the seasonal constellation of the Easter festival (see p.159), we may approach the essential mystery of this festival from the *yearly rhythm* itself.

And indeed, whereas all the previous festivals—Michaelmas, Christmas, Epiphany—are, through being immovable, more connected with the forces of the Earth, the festival of Easter, because of its movability and its direct connection with the three cosmic regions of the fixed stars, the Sun and the Moon, leads us above all to the great 'Cosmic Man' who bears within himself the entire cosmos, the forces of all the Hierarchies and who

---

* Regarding the point that a true knowledge of the Mystery of Golgotha is attained only through intuitive knowledge, see also Rudolf Steiner's words quoted on pp. 199–200.

through the Mystery of Golgotha was for the first time *born* within the being of the Earth:

> At the Turning Point of Time
> The Spirit-Light of the World
> Entered the stream of Earthly Being.

With this 'Cosmic Man', however, a further Mystery is connected. In the Foundation Stone Meditation and especially in the fourth rhythm of the Christmas Foundation Meeting, Rudolf Steiner refers to how all the sublime and multitudinous deeds of the divine-spiritual Hierarchies in our cosmos are brought into a unity and to a single, purposeful activity through their revelation in the sounding of the all-embracing Cosmic Word, the Logos.[4] What would otherwise be uncoordinated and inharmonious acquires through Him its integrity and completeness, receives its *highest form*. And this universal form is none other than the aforesaid 'Cosmic Man', the totality of the deeds of the Hierarchies as revealed in the sounding of the World Word. In a certain sense one could say that He (the 'Cosmic Man') is the true revelation of the Cosmic Word in our cosmos.

This Cosmic Word, this creative Logos of our cosmos, the hidden focus and source of the forces of all the higher Hierarchies, was at the Turning Point of Time borne by Christ in all its fullness into Earth-existence. For in Him 'the Word' truly 'became flesh'. The Logos itself united with man's physical body, with the earthly body of Jesus of Nazareth. Such is the nature of the third and final stage of God becoming man, such is the mystery of the night of Gethsemane and the Hill of Golgotha. But to this first part of the Mystery of Golgotha, which sums up the entire *past* of the evolution of the world and of humanity, is added after three days its second part, the fundamental mystery of all *future* evolution. The event of the Resurrection also directs us towards this mystery of the future. There indeed does 'flesh again become Word'. For through the working of the Logos in man's physical body it has been reunited with its archetype, with the great 'Cosmic Man', with the forces of the higher Hierarchies. This process could also be described as follows. Until the Mystery of Golgotha the whole of world-evolution was directed towards the cosmos becoming man. The spiritual forces of the seven planets had gradually to become the foundation in man of his fluid organism, while the spiritual forces of the starry sphere, of the whole twelvefold circle of the zodiac, became the foundation of his physical (solid) organization. Since the Mystery of Golgotha, world-evolution has taken the opposite direction. That which in former times became man's flesh and blood, the manifestation of the forces of his physical and etheric bodies, must, as a result of the working of the astral body and ego, enter upon the path towards a new union with the world of the stars and the world of the planets.[5] Herein lies also the ultimate fulfilment of the most secret strivings of the Sun Mysteries of antiquity, the Mystery of the living Christ: the Mysteries of death, which are expressed in the words 'and the Word became flesh', and the Mysteries of resurrection, which are connected with the words, 'and flesh again became Word'. In these two esoteric formulations we have, therefore, that sublime pronouncement of the truth whereby at the moment when the Mystery of Golgotha was accomplished on the Earth the leading Sun Archangel, the leader and inspirer of the Sun Mysteries, Michael, the Countenance of Christ, answers from the Sun, turning as he does to all the people of the Earth. 'The Word becoming flesh is the first revelation of Michael,' says Rudolf Steiner, 'and the flesh becoming Word must become the second revelation of Michael.'[6] In this way Michael bears the Sun-knowledge of Christ to mankind through the centuries and millennia.

Hence we may see that the entire relationship between macrocosm and microcosm, between Gods and men, changed quite fundamentally at the moment of the Mystery of Golgotha. Since that time the knowledge of the new order of the cosmic forces, their transformed relationships and interplay which entered into all things, represents for all future times the true content of esoteric Christianity. For Christ did not bring a new doctrine into the world but a single *deed*, the deed of Golgotha. Thus the gradual revelation of its telluric-cosmic significance, its all-embracing significance for the world of the Gods and the world of men, is the only 'doctrine' in Christianity, and its foundations were laid by the Resurrection of Christ Himself in the course of the forty days of His conversations with the Apostles. Furthermore, all esoteric knowledge of the Mystery of Golgotha has its ultimate source in these conversations. Rudolf Steiner speaks of this as follows: 'Besides this exoteric aspect [in the Gospels] there has always existed an esoteric Christianity for those who have made the effort to prepare their souls for this esoteric Christianity. What is most important in this esoteric Christianity is whatever one can come to know about the personal contacts of the Risen Christ—that is, the Christ who had experienced and overcome death—with those of His disciples who were able to understand Him.'[7] In another lecture we find these words: '... Now the time has come when man yearns for a deeper knowledge of the Mystery of Golgotha. This knowledge can be acquired only through Anthroposophy. It can come about only through the emerging of a knowledge which follows purely spiritual paths. Man will then attain to a fully human understanding of the Mystery of Golgotha. He will learn again to understand that the most important teachings were given to mankind not by the Christ, who lived in a physical body in the period *before* the

Mystery of Golgotha, but by the Risen Christ *after* the Mystery of Golgotha.'[8]

Thus we may define the principal content of the teaching of esoteric Christianity, together with the essential nature of the conversations of the Risen One with His disciples, as the knowledge of the new relation between macrocosm and microcosm, between the world of the Gods and the world of men, which came into being as a result of the Mystery of Golgotha. For these conversations revealed to the disciples the mystery of the whole of world-evolution *prior* to the Mystery of Golgotha as the cosmos becoming man, and the whole of future evolution as directed towards the aim that man might again become a cosmos, consciously entering the world-whole as the Tenth Hierarchy which represents the completion of our cosmos. Both these world-processes have found their full expression in the fundamental Mystery of the Christ in that He gradually made the transition from cosmic being to human being and that He then overcame the limits of all that is human. This last came to expression in Christ's victory over death, a condition which applies *only* to human existence on Earth, and in His ascent back into the macrocosm, into the realm of the Father, the realm of the higher Hierarchies—though now *together* with the redeemed human form that bears within it the *substance of humanity* (or in other words the quintessence of human existence) the principle of individual ego-consciousness.[9] The event of the Ascension at the end of the forty-day conversations reflected this reunion of the Christ with the macrocosm when, before the awakening imaginative gaze of the disciples, He took with Him into the spheres beyond the Earth the fully spiritualized human physical body which had become the purest image of His cosmic ego-consciousness. Thus the essence of the new relationship between macrocosm and microcosm was revealed as a spiritual vision to the inner experience of the disciples.

However, as the Fifth Gospel makes plain, not all the disciples of Christ Jesus were able to experience these conversations consciously.[10] For such a conscious perception demanded of them, as we have seen, an ascent into the sphere of world Intuition, a fructification by the world-wisdom of the Holy Spirit proceeding from Christ. And *before* the Whitsun Mystery only 'the disciple whom the Lord loved', who received the 'Sophia of Christ' into himself, as he stood beneath the cross on Golgotha, was capable of this.

The modern initiate on the Christian-Rosicrucian path of initiation who approaches a conscious meeting with the Christ in the sphere of Intuition and (in accordance with what was quoted from *Occult Science* at the beginning of the chapter) penetrates to a true knowledge of the Mystery of Golgotha, necessarily experiences, as a result, the content of what has been preserved in the Akashic Chronicle of the conversations of the Risen One. For in our time any *true knowledge* of the Mystery of Golgotha can be obtained only through the intuitively comprehended— here one could also use the word 'heard'—conversations of the Risen Christ. Hence we should say: everything which modern anthroposophically orientated spiritual science, as the bearer of the new knowledge of the Christ Being and the Mystery of Golgotha, now brings into the world, and also all that it contains of knowledge of the Christ Being and of the Mystery of Golgotha, which is surely also an expression of the new relationship between the world of the Gods and that of men which came about as a result of the Mystery of Golgotha—all this is none other than the transmission of the esoteric content of the forty-day conversations of the Risen One with His disciples[11] *in a form appropriate for modern times.*

This relationship can also be expressed as follows. Today, when, as a result of the 'repetition of the Mystery of Golgotha', the Christ who has again been 'resurrected' in the spiritual worlds is able to approach mankind in an etheric form,[12] the content of esoteric Christianity, the content of the forty-day conversations of the Risen One, must also be renewed and appear in a new form among mankind. The opportunity must again emerge, though now for all *mankind* and *in full consciousness*, to speak with Christ, to ask of Him and to receive from Him answers and elucidations regarding all manner of secrets of the world and of life. The language in which we may thus speak with the Etheric Christ, speak with Him as the Apostles once spoke with Him during the forty days from Easter until Ascension, is modern anthroposophically orientated spiritual science (see the words of Rudolf Steiner quoted on p.130), which in its esoteric nature represents, therefore, *the beginning of the rebirth of the teachings of the Risen Christ within humanity.*

Even the very composition of the word Anthropos-Sophia is an indication of this more inward, original source of modern spiritual science. In our study of the Mystery of Christmas we have already been able to describe the imagination that gave rise to this word: the form of Mary-Sophia, who holds in her arms the archetype of man, Anthropos, in the person of the heavenly being of the Nathan Soul who had descended to the Earth for the first time. Then we saw how this imagination, becoming filled with forces of Inspiration, directs us to the scene of the Baptism in the Jordan, when the Sun Being of Christ united for the first time with man's being, Anthropos, through the mediation of the Sophia or the Holy Spirit.[13] This is the second or 'inspirative' stage in the revelation of the imagination of Anthropos-Sophia. Finally, if we penetrate this imagination with forces of *Intuition*, we are led towards the Mystery of Golgotha, in the course of which the essential being of Anthropos, the ancient human archetype in the form of the imperishable Resurrection-body, is once more united with the entire macrocosm, and is thus permeated by the universal wisdom of the Hierarchies, the cosmic Sophia, who from the very beginning participated in His creation in the macrocosm.

From this it becomes clear that modern Anthroposophy is above all else the bearer of the all-embracing wisdom of the Mystery of the Resurrection, the wisdom of the true human Anthropos who has risen from the grave, who because of the presence of the macrocosmic Ego of Christ within him manifests the whole fullness of the forces of 'cosmic universal man' in the earthly sphere.

It can fill us with astonishment to become aware of the many indications which tell us that Anthroposophy serves especially to reveal the central Mystery of the Resurrection, that is, the content of the forty-day conversations which thus form its true centre. Furthermore, it is from a penetration into the secrets of this Mystery, which, we have seen, consists in a knowledge of the essential nature of the 'imperishable body' or Phantom which rose on the third day, that those three elements arise upon which the whole of Anthroposophy is founded, elements which we find engraved in Rudolf Steiner's books *Theosophy, Occult Science* and *Knowledge of the Higher Worlds: How is it Achieved?* What, then, do we know of the 'imperishable body' through modern initiation, and how is this knowledge reflected in the above books?

In the first place, we hear of the sevenfold nature of the human being. For a knowledge of the 'Phantom' discloses to us the secret of how Christ's Ego, which after the Baptism in the Jordan had united respectively with the astral, etheric and physical sheaths of Jesus of Nazareth, gradually transformed them in the course of three years into the higher members of human nature: into the Spirit Self, the Life Spirit and the Spirit Man (see p.115). This knowledge forms the first part of the book *Theosophy.*

In the second place we experience the evolutionary development of the Phantom from Saturn through Sun and Moon to the middle of the Earth-aeon, and also the participation in this development of all nine Hierarchies.[14] Then we learn of the injury which it sustains as a result of the entry of Lucifer and Ahriman into evolution and its resurrection in its former glory and strength through its being endowed by Christ with forces from the future development of the aeons of Jupiter, Venus and Vulcan. In this knowledge is contained the whole of world-evolution and the activity of all the hierarchic spirits that it encompasses; this corresponds to the principal content of *Occult Science.*

Finally, in the third place, we learn of the new path of initiation, which leads through a true knowledge of death (the meeting with the lesser Guardian of the Threshold) to a conscious ascent into the macrocosm (the meeting with the greater Guardian of the Threshold); this signifies, on the one hand, the attaining of a higher consciousness even while on Earth, in the physical body, and, on the other hand, the complete preservation of individual ego-consciousness in the ascent into the higher worlds after death.[15] Thus in this knowledge we have the true sources of what we then find set forth in *Knowledge of the Higher Worlds: How is it Achieved?* and in the second part of *Theosophy*. Also, in what directly concerns anthroposophical occult exercises (that is, in the indications for spiritual development), we always find, at the foundation, the development of those forces which lead to a gradual inner resurrection—whether it be a resurrection in the sphere of thoughts, in the sphere of feeling or in the sphere of will; for these resurrection-forces have in the deepest sense belonged to Anthroposophy from the beginning and cannot be separated from it.

2. The Mission of the Master Jesus in the Cycle of the Year

Before turning directly to the content of the forty-day conversations of the Risen Christ with His disciples, in so far as we can gain access to this on the basis of what modern spiritual science can tell us, we must still touch upon one purely supersensible aspect of these conversations which has a quite particular relationship to the principal theme of the present work, to the esoteric study of the cycle of the year that has been undertaken in the pages of this book. This 'supersensible' aspect of the forty-day period of teachings by the Risen One consists in this, that besides Christ Himself, and the disciples attending to His teachings, there were *three* individualities who were supersensibly present and who also took part in these conversations, even though they were *not incarnated* in physical bodies.

One of these individualities is the Nathan Soul, of whom we have already spoken many times and in various connections. As we know from the words of Rudolf Steiner quoted on p.174, this soul remains inseparably connected with the Christ Being even after the Mystery of Golgotha, surrounding Him in the spiritual world with what can be called a spiritual sheath which appears as a radiant aura of light. The second individuality is the spiritual being of John the Baptist who was connected with John the Apostle, and who united with him during his initiation as Lazarus.[16] After his death this spiritual being of John the Baptist also formed that aura which then came to encompass all the Apostles and which, according to Rudolf Steiner, worked among them as their 'group-soul'.[17] And finally, we should refer here to the supersensible presence in the conversations of the Risen One to one further individuality, who, as we have seen, has a quite particular significance. This is the individuality of *Zarathustra*. However, in order that we may have a better understanding of the particular character of this individuality's participation in the forty-day conversations, we need (albeit in brief) to recall the altogether special task with which it was entrusted by the world-rulership in the course of the events of Palestine.

It is known through spiritual science that at the beginning of the Christian era the individuality of Zarathustra incarnated on Earth as the Solomon Jesus-child—of whom the Gospel of St Matthew tells. When the child had attained the age of twelve, the ego of Zarathustra left him and united with the Nathan Jesus child—of whom the Gospel of St Luke tells—dwelling in him until his thirtieth year. The Solomon Jesus child, thus abandoned by the ego of Zarathustra, soon died, and his etheric body, which had been penetrated and spiritualized to a high degree, was borne away into the spiritual world by the mother of the Nathan Jesus child who had died at approximately the same time.[18] Thus in the course of the eighteen years, while the ego of Zarathustra dwelt in the sheaths of the Nathan Jesus, the etheric body of the Solomon Jesus remained in the spiritual world, because it had been transformed to so high a degree that it was not subject to the process of dissolution in the surrounding ether, which is what normally happens to a human etheric body after death. Furthermore, shortly before the Baptism in the Jordan, the ego of Zarathustra left the sheaths of Jesus of Nazareth and, passing through a kind of microcosmic 'ascension', entered the spiritual world, leaving the sheaths which he had prepared to the Sun Ego of Christ. We should understand this 'ascension' of the ego of Zarathustra primarily as a deeply sacrificial deed, in that he first sacrificed to the Nathan Soul all the treasures of wisdom which he had gathered in his ego in the course of all his previous incarnations,[19] and then left the physical plane, willingly renouncing the opportunity to witness the greatest earthly event of all—the appearance of Christ on the Earth. And so the individuality of Zarathustra was able to experience the three years of Christ walking the Earth only from the spiritual world, from the supersensible sphere that is nearest to the physical plane, where the *etheric body* of the Solomon Jesus-child also abided.

Now we must examine in further detail some of the more inward qualities of this etheric body, of which two in particular will be of importance as we take our investigations further. The first of these is connected with the general stream of human evolution, that is, with the condition of the etheric bodies of all human beings on Earth at the time of the events of Palestine, when the ancient wisdom, which man has brought in the course of his descent into the physical world as the content of his etheric body, had now—under the influence of the physical body, which had been having an effect on the etheric body over countless generations— become completely exhausted. Rudolf Steiner speaks of this as follows: 'In Atlantean times man plunged with his etheric body into the physical body. It was, so to speak, his misfortune when he was in a certain sense 'abandoned by God' that in this physical world he experienced the influences of Lucifer and Ahriman within his physical body. This was his fate. The consequence of this was that precisely through the influence of the physical body, through life in the physical body, the ancient treasure of wisdom became useless . . . [And by the time of the events of Palestine] he [man] no longer possessed it. And it then happened that, as man did not have in his body a source for the renewal of wisdom, every time, when after death he emerged from his physical body, there was less and less wisdom in his etheric body ... The etheric body became increasingly poor in wisdom.'[20]*

Thus at the time of the events of Palestine only initiates, and pupils of the Mysteries, were able to bring into their etheric bodies a certain amount of wisdom that was drawn either directly from the Mysteries themselves or from their memories of initiation-experiences in past lives. For the rest of humanity this had by the time indicated become wholly inaccessible. But now the question arises: was wisdom of this kind not accessible to the Solomon Jesus-child? If we look upon a more outer aspect of his life, we would wish to answer this question in the affirmative, in so far as we know that he bore within himself an unusually mature ego, permeated as it was with the results of his sublime spiritual achievements and experiences in past earthly lives. However, if we study this matter more deeply, we come at once to the opposite answer. For the main point here is that the ego of Zarathustra, as the bearer of the wisdom of all his previous incarnations, left the sheaths of the Solomon Jesus-child *before* the birth of his astral body, that is, before that moment when through the mediation of this astral body he could have transmitted all his wisdom to his etheric body, which was on the Earth very strongly dependent on the stream of heredity, as is described in the Gospel of St Matthew. (Such an event occurs with regard to the etheric body of the *Nathan* Jesus-child and comes to expression in the scene of Jesus's conversation with the scribes in the temple of Jerusalem, as described in the Gospel of St Luke.)

Hence we must say that the etheric body of the Solomon Jesus-child would not have received any special influx of *inner wisdom* either through the general course of evolution—that is, through the stream of human heredity—or from the ego of Zarathustra.[21] Herein lies the second essential quality. However, despite all that has been said, this etheric body was very strongly distinct from the etheric bodies of all other people. For although Zarathustra's ego was unable fully to incarnate in it before the twelfth year, nevertheless in the earlier years—as is indeed the case with everyone in early childhood—it continually worked upon him, though from without, that is, still largely proceeding from higher worlds.[22] And as the ego of Zarathustra was the ego of one of the great initiates, which had worked among mankind since ancient times, the etheric body which it penetrated 'from without' was—in Rudolf Steiner's words—'an etheric sheath of great value.'[23]

Thus we have here to do with an etheric body which, on the one hand, with respect to its content of higher wisdom is completely empty and, on

---

* Later in the same lecture Rudolf Steiner points to the direct connection that exists between the wisdom of the etheric body and its *life-forces*.

the other, with respect to its form had attained the highest fulfilment—inasmuch as this form was bestowed on it by the ego of Zarathustra which worked in the Solomon Jesus-child until his twelfth year, although largely from the higher worlds. Pictorially speaking, one could say that, in the case of this quite special etheric body, it is as though we are concerned with a wonderfully formed etheric cup which is, however, inwardly quite empty and awaits being filled with a new content, a new wisdom. Thus after the death of the Solomon Jesus-child it enters the higher worlds and is preserved there for almost *three seven-year periods* until the Mystery of Golgotha. When on the hill of Golgotha the blood flowed from the wounds of the crucified Saviour, a stream of new etheric life entered into the etheric sphere surrounding the Earth.[24] By this means it became *possible* for the etheric bodies of all people to receive the new wisdom, the life-wisdom of the Christ, into themselves in the future. Rudolf Steiner speaks of this in the following words: 'Let us now accept that at some suitable time something would occur whereby man acquired the capacity of withdrawing his etheric body from the physical body,★ of giving something to this etheric body, of re-enlivening it, permeating it once more with wisdom. Then the etheric body would also withdraw in future, but it would have new life, new strength—which it could employ for the enlivening of the physical body. It could send strength and life back into the physical body ... And so an impulse had to come to the Earth whereby what had been used up of the ancient wisdom might be renewed, whereby new life might be imparted to the etheric body ... it was precisely this new life that Christ brought into the etheric body.'[25]

These life-forces, which in this moment went forth from the hill of Golgotha into the etheric environment of the Earth,[26] entered as a result of Christ's Ascension with particular power into the etheric body of the Solomon Jesus-child which had been preserved in the spiritual world, and this etheric body was thereby able to unite in a new way with the ego of Zarathustra, which also abided in the spiritual world. This altogether special entity of the Zarathustra ego, which had united with the etheric body of the Solomon Jesus child, now enlivened as a result of the Mystery of Golgotha, was able to enter directly into the etheric sphere of the Resurrection and hence be present at and take part in (even though only in the etheric body) the forty-day conversations of the Risen One.[27] For the most important feature of the forty-day conversations of Christ with the

---

★ More will be said about the gradual withdrawing of the etheric body from the physical, a process which was initiated with the Mystery of Golgotha, in the chapter 'Easter, Ascension and Whitsun and the Essential Nature of the Foundation Stone of the Christmas Conference of 1923/24'.

disciples in which He participated in the Resurrection body was that they took place simultaneously *in two worlds*—the earthly world and the supersensible world bordering upon the Earth, while Christ could be both seen and heard in both worlds.

One consequence of this presence of the Zarathustra ego in the conversations of the Risen Christ was that the etheric body of the Solomon Jesus (which was initially quite 'empty' and devoid of Mystery-content) gradually became 'filled', while the ego of Zarathustra, which on its great sacrificial path had at first given the *whole* of its wisdom to the Nathan Jesus, now received it back completely transformed through the *wisdom* of the forty-day conversations of the *Risen Christ*.[28] It was with this content of new esoteric Christian wisdom that the new etheric body of Zarathustra was permeated during the time between Easter and Ascension. As the etheric body is at the same time the bearer of man's deep, 'living' memory, one can say that from this time the individuality of Zarathustra becomes the bearer or preserver of the entire fullness of the wisdom of the Risen Christ and the Mystery of Golgotha, that is, of the fullness of the wisdom of esoteric Christianity which has its source in the forty-day conversations. If we now recall that the principal content of these conversations was the revelation of the Mystery of the 'imperishable body' which had risen from the grave of Golgotha, the spiritualized physical body of man, this knowledge which was not ordinarily human but *livingly* substantial (for Zarathustra was in the spiritual world where all knowledge is of a substantial nature) was for him the source of those real forces through which he shortly afterwards acquired the possibility of fashioning a new physical body and of thus embarking upon the fulfilment of a still higher mission among mankind.[29] Rudolf Steiner refers to this in the following words: 'It [the ego of Zarathustra] was after a relatively short time able to build up a new physical body with the help of the etheric body that we have just described. Because of this, *that being was born for the first time* who thereafter appeared again and again, always appearing in such a way that relatively short periods of time elapsed between his physical death and a new birth[30] [for the Zarathustra ego was so mature that it was not necessary for it to pass again through Devachan].[31] And so when this being left his physical body at death, he soon appeared again on Earth in a new incarnation.'[32]

This new 'being born for the first time' has ever since secretly accompanied the whole history of the development of mankind as the great teacher of esoteric Christianity, as the 'Master Jesus', the preserver of the entire fullness of the wisdom imparted by the Risen One during the forty days, the bearer of the deepest *knowledge* of the great 'Event of Palestine'. Rudolf Steiner goes on to speak as follows about the subsequent activity of this being among mankind as the unfailing helper and inspirer of all who strive towards a deepened knowledge of the Christ Mystery: 'This being, who had sought and found the etheric body that he had relinquished in the circumstances indicated, then went on his way through human history. As you may imagine, he became *the greatest possible helper of those who have striven to comprehend the great Event of Palestine.* This individuality passes through the epochs of human evolution as the so-called *"Master Jesus"*. And so it was that Zarathustra, the ego of Zarathustra, again finding his etheric body, set forth upon his path through human evolution as the "Master Jesus", who since that time has lived on our Earth, incarnating again and again to give guidance and direction to that spiritual stream which we call Christian. *He is the inspirer of those who endeavour to understand Christianity in its living growth and development. In esoteric schools he has inspired those whose constant concern it was to nurture the teachings of Christianity. He stands behind the great spiritual images of Christianity, ever imparting the true meaning of the great Event of Palestine.*[33] (The second individuality, who is spoken of further below, is also a highly important teacher of this path.)

If we would sum up this brief study of the spiritual path of Zarathustra's individuality, we may say: Zarathustra has since ancient times, since the beginning of the Ancient Persian epoch and 'even since the Atlantean epoch, been the great servant of the Sun Spirit, of the Christ'. In the course of this service, over the extent of all his numerous incarnations, he has been able to gather a truly vast treasure of the highest initiation-wisdom in order that at the Turning Point of Time he might fully sacrifice it for the preparation of the descent of Christ Himself to the Earth, when he bestowed it over the course of eighteen years on the Nathan Jesus. Through making this high sacrifice, which reached its culmination when he relinquished the sheaths of Jesus immediately before the Baptism in the Jordan, Zarathustra acquired the possibility of witnessing the Mystery of Golgotha from the sphere of the spiritual world bordering upon the Earth and then, having united with the transformed etheric body of the Solomon Jesus, was able to participate directly in the forty-day conversations from this supersensible sphere. That Zarathustra experienced the Mystery of Golgotha from the spiritual world and that he went on to dwell there with the Risen Christ right until the Ascension, is the highest fruit of Zarathustra's entire spiritual path over thousands of years and is at the same time the beginning of his new, still higher, mission among mankind, the mission of the Master Jesus, of which we have already spoken.

In this sense the Resurrection of Eastertide and the forty days that follow are for the Master Jesus (Zarathustra) every time a microcosmic repetition of the macrocosmic events which had formerly taken place, events which he was worthy of experiencing directly from the higher worlds at the Turning Point of Time. Hence it is in accordance with a profound law that the Master Jesus, *regardless of whether he is incarnated in a physical body or not,* each year seeks the microcosmic repetition of those experiences through which he was *on one occasion* able to pass macrocosmically, in order that he might, in turn, transmit their fruits to those people who have prepared their souls for this and who will then bring the impulses of esoteric Christianity which they have thus received to all mankind. Furthermore, for all who are sincerely striving to deepen their understanding of the events of Palestine, this period (from Easter until Ascension) is the most suitable time in the yearly cycle to try to approach the Master Jesus on a meditative path, to become in a certain sense his esoteric pupils, in order through him to come in contact with the most sublime Christian wisdom, with the wisdom of the Risen Christ which he has preserved.

If ever and again, by renewing these endeavours from year to year at the time indicated, we are gradually able to bring them to the point of true spiritual experience, we will come to know for ourselves what Rudolf Steiner describes in the following words: 'Those who have the mission of working out of the spiritual-scientific movement, as executors for what streams into humanity from the Mystery of Golgotha, know that every year at Easter the Jesus who received Christ into himself seeks the place where the Mystery of Golgotha took place. *Regardless of whether Jesus is in the flesh or not,*★ he seeks this place every year, and the pupils who have reached [the corresponding] maturity can then abide with him.'[34]

Thus an esoteric study of the cycle of the year leads us to a knowledge of the great mission of the Master Jesus among mankind today. Once we have recognized this and have also learnt of one of the paths whereby he seeks its fulfilment, we may now—even in only a small way—touch upon the content of the forty-day conversations themselves, in so far as this is revealed to us in the spiritual-scientific investigations of Rudolf Steiner and in so far as this is connected with the direct inspiration of the Master Jesus.

As we have already seen in the previous chapter, we have in these conversations of the Risen One with His disciples the most profound and all-embracing knowledge of the Mystery of Golgotha and, above all, a knowledge of the transformation which it has engendered of the relationships between macrocosm and microcosm, between the world of the Gods and the world of men. We need now to look upon the Mystery of Golgotha, and with it upon the festival of Easter, from these two stand-

---

★ The first sentence of this quotation could be understood in such a way as to suppose that it is not about the Master Jesus but about the Nathan Soul. This possibility is, however, altogether excluded through the words in italics. For, if we speak of abiding in the flesh, that is, in physical incarnations, one can only have the Master Jesus in mind—though of course this does not rule out supersensible participation also of the Nathan Soul in these daily 'Easter conversations'.

points: from the standpoint of the world of the Gods and from that of men, in so far as these standpoints in all their inter-relationships are revealed to us ever and again in the cycle of the year through the threefold constellation of Easter in the macrocosm and the Resurrection of Christ as celebrated by people on Earth.

3. The Significance of the Mystery of Golgotha for the World of the Gods

The revelation of the *cosmic* significance of the Mystery of Golgotha, of its fundamental significance not only for people on Earth but above all for the highest Hierarchies, for the world of the Gods, forms part of the most profound knowledge which has been imparted to humanity in the twentieth century through Anthroposophy. Rudolf Steiner refers to this quite special mission of Anthroposophy in our time, when he characterizes the Mystery of Golgotha through supersensible knowledge of the teachings of the Risen Christ in the following words: 'This is a divine event: the Gods introduced the Mystery of Golgotha as a divine event into the evolution of the cosmos for the sake of their own destiny; the Gods allowed the Mystery of Golgotha to come about also for their own sake. While previously all events took place in the divine-spiritual worlds, now a God came down and a supersensible event took place on Earth and in earthly form. What was accomplished on Golgotha was therefore a spiritual event transferred to the Earth. *What is most important is what can be learned about Christianity through the anthroposophical spiritual science of today.*'[35]

Let us now try to penetrate somewhat more deeply into what Rudolf Steiner here calls 'most important'; into what can be learned about Christianity through the anthroposophical spiritual science of today. For this purpose let us turn again to the most ancient times of human evolution on Earth, to those times when, for the sake of man's future attainment of individual freedom, first the luciferic powers—at the end of the Lemurian epoch—and then the ahrimanic powers—in the Atlantean epoch—were allowed by the ruling Gods of the cosmos to gain entry into human evolution. Through the influence of these forces of opposition on earthly evolution, man gradually entered upon a path which led him further and further away from the world of the Gods, from the world of the higher Hierarchies. The consequence of this was the appearance of death on the Earth, the only event in human life to which none of the Gods had access. Just because a phenomenon had entered into human life to which even the highest Hierarchies had no access, there arose, in the course of time, the danger that the human race might fall away altogether from the spiritual world. In other words: the whole of world evolution which had been willed by the higher Gods became endangered, for this was inseparably connected with the destiny of mankind on Earth. In all other realms of

197

earthly life the Gods still had the possibility of helping human beings and guiding them in their evolution, inasmuch as everything else remained to a greater or lesser extent in the sphere of their understanding. Death alone was the one phenomenon in the domain of Earth-existence that was inaccessible to the Gods' understanding and, as a result, it had to remain a mystery even for the highest among them. One could also say that death gradually became the only 'place' in the whole world that was ever less and less accessible to the divine-spiritual Hierarchies. The opposing powers of Lucifer and Ahriman strove fully to take hold of this place, in order that they might thereby gain in time the opportunity of winning possession of all mankind, of finally separating humanity from the divine-spiritual worlds and of thus guiding the entire evolution of the Earth along a different course.

At approximately the time when the Mystery of Golgotha was to take place on Earth, this process had already advanced to the extent that a true knowledge of death had almost completely disappeared. Because of this, death increasingly appeared to human beings as something dark, gloomy and devoid of light. An ungovernable dread of death gradually spread among mankind, for people instinctively sensed that in death they were increasingly losing the possibility of uniting with their heavenly home and were becoming prisoners of the dark, spectral domain of Lucifer and Ahriman. The other world was felt to be a lightless realm of shades, even in the Graeco-Latin epoch, and death gradually became a wall that finally separated man, the microcosm, from his heavenly home, the macrocosm. Even for those who during their life on Earth had been able to find through the Mysteries, which had revealed certain secrets to them from the life before birth, the ever weakening thread connecting them with the spiritual world, death appeared before them as an altogether impenetrable, solid curtain, separating them for ever from the world of the Gods of Light. Not *even* the remnants of the most high wisdom of the ancient teachers of humanity, who belonged to the various ranks of the higher Hierarchies, could penetrate beyond this curtain.[36] For according to Rudolf Steiner, 'the first great teachers of humanity were spiritual beings, who in a spiritual way formed a connection with the first initiates and imparted to them the secrets of man's birth, the secrets of the living soul which has descended in an unborn state [to Earth] from the divine-spiritual worlds.'[37] And he goes on: 'These spiritual teachers of humanity were those who lived in the spiritual world and came down to people only as teachers who, however, did not take part in human destiny and *did not themselves know the Mysteries of death*. This is in itself a great Mystery, that in ancient times people received teachings from the higher world which concerned the Mystery of birth but not the Mystery of death' ... The divine-spiritual teachers of mankind knew about birth but not about death ... The Gods saw that, because they had previously been able to speak to earthly humans only about the Mystery of birth, the Earth was gradually being deprived of those forces which they themselves had placed within it, and *that death would take hold of the soul.*[38] Because the higher Hierarchies gradually lost their authority over mankind at the moment of death, the luciferic and ahrimanic powers took the opportunity to draw human souls into their domain, which had in the end to lead to the *death of the soul* together with the death of the body.[39]

This 'mood' of the Gods in the spiritual world, arising from the possibility that the whole of earthly evolution might succumb to death, is characterized by Rudolf Steiner as the great 'dread of the Gods',[40] the cause of which was that at the time of the Mystery of Golgotha the Gods of the higher Hierarchies had to say to themselves: 'It is becoming impossible for our servants to work in the souls of men. As we have been unable to suppress Lucifer and Ahriman, it has been possible for us to work through our servants only until this point of time. For *powers* are formed in human souls which cannot be ruled by Angels, Archangels or Archai. Human beings are falling away from us through the forces of Lucifer and Ahriman.'[41] These 'forces' under the sway of Lucifer and Ahriman, which arise in human souls and which the beings of the Third Hierarchy are no longer able to govern, are the forces of death.

Thus death appeared for the highest Hierarchies as that which in course of time had finally to separate people from the divine-spiritual world and create an unbridgeable gulf between macrocosm and microcosm (humanity) which would lead man in the end to the destruction of his soul. And so only a true knowledge of the Mystery of death, together with the penetration of this Mystery by the highest divine forces, could offer a means whereby the Gods might avoid losing hold upon earthly evolution and people might be led first to a real knowledge of the relationship between microcosm and macrocosm[42] and then to a new, conscious union with the macrocosm. This sublime knowledge of death, which was won through its having been fully overcome, was brought into the world by Christ, who, in passing as a God through human death on Golgotha was able to attain to, and then to communicate to *all* the higher Hierarchies, this *sole* aspect of knowledge which had remained beyond their reach. With this we touch upon the central Mystery of esoteric Christianity, which in our time is accessible only to the highest intuitive knowledge, and of which it is the most important task of anthroposophically orientated spiritual science to speak to mankind today: 'And it was decided in the realm of the Gods to send a God down to Earth, so that He, as a God, might suffer death and make the knowledge of death accessible to the divine wisdom [to the Hierarchies]. This is revealed *through an intuitive contemplation of the Mystery of Golgotha*, by which something took place not only for men but also for the Gods.'[43]

What was it which in a deeper sense happened for the Gods, for the higher Hierarchies, as a result of the Mystery of Golgotha? Until the Mystery of Golgotha the whole Hierarchic cosmos, including the most exalted of the Gods, was in a certain sense *incomplete*; for the one fundamental Mystery of earthly evolution, the Mystery of death, was unknown in the divine-spiritual worlds. But now that the world of the higher Hierarchies, which in its totality represents the whole macrocosm that is connected with the Earth, has encompassed this Mystery and has again won full access to man, as microcosm, the opportunity has opened up for the Gods to lead mankind forwards in the right direction. Moreover, it is only with the knowledge of this 'last Mystery' that the hierarchic cosmos has reached a final completion in its evolution. For the Mystery of Golgotha was that unique event in the whole of world-evolution which so shook the entire hierarchic cosmos to its foundations that it was able to ascend to a higher and more complete stage of its development.

Rudolf Steiner speaks in the following words about this sublime *event* in the world of the highest Hierarchies, which took place there as a result of the coming about of the Mystery of Golgotha on Earth: 'Now there is one thing which until that time the Gods had not attained and which already existed here on Earth in reflected form. What the Gods had not yet attained was the passage through death. This is a fact to which I have often referred. The Gods, in their various Hierarchies, stand above humanity and experience only transformations, metamorphoses from one life-form into another. The manifestation of death in life did not form part of the experience of the Gods before the Mystery of Golgotha. Death entered the sphere of life through the luciferic and ahrimanic influence, through retarded or over-hasty divine beings. But death itself was not something that existed as a life-experience of the Hierarchies. This began to be an experience for these higher Hierarchies at the moment when Christ passed through the Mystery of Golgotha, that is, through death: when Christ had united with the destiny of humanity to the extent that He wished to share with this earthly humanity the fact of having passed through death. Thus the Event of Golgotha is not merely an event of earthly life but an event for the life of the Gods. What took place on Earth, and what appeared in the human soul [*Gemüt*] as knowledge of the Mystery of Golgotha, is the reflection of something vastly more all-encompassing, sublime, powerful and exalted than anything that had taken place in the world of the Gods. For Christ's passage through death on Golgotha is the event through which the First Hierarchy [Seraphim, Cherubim and Thrones] reached a still higher domain. Hence I should always tell you: the Trinity lies essentially above the Hierarchies. But it has attained this only in the course of evolution. Evolution takes place everywhere.'[44]

Thus through the fulfilment of the Mystery of Golgotha on the Earth, a *twelvefold* hierarchic cosmos emerges out of what had hitherto been a ninefold cosmic order, that is, it attains its high, all-encompassing perfection, as reflected in the twelvefoldness of the zodiac.

In order that we may come nearer to an understanding of those truly soul-shaking words, we shall turn to the cycle of lectures about the life between death and a new birth given in 1914 in Vienna. In the second lecture of this cycle Rudolf Steiner puts the question: 'Is there something comparable to "religion" in the Spiritland, in the realm of the Hierarchies?' And then he says in answer: 'There stands before the Gods, as the goal of their creativity, the ideal of man, which is not as man is now but as the *highest soul-spiritual life of the fully unfolded predispositions of this physical man* [that is, the image of a human being who has fully realized in himself the principles of the Spirit Self, Life Spirit and Spirit Man]. Thus an image of humanity stands before the Gods as a high ideal, as the religion of the Gods. And, as though on the far shore of the world of the Gods, there stands before them the Temple which represents their sublime achievement: *the reflection of the divine in the image of man.*'[45]

One can say: the Hierarchies sacrificed their best creative forces for the fashioning of man in the aeons of Saturn, Sun, Moon and Earth in order that man might—as the culmination of his evolution—reproduce in himself the whole divine nature of the Hierarchies and thus realize the highest 'ideal of the Gods', forming as it does the very essence and the goal of their 'heavenly religion'.[46] Already in Lemurian times, however, there entered into this evolution first luciferic and then ahrimanic spirits. The consequence of this was that death came into the world as a phenomenon that was inaccessible to the understanding of the Gods. There now arose the danger that the Hierarchies would not be able to guide humanity in the right way; and this would mean that their highest aim, their ultimate idea, would not be attainable. Hence it was necessary for the Sun Being Himself, the Christ, to descend into the earthly world, that Being who was, in the course of the three years of His life, in the sheaths of Jesus of Nazareth, able fully to embody the principals of Spirit Self, Life Spirit and Spirit Man (see p.115) in order that, once death had been overcome in Spirit Man, this sublime idea of humanity might appear before the Gods: *the reflection of the divine in the image of man*, the reflection of the highest divine Trinity of the Spirit, the Son and the Father[47] as the aim of all world evolution—which was to appear not in the spiritual worlds but on the Earth, even in the realm of man.

When in *Occult Science* Rudolf Steiner referred to Christ as the great earthly Archetype of Man, he was pointing precisely to the very essence of the events that we have been considering. For the 'earthly man' who has inwardly developed all the soul-spiritual predispositions that have been established in him by the Hierarchies, corresponds to what is the 'religion of the Gods' in the spiritual world, and Christ appeared on Earth in the Mystery of Golgotha as its Archetype, *the Archetype of the highest purpose of the Gods*. Only through this truly cosmic event, which has occurred on Earth in the physical world, have the Hierarchies been able to acquire the forces and the knowledge which they will need for the fulfilment of this great ideal in the future.

Before the Mystery of Golgotha, the Hierarchies could experience this 'ideal' only in the Spirit-land, where it was revealed in the macrocosmic working of the Logos, in the fashioning of the great 'Universal Man'. Christ, however, brought the Logos down to the Earth; in Him 'the Word became flesh'—and *since then He has manifested the ultimate aim of the Gods upon the Earth*.[48] Now the higher Hierarchies had what one could call the most sublime mirror for their consciousness in the manifestation by Christ on Golgotha of 'the reflection of the divine in the image of man'. This then enabled them to ascend to the heights, to the summit of the whole Hierarchic cosmos, in order there to attain the entire fullness of the knowledge and the forces with whose help they might in future lead mankind, *begotten* by them in former times, through the overcoming of *death* to the final *Resurrection* in the spirit-worlds, to the fulfilment of that ideal which as the ultimate goal of world evolution was revealed to them in the physical world by the Christ-Logos, who passed through death and won it for eternal life.

After His Resurrection, when 'for forty days He appeared to their beholding souls and spoke to them of the Mysteries of the Kingdom of God',[49] Christ spoke to His disciples of this fundamental Mystery of the death on Golgotha (and also of its significance for the higher Hierarchies and for the whole evolution of humanity on Earth) as a deed whereby the world of the Gods and the world of men—macrocosm and microcosm—are again united. In the course of these days, He revealed to them that higher knowledge of the Mystery of Golgotha which is now being spread among mankind for the first time by anthroposophically orientated spiritual science. For in Rudolf Steiner's words, '. . . only through being guided by initiation-science can we gain insight into the event of Golgotha which has taken place within Earth-existence as something which has been laid into the Earth simultaneously *as a cosmic and as an earthly event*'.[50]

4. The Significance of the Mystery of Golgotha for the World of Men

Now that we have considered the macrocosmic significance of the Mystery of Golgotha, its significance for the world of the Gods, for the whole company of the higher Hierarchies, we must turn to the second aspect, to its significance for the microcosm, for the world of men. For the knowledge of death, which was attained on the hill of Golgotha, was, in truth, a deeply fundamental event also for the whole future evolution of humanity on Earth.

Through the fact that Christ, by passing through death, has reunited the world of the Gods with the world of men, He made it possible for mankind to enter into the Mystery of death in such a way that it would lead to a completely new *understanding* of the re-established connection of macrocosm and microcosm. It was this Mystery which Christ revealed to His disciples during the forty days after His Resurrection from death.

The essence of this Mystery is that, after the Mystery of Golgotha, death ceases to separate man from his home of origin, from the macrocosm, *but unites him with it*; no longer is it a bringer of death to the soul but a source of eternal, inexhaustible universal life. Rudolf Steiner speaks about this in the following deeply meaningful words: 'Thus through the innocent death on Golgotha, the proof was furnished—which people will understand little by little—that death is the ever living Father.'[51] Its outward aspect is Maya. Behind death man must seek the Father, the cosmic Father! ... thus he must learn to say to himself: death is the Father'[52]—that is, the whole great hierarchic macrocosm with which man will now again be united.[53] And Rudolf Steiner continues: 'But why does a false image of the Father appear before us in the physical world of the senses? Why does an image of the Father appear to us which is so distorted that it comes before us in the deceptive form of death? Because the Lucifer-Ahriman principle has intervened in our life! ... Death became a distorted image of the Father because of the interference of Lucifer and Ahriman in human evolution. Death was the consequence, the result of the influence of Lucifer and Ahriman.'[54] Hence 'the false image of death would never have gone from human life if its cause—Lucifer and Ahriman—had not been removed. But there was no earthly being who was able to accomplish this.'[55] Only the divine *Christ Being* belonging to the whole macrocosm, who, *in passing through death and overcoming it*, was able as a result of this deed to withdraw it from the authority of Lucifer and Ahriman and return again to the world of the higher Hierarchies, to the world of the Father: 'Now came this Being [Christ] to the Earth and at precisely the right moment despatched ... Lucifer and Ahriman, the cause whereby death came into the world. This could only be done by a Being who had had nothing to do with any of the aspects of the causes of death within humanity, nothing to do with all that made man suffer death, that is, all that was effected by Lucifer and later by Ahriman ... in other words, with the reason why human beings became sinful and succumbed to evil.'[56]

But how did Christ's victory over the forces of Lucifer and Ahriman during His life on Earth in the body of Jesus of Nazareth take place? Rudolf Steiner describes this process in the following way: 'In the moment of His life when His astral body had within it all that is capable of being veiled by the luciferic intervention, Christ Jesus began to come forward as a teacher of mankind. From this moment on, the capacity was implanted in human evolution of receiving the wisdom whereby the goal of the physical Earth can gradually be attained. At the moment when the Mystery of Golgotha was fulfilled, another faculty was instilled into mankind—the faculty whereby the influence of Ahriman can be turned into good. Out of his life on Earth, man can henceforth take with him through the gate of death that which will free him from isolation in the spiritual world. Not only for the physical evolution of mankind is the event of Palestine the centre and focal point; the same is true for the other worlds to which man belongs. When the Mystery of Golgotha had been accomplished, when the Death on the Cross had been suffered, then did the Christ appear in the world where the souls of human beings sojourn after death and set limits to the power of Ahriman. From this moment on, the region which the Greeks had called the "realm of shades" was shot through by a spiritual lightning-flash— announcing to its dwellers that light was now returning to it again. What was achieved for the physical world through the Mystery of Golgotha shed its light also into the spiritual world.'[57] Only through thus overcoming the power of Lucifer and Ahriman in the earthly and super-earthly worlds was Christ able to kindle the 'new Sun of Life' in Earth-existence and, in the light of this Sun, to manifest the true countenance of death to mankind: 'Christ Jesus wedded himself to death, He approached this death which became the characteristic expression of the Father; He united with this death. And out of Christ's marriage with death was born the beginning of the Sun of Life. It is a deception, Maya, an illusion, to equate death with suffering. Death—if people would learn in future to allow it to approach them as it approached Christ—is, in truth, the seed for [cosmic] life.'[58] And he goes on: 'The new Sun of Life would never have arisen if death had not come into the world and had not been allowed by Christ to win its victory.

Thus death, in its true aspect, is the Father. Christ came into the world because a false picture of this Father had arisen in death. He came into the world in order to create a true picture of the living Father God. The Son is the offspring of the Father, He reveals the true picture of the Father. Truly, the Father has sent His Son into the world[59] in order that the true nature of the Father might be revealed, that is, the *eternal life* which lies hidden behind temporal death.'[60] This thought is also expressed in the words of St John's Gospel: 'I came from the Father [the macrocosm] and have come into the earthly world [the microcosm]; again, I am leaving the world of the senses and going to the Father.'[61] These words already contain the seed of all the subsequent teachings of the Risen One. 'I have come from the macrocosm into the microcosm, I have experienced death, the central event of the microcosm, and now I am going once again into the macrocosm, to the Father: I am now going to the Father so that all who have received the Christ-impulse might also come thither in due time.'[62]

From this we may see wherein lies the significance of the Mystery of Golgotha for the two worlds, the divine and the human. Through His victorious passage through death, Christ has, we may say, thrust open for all future time the great gate which unites the two worlds so that, on the one hand, the Angels, Archangels and Archai, and through them all the other Hierarchies, may fully take over the rulership of earthly humanity,[63] and on the other hand, the path of a new conscious ascent into the higher worlds is opened up before human beings: 'Truly, truly, I say to you: you will see Heaven opened, and the Angels of God ascending and descending upon the Son of Man.'[64]

Such an understanding of the Mystery of Golgotha as the central event which directly unites macrocosm with microcosm was also instilled by Rudolf Steiner into that rhythm in which he read the Foundation Stone Meditation of the Christmas Conference *for the first time* on 25 December 1923: first the microcosmic sections of the three first parts, then the fourth part, 'At the Turning Point of Time ...' and in conclusion those same microcosmic sections, though now united with the macrocosmic parts.[65] And so this fundamental understanding of the Mystery of Golgotha, which forms the very essence of esoteric Christianity and has its source in the intuitively heard teachings of the Risen Christ, passes like a red thread through all the twenty-one-year development of Anthroposophy into the very substance of the Christmas Foundation Meeting.

VII

THE MYSTERY OF THE ASCENSION

1. The Ascension as an Indication of Christ's Participation in the Life of the Human Soul after Death

'I am the way, the truth and the life'—these words of Christ Jesus express with surprising accuracy the very essence of his forty-day conversations. In the light of what has been said above, they can be understood as follows: Christ is, in them, pointing to the fact that through the Mystery of Golgotha He Himself becomes the *way* leading to a knowledge of the *truth* about death which, in its present aspect, is none other than an image of the Father, the Bearer and Bestower of the macrocosmic forces of *life*. It is possible for man to enter His kingdom, the kingdom of the highest universal life, only through permeating himself with the Christ-impulse or—which is the same thing—embarking upon the path that leads to an experience of the words '*In Christo morimur*', to an experience of the truth that in Christ death becomes life. Christ concluded this teaching, which He had imparted to His disciples during the forty days after His Resurrection from the dead, by placing it before them as a living imagination in the scene of the Ascension. For in the Ascension, Christ raised the microcosm, the spiritualized human form (the physical and etheric bodies), up into the macrocosm before the spiritual sight of the Apostles and, hence, made manifest the relationships and correspondences which had long since been lost to mankind through the prevailing authority of the false image of death.

In spiritual-scientific terms this means that all the elements of which man's earthly being is composed have found the path and are able to unite again with those archetypes in the macrocosmic world whence they originally proceeded. This corresponds to the fifth stage in the modern path of initiation, described by Rudolf Steiner in *Occult Science* as follows: 'Man has evolved out of the world which most immediately surrounds him and every detail that is inherent in him corresponds to a process or a being of the outer world. At the corresponding stage of his development the spirit-pupil comes to recognize this connection of his own being with the wider world.'[1]

Let us take, for example, the human etheric body, which, according to Rudolf Steiner, has a constant inner tendency to aspire to its cosmic archetype, to the Sun.[2] If, however, it were to follow this basic tendency, it would—in entering the sphere of the Sun—completely dissolve in the world ether. Any kind of individual life would then be impossible for it, and it would never again be able to become a human etheric body. If on the other hand it were to be wholly divorced from its heavenly origin, from the forces of the Sun-sphere, it would also be unable to serve man in the right way, for, once deprived of the connection with its macrocosmic archetype, it would 'dry up'. In both cases man's life on Earth would become impossible and all earthly evolution would cease.

Through the Mystery of Golgotha and the *Ascension* that followed, Christ has saved man's etheric body from both these dangers. On the one hand, He enables the etheric body to pursue its aspiration to unite with its heavenly origin and, on the other, He Himself unites with this aspiration.[3] Because of this, even if it ascends into the macrocosm, man's etheric body will not lose its individual character—which alone makes it a *human* etheric body. This process could be imagined from the opposite viewpoint. One could say: through Christ's union with the Sun-aspiring human etheric body, it becomes possible for it to unite even in the earthly domain (that is, while fully preserving its individual, human character) with its archetype, the Sun. For Christ has, since the Mystery of Golgotha, extended the plentitude of Sun-forces to the earthly sphere, and has therefore made them accessible to the etheric body of every human being. Thus, as a result of this *completely new* union of macrocosm and microcosm, Christ has saved not only man's physical body—to which the Mystery of Golgotha essentially points—but also his etheric body. It is of this that the festival of the Ascension speaks.

In the lecture of 7 May 1923 in Dornach, which was devoted to a revelation of the esoteric significance of Ascension and Whitsun as festivals that represent a direct contribution of the impulse of the Mystery of Golgotha, Rudolf Steiner has, in particular, the following to say: 'Thus we may say: we allow the picture of the Ascension to pass before our souls. The disciples, *having become clairvoyant*, behold the natural tendency of the human etheric body to aspire towards the Sun. Christ unites with this aspiration, holding it back. This is a mighty picture: that of Christ rescuing the *physical and etheric bodies* of man in the Ascension.'[4] Thus in Christ's Ascension there stands before us first and foremost the union of man's physical and etheric bodies (that is, the human *form*) with their macrocosmic archetypes.

This esoteric content of the event of the Ascension has a further aspect, which has to do with the subsequent evolution of humanity. In order to understand this aspect, we should bear in mind that the old atavistic clairvoyance which people still had in ancient Atlantis and in the early post-Atlantean epochs was based on the fact that at this time the etheric body, especially in the realm of the head, was still *outside* the physical body and that in the course of post-Atlantean evolution the etheric body became increasingly united with the physical body, merging completely with it at the time of the events of Palestine.

Once it had passed through the deepest point of its immersion in matter, the human etheric body gradually started on its path out of the physical body into the spiritual world. This 'turning-point' in earthly evolution took place at that moment when Christ came to the Earth. The significance of this is, however, that the appearance of Christ in a physical body and His passing through the Mystery of Golgotha is the event which—from an occult point of view—laid the foundation for the gradual emerging of the etheric body from the physical body, for the process in which humanity is currently and will continue to be engaged for several thousands of years. And the aim of this process is a new and fully conscious reaching out into the spiritual world.

Rudolf Steiner once described this process as follows: 'Whereas the etheric body had formerly kept drawing ever more deeply into the physical body up to the coming of Christ, the time then arrived when the course of evolution changed. At the moment when Christ appeared, the etheric body began again to withdraw; and it is today already less bound up with the physical body than it was when Christ was present on Earth.'[4a]

Thus in so far as the etheric body is concerned it can be said that, through His appearance on the Earth and the overcoming of the power of death through the Resurrection, Christ prevented a great danger from befalling mankind—the danger that the etheric body would eventually become united with the physical body to the point of coming wholly to resemble it, and this would have led to its becoming completely dried up.

The warding off of this danger does, however, represent only the first stage of this whole process. For the future destiny of mankind depends not only upon the fact of the gradual loosening of the etheric body's ties but upon the *direction* that it takes in the course of its renewed union with the spiritual world. The *right*—that is, the *non*-luciferic—direction leads the etheric body into receiving the primordial forces of the Father, and this was made possible for it through Christ's union with it in the event of the Ascension.

The second stage can also be characterized in another way. In olden times, when the etheric body was still to a large extent outside the physical body, its direct connection with the spiritual world led to its being the bearer of cosmic primal wisdom in the form of the life-forces with which it was imbued. These primordial life-forces of the etheric body did, however, prove to be for the most part exhausted when it had become fully immersed in the physical body. This led to a new danger, namely, that when the etheric body began again to emerge from the physical body it would be inwardly empty, devoid of all the life-forces which it would need in order to prevent the physical body from disintegrating during earthly life as it withdrew from it. In other words, the etheric body needed new etheric forces if its emergence from the physical body were not to lead to the latter's decline (illness) and premature death. These new etheric forces that were necessary were given to the etheric body by Christ when He united Himself with it through the Ascension. 'Life was infused into the human etheric body by the Christ-impulse—new life, after the old life had been spent! And as man looks into the future he must say to himself: when my etheric body will ultimately have emerged from my physical body, I shall have to have developed in such a way that my etheric body is wholly permeated by the Christ. The Christ must live in me. In the course of my earthly evolution I must by degrees become completely imbued with the Christ *as regards my etheric body!*' The possibility of achieving this was given to mankind by Christ with His Ascension.

Thus Easter and Ascension are inseparably connected with one another and together determine the destiny of the etheric body and, with it, the future of mankind.

But this is not yet all, as this second stage is followed by a third stage. For just as Easter is inseparably connected with Ascension, so is Ascension with Whitsun—meaning that the human individual becomes *conscious* of this process. Without this growth of consciousness, all materialistically inclined human beings will be threatened with the loss of individual consciousness in the higher worlds when a new clairvoyance develops with the loosening of the etheric body. Such people will then, according to Rudolf Steiner, 'be in danger of what is called "spiritual death" . . . That is what it means to die in the spiritual world, something that threatens human beings if they do not bring with them when they enter the spiritual worlds the *consciousness* of this spiritual world.'[4b]

This 'consciousness of the spiritual world' can give the human individual that connection with the Spirit of Whitsun which furnishes a true *understanding* of the Mystery of Golgotha: 'And through this unique victory over death, *if it is rightly understood,* man is shown how he has to live in order to bring with him for all future times the awareness that there is a spiritual world. That is the union with the Christ.'

And so a threefold union with the Christ needs to be accomplished in the future: the union with His imperishable Resurrection body, the union with His cosmic life-forces, and the union with the light of the new spirit-consciousness which reveals the cosmic-earthly significance of the deeds of Christ.

With this we have already embarked upon the context of the following chapter, which must, however, be prefaced by a consideration of another aspect of the festival of Ascension.

For the festival of the Ascension is more than this. It is an indication to us not only of Christ's bearing the forces of the Sun-sphere, the forces of the macrocosmic kingdom of the Son, into Earth-existence, but also of His bearing into it forces proceeding from the sphere of the Father. Hence we read in St Mark's Gospel: 'So then the Lord Jesus, after He had spoken to them, was taken up into the heavenly spheres and *sat down at the right hand of the World-Father* as the fulfiller of His deeds.'[5] In order to understand these words of the Gospel we must recall how, as a result of the forty-day conversations of the Apostles with the Risen Christ, there gradually awoke through His teachings and, above all, through His immediate presence, the faculty of imaginative clairvoyance. In this special condition of consciousness the Apostles beheld the Risen Christ during the forty days and received His teachings. But this is not all. As we have already seen, the chief content of the conversations of the Risen One was the revelation of the Mysteries of the relationships between macrocosm and microcosm. Hence Christ concludes His teachings in such a way that the Apostles are led to a perception of those forces which are altogether able to awaken imaginative knowledge in man. Thus one can say: those forty days which the Apostles were still able to spend with the Risen Christ were for them a path leading to the primal sources of Imagination, to the primal sources of all true supersensible vision, to that highest sphere of the macrocosm which Rudolf Steiner in his lectures calls 'the world of the spiritual archetypes of all things.' 'It was this Mystery of the origin of their faculty of imaginative knowledge from out of the world of Archetypes, from that world whence—according to Rudolf Steiner—the Hierarchies 'derive their forces'[7] and where Christ is seated at the right hand of the World Father, that Christ revealed to them in the scene of His Ascension.

Let us at this point turn again to the words with which Rudolf Steiner describes these interrelationships: '... As soon as we can admit the idea that clairvoyant consciousness exists in the world, we have to say: therefore a world must also exist whence the forces for the organs of clairvoyance emanate—and this world is called in spiritual science the world of Archetypes. Whatever can appear before us as *Imagination* is ... a reflection of the world of Archetypes. Thus we pass into the macrocosm from stage to stage through the elemental world, the spiritual world, the world of Reason and the *world of Archetypes*.'[8] And in another lecture in the same cycle he continues: '... just as the eyes [and all the rest of man's sense-organs] have been formed out of the elemental world, the nerve system out of the spiritual world [lower Devachan], the human brain out of the world of Reason [higher Devachan], so are those organs that we call the higher sense-organs, which render us ever more capable of beholding the spiritual world, formed out of the world of Archetypes . . .'[9]

So we have the following picture: during the forty days the Apostles, with the help of the faculties of imaginative knowledge which had awakened within them, embraced with their consciousness the Risen Christ and His teachings about the heavenly realms, that is, about the spiritual worlds. This process lasted until the Apostles had advanced so far in their penetration into the mysteries of the new relationship between macrocosm and microcosm that they were able to grasp the secret of the origin of their own faculties of imaginative vision. Only now were they able to understand that the clairvoyance which they possessed, and which originated as a consequence of the working within man of forces proceeding from the world of Archetypes, *was awakened within them by the Christ Himself.* For it was Christ who now endowed them *on the Earth* with the entire fullness of the macrocosmic forces of the world of Archetypes which were arousing imaginative clairvoyance within them. This experience of Christ as the new source of imaginative clairvoyance, that is, as the bestower of forces from the world of Archetypes, was then expressed for the disciples in the picture of the Ascension of Christ into the world of Archetypes, into the divine Kingdom of the Father.

Thus a higher stage of knowledge of the relationship between macrocosm and microcosm was revealed in this event to the disciples: the origin of the faculties of imaginative knowledge which were awakening within man out of their macrocosmic source, from the world of Archetypes. Through this the last veil, hiding from view the true image of death which since the Mystery of Golgotha has taken on the aspect of the heavenly Father, was withdrawn from the consciousness of the Apostles. This came to expression in the scene of the Ascension in that it brought to manifestation the inner content of death as a revelation of man's higher, imaginative consciousness, which has its source in the kingdom of the divine Father and bears within itself the archetypes of all things and beings of the world.★ Hence the fact (to which allusion has been made by modern spiritual research) that from that time onwards one of the first experiences of every man after death has been a contemplation of Christ's Ascension, which conclusively reveals to him the true picture of death and indissolubly connects the spiritual world that lies nearest to the Earth with the highest

---

★ It will become clear from what is said later that, according to the Fifth Gospel, the Ascension was for *the Christ Himself* an event which is comparable only with death in human life. Hence the words quoted above from the Gospel according to Mark (see p. 213) are also an indication of how, at that moment, death was made manifest by Christ to the disciples in such a way that they beheld it *with their own eyes* as a process of union with the world of the Father.

sphere of the Father, with the world of Archetypes—this is deeply grounded in the new world-order which came into being as a result of the Mystery of Golgotha.[10] Rudolf Steiner speaks as follows about this experience which every human being has after death, an experience which is also associated with the gradual dissolution of his etheric body in the sphere of the Sun: 'And now we can add something·else to the picture of the Ascension. Spiritual visions such as came to the disciples on the day of the Ascension always have a bearing upon what man actually experiences in one or another state of consciousness. After death, as you know, the human being experiences the departure of his etheric body. At death he lays aside the physical body. For a few days he retains his etheric body which then dissolves and *is actually united with the Sun*. This dissolution after death is a process of uniting with the Sun-nature which permeates the space wherein lies the Earth. In this departing etheric body man has, since the Mystery of Golgotha, beheld also the Christ, who has become its saviour for future Earth existence, so that since the Mystery of Golgotha there has stood before the soul of every human being who passes through death the Ascension picture which the disciples were able to behold that day, on account of their particular soul-condition.'[11]

However, despite the fact that in our time *every* human being after death beholds the imagination of Christ's Ascension, there is here a fundamental difference between a person who has already on Earth striven towards a true knowledge of the Mystery of Golgotha and someone who has for one reason or other missed this opportunity in the incarnation in question. For one belonging to the first group '... this picture [of the Ascension] after death becomes the greatest consolation that he can possibly experience; for he now beholds the Mystery of Golgotha in all its truth and reality ... This picture of the Ascension tells him: you can with confidence entrust all your following incarnations to Earth evolution, for through the Mystery of Golgotha Christ has become the Saviour of Earth evolution.'

On the other hand, for those who miss such an opportunity for a true knowledge of the Mystery of Golgotha, the consequences of a picture of this kind will be altogether different: 'For one who does not penetrate with his ego and his astral body—that is to say, with knowledge and with feeling—to the essence of the Mystery of Golgotha, for him this picture is a *reproach*, and it will remain so until he has recognized that he too must learn to understand this Mystery of Golgotha.' As a result of such an experience after death and the soul-suffering connected with it, a resolve can arise in the soul: 'Endeavour to acquire for your next earthly life such forces as will enable you to understand the Mystery of Golgotha.'

In conclusion, one further aspect of the Ascension needs to be considered which directly concerns the Moon-sphere or the sphere of the

Holy Spirit—where the soul of one who has died experiences the imagination of this event shortly after death. Rudolf Steiner speaks in particular detail about this matter in a lecture of 15 September 1922 in Dornach: 'He who speaks today out of initiation-science must still add the following: yes, it is the Christ-impulse that works on after death, it is this impulse under whose influence man frees himself from the Moon-sphere, penetrates the starry Sun-sphere and, from the impulses given to him by beings of the starry world, is there able to work upon the forming of the physical organism for his next earthly life. But he is freed from the Moon-sphere through the forces which he has accumulated in his ego because of his inclination toward the Christ Being and the Mystery of Golgotha.'[12] While somewhat earlier in the same lecture Rudolf Steiner speaks of this process in yet another way: 'And just as one's outer life flows by under the influence of the physical light and warmth of the Sun, so after death is one's being gripped by the high Sun Being [Christ] who frees one from one's *essential destiny* and leads one into the starry spheres, so that one is able to work there under the guidance of one's Sun-leader on the forming of the spiritual part of one's future physical organism.'[13] What is of particular importance for our present considerations is that it is the power of Christ which '... works after death and wrests the soul from its essential destiny and from the Moon-sphere ...'[14] in such a way that 'through the guidance of the high Sun Being the human soul is purified as it makes the transition from the soul-world to the Spirit-land',[15] or (which is the same thing), from the sphere of the Moon to the sphere of the Sun.[16]

But how are we to understand what is meant by 'purified' or 'freed' from one's essential destiny? This 'essential destiny' or 'core of one's destiny', which also makes up a man's 'moral worth', must—in that it is the bearer of the karma that he has not yet lived out[17]—be left behind, after the death of the soul, in the Moon-sphere in order that its influences might not have a bewildering effect on the soul during its sojourn in the region of Sun and stars, for such a bewildering or darkening of consciousness in the higher spheres of cosmic being would make it impossible for it *rightly* to fashion a physical body for future life on Earth. After its sojourn in the Sun-sphere and in the starry worlds, the soul must, as it enters the Moon-sphere *for the second time*, thenceforth unite there with the 'karmic nature' that it left behind so as to work further upon its betterment in the course of the next earthly life. As, however, the aforementioned process of freeing oneself from this 'karmic nature' takes place after death in the Moon-sphere through the union of the human ego with the Christ-impulse while still on Earth, we must say: in freeing the soul of a dead person during Sun (and star) existence from the influence of the Moon-sphere and from the negative human karma remaining within it, Christ takes this karma upon

Himself for the whole period of man's life after death, thus enabling the soul to find under His guidance the path of the true Ascension, which leads from the Moon-sphere to the Sun-sphere and from there ever higher and higher to the world of the fixed stars.

Thus in the scene of the Ascension we have an indication of the all-encompassing influence of the Christ Being, after the Mystery of Golgotha, upon the sphere of life of the human soul after death. His influence embraces all *three* of the principal regions of the macrocosm through which the soul passes between two incarnations: the region of the Moon, the region of the Sun, and the region of the fixed stars, which are the reflections in our world of the super-hierarchic spheres of the Spirit, the Son and the Father. In the first region Christ manifests to the soul the rescuing of man's etheric body and helps it to separate itself for a time from the consequences of its bad karma, and also frees it from the Moon-forces which bind it to the Earth. In the second region Christ enables the soul rightly to enter the Sun-realm so that it may there transform all the experiences of the previous incarnation into faculties for the next earthly life. Finally, in the third region, that of the fixed stars, the kingdom of the Father, Christ guides the soul in its work of forming, out of the forces of the Divine Wisdom (the Sophia), the 'Universal Man', the cosmic Archetype of its future physical body. Thus the influence of Christ extends to all regions of the soul's existence after death, that is, to all those regions of the macrocosm whose forces Christ brought to the Earth through the Mystery of Golgotha and then connected, through His Ascension, directly with the life of every human soul. It was for this reason that when the Apostles, who had been prepared for this by the forty-day teachings of the Risen One, also experienced the Ascension, this was for them not merely the proof of the whole immeasurable significance of the Christ for the life of every human soul after death, but was at the same time the event through which they were able to attain the fullest and most all-encompassing *knowledge* of the new relationship between microcosm and macrocosm.

VIII

THE MYSTERY OF PENTECOST

1. The Transition from the Old to the New Initiation

As has already been mentioned more than once in this book, the teachings received by the Apostles and disciples from the Risen Christ during the forty days, together with the event of the Ascension itself, were—according to the Fifth Gospel—grasped by them in what was no more than a lowered, dreamily imaginative state of consciousness.[1] This means that those mighty secrets of the spiritual worlds which were buried in their souls had not yet come to a fully awake, clear day-consciousness. Although they had been able to experience Christ as the Bearer of the entire fullness of the macrocosmic forces in the earthly sphere, nevertheless these forces had not as yet found expression in them and had, even in the scene of the Ascension, remained *outside of them* in such a way that they were only able to contemplate the Ascension in, so to speak, a spiritually *outward* way.[2] For at this stage only the *knowledge* of the new relationship between microcosm and macrocosm was accessible to them and not the experience of being quickened by the macrocosm and becoming one with it. Herein also lies the reason why, in the Gospel of St John, Christ says to Mary Magdalene after His Resurrection: '*Do not touch me*, for I have not yet ascended to the Father Ground of the World.'[3] After His Resurrection from the dead and also at his Ascension, Christ was still outside the world of human beings; He had not endowed their individual ego-consciousness with those forces which He had already borne into Earth-existence through the Mystery of Golgotha. In order that this might come about, the festival of the Ascension had to be followed by the festival of Pentecost, the festival of the outpouring of the Holy Spirit, the Spirit of Universal Love, upon the Apostles. Only through such a quickening of the Apostles by the macro-cosmic Spirit, the Universal Spirit of Love, could there fully awaken in their earthly ego-consciousness what subconsciously resided in the depths of their souls, on account of their life on Earth with Christ Jesus, of their experience of the Mystery of Golgotha, and of the teachings imparted by the Risen One until His Ascension.

In the lectures devoted to the Fifth Gospel, Rudolf Steiner describes this awakening of the Apostles at Pentecost as follows: 'This awakening they [the Apostles] experienced in a particular way: they really felt as if something had descended upon them from the universe which could only be called the *substance* of an all pervading love. They felt as if they had been quickened from the dream-state into which they had fallen. It seemed to them as if they had been stirred by everything which, as the primal force of love, pervades the universe and permeates it with warmth, as if this primal force of love had come down into the soul of each one of them.'[4]

From now on the Apostles were people 'who had been stirred by the Cosmic Spirit of Love', who had experienced 'being quickened by an all-pervading cosmic love.'[5] And now all that had happened to them was revealed to them directly *as their own experience*. They were, for example, now able to say to themselves regarding the forty days which they had spent with the Risen One: 'And the Risen Christ was with us. As though unbeknown to us, He received us into His Kingdom; He went about with us and revealed to us the Mysteries of His Kingdom . . .'[6] For only from the time of Pentecost did Christ finally unite Himself *with the whole being of man* and bear into his very nature what had formerly existed only in the heights of the macrocosm. Rudolf Steiner speaks about this as follows: 'From the event of Pentecost onwards, the Christ Being experienced His entry into the sphere of the Earth, which signified for Him what the transition into the Spirit-land signifies for the human being. But instead of ascending—as is the case with a human being after death—to Devachan, to a spiritual region [that is, as far as the world of Archetypes], the Christ Being offered up His sacrifice *as though He were building His Heaven on the Earth*; He sought it on the Earth . . . It is a saying of immeasurable greatness if we express this Mystery in the following words: since the event of Pentecost the Christ Being has abided *with human souls* on the Earth; before then He did not abide with the souls of people on the Earth!'[7]

Only after this deeply significant moment in human evolution is it possible to speak of the great macrocosmic Being of Christ finally united with human souls on Earth, with the human microcosm. Since then, and for all future ages of the Earth, it has become possible for every man inwardly to experience the direct presence of the macrocosmic Christ through an inner experience of the new Holy Spirit who proceeds from Him, who quickens the soul of man with a universal, cosmic love, and reveals to his fully awake individual ego-consciousness a perception of the higher worlds so that he may become a conscious witness and servant of the Spirit. Through this, man has now attained a completely new connection with the spiritual world: the experience of becoming wholly at one with the macrocosm, of uniting with it in a purely *inward* way while fully preserving his individual ego-consciousness. This possibility of *a new, fully conscious clairvoyance* was prophetically implanted—as a seed for the entire future evolution of mankind—in the Mystery of Pentecost, which has since that time been the great archetype of the new initiation, which leads to man's conscious union with his spiritual home, with the macrocosm and even with the kingdom of the Father Himself. Rudolf Steiner describes this high state of consciousness, which will be attained only at the *sixth* stage of modern Christian-Rosicrucian initiation, in the following words: 'When the spirit-pupil has worked his way through this knowledge [of the relationship between macrocosm and microcosm], a new experience awaits him. He begins to feel as though he is growing together with the whole vast structure of the world, *while being aware of his complete independence*. This is a feeling of merging with the world, of becoming one with it, though *without losing his own separate existence*. In spiritual science this stage of development may be described as "becoming one with the macrocosm". It is *very important* not to think of this as implying that individual consciousness should cease and that human nature should flow out into the universe. Such an idea could arise only from an inadequately trained faculty of judgement.'[8]

In the concluding thought of this extract, Rudolf Steiner emphasizes as 'very important' this basic distinction between the new and the old paths of initiation leading to a union with the macrocosm. What necessarily came about on the old path only in the course of a deep, deathlike, mystic sleep, in a considerably lowered condition of human consciousness, can in our time be attained—while fully preserving one's individual, waking ego-consciousness[9]—through a direct relationship with Christ on the Earth. For in passing through death and the Resurrection and thus placing death's true image before all mankind, Christ was able to lay for the first time the foundation for the *immortality* of man's own, individual ego, endowing it with the forces of eternity, that is, with the capacity of preserving a clear, waking ego-consciousness at *all* stages of ascent into the spiritual cosmos. Rudolf Steiner refers to this in the following words: 'And this possibility, that death—which formerly meant annihilation—might now become the *seed* of eternal egohood, was given by the Christ-impulse. On Golgotha the true image of death was placed for the first time before mankind. By His union with death, Christ, the image of the Father Spirit, the Son of the Father Spirit, has made His death on Golgotha the starting-point of a new life and . . . of a new Sun. And now it is indeed so that, once man has gained for himself an ego for eternity, everything which is of the past and which, so to speak, belongs to the period of man's apprenticeship [the old path of initiation] can fall away, and man can enter into the future with his rescued egohood, which will to an increasing extent become a likeness of the egohood of Christ.'[10] If the rescuing of the human ego occurred as a result of the Mystery of Golgotha, the foundation for this ego becoming in its future development 'to an increasing extent a likeness of the egohood of Christ' was laid in the event of Pentecost, through the penetration of man's own ego by the new Holy Spirit proceeding from the Christ.[11] Hence Rudolf Steiner says: 'We have no better symbol of the penetration of the [human] ego by the Spirit than in the story of the miracle of Pentecost.'[12] In this sense the event of Pentecost is, in truth, the foundation stone of the new Christian initiation, which has its source in the Mystery of Golgotha and has come in place of the old initiation which was still connected with the pre-Christian stage of human evolution.

Let us examine at this point the transition from the old pre-Christian to the new Christian initiation in somewhat more detail, on the basis of the Ancient Persian path of initiation of which Rudolf Steiner spoke on a number of occasions.[13] There we find seven principal stages, with the following names:

1. Raven
2. Secret One or Hidden One
3. Fighter
4. Lion
5. Persian (the name of the folk to which the initiate belonged)[14]
6. Sun Hero
7. Father[15]

In the present work it is not possible adequately to pursue the continuity and, at the same time, the principal difference between the old path of initiation and the modern Christian-Rosicrucian path, which also consists of seven stages. Such an analysis would lead us too far from our theme. We shall therefore confine ourselves here to a comparison of only the *sixth stage* of both paths. In Christian-Rosicrucian initiation the sixth stage is called 'becoming one with the macrocosm', while in the Persian initiation it is that of the 'Sun Hero'. In his lectures on the Fifth Gospel, Rudolf Steiner describes this stage of the old initiation in the following words: 'What lived in the Sun Hero spread over the entire Earth. And just as an initiate at the fifth stage of the ancient Mysteries had to pass out of his body ... so did he who was to become a Sun Hero have to pass out of his body and, during this time of absence from his body, actually transfer his abode to the Sun ... Hence at this period of his initiation the Sun Hero lived in communion with the whole solar system. Just as an ordinary human being lives on the Earth as his own planet, so does the Sun Hero have the Sun as his place of abode ... In the ancient Mysteries this could be attained only outside the body. But when one came back into one's body *one remembered what one had experienced outside it* and was able to use this ... for the well-being of all humanity.'[16] Such was the experience of the initiate of ancient times at the sixth stage of Persian initiation. He was outside his body and, during the three days of his sleep in the temple, was in a state of rapture on the Sun. However, the most characteristic feature of this old form of initiation was that the initiate, in ascending to the sphere of the Sun, was in those times *unable* to preserve therein his individual waking ego-consciousness. The consequence of this was that what he experienced in the Sun-sphere entered his consciousness not directly at the moment of experience but only in the form of a 'memory of what had been experienced' after he had awakened from his sleep in the temple.

Precisely at this point there arose the greatest change in the Mystery life of humanity, a change which was wrought by the death and Resurrection of the Sun Being of Christ. Because of this decisive event and the subsequent union of Christ with earthly evolution, for the first time it became possible for humanity to reach the sixth stage of initiation not through an ascent to the sphere of the Sun, with the concomitant loss of individual ego-consciousness, but through becoming permeated, within the earthly realm itself, by the new Holy Spirit proceeding from Christ. It became possible to experience, *while remaining within one's physical body*, the entire fullness of Sun-life, to accomplish the ascent into the Sun-sphere while fully preserving one's individual, waking ego-consciousness. This is what happened to the Apostles at Pentecost. Since that time this festival has been a prophetic indication of that future condition of humanity when vast circles of human beings will rise to that degree of penetration into the higher world which is, in our time, accessible only through entering upon the modern path of Christian-Rosicrucian initiation and thereby attaining the sixth stage of this journey.

With particular emphasis Rudolf Steiner refers to this fundamental change in the Mystery-life of humanity in a description of the spiritual metamorphosis of the sixth stage of initiation through the Mystery of Pentecost: 'And what was it that the Sun Heroes experienced during the three and a half days of their initiation? What did they experience when they—as we may rightly say—roamed the Sun? They experienced communion with Christ, who before the Mystery of Golgotha was not yet upon the Earth. All the Sun Heroes of old had left for higher spiritual worlds because in olden times this was the only place where communion with Christ could be experienced. From this world [to which the initiates of old had to rise during their initiation], Christ descended to the Earth. And so we may say: what in ancient times could be attained for a few individuals through the whole procedure of initiation was in the days of Pentecost attained, as though through a natural event, by those who were Christ's Apostles. Whereas in former times people had to ascend to Christ, now Christ descended to the Apostles. And *the Apostles had* in a certain sense *become people who bore within them everything with which the ancient Sun Heroes had been endowed*. The power of the Sun had poured into the souls of human beings, working on henceforward in the evolution of humanity. In order that this might come about, the events of Palestine had to be accomplished, the Mystery of Golgotha had to take place.'[17]

Thus the Mystery of Pentecost is that event whereby the Christ-impulse, which through the Mystery of Golgotha and the Ascension was related to man's physical and etheric bodies, now finds a relationship to his soul-spiritual nature, to his astral body and ego. For Christ accomplished the Mystery of Golgotha in such a way '... that ten days after the event of the Ascension he sent people the means whereby their soul-spirit nature, their ego and astral body, might also become imbued with the Christ-impulse. This is the picture of the Whitsun festival: the permeation of the soul-spirit nature with a power capable of *understanding* the Mystery of Golgotha, which is the mission of the Holy Spirit. Christ accomplished His deed for all mankind. To the person who is to *understand* this deed, to such single human individuals, He sent the Spirit, in order that [man's] soul-spirit nature may gain access to the universal deed which concerns the whole of humanity. Through the Spirit, man shall make the Christ Mystery inwardly his own, in spirit and in soul. These two pictures stand one behind the other in the history of human evolution in such a way that the picture of the Ascension tells us: in so far as the physical and etheric bodies are concerned, the Mystery of Golgotha was accomplished for all human beings. But the individual human being must make it fruitful for himself by receiving the Holy Spirit. By this means the Christ-impulse becomes an individual [experience] for every single person.'[18]

And so the spirit who descended upon the Apostles at Pentecost is at one and the same time the Spirit of *Universal Love* and the Spirit of *Knowledge* of the Mystery of Golgotha, for in the macrocosmic Ego of Christ the whole world-wisdom of the past became love, active, cognitive love[19]—'The Event of Golgotha is a free cosmic deed springing from the Universal Love, and it can be comprehended only by human love.'[20]

As described in the Gospel and confirmed by modern spiritual research, the Holy Spirit descended upon the *heads* of the Apostles at Pentecost,[21] and this enabled Christ to speak from their *hearts*,[22] not annihilating but strengthening, heightening, their individual ego-consciousness.[23] With this the basis was laid for those new interrelationships within man of the forces of the Father, the Son (Christ) and the Spirit, which thenceforth and for all future ages form the foundation stone of all true Christian Mysteries, in so far as their goal is the final union of man, as microcosm, with the macrocosm—though *without* the loss of his individual nature. In this way the fundamental definition of Anthroposophy, as a path to the new Christian Mysteries, becomes understandable. For as Rudolf Steiner observes in the first 'leading thought': 'Anthroposophy is a *path of knowledge* which would lead the spiritual in man to the spiritual in the universe. It enters into man as a need of his *heart*, of his feeling.'[24] In other words: Anthroposophy is a path of knowledge inspired by the Spirit, which enters in freedom into the heads of human beings in response to a need springing from their hearts (where the Christ works)—to the need for the union of man's spirit with the Spirit of the Cosmos, of the individual human ego with the Kingdom of the Father—with the sphere of Cosmic Life.

From this it becomes clear that we should also seek the source of the *modern Christian Mysteries* in the event of Pentecost. Hence the fact—that in the founding of these modern Christian Mysteries only such a Foundation Stone could be laid as was formed of the spiritual forces that have worked in man's being since the first Whitsun—is deeply rooted in world evolution as a whole.

If we pass from the fifth stage of modern Christian-Rosicrucian initiation to the sixth, and in the yearly rhythm from the festival of Ascension to the festival of Whitsun, we unite ourselves with all that is hidden behind the words 'know thou thyself' as true *world-knowledge*. Rudolf Steiner speaks of this in the following way: 'With this we have touched upon the sixth stage, which is called "becoming immersed in the macrocosm". Whoever has thus come to know within himself the relationship of microcosm to macrocosm has reached out to a knowledge of the whole world. This is concealed behind the ancient dictum, "Know thou thyself!"'[25] These words may serve us now as the best introduction to understanding those forces, together with their activity in man's being, whence Rudolf Steiner formed the Foundation Stone of the new Mysteries at the Christmas Foundation Meeting: 'But if out of the signs of our time [that is, under the sway of the Time Spirit, Michael] we would rightly renew these words, we must say: O Soul of Man, *know thyself* in the weaving of thy being in spirit, soul and body. Then we have understood what lies at the foundation of the whole human being . . . this world-substance, in which there works and lives and flows the Spirit that streams from the heights and reveals itself in the human *head*; the Christ-force, which works everywhere in the periphery, which weaves with the *air* encircling the Earth, which works and lives in our *breathing system*; and the forces from the depths, from the interior of the Earth, which work in our *limbs*. And from these three forces—from the Spirit of the heights, from the Christ-force in the periphery, from the working of the Father, the creative Father-activity that streams from the depths—we would in this moment form in our souls the dodecahedral Foundation Stone which we immerse in the ground of our souls, in order that it may abide there as a mighty sign and in the sure foundation of our soul-life, and that in the *future* working of the Anthroposophical Society we may stand on this firm Foundation Stone.'[26]

When the forming of the Foundation Stone is described in this way, it is

227

not difficult to see that the very essence of the Mystery of Pentecost lies before our eyes. The Spirit that works in the heights descends, as the Spirit of knowledge, into the human head and from there pours forth into the heart. Through this the Christ-forces, which since the Mystery of Golgotha have worked in the environment of the Earth, penetrate the airy element[27] into the lungs and thence by way of the blood enter the *heart*, which can then itself be filled with the Christ-substance. Hence the Foundation Stone address continues 'And the true ground in which we must today lay the Foundation Stone is our *hearts* in their harmonious co-operation, in their *love-imbued good will together* to bear the *anthroposophical will* through the world.'[28] (In these words, as in the reference to the *future* in the previous quotation, one can feel with particular intensity the mood of Pentecost.) Finally, the Father-forces working from the depths penetrate our limbs with the *will*, with whose help we can turn *into deeds of goodness* all that descends as the light of knowledge to our heads and streams as the warmth of love towards it from our hearts:

> O Light Divine
> O Sun of Christ!
> Warm Thou our Hearts;
> Enlighten [with Thy Spirit] Thou our Heads;
> That good may become [that is, transformed into
> our deeds of goodness]
> What from our Hearts we would found,
> And from our Heads direct
> With single purpose.

Thus the forces of which the Foundation Stone of the new spiritual life was formed and laid into the hearts and souls of human beings at the Christmas Conference spring from the first Whitsun, which already, nearly two thousand years ago, marked the great transition from the old initiation to the new.

2. The Modern Experience of the Holy Spirit

The relationship between the Christmas Conference and the original Mystery of Pentecost (which we examined at the end of the previous chapter) reveals to us a quite particular aspect of its inner essence and its significance for mankind's evolution into the future. For the Christmas Conference is the first free and openly accomplished *deed performed* among mankind *purely out of the Spirit* in the epoch of the consciousness soul.

It follows from all that has been said, however, that such a 'deed out of the Spirit' is only possible *in our time* when the initiate himself has experienced the entire fullness of the esoteric content of the event of Pentecost, that is, the attainment by such a person of the *sixth stage* on the modern Christian-Rosicrucian path of initiation. And so we may at this point put a question which is of fundamental significance for our time: what does a *modern initiate* discover when he rises to the sixth stage of the Christian-Rosicrucian path of initiation and gains access to the essential nature of the Mystery of Pentecost out of his own experience? What does the modern initiate experience once he has reached the stage of becoming one with the whole macrocosm while fully preserving his individual, waking ego-consciousness? What can he impart to humanity? What can be told to mankind by a person who in the twentieth century has experienced with full consciousness the event of Pentecost in its totality and can, therefore, with full justice be designated in our time as one who 'is filled with the Holy Spirit'?[29] With what words can he tell of his experiences?

Let us hear some words of this kind, which tell us of the sublime experience of one particular human life, and hold out the greatest promise for our spiritless age. Let us hear these words of a man who lived in the midst of twentieth century mankind, and who for the first time in our age reveals for modern consciousness the secret of what a human being experiences who is 'filled with the Holy Spirit'.

Rudolf Steiner speaks of this approximately in the middle of the last full year of his earthly life, conveying in a few, bare words to all 'men of good will' the deepest experience of his inner life, thus revealing to humanity the truly boundless horizons of world evolution.

In the lecture given in Dornach on 4 June 1924, three and a half days before the festival of Pentecost, the last Whitsuntide in Rudolf Steiner's earthly life, we find these words: 'Yes, to His intimate disciples Christ spoke these words: "Behold the life of the Earth; it is related to the life of the cosmos. When you look out on the Earth and the surrounding cosmos, it is the Father whose life permeates this universe. The Father God is the God of space ... But I make known to you that I have come to you from the Sun, from time—time that receives man only when he dies. I have brought you myself from out of time. If you receive me"—said the Christ—"you receive time, and you will not be held spellbound in space. But you find the transition from one trinity—physical, etheric and astral— to the other trinity, which leads from the [macrocosmic] etheric and astral to Spirit-Selfhood. Spirit-Selfhood is not to be found in the cosmos. But I bring you the message from the cosmos, for I am from the Sun."

'Yes, the Sun has a threefold aspect. If one lives within the Sun and looks down from the Sun to the Earth, one beholds the physical, etheric and astral. Or one may gaze on that which is within the Sun itself; then one will continually behold the Spirit-Selfhood. One sees the physical if one remembers the Earth or gazes upon it. But if one looks away from the Earth one beholds on yonder side the Spirit-Selfhood. Thus one swings backwards and forwards between the physical and the substance of the Spirit-Self. But if one looks out into the great universe, the earthly vanishes away, and only the etheric, the astral and the Spirit-Selfhood remain. This is what you behold when you enter the Sun-realm between death and a new birth.

'And so let us imagine that the inner mood of a man's soul is such that he shuts himself entirely within this Earth-existence; he can still sense the Divine, for out of the Divine he is born: *Ex Deo nascimur.*

'Then let us imagine him no longer shutting himself up in the mere world of space but receiving the Christ who came from the world of time into the world of space, who brought time itself into earthly space. If a man does this, then in death he will overcome death: *Ex Deo nascimur. In Christo morimur.* But Christ has brought the message that when space is overcome and one has learned to recognize the Sun as the creator of space, *when one feels oneself transplanted through Christ into the Sun, into the living Sun,* then the earthly physical vanishes and only the [cosmic] etheric and the astral remain. Now the etheric comes to life, not as the blue of the sky but as the light-red radiance of the cosmos; and from out of the reddish light the stars no longer twinkle down upon us but *touch us with their love-radiant deeds.* If a man really enters into all this, he can feel himself *standing upon the Earth, having cast the physical aside;* he can feel the presence of the etheric, per-meating him with its rays and radiating out from him in its lilac-reddish light; he can feel the stars not as glimmering points of light but as love-filled radiance, like the caressing hand of a human being.

'But as we sense all this—the Divine within ourselves, the divine cos-mic fire flaming forth from within us as man's essential being, feeling ourselves within the world ether, experiencing the revelations of the Spirit in the cosmic astral radiance—there bursts forth within us the inner experience of the spirit-radiance which is man's high calling in the universe.

'And when those to whom Christ revealed all this had let these thoughts sink long and deep into their being, then the moment came when they experienced the working of these thoughts in the fiery tongues of Pentecost. At first they felt the falling away, the discarding of the earthly-physical, as in death. But then they felt: this is not death, for in place of the earthly-physical there now *ascends the Spirit-Selfhood of the universe: Per Spiritum Sanctum reviviscimus.*'[30]

This outpouring of the 'Spirit-Selfhood of the universe' from beyond the stars is experienced by the initiate whose consciousness has awakened in the sphere of the Sun. This 'love-filled radiance', this descent from the cosmic region that lies beyond the stars of the Holy Spirit, as the Spirit Self of the universe, is the experience which befell the Apostles at Pentecost and which John, 'the disciple whom the Lord loved', passed through even earlier, as he stood in full consciousness beneath the Cross on Golgotha (for the Mystery of Golgotha was for John a Whitsun event).[31]

Rudolf Steiner speaks (although in a somewhat different form) of this encounter with the Holy Spirit, as the fundamental experience of the modern Christian initiate, in the year 1908, in the last lecture of the Hamburg cycle devoted to the Gospel of St John: 'Through what a man receives during catharsis, he purifies and transforms his astral body into the "Virgin Sophia". And to the "Virgin Sophia" descends the cosmic Ego, the world Ego, bringing her enlightenment and surrounding man with light, spiritual light. This second power which becomes associated with the "Virgin Sophia" was known in Christian esotericism, and *is still known today*, as the "Holy Spirit". So according to Christian esotericism one speaks with absolute truth if one says that the Christian esotericist purifies his astral body in the initiation-process in such a way that it becomes the Virgin Sophia and is then illuminated, or, if you wish, *overshone by the Holy Spirit, by the Cosmic World Ego.* And one who has been thus illuminated, who has received in himself what esoteric Christianity would call the "Holy Spirit", speaks altogether differently from other people. How, then, does he speak? When he speaks about Saturn, Sun, Moon, about the various members of man's being, about the events of world evolution, he is not expressing his own opinions. His own views do not have any significance in all this. Henceforth, when he speaks about Saturn, it is Saturn that speaks through him; when he speaks about the Sun, it is the spiritual Being of the Sun that speaks through him [that is, the whole macrocosm]. He is the instrument; his [lower] ego has been eclipsed—which is to say, it

231

becomes impersonal at such moments—and the Cosmic World Ego speaks from it, using it as a tool.'[32]

Of this speak also the following words from the second part of the Foundation Stone Meditation:

> Where the surging
> Deeds of the World's Becoming
> Do thine own I
> Unite
> Unto the I of the World.

This experience of the Christian initiate of modern times is none other than the fulfilment in the most direct way and at the highest level of the Mystery-words 'Not I, but Christ in me', words which open the gates to a real experience of 'being filled with the Holy Spirit.'[33]

We can say that in our time Rudolf Steiner, as a man who has passed *personally* in his spiritual strivings through *all* the experiences that have been described, can with justice be called—and in the deepest esoteric sense of these words—*the modern Apostle of Christ Jesus.*[34]

IX

EASTER, ASCENSION AND WHITSUN

1. The Three Stages of Christ's Union with the Sphere of the Earth and their Reflection in the Festivals of Easter, Ascension and Whitsun

At the conclusion of our study of the three principal Christian festivals that fall in the period of the Earth's gradual outbreathing, namely Easter, Ascension and Whitsun, one further quality belonging particularly to them needs to be taken into account, and that is their direct connection with the macrocosm. All three festivals are *movable*, for the latter two are determined according to Easter, to the day which is calculated every year from the *starry script*, from the relative positions of the Sun, the Moon and the stars. This special feature of these festivals enables us to look at them as an isolated entity *within* the yearly cycle as a whole.

As such an interrelated whole they are also connected in a quite particular way with the three Rosicrucian dicta, which are usually associated with the yearly rhythm as follows: *Ex Deo nascimur*—Christmas; *In Christo morimur*—Easter; *Per Spiritum Sanctum reviviscimus*—Whitsun.[1] In the context, however, of the three movable festivals—in so far as they most directly concern *the destiny of the Christ Being in the earthly sphere*—these phrases acquire a somewhat different meaning. Here the following words from Rudolf Steiner's lecture of 3 October 1913, which relates to the content of the Fifth Gospel, may serve as a key: 'We should understand the Mystery of Golgotha as an earthly birth—that is to say, the death of Jesus is the earthly birth of the Christ; while we should seek His earthly life in the time after the Mystery of Golgotha, when Christ ... communed with the Apostles while they were in a different state of consciousness. This was what followed the real birth of the Christ Being. And *in so far as the Christ Being is concerned*, we should regard what is described as the Ascension [and the subsequent outpouring of the Spirit] in the same way as we are accustomed when a person dies to view his entry into the spiritual worlds. The further life of Christ in the earthly sphere *after* the Ascension or after the event of Pentecost is to be compared with what the human soul experiences when it dwells in what is called Devachan, in the Spirit-land.'[2]

From these words we may see that the three stages through which every human being passes in the cycle of his existence—birth in the earthly world, death, and the revelation of his higher consciousness in Devachan after death (which also find their reflection in the three Rosicrucian

235

dicta[3])—are expressed for the Christ Being in the three principal stages of His union with Earth-existence: the Mystery of Golgotha—*Ex Deo nascimur*,[4] Ascension—*In Christo morimur* (in Christ death becomes life)★; Whitsun—*Per Spiritum Sanctum reviviscimus* (Christ bearing the forces of higher Devachan and the World of Buddhi into earthly existence, whereby the human soul becomes capable of 'awakening in the world-thoughts of the spirit').

As the three stages of the Christ Being's union with Earth-existence are contained in these three phrases, we should now therefore ask: what is the spiritual reality which stands behind these three events? To some extent we have already touched upon this in the previous section. We shall try to examine them now in further detail. As a starting-point we may take the results of the modern spiritual research set forth by Rudolf Steiner in the thirteenth lecture of the cycle *The Gospel of St John in Relation to the Other Gospels*. In this lecture Rudolf Steiner refers in a quite particular way to the significance of the Mystery of Golgotha and its consequences for earthly evolution, which he describes in such a way that a distinct picture emerges of the three stages of that mighty metamorphosis which has subsequently been wrought within Earth-existence.

The first stage of this metamorphosis was the Mystery of Golgotha itself, whereby the seed of a higher cosmic life was implanted into Earth-existence, the seed of the new Sun which will gradually arise from the Earth. Rudolf Steiner speaks of this as follows: 'At the moment when the Cross was raised on Golgotha and the blood flowed from the wounds of Christ Jesus, a new *cosmic centre* was created ... Thus do new worlds arise! And we must understand that we are standing in the presence of *the birth of a new Sun* when we behold the dying Christ. Christ unites Himself with death, which has become the characteristic expression on Earth of the Spirit, of the Father. Christ goes to the Father and unites Himself with His expression, with death. And the image of death now becomes false. *For death becomes the seed of a new Sun in the universe.* Let us feel this deceptiveness of death; let us feel that, on the Cross, death becomes a seed whence springs a new Sun ...'[5]

Such was the first stage of this metamorphosis. The second followed it directly: 'But through the Earth being permeated [at the time of the Mystery of Golgotha] by a new power which laid the foundations for transforming the Earth into a Sun, the possibility arose whereby this power might also permeate human beings. The first impulse was given ... for *Christ's power to stream into the human etheric body.* And through that which

---

★ More will be said later about the relationship of the second Rosicrucian dictum to the esoteric meaning of the Ascension.

236

could then stream into it of an astral nature, the human etheric body became able to receive a new life-force which it will need for the distant future.

'And so, if you imagine *a certain time after the deed of Golgotha* and compare it with the time when the deed of Golgotha was accomplished, that is, if you compare a future condition of humanity with that moment when the deed of Golgotha actually occurred, you may conclude that, at the time of Christ's intervention, the Earth was such that it could no longer pour forth anything into people's etheric bodies. *But when a certain time had elapsed* [that is, a certain time after the Mystery of Golgotha] the etheric bodies of those people who had acquired a relationship to the Christ-impulse became filled with light; having understood Christ, they received into themselves a radiant power which has been within the Earth ever since, the new radiance of the Earth. They received the light of Christ into their etheric bodies. The light of Christ [that is, the substance of love, for "light is love", see p.141] streams into people's etheric bodies. And now, since from that time the light of Christ has always been present in a certain part of mankind's etheric bodies, what happens next? What happens with that part of a person's etheric body which has received the light of Christ? What happens with it after death? Moreover, what is it that has gradually come to indwell the human etheric body as a result of the Christ-impulse?

'Since that time it has become possible for something new to appear in human etheric bodies as an effect of the light of Christ, something which *exhales life*, which is immortal, which can never succumb to death ... Thus there has since then been something in the human etheric body which is immortal, which is not subject to the mortal forces of the Earth. This something which does not die, and which human beings will gradually win for themselves through the influence of the Christ-impulse, *now streams back, streams into cosmic space, forming—in proportion to its strength or weakness in a human being—that power which flows forth into cosmic space. And this power will form a sphere around the Earth, a sphere which is in the process of becoming a Sun. A kind of spiritual sphere is forming around the Earth of the etheric bodies that have become alive.*'[6]

This is the second stage of this mighty metamorphosis; and it is followed by the third, which completes the whole picture: 'Just as the light of Christ rays forth from the Earth, so do we have *in the Earth's surroundings a kind of reflection of the light of Christ. What is being reflected here as the light of Christ and which appears as a consequence of the deed of Christ is what Christ calls the Holy Spirit* [the third stage of the metamorphosis]. And just as it is true that the changing of the Earth into a Sun began with the deed on Golgotha [the first stage of the metamorphosis], so is it also true that from this time onwards the Earth begins to be creative and starts to form around itself a spiritual [etheric] ring which will subsequently become a kind of planet around the Earth [the second stage of the metamorphosis].[7]

And so in this process we have three majestic stages:

1. The Mystery of Golgotha—the beginning of the Earth's transformation into a Sun.
2. The enlivening of human etheric bodies, which after their death gradually form an 'etheric ring' around the Earth.
3. The reflection from the 'etheric ring' of the spiritual (astral) light which rays forth from Christ in the earthly sphere and the appearance of the Holy Spirit within this reflection.[8]

It is not difficult now to find the relationship of these three stages with the three festivals under consideration, Easter, Ascension and Whitsun. Thus the first stage is, as we have seen, the direct result of the Mystery of Golgotha, which was for Christ the moment of His birth in the earthly sphere (*Ex Deo nascimur*); while for human beings it became the source of the rescuing of the *physical body* through the Resurrection of His Phantom on the third day after the Mystery of Golgotha. One could also say that in the Resurrection we have to do with the 'birth' of man's new physical body.[9]

The second stage is the result of the event of the Ascension, which for the Christ was an experience comparable only with an ordinary man's passage through the gates of death and his subsequent separation from his etheric body: *In Christo morimur*—In Christ death becomes life. At this second stage the element of the new cosmic life sinks down into the human *etheric body*, which without being thus united with the power of Christ would be doomed to being completely dissolved in the world ether,[10] the consequence of which would be that at the end of Earth-evolution man would not have attained that degree of spiritualization which he would need for a right transition to the future Jupiter-stage.[11] However, this death-element which entered into the etheric body as a result of the Fall of man was once and for all overcome through Christ's union with the etheric body, as we learn from an esoteric understanding of the Ascension. Rudolf Steiner said of this: 'The etheric body is [after death] separated off from the soul like a kind of second corpse, but through the legacy of the Christ-impulse from the Mystery of Golgotha it is nevertheless in a certain sense conserved; it does not dissolve into nothing but is conserved.'[11a] Consequently, in such a conserved human etheric body the element of death pervading it was then fully transformed by Christ's power into the element of *life*. As a result of this the etheric body acquired the possibility of returning in time to its original state, to the state in which it was before the

Fall, before it was penetrated by the forces of death. This also allowed it to rediscover that condition which before the Mystery of Golgotha had been preserved only by one sole human being, the Nathan Soul. This is what became possible as a result of the Ascension—the awakening within every human being of *something* of the nature of the Nathan Soul, of the unfallen etheric body of primordial humanity.[12] For only through this overcoming of the element of death in man's etheric body did those parts of his being which had received the Christ-force, instead of withdrawing from the Earth and dissolving in the etheric distances of the macrocosm, remain in its surroundings, gradually forming the 'etheric ring' referred to above.[13] An initiate can even today observe the gradual formation of this 'ring' with the help of an imaginative knowledge permeated with inspirations.[13a] Rudolf Steiner speaks out of such spiritual considerations about a particular 'moral-ether-atmosphere', which has its origin in these processes and in which the entire Earth will in the future increasingly be 'bathed'.[14]

Lastly, the third stage is the result of the final deed of Christ, which found its expression at Pentecost, in the festival of the sending of the Holy Spirit. For the Christ Himself this third stage of His union with Earth-existence was an experience only to be compared with an ordinary man's ascent after death to Devachan, to where it borders upon the world of Buddhi.[15] However, in the case of the Christ Being something quite special takes place here. For Christ does not ascend to Devachan but, on the contrary, draws the forces of Devachan, and also of the world of Buddhi, the world of Archetypes, 'down' into the sphere of the Earth itself and endows human souls with them, as the forces of the cosmic Spirit Self from beyond the stars. This process is the macrocosmic archetype which stands behind the words *Per Spiritum Sanctum reviviscimus*—'In the Spirit's Universal Thoughts, the Soul awakens'. The soul here is man's astral body which awakens to Sophia-existence, to life in the universal thoughts of the Spirit of Wisdom, through the spiritualizing of the human ego by 'the Spirit-Selfhood of the universe'. And so Pentecost has to do with the rescue of the human ego and astral body, just as the Ascension is concerned with the rescue of the etheric body,[16] and Easter (the Mystery of Golgotha) with the rescue of the physical body.[17]

From all that has been said we may see that the three stages of Christ's union with Earth-existence arising as a result of His fulfilment of the Mystery of Golgotha, of the Ascension and of Pentecost, are at the same time the path on which the rescuing of the four members of man's organism—physical, etheric and astral bodies and ego—successively takes place. From the esoteric point of view, therefore, the substance of the third stage can be expressed in that the 'etheric ring' which has come into being at the second stage in the Earth's surroundings, and which receives into itself and preserves the human etheric bodies that have been permeated by the power of Christ, becomes able to reflect the Christ-light that has worked since the Mystery of Golgotha in Earth-existence. In the present time it is only visible to man's spirit-vision as *astral light*, while in the future, as the Earth approaches its goal of becoming a new Sun, this Christ-light will, according to Rudolf Steiner, gradually become an etheric light and will—still later—appear in a physical form: 'The deed of Golgotha permeated the Earth with *astral light*, which will gradually become etheric, and then physical, light ... The first impetus towards the transformation of our Earth into a Sun was given in that time when the blood flowed forth from the wounds of the Saviour on Golgotha. The Earth then began to shine, first astrally and, hence, visible only to a seer—but in future the astral light will become physical light and the Earth will become a radiant body, a Sun-body.'[19]

And this Christ-light, which in the present time works only astrally, begins from the moment of the event of Pentecost to be reflected by the 'etheric ring' which has been formed around the Earth as a result of the Ascension—a ring in which, as we have seen, are preserved the etheric bodies of those people who have received the Christ-impulse into these respective members;[19a] while the *extent of penetration* by the Christ-impulse of such etheric bodies is expressed in their capacity (to a greater or lesser degree) to *reflect* the Christ-light which rays into the earthly sphere—this means enabling the Holy Spirit, who awakens human beings in our time (from the twentieth century onwards) to a new imaginative experience of the Etheric Christ, to live and work (to a greater or lesser extent) in the Earth's surroundings.[20]

2. The Exoteric and Esoteric Working of the Etheric Bodies of the Great Initiates in the Twentieth Century

With the ending of the Kali-Yuga, Christ has strengthened the working of the Holy Spirit among mankind to such an extent that from the twentieth century onwards it is possible to behold Christ in a new, etheric form.[21]

What is of prime importance here, however, concerns the participation in this process of those individualities who have, during their lives, been able to permeate themselves sufficiently intensely with the Christ-impulse that their etheric bodies have not dissolved after death but, in the fullest sense, have 'passed from death to life',[22] that is, have united with that 'etheric ring' around the Earth which was spoken of in the previous chapter. For, as we have seen, in the reflection of what has been enkindled in the Earth's surroundings by this 'ring' through the Mystery of Golgotha there works, lives and weaves the new Holy Spirit whom Christ has sent, and who is now able to awaken every person to beholding Him in the etheric sphere.[23]

The etheric bodies of the great teachers of humanity stand out in this 'ring' like radiant diamonds amidst rock-crystals, and above all the etheric body of him who, according to the esoteric tradition of the West, bears the name of Christian Rosenkreutz. His quite particular initiation, which was enacted at a secret location in Europe around the year 1250 by a council of the twelve most advanced initiates of Christendom, has been described by Rudolf Steiner in many of his lectures. As a result of this initiation, which Christian Rosenkreutz received at that time as the thirteenth in the circle of twelve, his 'immortal' etheric body came into being, which through the fact that it was unusually strongly imbued with the Christ-impulse did not dissolve in the world ether but directly became part of the 'etheric ring' around the Earth and was preserved there. This information was given by Rudolf Steiner in the lecture of 27 September 1911: 'We must envisage the occult process in such a way that the fruits of the initiation of the thirteenth were preserved as the residue of his etheric body within the spiritual atmosphere of the Earth. This residue worked as an inspiration upon the twelve as well as upon the pupils that succeeded them, enabling them to found the occult Rosicrucian stream.' Thus it can be said: 'All the forces of the wonderful etheric body of the individuality of the thirteenth century remained intact, and nothing dispersed after death into the general cosmic ether. This was a permanent etheric body, which thereafter remained intact in the ether spheres.' Rudolf Steiner speaks of the nature of the working of the mighty etheric body of Christian Rosenkreutz, which is further strengthened by the work of generations of his pupils during the Middle Ages and modern times, in the following way in the same lecture: 'Through the works of the Rosicrucians, the etheric body of Christian Rosenkreutz became ever stronger, ever mightier, from century to century. It worked not only through Christian Rosenkreutz but through all those who have become his pupils. Everything that is proclaimed as spiritual knowledge strengthens the etheric body of Christian Rosenkreutz, and those who proclaim it are overshone by this etheric body, which is able to work upon them while Christian Rosenkreutz is in incarnation but equally when he is not ... Devotion to the mighty etheric body of Christian Rosenkreutz can lead people to a new clairvoyance and summon forth high spiritual forces. But this will be possible only for those who rightly follow the teachings of Christian Rosenkreutz. Until now an esoteric Rosicrucian preparation was necessary for this, but the twentieth century has the task of enabling this etheric body to become so strong that it is also able to work exoterically. Those who are overshone by it will be granted an experience of what Paul experienced before Damascus. This etheric body has hitherto been active only in the school of the Rosicrucians, while in the twentieth century an ever greater number of people will be able to experience this influence and thereby also Christ's appearance in an etheric body. The experience of the Etheric Christ has become possible through the work of the Rosicrucians. The number of those who become capable of beholding Him will grow more and more. We must attribute this new manifestation of the Christ to the great deed done by the twelve and the Thirteenth, in the thirteenth and fourteenth centuries.'★[24]

In the light of what we have already said we can understand these words of Rudolf Steiner as follows. Over the centuries the etheric body of Christian Rosenkreutz, which arose as a result of his initiation in the thirteenth century when he was to a quite unprecedented degree permeated by the Christ-impulse,[25] was subsequently strengthened to such an extent through the spiritual work of Christian Rosenkreutz himself and, in particular, by generations of his pupils in the Mystery-schools of Europe in the period from the fourteenth to the nineteenth centuries that it was in our time able to work among mankind also exoterically, that is, it was able gradually to extend its influence *beyond* the Rosicrucian schools. This work

---

★ This is a reference to the initiation of Christian Rosenkreutz in the thirteenth century, as described in the lecture of 27 September 1911, and to the founding by him, in his next incarnation in the fourteenth century, of the esoteric Rosicrucian schools and the Rosicrucian path of initiation, as described in the lecture of 28 September 1911.

of the *pupils* of Christian Rosenkreutz has been that, through employing the alchemical method of spiritual training, they have aspired so to permeate their own etheric bodies with the Christ-impulse that they might after their death enter the 'etheric ring' and be united with the etheric body of Christian Rosenkreutz which dwells there continually. This etheric body gradually attained thereby its unusual strength, expressed in its immense capacity to reflect the astral light of Christ which has pervaded the Earth's surroundings since the Mystery of Golgotha. And, as a result of this, the working of the Holy Spirit in this reflected light has intensified to such an extent that those who are overshone by it will, from the twentieth century onwards, be granted experiences of beholding Christ in the etheric sphere.

In this sense we may summarize the three stages of the forming of the etheric body of Christian Rosenkreutz:

1. Its initial formation in the thirteenth century as a result of the initiation of the Thirteenth in the circle of the twelve.
2. Its *esoteric* activity through the centuries in Rosicrucian schools that were strictly hidden from the outer world, among which were those who, in Rudolf Steiner's words, 'truly follow the teachings of Christian Rosenkreutz'.[26]
3. Its *exoteric* activity from the twentieth century onwards, through which it was able to overshine not only the pupils of Christian Rosenkreutz but also others, thus leading them to a new experience of the 'Event of Damascus'.

This development is not, however, confined *solely* to the etheric body of Christian Rosenkreutz. Something similar is in our time gradually taking place also with another etheric body, which from the second quarter of our century onwards has also belonged to the 'etheric ring', where it occupies a position of quite special, even outstanding, importance. This etheric body has also followed the path delineated above and in the course of the twentieth century it is to make the transition from its first stage to the second—that is, to begin to work ever more *esoterically* among the pupils of him who in his last earthly life was the creator of this outstanding etheric body, to begin to work among those who until this day 'truly follow his teachings'. This is the etheric body of one who has *in our time* attained the highest experience of Christ that is accessible to an incarnated human being and who is therefore *the great herald of the Etheric Christ in the twentieth century*. This is the etheric body of the man who, as a personal pupil of Christian Rosenkreutz,[27] had at the end of his path of initiation attained the stage of his teacher, and who placed into the world the Christmas Conference of

1923, the central spiritual event that has occurred on the physical plane in the twentieth century. This man is the founder of Anthroposophy—*Rudolf Steiner.*[28] His etheric body, which has in the highest degree been permeated by the Christ-impulse, was fully preserved in the 'etheric ring' surrounding the Earth.[29] This etheric body—further strengthened in subsequent years by the work of his pupils, who together form the General Anthroposophical Society with its centre in the School of Spiritual Science—must in the course of the twentieth century be given the possibility of beginning to work *esoterically* with ever greater intensity among anthroposophists who wish to be true pupils of Rudolf Steiner, that is, who remain *faithful* to the principal impulse which he brought into the world: the impulse of the Christmas Foundation Meeting,[30] the impulse of the new Mysteries of Michael-Christ.[31]

Hence we may say: it fully depends upon our work, as anthroposophists, whether the etheric body of Rudolf Steiner will be able to work among us at the end of the century, irrespective of whether at that time he is outwardly present among us or not. For the most important task that confronts anthroposophists at the end of the century is that through their spiritual work, *faithfully* carried out on the basis of the anthroposophical impulse, the etheric body of Rudolf Steiner will be able to attain a strength such as will enable his pupils, who are overshone by this etheric body, to be granted a direct experience of Christ. In other words: *that Christ Himself may, from the end of the twentieth century onwards, work through the etheric body of Rudolf Steiner amongst his pupils.* This will, however, become possible only when the *Holy Spirit*, having united with the reflection of the Christ-light by this etheric body, is able to enter the pupils' consciousness and thus awaken within them a direct experience of the Christ.

If, in connection with the end of our century, we can speak of the forthcoming culmination of the Anthroposophical Movement in the world on the basis of a renewed experience of Pentecost as a cosmic festival of knowledge[32] we should also add that, inseparably connected with this, the etheric body of him who in modern times was the main bearer and founder of 'the wisdom of the Holy Spirit concerning man', or *Anthroposophy*, is beginning to work esoterically among anthroposophists who are striving towards this culmination.

3.   Easter, Ascension, Whitsun and the Essential Nature of the Foundation Stone of the Christmas Conference of 1923/24

The Foundation Stone of the General Anthroposophical Society, which was laid into the hearts and souls of the anthroposophists who were present at the time, was formed by Rudolf Steiner at the Christmas Conference of 1923/24 out of the Father-forces rising from the depths, the Son-forces working in the periphery, and the Spirit-forces descending from the heights. Through this profound Mystery-deed, an altogether new relationship of the macrocosmic forces working within man (the thoughts of the Spirit revealed in the human head, Christ working in the heart, and the will of the Father fulfilled in the deeds of the limbs)[33] was made openly manifest, a relationship which, as we have seen, arose for the first time as a result of the event of Pentecost,[34] the third and final stage of Christ's union 'with the stream of Earthly Being'.[35] Hence we may say: this new form of interaction between the principal forces of the macrocosm, which came about as a result of the first Whitsun and was made manifest at the Christmas Conference, reveals to us the path to an understanding of the deep inner connection existing between the laying of the Foundation Stone of the new Mysteries and what has already been described in some detail in previous chapters regarding the three stages of the penetration of Christ, the Sun Being, into Earth-existence. This connection is something that we need to study here at greater length. As a point of departure we may take the communication of spiritual science that the principles of Father, Son and Spirit in our cosmos are represented above all by the activity of the three divine-spiritual Hierarchies. This means that we may speak of a threefold change in the activity of the higher Hierarchies, which came about in connection with the Christ Being's passing through the Mystery of Golgotha, the Ascension and Pentecost.

Thus through the Mystery of Golgotha the highest Hierarchy of the Seraphim, Cherubim and Thrones, which represents the Father-principle in our cosmos, was enabled to work out of the depths of the Earth not only in a 'natural way', forming its solid, liquid and gaseous elements from within outwards,[36] but also in the manner that it works and weaves in its own sphere, that of the fixed stars, whence it fashions and holds sway over the whole moral order of the cosmos. As a result of this, the Earth's natural order is in our time ever preparing to become a moral order, which on Jupiter will also become physically visible. This change in the activity of the First Hierarchy can also be expressed as follows. When the First Hierarchy works *directly*, as it does in the sphere of the fixed stars, it finds expression in the fashioning of a purely moral world-order, and when it works *in the manner of a reflection*, 'as an echo', it makes possible the arising of a natural world order, for then its forces, in descending from the heights, are, so to speak, reflected in the depths by what has within the Earth (and within man) already succumbed to death and has therefore become inaccessible to its understanding[37] (that is, has ceased to be 'transparent' for its forces).

We can also discern something similar with respect to the Second Hierarchy of the Dominions, Mights and Powers, which represents the Son-principle in our cosmos. The sphere of its original activity, where it participates with the First Hierarchy in the fashioning of the 'moral cosmos', is that of the Sun. There it can *directly* unfold all its creative forces. In the Earth's surroundings, however, its activity until the Turning Point of Time comes only indirectly to expression: thus it is chiefly the Powers (the Spirits of Form) who reveal themselves through the Sun's light and warmth; it is especially the Mights (the Spirits of Movement) who reveal themselves through the music of the spheres (the chemical or sound ether) proceeding from the Sun and planets; and finally, it is the Dominions (the Spirits of Wisdom) who reveal themselves through the life-forces (the life ether) radiating from the Sun. Consequently, all the three kinds of Spirits of the Second Hierarchy work in the Earth's surroundings not as they work in their own region of the Sun in a 'natural way' but *through the mediation* of the four varieties of world-ether,[38] in so far as the possibility of *direct* (i.e. moral) activity in the Earth's surroundings has remained closed to them on account of the presence there of death-forces, which by their nature have, as we have seen, always been inaccessible to their understanding.

This state of affairs has, however, changed in a fundamental way since the Mystery of Golgotha *and* the Ascension. For through His union in the Ascension with the Sun-aspiring human etheric body, Christ laid the foundation for the forming in the Earth's surroundings of that 'etheric ring' which, in Rudolf Steiner's words, is already today the beginning of the Earth's transformation into a new Sun.[39] In an esoteric sense this means that as a result of the event of the Ascension all three kinds of spirits of the Second Hierarchy have now acquired the possibility of working in the Earth's surroundings, or—to be more precise—in the 'etheric ring' encircling the Earth, not merely in a 'natural way', through the mediation of the world-ether, but also *directly*, as they have hitherto worked only in their own realm, in the sphere of the Sun. In so far as people living on the Earth are concerned, such a change in the manner in which the Second

Hierarchy works within Earth-existence is also of immense significance for them. For now the forces of this Sun Hierarchy can penetrate even to man's *etheric heart*, so that he can, in Rudolf Steiner's words, gradually learn to speak of 'an inner Sun' and '. . . to recognize that his own being that walks the Earth is *led by the Sun.*'[40]

Finally, we can also observe a similar fundamental change in the realm of the Third Hierarchy of the Archai, Archangels and Angels, which represents the principle of the Holy Spirit in our cosmos. According to spiritual science these three kinds of hierarchic beings have, since olden times, worked in human evolution not so much outwardly, in the forming of earthly nature, as *within* earthly beings themselves and above all within man. Thus through their influence upon man's astral body the Angels become the guides and guardians of individual human beings. Through their influence upon man's etheric body the Archangels become the leaders of the various peoples, while the Archai, through an influence which extends even to man's physical body, become the guides of whole historical epochs. With regard to the soul-life of man, these three categories of spiritual beings work formatively upon man's thinking, feeling and will and have determined to a significant degree—especially in former times—his whole soul-configuration. They have received the impulses for this activity from higher Hierarchies, who in the present cycle of evolution do not as yet work directly upon man's inner nature.[41] As Rudolf Steiner says: 'Guidance on the part of the higher Hierarchies is manifested in accordance with their powers, and to begin with it is the lowest who participate therein. Matters of earthly evolution are conducted in such a way that—although high beings (of the Second Hierarchy), and even the highest (the First Hierarchy), are active within it—they entrust the execution of certain tasks* to the Angels, Archangels and Archai who serve them, so that it is they who are the first to enter into earthly evolution.'[42]

With the approach to the Turning Point of Time, however, it came about that, as the death-forces introduced into human evolution by Lucifer and Ahriman became ever stronger, the higher Hierarchies—'even the very highest'—gradually lost all their capacity of influencing human souls through the mediation of beings of the Third Hierarchy (see Rudolf Steiner's words quoted on p. 199) and thus of rightly leading humanity in future to its intended goal. But when Christ had passed through the Mystery of Golgotha, through the Ascension and, finally, through the event of Pentecost, and was able as a consequence to send the Holy Spirit from the heights down to the heads of the people whose hearts he had thus

---

* Earlier in the same lecture, Rudolf Steiner speaks of how these 'tasks' have particularly been concerned with influencing man's inner being.

entered, it again became possible for beings of the Third Hierarchy to gain access to the inner being of each human individual. Since the first Pentecost, therefore, the Holy Spirit that works within man has also been that power which connects human beings with the sphere of the Third Hierarchy and, through it, with the higher Hierarchies, 'even the very highest'.[43] As a consequence of this new situation, it will in the future become evident that beings of the Third Hierarchy, in penetrating people's inner being through the mediation of the Holy Spirit, the bearer of the new consciousness, will be able to exert their influence upon man not only as was the case in deep antiquity, when such an influence was akin to a natural force which arose out of necessity in the depths of the soul, but will henceforth be able to work within man without extinguishing his clear, waking ego-consciousness, that is to say, while fully preserving his individual freedom.

Thus from our time onwards it is possible for all those who are, in the words of the Gospel, 'men of good will'[44] gradually to evolve towards a new, fully conscious and completely free communion with the Gods. For only on this path will they be able to form the foundation of a truly *moral order* in their souls which then can be extended to social relationships as a whole.

So we may see that, as a result of the Mystery of Golgotha and the events of the Ascension and of Pentecost that followed, it became possible for all three Hierarchies to work not only 'naturally' but also in a *moral* way *directly* into Earth-existence. Through this, the entire Earth is gradually prepared for the time when it will become the *moral Sun of the world*, a new 'cosmos of love' at whose foundation there will lie a purely moral world order, in the same way that at the foundation of our present Earth, which is a 'cosmos of wisdom', there lies a natural world order. Man was originally placed into this natural world order so that he might, through coming to know and master it, win for himself true inner freedom. This process of development has, to a significant degree, come to fulfilment in our epoch, as confirmed by the fact that it was possible for the Christmas Foundation Meeting to take place among humanity—an event which in its esoteric nature is none other than a call from the spiritual world itself to all 'men of good will' for a new partnership with the Gods, for a conscious participation in the fashioning of the new cosmos of freedom and love!

If we now recall that, according to Zeylmans van Emmichoven, the 'dodecahedral Foundation Stone of *love*'[45] was formed by Rudolf Steiner at Christmas 1923 out of the forces of all three Hierarchies, we can come significantly closer to an understanding of the very core of the Christmas Conference. Furthermore, we may then truly feel, with all the forces of our being, the inner impulse to aspire towards laying in our hearts this Foundation Stone, which in its hierarchic aspect corresponds to the new moral order of the cosmos and in its human aspect to that moral order which every man must establish in his own soul as the *moral order of Christ*, if he wishes to work in the modern world in the spirit of the new Christian Mysteries.

We can, however, enter into a still deeper understanding of the esoteric essence of the Foundation Stone of the Christmas Conference. For this purpose we need to return to the three stages of the Christ Being's union with Earth-existence, and examine them from another viewpoint. Let us now turn to the first of these stages. This first stage is, as we have seen, the Mystery of Golgotha itself. Rudolf Steiner characterizes it in a quite special way in his lectures on the Fifth Gospel: 'With the death of Jesus there was *born* for the Earth what had previously pervaded only the regions *beyond* it: an all-prevailing love, cosmic love ... Something was born for the Earth that had formerly existed only in the cosmos at the moment when Jesus of Nazareth died on the Cross. The death of Jesus of Nazareth was the birth of the all-prevailing cosmic love within the earthly sphere.'[46] Thus the first stage is '*the birth of the all-prevailing love within the earthly sphere*'—*Ex Deo nascimur!* And this cosmic love is what lives and weaves in that astral Christ-light which flowed into Earth-existence from the Cross on Golgotha, for 'light is love' (see p. 141).[47] Concerning this light of love, Rudolf Steiner goes on to say that it will in future become etheric and then physical. Then the whole Earth will shine forth in the universe like a Sun of love which will gradually become the creative centre of a new cosmos, the 'cosmos of love' which is referred to in the last chapter of *Occult Science*. Such is the esoteric aspect of the Mystery of Golgotha. For 'the Event of Golgotha is a free cosmic deed which springs from *universal love* and can be comprehended only by *human love*.'[48]

Let us now consider the second stage. It consists, as we have seen, in that human etheric bodies were permeated by the Christ-force in such a way that those parts of man's etheric body which have received this force into themselves no longer dissolve in the world-ether (i.e. they are not subject to death *as individual etheric bodies* but are preserved in the Earth's surroundings forming the 'etheric ring' to which we have already referred). However, such a metamorphosis of the etheric body can take place only if man really embodies in himself the principle *In Christo morimur—In Christ death becomes life.* Only in this case can the human etheric body acquire the new life-forces which Christ has granted and which enable it to avoid succumbing to death in the vast etheric spaces of the universe. But in what does this process of endowing man's etheric body with life-forces consist? What are life-forces for the etheric body? These forces are the *World*

Imaginations, those imaginations out of which it builds up and restores the physical body in the course of earthly life.[49]

Rudolf Steiner considers this theme in particular detail in the lecture of 21 April 1924, where he describes the gradual forming of man's etheric body by the Moon teachers of wisdom from the forces of the entire planetary system, in the course of which the substance of the etheric body is drawn from the Moon-sphere surrounding the Earth and is then individualized through the forces of the entire planetary system being imprinted upon it, forces which then become the foundation for the soul-physical human faculties that would subsequently develop therein: speech, movement, wisdom, love, soul-warmth and protective forces. Rudolf Steiner characterizes this process in the lecture indicated as follows: 'Everything that happens on the Moon—which also, moreover, happens in order that man might rightly acquire the forces that he needs for building up his etheric body—depends upon the results of *observation* arrived at by beings on the Moon, who, so to speak, live on the Moon and *examine* from there the wandering stars of our planetary system that surround them: Mercury, Sun, Moon and so forth.'[50] It is clear from this that 'observation' and 'examination' (at another point in the same lecture Rudolf Steiner speaks of 'contemplation' and 'beholding') relate to the Moon teachers receiving wisdom from out of the planetary spheres of *World Imaginations*, which they then imprint upon the newly formed human etheric body. In the course of his earthly life, man then augments these World Imaginations with *human imaginations*, which after his death (or during initiation) come before him as his living memory, as the imaginative panorama of his past earthly life. Thus as a whole we may say: the human etheric body is primarily the bearer of World and human Imaginations. However, by the time of the Mystery of Golgotha, the darkening brought about by Ahriman in the spiritual world adjacent to the Earth, together with his direct influence upon the forming of man's etheric body before its descent into the earthly world, had reached such an intensity[51] that the World Imaginations, drawn from the planetary spheres, were no longer equal to the task of preserving man's etheric body from gradually drying up. Thus the human etheric body was in need of a stream of new, far more intense life-forces, far more powerful World Imaginations, and this became possible through the Ascension of Christ that followed His deed on Golgotha, through His union with the etheric bodies of human beings and their permeation with the *archetypes of the imaginations* themselves,[52] that is, with the forces of the world of Buddhi, the world of Archetypes, which form these imaginations.

This process can, however, also be considered from the standpoint of evolution. Of fundamental importance here is Rudolf Steiner's indication that the ancient wisdom of mankind (that is, the clairvoyant experience of the World Imaginations) was associated with the fact that man's etheric body extended in olden times far beyond his physical head. Only from the middle of the Atlantean epoch did there begin the slow process of the etheric body's entry into the physical body, which was accompanied by the gradual loss by human beings of their old atavistic clairvoyance, of the old wisdom, of any real possibility of inwardly experiencing World Imaginations. Because of this the whole of humanity was confronted at the time of the events of Palestine by the possibility of finally losing all connection with the old wisdom, and hence with its source—the divine-spiritual worlds themselves. But evolution took a further course; and it was through the wisdom of world rulership that the process which had its beginning in the middle of the Atlantean epoch found its turning-point at the time of the events of Palestine. For 'at the moment when Christ appeared, the etheric body began again to depart ...',[53] that is, depart from the physical body. However, in order that this process might serve the good of mankind, the etheric body was not allowed to be drawn without wisdom, without World Imaginations, into the outer spiritual world; it was not allowed to go there deprived of life-forces.[54] For, as has been already observed, imaginations are the element of life for the etheric body. Hence '... it was necessary for an impulse to come to the Earth whereby the dwindling store of ancient wisdom might be replenished and new life instilled into the etheric body ... And it was Christ who brought it, who brought this life to [man's] etheric body'.[55] Thus we can say: only through such an enlivening of human etheric bodies did it become possible for the 'etheric ring' to form around the Earth; and it is this which is discerned by the clairvoyant consciousness of the initiate as the sum of life-permeated World-human Imaginations.

In conclusion, let us turn to the third stage of Christ's union with Earth-existence. In order rightly to understand this we first need to examine in greater detail the process of spiritual reflection that is associated with it and which has already been described above; and in order that we may gain insight into this we shall take as our starting-point the essential nature of the old form of initiation, the culmination of which was the immersing of the neophyte in a three-day, deathlike sleep in the temple. Until this moment the astral body had been prepared in such a way that organs of clairvoyance gradually developed within it; and through this it became able to have spiritual experiences. But in order that these experiences might be brought to consciousness within the pupil, it was necessary for all the new content that had been acquired by the astral body to be imprinted upon the etheric body. For this purpose the three-day, *deathlike* sleep in the temple was required, so that during this time not only the astral body (as is the case during sleep) but also the etheric body (as in death) was drawn to a

251

significant degree out of the physical. The significance of this somewhat dangerous procedure was that the content of the astral body was reflected in the course of its penetration into the field of ego-consciousness not by the physical body, as is the case with an ordinary man in everyday life, but by the *etheric body*, through which a man can consciously experience the world of Imaginations. A similar process takes place in modern initiation when, with the aid of exercises in meditation and concentration, a certain weakening of the connection between the etheric and physical bodies is called forth, and by this means, *though now on a purely inner path*, the same results are attained.[56] Hence in both cases, albeit on altogether different paths, there is *a transfer of the reflective capacity of the physical body to the etheric body*. The consequence of this is that it is not the dead, shadowy thoughts reflected by the physical body which enter the field of ego-consciousness but *the living thoughts* reflected by the *etheric body*, and these have the capacity of bringing to human consciousness the facts and events of the spiritual worlds.

Something similar, though on a macrocosmic plane, takes place at the third stage of Christ's union with Earth-existence. The 'etheric ring' that surrounds the Earth and which reflects the astral Christ-light, wherein is contained the substance of world Love, transforms the light in the process of reflection into a stream of spiritualized, life-filled World Thoughts, into a stream of the purest Intelligence which, as *reflected light*, is that element in which the Spirit lives and weaves.[57] And in these World Thoughts in which the Spirit works and weaves, the soul can now awaken—if it brings to them its own thoughts which have been spiritualized and enlivened by spiritual science, that is, human thoughts such as are truly capable of gaining access to the World Thoughts and, hence, of bringing the human soul to a real experience of the Spirit-impulse, to a true awakening in the Spirit, to a true Whitsun festival: *Per Spiritum Sanctum reviviscimus*—'In the world-thoughts of the Spirit the soul awakens.'

And so, in these three stages of the union of the Christ Being with Earth-existence, which came to expression in the events of Easter, Ascension and Pentecost, we may find the source of those forces which work in the earthly sphere as the substance of World Love, as life-bestowing World Imaginations, as light-bearing World Thoughts, which man can approach in experience only through inwardly generating spiritualized human thoughts, human imaginations and human love, *as inner organs of knowledge*.

If we now return to considering the essential nature of the Foundation Stone of the Christmas Conference, we may say: the 'dodecahedral Imagination-form of Love',[58] which was for the first time laid into the hearts and souls of anthroposophists at the Christmas Conference as the Foundation Stone of the General Anthroposophical Society, was formed by

Rudolf Steiner from the three forces of World Love, which can be comprehended only by human love; World Imaginations, which can be made alive only by human imaginations; and World Thoughts, which can be united only by spiritualized human thoughts—or, in other words, *from the forces of Easter, Ascension and Pentecost.*

Rudolf Steiner characterizes this 'dodecahedral Stone of Love'[59] on the second day of the Christmas Conference, 25 December 1923, during the Mystery of the laying of the Foundation Stone, as follows: 'Then the Foundation Stone will light up before the eye of our soul—that Foundation Stone which receives its substance from World-human Love; its living picture-quality,[60] its form, from World-human Imagination; and its resplendent light, which whenever we remember this present moment can radiate towards us with light which is warm but which awakens our activity, our thinking, our feeling and our will, from World-human Thoughts.'[61]

'That good may become ...' what we from the forces of Pentecost, which awaken our thinking, from the forces of Ascension, which enliven our feeling, and from the forces of Easter, which permeate our will, wish to bring through our deeds into the world, for the good of mankind's development.[62]

X

ST JOHN'S-TIDE

1.   St John's-tide: a Festival of the Future

As a conclusion to our study of the esoteric foundations of the cycle of the year, only a few words shall now be said about the last great annual festival, that of St John's Day. For not much can be said about this festival in the present epoch of human evolution, as in its deepest foundations it is a festival that points towards the future evolution of humanity; it is one which human beings will be able to celebrate in a full and conscious way only in the very distant future.

St John's Day, which in the cycle of the year follows shortly after the summer solstice, corresponds to the point in the life-cycle of the Earth when it is most fully breathing out. The whole inner being of the Earth at this time of year is immersed in a deep sleep, the outward expression of which is all the beauty and diversity of its plant life. However, the Earth's Soul now lies fully outside its physical planetary body. It ascends to the far reaches of the cosmos, to the sphere of the fixed stars, and abides there in the circle of the higher Hierarchies, immersed in blissful dreams, in the dreams which it will then recall throughout the winter, especially during the thirteen Holy Nights. This bliss which the Soul of the Earth experiences as it ascends to the highest spheres of the macrocosm can be felt—albeit as an outward, shadowy reflection—by any sensitive person who in summer's noon-tide heat gives himself up to an experience of his natural surroundings. It is indeed so that in such moments nature's condition cannot be described otherwise than by the word 'bliss'. But for the Soul of the Earth, which at this time experiences the deepest riddles of existence in the far reaches of the cosmos, this condition is—as has been observed—no more than a dream. The Soul of the Earth, as it abides in the highest spheres, cannot fully awaken to a *conscious experience* of that 'divine bliss', the bliss of being in the lap of the higher Hierarchies in which it now abides.

The same applies also to man. Man is unable consciously to follow the Soul of the Earth into the far reaches of the cosmos at this time of the year. He can only unite with it unconsciously in his nightly wanderings; it is not accessible to his modern waking consciousness.[1] And much time will still pass before it will become possible for man in the natural course of his evolution to follow the Earth Soul into the starry distances with full consciousness. Meanwhile he must be content with listening at Christmas-tide to the Earth Soul as it recalls its summer sojourn in the macrocosm.

However, even in our time there exists a path that can enable modern man to follow the Soul of the Earth into the far reaches of the cosmos and, as it were, to behold with the eyes of the cosmos the unspeakable mysteries of the starry worlds while fully preserving one's waking ego-consciousness. And although this path has become accessible to the whole of humanity only in our time, its foundations have been laid through the Mystery of Golgotha, when the Christ Being became the new Spirit of the Earth. It is for this reason that when the Earth breathes out, not only its Soul but also its Spirit takes leave of its physical body and unites with the world of the Sun and the stars. Thus one can say: at St John's-tide not only the Soul of the Earth but also the new Spirit of the Earth, Christ, in a certain sense takes leave of the planetary body and dwells out in the macrocosm, uniting there with His eternal Kingdom in the spheres of the Sun and the stars.

Rudolf Steiner speaks of this union of the Earth Spirit with the cosmos at St John's-tide as follows: 'The entire soul-nature of the Earth has been poured forth into cosmic space, it has given itself up to cosmic space. The soul-nature of the Earth has been permeated by the power of the Sun, by the power of the stars. Christ, who is deeply associated with this soul-nature of the Earth, also unites His strength with the power of the stars and the power of the Sun, which surge through the Earth's soul-nature thus surrendered to the cosmic All. This is St John's-tide, the season of St John's Day. The Earth has fully breathed out. In its outward aspect, with which it beholds the universe, the Earth manifests not its own forces, as at the time of the winter solstice, but reveals, rather, on its surface the reflected forces of the stars, the Sun and all that lies outside it in the cosmos.'[2]

If an individual has entered upon the modern path of Christian-Rosicrucian initiation, which leads him to a conscious union with the Christ Being, such a union can enable him at St John's-tide to rise with the Soul of the Earth into the macrocosm, and there behold with its eyes the divine Mysteries, feeling himself to be at the very heart of the divine-spiritual world and experiencing all this in full possession of his waking ego-consciousness. For man does not accomplish this ascent with the Soul of the Earth *on his own*, but with the Christ Being, who—alone of all the divine beings of the cosmos—is able to uplift and sustain man's individual ego-consciousness at *all* levels of world-existence.[3]

As a consequence of this, the deepest mystery of the Christ as the Spirit and guiding star of the whole Earth is revealed to the initiate.

In so far as such an experience of the macrocosm—of the planets, the Sun, and the whole world of the fixed stars *in union with the forces of the Earth Soul*—is something immeasurably greater than what we have already referred to as the 'union with the macrocosm', which merely issues from man's individual forces, it corresponds to that highest stage of Christian-

258

Rosicrucian initiation, which Rudolf Steiner defines in the words, 'divine bliss'. In *Occult Science* he writes of this as follows: 'After this stage [the sixth] something arises which may be defined in spiritual-scientific terms as "divine bliss". It is neither possible nor necessary to describe this stage of development more precisely. For there are no human words which have the power to describe what a man learns through this experience. And one can say with justice that it is possible to form an impression of the condition envisaged here only by means of a thinking which no longer requires the instrument of the human brain.'[4]

In this sense we may say: the summer festival of St John is, esoterically speaking, an indication of the most distant future in the evolution of mankind, of that future which in our time a person can make an inner reality only once he has reached the seventh and final stage of the modern Christian-Rosicrucian path of initiation.

Thus the festival of St John's, when rightly understood and celebrated, is a festival which anticipates that condition of the Earth when it will again be united with the Sun and—through it—with the whole of the starry world. Hence we may characterise the future festival of St John's as a true Earth-Sun festival.

2. The Modern Path of Initiation and its Reflection in the Seven Principal Christian Festivals

Let us sum up all that we have said. In the present work we have attempted to examine the cycle of the year from a more esoteric viewpoint, and to clarify the extent to which the fundamental elements of the modern Christian-Rosicrucian path of initiation lie at its foundation. This inner connection of its seven stages with the yearly rhythm is not fortuitous but corresponds fully with cosmic laws. For this path of initiation is in all its elements an exact reflection of the life of the macrocosm. Hence it is already contained, in a hidden form, in the yearly rhythm and only needs to become conscious within man. It is something quite objective, essentially independent of anyone's inclinations or sympathies.

This thought can also be expressed in another way: the whole world was fashioned by the Gods according to the laws of initiation. When a person embarks upon this path, he is merely making these laws *conscious* within himself, and through this he becomes able to enter in full consciousness into the great hierarchic whole. He becomes an instrument, a larynx for the Gods of the cosmos, and is henceforth a conscious bearer of those laws according to which the Gods once created the world.

In our investigation of the spiritual foundations of the cycle of the year we have been able to distinguish in particular *seven* Christian festivals, which introduce the sevenfold rhythm of the inner development of the human soul into the twelvefold rhythm of the year. These festivals are: Michaelmas, Christmas, Epiphany, Easter, Ascension, Whitsun and St John's Day. Although the aforementioned fundamental elements of the Christian-Rosicrucian path of initiation are not precisely fixed within the yearly cycle but maintain a certain mobility, in so far as they relate more to the 'festive periods' of the year whose culmination at any particular time is the corresponding festival, nevertheless we can, while being aware of the *relativity* of these relationships, endeavour to connect these seven principal Christian festivals with the seven stages of modern initiation in a more direct way. Such relationships do indeed follow quite naturally from all that has been said hitherto. It is necessary only to elucidate one further point in order to receive a full and final picture.

If we consider the cycle of the year as a whole, we do in fact have not one but *three* Christmases, or (to be more precise) *three* divine births. The first is, of course, Christmas as such, the birth on Earth of the *man*, Jesus of

Nazareth (the Nathan Soul), celebrated on 25 December. This birth is a *lunar* birth, in the sense in which the physical birth of *every* human being on Earth arises from the Moon-forces or, in modern terms, from the forces of heredity. In the cosmos it is principally the Moon Archangel, Gabriel, who rules these forces.[5] The time when his influence upon earthly events is particularly strong corresponds in the yearly rhythm to the period of the winter solstice, or Christmas.[6] Hence in ancient times, when the process of the conception and birth of the human organism was not yet fully under man's power but was still to a significant extent directed from the Mystery-centres, conception always had to take place in such a way that the child was born at Christmas-time,[7] so that it could descend to the Earth from the sphere of the Moon under the guidance of the Archangel Gabriel. The classic example of such a birth is the birth of the Nathan Soul on 25 December and its annunciation by the Moon Archangel.[8] In the case of the Nathan Soul, however, the influence of the Moon-forces was significantly strengthened by the circumstance that in it there descended to the Earth a *human* being for whom this incarnation at the Turning Point of Time was the *first* incarnation since the Lemurian epoch, which is itself the repetition in the Earth-epoch of the Old Moon condition of our planet. Moreover, the Nathan Soul was also the bearer of the purest unfallen substance of the human ego,[9] which was poured into man in the Lemurian epoch by the Moon Elohim, Yahveh, who was at the same time the chief antagonist of Lucifer in our cosmos,[10] that is, of the spirit who had remained behind on Old Moon, and who then brought about the Fall of man. Thus from various sides we have numerous indications of how *lunar* birth, birth which stands wholly under the sign of the Moon-forces, has a particular connection with the festival of Christmas.★

This distinctive quality of the festival of Christmas also gives rise to the fact to which we have already directed our attention in describing the Christmas Mystery in the rhythm of the year, namely, that an esoteric penetration into the nature of this festival is most accessible to an *imaginative knowledge* which for its part has a deep relationship with both the ancient and the modern Moon (that is, with the Moon-sphere surrounding the Earth). Hence the theme of Christmas has in Christian times always been a favourite theme for artists, not only because the art of painting is most closely associated with the world of imaginations but also because traces of the old atavistic clairvoyance were preserved in Europe until the beginning of the nineteenth century, while the faculties for inspirative and, still more

---

★ Of course, the Nathan Soul was also connected with the Sun (see the chapter entitled 'From Michaelmas to Christmas') but its *physical* birth on Earth, like the physical birth of any human being, stood under the sign of the Moon.

261

for intuitive, knowledge had almost completely disappeared by the fourth century of the Christian era.[11] Finally, according to modern spiritual research, the Gospel according to Luke, which contains the story of the Annunciation, was written mainly out of the forces of *imaginative knowledge*, and on the strength of this was always accessible to even the most simple and naive souls,[12] just as Christmas is the festival which in Europe has been the most understood and loved in the whole cycle of the year.

The second birth is celebrated at Epiphany, which is the festival of the descent of the Christ Being into the three sheaths of Jesus of Nazareth at the Baptism in the Jordan. Here we are concerned with a pure *Sun-birth*, with the incarnation on Earth of the Sun Spirit Himself, the Christ. Until His descent to the Earth, Christ belonged fully to the great sphere of the Sun, whence He ruled over the whole planetary evolution through mighty cosmic rhythms with the aid of the so-called 'music of the spheres', whose source is the Sun itself:

> The Sun, in ancient guise, competing
> With brother spheres in rival song,
> With thunder-march, his orb completing
> Moves his predestined course along.[13]

It is for this reason that in order truly to grasp the essential nature of the Baptism in the Jordan, the second, Sun-orientated, birth, there was a need not merely for imaginative but also for *inspirative* knowledge. In other words, it demanded not simply clairvoyance but a certain degree of initiation.[14] John the Baptist had reached this degree of initiation. According to spiritual science he had in his inner development attained the so-called 'initiation of the Waterman', which enabled him to receive direct inspirations from a certain being of the Hierarchy of the Angels. 'The gaze of John the Baptist was trained in such a way that he could look, at night, through the material Earth to the constellation of the Waterman; and when the Angel took possession of his soul, he was able to receive *that initiation* which bore the name of Waterman-initiation,'[15] as Rudolf Steiner says. Herein also lies the inner reason why John was sent into the world 'to prepare the way' for Christ Jesus. For, having penetrated through his initiation to the sphere of Inspiration, he was able to recognize in Christ the great Sun Spirit★ and, with the aid of *inspired imaginations*, to say of Him: 'And John bore witness, "I saw the Spirit descend upon Him as a dove from Heaven, and it remained connected with Him."'[16] And then:

★ That is, that Being who belongs to the cosmic sphere of the Son (which is the Sun-sphere). 'And I have seen and have borne witness that this is the Son of God' (John 1:34).

'And when he saw Jesus passing by, he said: "Behold, the Lamb of God."'[17]

In a lecture of 28 July 1922 Rudolf Steiner describes in detail the esoteric significance of these two utterances of John the Baptist, emphasizing especially their origin in the sphere of inspirative knowledge. This is what he says: 'And it is completely in accord with this that those who hearkened to inspirations imparted to the Holy Spirit the form of the dove. How are we to understand it in our time if the Holy Spirit is referred to in the form of a dove? We should understand this as leading us to say: those who spoke in this way were people who were inspired in the old atavistic sense. In that realm where the Holy Spirit appeared to them purely spiritually, they perceived it as an inspiration in this form. And how did these atavistically inspired contemporaries of the Mystery of Golgotha characterize the Christ? They saw Him in an outward way and hence saw Him as a man. In order to see Him as Man in the spiritual world, they would have to have possessed Intuition. But at the time of the Mystery of Golgotha there were no such people who could have seen Him as an Ego, in the world of Intuition; this they were unable to see. [Rudolf Steiner indicates later on that Lazarus-John was an exception in this respect.] However, they were still able to see Him in atavistic Inspiration. And so they employed animal forms when they wished to speak of Christ Himself. "Behold, the Lamb of God!" This is a language that is right for that time, a language with which we need to become accustomed if we would again come to an understanding of what Inspiration is and, hence, of what it is that is seen through Inspiration which is capable of appearing in the spiritual world in the form, "Behold the Lamb of God".'[18]

Apart from these words of Rudolf Steiner regarding the inspirative character of the Baptism in the Jordan, there is one further fact which has been established by modern spiritual research, namely, that Christ, in the course of His descent from the Sun to the Earth through the various ranks of the Hierarchies, reached only as far as the Hierarchy of the *Archangels* and then, by-passing the Hierarchy of the Angels (see Rudolf Steiner's words quoted on p. 235), that is, in a certain sense 'by-passing' the entire sphere of the Moon, incarnated directly into the sheaths of Jesus of Nazareth.[19] And so those words, which sounded like the harmony of the spheres from the far reaches of the universe at the moment of the Baptism in the Jordan, 'Thou art My beloved Son, today I have begotten Thee,'[20] became accessible to the ears of earthly humans only through their connection with the sphere of the Archangels, the great inspirers of human speech.[21]

To conclude this characterization of the Mystery of the Baptism in the Jordan, it should be observed that its inspirative character also comes to expression in that it is particularly music's task to reveal the essential nature of the divine birth of the Christ Being in Jesus of Nazareth. In his lecture of 22 August 1924, Rudolf Steiner even indicates that it will be music's most important task in the future evolution of humanity to transmit the Mystery of the incarnation of Christ Jesus. For just as the Jesus-impulse can best be transmitted through the medium of the figurative arts, so in the future will it be the case that 'the Christ-impulse can be found in [the element of] music'.[22]

Finally, we have the third birth in the Mystery of Golgotha. This is, properly speaking, the birth of the Christ Being in the spiritual sphere of the Earth (see Rudolf Steiner's words quoted on p. 235). In the lecture cycle *From Jesus to Christ*, Rudolf Steiner also defines this as '... the birth of a new element in human nature: the birth of the imperishable body',[23] or (in more spiritual-scientific terms) of the 'Phantom' of man's physical body. And in so far as '... what one might call the *foundation stone*, the first rudiments of this Phantom, was laid in the *Saturn epoch* by the Hierarchy of the Thrones ...'[24] it follows that the Phantom is related, on the one hand, to present-day Saturn, the outermost planet of our solar system[25] and, on the other, to the whole starry cosmos, to which belong the beings of the First Hierarchy, among whom are the Thrones.★[26]

In the course of considering the Mystery of Easter, we spoke of how the Phantom of man's physical body, which rose from the grave of Golgotha, is connected with the entire starry cosmos and also with the highest goal of earthly evolution, with the manifestation of the principle of Spirit Man in the final condition of Vulcan, the counterpart of the ancient condition of Saturn. Thus on the basis of what has been said already, we have full reason to say: this third birth can truly be called a *Saturn-* or *starry-*birth in the same way that the Baptism in the Jordan can be called a Sun-birth,[27] and Christmas, as described in St Luke's Gospel, a Moon-birth. However, the sphere of the fixed stars, the sphere of the great macrocosmic Man, Adam Cadmon, is (as we have seen) at the same time the sphere of activity of the universal Logos, the World Word, the highest aspect of the all-encompassing Being of the Christ. And so in order that man may penetrate this sphere, in order that he may comprehend the cosmic Mystery of the Word and thereby also the Mystery of Golgotha itself, he needs to rise to an experience of Intuition, to intuitive knowledge. The art best suited to bring to earthly life something of the Mystery of the Logos is the art of the word, which attains its highest expression in the Gospel written by John the Apostle, who alone of the disciples of Christ Jesus was able to stand in full consciousness (that is, with the highest intuitive consciousness) beneath

---

★ This is why the Phantom of man's physical body, resurrected by Christ, can also be called the *starry body*.

264

the Cross on Golgotha. Regarding the supersensible character of the spiritual sources of the fourth Gospel, Rudolf Steiner has this to say: 'If from this standpoint [that is, from the standpoint of modern imaginative, inspirative and intuitive knowledge] we now turn our attention to the four Gospels, we may say that the Gospel of St John is written from the viewpoint of an initiate who was able to fathom world mysteries to the degree of Intuition. He described the Christ-event out of a perception of the supersensible world that extended to Intuition ... Hence with regard to the Christ-event we can call the author of St John's Gospel the herald of what is perceived by a man who is possessed of the "inner word" to the level of Intuition. Thus the author of the Gospel of St John essentially speaks in such a way that he characterizes the mysteries of Christ's Kingdom as being endowed with the inner Word, or Logos. An inspired intuitive knowledge lies at the foundation of the Gospel of St John.'[28]

We can now sum up all that has been said in the following words. There are three births in the cycle of the year—of the Moon, the Sun, and of Saturn (or of the stars), corresponding to the festivals of Christmas, Epiphany and Easter. From the standpoint of a modern initiate, this thought could also be expressed as follows:[29] in order truly to understand the festival of Christmas, one needs *to be born* in one's consciousness in the sphere of Imagination; in order to understand the festival of Epiphany, one needs *to be born* in the sphere of Inspiration; while for an understanding of the Mystery of Golgotha itself the requirement is *birth* in the sphere of Intuition.[30] '*At all stages* of supersensible knowledge we encounter the great secrets which are connected with that event which we refer to as the manifestation of the Christ; thus imaginative knowledge, inspirative and intuitive knowledge tell us much, infinitely much, about the deeds of Christ.'[31]

In conclusion, we shall return once more to the autumnal festival of Michael and consider one of its qualities which distinguishes it in a fundamental way from all the other yearly festivals. While the other six festivals, in their Christian form, have existed within humanity for almost two thousand years and were merely renewed through anthroposophically orientated spiritual science, the festival of Michael was actually *founded* for the first time in the twentieth century* and added *as a new Christian festival* to the others, thus enabling them to arise as a completed whole in the cycle of the year, a totality which finds esoteric expression in the number *seven*.

Rudolf Steiner speaks thus about the establishing of this new Christian festival, the festival of Michael: 'But when, if people will again come to

---

* It was founded in 1923, forty-four years after the beginning of the new rulership of Michael among mankind.

understand the festivals which today they celebrate without really understanding them, they will have the strength to establish, out of a spiritual understanding of the year's course, a festival which has a real significance only for modern man ... If in our time people were to resolve in a worthy way to establish a festival of Michael at the end of September, this would be a deed of great significance. For this the courage must be found not merely to discuss external social arrangements and the like, but to accomplish something *which unites the Earth with the Heavens, which again unites earthly circumstances with heavenly circumstances.* Then indeed, as the spirit would thereby be drawn into earthly affairs, something could come about among people which would represent a mighty impulse for the further advance of our civilization and our entire life. There is insufficient time to present to you a picture of what this would mean for all scientific, artistic and religious ideals—as was the case for the older festivals—to establish such a *new festival* on a grand scale out of the spirit, and to what extent this creativity arising out of the spiritual world would be more important than all manner of gimmicks in the social field.'[32] For '... then not merely a human will but the will of Gods and the will of the Spirit would be revealed through the forming of such a festival. Then would the Spirit again be present among people! ... Then we shall not merely think about the meaning of the old festivals, but we shall ourselves become socially creative through being able to create festivals out of the yearly cycle.'[33] This, of course, demands more from people than merely elucidating the festivals that were established in the past. But this, too, is real Anthroposophy, *a higher Anthroposophy.*'[34]

As we have already seen from our study of the nature of the Michael festival in the earlier chapters of the present work, this festival corresponds to the first stage of the modern Christian-Rosicrucian path of initiation. In *Occult Science* Rudolf Steiner defines this stage as 'the study of spiritual science, in the course of which man employs in the first instance the faculty of judgement which has been acquired in the physical world of the senses'.[35] In the last foreword to the book, written on 10 January 1925, he adds: 'I quite consciously refrained from giving a "popular" account but wrote in such a way that necessarily demands a true *exertion of one's thinking* in order to enter into the content. By this means I endowed my books with a character such that the reading of them is already the beginning of spiritual training.'[36] In a certain sense the Michaelmas festival also has this particular quality. For although it is established out of the Spirit, it is nevertheless to a large extent accessible to purely human understanding. And as it is being established in an age when an overwhelming majority of people do *not* as yet possess clairvoyant powers but, at most, forces of thinking, it is directed out of the spirit of the time not so much towards a clairvoyant experience of the spiritual as towards an 'experience of the spiritual through thinking alone'.

In a lecture given in Vienna on the eve of Michaelmas day 1923, Rudolf Steiner speaks of this as follows: 'In this way we may indicate what must appear in man if the Michael-*thought* is to become alive again. Man really must be able to have an experience of the spiritual. He must attain this experience of the spiritual not, initially, out of some sort of clairvoyance *but out of thoughts alone*. It would be a bad thing if everyone had to become clairvoyant in order to have this confidence in the Spirit. This confidence in the Spirit can be had by everyone who is at all *receptive* to the teachings of spiritual science.'[37] It is for this reason that (as has been said) the study of what has been imparted by spiritual science forms the beginning of the modern path of initiation, which is today, as the Christian-Rosicrucian path, pre-eminently an *initiation of the will*, which is to say, it demands in the first instance a real inner *courage* if it is to be rightly followed.

There are at present two principal obstacles which hinder modern man from embarking upon this path, 'two evils which must be overcome within the Anthroposophical Society. One is the *fear of the supersensible* . . . That is one aspect. The other aspect is—for all the many manifestations of will, which are for the most part really only a form of camouflage—*weakness of will*, the inner paralysis of the will of contemporary humanity.'[38] It follows from this that the *very first* thing modern man needs to do in order to embark upon the path of initiation, corresponding to the spirit of the age, is to overcome these two evils, without whose conquest spiritual development is altogether impossible. As a means of helping modern man in this inner struggle and, hence, of enabling him to embark upon a path of true spiritual training, the autumnal Michael festival was established in our time as a gateway to, and also as the first stage of, modern initiation.

In this connection we shall cite two observations of Rudolf Steiner, already quoted in part, which characterize the Michael festival, the Michael-thought, in the manner indicated. Thus in the lecture of 1 April 1923 he says: 'In the festival-thought of the autumn equinox, the soul must feel its own strength, appealing not to its faculty of perception but to its will: take up into yourself the Michael-thought that can conquer the ahrimanic forces, that thought which gives you the power to acquire spirit-knowledge here on Earth in order that you can overcome the forces of death . . . Thus does this thought relate to the will-forces: to take hold of Michael's power is to take hold of the power of spiritual knowledge with the forces of one's will.'[39] While in the lecture of 8 April in the same year we read: 'But what comes especially into consideration in the festival of Michael is that there needs to be a festival in honour of human courage, of the human manifestation of the courage of Michael. For what is it that now

267

holds people back from spirit-knowledge? Lack of soul courage, if not to say soul cowardice . . . This inner courage must find its festival in the festival of Michaelmas. Then from this festival of courage, from this festival of the inwardly courageous human soul, there will ray forth *something which will also give true content to the other festive periods of the year.*'[40]

This concluding thought can also be expressed in the following words: if the Michaelmas festival, which was established in our time simultaneously with the new Christian initiation,[41] is celebrated in the right way, if it really becomes the gateway which leads modern man on to the path of inner development because it is passed through as the first stage of this path, then the *whole* of the yearly cycle will be revealed as the great sevenfold path of initiation which was born from Michael's inspiration. The individual stages of this path can be related to the principal Christian festivals as follows:

1. The study of spiritual science, in the course of which man employs in the first instance a faculty of judgement that has been acquired in the physical world of the senses—Michaelmas
2. The attainment of imaginative consciousness—Christmas
3. The reading of the occult script (corresponding to Inspiration)— Epiphany[42]
4. Working upon the stone of wisdom (corresponding to Intuition)[43]— Easter
5. Knowledge of the relationships between microcosm and macrocosm— Ascension
6. Becoming one with the macrocosm—Whitsun
7. Divine bliss—St John's Day

It should be observed in connection with these relationships that they are in the first instance an indication of those stages of the path of initiation which must be reached if the corresponding festivals are to be inwardly understood. As man now lives in the epoch of freedom, which is at the same time that of the greatest degree of separation from the laws of the macrocosm, it is not absolutely necessary that in the process of higher development all the stages are passed through strictly one after the other, that is, as they are placed in the cycle of the year. It is in this sense that we should understand the following words of Rudolf Steiner: 'But these stages should not necessarily be thought of in such a way that man passes through them successively one after the other. On the contrary, training can proceed in such a way that, depending on the individual character of the pupil, an earlier stage may have been passed through only in part when he begins to undertake exercises corresponding to the next stage. It may, for example, sometimes be perfectly right that once he has had but a few genuine imaginations the pupil begins at the same time to undertake exercises which bring Inspiration, Intuition or a knowledge of the connection between microcosm and macrocosm into the sphere of his experience.'[44]

On the other hand, although certain of these stages can indeed be passed through 'only in part' in the course of inner development, it is nevertheless so that there is not one stage that can be omitted altogether.[45] In this sense we can speak in connection with the cycle of the year about an *organism of initiation*, which while indeed being completely mobile is nonetheless a self-contained whole. For *knowledge* of the respective festivals it is a matter of having a strict relationship to the course of the year. For a path of initiation through the yearly rhythm—as with all that has been discussed in the present work—there is a need for considerable mobility; it is a question of *the most suitable periods of the year* for passing through particular stages of the modern path of initiation. For instance, the most suitable time for Preparation, Enlightenment and even the first elements of initiation is the period from the summer solstice until Christmas. While the time that is most suitable for imaginative, inspirative and intuitive knowledge is the period from Christmas until Easter, or in a wider sense the entire half-year from Christmas until the summer solstice—although this does not rule out the possibility that the spirit-pupil, at the stage of Enlightenment and, even more, in connection with the first experiences of initiation, may also attain certain imaginations during the other half of the year. Thus what has been indicated here are only the *objective* spiritual laws working in the cycle of the year, which, however, should in no sense be employed in a dogmatic way.

There is, finally, one further question: why does it become necessary to make a connection between the modern path of initiation and the cycle of the year? At this point we must turn once more to the inner life of the human soul. This life of soul, in so far as its course flows in connection with outer nature, is supported by the forces of space and its twelvefold law. If, however, the soul embarks upon a path of inner development, it thereby enters the realm of time, the sphere of moral life, and makes the transition from the law of twelve to the sevenfold path of initiation.[46] For in *the rhythm of seven*, in the rhythm of initiation, there lives in man his spirit, his true ego; Christ Himself lives in him.[47] On the other hand, the outer life of the Earth has from ancient times also run its course according to the twelvefold law of the natural course of the year. Since the Mystery of Golgotha, however, Christ has been united with Earth-existence and has since that time worked as the new Spirit of the Earth. In so doing He brings to the domain of natural law the moral law, the sevenfold law of initiation, which comes to expression in the seven principal Christian festivals forming the spiritual rhythm in which the Spirit of the Earth, its Ego, Christ Himself, lives in the cycle of the year. Thus if the individual, as a pupil of anthroposophically orientated spiritual science, strives in the course of this path of initiation to unite in his inner experience its individual stages with the corresponding festive periods of the year, he is then working in a direct way towards the chief task of Anthroposophy in the modern world, a task which Rudolf Steiner defines in the following words: 'Anthroposophy is a path of *knowledge* which would lead the spiritual in man to the spiritual in the universe.'[48]

XI

THE PATH OF CHRIST AND THE PATH OF MICHAEL IN THE CYCLE OF THE YEAR

1. The New Path of the Shepherds and the New Path of the Magi

Now that we have completed our study of the cycle of the year in relationship to its sevenfold rhythm, which finds expression in the seven principal Christian festivals, let us in conclusion survey the cycle of the year *in its entirety*, paying particular attention to the more general laws which rule therein. As with our previous studies, we can use as a starting point the knowledge that the yearly rhythm of the Earth, *as a living organism*, divides naturally into two life-cycles—in-breathing and out-breathing—which are associated with the two halves of the year: from St John's Day until Christmas, and from Christmas (or, to be more precise, from Epiphany) again to St John's Day, each having its own specific character.

These two phases of the Earth's life-cycle also have a correspondence with two fundamental aspects of the old initiation: the path to the spirit through immersion in one's own inner being, and the path to the spirit through going out into the macrocosm. In ancient times these two aspects of initiation, which have their sources in the Mysteries arising from the southern and northern migratory streams from Atlantis, were kept strictly separate from one another. Only since the appearance on Earth of the Spiritual Sun, the Christ, did the possibility arise for the uniting of both streams in the single all-embracing Christian initiation, which has its foundation in the principal Mystery of Earth-evolution, the Mystery of Golgotha. 'Only in the figure of Christ do the two aspects [of initiation] unite. And only the knowledge of this makes it possible rightly to understand the image of Christ,'[1] says Rudolf Steiner. Furthermore, from the time when Christ became the new Spirit of the Earth, living with the *full cycle of the year* has become our best opportunity for uniting these two paths in a natural way.

We have a prophetic indication of the union of these two streams in the single Christ Mystery in the descriptions in two of the Gospels of the appearance of the Shepherds and the Magi from the East wishing to participate in the twofold Mystery of Christmas. Here, the Shepherds are the representatives of the 'southern stream', whose leading initiate appeared to them in the field in the form of the 'heavenly host', while the Magi from the East are the representatives of the 'northern stream', who had come to pay their respects to the new birth of the greatest initiate of their Mysteries.[2]

According to modern spiritual science, however, the whole character of initiation—as expressed in the images of the Shepherds and the Magi—acquired a completely new direction after the union of the Christ Being with Earth-existence. From this moment the path of the Shepherds consists in finding the way from experiencing the spirit within to experiencing it in the outer world in the macrocosm, while the path of the Magi now amounts, in contrast, to making the transition from experiencing the spirit in the far widths of space to experiencing it in their own inner being.[3] This metamorphosis of both paths, which came about as a consequence of the Mystery of Golgotha, is the result of the Christ Being's entry into Earth-evolution. Thus if we turn again to the cycle of the year, we can say: the one half, from Epiphany until St John's Day, which is connected with the Earth's out-breathing, corresponds in the epoch since the Turning Point of Time to the *new* path of the Shepherds from within outwards; while the other half, from St John's Day until Christmas, connected as it is with the Earth's in-breathing, corresponds to the *new* path of the Magi, which now leads from without inwards.

These observations can be further deepened if we recall that, as is evident from the fourth part of the Foundation Stone Meditation, the Shepherds were more the bearers of the heart-impulse, the impulse of *love*, while the Magi from the East were the bearers of the head-impulse, the impulse of *wisdom*. When the two streams are thus delineated, there is one further aspect elucidating the relationship of the two halves of the year which, according to Rudolf Steiner, can be united with them, namely, that while the one half is associated with the deeds of Christ which establish the kingdom of *freedom and love* on the Earth, the other is related to the realization in human life of world-karma, which comes about through the *wisdom*-filled deeds of the higher Hierarchies. In this sense, Rudolf Steiner characterizes the two halves of the year as follows: 'And there remains the other half of the year [from St John's to Christmas]. If this is also to be understood, the other side of man's life must needs come before one. If one understands the relationship of man's physical nature to the soul and supersensible aspects of his being, that relationship which contains within itself the freedom in which earthly man participates on the Earth, then in the interrelationships between the festival of Christmas, the festival of Easter and the festival of Whitsun one understands *the free human being upon the Earth*. And if one understands this out of these three thoughts, the Christmas-thought, the Easter-thought and the Whitsun-thought, and is thereby enabled to call forth an understanding of the rest of the year, then the other half of human life comes forth, that to which I pointed when I said: *if you look upon human destiny, the Hierarchies appear behind it; the activity, the weaving of the Hierarchies*. Hence it is so wonderful to behold human destiny, because you then see how *all* the Hierarchies stand behind it.'[4]

And so we have in one half of the year, we may say, a memory of the union which the Christ Being, the bearer of *cosmic love*, forged in former times with Earth-existence, whereby the whole of earthly evolution received the impulse towards a new *ascent*. This process of ascent begins at Epiphany and then extends through Easter to Whitsun. Here we also have an affirmation of true *freedom* in the evolution of humanity. For in uniting Himself in this way with human souls, Christ endows them with the impulses of love and freedom, with those impulses which will only in the distant *future*, as the consequences of the whole of human evolution, enable humanity to attain the divine purpose that is set before it—to become the Tenth Hierarchy in the cosmos, the Hierarchy that will act solely out of the purest principles of freedom and love.

During the other half of the year different influences come to the fore,★ namely, those deeds of the higher Hierarchies that govern the karma of the Earth and of man. In this karma is contained the entire *past* of human evolution, and also that world-wisdom which enabled the Earth to become what it is now: a cosmos of wisdom, which will only be transformed into a new cosmos of freedom and love to the extent that humanity becomes the Tenth Hierarchy.[5]

These processes can also be characterized as follows. One half of the year indicates to us the path on which, according to the extent of his development, man, as he becomes ever more and more permeated by the Christ, progresses gradually towards the forming of a new cosmos, and ascending with Christ into ever higher spiritual spheres creatively transforms them out of the principles of freedom and love. Of this *future* we have a prophetic indication in the annual ascent of the Christ Being, as the new Spirit of the Earth, together with the Soul of the Earth into the cosmic distances, into the far widths of the macrocosm, which He reaches at the time of St John's Day, revealing at that moment to the initiate the cosmic religion of the Gods, their cosmic purpose—the most sublime ideal of humanity, the Mystery of the Tenth Hierarchy. Thus the season of St John's corresponds in the rhythm of the year also to the goal of the *new* path of the Shepherds, which Rudolf Steiner characterizes in these words: 'Then will the growing plants, the rushing river, the murmuring stream, the lightning and thunder from the clouds, not merely speak to us in an indifferent way; rather from all that the flowers speak, from all that the radiant stars and the shining Sun speak, as the result of every observation of nature, there will stream into

---

★ For one can never say that these influences completely disappear. One rather speaks simply of the *predominant* effect of one or the other influence during particular times of year.

our eyes, into our ears, into our hearts, words which proclaim nothing else than this: God reveals Himself in the heavenly heights, and peace must reign among men on Earth, among men who are of good will.'[6]

In contrast, the other half of the year shows us an image of the cosmos becoming man, that is, an image of the whole of evolution hitherto, which during the thirteen Holy Christmas Nights reveals to the initiate with particular intensity the fundamental mystery of *world-evolution*, the mystery of the whole hierarchic cosmos as the great Anthropos, the universal 'Adam Cadmon', the fullness of whose forces were brought into Earth-existence through their being united with the Christ Being. The gradual approach of the Christ Being during this period of the year from the cosmic distances to the Earth, which is a repetition in the rhythm of the year of the path formerly traversed by Him from the widths of space to incarnation in a human body so as to pass through the Mystery of Golgotha, is also an indication of this profound mystery of the *past of our cosmos*. In this sense the season of Christmas also corresponds to the goal of the *new* path of the Magi, which Rudolf Steiner defines in these words: '... we must be in a position to bring forth an astronomy, a solution to the world-riddle *that proceeds from out of man's inner nature* through Imagination, Inspiration and Intuition. A spiritual, or occult, science which is created out of man's inner nature must arise for us. We must examine what constitutes man's true nature. *And man's true nature must speak to us of the world's becoming* through the Mysteries of Saturn, Sun, Moon, Earth, Jupiter, Venus and Vulcan. We must feel the arising of a whole cosmos within us.'[7]

Both these processes, which together encompass the *entire* cycle of the year, may best be expressed in the words of the following meditative formulation of Rudolf Steiner:

> If you want to know yourself,
> Behold the world that lies around.
> If you want to know the world,
> It is your own soul you must sound.[8]

2. The Working of the Forces of Lucifer and Ahriman in the Cycle of the Year

The two principal paths into the spiritual world that we have examined in the previous chapter also reveal the different character of those temptations through which the spirit-pupil must pass who wishes, in the sense of modern initiation, to achieve the union of those paths through an esoteric experience of the cycle of the year. For the working of the opposing forces of Lucifer and Ahriman is also of a different nature on the *new* paths of the Magi and the Shepherds or, similarly, in the two halves of the yearly cycle.

Thus in the period from St John's Day until Christmas it is more the forces of Lucifer that work within man, enabling Ahriman to hold sway in the outer world, from which he will then strive fully to eradicate all forces of *love* and instead to strengthen on the Earth only the powers of darkness, hatred and death. This struggle of Ahriman for rulership over the Earth at this time of year is expressed in outer nature in the gradual transition from summer through autumn to winter. Ahriman strives in this season to establish his authority over the Earth forever by trying to prevent Christ—who, as the new Spirit of the Earth, leaves it in the summer to accompany the Soul of the Earth on its journey into the macrocosm—from reuniting Himself with the Earth. In other words Ahriman strives at this time of year, with all the means available to him, to prevent the coming of Christmas, the entry of Christ, the bearer of the Sun of love, into the darkness of Earth-existence. At this point, however, Michael, the Countenance of Christ, advances against the forces of Ahriman, cleansing the Earth in autumn from the ahrimanic spirits, so that Christ may again be born without hindrance at Christmas. Rudolf Steiner speaks of this as follows: 'Before the yearly cycle is ended and December comes, which is when it is possible for the Christ-impulse to be born in the ensouled Earth, the Earth must through a spiritual power be purified from the dragon, from the ahrimanic forces.'[9] Only he rightly understands the significance of this half of the year who can say: 'Michael has purified the Earth so that at Christmas-time the birth of the Christ-impulse might come about in the right way.'[10] Thus Michael helps the human soul at this season to overcome the forces of Ahriman working from without in order that, without losing hope amidst all the forces of hatred and death, it may nevertheless be able to find the path to Christmas, to the Sun of love burning in the darkness and cold of winter's night.

But Michael does not only help man at this time of year in his battle against Ahriman. He also helps him in his inner battle against Lucifer. For, working in the human soul, Lucifer tries to confuse man through all possible kinds of illusions with regard to his own inner nature in order ultimately to prevent him from achieving true *self-knowledge* (founded as it is always upon a true knowledge of his past), which in the course of rightful development will come objectively before the spirit-pupil in the period around Christmas in the form of the lesser Guardian of the Threshold. Here too (as has been said), Michael comes to the aid of the human soul: for 'the manner in which Michael brings the past to manifestation in human life in the present is in complete correspondence with the right spiritual progress of the world and has nothing luciferic about it.'[11] Through thus bringing the past into the present in an objectively right way, Michael strengthens the impulse of wisdom within man which then enables him—with the help of this wisdom—to catch, in the death that seemingly surrounds him everywhere from without, a breath of the approaching cosmic love, the breath of the Christ Being entering Earth-existence.

The activity of the forces of opposition during the other half of the year, from Epiphany until St John's Day, comes to manifestation in a different way. Now it is the forces of Ahriman that penetrate into man's inner nature, arousing in him various kinds of illusion with regard to the pos-sibility of having knowledge about the outer world—awakening in him an inclination towards a materialism that is either openly evident or con-cealed, or inwardly nurturing thoughts and feelings that are incapable of approaching anything spiritual—in short, trying as hard as possible to make man's inner world like the natural world that surrounds him. All this is necessary for the ahrimanic powers in order that they might prevent man from gaining a true *knowledge of the world*, a knowledge of the macrocosm, at whose gates the meeting with the greater Guardian—that being who also reveals to him the secrets of the future—awaits the spirit-pupil at the time around Epiphany. The ahrimanic powers are especially directed against this *true* knowledge of the impulses of the future. Here, however, the Christ-impulse comes to man's aid. For 'Christ bears within Himself the future impulses of humanity in a cosmically just way.'[12] Hence 'rightly forming a connection with Christ means also rightly defending oneself against the influences of Ahriman'.[13]

While at this time of year Ahriman threatens man's inner nature, Lucifer strives all the more forcefully to extend his authority over outer nature. Working in the forces of the growth and flowering of plants, in the glory of summer's starry sky, he tries to call forth in man the illusion that only natural laws foreign to the spirit exist in the world, in order thus to deprive him of the true *wisdom* that is capable of approaching an understanding of the spiritual-moral principles in the world that surrounds him. For, in Rudolf Steiner's words, 'with Lucifer all interest is focused upon isolating the moral element as such—which being ever present has great significance because it works as a seed for world-creativity in the future—from one's picture of the world and allowing only natural necessity to appear in this world-picture. Thus before the impoverished human being of modern times there is presented a world-wisdom which at the same time offers a picture of the world where the stars move according to an amoral, purely mechanical necessity, where the stars move in such a way that we cannot associate any of the moral meaning of the world's order with their movements. This is a purely luciferic picture of the world [for the world-wisdom contained in it has been completely distorted].'[14]

However, through receiving the Christ-impulse into himself at Christmas (Epiphany) and becoming inwardly strengthened through the experience of Easter, man can fill himself with the forces of cosmic love. With this power he is able to confront the amoral, and hence profoundly false, luciferic picture of the world. And then, once penetrated by the love of Christ, this false picture of the world can again be filled with the moral forces that are able to overcome the power of Lucifer and thus manifest the archetypal divine wisdom inherent in the world *in its true aspect*.

In this way it becomes clear that the opposing powers of Lucifer and Ahriman are in the end, in their ceaseless interaction throughout the yearly cycle, striving to attain similar goals: to seduce man during one half of the year in such a way that he cannot recognize the presence of love in the world, and during the other half, the presence of wisdom.

3. The Quest for Isis-Sophia and the Quest for Christ

We know from various communications of spiritual science that the principles of love and wisdom in our cosmos are personified in two beings: love in the being of Christ, and wisdom in the being of Sophia. Hence one can formulate the two dangers which threaten man in the yearly cycle from Lucifer and Ahriman also as follows: during the one half of the year (from Epiphany until St John's) man is threatened by the danger of losing his inner connection with the Sophia, while during the other half of the year the danger is that of losing his inner connection with Christ.

In our studies, however, we could also point to those two forces which are capable of helping man in withstanding both these dangers: one is the power of Michael, with which he can unite especially at the time of the Michael festival in the autumn, and the other is the power of Christ, which enters into man at Epiphany and attains its full manifestation through the experience of Easter.[15]

As we have already observed in the previous chapter, in the period from Epiphany until St John's we are concerned, on the one hand, with an ever deeper penetration of the Christ Being into the inner regions of the human soul and, on the other hand—on account of the influence of the opposing powers—with the gradual loss of the old natural wisdom, of the capacity of beholding the spiritual-moral forces behind the Maya of the outer world. This comes to manifestation with particular clarity in modern astronomy of which Rudolf Steiner says that it is a picture of *the being of the new Isis, the Divine Sophia, killed by Lucifer and carried out into the cosmos.*[16] In this sense his words quoted below can with justification be related to the half of the year that we are now studying: 'It is not the Christ that we lack; the knowledge of Christ, the Isis of Christ, the Sophia of Christ, is what fails us.'[17]

However, the forces that can help us avoid succumbing to this danger and rather enter with all inner activity upon the quest for the new Isis in order to rediscover for oneself the divine wisdom, the Sophia, are given to us in the Mystery of Golgotha, in the festival of Easter. For, through the inner penetration of the human soul into this central event of earthly evolution, the possibility now opens up before *each* human individual of significantly strengthening within himself the Christ-impulse, which enters into his soul at Epiphany, in order that the quest for the new Isis-Sophia might be consciously begun, so as to achieve what Rudolf Steiner characterizes in the following words: 'We must with that *which we do not understand* but which abides in us, the power of Christ, the new power of Osiris, go out into the world and search for the dead body of the modern Isis, the dead body of the Divine Sophia. We must approach luciferic natural science and seek the coffin of Isis; this means that we must find in what natural science gives us something that inwardly stirs us to Imagination, Inspiration and Intuition. For through this we discover within us the help of Christ, who would remain obscure to us, remain in shadow, if we did not illuminate Him with divine wisdom. Armed with this power of Christ, the new Osiris, we must set forth upon the quest for Isis, the new Isis.'[18] For finding in this sense the new Isis, the Divine Sophia, we need to embark upon the new path of the Shepherds in order that, imbued with the Christ-impulse, the impulse of cosmic love, we may open ourselves up to the outer knowledge of nature that comes towards us. For 'we must become as pious *in our relationship to nature* as the Shepherds were in their hearts.'[19]

Only such a search full of a real inner self-surrender for the new Isis, the Divine Sophia, can—if the Christ-impulse has become sufficiently alive in the human soul—lead to a true experience of the festival of Whitsun, the festival of the descent of the Holy Spirit, which testifies to man's acquiring of a relationship to the new cosmic *wisdom*, the new Sophia of Christ. And with this newly won relationship with the Sophia, which has been found through the outward contemplation of nature (and also modern natural science) being inspired and permeated by the forces of the heart, man can, as he progresses onwards in the rhythm of the year, make the transition to its other half, to that half where a second danger threatens him—that of inwardly losing the Christ-impulse. This second danger arises in the cycle of the year because, in the period of St John's-tide, Christ, as the new Spirit of the Earth, abides with the Soul of the Earth *outside* its physical body, an opportunity which the opposing powers try ever and again to make use of in order to prevent Him from finding the way from the cosmos into the earthly sphere, which is to say into human souls. If this is not to happen, man must at this time of year embark, out of his own initiative, upon the quest for Christ in Earth-existence. And that power which can help him in this is the power of the Sophia, of the divine wisdom of Christ, which he has gained at Whitsun.

Rudolf Steiner tells us in the following words of the necessity for such a quest for Christ with the help of the Sophia-forces, a quest which must find its completion at Christmas-time: 'The new man must also learn to understand the Christmas Mystery in a new sense. He must understand that he must *first* find Isis [the Sophia] if the Christ is to be able to appear to him.'[20] And somewhat earlier in the same lecture Rudolf Steiner formulates this thought in this way: 'Then in this capacity to see into the universe, the power of Isis [which is now the power of the Divine Sophia] will again be found and, with the help of this newly acquired power of Isis [acquired during the period of the Earth's out-breathing], Christ [who since the Mystery of Golgotha has been united with Earth-existence] also attains a right influence within human beings, because they shall truly know Him.'[21] Here we are really entering upon the *new* path of the Magi, on which we need to permeate ourselves with the Sophia-impulse, the impulse of cosmic wisdom, and so enter into our own inner nature, in order at Christmas-time to be able again to receive Christ into our souls. For 'we must become as wise in our *inner* contemplation as the Magi became in observing the planets and stars in space and time.'[22]

If, however, man is to acquire such a new and fully *conscious* relationship to the Christ Being at Christmas, he needs a certain measure of help.[23] For just as in the ascending half of the year, in his quest for Isis-Sophia, he was in need of the strengthening power of the Christ-impulse that entered his soul at Epiphany, and whose source was Easter, so now, upon entering consciously upon the new quest for the Christ Being with the help of the forces of the Sophia, the cosmic wisdom, he stands in need of the strengthening power of this wisdom within himself—and the source of this is the autumnal festival of Michael.

Thus in Easter we have a festival which strengthens the Christ-impulse, the impulse of cosmic love, within us to such an extent that we can with its help rediscover the Divine Sophia in our experience of Whitsun. This is the Christ-path, which leads us from death to resurrection, *from Christ to the Sophia* (to the spirit).

In Michaelmas, however, we have a festival which is capable of strengthening in us the Sophia-impulse—the impulse of cosmic wisdom[24] that we received at Whitsun—to such an extent that by Christmas we are able to find Christ again in our inner being. This is the path which leads us from resurrection in the spirit to a right encounter with the death-forces in nature, behind whose threshold we can, with the power of the Sophia, again find the Christ. This is the path *from the Sophia to the Christ*, this is the path of Michael. Hence the fact that Michael is the cosmic Spirit who is especially able to strengthen in us the Sophia-forces, the forces of cosmic wisdom, is not fortuitous. For since ancient times he has worked in the universe as the great ruler of the cosmic Intelligence, the divine thoughts of the Hierarchies which form the radiant garment of the heavenly Sophia. It was on account of this connection between the Sophia and Michael in the Mysteries of Ancient Chaldea and, in the still more distant past, in the Mysteries of Ancient Persia that Marduk-Michael was everywhere worshipped as the *Son* of the all-permeating world-wisdom *Soph-Ea*, Sophia.[25]

Finally, if we bring together all that we have said about the activity of the two spheres of opposing forces in the yearly cycle, we can say: in one half of the year we have a path that leads from within outwards, the Christ-path, on which the power of Christ overcomes Ahriman within and Lucifer without; while in the other half of the year we have the Michael-path, leading from without inwards, on which the power of Michael overcomes Ahriman without and Lucifer within.

It appears that the festival of St John alone stands outside the yearly cycle, but this is not really the case. For if, *on the basis of what we have now established* we can associate the words *Ex Deo nascimur* with Christmas, *In Christo morimur* with Easter and *Per Spiritum Sanctum reviviscimus* with Michaelmas,[26] this Trinity of the forces of Father, Son and Spirit, raying out from the foundation and from the right and left sides of the great cross of the year, unites at its 'tip' in St John's Day, and so forms in the cosmos at this time of year the sublime imagination of the Holy Trinity.[27]

4. The Cycle of the Year as a Path Leading to a New Experience of the Christ Being

We have arrived at the goal of our studies. Now we may see what a meaningful picture appears before us in the cycle of the year when this is examined from an inward, esoteric standpoint. It contains not only *all seven* stages of the new Christian-Rosicrucian path of initiation but also a mighty image of the interaction of Christ, Sophia and Michael. Starting at Christmas, from the birth of the Christ-impulse in Earth-existence, the cycle of the year leads us from Christ to the Sophia, to the festival of the coming of the Holy Spirit, and then from the Sophia through the Michael festival back to Christ—though now not to Christ in the aspect in which He entered into earthly evolution at the Turning Point of Time and then finally united with it in the Mystery of Golgotha, but *in a new, supersensible aspect* in which He appears among mankind from the twentieth century onwards.

In the following words Rudolf Steiner, the great herald of the Etheric Christ in the twentieth century, speaks of this in a lecture given in the Goetheanum in Dornach at Christmas 1920: 'We shall only be looking rightly at the manger when we allow what surges there through space to work in a particular way within our feelings and then turn our eyes to that Being who came into the world through the child. We know Him, we bear Him within us, but we must bring our understanding towards Him. And so, *just as an Egyptian looked from Osiris to Isis,* we must learn to behold the new Isis, the Holy Spirit [the path of the ascending half of the year, from Christ, the new Osiris, to the Sophia]. Not only through something entering in from without will Christ appear in His spiritual aspect in the twentieth century, but through *people finding that strength which is given by the Holy Sophia* [this is the path of the other half of the year, from the newly won Sophia to the Christ].'[28]

These thoughts can be taken further if we consider certain indications given by Rudolf Steiner in a lecture of 20 February 1917 and to which we have already referred in the chapter entitled 'The Uniting of the World-Impulses of Wisdom and Love in the Experience of Christ'. From this lecture, which speaks of the three meetings of the human soul with the cosmic principles of the Father, the Son and the Spirit, the connection of the principle of the Son (Christ) with the cycle of the year comes before us with particular clarity. We shall now examine this relationship in greater

284

detail. Rudolf Steiner speaks of this as follows: 'Hence the second meeting is connected more with the great macrocosmic order. This second meeting is connected with the course of the year in the same way that the first is with the course of the day.' Then Rudolf Steiner refers to how, during the descending half of the year (autumn and winter) and especially in the time just before Christmas, all outward sense-impressions gradually withdraw, and how there arises in the soul an ever-growing longing to behold the spiritual sources of all that is physically visible: 'Then man has in a certain sense an experience of a realm where the spirit comes near to him. And *the consequence of this* is that at around Christmas-time, approximately at the time of our modern New Year, man experiences ... a meeting of his astral body with the Life Spirit ... And upon this meeting with the Life Spirit depends his nearness to Christ-Jesus ... Hence through this meeting, in its relationship to modern evolution from the Mystery of Golgotha onwards, we draw near to Christ in a quite special way, so that we may also call the meeting with the Life Spirit a meeting with Christ *in the deepest foundations of our soul* ... Now if man deepens and inspires his feeling-life[29] ... he ... experiences the *after-effects* of the meeting with the Life Spirit, or, as one could also say, with Christ. And it is indeed the case that *during the time that follows this Christmas-period and extends until Easter we have particularly favourable conditions for bringing man's meeting with Christ-Jesus to consciousness.'

And then, turning to the nature of the time of Easter, Rudolf Steiner concludes his description of this process with these words: 'And the great Mystery, the Mystery of Good Friday which unfolds the Mystery of Golgotha before man at this Easter season, signifies—among many other things—*that Christ, who has, so to speak, been walking beside us during the time that I have described* [that is, from Christmas until Easter], *now comes particularly close to us, or to put it rather crudely, disappears into us, permeates us in such a way that He can remain with us for the time that follows the Mystery of Golgotha*, for what now comes as the season of summer, during which in the ancient Mysteries human beings aspired at St John's-tide to union with the macrocosm, though in a manner different from what would have been the case after the Mystery of Golgotha.'[30]

In these words of Rudolf Steiner we can with full clarity distinguish a *threefold* division in the cycle of the year. First, there is the yearning that grows within man during autumn and winter to behold the spiritual sources of the physical world of the senses. This yearning is called forth by the fact that at this time of year the Earth's natural surroundings manifest to him a picture of the gradual dying of all that is physically perceptible. Man feels himself to be abandoned by outer nature and has a strong experience of solitude which, in turn, strengthens his wish to return to his spiritual home whence in ancient times he descended into this land of death: 'He

[man] is separated [at this time of year] from his own spiritual surroundings—from himself and from the Earth—and is more connected with the spiritual world, with the whole spiritual environment.'[31] However, this spiritual ground or spiritual world which lies directly *behind* man's natural surroundings has since ancient times been known to all peoples as the primordial Kingdom of the Father-God. 'These peoples,' says Rudolf Steiner, 'have felt, at any rate in their teachings of wisdom, that the cosmos is wholly permeated by divine powers and that this divine element must necessarily be distinguished from what exists on the Earth, in the physical world that lies around us.'[32] Christ also speaks of this to His disciples after His Resurrection from the dead: 'In so far as you behold the Earth and the cosmos that surrounds it, it is the Father who permeates this universe with life. The Father-God is the God of space.'[33] Hence we may say: it is this descending half of the year, which also presents to us a picture of the whole of human evolution before the Mystery of Golgotha, that reveals to us the Kingdom of the sole Father of all being, the domain of the primordial spirituality that creates and sustains the entire physical world of the senses. And if man has at this time of year more or less unconsciously the yearning to return to the sphere of the Father, the initiate can use this period of the yearly cycle for consciously uniting with this sphere and for penetrating more deeply into its secrets.

This process of development culminates at Christmas-time in the experience of the spiritual meeting with the Christ as Son-principle. This meeting first occurs only 'in the deepest depths of the soul', and only later, in the time until Easter, 'is made conscious' by the human soul, which then learns first to feel and thereafter to behold Christ as a Being who thenceforth 'walks *beside* it'. Now it is that man fully abides in the domain of the Son, and this spiritual existence beside Christ forms the second element in the cycle of the year.

The third element comes into its own at Easter. At this season, according to Rudolf Steiner, Christ 'comes particularly close to us', and then 'disappears into us', 'permeates us'. This direct entry of the Christ Being into the human soul is, however, possible in our time only through the mediation of the impulse of the Holy Spirit. For if Christ were to enter into man's inner being without the Spirit's mediation, the consequence for the individual human ego would be its complete extinction, in that in the present cycle of evolution there is not a single earthly ego that could endure the direct presence of the Christ Being within it.[34] 'Thus the Holy Spirit is indeed he whom Christ was to send in order that man might preserve his ego-consciousness and that Christ might dwell within man without his being aware of it.'[35] Thus at this third stage we have a process which begins at Easter and reaches its conclusion at Whitsun, when every year there can be repeated what occurred for the first time at the Turning Point of Time—when the Christ-impulse, after it 'had [inasmuch as it was manifested in outward visible sheaths] disappeared into the undivided totality of the spiritual world at the Ascension, emerged again after ten days *from the hearts* of the particular individualities of those who first understood it [the Apostles]'.[36] That is the moment when a new spiritual consciousness awakens within man, a consciousness of which Rudolf Steiner says in another lecture: 'The power of the Spirit who thus enters into people's bodies opens up their spiritual eyes in order that they may see and understand the spiritual worlds,' that 'in the physical body, too, the best forces of the soul, which have the capacity of beholding the spiritual worlds, may become ever more and more awakened.'[37]

Rudolf Steiner describes in the following words what is then gradually revealed to man: 'If, however, we allow Christ to accompany us, if we bear our dead thoughts in company with Christ into the world of the stars, into the world of Sun and Moon, clouds, mountains, minerals, plants and animals, if we bear them into the physical world of human beings, everything becomes alive as one beholds the natural world, and then, as from a grave, there arises from all the beings of nature the living, healing Spirit, the Holy Spirit, that awakens us from death.'[38]

This process does not, however, cease there. For the union of the Christ Being with man continues on, in the cycle of the year, until St John's Day, the consequence of which is the gradual and—in contrast to the ancient Mysteries—fully conscious growth of man into the macrocosm. And that which in such a case can become accessible to man will—among much else—be an experience of Earth-existence reaching right back to Old Saturn, whose last natural reflection is the warmth of summer that surrounds the Earth at St John's-tide like an enveloping sheath. This inner condition that Rudolf Steiner in a lecture of 31 October 1911 initially defines as a perception 'of the power of the Holy Spirit in the world ... through whom man can comprehend the spiritual world directly from spiritual impressions', he then describes as follows: 'What man can at first only imagine becomes a present reality in clairvoyance. Imagine that you are immersed in the sea, though now as a spiritual being *who feels himself at one with the Christ Being*, borne by the Christ Being, and you swim, though now not in a sea of water but in a sea of ... flowing courage, flowing energy, that fills the infinity of space.'[39] In these few words we have one example of what a Christian initiate of modern times (in this case Rudolf Steiner) can experience when Christ 'comes close' to him and 'permeates' him through the mediation of the Holy Spirit.[40] But what is revealed to the initiate when thus contemplating Old Saturn concerns not only the distant past of our Earth but also its most immediate present. For '... if we search for what still remains of the forces which ... were natural forces in the evolution of Old Saturn, we must turn to the laws of our personal karma ... And if we try to bring [our] personal karma into a relationship with the constellations which relate to the *signs of the zodiac,* we are living more or less in that sphere of world-observation which would have been adapted to the laws of the ancient epoch of Saturn.'[41]

We may now understand the meaning of the words quoted on p.285 regarding the ascent in the period of St John's-tide into the far reaches of the macrocosm. For only through rising to the world of the fixed stars and experiencing there the 'purely spiritualized'[42] existence of Old Saturn can the modern initiate approach a direct understanding of the law of karma, the law of human destiny. And it is this that is revealed to him at St John's-tide when, 'feeling himself at one with the Christ Being', he ascends into the sphere of the fixed stars, where ... 'Christ becomes our Guide ... through the intricate events of the zodiacal circle.'[43] Then does the new Holy Spirit, streaming into his soul, reveal to the initiate an all-embracing picture of the working of world-karma.[44]

And so we have, summarizing what has been said so far, initially the following three stages in the cycle of the year:

1. The time from St John's until Christmas. The ever-growing longing of man to perceive the spiritual world lying immediately behind the physical world of the senses. Man receives the impulse for union with the realm of the Father. (For the initiate this longing is transformed into an actual contemplation of this sphere.)
2. The time from Christmas until Easter. Man's entry into the realm of the Son. The experience of the Christ Being 'walking beside' one.
3. The time from Easter until St John's. The penetration of the Christ Being into man through the mediation of the Holy Spirit whom He has sent. The contemplation of the working of world-karma.[45]

The modern Christian initiate can experience all these three stages, which have been contained in the yearly cycle since the Mystery of Golgotha, with full consciousness. It is the result of such an experience that forms the content of the lecture of 20 February 1917 quoted above. However, the knowledge regarding the working of the forces of Father, Son and Spirit in the course of the year is remarkably important also for someone who has no more than set forth upon the path of spiritual development in the sense of modern anthroposophically orientated spiritual science, for such knowledge can prepare him in the best possible way for an experience of the Etheric Christ. And at this point we touch upon a deep secret to which Rudolf Steiner once referred when speaking to Friedrich Rittelmeyer, when he told him that the best path leading to a perception of the Etheric Christ is a meditative immersion in, and a spiritual experience of, the cycle of the year.[46]

If, as has been the case in the pages of this book, we take autumn as the beginning of the yearly cycle, this season can by its very character also be seen as especially suitable for an intensive study of anthroposophical spiritual science. This study would have to be carried out in such a way that by the time of Christmas one principal theme, that of *Christology*, would, as though out of itself, come to the fore. The following period, approximately from Christmas until Easter, would then be devoted to this particular study, and in the course of this time there would arise in all intensity the consciousness and the feeling that modern spiritual science has as its task principally that of 'letting flow into what is humanly comprehensible all that streams from the spiritual worlds through Christ'.[47] Only if this feeling has gripped the soul with full force can the student take the next step of becoming a real pupil of spiritual science and embark upon working with the occult exercises as have been given in the various works of Rudolf Steiner. These exercises are especially effective in the period from Easter through Whitsun and until St John's.[48]

If we now relate these three stages to the course of the year, we can also experience in them the threefold working of the spiritual forces that give it form:

The study of Anthroposophy   — Forces of the Father
Christology (relationship to Christ in thought) — Forces of the Son
Occult praxis (meditation)   — Forces of the Spirit

With this the following can come about. If the second of these stages is—during the period from Christmas until Easter—passed through with such intensity that the experience of the Christ Being in thought does not remain a mere dry intellectual theory but embraces the *whole* human being, that is, not only his thinking but also his feeling and will, the Christ-impulse filling such a person (even if for the time being it does so unconsciously) can, in its turn, have an effect upon the entire course of his meditative exercises, or in other words it can strengthen the Spirit-impulse within him. If this happens, if the Spirit-impulse within the meditant is strengthened by the Christ-impulse to such an extent that it can penetrate *beyond* the realm of its original activity, if, that is, it can penetrate *beyond* St John's Day in the course of the year, then, as it begins to permeate the second, descending half of the year, this Spirit-impulse will be able to transform its more or less unconscious striving towards the contemplation of the spiritual world into a real vision of the spiritual facts and beings lying behind the processes and objects of the visible world. Then 'we will feel the living, healing Spirit speaking from all the beings of this world', because 'our knowledge will remain dead ... if we are not awakened by Christ in such a way that from all nature, from the whole of cosmic existence, the Spirit, the living Spirit, again speaks to us'.[49] And this experience will then be none other than the real penetration of the new Christ Being into the world of the Father, into the being of nature. Then in the course of autumn and winter we will, simultaneously with the outward death-process in the natural environment, experience the birth within us of a spiritual awareness that endows us with the faculty of a new etheric clairvoyance in the elemental world, the first glimpse into the all-embracing spiritual domain of the Father.[50]

And if, led onwards by the Spirit-impulse, we are able to make this new world opening up before us our own during autumn and the beginning of winter, the Etheric Christ will be able to approach our inner being at Christmas-time. His gentle form, filling our whole soul-existence with forces of love, life and light, will arise before us as though out of a surging sea of imaginative pictures. And then He will accompany us during the ensuing period from Christmas until Easter and even right up till the time of the Ascension, in order that He may finally unite with us, 'permeate us', and thus give us access to the impulse of the Holy Spirit whom He has sent—the Spirit who reveals to us in direct clairvoyant vision all the karmic consequences of the deeds that we have accomplished, and also our life-tasks that derive from this clairvoyant vision. Thus we can again distinguish three stages corresponding to the second yearly cycle:

The etheric contemplation of the elemental world	— Forces of the Father
The beholding of the Etheric Christ	— Forces of the Son
The clairvoyant perception of the consequences of one's deeds	— Forces of the Spirit

However, this whole process can be carried yet another yearly cycle further. Then the next stage is not merely contemplation of our own karma but includes also the opportunity for the conscious *fulfilment* of its demands. For we should not only perceive what has been revealed to us by the Spirit but also find within ourselves the *will-forces* to make what we have perceived real in our earthly lives. And for this we need the help that can flow forth for us only from the domain of the Father. We have need of a new influx of will-forces from His sphere for the fulfilment of the tasks beheld in the Spirit. This can come about when, as a result of our deep devotion to the Etheric Christ, the Spirit-impulse becomes so strong in us that it leads us in the further course of the year into the sphere of influence of the Father-forces, with whose help we will then be able to find the right path from the spiritual back to the earthly realm.

The further process of development will consist in this, that the fruits of the earthly deeds fulfilled in the manner described are received by the Christ Being into His sphere and are from there introduced into the karmic development of mankind as a whole. For, from our time onwards, Christ's becoming the Lord of Karma signifies that He will rule over the consequences of our karma-balancing deeds in such a way as to bring about the greatest good for the world and for humanity:

> That *good* may become
> What from our Hearts we would found,
> And from our heads direct
> With single purpose.

'To ensure that in future our karmic account may be balanced out, that is, when in the future we have found our way to Christ, it will be so placed into the cosmic order that the process of compensating for our karma may serve the greatest possible good of mankind for the rest of human evolution—this will be the concern of Him who from our time onwards will be the Lord of Karma, this will be the concern of Christ.'[51]

Through this means the Earth's *karmic liberation*, which is necessary for its future transition to the Jupiter-condition, is being gradually prepared during the present Earth-condition. Hence the spiritual path that we have been considering can be pursued yet one stage further, and this would then represent the completion of the *third* yearly cycle and the whole evolutionary process that has been described. This stage consists in that the higher experience of Christ, as Lord of Karma, will again (now for the third time) strengthen in us the Spirit-impulse, which will thereby be enabled to become *spiritually creative* within us. This sublime spiritual impulse, as it becomes manifest in physical existence, will then lay the foundation for the actual *spiritualization of the Earth*, for its becoming a new Sun, through the power of the new *creative Spirit* working within man.

The fulfilment of karma	— Forces of the Father
The introduction of the fruits of individual karma into world karma	— Forces of the Son
The beginning of the spiritualization of the Earth	— Forces of the Spirit.[52]

Thus the cycle of the year is gradually transformed for us into a living, indivisible spiritual whole. Through inwardly experiencing and participating in this in the course of three yearly cycles[53] we may comprehend the threefold transforming activity of the Christ Being, firstly out of the sphere of the Father, then from His own sphere, that of the Son, and finally from the sphere of the Spirit, whereby the first of the three yearly cycles corresponds to the working of the forces of the Trinity in man's 'bodily' nature, the second cycle to their working in his 'soul' nature and the third in his 'spiritual' nature.[54]

Thus a meditative immersion in the esoteric aspect of the cycle of the year becomes for us a real path leading to a new, and direct, experience of the supersensible Christ.

5. The Cycle of the Year as a Social Reality that Unites Human Beings. The Working of the Christ Being in Social Life

There is one further aspect of the cycle of the year that needs to be considered here. This is its significance for the social life of mankind. Rudolf Steiner refers to this when he says: 'Social science ... social ideals ... all these things must be fructified, and they will be fructified by what arises within man as he himself again endows the course of the year with a spiritualizing element. For when, in a certain way parallel to the course of the year, one experiences every year as a reflection of the Mystery of Golgotha, one is in turn inspired with social life, social feeling ... If the cycle of the year generally comes to be experienced in such a way that it is felt to be inwardly connected with the Mystery of Golgotha, a real social feeling will be spread over the Earth as a result of placing human feelings within the context of the cycle of the year and of the secret of the Mystery of Golgotha. Then will be found the true solution or at least the further progress of what is called today ... the social question.'[55]

These words place before us an essential question: in what way can the spiritual content of the yearly cycle, as depicted in the present work, contribute towards the resolution of the most acute problem of modern times, namely, the social problem? The answer arises with full clarity from the fact that in the cycle of the year we are concerned above all with two things: with the sevenfold path of Christian-Rosicrucian initiation and with the seven principal Christian festivals. In the first case it is largely a matter of the spiritual development of the individual, and in the second of the social interaction of many people, which comes to expression in the *common* celebrating of the yearly festivals. For if modern Christian initiation has as its goal the realization of the fundamental formula of the new Mysteries, 'Not I, but Christ in me',[56] then the goal of the socializing impulse of the principal yearly festivals is the fulfilment of the words: 'For where two or three are gathered together in my Name, there am I in the midst of them.'[57]

In such a spiritual union in the yearly rhythm of individual and social impulses we may find that we have a firm foundation and a true path towards the solving of the most urgent social problems of both present and future. In the process of bringing to realization the first formula in modern initiation, despite the significant strengthening of the forces of one's ego-consciousness, one is—if, of course, the spiritual path is being traversed in the right way—very far from becoming shut up in oneself but will, on the contrary, extend one's strengthened ego-consciousness in such a way that, instead of limited, personal interests, it is the interests of the whole of humanity 'in as far as the Christ-impulse is working within it' that are encompassed. On the other hand, as one fulfils the second formula in the shared experience of the festivals, one is united with other people and in a certain sense even with the whole of humanity, though without losing sight of the human individual, for whom one acquires a greater interest. For in the complete sequence of the annual festivals, what comes ever more to the fore is the gradual emergence and activity among mankind of the primordial man-*Anthropos*, so that the fruit of their being rightly celebrated is '. . . the growing together of an experience in and with Christ with an experience of true humanity. "Christ endows me with my humanity"—this is the basic feeling which will permeate the soul.'[58]

One could also say: as we unite ourselves with others in the festival periods of the year, we come to know ever more deeply our own individual being, the primordial Anthropos that lies hidden within us. And on the other hand, as we pursue the modern initiation path, we come increasingly to understand the meaning of the evolution of the Earth and of humanity that dwells upon it.

Here we have the beginning of the arising of the new social ethic of mankind, which not only 'reconciles' the fundamental social antithesis between the individual and society, but in a spiritual sense makes their rhythmical interplay a *true* reflection of the supersensible life of the soul between death and a new birth, that life which flows in constant oscillation between being caught up in itself (which is associated with the strengthening of individual consciousness) and giving itself up to the surrounding spiritual world.[59]

Social and antisocial impulses form a reflection of these two polar conditions of life after death[60] (Rudolf Steiner also characterizes them as impulses of subconscious falling asleep and waking[61]), and their harmonious interaction and gradual transformation in the Christ Spirit is a possible consequence of experiencing the cycle of the year in the manner indicated. For inasmuch as human souls consciously gain access to it, the Christ-impulse working in the yearly cycle leads to a situation whereby the coming together of human beings does not extinguish the individual principle within man but, as is the case during the festive periods of the year, serves to further his social development. On the other hand, the individual principle does not destroy the social, for this is quite out of the question if the modern path of initiation is being rightly followed. Serving as the foundation for such an interaction between the two chief tendencies in social life is one highly important quality of the Christ-impulse; for 'the Christ-impulse can be the same for all humanity and nevertheless a personal affair for every human individual.'[62]

This quality of the Christ-impulse can also be expressed as follows. Christ after the Mystery of Golgotha is both the true ego of the human individual and the higher Ego of all mankind.[63] And these two high ideals are also the goal of the two kinds of spiritual activity that we have described as taking place in the course of the year. Thus on the individual path of initiation man strives towards a conscious experience of Christ in his true ego, while on the path of spiritually living with the yearly festivals he strives in social oneness with other human beings to experience Christ as the higher Ego of all mankind. For 'that which can be born in every human soul as the higher ego is an indication to us of the birth of the divine Ego in the evolution of humanity through the events of Palestine. And as in every individual there is born his higher ego, so in Palestine there is born the higher Ego of all mankind, the divine Ego.'[64]

Thus we may see that living with the cycle of the year in a manner corresponding to the spirit leads to the gradual union of all mankind in one spiritual whole, without in the least degree harming individual human development and—seen from this point of view—at the same time furthering the emergence of that 'immortal individuality' which has already been spoken of in the chapter, 'The Spiritual-scientific Idea of God-manhood and its Reflection in the Apocalypse and in the Gospel of St John.'

There is, however, something else that is connected with this theme. If social impulses really proceed from a spiritual experience of the cycle of the year and of the forces of the Christ Being working within it, they then, in the course of their manifestation among human beings, take on a truly *cultic* character. Arising from the spiritual ground of the yearly cycle, they become the foundation for a real *social religious rite*, a sacrificial ceremony among mankind, as a result of which Christ will gradually be able to enter into humanity in such a way that the deeds and actions of people in social life can be fashioned directly 'at His behest'. And this is the beginning of what one may denote as the true penetration of the world by Christ. Rudolf Steiner speaks of this as follows: 'Who will be the great reformer of social life who will bring it about that the deeds taking place among human beings are at the outset carried out in social life at the behest of Christ, that the world is penetrated by Christ? ... Only the Christ will be such a one as can enable people to have a social life together which *at certain moments of life* becomes a religious rite, where as they look upon Christ they will say not "I" but: "If only two or three or many are gathered in Christ's Name, then Christ dwells among them". Then will social activity become a sacrificial religious rite, it will be the continuation of the old cultic acts. Christ must, if He works in a living way within man's being in our time, Himself become the great social reformer.'[65]

After all that has been said in this chapter, we can with full confidence relate the words '... *at certain moments of life*' above all to the chief festive periods of the year, in the rhythmical experience of which in the yearly cycle we have the best opportunity to work within social life 'at Christ's behest', in order that through our conscious anthroposophical activity we may lay the foundation of the social culture of the future, the social relationships of the sixth cultural epoch, which will be the first precursor of the future Jupiter-condition.[66]

We can, however, examine this final thought in more detail. For the 'social sacrificial religious rite which is the continuation of the old cultic acts' has one further highly important consequence for Earth-evolution as a whole.[67] It is a familiar fact that an essential aspect of any true cultic act is that its spiritual-moral impulses penetrate to the very supersensible foundations of the physically visible world. From an occult point of view this means that the higher spiritual-moral principle is not limited in its transforming activity merely to the soul-spiritual realm but also encompasses and transforms the physical, material principle of the world, thus imprinting upon it moral (spiritual) laws that lie beyond the natural order.

In the cycle of the year this process or transition is manifested through the fact that through celebrating the principal festivals together, we bear into the natural twelvefoldness of the year a new moral order in full consciousness. By this means we bring about the gradual Christianizing of the Earth, its complete dedication to the Christ Being, in order that the Christ Being, who has been connected with it since the time of the Mystery of Golgotha, might fully take possession of it, penetrating and transforming it even to the extent of its physical substances.[68] In this way a new world order is being gradually prepared in the present Earth-condition, for, in Rudolf Steiner's words, 'the moral world order of today is the germinating power of the natural order of the future—that is the most real thought that can possibly exist. The moral sphere is not something that is merely thought out; it exists now, if only it is imbued with reality,[69] as the seed of subsequent external realities.'[70] Then does the Christ receive into His sphere the deeds that we have accomplished in freedom and love through being permeated by the Christ-impulse, and prepares them in such a way that they become the new natural order, the condition of Jupiter, when love and morality will ray forth from the natural world just as there now shines from it the world-wisdom that represents the cosmic consequence of Old Moon.[71]

Thus in the transition from the individual to the social and from the social to the transformed natural world is to be found the principal direction of the activity of the Christ-impulse on Earth. And if we become conscious of this, we then can add to the sayings 'Not I, but Christ in me' and 'There where two or three are gathered together in my Name ...' a third saying, which expresses the most deeply hidden meaning of the cycle of the year and at the same time of the entire evolution of the Earth: 'Heaven and Earth will pass away, but my words will not pass away.'[72] In the sense of the above, this saying of Christ can be understood as follows: 'Heaven and Earth will pass away [that is, the old natural order] but my words will not pass away'—for they will become the foundation of the new natural order on Jupiter.

This latter saying bears a direct connection with the first words of the twenty-first chapter of the Apocalypse: 'Then I saw a new Heaven and a new Earth; for the first Heaven and the first Earth had passed away ...' These are words which proclaim the transition to the new world aeon.[73] But the preparation for this transition begins even in our time. For through anthroposophical participation in the sevenfold cycle of the festivals, where this is fulfilled in the spirit of service to the Christ-impulse, we gradually fashion within us that *spiritual-moral substance* out of which Christ will in future be able to form the new natural foundation for the future aeon of Jupiter.

Thus when the cycle of the year is experienced as a community-building social reality it leads us towards the gradual forming of the Foundation Stone of the New Jerusalem in human hearts and souls.

XII

THE MODERN MYSTERIES OF THE ETHERIC CHRIST

1. The Vidar Mystery

In the previous chapter, which represents in a certain sense the summation of all our studies, we were able to demonstrate the quite special significance of entering in our time into the essential nature of the yearly cycle, revealing as it does a path that leads to a direct experience of the Etheric Christ. It is therefore the case that in our investigations the motif of the new Advent—or Second Coming—arises quite naturally from the principal theme, namely, the esoteric understanding of the cycle of the year, to which the present work is devoted. And this, in turn, enables us at the conclusion of our studies to dwell at greater length upon this fundamental spiritual event that has been taking place from our twentieth century onwards in the supersensible regions lying closest to the physical plane.

From the outset, however, it is necessary to emphasize that this event is really extraordinarily complex. For although the Christ Being occupies the central place in this event we can discern in it also the participation of other beings associated with His sphere of the Sun. Thus, on the basis of what has been imparted by modern spiritual science, we can speak of the participation of the Nathan Soul (see p.174), and also of the ruling Spirit of our age, Michael.* But there is yet a third being in the spiritual world who plays an extremely important part in the new appearance of Christ. And indeed, without his participation this supremely important event of our time would to all intents and purposes not be able to come about. And so before turning to a study of the Mystery of the new appearance of Christ in the etheric we must attempt to lift the veil of the secret that enshrouds this enigmatic being, for without a knowledge of this secret we will never be able to understand either the significance or the role of this being in the new Advent, or, indeed, this new Advent itself.

As the starting-point of what we are about to consider we shall take certain facts from this history (already explored here) of the relationship between the other two beings who also participate directly in the new Christ event: the Archangel Michael and the Nathan Soul. The essence of their relationship, as we have seen, consists in this: in the great sacrificial service of the Nathan Soul to the Christ Being in the spiritual worlds, this soul received help, from the very beginning, from the leading Sun

---

* More will be said about Michael's participation in the new Christ event in the final chapter.

Archangel Michael. For this reason we were able to point to the Archangel Michael as that high Spirit who was a kind of heavenly 'guardian' of the Nathan Soul in that he participated in its three heavenly sacrifices. While during the fourth sacrifice, for the fulfilment of which the Nathan Soul had to incarnate on the Earth itself, it was left fully to its own devices, as the being who was accompanying it, namely, the Archangel Michael, remained above in the sphere of the Sun. However, this inner solitude of the Nathan Soul, his sense of abandonment on the Earth, became the foundation from which people can in future follow him, out of full freedom, to the new Mysteries. With regard, however, to the three future sacrifices of the Nathan Soul in our time and in the course of the sixth and seventh cultural epochs, one may justly ask: *who* is now the *new* 'guardian' in the spiritual worlds of the Nathan Soul, the *new* participator in its supersensible path? Here we must take fully into account that this 'guardian' can no longer be the Archangel Michael, in that, as we know from spiritual science, he had by 1879 fully completed his ascent from the rank of the Archangels to the rank of the Archai or Time Spirits. These, however, have to do not with individual human beings or with individual nations but with humanity as a whole. Thus they work in the world not through the principle of the Life Spirit (the cosmically transformed etheric body), but through the principle of the Spirit Man (the cosmically trans-formed physical body). They acquire the faculty of encompassing the *whole* of man's being, even to the extent of his physical sheath, within their sphere, and of extending in this way their influence over the whole of Earth-existence. On account of this, the Archangel Michael, who works now as the ruling Spirit of our age, was able in the present epoch of his rulership and after the ending (in 1899) of the dark period of the Kali-Yuga to found on Earth the new Christian Mysteries, which have a decisive significance not for any particular individual or human group but for *the whole of humanity*, irrespective of how many people want to know about this.[1] For since the last third of the nineteenth century Michael has, with respect to the world of human beings, been the guardian of the modern path of initiation,[2] the new guide of mankind towards Christ.[3]

We can also observe a significant extension of his spiritual sovereignty with respect to the macrocosm. Henceforth he works therein not only as the 'Countenance of Christ' but also as the new ruler of all the spiritual forces of the Sun. In ancient times the highest ruler of the Sun-realm was the Christ. At the time of the Mystery of Golgotha, however, He aban-doned the region of the Sun and left in His stead Michael, the bearer of His 'countenance', who then almost two thousand years later reached the stage which enabled him to become Christ's fully empowered *representative* on the Sun,[4] that is, the new ruler of the Sun-forces. Rudolf Steiner speaks of this as follows: '... The most important spiritual beings who, so to speak, radiate the spiritual from the Sun, just as sunlight rays forth in a physical or etheric sense, are all grouped around a certain being. According to Christian-pagan, or Christian-Judaeo, terminology, we may designate him as the Michael being. Michael works from the Sun. And what the Sun gives spiritually to the world can also be said to be given by Michael and his hosts to the world.'[5] But once he had attained this high office, Michael was (as we have seen) unable to remain the 'guardian' of the Nathan Soul. For the Nathan Soul is in its inner essence an etheric being, the bearer of the unfallen etheric forces of Adam. As an etheric being, it is inwardly connected more with the forces of the sphere of the Archangels than with those of the Archai, more with the forces of the Life Spirit, the transformed etheric body, than with those of the Spirit Man. It is further connected with the sphere of the Archangels because of its sojourn in their sphere during the Fall and also in the times that followed, when it had been separated from the rest of humanity, which, in succumbing to the luciferic temptation in the sphere of the Angels, then descended into the region that belongs especially to human evolution, the physical material world.[6]

And so there must have been some *other* spiritual being, belonging originally to the Hierarchy of the Angels but having in his evolution already attained the rank of *Archangel*, who from the year 1879 began to fulfil that mission with regard to the Nathan Soul formerly undertaken by the Archangel Michael. Moreover, as is clear from what has just been said, this could not simply be *any* being from the Hierarchy of the Archangels but only such a being who through his ascent to the rank of the Archangels could really *replace* Michael in his office as the leading *Sun* Archangel and 'guardian' of the Nathan Soul. This means that this being from the Hierarchy of the Angels must have surpassed the other beings of this Hierarchy in his spiritual development to the same extent that Michael surpassed the other Archangels, or—setting this in a human context—that Buddha, for example, surpassed other human beings. In other words: one is speaking of a being who, around the year 1879, when Michael had completed his ascent to the rank of Archai and had left his position of *Sun* Archangel vacant, had to occupy this position and hence take upon himself part of the responsibilities of his predecessor.[7] And this meant, on the one hand, that this being could take up the continued 'protection' of the Nathan Soul in the spiritual world, and, on the other, the possibility of directly participating—by virtue of his Archangel-like etheric nature—in the new appearance of Christ in an etheric body, an event that was to begin in the thirtieth year of Michael's period of rulership as the new Time Spirit.[8]

We shall now express the question that appears before us in the words of Rudolf Steiner: 'If an advancement of Michael has come about, if he has become the guiding Spirit of western culture, *who will take his place?* The position must be filled. Everyone must say to himself: hence there must be an Angel who has also experienced elevation or advancement and must enter the ranks of the Archangels. Who is this?'[9] And, having placed this question before us, Rudolf Steiner then, in answer, unfolds before us the secret of this quite special angelic being: 'As long as man dwells on the Earth, however high he may rise, it is always possible to speak (with respect to such a human being) of the individuality who guides him from incarnation to incarnation. The individual guidance of a human being is given over to an Angel, an Angel being. And when a man passes from the stage of Bodhisattva to that of Buddha, then his Angel becomes free. It is therefore such Angel beings who, after the fulfilment of their mission, ascend to the realm of the Archangel beings. *Thus up to a certain point we may gain a real understanding of an Archangel's ascent to the rank of Archai and an Angel being's ascent to the nature of an Archangel* if we can truly understand how we may penetrate ever more deeply into the supersensible evolution that lies behind the evolution of the sense-perceptible world.'[10]

We shall now, on the basis of the above words of Rudolf Steiner regarding the connection of this Angel being with the evolution of the individuality of the future Gautama Buddha, endeavour to trace certain moments in the spiritual activity of the latter. Here one needs to bear in mind that all the deeds which he accomplished had their sources, in the first instance, in the direct inspirations of his Angel.

Thus in describing his deeds, we at the same time touch upon the path of development of this Angel being. We shall begin from the fact—communicated by spiritual science—that in the Hyperborean epoch, at the time of the separation of the Sun from the Earth, the future Gautama Buddha, who was then still at the Bodhisattva stage, did not remain on the Earth with the rest of humanity but was, because of his former evolution, able to follow Christ to the Sun and to remain there until the planet Venus separated from it. This deed was accomplished by him under direct guidance from his Guardian Angel, who even then had a quite particular connection with Christ and with the entire Sun-sphere. Herein also lies the reason why the Gautama-Bodhisattva was, from the Lemurian epoch onwards, able to enter into the evolution of humanity as a forerunner and preparer of the earthly activity of Christ, firstly on the planet Venus (the esoteric Mercury) and then on the Earth, where he accomplished his mission *before* the Mystery of Golgotha and so did not come into contact with the Christ-impulse on the physical plane.[11] All this the Gautama-Bodhisattva owed to his Guardian Angel who, during his early sojourn on the Sun, had taken in the Christ-impulse★ with such remarkable intensity that he was able to fulfil the mission entrusted to him by the Christ,[12] and so ascend to the dignity of Buddhahood some six centuries before the events of Palestine. Such was the activity of the Gautama-Bodhisattva during the Hyperborean and Lemurian epochs. As regards his activity during the Atlantean and post-Atlantean ages, his appearance among the old Germanic peoples under the name of Wotan or Odin at this point requires our foremost attention.

'This individuality of Wotan … this individuality who, indeed, as Wotan, taught in the Mysteries of the Germanic peoples, is the same as he who later appeared on the same mission under the name of Buddha,'[13] says Rudolf Steiner in Stuttgart in the year 1908. And when he returns to this theme once more in Leipzig, he adds the following highly important detail: 'If we know of this phenomenon [the penetration of the astral or etheric bodies of a human being by a higher hierarchic being], we shall no longer think of incarnation in so simple a way. It may be that there is a person who is the reincarnation of a human being who has purified his three bodies to the extent that he is now the vessel for a still higher being. *In such a respect was Buddha a vessel for Wotan.* That being who in the Germanic myths was named Wotan appeared again as Buddha. Buddha and Wotan are even related semantically.'[14] Thus when we speak of the chief divinity of the old Germanic peoples, we may distinguish between the earthly and the heavenly aspects of his nature, between the human bearer and his supersensible inspirer. We have already referred to the former as the individuality of the Gautama-Bodhisattva, while by the latter is meant a mighty being of the Hierarchy of the Archai who has for the sake of the further evolution of mankind made the sacrificial resolve to remain behind at the previous stage of his development and who since that time has worked in the world *as an Archangel.* Rudolf Steiner, in the course of characterizing the soul-condition of the ancient Teuton, refers to this in the following words: 'At first he [the ancient Teuton] beholds archangel beings, who work upon his soul while endowing him with what are to become his soul-forces, and in their midst he finds the greatest of these Archangels, Wotan or Odin … He learns to know him as one of those Archangels who have come to the decision of renouncing their ascent to higher stages. He learns to see in Odin one of the Archangels of abnormal development, one of the great renouncers of ancient times, who have preserved their Archangel nature in taking on the important mission of working upon the human soul.'[15] Only

---

★ Other Angels, who guided the remainder of mankind, were able to take up the Christ-impulse only considerably later, during the time of the third post-Atlantean epoch. See *The Spiritual Guidance of Man,* Chapter 3.

because of this sacrifice was the Archangel Wotan, through the 'earthly Wotan' (that is, the individuality of the Gautama-Bodhisattva) whom he was inspiring, able to endow the souls of the old Germanic peoples with the gift of *speech* and *runic script*,[16] for the impulses for human speech and for the word proceed from the realm of the *Archangels*.[17]

At this point we need briefly to recall the nature of the relationship between a Bodhisattva-being and the two Hierarchies immediately above it, the Angels and the Archangels; for herein lies the principal differences of such a being from other people. If we bring together the various observations of Rudolf Steiner on this theme, the relationship referred to above can be defined as follows. A Bodhisattva is still a human being connected with earthly evolution who is, however, capable of working *in full consciousness* with his Angel upon transforming his astral body into the Spirit Self, while receiving inspirations for this work from a still higher being of the Hierarchy of the Archangels,[18] in this case from an especially mighty Archangel (Wotan) who as regards his inner development actually belongs to the Hierarchy of the Archai.[19] Hence Wotan, who endowed northern humanity with the faculties of speaking and writing, may be called the 'Bearer of speech', the *speaking Archangel*, in contrast to the Angel of the Gautama-Bodhisattva, who may be called the *silent* Spirit, inasmuch as in belonging to the Hierarchy of the Angels he does not have a direct access to the element of language, the word.

On the other hand, the Angel of the Gautama-Bodhisattva can also be called the 'son of Wotan', for according to Rosicrucian esoteric tradition the Angels are always called 'sons' of Archangels. For example, in *Occult Science* Rudolf Steiner calls the Angels the 'Sons of Life'.[20] Life is a quality belonging especially to the etheric body, and it belongs in the greatest measure to an etheric body that has been fully transformed into the Life Spirit, which is fully developed only in beings of the Hierarchy of the Archangels and upwards. In this sense the latter may be called the 'Bearers of Life',[21] while the beings of the Hierarchy of the Angels are 'their sons'. Thus as we gather together all the observations that we have quoted concerning the Angel of the Gautama-Bodhisattva, we can say: 'He is the silent son of Wotan, the silent Aesir.'

All this has been handed down with remarkable accuracy in the stories and the genealogy of the gods of Teutonic Mythology. Rudolf Steiner gives a general characterization of them in connection with the distinction between the two races of the gods, the 'Vanir' and 'Aesir': 'But the ancient gods, who directed affairs before those gods who were by now [in the post-Atlantean epoch] visible and accessible to mankind, had entered into people's souls—those divine beings of the far distant past of ancient Atlantis were called the 'Vanir'. Then human beings came forth from the age of ancient Atlantis and beheld the weaving of Angels and Archangels; these they called the 'Aesir'. These were the beings—Angels and Archangels—who were concerned with man's ego, which now awoke at a rudimentary level. They guided these peoples and directed them.'[22] From this characterization we may see that in Teutonic mythology three kinds or races of gods are clearly to be distinguished.

In the first place there are the 'Vanir', divine beings who were active in the epoch of ancient Atlantis and were still connected with the realm of the Archai (as was, for instance, the god Niord). Then there are the 'Aesir', consisting of two 'generations': Archangels and Angels. To the older generation of gods (that is, the Archangels) belong Odin (who in his inner qualities is already one of the Archai), Vili and Ve (the *brothers* of Odin) and Honir and Lodur (who are *brothers* of Odin but nonetheless appear as normally evolved Archangels). Finally, in the third place, there are the gods belonging to the younger generation of the Aesir (that is, the Angels), these being for the most part *sons* of Odin. Among these are Thor—who in his inner qualities is already an Archangel, but has made the sacrifice of remaining at the Angel stage so as to endow the Teutonic peoples with the ego-principle—and also Baldur, Vali, Vidar and Hodur.[23]

We shall now return to further consideration of the spiritual path of the Gautama-Bodhisattva and the Angel being who accompanies him. It is a familiar fact that the Gautama-Bodhisattva, who in the sixth century before the birth of Christ proclaimed to mankind the great 'teaching of compassion and love' in the form of the 'eightfold path', in this way fulfilled his earthly mission and, in ascending to the plane of Buddhahood, no longer needed to incarnate further upon the Earth. Henceforth he participated in earthly evolution in a more refined spiritual body. In the East this is called 'Nirmanakaya', and is according to spiritual science none other than the substance of a human astral body which has to a sufficient degree been transformed into the Spirit Self.[24] Through this fulfilment by the Gautama-Bodhisattva of his mission on the Earth, his Guardian Angel, who had until then worked in his astral body, reached the peak of his evolution as an Angel and was fully prepared for his ascent into the realm of the next Hierarchy, that is, for appearing among the ranks of the Archangels. This did not, however, take place, for the case in question is one of a quite particular kind.

After the completion of his evolution as an Angel, the Angel of the Gautama-Bodhisattva forgoes his ascent to the rank of Archangel and, while thenceforth manifesting the inner qualities of an Archangel (that is, in possessing a full Spirit Self, which he had gradually attained in guiding the Gautama-Bodhisattva in his evolution), he remains at the Angel-stage *as a sacrifice* and continues to work on as such in the spiritual world. This sacrificial renunciation of any further ascent lasts for a long time. It lasts one twelfth of a Platonic year—for the entire fourth post-Atlantean epoch, which stands under the sign of the Ram, and even for part of the fifth post-Atlantean epoch. However, the Archangel who remained at the Angel stage was, as a result of this period of *sacrificial waiting* which lasted about 2500 years, able at its conclusion to attain the highest goal. He was, in Rudolf Steiner's words, able in around 1879 to take the place of Michael in the realm of the Archangels, that is, to become in a certain respect *the new Sun Archangel*. In this sense we may say: the Guardian Angel of the Gautama-Bodhisattva, who had in the sixth century before the birth of Christ completed his Angel mission and had *only in the year 1879* ascended to the rank of Archangel, can justly be called a '*young Archangel*'.

And so we may see that the Angel of the Gautama-Bodhisattva was already in the sixth century before the birth of Christ sufficiently mature in his inner development for the ascent to the rank of Archangel, but because he made the sacrifice of renouncing this ascent he was, in working as an Angel, subsequently able to remain connected in a far more intimate way with all earthly events and above all with the future destiny of the Nirmanakaya of Buddha, which abided principally in the Angel-sphere, in the spiritual world directly bordering upon the earthly world, where the Buddha also continued to work in his supersensible body. For this reason we should seek the traces of the Angel of the Gautama-Bodhisattva wherever we find the Nirmanakaya of Buddha in action. This we find in Luke the Evangelist's description of the birth of the Nathan Jesus (that is, the Nathan Soul), the guardianship of whom was in future to be entrusted to the Angel of the Gautama-Bodhisattva in place of the Archangel Michael. In order that we may see how this comes about we shall now turn to the Gospel of St Luke itself.

Luke the Evangelist, who was a direct pupil of Paul the Apostle, reveals to us in his Gospel the deepest mystery of the Nathan Soul. He received his knowledge from his teacher, who during the event of Damascus was able to experience the Risen Christ surrounded by the radiant light-aura in which the Nathan Soul was manifested. Hence it becomes understandable that it was through Paul that the Nathan Soul inspired Luke to write his Gospel. And so it is that we find in this Gospel the tidings of the birth of the Nathan Soul and also the genealogy, reaching right back to Adam and even to God. On the other hand, we have already observed that it is this Gospel that contains the most direct indications regarding the participation in the events of Palestine of the Nirmanakaya of Buddha, which as we know from modern spiritual science appeared to the Shepherds in the field in the form of the 'heavenly host'.[25] This is also one of the reasons why Rudolf Steiner characterizes this Gospel as the one that contains all the fundamental truths of Buddhism, though in a wholly new and higher form.[26]

On the basis of this knowledge of the part taken by the Nirmanakaya of the Buddha in the events of Palestine as described in this Gospel according to Luke, we shall now also try to discover in this Gospel allusions to the participation of the Angel of the Gautama-Bodhisattva in these events. We shall begin with the scene where the birth in Bethlehem of the Jesus of the Nathan line of the House of David is proclaimed to the Shepherds in the field. This birth is described by Luke the Evangelist in the following words: 'And in that region there were shepherds out in the field, keeping watch over their flock by night. And an Angel of the Lord appeared to them, and the glory of the Lord shone around them, and they were filled with fear . . . And the Angel said to them, "Be not afraid; for behold I bring to you good news of a great joy which will come to all the people; *for to you is born this day in the city of David a Saviour, who is Christ the Lord.* And this will be a sign by which you shall know Him: you shall find a babe wrapped in swaddling clothes and lying in a manger." And suddenly there was with the Angel *a multitude of choirs of heavenly Angels*[27] praising God and saying: "Glory to God in the highest and on Earth peace among men who are of good will." '[28] Rudolf Steiner makes the following observations about this supersensible experience of the Shepherds: 'And when the most important of all earthly events was being prepared and the Shepherds were in the field, *an individuality appeared to them out of the heavenly heights* and proclaimed to them what was recorded in the Gospel of St Luke: And then a "heavenly host" appeared *with the Angel.* Who was this? What the Shepherds saw in their visions was the Bodhisattva of ancient times, the "enlightened Buddha", the spiritual form of that being who in the course of many thousands of years had brought to mankind the message of love and compassion. Now that his last incarnation on the Earth had come to an end, he soared into the spiritual heights and appeared in the heavenly heights to the Shepherds *beside the Angel who had previously brought tidings of the event in Palestine.*'[29] And somewhat later Rudolf Steiner adds: 'Thus we may say that the Nirmanakaya of the Buddha appeared to the Shepherds in the form of the Angel hosts.'[30] And so we can see that, in the scene where the Nirmanakaya of Buddha appears to the Shepherds in the form of 'the heavenly host', this is preceded by the appearance of the *Angel* who gives them tidings of the birth in Bethlehem of the Nathan Soul, the human being who would subsequently receive the Christ into his own being. And this Angel is none other than the Angel of the Gautama-Bodhisattva, who had prepared for his future mission of guarding the Nathan Soul by bringing tidings of its birth on the Earth.

If we now follow the further participation of the Nirmanakaya of

Buddha in the events of Palestine, we can find another instance of the presence therein of the Angel of the Gautama-Bodhisattva. Among the many indications of spiritual science we find an allusion to the quite special connection existing between the Nirmanakaya of Buddha and the individuality of John the Baptist. Rudolf Steiner defines this connection as follows: 'Now again a spiritual being was present who, as the Nirmanakaya of Buddha, hovered above the Nathan Jesus; it worked upon Elisabeth when John was to be born, bringing into movement the embryo of John within her body in the sixth month of pregnancy and awakening his ego. But as this force was now nearer to the Earth it called forth not merely an inspiration but actually gave form to the ego of John the Baptist ... Thus the Nirmanakaya of Buddha exerts an awakening influence—extending even to the physical substance—upon the ego of the former Elijah, now the ego of John the Baptist ... What resided in the Nirmanakaya of Buddha flowed into the ego of John the Baptist as an inspiration. What was proclaimed to the Shepherds, what hovered above the Nathan Jesus, poured its forces into John the Baptist.[31] And the preaching of John the Baptist is, therefore, the reawakened preaching of Buddha.'[32]

However, the influence of the Nirmanakaya of Buddha upon the awakening ego of John the Baptist was only one of the influences working upon him from the spiritual world. A further influence, which arose somewhat later but was nevertheless even more powerful and long-lasting, is referred to in words of the prophet Malachi that stand at the beginning of the Gospel of St Mark: 'Behold, I send my *Angel* before thy face who shall prepare thy way.'[33] Thus here we again find, alongside the Nirmanakaya of Buddha, the working of *a certain Angel* who speaks through John the Baptist.[34] In his observations upon these words from the Gospel of St Mark, Rudolf Steiner defines the prophetic character of this Angel: 'The *messenger*, the *Angel*, had to proclaim to man that he will in future become an ego in the full sense of the word. Former Angels had the task of showing the spiritual world to man; now a *particular Angel*[35] has received the *particular task* of bringing further revelations to mankind. He must say to people that they must penetrate into their ego, whereas the revelations of former Angels were not directed towards the ego. And the prophet Isaiah[36] refers to this when he says: 'The time is coming for the receiving of the Mystery of the ego, and one will be chosen from the Angel-hosts who will show you that this Mystery is coming! Only in such a way can we understand the meaning of the words: the Angel, the messenger, will be sent on before.'[37] But before whom will he be sent? We may find the answer to this question in the words that the Angel addressed to the Shepherds in the field: '... for to you is born in the city of David a Saviour, who is Christ the Lord.'[38]

As regards John the Baptist, Rudolf Steiner speaks as follows about the special character of his initiation: 'The gaze of John the Baptist was trained in such a way that he could look, at night, through the material Earth to the constellation of the Waterman [that is, the constellation associated with the Hierarchy of the Angels, see p. 111]; and when the Angel took possession of his soul he was able to receive the initiation referred to as the "initiation of the Waterman". Thus in knowing and feeling all that he did, John the Baptist was able to place at the Angel's disposal all those faculties whereby the Angel could give expression to the Waterman-initiation in all its fullness and point towards the future manifestation of the dominion of the ego, *Kyrios*, the Lord, within the soul.'[39] And in another lecture Rudolf Steiner speaks of this connection of John the Baptist with a certain being from the Hierarchy of the Angels in an even more impressive way: 'The Bible views the personality of John as Maya. In John there lives an Angel-being who takes possession of his soul and *leads people to Christ.*[40] He is a sheath for the revelation of the Angel-being. The Angel was able to enter into him because the reborn Elijah was ready to receive the Angel. Then the Angel who was sent spoke through him. He merely used John as an instrument. With such precision does the Bible speak.'[41]

The following words from the prologue of the Gospel of St John are also an indication of *what* the Angel was to proclaim to mankind through John the Baptist: 'There was a man sent from God, whose name was John. He came for a testimony, *to bear witness to the light,* that all might believe through him. He was not the light, but came *to bear witness to the light.*'[42] Finally, we know from Rudolf Steiner's spiritual-scientific research that John himself spoke in the following way about his mission in the intimate circle of his pupils: 'Through the Waterman-initiation I can only make those forces available to my Angel with whose help *he can proclaim* that *Kyrios*, the Lord, is coming . . .'[43] And so this 'bearing witness to the light', this 'proclaiming that *Kyrios*, the Lord, is coming', is the true meaning of what the Angel prophesies through John the Baptist, a prophecy which he has already made not through the mouth of a human being but directly from the spiritual heights to the Shepherds in the field, appearing to them *beside* the 'heavenly hosts', that is, with the Nirmanakaya of Buddha.[44]

Let us now turn to one further highly important aspect of the super-sensible activity of the Angel of the Gautama-Bodhisattva, one which can also appear before us in connection with the future destiny of the Nirmanakaya of Buddha. In the lecture-cycle devoted to the Gospel of St Luke, Rudolf Steiner describes in detail how, with the coming of the twelfth year, at the moment when the astral body of the Nathan Jesus was born, the maternal astral sheath separated from him and united with the Nirmanakaya of Buddha. He says: 'What shone down from the heights in the Angel hosts united with the astral sheath that had separated from the twelve-year-old boy, united with all those *youthful forces* from the period between the *change of teeth* and *puberty*. The Nirmanakaya of Buddha, which had shed its light over the Jesus-child at his birth, now became one with the youthful astral sheath that had separated from this boy at puberty; it received all this, united with it, and became thereby *rejuvenated.* Through this rejuvenation it became possible for what the Buddha had formerly given to the world to reappear in the Jesus-child in a new form, in the innocence of childhood.'[45] For '... in the meantime the Buddha had himself advanced! He had absorbed the forces of the maternal astral sheath of the Jesus-child and had thereby acquired the capacity of speaking in a new way to the hearts of human beings. Thus the Gospel of St Luke contains Buddhism in a new form, *as though washed in a fountain of youth*, and hence gives expression to a religion of sympathy and love in a form that is comprehensible to the simplest of souls. This is something that we may read. The author of St Luke's Gospel has placed it there.'[46]

At this point, however, a fundamental question arises: if the maternal astral sheath of the Jesus-child that had been thus separated off could have such a transforming and *rejuvenating* effect on the Nirmanakaya of Buddha, this would suggest that the separation of his maternal *etheric* sheath—an event which corresponds to the birth of the independent etheric body—between his fifth and seventh years[47] must have been an even more significant event that was able to have a still greater influence upon the spiritual environment, for the essential mystery of the Nathan Soul was that it was the bearer of the unfallen *etheric body* of ancient humanity. In the sixth lecture of the cycle devoted to the Gospel of St Luke, Rudolf Steiner refers to this as follows: 'We know that in the *etheric body* of this boy who was of the Nathan line of the House of David there lived an as yet untouched part of that *etheric body* which had been withdrawn from humanity with the event known as "the Fall". Thus this etheric substance, which had been drawn forth from Adam before the Fall, was preserved and submerged in this child ..: But this etheric substance was as a result still united with those forces which had worked upon Earth-evolution *before the Fall* and so now generated an immense spiritual power within this child.'[48] One can sense from these words that the etheric body of the Nathan Jesus must have had even mightier forces of youthfulness and rejuvenation than his astral body, which was able to bear these forces within itself only as a reflection of this unique etheric body. Rudolf Steiner speaks further of this when he says: 'This child, who had a soul which was the mother-soul of humanity and which had remained youthful through the ages, lived in such a way that it radiated all its pristine forces into the astral body; and this then separated off, rose upwards and united with the

Nirmanakaya of Buddha.'[49] While the following words refer to the fact that by 'the mother-soul of humanity' is meant in this case that being who was directly connected with the etheric body of Adam preserved untarnished by the Fall: 'This [the words in the Bible about the Tree of Life] means that *a certain portion of the forces of the etheric body* was held back, and these forces were not handed down to the descendants. Thus in Adam a certain portion of forces had been removed before the Fall. This innocent part of Adam was preserved in the Mother Lodge of humanity, where it was lovingly protected and nurtured. This was, so to speak, the Adam-soul that was as yet untouched by human guilt, that was not as yet entangled in what had led man to the Fall.'[50]

It becomes clear from these observations of Rudolf Steiner that these mighty etheric forces from the primal youth of mankind must also have been to a very high degree contained in the *maternal etheric sheath* which accompanied the Nathan Jesus until approximately the beginning of his seventh year. For it is necessary to take into account that these forces were present within the individuality of the Nathan Jesus only because it had since Lemurian times never incarnated on the Earth. Hence its *first* incarnation, as described in the Gospel of St Luke, signified to some extent the loss of these primordial forces of youth or, to be more precise, their *emanation*, their transference to the departing maternal etheric sheath.[51] And so between the fifth and seventh years of the life of the Nathan Jesus a unique etheric sheath, bearing within itself *the quintessence of the life-forces of all humanity*, separates from his altogether special etheric body. In order, however, that this great treasure might not be lost for the further evolution of humanity, it was not allowed simply to be dispersed in the surrounding cosmos but was embraced and preserved (as with the maternal *astral* sheath of the Nathan Jesus). This could be achieved only by a particular being of the spiritual world, a being whose task it was to accomplish at a higher stage what the Nirmanakaya of Buddha had to fulfil *at a later time*.[52] And so this being had, on the one hand, to be in the region of the spiritual world most immediately adjacent to the physical world (namely, the Angel- or Moon-sphere) and, on the other, to belong *in its inmost essence* to the rank of Archangel, that is, bearing within itself a fully developed *Life Spirit*, a fully spiritualized etheric body, thus enabling such a being to have a particularly intimate kinship with everything of an *etheric* nature in the world.[53] It follows from all that has been said hitherto that such a being could only be the Angel of the Gautama-Bodhisattva, who directly *before* the appearance of the Nirmanakaya of Buddha to the Shepherds brought tidings of the birth of the holy child. And this Angel of the Gautama-Bodhisattva, who works in the supersensible world as an Angel, but at the same time bears within himself in a veiled form the nature of an Archangel (the Life Spirit),

313

now *embraces and preserves in his Life Spirit the boundlessly youthful forces of the etheric body of the Nathan Jesus.* From this moment he is the guardian of the primal youth-forces of humanity in the supersensible world!

All that has just been said can shed some light upon a particularly important detail mentioned in the Gospel of St Luke in the scene of the 'prayer about the cup' in the Garden of Gethsemane. This detail is contained *only* in the Gospel of St Luke. Its omission in the other Gospels is merely one further indication that Luke had been initiated in a particularly profound way through the Apostle Paul into the mystery of the Nathan Soul, into the nature of its ancestry, its birth and also its connection with the Nirmanakaya of Buddha and with the Angel of the Gautama-Bodhisattva.

However, before approaching this deeply significant point in the twenty-second chapter of the Gospel of St Luke, it is necessary to touch (albeit in brief) upon the spiritual significance of the whole scene of the 'prayer about the cup'. As a point of departure we can avail ourselves of the description given by Emil Bock in his book *The Three Years*. In his chapter on Good Friday, Emil Bock sees in this scene the evidence of the struggle that Christ Jesus has in the Garden of Gethsemane with the forces of death. Emil Bock writes: 'The secret of the conflict in Gethsemane lies in the fact that death wants to outwit Jesus. It wants to wrest Him away too soon [from life], before He has ended His work and filled the last vestige of the earthly vessel with His Spirit. For three years the fire of divine Egohood has burned in the body and soul of Jesus. The human vessel—from within outwards—has thus already been consumed almost to ashes. What still has to be suffered and completed demands so much strength from the earthly sheath that there is a real danger of premature death. Ahriman lies in wait and hopes to make use of this moment.'[54] The Evangelist Luke, a doctor by profession, describes this scene in words which characterize with complete precision (also from the medical point of view) the physical condition of Christ Jesus at this moment. According to Emil Bock, the original text runs as follows: ' " And being *in agony* ..." When St Luke adds, "and His sweat was as it were great drops of blood falling down to the ground", he adds exact symptoms of the agony of death.'[55]

Thus in the scene of the 'prayer about the cup' in the Garden of Gethsemane, Christ is exposed to the greatest danger since His descent into the sheaths of Jesus, the danger of being prematurely carried away by death. His physical and etheric bodies are completely exhausted. All His life-forces have dried up. What can help Him in this situation? He, who has sacrificially renounced His macrocosmic etheric forces, His divine majesty and power, so as to become the Son of Man from the Son of God,[56] no longer has any forces left in His human etheric body, which has been 'burnt up' by the presence of the World Ego.* In this moment He is in need of help. It is not the Christ Being who needs help but His human etheric body. And what can now furnish Him with this help is an influx of new, fresh and eternally youthful etheric forces. Such a stream of forces can proceed again only from that being who, on the one hand, is as an Angel being able fully to approach the earthly world and, on the other hand, also bears within himself a higher archangelic nature, the nature of the Life Spirit, which as the spiritualized etheric body has a kinship with everything of an etheric nature in the world. But this is not all. In the spiritual world there is no such thing as death. Hence those etheric forces that go to make up the etheric body of an Archangel, his Life Spirit, are essentially of a completely different nature from the forces of a human etheric body. It is for this reason that Rudolf Steiner even once said that 'life' in the human sense (that is, as an antithesis to death), does not exist in the spiritual world. Thus the etheric forces of even a fully evolved Life Spirit were not able directly to help Christ Jesus at the moment of His struggle with death in the Garden of Gethsemane. His human etheric body was in need of something different. It needed those unfallen forces of primal youth which were initially contained in the maternal etheric sheath of the Nathan Jesus and then separated with it from him before he had attained his seventh year of age.[57] These were the purest *human* etheric forces, preserved from the epoch *before* the Fall of Man, that is, before the power of death had entered into the earthly world for the first time.[58] Only these forces were capable of streaming into the etheric body of Christ Jesus where, withstanding the power of death, they averted the danger of a premature parting with the physical body.[59] In this we have the answer to our question as to which being was able to come to the aid of the etheric body of Christ Jesus: this being was the Angel of the Gautama-Bodhisattva, the heavenly guardian of the ancient youth-forces of the maternal etheric sheath of the Nathan Jesus. It is he who appears in this profoundly dramatic scene, and it is not surprising that Luke *alone* knows of this secret of his presence and refers to it in his Gospel. There, in the twenty-second chapter (vv. 40–44), we read: 'And when He came to the place He said to them, "Pray that you may not enter into temptation." And He withdrew from them about a stone's throw, and knelt down and prayed. "Father, if thou art willing, remove this cup from me; nevertheless not my will but thine be done." *And there appeared to Him an Angel from heaven, strengthening Him.* And when the struggle with death began,[60] He prayed more earnestly; and His sweat

---

* If we would characterize this condition more precisely, we would say that the physical body was 'burnt up' and the etheric body *exhausted* to the extent that it could no longer prevent the physical body from succumbing (to death).

become like great drops of blood falling down upon the ground.' Thus in these words we have the *third* allusion in the Gospels to the participation of the Angel of the Gautama-Bodhisattva in the events of Palestine.

We shall now draw all this together. According to Rudolf Steiner, around the year 1879 the Angel of the Gautama-Bodhisattva ascends into the sphere of the Archangels. There he takes the place vacated by Michael, who at this time completes his ascent to the rank of Archai.

The Angel of the Gautama-Bodhisattva is deeply connected with the being of the Nathan Soul. He is the guardian of the *ancient youth-forces* of the maternal sheath of its etheric body, that is, the *ancient youth-forces of all mankind*.

After the Gautama-Bodhisattva's Angel ascends to the rank of the Archangels, the fully evolved Life Spirit with which he has been endowed since the last earthly life of Gautama Buddha (although he has continued to work as an Angel) comes into the light of day, and from this moment the Angel of the Gautama-Bodhisattva is able to replace Michael as the 'guardian' of the Nathan Soul in the spiritual world.

Because of his exceptional path of development, the Angel of the Gautama-Bodhisattva is able to take upon himself one further task in the twentieth century, one that is directly connected with the new appearance of Christ in the etheric, who—as the Apostle Paul had already prophetically experienced on the road to Damascus—from our time onwards passes through the supersensible world closest to the Earth in the garment of the Nathan Soul.

Finally, on the basis of an esoteric understanding of the occult terminology in Teutonic mythology, we can, as we have seen, call this being, this Angel of the Gautama Bodhisattva, the 'son of Wotan', the 'silent Aesir'.

All these assembled facts together reveal to us the profound mystery of this unique hierarchic being, who has—like Michael himself—a quite particular relationship to the work carried out on Earth in the twentieth century in the name of anthroposophically orientated spiritual science; for this being is none other than he who appears before us in Teutonic esoteric wisdom under the name of *Vidar*!

If we turn now to what Rudolf Steiner has to say about Vidar, we find a complete correspondence with what has been set forth in the preceding pages. Thus in the lecture of 21 December 1913, given in Bochum on the occasion of the inauguration of the 'Vidar' branch in that town, Rudolf Steiner speaks as follows: 'To the name of that divinity who is in the North regarded as the divinity who will once again bring *the forces of youth, the spiritual forces of childhood*, to an aging humanity, to whom northern souls bow down when they wish to speak of *what from the wellsprings of the Being of*

Christ Jesus can bring a new message of rejuvenation to mankind, to this name do our friends wish to dedicate their work and their branch; "Vidar branch" is what they want to call it. May this name be *filled with promise* . . .'[61] These words come at the end of a lecture whose subject matter ranges from, on the one hand, the cycle of the year, its festivals and our souls' experience of them, to, on the other, the mystery of the two Jesus children and especially the mystery of the Nathan Soul. Thus the lecture as a whole refers not only to the connection of Vidar with the Christ-impulse and with the primal youth-forces of mankind, but also to his connection with the Nathan Soul.

In another lecture (given three years earlier, 17 June 1910, in Christiania) as a conclusion to the lecture-cycle entitled *The Mission of Folk Souls,* Rudolf Steiner spoke in a profoundly meaningful way about the relationship between Vidar and the etheric manifestation of the Christ, and also about the emergence from our time onwards of a new clairvoyance which will have to wage a hard battle with the atavistic clairvoyance of Lucifer and Ahriman, now inspired from the astral plane by the Fenris Wolf. So that we may rightly understand the character and particular qualities of this new clairvoyance and also its relationship to the Vidar-impulse and to the new manifestation of the Christ, we need to consider certain facts regarding the combined work of the individuality of the Gautama-Bodhisattva and the Angel being (Vidar) who inspired him.[62]

The present epoch, the fifth cultural epoch in the post-Atlantean age, has as its principal task the cultivation of the *consciousness soul.* At the same time this epoch is in a certain sense a repetition of the third, the Egyptian-Babylonian-Assyrian-Chaldean epoch,[63] which chiefly cultivated the sentient soul. The mighty ancient clairvoyance that existed at that time among the peoples of the European North was to a significant degree inspired by the Archangel Wotan, who led these peoples and worked through his earthly representative and helper, the future Gautama-Buddha. Then in the course of the fourth post-Atlantean cultural epoch, that of the intellectual or mind soul, this ancient clairvoyance gradually dried up and was first replaced by the inspired thinking of the Greeks and then increasingly by the independent thinking of individual human beings.[64] The last earthly incarnation of the Bodhisattva who rose therein to the stage of Buddha took place at the threshold of the third and fourth cultural epochs. It was then that he attained that goal to which he had been led by his Guardian Angel in the course of his numerous lives on Earth as a Bodhisattva. This goal consisted of imparting the teaching of compassion and love in the form of the 'Eightfold Path'. Already at that time (the sixth century BC), however, this teaching was to be imparted to mankind not from the forces of the intellectual or mind soul but from the forces of the *consciousness soul.* This was the great and deeply prophetic deed of Buddha.

317

'... The task of Buddha in the fifth and sixth centuries before our era was to instil the consciousness soul into the human organization,'[65] as Rudolf Steiner says. Shortly before this he refers to the fact that it is the present epoch that bears within it a true understanding of all that was accomplished by Buddha: 'Now does man through his consciousness soul, according to the measure of its development, gradually mature to an independent realization of the mighty impulse of Buddha. Buddha had to develop the consciousness soul at the time when human beings had only developed the intellectual or mind soul.'[66]

And so we have the following picture: in the sixth century the Buddha lived with the rest of humanity at the beginning of the intellectual-soul epoch. He drew his clairvoyance from the inspirations of the Archangel Wotan, who worked through his sentient soul, and evolved towards the consciousness soul through his own forces under the guidance of his Guardian Angel. As a result of Buddha's attainment of his goal, his Guardian Angel—that is, the Vidar of Teutonic mythology—was, already in the sixth century before the birth of Christ, fully prepared for working among people of the fifth post-Atlantean cultural epoch, that is among people who develop the consciousness soul as a matter of course. For it was out of the forces of this member of man's being that the teaching of compassion and love, together with the eightfold path, was given to people at that time.[67] And now, when for the first time in the entire Earth-evolution the mature, free individual human ego can unfold, it is from the forces of this member of man's being that the development of a new clairvoyance must begin. And Vidar is the being who can best help mankind in this respect. For apart from having a profound knowledge of the nature, character and particular qualities of the consciousness soul, Vidar, as Michael's closest follower in the sphere of the Archangels, also has a direct relationship to the heavenly Intelligence of Michael and is thereby best fitted to inspire human beings to that clairvoyance which, in proceeding fully from the consciousness soul, is wholly permeated by the light of the spiritualized Intelligence. This new clairvoyance will gradually unfold amongst mankind from our time onwards, that is, in the first post-Christian epoch of Michael's rulership, and at the conclusion of the dark age of the Kali-Yuga in 1899.

The fact that such a special constellation was necessary for the awakening of the new clairvoyance can also shed light upon the deeper grounds for Vidar's sacrificial renunciation of his ascent to the rank of the Archangels in the sixth century BC. For, as we have seen, he had progressed in his own development so far that after the Buddha's enlightenment under the Bodhi tree he was ready to rise to the rank of Archangel and as such to awaken the forces of clairvoyance in man's consciousness soul. At that time, however,

318

which was at the very beginning of the fourth cultural epoch, there were—apart from the Buddha and a few other initiates—no human beings with a developed consciousness soul. Hence Vidar, now an Archangel, would then, like Wotan, have been able to bequeath forces of clairvoyance only to the sentient soul, which in the epoch of the intellectual or mind soul, when man gradually had to lose a direct connection with the spiritual world, would have been unwarranted and in contradiction to world evolution as a whole. For this reason Vidar had to renounce his ascent and remain for almost 2500 years as 'the silent Aesir', waiting for the right time for his task, the fifth post-Atlantean epoch.

It is clear from the above that in this modern, fifth, post-Atlantean epoch, which is the rebirth of the third, Egyptian-Babylonian-Assyrian-Chaldean epoch, the clairvoyance that existed then must, after the 'period of silence' of the fourth, Graeco-Latin, epoch, come to life again. Hence today it is, on the one hand, possible to develop—through the connection with the impulse of Michael-Vidar—a new clairvoyance, which will arise at the border between the consciousness soul and the Spirit Self. On the other hand, it is also possible in our time—and we can everywhere already observe the first symptoms of this—to acquire forces of clairvoyance in an old form *as though* 'from the inspirations of Wotan' through the sentient soul and even through the sentient body.

While the inspirations of the Archangel Wotan were absolutely justified and even necessary in the third post-Atlantean epoch (and in the northern regions of Europe this was still the case in the first centuries after the birth of Christ), they now, if introduced into our own age, become especially hostile to a true path of evolution.

The reason for this is that a demonic astral being, whose name in northern mythology is the Fenris Wolf, has appeared in Wotan's place; whereas the Archangel Wotan, having fulfilled his mission as the leader of the Teutonic tribes, has risen to higher realms of the spiritual world in order after a certain time to undertake a more extensive task in the rulership of the earthly evolution of humanity as a whole.[68]

As for the Fenris Wolf, he wants to endow man with a clairvoyance that arises not through the development of the free, individual ego within a consciousness soul that seeks the path to the Spirit Self, but through stifling this ego in the impenetrable waves of the sentient soul. Thus the deeper meaning of the victory of the Fenris Wolf over Wotan in the 'Twilight of the Gods' is that in our time the power which in the past stemmed from Wotan and worked with full justification on the sentient souls of the ancient Teutons no longer derives from Wotan but from the demonic being of the 'Fenris Wolf' and works—in a way that is no longer appropriate—on the sentient soul, by-passing the consciousness soul. As a result the Fenris Wolf enters into battle against the forces of true evolution led by Michael—against the impulse of the new clairvoyance, which will become widespread as human intelligence is permeated by the light of the Spirit. For the new clairvoyance cannot be won by evading human intelligence through the impulse of the Fenris Wolf, but by spiritualizing it through completely overcoming the ahrimanic power of the Wolf by the forces of Michael-Vidar. This overcoming of the power of the Wolf is referred to in the esoteric traditions of the European North, where Vidar conquers it by tearing its jaws apart, that is, by depriving it of the capacity of speech. For the old clairvoyance should no longer 'speak' among people, but rather the new. The Wolf must be silent, while Vidar, hitherto the 'silent Aesir', must now lift his voice aloft for the first time.

In our time this victory of Vidar over the Wolf must be won in *every* human soul, otherwise humanity will be threatened with the danger of succumbing to the forces of an atavistic clairvoyance devoid of the light of Intelligence, where the Fenris Wolf is seen as none other than the first emissary of the 'ahrimanic spectre' which has already been spoken of here. This 'ahrimanic spectre' has hitherto *only* appeared as an etheric being on the astral plane where it stands as the chief antagonist of the Etheric Christ and as a terrifying symptom of the approaching incarnation of Ahriman himself at the beginning of the next millennium.[69]

Rudolf Steiner refers to all these facts in his lecture of 17 June 1910 in Christiania. Thus in conclusion we shall draw fully upon the esoteric characterization that he gives there of the being of Vidar, as this is revealed to the spiritual researcher on the basis of a true understanding of his mission in the 'Twilight of the Gods' and in our age: 'All these details of the Twilight of the Gods have their counterpart in a new etheric vision which will come before mankind as a pointer towards the future. The Fenris Wolf will remain. That the Fenris Wolf prevails in the struggle against Odin hides a deep, deep truth. In the immediate future, instead of developing new forces of clairvoyance, man is imperilled by the danger of succumbing to the attraction of remaining with the old astral clairvoyance of antiquity, which would continue to entice him with such soul-pictures as, for example, the Fenris Wolf. This, again, would be a severe test for what must grow from spiritual science. If, for example, there were to arise from within this spiritual science an inclination towards any unclear, chaotic clairvoyance, a tendency would come about to value more highly not that clairvoyance *which is illuminated by reason and scientific thinking* but the old clairvoyance that lacks these advantages. The relics of this old clairvoyance, which have the power to confuse human consciousness with all manner of chaotic forms, would wreak a terrible vengeance. It is impossible to confront such clairvoyance with those capacities which themselves have their origin in forces of the old clairvoyance; it can be met only with what has matured in the course of Kali-Yuga as a healthy impulse towards a new clairvoyance. Neither the power given by the old Archangel Odin nor the old clairvoyant powers can be of any avail; something quite else must come about which is, however, known to Teutonic mythology; it knows of its existence. It knows of *the life of the etheric form in which that principle that we shall come to see as the etheric form of Christ will incarnate.* He alone will succeed in driving away what would confuse and befog mankind with an impenetrable clairvoyant power if Odin does not destroy the Fenris Wolf, which is none other than what is left of the old clairvoyance. Vidar, *who has remained silent throughout,* will overcome the Fenris Wolf. This, too, is spoken of in the "Twilight of the Gods".

'*Whoever recognizes Vidar in all his significance and feels him in his soul will understand that in the twentieth century the capacity to behold the Christ can again be given to man;* Vidar, who is close to all of us in northern and central Europe, will again stand before him. He was held secret in the Mysteries and occult schools as the god *who will receive his task only in the future.* Even his image has only been spoken of in a vague way. This is evident in that a sculpted form has been found in the vicinity of Cologne whose identity no one knows and which could only be a likeness of Vidar.★

'During the Kali-Yuga forces have been developed which can endow man with the capacity to behold the new appearance of Christ. Those who are called upon to interpret from the signs of the time[70] what will come about know that *the new spiritual research will restore the power of Vidar which will banish from human souls all the residues of the forces of the old chaotic clairvoyance, bringing as they do such confusion, and will arouse within the human breast, within the human soul, the clairvoyance that is newly unfolding.*'[71]

From these words of Rudolf Steiner we may see that Vidar is a hierarchic being who will 'only in the future', that is, in that future which begins in our epoch (the twentieth century) 'receive his task', a task which is directly connected with the new appearance of Christ. For Vidar now fashions for Christ the 'etheric form', the etheric sheath in which Christ 'will incarnate' in the elemental (astral) world bordering upon the physical earthly world. And in as much as 'new spiritual research' (in the first place, anthroposophically orientated spiritual science) proclaims to mankind this new supersensible beholding of Christ[72] and makes people ready for it, it will restore the power of Vidar, which then 'will banish the residues of the old chaotic clairvoyance' proceeding from the atavistic forces of the sentient soul.[73] It will then be the power of Vidar which 'will arouse within the human soul the clairvoyance that is newly unfolding', that clairvoyance

---

★ See Appendix 3.

which springs from the light-filled spirit of the intelligence, from the consciousness soul that is ascending to Spirit Self:

Where the eternal aims of Gods
World-Being's Light
On thine own I
Bestow
For thy free Willing.

These words of Rudolf Steiner are also an indication of the profound connection between Vidar and the Nathan Soul, who accompanies the Risen Christ after the Mystery of Golgotha. For the fact that Vidar fashions the 'etheric image' in the supersensible world for the Christ, who is surrounded by the light-aura of the Nathan Soul as though by a 'soul-sheath',[74] is inseparably connected with his having taken on the mission concerning the Nathan Soul which was formerly administered in the cosmos by the Archangel Michael. And just as Michael in the past 'supported and protected' the Nathan Soul in its three heavenly sacrifices to the Christ Being—when on three occasions in three worlds it presented itself as the archetype of a Christ-bearer—so from now onwards does Vidar take his place, so as henceforth to be the 'spiritual-guardian' of the Nathan Soul in its three new supersensible sacrifices to the Christ—when again thrice in three worlds it will reveal itself as the archetype of a Christ-receiver, *as the archetype of a man who is wholly permeated by Christ.*[75]

From all this we may see the deep connection and continuity that exists between the cosmic deeds of Michael and the future deeds of Vidar. In a certain sense it is even possible to say that Vidar carries the impulse of Michael forward, or that Michael works through Vidar, who acts as his messenger, his herald. So the three deeds of Michael with respect to the Nathan Soul in the past now appear again in a new, metamorphosed form—permeated with the fullness of the forces springing from the Mystery of Golgotha—in the three future deeds of Vidar. And just as the three 'descending' deeds of the past and the three new 'ascending' deeds in a certain sense reflect one another, *so the first* deed of Vidar—which is taking place already in our own time—can be seen as a metamorphosis of the *last* deed of Michael.

At the end of the Atlantean epoch, Michael, through the Nathan Soul, conquered the Python Dragon which, working in the human astral body, wanted to bring the three soul-forces of thinking, feeling and willing into such a state of disorder that man could never ever attain to the free, individual ego which alone is able to receive the Christ-impulse into itself.[76] In our time, in place of the Python Dragon comes the Fenris Wolf, causing modern man to become *possessed* by the old atavistic clairvoyance, which is able to darken human consciousness with such chaotic and deceptive images and voices that everything that has been achieved by way of the evolution of the free, individual ego is again lost and man is therefore unable to attain a *conscious* relationship to the Christ.

Now, however, Vidar, the 'silent Aesir', confronts the Fenris Wolf—Vidar, who works in the spiritual world together with the Nathan Soul and reveals to people the *right* path, the path which leads to a true supersensible experience of the Etheric Christ.

2. The New Appearance of Christ in the Etheric Realm

The new appearance of Christ in the etheric realm is to be seen as the most significant event taking place in the supersensible world nearest to the Earth in the twentieth century. According to indications given by Rudolf Steiner, this event began in the year 1909,[77] the year at the end of which the mysteries of the Fifth Gospel and—in the cycle on the Gospel of St Luke—the mystery of the two Jesus children, were revealed for the first time.

In the years that follow, this new pronouncement passes (from January 1910 onwards) like a red thread through the entire lecturing activity of Rudolf Steiner until the beginning of the First World War, and then continues with greater or lesser intensity until 1920, when in October and December the final indications regarding this event are given in the last two lectures of the cycle *The New Spirituality and the Christ Experience of the Twentieth Century*, and also at the end of the second lecture of the Christmas cycle, *The Search for the New Isis, the Divine Sophia.*[78]

Rudolf Steiner speaks about this seminal event in words of far-reaching significance (already quoted in part: see p.130) in the lecture of 6 February 1917 in Berlin, where he defines *all* that he has elaborated by way of spiritual science as that language whereby twentieth-century man can speak with the Christ as He enters into human evolution in a new, etheric form: 'But humanity must learn to consult Christ. How shall this happen? It can happen only if we learn His language. Anyone with insight into the deeper meaning of what our spiritual science would achieve sees in it not merely theoretical knowledge about all manner of humanity's problems, about the members of man's being, about reincarnation and karma, but seeks in it an altogether special language that is capable of expressing spiritual things. We must learn, with the help of spiritual science, inwardly to speak with the spiritual world in our thoughts; this is much more important than merely acquiring theoretical thoughts. For Christ is with us every day until the end of earthly time. We must learn His language. And with the help of this language, however abstract it may seem, a language through which we hear about Saturn, Sun, Moon and Earth and about other mysteries of evolution, through this so-called teaching we ourselves learn that language in which we can clothe the questions that we address to the spiritual world. If we learn rightly to speak this language of spiritual life, then, my dear friends, Christ will stand beside us and give us an answer . . .

Let us try to make spiritual science our own not merely as a teaching but as a language and then await the moment when we shall find those questions which we may address to Christ. And He will answer, yes, *He will answer!*'[79]

Thus in these words which we have quoted there appears before us the fundamental spiritual requirement of that new epoch into which we have entered in our time: to learn to *ask* Christ about all our problems and to *receive His answer*, for '... if only this would be sought, it would now be wholly possible to be near Christ, to find Christ in an altogether different way from how He was found in former times.'[80]

This special sense of *inner closeness* to Christ that becomes possible in our time is an immediate foretaste of what will subsequently become manifest as the consequence of His new appearance in the etheric realm. There are three such consequences.

Firstly, the gradual awakening of the new etheric clairvoyance. Beginning with the twentieth century and throughout the next 2500–3000 years, ever wider circles of people will acquire the capacity of imaginative vision in the supersensible world nearest to the physical realm; the sphere of the elemental beings of nature will become accessible to them, and they will be able to behold the etheric bodies of plants, animals and human beings.

Secondly, to these etheric experiences is added the contemplation of that 'etheric form' in which the Christ Himself approaches.[81]

And thirdly, as a further consequence of the new appearance of Christ, human beings will gradually develop the capacity consciously to recognize and experience their own karma. This is initially expressed in the capacity directly to behold the consequences of one's own deeds, of one's unresolved karma, which in its turn is the first consequence of Christ's having taken upon Himself the role of karmic judge in the twentieth century.

To these three purely spiritual experiences it is necessary to add certain facts from mankind's spiritual history which made possible that particular constellation which preceded the new Christ event. Here again three facts may be discerned.

1. The inception in the year 1879 of the new rulership of the Archangel Michael, which is associated with his ascent from the rank of Archangel to the rank of Time Spirit and with his deed of casting the ahrimanic spirits of darkness, who belonged to the Hierarchy of retarded Angels, down from Heaven to Earth, thus cleansing the supersensible world nearest to the Earth from the opposing spirits and preparing it for the new Christ event.
2. The ending in the year 1899 of the dark age of the Kali-Yuga, and the gradual preparation in the incipient age of light of a spiritual ground for

the development of new supersensible faculties among mankind. For from this time gradually the higher worlds will again 'quite naturally' become accessible to human beings.

3. The emergence of anthroposophically orientated spiritual science, which commenced at Michaelmas 1900 with the first spiritual-scientific lecture of Rudolf Steiner on 'Goethe's Secret Revelation'; the dawning ray of the new revelation of Christ-Michael, which was to become accessible to human consciousness in the new age of light.

To these two aspects of the new Christ event in the twentieth century, the spiritual and the spiritual-historical, a third should be added to which reference has already been made at the beginning of the previous chapter, namely, the participation in this event of three spiritual beings in particular who act as helpers and servants of Christ in His new manifestation to mankind. These beings are: the ruling Spirit of our time, Michael, the Archangel Vidar and the Angel being (or the Angel-like being) of the Nathan Soul.

We now need to consider in somewhat more detail the relationship of these three spiritual beings to, and the nature of their participation in, the new Christ event.* For only such an examination will reveal to us the path towards a real understanding of this event.

Let us begin with a consideration of the Nathan Soul. As has already been observed, after the Baptism in the Jordan, the Nathan Soul became for all future ages the great archetype of a human being who has in the fullest sense 'received Christ into himself'. And then after the Mystery of Golgotha, it appears in the spiritual world as the 'soul sheath' of Christ, as the radiant aura of light that surrounds Him.[82] This means, however, that, in continuing to be connected with Christ in the spiritual world after His 'Resurrection from the dead', it becomes the true bearer of *Christ's consciousness* in the supersensible sphere nearest to the Earth, that is, the sphere of the Angels. By this inner permeation with the consciousness of Christ, as though raying forth the entire fullness of the Angel-like consciousness of Christ in streams of spiritual light, the Nathan Soul appears to Paul the Apostle in the event of Damascus. Thus it works on even to our own time, for, as Rudolf Steiner has often pointed out, Paul's experience before Damascus was at the same time a prophetic indication of the appearance of the Etheric Christ in the twentieth century.[83] However, in order that we may grasp these relationships more concretely, we should add to what has

---

* It should here straightaway be emphasized that there are other spiritual beings who take part in this seminal event in the spiritual life of our time. However, modern spiritual research speaks of the especially intimate and direct participation of these *three* beings.

been said certain highly important facts given by Rudolf Steiner in the lecture held in London on 2 May 1913. In this lecture, we find a direct indication to the effect that the appearance of the Etheric Christ in the twentieth century was preceded by a kind of *supersensible repetition of the Mystery of Golgotha* in the nineteenth century. If, then, we make a direct comparison between the events preceding the new appearance of Christ and the Mystery of Golgotha that took place upon the Earth in that former time, we may see the signs not only of a supersensible process of death and resurrection but also of the participation in this process of not one but *two* spiritual beings: the macrocosmic Being of the Christ and the Angel-like being of the Nathan Soul, just as was the case with the original Mystery of Golgotha. For just as the Christ Being formerly experienced death in the sheaths of Jesus of Nazareth (the Nathan Soul), so in the spiritual worlds did *that part of Christ's consciousness* which had continued to be connected with the Nathan Soul experience a kind of extinction in the Angel-sphere that borders upon the Earth, in order to rise again in the sphere of human beings as a new Christ-consciousness, as a new opportunity for *each* person to experience directly his connection with Christ.

Let us now turn to the words of Rudolf Steiner himself. In the lecture that has been referred to he says: 'Although Christ came into the old Hebrew race and was led to His death within it, nevertheless the Angel being who *from that time onwards* [since the Mystery of Golgotha] *has been the outer form of Christ* experienced an extinction of consciousness in the course of the nineteenth century as the result of the opposing materialistic forces which—because of the materialistically inclined human souls passing through the gates of death—had entered the spiritual world. And from this loss of consciousness that has taken place in the spiritual worlds there will arise the resurrection of the consciousness of Christ in human souls on Earth between birth and death in the twentieth century. Thus, in a certain sense, one can foretell that from the twentieth century onwards the consciousness humanity has lost will surely arise again as clairvoyant vision. At first only a few and then an ever increasing number of people will in the twentieth century be able to perceive the appearance of the Etheric Christ, that is, Christ in the form of an Angel. For the sake of mankind, this annihilation of consciousness, as one may call it, took place in the worlds which lie immediately above our earthly world and in which Christ was visible during the time between the Mystery of Golgotha and our own age ... Just as the few—who in those days were able to read the signs of the times—were in the position of viewing the Mystery of Golgotha in such a way that they could understand that a great, mighty Being had descended from the spiritual worlds to live on Earth and pass through death so that, through His death, the substances of His Being might be united with the

Earth, so we are able to perceive that in certain worlds (lying immediately behind our own) a spiritual death and resurrection of consciousness—and hence a repetition of the Mystery of Golgotha—has taken place in order that a reawakening of the hitherto concealed Christ-consciousness might come about in human souls on Earth.'[84]

This indication regarding the supersensible *repetition* of the Mystery of Golgotha prior to the etheric manifestation of Christ permits us to speak of the extinction and resurrection of the Christ-consciousness within the Nathan Soul, within that Angel-like being who since the Mystery of Golgotha has accompanied Christ as His radiant soul-sheath.[85] To express this process more imaginatively, we could say that the spiritual (astral) light which Paul the Apostle beheld around Christ at the event of Damascus became gradually extinguished with the onset of the materialism of modern times. Then, after passing through the metamorphosis of death and resurrection, it began to shine again, though now not only outwardly as astral light but also inwardly within people's souls, in their etheric bodies, as *etheric light*, with the capacity of awakening in them a life in purely spiritual thoughts, in the thoughts of spiritual science, which gradually lead towards a new conscious experience of the Christ Being.

Here, however, a basic question arises. If, in passing through the process of the extinction of its Christ-consciousness in the nineteenth century, the Nathan Soul was able to send the light of this consciousness into human souls, thus awakening the first sense of this Christ-consciousness among people, what would then happen with the Nathan Soul? At this point we touch upon a secret that is connected with the *modern* Mysteries of the Nathan Soul. In order to come near to an understanding of this, we need to dwell once more upon the fact that Rudolf Steiner characterizes this entire process as a kind of spiritual *repetition* of the Mystery of Golgotha. This means: when the Nathan Soul passed with Christ through the death on Golgotha at the Turning Point of Time, it also, because of its close connection with Christ and the complete permeation of its being with the forces of the *Ego of Christ*, experienced the Resurrection that followed. Only through such a participation in Christ's Resurrection was the Nathan Soul able to become the bearer of His consciousness in the spiritual world closest to the Earth in the sphere of the *Angels*.

This Christ-consciousness, of which the Nathan Soul has been the bearer for almost two millennia, it now sacrifices to humanity, just as at the time of the historical Mystery of Golgotha it sacrificed its Christ-permeated physical body. As a result of this sacrificial deed, which could also be called the *fifth* sacrificial deed of the Nathan Soul, it passes through what has to be described as a period of unconsciousness in the spiritual world (for, as we have seen, the forces of its Christ-consciousness have now abandoned it

and have passed over to human beings). After some time it is again awakened from this state of unconsciousness by Christ, but now it is awakened
not through a union with the forces of Christ's Ego, as was the case after
the historical Mystery of Golgotha, but through the forces of the next
higher member of Christ's Being, His *Spirit Self*, with which He had
Himself entered into Earth-existence at the Turning Point of Time.[86]
After this second resurrection in the higher worlds, the Nathan Soul must
yet again fashion for the Christ—who in our time journeys among mankind in etheric form—a garment of light. This time, however, it can be
woven only from the light of spiritual thoughts which, born from the
working of the Christ-consciousness in man, human beings are able to
carry through the light-ether into the astral light. It is from such a transformed astral body that the Nathan Soul now fashions a new garment of
light for the Etheric Christ. And we may consider Rudolf Steiner's revelation, in September 1909, of the Mystery of the Nathan Soul in his lecture-cycle on the Gospel of St Luke, as an indication of the beginning of
this process in the supersensible worlds nearest to the Earth.

The second being who takes a direct part in the new Christ event is the
Archangel Vidar. According to what has already been quoted here from
Rudolf Steiner (see p. 321), he is now fashioning, in the spiritual world
closest to the Earth, that 'etheric form' in which 'the principle that we shall
come to see as the etheric form of Christ will incarnate'. Vidar fashions this
etheric form from the most refined etheric forces in the 'etheric ring'
around the Earth and also from that purest etheric substance of mankind's
primal youth, whose guardian he has been in the spiritual worlds since the
events of Palestine—in other words, from the etheric forces that are fully
permeated by the Christ-impulse and the etheric forces of the unfallen
macrocosmic universal *life*,[87] both of which he condenses to an *imaginative
shape*, an imaginative form, wherein the Etheric Christ may work amongst
mankind.[88] And inasmuch as Vidar is the new guardian of the Nathan Soul
and also the protector of the etheric forces of mankind's primal youth, so
now his task is to awaken in the souls of human beings those new clairvoyant faculties which can rightly apprehend the Christ event.

Thus, in the present epoch of human evolution, the Archangel Vidar
not only participates in the manner described in the new Christ event in
the external spiritual world but also directly participates in the awakening
and enlivening of those forces in the human soul which can enable it
consciously to perceive this event. Vidar fulfils this latter function in that he
prepares and strengthens that part of the human soul in which the birth of
the new Christ-consciousness is to take place and in which the primordial
forces of the Nathan Soul are to be awakened to conscious activity. But
where within man does this awakening of the Christ-consciousness, borne

by the Nathan Soul, come about? Rudolf Steiner answers this question with these words: 'One should, however, pay heed to what has remained of a childlike nature within man, in that in a roundabout way it is through this legacy of childlike qualities that the Christ forces will again bring warmth to the other faculties. We must *make our childlike nature bright* so that a certain *brightness* may be imparted to our other faculties. There lives a childlike nature in every human being, and if *it is activated* it will be responsive to union with the Christ principle.'[89] It is to this *permeation* of man's childlike nature with *brightness* and its activation in order that it may unite with the Christ principle that Vidar would lead mankind. For these childlike forces form that maternal ground whence Vidar can enable the flowering, in our time, of the new clairvoyance—not the old chaotic clairvoyance but its new counterpart, 'illumined by reason and knowledge'. Hence Vidar and the Nathan Soul now work together amongst mankind. Vidar activates and permeates with reason the childlike part of every human soul, thus awakening the primordial soul-forces that are related to the Nathan Soul, which then 'resurrects' within man and endows him with that inner light of the angelic Christ-consciousness, a quality which Vidar can transform into the forces of the new imaginative clairvoyance. This process can also be described as follows: the Nathan Soul imparts to the human soul the new Christ *light*, while Vidar, through activating those parts of the soul which can serve as the foundation for new supersensible faculties, endows it with the possibility of *living in Imaginations*.

This combined activity of Vidar and the Nathan Soul can be viewed with particular clarity if one considers the further metamorphosis of the human faculty of memory. We have already spoken (see p. 56) of how the forces for the right use of this faculty, so intimately connected as it is with the essential nature of human ego-consciousness, entered into humanity through the fourth sacrifice of the Nathan Soul at the Turning Point of Time. The right development of the faculty of memory was at that time a prerequisite for the entire development of ego-consciousness. Now, however, when this ego-consciousness has to a large extent been attained by human beings, a further metamorphosis must take place. Man must *in full consciousness* permeate his faculty of memory with the forces of Christ, an endeavour which in its turn is directly associated with the development of the new clairvoyance.[90] And as the faculty of memory is rooted in the etheric body, one is therefore initially speaking of the union of the Christ-impulse with those parts of it where the forces related to the Nathan Soul still prevail, and then of its influence upon the other parts of the etheric body.[91] These forces related to the Nathan Soul, which in ancient times were in accordance with the purposes of world rulership kept back from the Fall, from being penetrated by luciferic and then by ahrimanic influences, are, as we know from Rudolf Steiner, connected with the particular part of the two higher kinds of ether that make up man's etheric body: the 'sound-ether' and the 'life-ether'.[92] It is the forces of these two kinds of ether—untouched as they are by the Fall—that the Nathan Soul has brought to the Earth in the course of its incarnation so as to immerse the forces of the ancient primal memory of Paradise in the stream of human evolution. Thus in the etheric body of modern man we have a higher memory which bears recollections of the life of the human soul in the higher worlds before the Fall (this memory is rooted in the sound- and life-ethers) and ordinary earthly memory, which is connected more with the light- and to some extent also with the warmth-ether. The process which in our time is to take place in the manner indicated within human souls, as a result of the combined activity of Vidar and the Nathan Soul, consists in this: that with the co-operation of Vidar, the forces of the Nathan Soul (which bear the consciousness of Christ) need to be awakened in the sound and life 'regions' of the etheric body, in order that they may to some extent also penetrate its light 'part' (and in the future even its 'warmth' part), thereby opening up the path to a direct penetration by the Christ-impulse. Rudolf Steiner speaks about this as follows: 'The new Christ event, which now no longer takes place physically but etherically, is connected with the first unfolding of the faculty of memory, with the first unfolding of what one may describe as a faculty of memory that is permeated by Christ; this new Christ event will be of such a nature that Christ will approach human beings as an *Angel-like Being*. For this we must prepare ourselves.'[93]

As to *how* this enlivening of memory, which is to lead in our time to a new etheric clairvoyance, will take place or, in other words, *how* the forces of Vidar and the Nathan Soul as they work together in our present age—once they have been stirred into life within the 'sound' and 'life' regions of the etheric body—can penetrate from thence into its 'light' region, we may learn from the lecture given by Rudolf Steiner on 2 January 1916. There the actual process of earthly memory, which is associated with the light part of man's etheric body, is set before us; Rudolf Steiner speaks in the same lecture of the gradual overcoming of the luciferic and ahrimanic forces that work within it.

Christ once spoke prophetically about this inner 'mystery of light' within man's being in the narrow circle of His disciples during the forty-day conversations after His Resurrection from the dead. And he concluded this revelation of the 'mystery of light' when He gave to the disciples a mantric text, which, in the form in which Rudolf Steiner was able to draw it forth from the Akashic Chronicle, is a most highly significant mantram that can, if rightly studied, awaken within people of modern times the forces of the new etheric clairvoyance that leads *to the contemplation of the etheric image of Christ as it is reflected in one's own etheric body.* This mantram runs as follows:

> O, you powers in the spiritual world, let me be conscious in the world of light out of [the forces of] my physical body, [let me] be in the light, in order to observe my own body of light, and do not let the might of the ahrimanic forces gain such power over me that it becomes impossible for me to behold what takes place within my body of light.[94]

(In the sense of the above, we may imagine the Nathan Soul, Vidar, and, as we shall see, the ruling Spirit of our age, Michael, to be among those to whom we in our time would initially turn with this plea for help.)

The following picture emerges of what is revealed to the human soul in the event of such an immersion in the contemplation of one's own body of light. We have already seen that the new appearance of Christ in the twentieth century was preceded by the extinction of the Christ-permeated consciousness of the Nathan Soul in the spiritual world nearest to the Earth, and then by its new enkindling within the souls of human beings. To be more precise, this process was expressed in the gradual extinction of the astral light that shone forth from the Nathan Soul and its simultaneous transformation, its 'condensation' into *etheric light.* By means of the life and sound parts of the human etheric body which had been enlivened by Vidar, his *etheric light* could penetrate into the light part of the human etheric body[95] which is where man can then behold his memory as per-meated with the forces of Christ.

If we now recall that the astral light is in a certain sense the astral memory of the cosmos,[96] while the light part of the human etheric body is the bearer of man's individual earthly memory, the whole process can also be defined as follows. This process is a fructifying of human memory by the cosmic memory that is imbued with the direct presence of Christ and is the beginning of the mystery of the gradual entry of the Christ-impulse into human memory, thus leading man towards the new vision of the Christ in the spiritual world nearest to the Earth.[97] In the sense of the lecture referred to, this corresponds to the process of the *enlivening,* and at the same time the *enlightening,* of the ordinary human memory, which is none other than light-filled movements of the human etheric body that have become immersed in darkness.[98] In this connection, the following words from the lecture of 2 January may be cited: 'Demons [the spirits that serve Ahriman] continually keep man's body of light in the darkness. This comes about through the treatment to which Ahriman subjects the physical and also, moreover, the etheric bodies [of man].'[99] With this it now becomes clear that the entry of the Christ-impulse into a light region of the human etheric body in the course of enlivening the faculty of memory makes possible not only the awakening of the new clairvoyance but also something even more significant, which Rudolf Steiner emphasizes in the lecture that has been referred to. He goes on to say: 'Hence we may say, and I shall write these words on the blackboard because they are so important: If it becomes possible for the human soul to observe from out of the light the processes in its own body of light, this means that the soul has freed itself from the ahrimanic forces which would normally darken the processes in the body of light.'[100]

Thus, at the end of the dark age of the Kali-Yuga, the opportunity will arise not only for initiates or for those who find themselves in a special position such as being direct pupils of Christ Jesus, but also for ever wider circles of people, to come—on the basis of the Christ-consciousness that has been born within human souls through the power of Vidar—to attain a new etheric clairvoyance which is attainable only because a victory (albeit partial) over the ahrimanic powers in the human etheric body has taken place. We may find the archetype of this event in the victory of Vidar over the Fenris Wolf, over those ahrimanic forces which would also awaken a certain clairvoyance in people of our time but in such a way that it leads not to a contemplation 'out of the body of light into the light' but only to an even greater darkening.[101] For the 'clairvoyance' of the Fenris Wolf will rest not upon the freeing of the light-ether from the ahrimanic forces[102] but upon the extending of their authority over the chemical- and life-ethers.[103]

We are now ready to consider in greater detail the nature of the part played in the new Christ event by the ruling Spirit of our age, Michael. Rudolf Steiner refers repeatedly in his lectures to the direct connection that exists between the Second Coming and the activity of Michael since 1879. We find particularly significant indications of this in the lectures of the years 1913, 1914 and 1915, where two aspects of our theme come especially to the fore.

The first aspect concerns Michael's ascent in the fifth decade of the nineteenth century from the rank of Archangel to that of Archai,[104] thus enabling him to serve the Christ Being at a higher level,[105] a task which had of course begun for Michael at the time of the Mystery of Golgotha, when he changed from being an envoy of Yahveh to being an envoy of Christ.

Since the 1840s, however, while he was preparing the epoch of his first rulership in Christian times, Michael had to connect himself deeply with the sphere in which the Christ-impulse works directly. Rudolf Steiner, in the lecture of 20 May 1913, relates the transition that Michael makes—from serving Yahveh to serving Christ—to the year 1879 and even, in a certain sense, to the beginning of Christ's appearance in the etheric realm:

'If in the twentieth century it is possible for souls to evolve towards an understanding of the Mystery of Golgotha [it will be seen that] this has its origin in that event whereby Christ was, through a conspiracy of materialistic souls, driven out from the spiritual worlds and placed into the world of the senses, into the world of human beings, so that a new understanding of Christ might arise also in this world of the senses. Because of this, Christ was connected even more intimately with the destinies of human beings on Earth. And just as it was once possible to look up to Yahveh or Jehovah and to know that he is that being who has sent forth Michael to prepare the way for the transition of the age of Yahveh to the age of Christ [just as it was formerly Yahveh who sent Michael], so *now* it is Christ who sends Michael to us. This is the new fact of great significance which we must transform into a feeling. Just as it was previously possible to speak of Yahveh-Michael as ruler of the age, so *now* we can speak of Christ-Michael. *Michael has been exalted to a higher stage—from Folk Spirit to Time Spirit—inasmuch as from being the messenger of Yahveh he has become the messenger of Christ.* Thus we are speaking of a right understanding of the Christ-impulse when we speak of a right understanding of the Michael-impulse in our time.'[106]

The following words of Rudolf Steiner, taken from the lecture of 2 May 1913 and representing the conclusion of the description of the Second Coming that he gives there, address this question even more clearly: 'Christ has already been crucified twice: once physically [in the physical world], at the beginning of our era, and a second time [as has been described] spiritually, in the nineteenth century. It could be said that humanity experienced at that former time the resurrection of His body [that is, the body of the Nathan Soul], and that it will experience the resurrection of His consciousness [that is, the Christ-permeated consciousness of the Nathan Soul] from the twentieth century onwards. What I have only been able to indicate in a few words [i.e. the description of the Second Coming] will gradually enter into human souls, and the mediator, the messenger, will be Michael, who is *now* the ambassador of Christ. And just as he formerly guided human souls in such a way that they might understand the direction of His Life as from Heaven to Earth, so is he now preparing humanity to experience the consciousness of Christ as it proceeds from the realm of the unknown to that of the known.'[107]

Here we have a further sign of the entirely new relationship that has come about between Christ and Michael as a result of the dawning of the new epoch of the Sun Archangel's rulership among mankind and Christ's passage through the repetition of the Mystery of Golgotha.[108] However, these two events may be seen as being still more intimately related if we consider the following.

The essential quality of the new rulership of Michael that began in the last third of the nineteenth century was that it was achieved as the result of the hard struggle with, and final victory over, certain ahrimanic beings belonging to the Hierarchy of the Angels (Rudolf Steiner also calls them the 'spirits of darkness'), who around 1879 were cast down to the Earth into the souls, into the *minds*, of human beings.[109] Through Michael's heavenly victory one could also say that the supersensible horizon, the celestial sphere which lies adjacent to the earthly world, was fully purified from the spirits of opposition, and this made it possible for a new spiritual revelation to stream forth upon the Earth, a revelation which at the beginning of our century took the form of anthroposophically orientated spiritual science. This meant that, while Michael has since that time remained in the spiritual sphere that he has purified, down on the Earth in the world of human beings an ever greater darkness has held sway. This state of affairs, however, changed quite fundamentally in the year 1899 with the ending of the dark age of the Kali-Yuga, resulting in an entirely new possibility of relating to and participating in the events of earthly, and in particular human, evolution emerging for all the beings of the spiritual world. Thus by the beginning of our century we have the following picture: in the heights, Michael in the purified spiritual world; in the depths, humanity with the fallen spirits of darkness in its midst, and between the two worlds a gate which, since 1899, is no longer closed but wide open, a freely accessible path for intercourse between spiritual and earthly beings.

Into this spiritual situation, from 1909 onwards, there then enters Christ in that etheric form which the Archangel Vidar, together with the Nathan Soul (who has accompanied Him since the events of Palestine), has fashioned for Him. For just as the foundation for the 'first' Mystery of Golgotha was the descent of Christ into the physical world to rescue man's earthly form, the Phantom of his physical body (in other words, the physical body of the Nathan Soul as the archetype of mankind), so at the foundation of the 'second' Mystery of Golgotha in the supersensible worlds—which culminates in the appearance of Christ in a new etheric form—we have Christ's sacrificial resolve to remain with humanity, that is, to enter that sphere to which, thirty years earlier, the opposing forces of darkness had been despatched by Michael. Thus Christ has willed to remain with humanity and with its destiny on Earth *until the very end*. This could be expressed more imaginatively as follows. As a result of Michael's victory in the heights, a new light has dawned in the supersensible world surrounding the Earth; while down on the Earth the darkness has intensified further—a darkness into which Christ has since the year 1909 begun to descend from the light above. Since this time two completely contradictory impulses have been working simultaneously in the very foundations of Earth-existence and also in the depths of human souls: the impulse of Christ and the impulses of the ahrimanic spirits of darkness. The following deeply significant words of Rudolf Steiner speak of this: 'But Christ will be there; through His great sacrifice He will live in that same sphere which Ahriman also inhabits. And man will be able to choose between Christ and Ahriman.'[110] In our time (as in the time that immediately follows it), ever greater numbers of people will have to make the choice, in full consciousness, between the newly awakening power of conscious clairvoyance, which leads to a Sun-borne vision of the Etheric Christ, and the old power of chaotic 'dark clairvoyance' that is engendered by the Fenris Wolf.[111]

And now we have to ask: what is the relationship of Michael, who has thus remained 'above',[112] to all the events that are being prepared and are taking place 'below' and what part does he take in them? According to the indications of modern spiritual science his task consists in making it possible that Christ, who is now living among people in the etheric form that Vidar has fashioned for Him, and the Nathan Soul, who enshrouds Him with a new aura of light, may *rightly and truly* be perceived by human beings on Earth. And at this point we touch upon an essential secret of our age.

In his lectures of the years 1914–15, Rudolf Steiner touches upon this mystery on three occasions, associating it with the tragic events of those war years. However, we should bear in mind that, inasmuch as these supersensible events are connected not only with the world of human beings but also with the sphere of activity of Michael-Christ, they have a far wider significance in the evolution of humanity; they retain their significance to this day, albeit in a metamorphosed form. Thus Rudolf Steiner addresses the question that concerns us most pertinently in three lectures, those of 9 November and 3 December 1914, and 14 February 1915.[113] These three lectures have as their principal theme the supersensible foundations of the First World War in their connection with the 'spiritual war' between East and West, together with the particular, and difficult, karma of Middle Europe, squeezed as it is between these two polar-opposite forces. In these lectures, however, Rudolf Steiner in a surprising way connects these events that are limited by place and time with what is of *general human significance*, and in particular with the new appearance of Christ[114] and with Michael, who strives for its *right* fulfilment; here we find a thoroughly concrete indication of Michael's preparation for and participation in the events of the Second Coming. Thus in the lecture of 3 December we read: 'So now, as I have often pointed out, we stand before the great event of future times, before the manifestation of Christ in a quite special guise ... Since the last third of the nineteenth century that Spirit whom we call Michael has gone on before as the warrior who prepares people for the Christ event, as the warrior who is the precursor of the Sun Spirit.'[115] In the lecture of 14

February: 'It has already been shown in a number of instances that this appearance of Christ to those people who are able to behold it has been in preparation since the last third of the nineteenth century, in that the ruling Time Spirit is a different one from before. In the course of the preceding centuries Gabriel was the ruling Time Spirit, while Michael has been the ruling Time Spirit since the last third of the nineteenth century. It is Michael who in a certain sense has the task of preparing the manifestation of Christ as an etheric Being. But all this must be prepared, all this must be furthered in evolution, and it will be furthered. It will be furthered in the sense that Michael to some extent wages the battle on behalf of the manifestation of Christ; he prepares the souls that are passing through experiences between death and a new birth for what is to take place in the aura of the Earth.'[116] And in the lecture of 9 November this thought is expressed as follows: 'This event of Christ's appearance ... can take place only if the rulership of Michael is extended ever more widely. This is still a process occurring in the spiritual world. Michael, it would seem, is campaigning on that plane which borders upon our world for the coming of Christ.'[117] Of what does this battle which Michael wages 'for the coming of Christ' consist? In the lectures under consideration, as we have said, the answer to this question is given more in connection with the tragic events of the beginning of the century. However, the spiritual processes that lie at the foundation of these events belong to a far higher spiritual sphere and hence, in a certain sense, continue to have significance in our time. With this in mind we shall consider them more closely.

As we may see from what is imparted by spiritual science, the whole of western civilization has in recent years gradually taken on a character in its development that works very strongly indeed upon man's etheric body. Owing to its influence, the etheric body has, on the one hand, become less and less malleable and, on the other hand, received an ever more concrete imaginative impression from its immediate environment. In the course of time the result of this was that the etheric body of a modern western person acquired to a high degree the tendency to resist the process of its dispersal after death. Because of this, there arose in the spiritual world from the end of the eighteenth century, and especially throughout the nineteenth century, an ever growing number of souls that bore, in their etheric bodies, the strong impulses of modern materialistic civilization in the form of dense imaginations which, on account of their sense of estrangement from the surrounding spiritual world, were ill suited to dissolve. It could be said that through these 'materialistic imaginations' these etheric bodies became dark, impenetrable and even dried up, and were no longer able rightly to unite with the streams of the light-ether raying forth into the universe. As a consequence of this accumulation of the etheric bodies of dead people, filled with 'dark imaginations', in the spiritual world nearest to the Earth during the nineteenth century, the great danger arose that the etheric image of Christ, which from the twentieth century onwards has been approaching human souls, would appear in a distorted form. Thus it was necessary in a particular way to hasten their dissolution in the far reaches of space, so as to enable the etheric form of Christ *rightly* to approach human souls on Earth. This hastening of the process of dissolving those etheric bodies, belonging for the most part to souls that had passed through modern western materialistic civilization, is 'Michael's battle for the coming of [the Etheric] Christ.' In this battle (as we learn from the three lectures under consideration), souls that have passed through their last incarnation in Eastern Europe stand by Michael's side. For through the childlike openness to the spirit that has characterized the large majority of the inhabitants of this area in the eighteenth, nineteenth and early twentieth centuries, life in these regions has not exerted a powerful influence on their etheric bodies, which therefore have the tendency to dissolve rapidly in the spiritual world after death.[118]

Such was the state of affairs in those years. *In our time* certain additional elements have been introduced into the spiritual situation that had arisen at that time. Above all it should be observed that, with the further spread of materialism in the course of the twentieth century, the number of etheric bodies ill-adapted—through their burden of dark 'materialistic imaginations'—to dissolve has greatly increased. The reason for this is, on the one hand, the general growth of materialism amongst civilized people of today and, on the other, the most intense penetration of materialism in the last half-century among the souls of those who inhabit the regions of Eastern Europe. Thus now, as at the beginning of our century, it is possible to speak of a battle, and even of a still harder battle, which is being waged by Michael behind the scenes of outer Earth-existence for the right reflection of the etheric form of Christ in the souls of people of today. Michael's position thus becomes all the more difficult as a greater number of etheric bodies ill-adapted to dissolving, through their materialistic impulses, enter the spiritual world, and also as there is an ever smaller number of inhabitants of Eastern Europe whose spiritual forces can give him help. Out of the background of this new state of affairs we must speak today of the great battle that is being waged behind the scenes of Earth-existence not so much between West and East (in the sense of spiritual geography) as between the spiritual and anti-spiritual impulses within the context of humanity as a whole, of a battle in which Michael receives help principally from two categories of human souls: from martyrs and from men and women who consciously strive towards spiritual development.[119] It is they who now form Michael's new retinue as he battles for the *right* entry of the

Etheric Christ into Earth-existence. *For this battle is by no means over! Moreover, it is only now, as the end of the century draws near, that it enters its most heightened and intense phase.*

To summarize, we may say that the aforesaid lectures refer first and foremost to the natural course of evolution that has taken shape in approximately the last four centuries, in the course of which human etheric bodies have, through the gradual growth of materialism in the entire civilized world, developed an ever greater difficulty in dissolving after death and have by the end of the nineteenth century become a real hindrance to the entry of the Etheric Christ into Earth-existence. This general and, so to speak, natural course of evolution could not have worked so destructively if something else had not combined with it; we shall now consider this. For alongside the general or, as one could say, lawful, growth of materialism in our time there exists an activity proceeding from certain occult circles which is directed with *full consciousness against* the spreading of the Christ-impulse among contemporary humanity. The passage from Rudolf Steiner's lecture of 2 May 1913 that has already been quoted in full on p. 334 contains an indication of this: 'If in the twentieth century it is possible for souls to evolve towards an understanding of the Mystery of Golgotha [it will be seen that] this has its origin in that event whereby Christ was, through a conspiracy of materialistic souls, driven out from the spiritual worlds . . .'

Somewhat earlier in the same lecture Rudolf Steiner speaks of this as follows: 'Materialism has seized people's souls and has taken roots within them. Materialism has become in many respects the fundamental impulse of the epoch that has just gone by. A large number of souls have died who have passed through the gate of death with a materialistic outlook. Never in any previous age have such a large number of souls with a materialistic outlook passed through the gate of death as has been the case in the epoch that has just elapsed. And these souls have gone on to live during the time between death and a new birth in the spiritual world without knowing anything about the world in which they were now living. Then a certain Being came towards them. This Being they perceived in the spiritual world. They had to perceive Him because this Being had united Himself with Earth-existence, even though for the present He reigns invisibly in the sense-perceptible realm of the Earth. *And these souls that had passed through the gate of death have succeeded through their exertions—and we cannot express it otherwise—in driving Christ out of the spiritual world.* Christ has had to experience a kind of renewal of the Mystery of Golgotha, although not in the same magnitude as before. Then He passed through death; now He has had to suffer banishment from His existence in the spiritual world.'[120]

From these words we may sense that the concern here is not merely with the ordinary materialists of our time but rather with a single-minded and widely planned occult machination. For one is speaking of 'a *conspiracy* of materialistic souls', of 'the exertions . . . of souls that had passed through the gate of death . . .', of 'a conspiracy' and 'exertions' directed against the Christ-impulse. At this point we again touch directly upon what is perhaps the most important aspect of the activity of certain occult societies which Rudolf Steiner examines more closely in the three lectures that he gave in Dornach on 18, 19 and 25 November 1917.[121] There he speaks of those secret societies of the East and the West where a conscious and centrally directed campaign is waged against the Christ-impulse as a whole and, in our time, against, in particular, His new appearance in the etheric realm. We have already referred to these secret societies.* But what is of principal importance for us here are the practices and methods of the *western* societies,[122] which we shall now dwell upon in greater detail.

According to what Rudolf Steiner says in the lecture of 18 November, the essential aim of these western secret societies or 'brotherhoods' is to work by all conceivable means for the growth and spread of materialism in the world. For through spreading it in this way they will, as we have seen, not merely make the dissolving of the etheric bodies of materialistically inclined human beings more difficult but will bring it about that: 'Many of those [people] who . . . have resisted the receiving of spiritual under-standing here on Earth, or have been deprived of the possibility of doing so, remain connected after death with the earthly sphere, where they roam aimlessly about. And so it is that the soul of such a human being, now no longer shut off from the surrounding world by his body, which can no longer prevent it from working destructively, becomes—in living in the earthly sphere after death—a centre of destruction.'[123] Thus 'at the present time there are misguided materialists who believe that the material life is all, but there are also initiates who are materialists and who disseminate materialistic teachings through brotherhoods . . . But what do such initiates really want? For although they know perfectly well that the human soul is a purely spiritual entity that is utterly independent of its corporeality, they nevertheless nourish and foster materialistic attitudes among people. These initiates have the wish that there be as many human souls as possible that will, between birth and death, only be receptive to materialistic concep-tions. Such souls will be prepared by remaining in the earthly sphere after death. They will in one way or another be held back in the earthly sphere. Just imagine that there are indeed brotherhoods which know all this to perfection. These brotherhoods prepare certain human souls in this way *in order that they might after death remain in the realm of matter.* Then these

---

* See the chapter, 'The Virtue of Faith and the Fifth post-Atlantean Epoch'.

brotherhoods bring it about—and this does indeed lie within the scope of their infamous power—that such souls are led after death into the sphere of influence of the brotherhoods. Through this means the power of such brotherhoods grows immeasurably . . . Now let us suppose that here lies the realm of such a brotherhood, that this brotherhood disseminates materialistic teachings, that it sees to it that human beings think materialistically. By this means it furnishes itself with souls that remain in the earthly sphere after death. Such souls become a spiritual clientele for this lodge; which is to say, this lodge has thereby fashioned for itself dead souls who, instead of leaving the earthly sphere, remain close to the Earth. And if things go as planned, souls are held within the lodge. Thus lodges are formed which include both living and dead people, but such dead *as have become related to earthly forces.*'[124]

And so we have, on the one hand, the ordinary modern materialists, who after their death are in the normal course of events compelled to work within these lodges, and, on the other hand, the initiates who rule these lodges together with their followers, that is, those who are at various stages of initiation into the mystery of the inner purposes of these lodges. Now the question arises: what is it that these 'initiate-materialists' and their retinue hope to procure?

We may find an answer to this question if we take into consideration what Rudolf Steiner says about these matters in the lecture of 18 November 1917, which has already been quoted, and the lecture of 20 January 1917.[125] These lectures, in a certain sense, complement one another. In the first, the principal aim of the initiates who lead the secret brotherhoods is defined as follows: 'Yes, those brotherhoods . . . that wish to confine human souls within the materialistic sphere try their utmost to ensure that Christ passes by unnoticed in the twentieth century, to render His coming as an etheric Individuality imperceptible to mankind. And they unfold their aspirations under the sway of a quite definite idea, of a quite definite impulse of will, namely, *to win that sphere of influence into which the Christ should enter in the twentieth century and beyond . . . for another Being.* There are western occult brotherhoods which yearn to make the Christ-impulse a matter of dispute and to place in Christ's stead another individuality *who has never as yet appeared in the flesh on Earth but is only an etheric individuality with a purely ahrimanic nature.* All those manipulations with the dead (of which I have just spoken) have as their final aim that of drawing people away from the Christ who has passed through the Mystery of Golgotha, and handing over the rulership of the Earth to another individuality. This is not some sort of abstract idea or what have you but an utterly real battle, a battle with the aim of setting up another being in place of the Christ Being to carry human evolution through the rest of our fifth epoch and also through the entire period of the sixth and seventh epochs of our post-Atlantean age.'[126]

And then this ahrimanic being will, according to the way of thinking of these brotherhoods, not—like Christ—lead mankind in full consciousness during the fifth, sixth and seventh epochs into ever higher spheres of the macrocosm but will, on the contrary, conjure forth a spectral realm which will—in accordance with the intentions of this being—be formed immediately beneath the surface of the Earth in the region of its solid and liquid elements.[127] Bringing such a spectral realm, inhabited by a subhuman humanity, into being is a principal aim of these brotherhoods. In the lecture of 20 January 1917, Rudolf Steiner calls this second aim of theirs 'the attainment of ahrimanic immortality'; and the lecture contains a description of the methods employed to achieve it. Their essential nature is as follows. Through the special forms of ceremonial magic practised in such lodges, the intention is to work upon human sheaths in such a way that when a member of the secret lodge dies he is not only enabled to remain for a long time within the earthly sphere, as are the souls of ordinary materialists, but is also granted the possibility of participating further in all the affairs of the lodge, of continuing to work towards furthering its goals, though now directly from the spiritual world. The members of these lodges seek the spiritual help and spiritual protection necessary for such ceremonial acts as these especially among ahrimanic Angel beings who remained behind at the time of the Egypto-Chaldean epoch and who now inspire human beings with all manner of materialistic ideas.[128] This latter thought can also be expressed differently. One could also say: these retarded ahrimanic Angels, who are in their nature especially akin to the spirits of darkness cast down by Michael around the year 1879,[129] have since those times worked with particular intensity in such brotherhoods which serve as the earthly instruments whereby they spread thoroughly unpleasant forms of materialism among mankind. Herein also lies the reason why the members of these brotherhoods, as they seek immortality on the ahrimanic path, do not fear the thought of losing *true* immortality after their death. For under the influence of the retarded ahrimanic Angels they come to feel that the world of ahrimanic forces is superior to Christ. The retarded nature of these Angels revolves around the fact that, in contrast to the normally evolved Angels, they refused to receive the Christ-impulse in the Egypto-Chaldean epoch.[130] Rudolf Steiner characterizes the attitude of the members of these lodges in such a way that they would say to themselves: 'We no longer want as leader the Christ who is the leader of the normal world;[131] we want to have another leader, we want to enter into opposition to this normal world.' And then commenting upon these words, Rudolf Steiner continues: 'Through the preparations that

342

they make, which are called forth by ceremonial magic, they receive the impression that their own world of ahrimanic forces is a far more powerful spiritual world [than the world of Christ], that they can above all else continue what they have made their own here in physical life, that they can make the material experiences of physical life immortal.'[132]

We shall now consider in somewhat more detail the way in which these secret societies work within human sheaths, for this will help us towards a better understanding of the nature of that immortal state, defined by the words 'ahrimanic immortality', to which they aspire. In his descriptions of the practice that is manifested in the various brotherhoods of a freemasonic orientation (which are often far from having such dark goals as the aforesaid societies that seek 'ahrimanic immortality'), Rudolf Steiner indicates on several occasions[133] that what they try to do is work in a transforming way upon the human *etheric body*. This comes about in such a way that the neophyte repeatedly takes part in certain symbolic, ritualistic acts which have the capacity to wield a powerful influence upon his etheric body but whose meaning and content remain totally beyond his comprehension. As a result, human beings appear in the world who have in their heads the ideas and conceptions that are normal for their time but who in their subconscious, in their etheric bodies, are filled with an all-embracing cosmic wisdom; this is how things work in the 'ordinary' brotherhoods.[134]

In the brotherhoods of a so-called 'left' inclination, on the other hand, where the attainment of 'ahrimanic immortality' becomes a goal to be striven for, the aim is to supplement this with the aid of special methods and rituals of ceremonial magic so as to influence not merely the etheric but also the physical body; and so those faculties, with whose help the attempt is made to extend an influence to the physical body, gradually lead in turn to a particularly powerful materializing of the etheric body.★ Such a powerful impression of purely 'materialistic imaginations', associated with the life of the physical body, is then made upon it that such an etheric body, after the death of a person of this kind, totally loses the capacity of dissolving in the world ether. It becomes poisoned to so great a degree by 'materialistic imaginations' that the etheric cosmos simply refuses to receive it, spurns it, and as a result it remains for a long time in the vicinity of the Earth. This is, however, the aim not merely of these secret brotherhoods but above all of the ahrimanic Angels who inspire them. And whereas Rudolf Steiner said even of the etheric bodies of people who are strongly

---

★ The aim in these lodges is to densify, to compress, the etheric body to the extent that it approaches as fully as possible the functioning that is natural to the physical body, as the result of which the soul necessarily becomes chained to physical matter (see Rudolf Steiner's words quoted on pp. 339–40).

inclined towards materialism: 'Such etheric bodies take a long time to dissolve [after death], they continue to exist for a long time as spectres' (that is, as phantoms, see p. 137),[135] The etheric bodies of the members of these brotherhoods that are worked upon in this way become *phantoms* that work with exceptional power in the spiritual world bordering upon the Earth, where they are gradually prepared for a quite special task.

In order that we may characterize the processes that arise here, we need to recall that the materialistically inclined souls who are compelled by such occult brotherhoods after death to serve their goals, and also the members of these brotherhoods themselves who continue to participate in the lodges after their death, are as a general rule dwelling not in etheric bodies but in *astral bodies*. However, because this is so, the 'ahrimanic immortality', which the members of these brotherhoods strive towards, remains essentially unattainable. For from the moment when a soul dwells in the spiritual world in an astral rather than in an ether body, it ceases to be able to remain for any length of time in the immediate vicinity of the Earth. Sooner or later—even if this sometimes takes place after a fairly long time—it must, in accordance with the spiritual laws that govern our cosmos, rise higher and so depart, even if only temporarily, from the immediate sphere of influence of these brotherhoods. On the other hand, it is of the nature of 'ahrimanic immortality' that a soul that dwells after death in the spiritual world in its astral body is given—by certain elemental ahrimanic spirits who are under the direct authority of retarded ahrimanic Angels—the opportunity of building for itself a new etheric body, though not in the way this ought to take place, that is, out of the forces of the cosmic ether, but out of the substance of the undissolved etheric bodies which have been prepared in occult lodges. This special secret, that after death a soul cannot ascend into higher spiritual spheres while still retaining its etheric body,[136] was well known in antiquity and was employed by the Egyptians in the process of mummification. For this reason these brotherhoods seek inspiration from retarded Angels of the Egyptian epoch, since they are best able to further this occult mummificatiorr of etheric bodies. And if they were once to succeed, if these brotherhoods were in some distant future to succeed in their object *that a person who has died and who has remained after death in his astral body within the sphere of such a lodge is able to incarnate in the substance of undissolved, densified etheric bodies that have been worked upon in the aforesaid way, a kind of 'ahrimanic immortality' would have been achieved!*

Through this the foundation would be laid for the achieving of Ahriman's goals in earthly evolution, a goal of which Rudolf Steiner speaks in some detail in the lecture of 3 December 1922. There he points to how already in our time the ahrimanic powers make ceaseless efforts in this direction during man's sleep-life. For when the physical and etheric bodies are left in bed at night and the individual ascends into the spiritual world arrayed in his astral body, the ahrimanic spirits try unlawfully to furnish him with a new false etheric body consisting not of a cosmic but of *earthly* ether.⋆ In the lecture referred to above, Rudolf Steiner speaks about this as follows: 'These beings are identical with those that I have always assigned to the category of the ahrimanic. They have set themselves the aim of keeping man on the Earth by all possible means. You know from the book *Occult Science* that the Earth will one day vanish away and will pass over into the Jupiter condition. This is what these beings want to prevent. They want to prevent man from evolving in a right way with the Earth until it comes to an end, and from passing over into the Jupiter condition in a normal manner. They want to preserve the Earth in its present state; they want to hold onto the Earth and keep the human beings only for the Earth. Hence these beings work ceaselessly and with great intensity to achieve the following.'[137] They endeavour '... *to give man during sleep an etheric body composed of the Earth's ether*, but they hardly ever succeed. *In rare cases, of which I shall speak later, they do succeed*,[138] but this almost never occurs. Nevertheless they do not desist from such attempts, on the presumption that at some time their efforts will yield results and that they will be able to surround, to permeate man while he sleeps, and has left his etheric body in bed, *with* [another] *etheric body formed of the Earth's ether*. This is what these beings want. If such ahrimanic beings actually managed to introduce an entire etheric body [from the Earth's ether] step by step into a man while he was asleep, such a person would be able after death, living in his etheric body, to remain within this body. Generally speaking, the etheric body dissolves after a few days. *But a human being—to whom what has been described above had happened—would be able to remain within his etheric body, and after a certain time a whole race of etheric human beings would have arisen*. This is what is wanted from this corner of the spiritual world. Then it would be possible to preserve the Earth. And it is indeed so that *in the solid and liquid parts of the Earth* hosts of such beings can be found *whose wish it is gradually to transform humanity into pure phantoms, into etheric phantoms, until the end of earthly evolution, so that the goal, the normal goal of the Earth's evolution, could not be attained.*'[139]

As has been said, this is not as yet attainable for these ahrimanic beings and their earthly followers, those human beings who seek 'ahrimanic immortality'.[140] But if something of the kind were once able to happen

---

⋆ That is, the ether that has been appropriated by Ahriman through his having torn it from the etheric cosmos as a result of the systematic imprinting of laws that belong to man's physical body (the earthly world) upon his etheric body. (See Rudolf Steiner's words on p. 339.)

(even though this would for the time being only come about in individual, 'rare' cases), a whole 'host of phantoms' would be created in this way, and this would then form the appropriate 'retinue'[141] for that being of 'purely ahrimanic nature' who, with the help of the aforesaid brotherhoods, will attempt to take the place of the Etheric Christ in the supersensible world nearest to the Earth '. . . for the entire remainder of our fifth post-Atlantean epoch and also for the full extent of the sixth and seventh [epochs].'[142]

Thus in certain secret brotherhoods of the west there is the aim to create—with the help of 'ahrimanic immortality'—in future times (which are already being prepared in our own age) a whole subhuman humanity in order to bring about as soon as possible the rulership of that being who as an 'ahrimanic spectre' now wishes to question the right of the Etheric Christ to hold sway over mankind. In other words, these secret brotherhoods are even now striving '. . . gradually to fulfil their ideal . . . of living in future periods of Earth evolution as spectres, of inhabiting the Earth as spectres.'[142a] Herein we have in a certain sense the final goal of this line of development. But as in our time the 'incarnation' of the dead in the substance of undissolved etheric bodies is still impossible on any great scale, the principal battle against such a future is being waged on a somewhat different front, directed as it is towards the rapid dissolution in the spiritual world of the mummified etheric bodies that are gathered there. For the danger that comes from their excessive accumulation in the Earth's surroundings is that, with time, they can form a sort of 'etheric anti-ring'[143] (see further regarding the 'etheric ring' on pp. 237–8), as a result of which a *distorted reflection* may arise of that etheric form in which Christ is to work now among human beings. If this were to happen, humanity would be thrust into the danger which confronted the Apostles in the scene of the walking on the waters—the danger of confusing the Etheric Christ with the ahrimanic spectre. In this event, with the awakening of clairvoyant faculties among people, it would not be the new clairvoyance of Vidar, 'illumined by reason and scientific thinking' and leading to an experience of the Etheric Christ, that would triumph but the chaotic clairvoyance of the Fenris Wolf which would fill the modern world with countless spectral visions so as to ensure that human evolution is eventually directed along an ahrimanic channel.

And so spiritual energies are focused upon mankind today from two opposite sides. On the one hand there is the activity that is directed towards strengthening the 'etheric ring' that has surrounded the Earth since the Mystery of Golgotha, a ring whose forces contribute especially to the right fulfilment of the new appearance of Christ; for this can come about in the right way '. . . only if work is done in the spiritual world upon the purity of the preparations that are made for the future appearance of the Etheric

Christ, who is to appear to people as an etheric form.'[144] On the other hand, the aforesaid secret brotherhoods and the ahrimanic beings that inspire them, who are working out of etheric bodies that are strongly impregnated with materialistic imaginations and unspiritual ideas, are trying to create, one can say, an 'etheric anti-ring', for '. . . the strongly impregnated etheric bodies that are around us everywhere in the elemental world would ever seek to work obstructively in that time which is to come, when this etheric form which the Christ must adopt is to become visible in a pure way.'[145]

Against this second kind of activity, which has begun since the last third of the nineteenth century, Michael fights in company with those human souls that are especially suited for this task, with the souls of those human beings who have, even if only to a certain extent, received the Christ-impulse into their etheric bodies on Earth, in order that this part of their etheric bodies might after their death strengthen the power of the 'etheric ring' around the Earth, and the remaining parts dissolve as soon as possible in the surrounding ether. From this point of view, an etheric body which has been especially strongly permeated by the Christ-impulse can also be thought of as being possessed by a human being who is after death enabled to connect himself especially deeply with the being from the Hierarchy of the Angels who guides him.[146] In contrast, a soul that brings into the spiritual world after death an etheric body that is filled with 'materialistic imaginations' and is as a consequence compelled to remain for a long time in the vicinity of the Earth acquires the tendency to distance itself even further from its Angel and to enter the sphere of influence of an ahrimanic Angel—a being who had remained behind in the Egypto-Chaldean epoch. The souls of the first kind are, therefore, in Rudolf Steiner's words, '. . . quite especially suited to the generating of the forces whereby the image through which the Christ is to become manifest may appear in purity.'[147] For it is 'in order that He does not appear in false form, in the subjective imaginations of human beings, but rather in His true image that Michael must wage his battle . . . [And] he must wage it in particular with the help of those souls that by their nature bear within themselves this Angel-consciousness.[148] Through this they are especially well prepared and because their etheric bodies dissolve easily, they have nothing in their etheric bodies which might make Christ appear in a false form, in false imaginations.'[149] On the other hand, etheric bodies that have a strong tendency to become hardened and might hence further the arising of the 'anti-ring' in the spiritual world nearest to the Earth must be fully dissolved as rapidly as possible in the world ether with the help of external forces. For this is a necessary prerequisite for the new appearance of Christ: '. . . it is necessary to work upon the dispersal of these etheric bodies in the universal world ether so that a false image of the appearance of Christ does not arise.'[150]

The following deeply prophetic words of Christ Jesus from the Gospel of St Luke refer in a remarkable way to the necessity for such a rapid dissolution of dead, mummified etheric bodies: 'And they answered and spoke to Him: 'Where, Lord? And He said to them: Where the corpse is, there the eagles gather.'[151]

As the number of souls that are *naturally* predisposed to ally themselves after death with the hosts of Michael and under his guidance to participate in the dissolving of the mummified etheric bodies is, because of the general spread of materialism, becoming ever smaller (even in Eastern Europe), the *conscious* work of human beings in the direction indicated becomes ever more necessary. Modern spiritual science exists in the world precisely in order to prepare human beings for this work, which must be carried out today principally in two directions.

Firstly, the new Christ-knowledge that is contained in anthroposophically orientated spiritual science must in the present time be embraced with all possible intensity, so that it permeates not only our astral body but is also enabled to penetrate through to the etheric body, to the particular qualities of our character and our most intimate and inward relationships to the world and to other people. For we must now learn to let Christ rule not only in our inner being, in our soul-forces, but also in our outward social relationships, which are connected not only with the astral but also with the etheric body.

Secondly, in our modern age we need to develop a right relationship to the new revelation of Michael and to his present position in the world and among human beings, as expressed in the great imagination of his battle with the ahrimanic dragon. However, in order to prepare ourselves aright for this second task, it is necessary not merely to 'know' the great imagination of Michael in a theoretical way but rather, with the entire inner strength of our soul, in full, selfless devotion and trust with respect to his great task as it is revealed to us in modern Anthroposophy, to imprint this imagination within ourselves as a living power that works even into our etheric body.

In the period of time that preceded the last third of the nineteenth century, such an imprinting of the Michael imagination into the etheric body could occur only to a very small degree. By the year 1879, however, a significant change took place in this respect. Rudolf Steiner describes—from the standpoint of the Michael-sphere—the wholly new spiritual situation that had arisen: 'Towards the end of the nineteenth century it came about that Michael was able to say: now the *image* [Michael with the dragon] has *become condensed* in man *to such an extent* that he can receive it inwardly, he can feel the dragon-conqueror in his soul, *at any rate he can sense some meaning in the image.*'[152] And then Rudolf Steiner continues, in explanation: 'But in the last third of the nineteenth century it was so that the image of Michael became so strong within man that it came, so to speak, to depend upon nothing more than his good will that he should raise his own feelings aloft and so be able consciously to rise to the image of Michael. And there appeared before the eye of his soul, on the one hand, the image of the dragon, as a feeling experience devoid of light, and then, on the other hand, in spirit vision and yet discernible by ordinary consciousness, the radiant image of Michael.'[153]

This experience of Michael fighting his battle, which the soul has acquired through conscious effort, must then be imprinted—with all the inner strength that stems from the deepest devotion to his work in the world—into man's etheric body, so that it may in a real sense become a vessel for what, for example, the most enlightened minds of the eighteenth century could conceive of in no more than a symbolic way: 'The outer human form is, in its lower animalistic regions, a dragon that writhes and entwines even the heart. But then, in a certain sense from behind man—for man sees what is higher with the back part of his head—there appears the outward cosmic form of Michael, exalted, light-bearing, retaining his cosmic being but nevertheless transmitting a reflection of this being of his to man's higher nature in such a way *that man's own etheric body becomes a mirror-image of the cosmic form of Michael.* And then the power of Michael vanquishing the dragon would become visible in this human head and would work through to the heart, so that its blood flows from the heart down to the man's limbs.'[154] Only if this can take place *as a reality* in man's inner being can '. . . Michael become the conqueror of the dragon in the manner described. In this image . . . Michael is cosmically behind man. *In man there lives an etheric reflection of Michael* which wages the battle within man and through which man can gradually become free in this battle of Michael; for it is not Michael who wages the battle but human devotion and *the reflection of Michael* [in the etheric body] that is called forth thereby.'[155]

All that has been said points, therefore, to two fundamental demands of our time, which the spiritual world has placed before us through modern spiritual science. In the first place, there is the need for us to receive the new Christ-knowledge into our etheric body, whereby at least a part of our etheric body can pass after death over into the 'etheric ring' and so contribute towards the strengthening of the forces of the Etheric Christ in the Earth's surroundings. And in the second place, the modern imagination of the great battle of Michael with the dragon must be strongly imprinted into our etheric body, so that—to an extent that will correspond to our devotion to Michael—we may achieve as rapid a dissolution as possible of the remaining parts of our etheric body after death so as then to enter into the company of Michael's heavenly host and become therein an active participant in the fulfilment of the work of Christ amongst mankind.

To conclude this description of Michael's participation in the new Christ event, we should observe that just as the Nathan Soul leads, through awakening within man the new Christ-consciousness, to a more inward and intimate sense of the constant presence of Christ within the human soul, and Vidar reveals to man through the development of new clairvoyant faculties the path of beholding Christ in etheric form, so does Michael bring about the third revelation of the Etheric Christ (see p. 326), becoming His servant in that sphere where He works in our time as the Lord of Karma. For even as the revelation of Christ in the etheric appears through Vidar, so does the new revelation of Christ as Lord of Karma come about in our time through Michael.

It is for this reason that the beginning of the karma studies and also the revelation of their fruits took place in that period of Rudolf Steiner's life when he was most deeply immersed in the sphere of Michael,[156] although he had already spoken considerably earlier about the beginning of Christ's activity as Lord of Karma.[157] Thus Rudolf Steiner speaks in his karma lectures concerning the impulses of Michael as follows: 'But the impulses of Michael are strong and powerful and from their spiritual source they work throughout man's being; they work within the spiritual aspect, thence within his soul-nature and then on into his bodily being. And in karmic connections there are always these super-earthly forces at work. Beings of the higher Hierarchies are working with man, upon man; and it is through this that karma is shaped. And so because they work *upon man in his entirety* the Michael forces also exert a very considerable influence upon human karma.'[158] In what direction do the impulses of Michael influence the karma of people of the present day and especially of those people who through their destiny have now found their way to Anthroposophy, to the new embodiment of Michaelic wisdom among mankind? If we proceed from the content of the Michael Mystery, as it is disclosed in Rudolf Steiner's karma lectures and in particular in those of 3 and 8 August 1924,[159] this question can be answered with a certain amount of precision. Michael strives in our time with great intensity to bring about as soon as possible an equilibrium within, and an ordering of, the karma between human individuals, and especially between those who even only in some measure belong to the Michael stream in the world, so that in this way a foundation may be laid for the overcoming of the chaos in the karmic connections of humanity which has come about since the year 869 when a whole series of Angel beings fell away from the spiritual sphere of Michael. In other words, Michael, who around 1879 took upon himself the spiritual rulership of the present epoch, strives first and foremost to restore harmony between the karma of the human individual and world karma, the karma of mankind.[160] And this means that he is working in the same direction in which Christ has from the twentieth century onwards been working among people as the Lord of Karma, directing the process whereby the human individual brings his individual karma into equilibrium in such a way that this process can best serve the further evolution of all mankind.[161]

As is well known from what has been imparted by spiritual science (to which reference has already been made), in ancient pre-Christian times a person who had died had an encounter immediately after his death—in the spiritual world nearest to the Earth—with Moses holding the tablets of the law, and with the figure of the Cherubim with the flaming sword, the principle of the cosmic conscience. These two figures appeared at that time before the human soul and revealed to it the objective judgement of the spiritual world regarding its earthly life that had just passed. From our time onwards the place of Moses in this supersensible encounter will with ever greater frequency be occupied by Christ as Lord of Karma, imparting to the human soul the right moral, karmic impulse for the whole of its subsequent life after death.

However, this direct participation of Christ in the karmic destiny of the soul is not limited solely to what has been said so far, for it does not merely stand out as one of man's first experiences *after* death but also becomes his most important experience in the period that precedes his new incarnation on the Earth. We have already spoken (see p. 147) of this meeting of the human soul with the Christ *before* its earthly incarnation, and it was also said that Michael participates in this meeting as the Spirit who walks before Christ in that world in which He reveals Himself today in His etheric form, and where the human soul dwells immediately before its incarnation, already possessed of an etheric body and preparing for the coming union with the physical body designated for it. All these facts therefore enable us to approach a fundamental mystery of our time, namely, that the figure of 'the Cherubim with the flaming sword', which in ancient times man experienced immediately after his death as an image of cosmic conscience, representing the karma of all mankind (in contrast to the figure of Moses, who stood as the judge of individual karma), is gradually transformed into the figure of the ruling Spirit of our age, Michael. For when he ascended to the rank of Time Spirit, Michael in so doing attained in his development the stage of Spirit Man and therefore became able, on the one hand, to influence not only man's soul-spiritual nature but also his physical being and, on the other, acquired a far more direct relationship to the beings of the First, and highest, Hierarchy, who work within man's physical body and who determine from thence his karma.[162] Hence in our modern epoch we must increasingly reckon with the fact that not only will an ever greater number of people experience a direct encounter with Christ— prepared by an encounter with the ruling Time Spirit—before their descent to the Earth, but that something similar will also take place all the more frequently after death, when man will have an experience of Christ and Michael appearing before him: Christ in place of the old figure of Moses, and Michael as the new representative of cosmic conscience, as the representative of the karma-weaving beings of the First Hierarchy, appearing among people in a form that is truly akin to 'the fiery Cherubim with the flaming sword'.[163]

Thus humanity is living today in an epoch when the karmic task of every human being in his forthcoming incarnation will be revealed to him from the spiritual sphere of Michael-Christ[164] before his birth on Earth, while immediately after completing his earthly path he will be shown to what extent he has fulfilled his task and to what extent the fruits of his work can be incorporated into the positive karma of the world and of humanity. In this way the *karma* of man and humanity will be guided and ruled in our epoch by both Christ and Michael together.[165]

3.   The Imagination of the Etheric Christ

Now that we have considered the nature of the part played by the three spiritual beings in the most significant supersensible event of our time, let us in conclusion bring together all that has been said, so as to present a single picture of the majestic, cosmically human imagination which is being enacted in the spiritual world nearest to the Earth, and also to indicate the direct connection that exists between the theme of the Second Coming and the principal theme of this book, the esoteric foundations of the cycle of the year.

These three spiritual beings, who were later to participate in such a significant way in the supersensible Christ event, ascended to their mission in three preparatory stages. These are the Nathan Soul, who is at once of divine and human nature and who as a result of its fifth sacrifice was able to attain to a certain degree the Angel stage of its evolution;[166] the Angel Vidar, who around the year 1879 ascended to the stage of Sun Archangel; and finally Michael, who had by this time completed his ascent to the rank of the Archai, or Spirits of Time.[167] In more general terms in order that the new Advent might come to fulfilment for mankind in the twentieth century, it had to be preceded in the spiritual worlds by a human being becoming an Angel, an Angel becoming an Archangel and an Archangel becoming one of the Archai.[168]

A still deeper understanding of this threefold ascent can be gained from Rudolf Steiner's lecture of 27 August 1924 in London, where he speaks of *Christ's Spirit Self* with which the Nathan Soul was united *after* it had sacrificed to human beings the Christ-consciousness which it had borne since the Mystery of Golgotha. It was owing to this union with Christ's Spirit Self that the consciousness of the Nathan Soul could rise again. In this lecture Rudolf Steiner also refers to *Christ's Life Spirit*, which in the course of His descent to the Earth Christ had left in its surroundings, in its spiritual-etheric atmosphere. According to Rudolf Steiner, in the year 869 there occurred in the spiritual world nearest to the Earth a meeting of these two principles. How the principle of Christ's Life Spirit worked until then in the Earth's surroundings is indicated in this lecture: 'Something quite sublime and wonderful is taking place behind the scenes of world history. From the West comes pagan Christianity, the Christianity of Arthur, *which also appears under another name and in another form*, and from the East comes Christ in the hearts of human beings. A meeting takes place: the Christ, He who had come down to the Earth, meets His image,[169] streaming towards Him from West to East. The year 869 marks the time of this meeting. Until that year we can clearly distinguish one stream which spreads from the North through central Europe and relates to Christ wholly as a Sun Hero, whether He was called *Baldur or something else,* and ... another stream— inwardly rooted in the heart—which became the Grail stream ...'[170] We have in these words an important reference to the connection of the name of Baldur with the Life Spirit of Christ, and also to the fact that this Life Spirit had been revered by the Norsemen through the mediation of *other gods* and in another form than in the circle of the Knights of King Arthur where this mood of reverence was exalted to its highest form through the Sun Archangel, Michael. Amongst these *other gods* is to be included principally the 'brother' of Baldur, the Angel Vidar, a being who already at that time tacitly bore the nature of an Archangel (that is, the Life Spirit) and was, of all the Teutonic gods, most closely connected with the sphere of Michael, which is to say, with the sphere of activity of Christ's Life Spirit. Only in the year 1879, after a long period of waiting and preparation, did Vidar finally enter the sphere of the next Hierarchy, where he took up the position of *Sun* Archangel which had been vacated at that time. As a result of this ascent he was also able finally to unite with the forces of Christ's Life Spirit, that is, to become to a certain extent its bearer in our cosmos (just as Michael had been hitherto), in order thereby to attain such a relationship to Christ as might enable him to fulfil the essential role in the new manifestation of Christ that had been assigned to him by the world rulership, namely, to create for Him in the spiritual world nearest to the Earth the etheric form in which He might then approach mankind.

Finally, when Michael had risen from the stage of Sun Archangel to that of *Sun* Archai, when, that is, he had become a being who bore the fully evolved 'Sun-Spirit Man', he acquired a quite special relationship to *Christ's Spirit Man,* which—according to the lecture of 27 August 1924— Christ in the course of His descent to the Earth had left on the Sun. It was this intimate relationship to the Spirit Man of Christ that enabled Michael in the new epoch of his rulership to become the true 'Representative of Christ on the Sun' and also to manifest himself to the world as the Countenance of the new Lord of Karma, as a Spirit who brings an ordering influence into the karmic connections of human beings.

If we would characterize this particular cosmic situation in a more general way, we could say: in order that these three beings might participate in the new Christ event, it was necessary for them to attain such a level in their individual development as might enable them to become the bearers of Christ's Spirit Self (the Nathan Soul), of His Life Spirit[171] (Vidar) and of His Spirit Man that had been left behind on the Sun (Michael).

We are now ready to consider the great cosmic-human imagination of the Second Coming in its two aspects: macrocosmic and microcosmic.

Let us first turn to its human, that is, its microcosmic aspect. There we have a picture of how the three cosmic servants of Christ work today in man's inner being. Thus there is the Nathan Soul, fading into oblivion in the course of the nineteenth century in order, by its sacrifice, to create a bridge between the astral light of the cosmos and the etheric light of the human etheric (life) body. One could also say: the Nathan Soul immerses itself sacrificially into man in order therein to kindle the light of the new Christ-consciousness, and it then resurrects in still greater glory and magnificence, wholly permeated by Christ's Spirit Self, just as in former times, at the Turning Point of Time, it resurrected through being permeated by His Ego. It now abides in the spiritual worlds in union with Christ's Spirit Self, and it will gradually fashion (and is already fashioning) a new garment of light for the Etheric Christ out of all those human thoughts which, because of the working of the new Christ-consciousness within people, are able to ascend into the spiritual world.[172]

And then, in man's inner being, there works Vidar, who is able to strengthen this light of Christ's consciousness to the point of forming imaginations, an activity which will lead in time to the complete enlivening of the etheric body (for imaginations are a source of life for the etheric body). This will then serve as the foundation for what Rudolf Steiner describes in the following words: 'Now must the etheric body be again enlivened, and this is associated with the new appearance of Christ in the etheric realm. Etheric bodies re-enlivened will behold the Christ. But, you see, an enlivening, a revitalizing of the etheric body must needs take place.'[173] This enlivening, this revitalizing, is to be brought about by Vidar, by that Spirit who, '... issuing from the Being of Christ Jesus [that is, Christ *and* the Nathan Soul], can bring the new tidings of rejuvenation to our humanity.'[174]

We can, however, describe this process still more concretely if we recall the words of Rudolf Steiner quoted on p. 328, where he speaks of how the repetition in the nineteenth century of the Mystery of Golgotha in the spiritual worlds was to have brought about '... a reawakening of the hitherto concealed Christ-consciousness in human souls on Earth'. 'Hitherto concealed ...'—this refers to what has since the Mystery of Golgotha secretly abided in the subconscious depths of every human being on the Earth. But in what form does the Christ-impulse abide within the human soul? The answer to this question may be found in Rudolf Steiner's lecture *The Etherization of the Blood*, where he speaks of how from the time of the Mystery of Golgotha there has in every human being, alongside the stream of his own etherized blood rising from heart to head, also ascended the stream of the etherized blood of Christ, the consciousness of which (through the coming together of the two streams) leads, according to Rudolf Steiner, to a clairvoyant experience of the Etheric Christ.[175]

And so, the following process, which is now taking place in the human etheric body, comes like a sublime picture before us: *the etherized blood of Christ working within man, which in its esoteric nature is revealed as the purest SUBSTANCE of sacrificial LOVE, is gradually encompassed, as by a formative element, by the IMAGINATIONS*[176] *awakened by Vidar and is overshone by the LIGHT OF THOUGHT of the Christ-consciousness within man, which radiates out from His blood etherizing in the heart as etheric light, kindled by the Nathan Soul as a result of its fifth sacrificial deed. And the whole of this process comes to fulfilment against the background of the figure, imprinted in the human etheric body, of the Michael Spirit, who drives the ahrimanic dragon away from the region of the heart (where the events that are being described take place) down into the region of the limbs and metabolic system* (see p. 349).

And once this inner, *microcosmic* process has attained such an intensity within man that it can also enter into his waking consciousness, there will be revealed to his personal spiritual experience what in the outer, objective spiritual world is taking place as the corresponding great *macrocosmic* process. *There appears the figure of the Etheric Christ, the divine Bearer of the SUBSTANCE of cosmic LOVE, who now approaches man in an etheric (IMAGINATIVE) FORM fashioned by Vidar out of the purest and most spiritualized etheric forces,*[177] *surrounded by the radiant aura which has gradually been woven for Him by the Nathan Soul out of the THOUGHT-LIGHT of the most spiritual thoughts of human beings, in whose radiance Christ will be revealed ever more and more to mankind. And all this takes place against the background of the all-embracing activity of the Michael SPIRIT, who goes before the Sun of Love and 'fights for the purity of the spiritual horizon'*[178] *against the human etheric bodies that dissolve only with difficulty, those etheric bodies which are strongly drawn to distorting the reflection of the etheric image of Christ and are preparing to enter the company of the 'ahrimanic spectre'.*

Thus the Etheric Christ now passes through the world; '... He has since the last third of the nineteenth century been preceded by the fighter who prepares people for the Christ event, by that Spirit whom we call Michael, who goes before the Sun Spirit as His champion.'[179]

Michael now appears before mankind as its great leader towards the Sun of Love. For being by virtue of his inner nature a son of the Sophia[180] and having an age-old connection with the *light* of the heavenly wisdom,[181] he brings this love to people from our time onwards in its most exalted and most selfless form in his capacity of being the Countenance of Christ, the Countenance of Cosmic Love. 'Michael goes with *love* on his way through the world, with all the earnestness of his nature, his attitude and his deeds.

Whosoever follows him cultivates love in relation to the outer world. And love must be unfolded from the outset in relation to the outer world, otherwise it will become self-love. If this love in the spirit of Michael is truly present, then one's love for others can radiate back into one's own self. The self will then be able to love without loving itself. Only on the paths of this love can Christ be found by the human soul.'[182]

If, standing as we do on the ground of modern spiritual science, we say today that the essence of what Christ has brought into the world may be summed up with the words *light*, *life* and *love*,[183] in the new etheric Advent of Christ that is now taking place these gifts are brought to mankind by those who work with Him: the Light of Christ by the Nathan Soul, the Life and the Imagination of Christ by the Archangel Vidar, and the Love of Christ by Michael, the Spirit of our time![184]

All that has been said on the preceding pages is also in full accord with the esoteric understanding of the cycle of the year, to which this book is devoted. Indeed, if we first take the 'Michaelic' half of the year—the time from the summer solstice until Christmas—it is, as we have seen, apparent that the characteristic feature of this period is the ever-strengthening activity of Michael in the Earth's surroundings, to which is then united the activity of his 'younger brother', the Archangel Vidar. The former works right into the supersensible foundations of physical existence,[185] while the latter works more in the purely etheric sphere. Rudolf Steiner unfolds the significance of the participation of these two beings in the cycle of the year as follows: 'As the Earth breathes out in summer, it becomes ahrimanized. Woe, if the birth of Jesus had occurred on this ahrimanized Earth! Before the cycle of the year has ended and December arrives [when the Christ-impulse may be born within an Earth that is, again, ensouled], the Earth has to be purified, through spiritual forces, from the dragon—from the ahrimanic powers';[186] this is the deed that Michael accomplishes. Every year, going on *before* the Christ Being, Michael cleanses the Earth's surroundings from the ahrimanic spirits; every year he conquers the dragon, thus enabling the Christ, together with the Nathan Soul, rightly to enter into Earth existence. And at his side goes Vidar, battling with and conquering the Fenris Wolf, that retarded clairvoyant power which tries to seduce human souls by false spiritual experiences (especially at the season of Advent), so as to prevent a *true vision* of the birth in the earthly sphere of the Nathan Soul on 25 December and of the Christ Being on 6 January. And then at the end of the Christ season, Christ and the Nathan Soul begin to make their way through the other half of the year, just as was the case at the Turning Point of Time, when from the moment of the Baptism in the Jordan they began their journey *together* in Earth existence through to the Mystery of Golgotha and on into the spiritual worlds through the

Ascension and Pentecost, until they appeared together to Paul the Apostle during the event of Damascus. Michael and Vidar remain very closely connected with Christ and the Nathan Soul also during the other half of the year, except that then they do not go before them but follow on *behind*.[187] Thus we see that the cycle of the year, when viewed as a single whole, contains in the deepest sense the mystery of the new Advent of Christ and also the mystery of the relationship to this new Advent of those exalted Spirits allotted by the world rulership to participate directly in it.

In deep antiquity, in the epoch of atavistic clairvoyance, man was still connected through all the forces of his soul with the supersensible worlds. This connection came to expression particularly in his living and purely spiritual relationship to the mysteries of the year; and through living with these mysteries he found the path out into the macrocosm, the path to the higher Hierarchies, to his ancient spiritual home. Subsequently, in order to develop freedom and individual ego-consciousness, man had to distance himself from the supersensible worlds and had as a result to lose almost completely his true understanding of, and inner connection with, the spiritual essence of the year. While now, as he passes through the 'darkest' period of his evolution, he can begin—furnished with a fully evolved individual ego—gradually to grow once more into the higher worlds, into the macrocosm. In the first instance he will find as a result of this a new, *conscious* and now *deeply Christian* relationship to the yearly cycle as a path which leads to a real revelation of the modern mysteries of the living Christ.

> O Light Divine,
> O Sun of Christ!
> Warm Thou
> Our Hearts,
> Enlighten Thou
> Our Heads.[188]

Conclusion:
The Spiritual Experience of the Cycle of the Year Viewed as the Beginning of a Cosmic Cultus Appropriate to the Needs of Present-day Humanity

If we survey Rudolf Steiner's manifold Christological research, we find just two different indications of how it is possible for man to have a direct personal experience of the Christ Being.

One of these found its classic formulation in the penultimate chapter of *Occult Science* (1909), where, in the course of a consideration of the sevenfold Christian-Rosicrucian path of initiation, Rudolf Steiner speaks of the meeting with the Christ at the fourth stage, that of *initiation*, through which only the last three stages can be traversed in the right way.[1] Such a meeting with the Christ can only be attained in our time by an individual who is adhering strictly to the path of spirit-pupilship and who has achieved true initiation on this path, that is, a conscious ascent into the higher worlds and an experience therein of the Christ Being in His macrocosmic aspect as the universal Logos, who is revealed only in man's 'true ego'.

The second kind of meeting, of which Rudolf Steiner speaks for the first time in January 1910, consists in perceiving the Christ Being in *Imagination*, as the Etheric Christ. This experience, which Rudolf Steiner has on several occasions compared with the prophetic event experienced by Paul outside Damascus, will, in contrast to the meeting of the first kind, from our time onwards and for the next 2500–3000 years gradually become accessible to an ever greater number of people who *are not* in the strict sense of the word *following* the modern path of spirit-pupilship. Rudolf Steiner openly referred to the possibility of this second way of experiencing the Christ, which has newly and 'quite naturally' appeared among mankind, in his little book *The Spiritual Guidance of Man*: 'When Paul became clairvoyant before Damascus, he was able to recognize that what had formerly been in the cosmos had passed over into the Spirit of the Earth. Of this everyone will be convinced who can lead his soul to an experience of the event of Damascus. In the twentieth century there will appear the first people who will experience spiritually the Christ experience of Paul. Whereas until now this event has been experienced only by those who have gained clairvoyant powers with the help of esoteric training, it will in future

359

become possible through the natural course of human evolution for the more advanced powers of the soul to behold Christ in the spiritual sphere of the Earth.'[2]

Thus in the present epoch two sources of a direct knowledge of Christ are available to mankind: to experience Him in the sphere of imagination, and to experience Him in the sphere of intuition, that is, in the two spheres corresponding, respectively, to the elemental world nearest to the Earth and to the world of the highest cosmic spirituality which lies *above* the Hierarchies and has its reflection only in the 'true ego' of every human being.[3] These two possibilities of a personal meeting with the Christ in the spiritual worlds are the consequences of the central Mystery of our earthly evolution, the Mystery of Golgotha, and its repetition in our own time in the immediate supersensible environment of the Earth as the necessary precondition for the new appearance of Christ.

'And lo, I am with you always, until the end of earthly time'[4]: these words of the Risen Christ have been since the time of the events of Palestine—and will continue to be until the very end of earthly evolution—the surest possible testimony that Christ has united Himself with the Earth, that He has become the new Spirit of the Earth. They speak at the same time of the fact that He has united Himself with each individual member of earthly humanity. Hence these two processes, the process of the union of the Christ Being with the Earth and the process of His union with each human individual, correspond to each other in a profound way. We find a particularly clear description of the spiritual correspondence between these processes, *which have a common source in the Mystery of Golgotha*, in a lecture to which we have already referred on more than one occasion, namely, *The Etherization of the Blood*: 'Just as in the region of the human heart there is a constant transforming of blood into etheric substance, so is there a similar process taking place in the macrocosm. We may understand this if we direct our minds to the Mystery of Golgotha, to that moment when the blood of Christ Jesus flowed from His wounds ... What happened to this blood in the ages that followed? Something akin to what normally takes place within the human heart. In the course of earthly evolution this blood has undergone a process of etherization. And just as our blood streams upwards from the heart as ether, so has the etheric blood of Christ Jesus lived in the ether of the Earth since the Mystery of Golgotha. The etheric body of the Earth is permeated by what has become of the blood which flowed on Golgotha ... Because the etherized blood of Jesus of Nazareth is present in the etheric body of the Earth with the etherized blood of man that streams from below upwards, from heart to head, there streams the etherized blood of Jesus of Nazareth, so that ... in man ... the human bloodstream unites with the bloodstream of Christ Jesus.'[5]

Thus a complete spiritual correspondence exists between the flowing and the subsequent etherization of the blood of Christ Jesus within the body of the Earth as an etheric-physical sign of His union with it, and the process whereby this etherized blood has thenceforth worked within the human heart (whence it continually streams upwards to the head) with the stream of the etherized blood of man himself. Moreover, seen from a spiritual point of view the one etheric mystery cannot be separated from the other, for it is in their inner connection that the real presence of the Christ Being in Earth existence can be recognized. This means that we cannot rightly comprehend the working of the Christ within man's being without at the same time understanding the nature of His activity in the organism of the Earth, and vice versa.

The path to such an understanding, which leads from an experience of the working of the etherized blood of Christ in the etheric sphere of the Earth and the *reflection* of this activity in the cycle of the year to the per-ception of these effects in the inner regions of man's being, in the etheric stream flowing from the heart to the head, is contained in Rudolf Steiner's *Calendar of the Soul*. For the soul-spiritual processes described therein and man's capacity to experience them were altogether unattainable before the Mystery of Golgotha, when the blood of Christ had not yet permeated the etheric organism of the Earth or the human heart.[6] So although the name of Christ is nowhere mentioned in the *Calendar of the Soul*, meditative work with these verses is in our time an effective way of achieving a personal experience of the etheric mystery of Christ—as Rudolf Steiner himself has indicated on more than one occasion.

And just as the one path of the human soul to Christ consists in the sevenfold path of initiation, so the *seven* principal Christian festivals, which express the inner essence of the cycle of the year, are really the *seven stages of the initiation of the Earth itself* through which it has begun to pass since the Turning Point of Time, when it entered upon the path of becoming a new Sun. Thus there is a connection of the deepest kind: a person who follows the modern path of initiation finds the Spiritual Sun within. He finds Christ in his ego and fulfils the sublime words of the new Mysteries: 'Not I, but Christ in me'. He himself becomes a Sun. Similarly the Earth, as it passes like a living being ever and again in the twelvefold rhythm of the yearly cycle through all the seven stages of the principal Christian festivals, approaches its goal of becoming in time, even in its physically visible substance, the reflection of its new Sun Spirit. This thought can also be expressed in another way. Through the Mystery of Golgotha the Earth receives the Christ into its ego as the new Spirit of the Earth and is thereby enabled to pass in the *twelvefoldness* of the year through a *sevenfold* path of initiation which finds its reflection in the seven yearly festivals. And man, who as a result of the Mystery of Golgotha has received Christ into his ego, acquires the possibility of traversing the new sevenfold path of initiation (promulgated for the first time in Rudolf Steiner's *Occult Science*), in order eventually to attain a conscious meeting with Christ, who will then appear as the inner Sun of the soul surrounded by the twelvefold countenance of the world-embracing human ego (see pp. 108–9).

And furthermore, if from our time onwards man can gradually, and in a 'natural way', approach the new experience of Christ in the etheric through *uniting* in himself the two streams that flow from heart to head—the stream of the etherized blood of Christ and his own etherized blood[7]—we must also seek something in the macrocosm, in the life of the Earth itself, that corresponds to this process. We have, however, already referred to this process when we said that the Christ-forces which participate in the yearly cycle are, in our time, *becoming united* in a completely new way in the etheric sphere of the Earth with the working of the three spiritual beings who bring to people the Light, Life and Love of His revelation in the etheric sphere, and are paving the way for Him now to approach mankind in a new form. Thus in the yearly rhythm we find a reflection of the two paths to the Christ that are accessible to present-day humanity, and so the yearly cycle becomes for us the true archetype and goal of our most inward and heartfelt aspirations.

Moreover, if with all the sensibility and understanding that we have attained we turn to an experience of the cycle of the year as set forth in this book, we shall see that, through immersing ourselves in it in this way, it is possible to take the first steps towards *a life in partnership with the course of cosmic existence*. In Rudolf Steiner's words: '... Living with the course of cosmic existence★ becomes for him [man] a cultus, and there arises the cosmic cultus in which man can participate at every moment of his life. Every earthly cultus is a symbolic picture of this cosmic cultus. This cosmic cultus is higher than any earthly cultus.'[8]

And if through the first Mystery, that of Golgotha, Christ brought to mankind forces for the future spiritualizing of physical existence in its entirety, introducing into the twelvefold principle of space the sevenfold principle of time,[9] through His second, supersensible Golgotha, which introduced into the sevenfold principle of time (the etheric body) the twelvefold principle of spiritual space,[10] He laid the foundations of a new imaginative vision among mankind,[11] the basis for man's conscious growth into the spiritual worlds.[12] In this sense the inner immersion in the spiritual essence of the cycle of the year becomes the beginning of a true cultus

---

★ In the sense of the lecture from which these words are taken, by 'cosmic existence' is meant initially man's connection with the cycle of the year.

appropriate to the needs of present-day humanity. For the rhythmic experience of spatial and temporal laws in the course of the year, the laws of twelve and seven, which have their ultimate source in the connections and interrelationships of the fixed and the moving stars, leads to the gradual strengthening—on the foundation of a true spiritual knowledge of man and cosmos—of human will and human feeling so that they become capable of entering upon the path of a *true imitation of Christ*. This path, which is none other than a path of *sacrificial service* in the great temple of the cosmos—the divine temple of the cycle of the year—becomes the beginning of a real *cosmic-human cultus*; and those who lead this to fulfilment will be those spiritual beings who now bring the Light, Life and Love of the Etheric Christ to the altar of humanity. At such a time those words with which Rudolf Steiner concluded the last lecture he gave in the First Goetheanum[13] on the eve of the building's annihilation in the flames will gradually become a reality. This lecture was devoted to a consideration of the spiritual relationships between the cycle of the year and the life inherent in man's being, and also to the birth of a new cosmic ritual out of a knowledge of these relationships—of a new cultus in which all the future promise of our Earth is contained.

Rudolf Steiner says in this lecture: 'When he is thus placed [in the world], man can experience himself in his will and in his feeling. Surrendering himself to the all-permeating life of the world being, the cosmic being, that surrounds him, he is able to experience the act of transubstantiation that takes place through him in the great temple of the cosmos, as he stands within it as one who is fulfilling a sacrifice in a purely spiritual way.[14] What would otherwise be no more than abstract knowledge achieves a relationship of will and feeling to the world. The world becomes a temple, the world becomes the house of God. And the man with *understanding*, who summons up his powers of *feeling* and of *will*, becomes a *sacrificing being*. His fundamental relationship to the world rises from knowledge to a *world cultus*, a *cosmic cultus*. *The first beginning of what must come to pass if Anthroposophy is to fulfil its mission in the world* is that all that pertains to our relationship to the world must be recognized initially as a cosmic cultus.'[15]

This 'cosmic art of consecration', this new cosmic-human cultus, is in all its principal elements already tacitly present in the cycle of the year, when it is rightly understood and inwardly experienced. It has been the purpose of this book to further such an experience of the yearly cycle and thereby to contribute towards the establishing of the new cultus.[16]

APPENDICES

1. Christmas and Epiphany
(one aspect)

The fact that the most suitable time in the yearly rhythm for experiencing a meeting with the Lesser Guardian (and, after a certain time, with the Greater Guardian of the Threshold) is at the festivals of Christmas and Epiphany (the Baptism in the Jordan) is a matter of profound significance. This becomes especially clear if we turn to what Rudolf Steiner has to say about these meetings in his book *Knowledge of the Higher Worlds: How is it Achieved?* and compare these descriptions with the spiritual nature of these festivals. According to Rudolf Steiner, the spirit-pupil experiences in the image of the Lesser Guardian of the Threshold the first encounter with his higher or 'other' ego, which initially appears to him enshrouded by his 'still unredeemed karma', or, in the sense of our present studies, by his 'higher memory', which embraces all his previous incarnations and connects them by means of the laws of karma into a single whole. Thus does the Guardian speak to the spirit-pupil who has attained a conscious meeting with him: 'And I am that very being who *has formed a body* out of your noble and ignoble doings. My spectral form is woven out of the entries in the ledger of your life ... I must become *a perfect and splendid being in myself* if I am not to fall prey to corruption ... Only when *you have made good all your past misdeeds and have so purified yourself that all further evil is impossible for you, only then will my being be transformed into radiant beauty*. Then, too, I shall again be able to unite with you for the blessing of your future activity.' From these words it is evident that the Guardian of the Threshold is here directing the pupil towards *a definite moral ideal* which must be attained if the Guardian is to be transformed into a 'splendid being' filled with 'radiant beauty' and then be united in this transfigured guise with the spirit-pupil: 'that you,' says the Guardian to the pupil, 'may become wholly united with me and pass in union with me into immortality.'★ The fulfilment of this moral ideal is, therefore, the inner goal which necessarily stands before the evolving soul as a result of the meeting with the Lesser Guardian of the Threshold. And it is precisely this ideal which—though now not within the knowl-

---

★ The original sentence at this point runs as follows: 'Only by thus unconsciously transforming me to perfection through ever-recurring earthly lives could you have escaped the Powers of Death and passed into immortality united with me' [translations from the sixth English edition].

edge-seeking soul but as a fact of world history—is manifested to all mankind at Christmas in the person of that being who was born on Earth for the first time and was untouched by the consequences of the Fall, the Nathan Soul. If we contemplate the birth of this being on the Earth, we are at the same time directing our attention to that ideal which is placed (in the words quoted above) before the spirit-pupil by the Guardian of the Threshold. For in the person of the Nathan Soul we are concerned with an individuality who came directly to the Earth from the cosmic sphere of immortality and had as yet no real earthly karma, so that with respect to this individuality the Guardian of the Threshold *already appears* as that splendid, radiant being which he is to become for every human individual in the distant future. He is united with the Nathan Soul in such a way that the festival of Christmas can become for the spirit-pupil the archetypal picture of the most inward and most intimate aspirations of his soul, the most directly accessible ideal of perfection, which comes before him objectively as the fruit of true occult *self-knowledge.*

The meeting with the Greater Guardian of the Threshold has an altogether different character for the spirit-pupil. Here, too, a definite *moral ideal* is placed before him, though now an ideal of a higher order, for it concerns not only the relationship of the individual knowledge-seeking soul to its own evolution but its relationship to the spiritual progress and perfecting of humanity as a whole. The Greater Guardian of the Threshold speaks of this to the soul in the following words: 'You have released yourself from the world of the senses. Your right to a home in the supersensible world has been won. You can now work from out of this world. For your own part you no longer require your physical bodily nature in its present form. If your intention was merely to acquire the capacity to dwell in this supersensible world, you need no longer return to the sense-world. But now, gaze on me. See how immeasurably I am raised above all that you have made of yourself until now. You have attained your present degree of perfection through the faculties you were able to develop in the sense-world as long as you were still dependent upon it. But now there must begin for you an era when your liberated powers will work upon this world of the senses. Hitherto you have only realized yourself, but now, having yourself become free, you can liberate all your companions in the sense-world. Until today you have striven as an individual; now make yourself a member of the whole, so that you may bring into the supersensible world not yourself alone but everything else that exists in the world of the senses. You will some day be able to unite yourself with me, but I cannot find blessedness as long as others are still unredeemed.' (*Knowledge of the Higher Worlds. How is it Achieved?*)

Then Rudolf Steiner continues: 'An indescribable splendour radiates from the second Guardian; union with him lies as a far distant ideal before the eye of the soul. Yet there is also the certainty that this union will not be possible until all the powers that have come to the initiate from this world are applied by him to liberating and redeeming this world. If he resolves to fulfil the demands of the higher being of light, the initiate will be able to contribute to the liberation of the human race. He brings his gifts to the altar of humanity.' This is one of the most significant experiences that the spirit-pupil has on his path into the higher worlds, when he is faced with the challenge to unite his own personal aims with the aims of all humanity on Earth. At this stage he has to take the most important decision not only for his present life but also for his future earthly lives. And he can receive the greatest measure of help and the highest example for this resolve, with all its many consequences, from the event of the Baptism in the Jordan, when the Sun Being of the Christ, solely out of the purest love for mankind and without needing to do so for His own evolution, made the resolve to sacrifice to earthly humanity all the spiritual forces that had been His from the beginning, even to sacrifice His own Being, in descending to the Earth and becoming united at the Baptism in the Jordan with the earthly sheaths of Jesus of Nazareth. Rudolf Steiner speaks of this as follows: 'When this descent of humanity [which had originated in the intervention of Lucifer] had reached its lowest level, the need arose for a powerful ascending impulse. This could come about only because that Being of the highest Hierarchies, whom we designate as the Christ, formed a resolve in the higher worlds that He had no need to make for His own evolution; for Christ would have attained His evolutionary goal if He had taken a path lying far, far above any path that mankind was on. Christ could have passed far above the evolutionary path of mankind. But if the impulse for an ascent had not been given, human evolution would have had to continue following a downward path. The ascent of Christ would have had as its counterpart the inevitable descent of humanity.' (Lecture of 14 October 1911 in GA 131.) However, Christ made His resolve. He united Himself with human evolution on Earth for all future ages. And the Baptism in the Jordan was the historical expression of this divine resolve. 'Christ accomplished something which He had absolutely no need to do. What kind of a deed was this? It was a deed of *divine love*! We must clearly understand that no human heart is as yet capable of feeling the intensity of love that was necessary for a God to form the resolve, which He had no need to make, to work upon Earth in a human body.' (Lecture of 14 October 1911.)

Thus, for the spirit-pupil who is at the stage of development described, the event of the Baptism in the Jordan can become a macrocosmic-historical archetype of his own individual resolve. If this resolve is made, then from the moment of his encounter with the Greater Guardian of the Threshold the pupil is on the path of active *imitation* of Christ Jesus. For at this stage of development, this path is the *only* white path, which is why Rudolf Steiner says of the occultists of the white path that '... they value devotion and readiness for sacrifice above all other attributes'.

The most suitable time in the yearly cycle for pursuing this path of spiritual, selfless love and sacrifice is the time which immediately follows the festival of the Baptism (Epiphany) and continues until Easter. This time corresponds to the three years of Christ's life on Earth in the three sheaths of Jesus of Nazareth, and is that time in the yearly rhythm when man is called to bring to the altar of humanity, out of the forces of love working within his ego, all the fruits of individual spiritual development, all the treasures of spiritual wisdom, that he has gathered in his sheaths during the descending half of the year ending with Christmas.

Thus, in the course of the year, the possibility arises again and again for every spiritually striving human being not only of inner preparation for the meeting with the Lesser and Greater Guardians of the Threshold but also of a serious self-examination: will he at the appropriate moment be able to take the right decision and enter upon the white path? For in the course of the yearly cycle he is placed each time before this question at Epiphany, and the possibility arises each time for him to test whether or not he has the strength to pursue this path during the ascending half of the year that follows this festival.

2. The Mystery Temple of the Year

The observations in the fourth chapter of Part III regarding the impulses of wisdom and love in the cycle of the year can be deepened quite considerably if we recall that since ancient times wisdom has always been associated with the *revelation* of world thoughts, while love, in so far as it has been able to become a 'formative power' in man, that is, to embrace his will, has worked in the world as a magical *life-germinating* power.

In this sense the entire yearly cycle can be seen as standing before us in the form of the two mighty columns which once stood at the entrance of the celebrated Temple of Solomon, of which Hiram was the builder: 'the column of wisdom' and 'the column of life [love]'.[1] Then the goal of a spiritual experience of the year can be expressed in Rudolf Steiner's words as follows: 'Today both are separated'—he refers to the two columns and in our case this may be taken as referring also to the two halves of the year—but 'they would demand of us that we overcome the present condition of humanity, they would guide our path to the point where through the widening of our consciousness they become merged in a manner that is known as Yakim and Boas.'

In these words of Rudolf Steiner we have an indication of the path leading to such a 'widening of consciousness', whereby man may come to experience the cycle of the year as a single whole, that is, to behold the *high spiritual Being who indeed works behind* its ever-alternating life-cycle!

Later in the same lecture Rudolf Steiner associates these two columns with two mantric verses, which express with remarkable exactitude the essential nature of the two halves of the yearly cycle. The first of these can be related to the descending (autumnal) half of the year, and the second to the ascending (spring) part:

> *Yakim*
> In purity of *thought* you find the self
> That holds itself in check.
> If you transform your thoughts into an image,
> You experience creative *wisdom*.

> *Boas*
> If you condense your *feeling* into light,
> You manifest a forming power.
> If you actualize your *will* in being,
> Then do you create in world existence.

The revelations of world thoughts streaming in the showers of meteors to the Earth at autumn time endow man with a sharp ego-consciousness. If, in the sense of the autumn festival of Michael, man is able on the modern path of initiation to 'transform his thought into an image', that is, to transform thoughts into Imagination, he will come to perceive in the course of the descending half of the year 'the creative wisdom' from whose substance the true, higher man can be born in his soul at Christmas and come to full expression at Epiphany.

In the course of the other half of the year, which is associated with the ascendancy of the forces of love, man must 'condense' this 'feeling' of love into light, and it will be revealed to him as 'a forming power' which will then by Easter-time give rise, in the sphere of his human *will*, to a new being, capable of becoming creative in world existence at Whitsun.

In the lecture of 27 May 1910,[2] Rudolf Steiner speaks of how the foundation of everything in the world that relates to the soul, and especially to the human soul, is love and how the foundation of the material world, and also matter as such, is light. Hence the process, referred to in the verse, of condensing feeling into light is a creative process in which the spiritual substance of the soul becomes a formative power that is able to work in a transforming way down to the very foundations of the material world.

Rudolf Steiner then proceeds to express in general terms the meaning of these verses. He says: 'The one verse has to do with knowledge, the other with life [death-bearing knowledge is associated with one half of the year, life with the other]. The formative power at first *reveals* itself in the sense of the first verse. The ascent from mere cognitive activity to magical effect lies in the transition from the power of the verse on the first column to that of the verse on the second.'

Thus the revelation of world wisdom leads man during the descending half of the year to true self-knowledge and hence to a meeting with the Lesser Guardian of the Threshold.[3] The Greater Guardian of the Threshold, however, leads him into the second, ascending half of the year. And as a result of the meeting with this being he acknowledges that what he '... will receive in the higher regions of the supersensible world is nothing that comes to him, but entirely something that goes out from him: love for the world and for his fellows'.[4] The person who works in the manner indicated has overcome all that is egoistic in himself; he has renounced the 'black path' and chosen the 'white path' of the new Mysteries. Henceforth his love-permeated will can work magically in the world. From now on '... he will be able to contribute to the liberation of the human race. He brings his gifts to the altar of humanity.'[5]

And so the cycle of the year is revealed to us in its entirety as a sublime gate, wrought by the Gods, into the spiritual world, a gate that is forged out of the two columns, out of the differing experiences of the soul in the course of the two halves of the year. Only through uniting both these experiences in a higher unity can the soul enter in full consciousness into the great spiritual temple of the year where Anthroposophy is seen as the key to a new, spiritualized perception of the universe, as the foundation of a true *Cosmosophy*.

3. Concerning a Representation of Vidar

In the passage quoted on p. 321 where Rudolf Steiner characterizes the esoteric nature of Vidar, we find the following indication: 'Even his image has only been spoken of in a vague way. This is evident in that a sculpted form has been found in the vicinity of Cologne whose identity is known to no one and which could only be a likeness of Vidar.'

It is quite possible that what is meant here is the so-called Frankish gravestone that was found at Niederdollendorf *near Cologne* in 1901 and was in that same year placed in the Bonn national museum, where it now remains.★ (It is thought that it dates from not later than the seventh century AD.)

We shall now attempt briefly to elucidate the significance of its images.†

On the 'front' side of the stone we find a representation of a human figure withstanding the assaults of a dragon-like or snake-like animal with three heads descending upon him from all sides, the most striking characteristic of which is the widely open jaws that are seeking to swallow the human figure in the centre. The very fact that we would never encounter such a three-headed animal in the natural world is an indication that we have here an imaginative scene taking place in the supersensible world and that the figure in the centre is a *spiritual being*. Furthermore, it is fully evident from the relative position of the three heads of the animal that what is being indicated here are the dangers which threaten the three realms of man's being: his head, rhythmic (heart and lung) and metabolic-limb systems—the physical foundation of his soul-faculties of thinking, feeling and will.

Thus one of the heads of the animal is trying to swallow with its open jaws the man's head, which is depicted on the stone in the form of a round, Sun-like disc. The second mouth of the animal is trying to devour the man's left shoulder and left arm, those parts of the physical body which will in the future come to be most directly connected with his heart.[1] And, finally, the third mouth of the animal threateningly assaults the man 'from

---

★ See the reproduction of the pictures of the stone on pp. 378–80.

† See the article by Herbert Seufert, 'Über den Vidar-Stein' in *Das Goetheanum*, 65th year No. 20, 11 May 1986. It was Herbert Seufert who made the author of the present work aware of the existence of this stone and of its possible connection with the 'unidentified representation' of Vidar referred to in the lecture quoted above.

below', from the sphere of the will or, to put it more physiologically, from the region of the metabolism.

The human figure resists this threefold assault by means of inner forces, which are represented by three objects: a comb, a sword and a vessel of water. The first object (the comb) is held by the man in his right hand and is used to parry the animal's assault on his head system. The combing of hair has, since ancient times, been a ritual act serving to strengthen man's connection with certain forces of the macrocosm. The hairs themselves were organs of perception in both the sense-perceptible and the super-sensible worlds, a kind of 'receiving-apparatus' with whose help people of olden times stored up the spiritual forces of the Sun and 'trapped' inspirations from the higher worlds (in this connection one may recall the biblical story of Samson). Hence in ancient times—and in the East this tradition has to some extent continued until this day—the priest or holy man was required to wear a beard and long hair. (For the same reason it is not recommended to cut children's hair until they have reached three years of age.)[2] Thus long hair was once a means of helping man to receive from without, from the spiritual macrocosm, or, to be more precise, directly from the sphere of the Sun, the World Thoughts, the inspirations of the cosmic Intelligence, which at that time did not as yet belong to man but was ruled from the cosmos by the leading Sun Archangel, Michael. Combing the hair with the aid of a comb was an occult Mystery-act, the significance of which was to put man's connection with the sphere of the cosmic Intelligence 'in good order'* to ensure that it was rightly perceived and used and that the power of the jaws of the animal's first head was overcome.

The second object is a short, one-edged sword. The human figure portrayed on the stone clasps it with his left hand—associated with the heart—to his breast, with the hand which the second set of jaws of the animal is trying to swallow. In the image of the sword we have an indication of the power of *courage*, which works in man's rhythmic system and is rooted in his heart, and it is this power that is able to overcome the assault of the second head.

The third object is the water-bottle standing at the man's feet with the sign of the Sun engraved upon it. Water is here to be regarded as an image of the purified etheric forces which must permeate the entire system of man's limbs and metabolism if he is to be able to vanquish the third set of gaping jaws that threatens him 'from below'.

Thus on this 'outer' side of the stone we have an imaginative repre-

---

* The memory of this extended even to recent times, for example in the legend of the Lorelei.

sentation of the being of Vidar in his 'Michaelic aspect' working through a human form and, in opposition to him, of an animal of dragon-like (i.e. anti-Michaelic) nature with the feature that most especially characterizes the Fenris Wolf, its wide-open jaws. For, as Rudolf Meyer has observed, the entire strength of the Wolf is concentrated solely in its jaws,[3] against which Vidar, in contrast, opposes his silence, this being expressed in the present instance through the image of the ritual combing of the hair, which is how the connection with the forces of the cosmic Sun-forces of wisdom is strengthened. A further attribute of Vidar is the sword, which the being depicted on the stone holds in his left hand near the heart. In the Twilight of the Gods, Vidar thrusts this sword into the Fenris Wolf's open jaws, penetrating to its heart. Finally, beside his feet we find the water-bottle. According to the Norse legends the most important attribute of Vidar is the 'iron shoe' which has been sewn from all the scraps which people have cast aside from the heels and toes of the shoes that they have made. This image of the shoe—quite apart from the role which it plays in Vidar's battle with the Wolf[4]—points to yet another aspect of Vidar, to Vidar the wanderer, who has resolved to unite his destiny with those of human beings on Earth and who accompanies them on the paths of their earthly destinies.[5] In olden times, alongside the 'indestructible' shoe as a symbol of the wanderer, there was also the image of the water-bottle with the sign of the Sun as a symbol of his more moral aspect—where wandering is depicted as a quest for the sources of the living, Sun-filled waters through a process of spiritual purification.

Thus Vidar stands before us in this representation as he who endows man's thinking with wisdom, his feeling with courage and his will with purity, as the true servant and follower of Michael, who provides man with the spiritual forces that enable him to overcome the three-headed, dragon-like animal (the Wolf) in the Twilight of the Gods.

One could also say that the images on this side of the stone testify to the destiny of the dead Frankish warrior, who after death would have joined forces with Vidar,[6] in order with the help of his three gifts to overcome the forces of the Wolf, now chained to the Earth, and hence to find the path to the new aeon to which Vidar, the victorious god, would lead him.

This new aspect of Vidar's nature is depicted on the other side of the stone. In its almost graphic severity, its economy of artistic means and at the same time the rich imagery with which it addresses the soul, it scarcely has an equal among the works of art of the old Germanic peoples.

If the image on the 'façade' of the stone, which we have already considered, shows Vidar in his 'Michaelic' aspect, as associated more with his victory in the Twilight of the Gods, then the mystery of Vidar's relationship to the realm of the Sun and to its most exalted leader, the Christ, is revealed at the reverse side. It is a prophetic indication of the nature of Vidar's activity *after* the Twilight of the Gods, in that new 'Sun' aeon of world-evolution which has been inaugurated as a result of the Mystery of Golgotha taking place on Earth.

Before us there stands the image of a high spiritual being of the Sun. Around his head there is a Sun aura. On his breast is a circle, the sign of the Sun, whose forces he bears in his heart. And from it there radiate streams of light, which illuminate the whole surrounding space with the Sun forces of the light-ether, these being portrayed in the form of an expanding series of triangles.[7] These streams of light, focused in triangular forms, both above and below, around the central figure, create a 'rhombic' (i.e. as though consisting of two triangles joined together) aura, like an etheric garment, an etheric form.

In his right hand Vidar holds, instead of a comb, the emblem of the Intelligence that is still being directed from the cosmos, a lance which is an image of the purified and liberated thinking that has now fully become man's own and is directed with full consciousness up into the etheric sphere of the cosmos. (At this point one may recall that for imaginative vision man's strong, goal-directed thinking frequently appears on the astral plane in the form of something akin to an arrow or a lance. The latter image is sometimes used in ancient times as a symbol of magical, spiritual power.)[8] Immediately below the central figure we have a picture of the metamorphosis to which the dragon-like animal was subjected as a result of its conquest by Vidar. Since then it has been banished to the depths of the Earth and is fettered there by the forces of the light-ether (the triangles of light surround it not only from above but from below), as a result of which it so completely loses its spiritual strength that this is directed by the power of light to the service of good, and it then becomes the foundation upon which the light-bearing image of Vidar the victorious arises.

Both motifs can also be discerned on the left and the right sides of the stone. On the left of the 'façade' there is the motif of the animal in the form of a two-headed, snake-like being, and on the right an ornamental motif indicative of the River Thund, which separates the world of the Gods from that of men, yonder world from that of the here and now, on whose banks the decisive battle of Vidar and the Fenris Wolf takes place.[9]

Thus the gravestone from Niederdollendorf shows us two fundamental aspects of Vidar, corresponding to the two significant epochs in the evolution of mankind, at whose threshold there took place the most important event in the whole of earthly evolution—the Mystery of Golgotha.

379

4. When Should the Festivals be Celebrated in the Southern Hemisphere?

When should the festivals be celebrated in the southern hemisphere? Without becoming aware of the spiritual geography of the southern part of our Earth by spending a certain amount of time there, any answer to this question can only be of a provisional nature. But spiritual science enables us to contribute one observation to this theme.

Because of the physical and etheric configuration of our earthly planet, it is the case that certain soul-spiritual processes within man are in harmony with the yearly rhythm of nature in the northern hemisphere but not in the southern hemisphere. All the relationships between land and water, that is, between the physical and etheric elements, are different in the southern hemisphere from that in the northern hemisphere and in many respects quite opposite. Thus in the northern hemisphere there is a considerable preponderance of land over water, while in the southern hemisphere it is the other way round.

According to the spiritual-scientific teaching of the ethers, water is connected more with the working of the sound-ether and dry land with the life-ether. As, on the other hand, the sound-ether has a relationship with the Moon and the life-ether with the Sun,[1] the northern hemisphere, with its centre at the North Pole, can be regarded as *Sunlike* and the southern hemisphere with its centre at the Antarctic as *Moonlike*. Thus in the 'North' we have a more formative principle and in the 'South' a tendency towards formlessness. This is manifested in the considerably smaller degree of contrast between summer and winter (and between the seasons in general) in the southern hemisphere than is the case in the northern hemisphere, where there are distinct seasons and greater variations in temperature.

We can also observe the effect of these respectively more formative and more amorphous tendencies in the cultural evolution of the northern and southern hemispheres. For this reason the evolution of mankind has, from the age of Atlantis and until our present time, taken place largely in the northern half; this was the case until the greatest event of Earth history, the Mystery of Golgotha.

Viewed historically, the people of the northern hemisphere had the task of mastering the material world, of becoming engrossed in it, in order then, having become completely separated from the divine-spiritual world, to come to an experience of individual freedom. We have now reached this 'deepest' point of evolution. And the appearance of Anthroposophy corresponds today to the world-historical necessity that mankind ascends again into the spiritual world, though now *fully conscious*, on the ground of this newly attained experience of freedom.

Northern humanity can gain support for this immensely demanding task from the yearly cycle, if certain processes of soul-spiritual evolution can be brought into harmony with it in the manner described in this book. Furthermore, in the immediate future the ascent into the spiritual world will hardly be possible for mankind without the support of the cosmic forces that are manifest in the cycle of the year. For the hindrances against this ascent originating from the materialistic civilization of the present are so considerable in our time that human beings will need this support to an ever-increasing extent if they are to fulfil their task of leading the way from the fifth post-Atlantean epoch to the sixth, when a purely spiritual culture will blossom on the Earth. The most perfect harmony between the human soul and the working of spiritual-cosmic forces in the cycle of the year will then be attained, for this spiritual culture of the sixth epoch will, to a significant extent, consist in the bringing about of such a harmony between man and nature (the cycle of the year). Man will then develop inwardly to such a degree that the highest spiritual forces will flow towards him from his intercourse with nature. Michael's demand to people of today that they 'learn to read in the book of nature'[2] represents the first beginnings of this. Such a possibility of bringing the soul-spiritual in man into harmony with the spiritual-cosmic in nature will not always exist, but it is of decisive importance that, so long as this is still possible, the bridge to world spirituality is formed.

As has been said, this possibility will only exist until approximately the end of the sixth (Slavic) cultural epoch, for already in the seventh (American) cultural epoch quite different natural and spiritual conditions will enter into earthly evolution. Rudolf Steiner describes the mighty change which will come about at that time in the following words: 'Now you know that the Moon will again become united with the Earth. This moment when the Moon will again become united with the Earth will be set by those astronomers and geologists who live in abstractions thousands of years into the future, but that is mere delusion. The truth is that this moment is not so very far away . . .'[3] And then Rudolf Steiner goes on to say that this moment will come in the seventh or eighth millennium after the birth of Christ.★

★ The *temporal* mid-point of earthly evolution lies in the fourth Atlantean cultural epoch, whereas the *spiritual* mid-point lies in the fourth post-Atlantean epoch. The departure of the Moon at the beginning of the Lemurian age has, according to the law of reflection, a correspondence to this temporal mid-point with a re-entry at the end of the whole post-Atlantean age, i.e. of the seventh cultural epoch.

'And so, just as this departure of the Moon [in Lemurian times] was an event of striking importance, in the same way the Moon's re-entry will be an event of similar magnitude.' And in the description of the Moon's departure in his book *Cosmic Memory*,[4] Rudolf Steiner writes: 'Thus the contemplation of the Akashic Chronicle has advanced to the point shortly *before that cosmic catastrophe* which was brought about by the departure of the Moon from the Earth.'

In the lecture of 31 December 1910[5] Rudolf Steiner refers to a quite particular rhythm in Earth evolution which lasts from 'six to seven to eight millennia' and is revealed in manifestations of a polar opposite nature. These manifestations are associated with the activity of the Spirits of Form (the Exusiai), who now work outwardly into the physical relationships of the Earth, and inwardly into the souls of human beings. The last outward manifestation was at the time of the great Atlantean catastrophe. The strongest inward manifestation, on the other hand, was around the year 1250.[6] The next great penetration into outward physical conditions will take place around the eighth millennium, when through the activity of the Spirits of Form together with the mightiest of them, Yahveh, the Moon will be reunited with the Earth—an event which will be associated with a change in the position of the Earth's axis.

This means, however, that through the Moon being received again into the Earth the combined spiritual and etheric nature-orientated processes which come to expression in the cycle of the year will be completely changed. The cycle of the year in the form in which it is known to us today will then no longer exist. But if man can bring the spiritual forces of the Moon under his rulership in the right way he will be able to work upon nature in a magical way, thus causing the new processes to arise within it which will then correspond to the yearly cycle of today.

According to the statements of Rudolf Steiner, in Lemurian times the Moon was drawn forth from the southern hemisphere of the Earth,[7] which was the cause of the relationships between water and land (between the physical and the etheric) in the southern hemisphere becoming so different from those in the northern hemisphere. This region is predestined to prepare in our time the Moon's return into the Earth in the seventh cultural epoch. One may also say: the entire etheric-physical configuration of the southern hemisphere is an indication of the past and future conditions of the Earth that have been described (the departure and re-entry of the Moon). The cultural evolution of the northern hemisphere has the ultimate task of bringing the Sun Mystery of the Christ to full manifestation over the whole Earth, and thereby of forging the transition, of building the bridge, between these two cosmic-earthly events that are associated with the southern hemisphere.

383

Thus we see that the ideal of the sixth epoch is to come into complete spiritual harmony with the spiritual-cosmic aspect of nature so as to be able to derive from it the highest cultural impulses. The ideal of the seventh cultural epoch is, however, to determine natural processes magically out of one's own resources. In other words: if in the sixth epoch the bridge to the spirit cosmos is fashioned, in the seventh epoch man will be in a position to bring forth out of himself, out of *his own heightened spiritual power*, that which will be necessary for the further evolution of humanity and of the Earth, and which in the previous (sixth) epoch he had himself fashioned from nature.

From this we may become clearer as to the nature of the task facing human beings who through their karma live in the southern hemisphere—as distinct from those living in the northern hemisphere—with respect to the yearly cycle and its festivals.

According to Rudolf Steiner's words quoted above, the time of the Moon's re-entry is not very far away—between the seventh and the eighth millennium, that is, in the final third of the seventh cultural epoch. As, however, this process of the re-entry of the Moon, together with the associated change of all natural laws on the Earth, will happen only gradually, one can also say that to a certain extent the entire seventh cultural epoch will stand under the sign of this process which comes to a conclusion at its end.

As already said, this can also be viewed from the standpoint of cultural history. In the 'South', because of the considerable excess of water over solid land, there is a sense of seclusion in the landscape, of cosmic expectation for what will one day take place there. It is due to this particular quality that, while in the 'South' there are indeed the relics of ancient cultures, there is no consequential *cultural evolution* as in the 'North' (e.g. the evolution through the succession of the post-Atlantean cultural epochs).

Since modern times the lands in the 'South' have become participants in the Christian cultural evolution coming from the 'North', and have had their true spiritual task set before them: that of forming the Christian festivals *solely out of inner human power* and without seeking any support in nature, in order thereby to prepare for the already mentioned distant future age. Human beings who live in these regions can, in so far as they belong culturally to the great Christian stream of evolution, in this way begin to prepare in the fifth post-Atlantean epoch the foundation for that stage of evolution which, in the seventh post-Atlantean cultural epoch, will be the destiny of all mankind.

It follows from this that there are basically two possible paths for the southern hemisphere. The difference between them is that in the one case

384

the sixth epoch and in the other the seventh is being prepared for; and the task of the southern hemisphere on behalf of humanity is essentially connected with the latter.

Here the following thoughts may also be taken into consideration. The present fifth post–Atlantean cultural epoch derives its principal characteristics from the development of human *thinking*; whereas the spiritual characteristic of the sixth epoch will be the development of *feeling* and that of the seventh of *will*.[8] Thus for those people who live in the southern hemisphere, it is possible either to connect themselves in a more feeling way with the life of the natural world around them or to follow wholly new untrodden paths out of their inner independent will-impulses.

There is, moreover, the great mystery which only spiritual science can reveal to us today, namely, that the whole of the natural world which surrounds us only bears within itself the forces of the past. If, however, we are searching for the forces of the future, we must turn towards man's inner being, where in his astral body and ego he is able to unfold his free, creative nature in complete independence from the course of the natural world.

Here begins the task whose fulfilment will be striven for until the end of earthly time. Rudolf Steiner addressed this theme with the following words: 'If, therefore, external nature is not to perish, it must be given that which man has through his astral body and his ego. This means that, as man through his astral body and his ego has self-conscious ideas, he must—if he wants to ensure a future to this otherwise dying Earth—bring to it what lives in him of a supersensible and invisible nature.'[9] In other words, the entire Earth which surrounds us—in so far as it is physical and etheric in substance, that is, belongs to what we regard as natural existence—in itself no longer has any future. Thus in the much wider perspective of spiritual and natural circumstances extending over the sixth and seventh cultural epochs, the Earth can only be rescued from physical death through human individuals bringing to it out of their own freedom what is 'of a supersensible and invisible nature' in them. This has, to begin with, nothing to do with the natural world as such, since it derives from the human astral body and ego, but it must penetrate into it as a transforming and redemptive power. For 'only when we are able to place into the Earth what it does not have [as a purely natural entity] can an Earth of the future arise'.

It is of course extremely difficult to celebrate the Christian festivals without having the support of nature's yearly cycle. In order, for example, to celebrate the Christmas festival at mid-summer one should not seek to imitate conditions in the northern hemisphere (snow, etc.) but rather find altogether new forms for the celebrations, stemming more from a spiritual-occult background.

This will be true pioneer work, which can, however, find support in the thought that through this means the whole of mankind will gradually be prepared for a future even more distant than that whose preparation remains the particular task of 'northern' humanity.

Only if this task is fulfilled by 'southern' humanity (and this must happen to some extent during the fifth post-Atlantean epoch) will mankind continue to live on Earth as *a spiritual entity* passing together through the Christian festivals. For the deeper meaning of the simultaneous celebrating of the festivals over the entire Earth is that after the Mystery of Golgotha these festivals come to represent the stages of the union of the Christ Spirit with the Earth. Thus through this simultaneous celebrating of the Christian festivals by all people on the Earth, a real vessel can be fashioned for the great Ego of humanity, the Christ, who will then lead mankind towards the great ideal of God-manhood.

What has been said here does not seek to lay claim to being the total answer to the question under consideration, but rather to indicate the consequences that may arise for a reader of this book who lives in the southern hemisphere of our Earth.

A further aspect of this problem is associated with working on Rudolf Steiner's *Calendar of the Soul*,[10] where the relationship of the soul to the spiritual-cosmic processes of nature is far more a *necessity*. For this reason, Rudolf Steiner answered Fred Poeppig's question as to how one should work with the weekly verses in the southern hemisphere as follows: 'The weekly verses of the Soul Calendar must be switched round, that is, they should be used in accordance with the seasonal rhythms of the particular locality.'[11] Of course, if one works in this way with the verses, the nature-rhythms do not correspond with the four yearly festivals. In order to restore this correspondence, the opposite verse must then be included, which is what many anthroposophists living in the northern hemisphere do already. In this way the unifying element in human evolution can also be retained in meditative work with the *Calendar of the Soul*.

5. Some Words about the Icon
The Council of the Holy Archangel Michael

The eighteenth-century Russian icon *The Heavenly Council of the Holy Archangel Michael*★ portrays a circle of twelve Archangels. Above, in the middle of the circle, the Archangel Michael himself is depicted as the leader and ruler of the 'Heavenly Council', the *thirteenth* in the circle of the twelve. He is the representative of the impulse of the Sun, surrounded by twelve stars. As 'the Countenance of Christ' he holds in his hands two fiery spheres on which are written the inscriptions 'JS' and 'CS' (meaning 'Jesus' and 'Christ'). With a gesture of his hands Michael blesses the central figure of the icon, who occupies a position directly below him: the young Jesus (the Nathan Soul) before his Baptism in the Jordan.

The whole circle of Archangels is positioned in such a way that two of them come especially to the fore who, with the gestures of their hands, seem to be supporting the figure of Jesus. Dressed in raiments of red and blue, they are like the two columns of Yakim and Boas that once towered at the entrance to the Temple of Solomon. In heading the two groups, with six Archangels in each, they at the same time symbolize the two halves of the year and so together represent its full cycle (see Appendix 2).

The youthful figure of Jesus (the Nathan Soul) at the centre of the composition is placed against the background of a double Sun-like disc on which stand the words 'The Lord the all-preserver'. Its outer, more radiant ring is indicative of the etheric aura of the Sun, while its darker inner ring is related to the astral aura. Both auras are permeated and unified by golden rays, symbolizing the third, purely spiritual aura. On the halo of Jesus is a cross with the Greek letters ὄου. Together they form the Greek word δὼυ which means 'that which has being', and they represent an abbreviation of the Old Testament phrase 'I am that which has being' or 'I am the I am' (or, in Hebrew, '*Ehjeh asher ehjeh*' (Exodus 3:14). These three letters, which are encountered in many other Russian and Byzantine icons, and most frequently where Jesus is portrayed in childhood or youth (before the Baptism), refer to that mystery which is concealed in the sources of his genealogy as recorded in the Gospel of St Luke, where Jesus is spoken of as having descended from Adam, and *hence also from God* (3:38), from God who is the 'I am'.[1] The figure of Jesus (the Nathan Soul), who is visible

---

★ See the reproduction in the Frontispiece.

only as far as the waist, rests upon three fiery six-winged beings bearing an affinity in their appearance with the Seraphim. They symbolize the three kinds of hierarchic Spirits (the Second Hierarchy) who inhabit the sphere of the Sun: the Powers, the Principalities and the Dominions.

In a compositional sense the icon can be divided into three parts. At the bottom there are thirteen bluish-white clouds (according to the number of Archangels). Directly above them are three light-green hemispheres, covered with stars, and in the middle, grouped around the figure of Jesus, are the thirteen Archangels with Michael at their head in their many-coloured garments. And in the upper part of the icon their halos—almost merging into one another—move gradually into the sea of golden light that fills the entire space. These three elements—the thirteen bluish-white clouds (one for each Archangel), the greenish star-studded semicircle above them together with the many-coloured garments of the Archangels, and their halos, seemingly dissolving in the golden background—correspond to the etheric, astral and purely spiritual regions of the super-earthly world. For it is in these three spheres in particular that the Archangels work for the evolution of mankind. They unfold their will in the etheric world, their feeling weaves in the astral or starry world, and their thoughts penetrate the world of spirit.

Among the beings of the Third Hierarchy the Angels are more connected with the world of imaginations, the Archangels with the world of inspirations and the Archai with that of intuitions. For this reason all thirteen Archangels (at any rate those whose heads are fully shown) are depicted in a state of constant divine *Inspiration*, of which the spiral streams, seemingly flowing into their ears from without, are an indication. Each of the Archangels (other than Michael) holds in his hands a lance ending in a trident. This is a symbol of those spiritual forces with whose help the Archangels direct the inspirations which they have received from above down to the Earth, where their task is to fructify people's thinking, feeling and will throughout the *entire* twelvefold cycle of the year.

So we have in the images of this icon a remarkable illustration of some of the most important aspects of the cosmic-earthly mystery of the Nathan Soul: its relationship to the Archangel Michael, its heavenly protector (see Part II, Chapter 2), and also its connection with the Sun-sphere as a whole, which was from the very beginning the place where it lived and worked in the spiritual worlds until its incarnation on Earth at the Turning Point of Time (see Part I, Chapter 3).

Moreover, in the three principal motifs of the icon the three most central themes of the present work have found their artistic expression: the twelve Archangels who are at the same time the rulers of the twelvefold cycle of the year and also of the twelve Holy Nights, in so far as they form a small-scale spiritual reflection of it; the Archangel Michael, who appears in our time as the highest cosmic protector, helper and inspirer of the modern Christian-Rosicrucian path of initiation; and the Nathan Soul portrayed in the sphere of the Sun, who manifests in its cosmic-earthly deeds (to the description of which many chapters of the present work have been devoted, see Parts II, V and XII) the archetypal image of a human being who has attained the fullest and most all-embracing *experience* of the Christ Being.

6. Foundation Stone Meditation

(I, 1)   Soul of Man!   (1)
Thou livest in the Limbs
Which bear thee through the world of Space
Into the ocean-being of the Spirit.
Practise *Spirit-recollection*   (5)
In depths of soul,
Where in the wielding
World-Creator-Life
Thine own I
Comes to being
Within the I of God.   (11)
Then in the All-World-Being of Man
Thou wilt truly *live.*

(I, 2)   For the Father-Spirit of the Heights holds sway
In Depths of Worlds, begetting Life.   (15)
Seraphim, Cherubim, Thrones!
(Spirits of Strength!)
Let there ring out from the Heights
What in the depths is echoed,
Speaking:
Ex Deo nascimur.   (20)
(From God, Mankind has Being.)
The Elemental Spirits hear it
In East and West and North and South:
May human beings hear it!

(II, 1)   Soul of Man!   (1)
Thou livest in the beat of Heart and Lung
Which leads thee through the rhythmic tides of Time
Into the feeling of thine own Soul-being.
Practise *Spirit-mindfulness*   (5)
In balance of the soul,
Where the surging
Deeds of the World's Becoming
Do thine own I

390

Unite
Unto the I of the World. (11)
Then 'mid the weaving of the Soul of Man
Thou wilt truly *feel*.

(II,2) For the Christ-Will in the encircling Round holds sway
In the Rhythms of Worlds, blessing the Soul. (15)
Kyriotetes, Dynamis, Exusiai!
(Spirits of Light!)
Let there be fired from the East
What through the West is formèd,
Speaking:
In Christo morimur. (20)
(In Christ, Death becomes Life.)
The Elemental Spirits hear it
In East and West and North and South:
May human beings hear it!

(III,1) Soul of Man! (1)
Thou livest in the resting Head
Which from the ground of the Eternal
Opens to thee the Thoughts of Worlds.
Practise *Spirit-vision* (5)
In quietness of Thought,
Where the eternal aims of Gods
World-Being's Light
On thine own I
Bestow
For thy free Willing. (11)
Then from the ground of the Spirit in Man
Thou wilt truly *think*.

(III,2) For the Spirit's Universal Thoughts hold sway
In the Being of all Worlds, beseeching Light. (15)
Archai, Archangeloi, Angeloi!
(Spirits of Soul!)
Let there be prayed in the Depths
What from the Heights is answered,
Speaking:
Per Spiritum Sanctum reviviscimus. (20)
(In the Spirit's Universal Thoughts, the Soul awakens.)
The Elemental Spirits hear it

In East and West and North and South:
May human beings hear it!

(IV, 1)   At the Turning Point of Time   (1)
The Spirit-Light of the World
Entered the stream of Earthly Being.
Darkness of Night
Had held its sway;   (5)
Day-radiant Light
Poured into the souls of men:
Light
That gives warmth
To simple Shepherds' Hearts,   (10)
Light
That enlightens
The wise Heads of Kings.

(IV, 2)   O Light Divine,
O Sun of Christ!   (15)
Warm Thou
Our Hearts,
Enlighten Thou
Our Heads,
That good may become   (20)
What from our Hearts we would found
And from our Heads direct
With single purpose.

Grundstein-Meditation

(*I, 1*)   Menschenseele!   (1)
          Du lebest in den Gliedern,
          Die dich durch die Raumeswelt
          In das Geistesmeereswesen tragen:
          Übe *Geist-Erinnern*   (5)
          In Seelentiefen,
          Wo in waltendem
          Weltenschöpfer-Sein
          Das eigne Ich
          Im Gottes-Ich   (10)
          Erweset;
          Und du wirst wahrhaft *leben*
          Im Menschen-Welten-Wesen.

(*I, 2*)   Denn es waltet der Vater-Geist der Höhen
          In den Weltentiefen Sein-erzeugend.   (15)
          Seraphim Cherubim, Throne!
          (Ihr Kräfte-Geister)
          Lasset aus den Höhen erklingen,
          Was in den Tiefen das Echo findet;
          Dieses spricht:
          Ex Deo nascimur.   (20)
          (Aus dem Göttlichen weset die Menschheit.)
          Das hören die Elementargeister
          Im Osten, Westen, Norden, Süden:
          Menschen mögen es hören.

(*II, 1*)   Menschenseele!   (1)
          Du lebest in dem Herzens-Lungen-Schlage,
          Der dich durch den Zeitenrhythmus
          Ins eigne Seelenwesensfühlen leitet:
          Übe *Geist-Besinnen*   (5)
          Im Seelengleichgewichte,
          Wo die wogenden
          Welten-Werde-Taten
          Das eigne Ich

Dem Welten-Ich (10)
Vereinen;
Und du wirst wahrhaft *fühlen*
Im Menschen-Seelen-Wirken.

(II, 2)   Denn es waltet der Christus-Wille im Umkreis
In den Weltenrhythmen Seelen-begnadend. (15)
Kyriotetes, Dynamis, Exusiai!
(Ihr Lichtes-Geister)
Lasset vom Osten befeuern,
Was durch den Westen sich gestaltet;
Dieses spricht:
In Christo morimur. (20)
(In dem Christus wird Leben der Tod.)
Das hören die Elementargeister
Im Osten, Westen, Norden, Süden:
Menschen mögen es hören.

(III, 1)   Menschenseele! (1)
Du lebest im ruhenden Haupte,
Das dir aus Ewigkeitsgründen
Die Weltgedanken erschließet:
Übe *Geist-Erschauen* (5)
In Gedanken-Ruhe,
Wo die ew'gen Götterziele
Welten-Wesens-Licht
Dem eignen Ich
Zu freiem Wollen
Schenken;
Und du wirst wahrhaft *denken*
In Menschen-Geistes-Gründen.

(III, 2)   Denn es walten des Geisten Weltgedanken
Im Weltenwesen Licht-erflehend. (15)
Archai, Archangeloi, Angeloi,
(Ihr Seelen-Geister)
O lasset aus den Tiefen erbitten,
Was in den Höhen erhöret wird;
Dieses spricht:
Per Spiritum Sanctum reviviscimus. (20)
(In des Geistes Welgedanken erwachet die Seele.)
Das hören die Elementargeister

Im Osten, Westen, Norden, Süden:
Menschen mögen es hören.

(IV, 1)   In der Zeiten Wende   (1)
          Trat das Welten-Geistes-Licht
          In den irdischen Wesensstrom;
          Nacht-Dunkel
          Hatte ausgewaltet,   (5)
          Taghelles Licht
          Erstrahlte in Menschenseelen;
          Licht,
          Das erwärmet
          Die armen Hirtenherzen;   (10)
          Licht
          Das erleuchtet
          Die weisen Königshäupter.

(IV, 2)   Göttliches Licht,
          Christus-Sonne,   (15)
          Erwärme
          Unsere Herzen;
          Erleuchte
          Unsere Häupter;
          Daβ gut werde,   (20)
          Was wir
          Aus Herzen gründen,
          Aus Häuptern
          Zielvoll führen wollen.

Notes and Additions

All works by Rudolf Steiner are referred to by the *Gesamtausgabe* (GA) volume number from the catalogue of the collected edition of Rudolf Steiner's works in the original German (published by *Rudolf Steiner Verlag*, Dornach, Switzerland). For information on the published English language translations see the list on page 481.

Foreword

1. The question was put to Rudolf Steiner by Friedrich Rittelmeyer at the time of the preparation for, and founding of, the Christian Community. See Emil Bock, *Rudolf Steiner. Studien zu seinem Lebensgang und Lebenswerk* (Studies in his Life and Works), lectures of 27 February and 15 December 1949.
2. GA 223, lecture of 31 March 1923.
3. GA 175.
4. S.O. Prokofieff, *Rudolf Steiner and the Founding of the New Mysteries*, Temple Lodge 1994, Part I, 'The Mystery of the Path of Rudolf Steiner's Life'.

Introduction: The Living Being of the Year and its Principal Festivals

1. GA 223, lecture of 31 March 1923.
2. GA 40.
3. GA 26.
4. GA 226, address of 17 May 1923.
5. GA 236, lecture of 4 June 1924.
6. Revelation 4:5.
7. In the lectures devoted to a description of the cosmic imaginations of the four festivals that comprise the cross of the year, Rudolf Steiner begins with the Michaelmas Imagination (see GA 229). From the further content of this book it will become clear that only *such* an order of studying the festivals may serve as a foundation for a real understanding of the esoteric nature of the *whole* yearly cycle.

Part I: The Festival of Michael as a Gate of Modern Initiation

1. GA 26, 'At the Dawn of the Michael Age', 17 August 1924.

2. Ibid, 31 August 1924.
3. GA 187, lecture of 22 December 1918.
4. GA 217, lecture of 15 October 1922.
5. GA 243, lecture of 13 August 1924.
6. Rudolf Steiner also speaks about this 'descent' of Michael in the following words: 'Shortly before the middle of the nineteenth century ... the Archangel Michael began his gradual ascent from a mere Archangel to a Time Spirit, so as to attain such a stage of development as would allow him to influence the lives of human beings not only from the supersensible world but directly from the earthly realm. The Archangel Michael had to prepare himself for this descent to the Earth by, to some extent, living in accordance with the great deed of Christ Himself, by living in accordance with the great process of taking the Earth as his point of departure and working on from this earthly standpoint.' (GA 174a, lecture of 17 February 1918.)
7. GA 13.
8. GA 40.
9. GA 240, lecture of 19 July 1924.
10. GA 219, lecture of 17 December 1922.
11. GA 240, lecture of 19 July 1924.
12. S.O. Prokofieff, *Rudolf Steiner and the Founding of the New Mysteries*, Chapter 6: 'The Foundation Stone Meditation'.
13. GA 219, lecture of 17 December 1922.
14. Ibid.
15. GA 119, lecture of 29 March 1910.
16. Ibid., lecture of 30 March 1910.
17. GA 26, 'At the dawn of the Michael Age' (17 August 1924).
18. See Note 12.
19. These lines from the Foundation Stone Meditation can also be compared with the following words from the lecture of 2 May 1913 in London: 'Michael can give us a new spiritual light, which we may regard as the transformation of that light which was given through him at the time of the Mystery of Golgotha, and in our time people may place themselves within this light' (GA 152).
20. GA 26, 'Man in his Macrocosmic Nature' (March 1925).
21. Ibid.
22. GA 219, lecture of 24 December 1922.
23. GA 26. In a lecture given almost eleven years previously, Rudolf Steiner speaks of this in the following words: 'Nevertheless, many people will recognize what is now beginning to rise like a dawning light and will in the course of the coming centuries pour into human souls like a Sun—for Michael can always be compared with a Sun. And even if many people do not acknowledge this new Revelation of Michael, it will nonetheless spread out amongst mankind' (GA 152, lecture of 2 May 1913).
24. GA 240, lecture of 19 July 1924.
25. GA 223, lecture of 1 April 1923.

26. If we would define somewhat more precisely the process of the union of the Soul and Spirit of the Earth with its etheric and physical bodies at Christmas-time, we could say the following. In winter the Soul of the Earth fully penetrates the plant kingdom and the Spirit of the Earth the mineral kingdom. Because of this, the consciousness of minerals can interpenetrate with the consciousness of plants (see the lecture of 31 December 1915, GA 165), that is to say, the Earth as a whole can for a short time rise half a step higher in its evolution and take up an intermediate position between the mineral and plant kingdoms.

27. GA 10. (The chapter entitled 'Inner Tranquillity'.)

28. Ibid. 'Control of Thoughts and Feelings'.

29. Ibid.

30. Ibid.

31. Ibid.

32. Regarding the power of the ahrimanic dragon in modern civilization, see especially the lecture of 15 October 1922 (GA 217).

33. GA 238, lecture of 28 September 1924.

34. GA 223, lecture of 1 October 1923.

35. See the description of the cosmic Michael imagination in the lecture of 15 October 1923 (GA 229).

36. GA 223, lecture of 8 April 1923.

37. Ibid.

38. Ibid.

39. GA 131, lecture of 12 October 1911.

40. GA 114, lecture of 18 September 1909.

41. Genesis 2:7.

42. GA 152, lecture of 2 May 1913.

43. Ibid.

44. There are a whole series of Rudolf Steiner's references concerning how Michael participated in 'the creation of man'. For example: 'But he [Michael] wanted to do all this only in the sense of serving, both then and in the future, those divine-spiritual powers with which he has been connected from his own, *and from man's*, distant past . . . for Michael bears in himself *all the primal forces* both of his Gods *and of human beings*' (GA 26). This is confirmed by an indication which Rudolf Steiner gave in a lecture of 1 November 1904 (not published) concerning how, in the middle of the Lemurian epoch, Michael 'fashioned the human form' in which he (man) subsequently incarnated on the Earth. Thus Michael is also called 'the moulder of the human form' or 'the Angel of form', in the sense of his activity as the servant of 'the ruling powers of Earth-existence', the 'Hierarchy of the Spirits of Form' (GA 105, lecture of 10 August 1908) and particularly of the foremost of these Spirits, Yahveh-Elohim (GA 194, lecture of 22 November 1919). This ideal human 'form' or 'image' (Rudolf Steiner uses both words in this connection), with which man was endowed by the Archangel Michael, was later (in the Lemurian epoch) to undergo a temptation on the part of luciferic and

ahrimanic forces—which led to the necessity for the first pre-earthly stage of the Mystery of Golgotha (see further about this in the chapter 'The Three Supersensible Deeds of the Nathan Soul'), as a result of which there arose a 'human-etheric form' in the region of the spiritual world closest to the Earth, the 'etheric *image* of man' was fashioned which could now radiate its forces into 'man's physical earthly *form*', thus enabling it 'to be protected' from destructive influences (GA 152, lecture of 7 March 1914).

If one compares Rudolf Steiner's description of this first preparatory deed with the content of the esoteric lesson to which reference has been made, Michael's direct participation in this combined working of Christ and the Nathan Soul becomes clear. For Michael, as the creator of the human image (form), was connected from the start with its entire earthly as well as its heavenly destiny. Furthermore, he is that being under whose guidance man is to embark upon the path leading to the conscious realization of this human image (form), the high ideal which has its archetype in the first pre-earthly deed of the Mystery of Golgotha. 'Greatest purity must have been attained in the human form; with regard to this human form, man must have reached his goal. Everything of a hindering nature must have been overcome,' says Rudolf Steiner on 1 November 1904. (Compare with the chapter 'Of Michael's Participation in the Supersensible Deeds of the Nathan Soul'.) This relationship between Michael and the Nathan Soul is expressed in an altogether different way in the *Bhagavad Gita*, which, as regards its contents, is deeply permeated with a Michaelic element. The teaching which Krishna imparts to Arjuna has the purpose of awakening in him a truly Michaelic mood, which he needs for this struggle against the anti-Michaelic powers threatening his soul. The outer reflection of his struggle is the battle on the field of Kuru.

45. See GA 26, articles of 18 and 25 January 1925.
46. See Note 19 to Part II. In the lecture of 7 March 1914 we find the following observation: 'And so one may say: there were, so to speak, *three* Angel-lives in the spiritual world. The being who led this *Angel and Archangel* life was indeed the same being who was subsequently born as man and is described as the Luke Jesus-child.' (GA 152.)
47. GA 11.
48. GA 131, lecture of 12 October 1911.
49. Ibid.
50. In the lecture of 30 December 1913 (GA 149), Rudolf Steiner refers more than once to the fact that the Sun-sphere was the original dwelling-place of the Nathan Soul. (See footnote on p. 28.)
51. See GA 146, lectures of 28 May and 1 June 1913.
52. GA 142, lecture of 30 December 1912.
53. GA 194, lecture of 22 November 1919 (see note 44). See also GA 112, the lecture of 7 July 1909.
54. See, for example, the lecture of 7 March 1916 (GA 167).

1. GA 152, lecture of 5 March 1914.
2. GA 152, lecture of 7 March 1914.
3. See GA 102, the lecture of 6 January 1908, and the description of the evolution of Old Saturn in the chapter 'The Evolution of the World and of Man' in GA 13.
4. In the majority of the lectures devoted to the supersensible deeds of the Nathan Soul, the first deed is, as a rule, associated with the luciferic temptation, while the second and third are associated with the temptation issuing from Lucifer *and* Ahriman. (The lectures of 30 December 1913, GA 149, and 7 March 1914, GA 152, are exceptions.) This is confirmed by the fact that, according to further information imparted through spiritual science, Lucifer approached man in the Lemurian epoch, while Ahriman did so only on Atlantis.
5. There exists a definite connection between man's twelve senses, whose foundations were laid on Ancient Saturn, and the twelvefold membering of man's being emerging in the Earth-period of evolution. However, a more detailed examination of these relationships would lead too far from our present theme. (Compare with what is also conveyed through the content of the two blue windows of the Goetheanum, North and South.)
6. GA 152, lecture of 7 March 1914.
7. Ibid.
8. See also the lecture-cycle of March 1911 (GA 128).
9. Genesis 2:19–20.
9a See GA 152, lecture of 7 March 1914.
10. GA 10, Chapter 10: 'Division of the Personality During Spiritual Training'.
11. See also the lecture of 10 June 1912 (GA 136).
11a See GA 152, lecture of 7 March 1914.
12. GA 152, lecture of 1 June 1914.
13. Ibid.
14. See, for example, the lecture of 30 December 1913 (GA 149).
15. GA 148, lecture of 10 February 1914.
16. GA 152, lecture of 27 May 1914.
17. GA 152, lecture of 1 June 1914.
18. GA 149, lecture of 30 December 1913.
19. If one examines a wider circle of Rudolf Steiner's utterances about the earthly destiny of the Nathan Soul, one may provisionally divide them into three categories. To the first belong those observations where the Nathan Soul is characterized as a being who belongs to *human* evolution and who in the Lemurian epoch appears as the sister soul of Adam. We find such references, for example, in the fourth lecture of GA 114 (18 September 1909), in the eighth lecture of GA 131 (12 October 1911) and in the seventh lecture of GA 146 (3 June 1913), and also in a number of individual lectures devoted to the theme of Christmas, for example the lectures given on 21 and

26 December 1911 (GA 127), and on 21 and 23 December 1913 (GA 150). The second category of observations are connected with the theme of the preparatory stages of the Mystery of Golgotha. These generally refer to an Angel- or Archangel-like being, though they sometimes include indications concerning the 'human' character of the Nathan Soul (for example, in the lectures of 30 December 1913 and of 5 March 1914), while in, for instance, the lecture of 30 March 1914 (GA 152) there is a reference to the 'Angel-being'. And finally, as a third category, there is the thoroughly clear indication of the participation of a certain being from the Hierarchy of the Archangels in the 'preparatory stages of the Mystery of Golgotha'. Thus in the lecture of 1 June 1914 we read: 'This [the third danger at the end of the Atlantean epoch] was averted through the third Christ event, when Christ for the third time, as Christ Being, in-dwelt the outer soul of an Archangel, *a being from the Hierarchy of the Archangels.*'

20. In the lecture of 30 March 1914 (GA 152) Rudolf Steiner says: 'The first and second preparatory stages took place in the world of Devachan [i.e., in the sphere of intuition and inspiration], while the third was in the astral word [i.e., in the sphere of imagination] and the event of Golgotha in the physical world.'

21. GA 150, lecture of 21 December 1913.

22. In the lecture. of 5 June 1913, Rudolf Steiner says: 'To understand the Christ-impulse means not only to strive towards perfection but also to receive into oneself something which may be defined in the words of Paul: "Not I, but Christ in me". "I"—that is the word of Krishna [the Nathan Soul]; "Not I, but Christ in me"—this represents the Christian impulse.' (GA 146.)

22a See the lecture of 10 January 1915 (GA 161).

22b See the lecture of 7 March 1914 (GA 152). The next quotation is from the same source.

23. See GA 240, lecture of 19 July 1924.

23a See further regarding the descent of the cosmic Intelligence of Michael to the Earth in the lecture of 19 July 1924 (GA 240).

24. Already in the epoch of Old Sun, the being whom we now call the Archangel Michael and who was then passing through his 'human' stage was able to unite himself in a particularly profound way with the Sun Spirit of the Christ and hence become, to a certain extent, the leader of Old Sun humanity. This connection of Michael with the great Sun Spirit, going back as it did to the epoch of Old Sun, enabled him in the Earth-epoch to become not only primarily a Sun Archangel but also to attain a quite particular relationship to the Christ and the hierarchic cosmos as a whole.

25. See GA 112, lecture of 24 June 1909.

26. GA 194, lecture of 22 November 1919.

27. GA 26, 'Michael's Mission in the Cosmic Age of Human Freedom' (9 November 1924).

28. See GA 223, the lecture of 1 April 1923.

29. GA 130, lecture of 1 October 1911.
30. GA 26.
31. See GA 223, lecture of 31 March 1923.
32. See the words of Rudolf Steiner quoted on pages 21–22.
33. GA 152, lecture of 30 March 1914. These words of Rudolf Steiner can help us gain a better understanding of the connection mentioned in the first chapter (of Part II) between the third sacrifice of the Nathan Soul and the rescuing of the primordial, as yet still clairvoyant, thinking. For as Rudolf Steiner shows, the impulses for human thinking come directly from the astral world, whereas the impulses for feeling derive from lower Devachan and those for will from higher Devachan (see the lecture of 4 November 1911, GA 130), that is, from those supersensible realms where all three cosmic 'preparatory stages' of the Mystery of Golgotha took place.
34. See GA 152, lecture of 7 March 1914.
34a See GA 9, 'Body, Soul and Spirit'.
34b See the lecture of 13 July 1914 (GA 155).
34c In accordance with the point of view from which he was addressing the subject, Rudolf Steiner sometimes referred to the three events individually as three ascending stages of one and the same cosmic-earthly process and at other times he united them with the one central concept of the Mystery of Golgotha, as, for example, in the following words: 'It is good if we study the Mystery of Golgotha—and the Christmas Mystery is indeed part of it—from points of view which can in a certain sense enable the meaning of the entire evolution of man to shine forth within it' (lecture of 24 December 1920, GA 202). Epiphany, which betokens the three years of Christ's life on Earth, forms part of the Mystery of Golgotha to an even greater degree than the birth of the Nathan Jesus. Thus Rudolf Steiner said in a lecture: 'In the Mystery of Golgotha the divine Christ Being unites with the man Jesus of Nazareth...' (lecture of 26 December 1921, GA 209).

If, however, one considers these three stages from a differentiated aspect, it is possible to point towards a further development of this process. Thus in the future, which, however, begins already in our time in connection with the reappearance of Christ in etheric form (see Part XII), this process will develop further, though now by awakening new supersensible faculties in every human being in mirror-image succession. If we take the redemption of the individual ego through the Mystery of Golgotha as the centre or principal axis of earthly evolution, the stage of the new, conscious clairvoyance in human evolution makes its presence felt to begin with in man's individual (inner) thinking, the consequence of which is that Christ is experienced in etheric form (see Rudolf Steiner's words quoted on p. 124. Later—and this too is being prepared in our time—Christ will, in addition, enter into the human faculty of memory, the effect of which will be that the full significance of the Mystery of Golgotha will be disclosed to humanity at the beginning of the sixth great epoch of evolution. For just as mankind had a wonderful clair-voyant memory in ancient Atlantean times (the fourth great epoch), this will, after its extinguishing in the post-Atlantean (or fifth) great epoch, return in a new form and on a far more conscious level through Christ's entering into the faculty of human memory. Rudolf Steiner has described this as follows: 'A time will come for humanity which is now being prepared but which will only be fulfilled *in the sixth great period* of human evolution, when people will look back upon what they have lived through and experienced, upon what lives within them as memory; and they will be able to see that Christ is present in the power of memory ... And through Christ entering into his power of memory ... man will know that until the Mystery of Golgotha Christ worked in the regions beyond the Earth [i.e. all three cosmic preparatory stages of the Mystery of Golgotha will at such a time be revealed to every individual in his own spiritual experience], that He prepared for and went through the Mystery of Golgotha and that He works on further as an impulse in history' (lecture of 7 March, 1914, GA 152). Rudolf Steiner goes on to say that 'it will not be possible inwardly to survey the earthly evolution of humanity otherwise than by seeing the Christ-impulse as the central point'.

But just as at the Turning Point of Time only a few decades separated Christmas (the birth) and Epiphany from one another, so must the beginning of Christ's entering into the human powers of memory follow directly today upon the entry of Christ into human thinking. 'Our thinking is [today] as yet permeated by the Christ-impulse in the barest measure, and already this impulse is approaching our memory.'

35. See, for example, the lecture of 10 February 1924 (GA 234), and also GA 13, the chapter entitled 'The Nature of Man'.

35a Lecture of 28 August 1912 (GA 138).

36. Epiphany and Easter are also connected with the fourth deed of the Nathan Soul. But while at Christmas the Nathan Soul, who at his birth is only over-shone by the Spirit Sun of Christ, is at the centre of events, at Epiphany and Easter the central position comes to be occupied by the *Christ*, who has united Himself with the Nathan Soul. Thus as we are here giving an account of the destiny of the Nathan Soul, we shall confine ourselves, for the time being, to simply mentioning these other festivals (of which more will be said later on).

37. Rudolf Steiner refers on several occasions to the connection of the human etheric body with the principle of time and with human memory. For example, in a lecture of 16 May 1923 (GA 226), he calls it the 'body of time' (*Zeitleib*).

38. GA 223, lecture of 8 April 1923.

39. GA·223, lecture of 1 October 1923.

40. Rudolf Steiner speaks of how the time from the height of summer until Christmas corresponds to human evolution *before* the Mystery of Golgotha in, for example, the lecture of 21 December 1913 (GA 150).

41. See GA 137, the lecture of 12 June 1912.

42. GA 93a, lecture of 11 October 1905.

43. GA 232, lecture of 2 December 1923.

44. Regarding the significance of the cultivation of thinking for spirit-pupilship,

see also GA 17, the chapter 'Of the Guardian of the Threshold and Certain Matters of Clairvoyant Consciousness'.

45. The significance of thinking in modern initiation also derives from the fact that Rudolf Steiner, in contrast to the traditional spiritual path (which extends only as far as the Moon-sphere), was able to penetrate to the Sun and to Saturn. According to what he says in a lecture of 20 August 1924, GA 243, this was due to the circumstance that he was able to bear the thinking faculties which he had developed through this absorption in natural-scientific thinking into supersensible realms.

46. GA 13, chapter 'Knowledge of Higher Worlds'.

47. Ibid. The word '*pure*' (path) is included in the sixth edition but omitted by Rudolf Steiner in the twentieth.

48. Ibid.

49. See, for example, the lecture of 13 September 1922 (GA 215).

50. GA 10, 'The Guardian of the Threshold'. [Quotations follow English edition of 1969.]

51. Ibid.

52. Ibid.

53. GA 13, 'Knowledge of Higher Worlds'.

54. Ibid.

55. GA 10, chapter 'Some Effects of Initiation'.

56. Ibid.

57. GA 13, 'Knowledge of Higher Worlds'.

58. GA 10, 'The Guardian of the Threshold'.

59. Ibid.

60. GA 146, lecture of 29 May 1913.

60a Lecture of 27 March 1913 (GA 145).

61. GA 10, chapter 'Initiation'.

62. Ibid.

63. Ibid.

64. Ibid.

65. Ibid.

66. Ibid.

67. Ibid.

68. Ibid.

69. Ibid.

70. Ibid.

71. Ibid.

72. Ibid.

73. Ibid.

74. Ibid.

75. See further about this spiritual law in the book *Rudolf Steiner and the Founding of the New Mysteries*, Chapter 7.

76. Matthew 4:3. [In the Russian text, the author in these quotations follows the German translation of Emil Bock in drawing out the meaning inherent in the

Greek words more fully than in any extant English version. Translator's note.]

77. Matthew 4:4.
78. GA 10, 'Initiation'.
79. Matthew 4:6.
80. Matthew 4:7.
81. GA 10, 'Initiation'.
82. Ibid.
83. Ibid.
84. See Matthew 4:8–9. A more precise description may be found in St Luke's Gospel, 4:5–6.
85. Matthew 4:10.
86. GA 10.
87. Ibid.
88. Ibid.
89. GA 13, 'Knowledge of Higher Worlds'.
90. All that has been said in the present chapter may give rise to a question in the mind of the reader: how do the three temptations of Christ Jesus in the wilderness described therein, taken in this case from the Gospel according to Matthew, relate to the description of the same scene given in the Fifth Gospel which is preserved in the spiritual memory of the world or in the so-called Akashic Chronicle?

It follows from Rudolf Steiner's indications in a lecture of 2 November 1909 (GA 117), that the Gospel of St Mark is a reflection of the will of Christ Jesus, the Gospel of St Luke a reflection of His feeling, and the Gospel of St John a reflection of His thinking. We could also say that these three Gospels are written out of a clairvoyant perception of cosmic will, cosmic feeling and cosmic thinking (the Sophia). In a lecture of 14 November 1909 (GA 117), Rudolf Steiner compares these three aspects with what the spirit-pupil experiences as the process of the 'division of the personality' (as described in GA 10). Just as the thinking, feeling and will of the pupil free themselves at a certain moment of spiritual evolution from the connection that has naturally subsisted between them and can be experienced independently one from another as three completely different regions of the soul, so we have something similar—albeit at a much higher level—in the case of these three Gospels.

However, the stage of the 'division of the personality' is, in the context of spiritual development, no more than a transitional stage that both precedes and follows—though, it is true, on two altogether different levels—a condition which could be defined as a working together of thinking, feeling and will within man. At the stage that precedes the 'division of the personality', thinking, feeling and will are united through the presence of the *physical body*, which regulates their mutual interaction and at the same time *weakens* them with respect to that original force which they possess when they work independently of one another. The second possibility of achieving a right mode of interaction of these three forces has to do with the stage of spiritual development which comes *after* the 'division of the personality'. This is the stage when thinking, feeling and will, having become independent from one another, are ruled 'from above' by the spirit-pupil's higher ego, which is, if necessary, able to unite them again in a higher unity, transforming them in the process into an organ for perceiving the higher worlds which is capable of reading in the Akashic Chronicle. We have something similar—though again, at a far higher level—in the case of the Gospels. Thus the Matthew Gospel, in Rudolf Steiner's words, presents a kind of 'harmonious union' of impulses of the will, feeling and thinking of Christ Jesus. As, however, these are united into a whole through the form of the physical body—to which Matthew, in contrast to the other Evangelists, was particularly drawn—they undergo a process of weakening, they grow 'pale'; and in this weakened form they bring to manifestation what Christ was as a man on Earth. Thus 'in the Gospel of Matthew the form of Christ Jesus comes before us in an altogether human way, as the solitary man of the Earth' (GA 123, lecture of 21 December 1909).

The Fifth Gospel represents a complete contrast to this. Here, too, there is a coming together of the impulses of will, feeling and thinking of Christ Jesus but this does not happen 'naturally', by means of the physical body, but rather through the higher Ego working in the Spirit. Such is the content of the Akashic Chronicle, wherein the cosmic will, feeling and thinking of Christ Jesus were inscribed by Him as a result of the activity of His World Ego. Hence, the following overall picture arises:

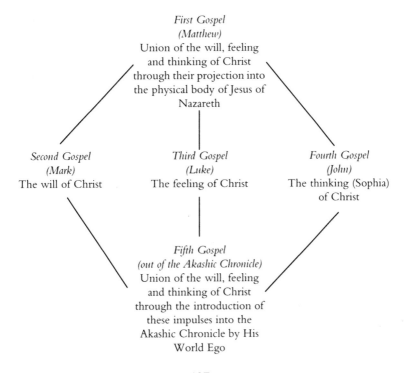

First Gospel
(Matthew)
Union of the will, feeling
and thinking of Christ
through their projection into
the physical body of Jesus of
Nazareth

Second Gospel
(Mark)
The will of Christ

Third Gospel
(Luke)
The feeling of Christ

Fourth Gospel
(John)
The thinking (Sophia)
of Christ

Fifth Gospel
(out of the Akashic Chronicle)
Union of the will, feeling
and thinking of Christ
through the introduction of
these impulses into the
Akashic Chronicle by His
World Ego

This is how the five Gospels in general terms relate to one another. It follows with total clarity that the first and the fifth of these form a certain polarity, and this comes to expression in—among many other instances—the order of succession of the three temptations in the wilderness. For the Gospel of Matthew, being connected mainly with the history of the arising of the *physical* body of Jesus of Nazareth, is to a significant degree concerned with the past of world evolution. Thus the description of the temptations here follows the line of development of the physical body: Saturn, Sun and Moon—physical body, etheric body and astral body.

Moreover, Christ is depicted in the Gospel according to Matthew as 'resolving' the first question of the tempter concerning the transformation of 'stones into bread', in that in the past three aeons mankind did not yet possess its own ego and was therefore still removed from the sphere of temptation (which always presupposes the presence of an ego). Similarly, we have in the three preparatory stages or steps leading to the Mystery of Golgotha a reflection of the ancient planetary conditions of the Earth, inasmuch as humanity is in these situations saved from temptation not through its own efforts but through cosmic help from without (the three supersensible deeds of the Nathan Soul).

In contrast, the Fifth Gospel is wholly connected with the future aeons of world evolution: with Jupiter, Venus and Vulcan (the transformations of the astral, etheric and physical bodies through the World Ego of Christ). And so if the Gospel of Matthew represents the normal stream of time, from past to future, the Fifth Gospel is associated with the reverse stream of time, from the future to the past, this being the stream which is characteristic of all events contained within the Akashic Chronicle. (When he first spoke of the Fifth Gospel, Rudolf Steiner gave all the events in their reverse order—see GA 148, 2 and 3 October 1913—while in connection with the third temptation he refers to the aeon of Vulcan as an indication of a reversed flow of time—18 December 1913, as above.) As, however, the free human ego will play an ever greater part in all the events of the future aeons of evolution, Christ includes man as a free ego-being in the struggle for the future destiny of earthly evolution through leaving the tempter's third question incompletely resolved: 'If Christ was truly to help man on Earth, He had to allow Ahriman a sphere of influence ... Ahriman's activity had to remain unconquered by Christ' (GA 148, 18 December 1913).

In so far as what has been said in the present part of this book relates to the descending half of the year, which is to say, that which is connected with the past evolution of the Earth and humanity, it would be appropriate to turn to the description of the temptations as they are given in the Gospel according to Matthew. On the other hand, for an examination of the consequences of the threefold temptation of Christ in the wilderness for the future evolution of the Earth and humanity—which corresponds to the second, ascending half of the year, the reflection of the three years of Christ's life on the Earth—it would be necessary to take as a foundation not the First but the

Fifth Gospel. For with these questions it is always necessary to keep in mind that we have in the four Gospels *four different points of view* of the events of Palestine and in particular of the 'temptation scene' which, as a result, is described *differently* in each of the first three Gospels (it is omitted from St John's Gospel for a definite reason). Rudolf Steiner refers to this in his lectures on the Fifth Gospel, in that he prefaces his description of the 'temptation-scene', as it is contained in the Akashic Chronicle, with the following words: 'The temptation-scene appears in various Gospels. *But they recount* [it] *from various viewpoints.* I have often pointed this out' (GA 148, 6 October 1913).

91. GA 10, chapter 'Initiation'.
92. Ibid.
93. Ibid.
94. GA 13, chapter 'Knowledge of Higher Worlds'.
95. GA 10, chapter 'Initiation'.
96. GA 13, chapter 'Knowledge of Higher Worlds'.
97. Ibid.

Part III: The Mystery of Christmas

1. These words of Angelus Silesius are quoted from a lecture given by Rudolf Steiner on 23 December 1913 in Berlin (GA 150). We may append to these words the following observation of Rudolf Steiner, which is at one and the same time their modern metamorphosis and an indication of the meaning and purpose of modern spiritual science (Anthroposophy): 'And again, what we need to wish for is a sort of world-Christmas in a spiritual context. Christ must be born anew in spiritual form, at any rate for human understanding. And this whole endeavour within spiritual science is really a kind of Christmas festival, *the birth of Christ in human wisdom*' (GA 165, lecture of 27 December 1915).
2. See the book, S.O. Prokofieff, *Rudolf Steiner and the Founding of the New Mysteries*, Chapter 5, 'The Christmas Conference of 1923–24'.
3. Words spoken at the laying of the Foundation Stone of the General Anthroposophical Society, 25 December 1923 in Dornach.
4. GA 146, lecture of 5 June 1913.
5. In the lecture of 7 March 1914 Rudolf Steiner speaks of this as follows: 'The path which is laid out before man is to make the words "Not I, but Christ in me" ever more real; and the way will be cleared through the Christ-impulse becoming gradually wedded *to the faculty of remembering*.'
6. Ibid.
7. GA 146, lecture of 5 June 1913.
8. In the penultimate chapter of *The Threshold of the Spiritual World* (GA 17), 'Summary of Certain Aspects of the Foregoing', we find the following characterization of the 'three' egos of man in connection with the

description of his various sheaths: 1) The physical body in the physical world of the senses. Through this man recognizes himself as an independent isolated entity (as an 'I'). 2) The refined etheric body in the elemental environment. Through this man recognizes himself as a member of the Earth's elemental or life-body. 3) The astral body in a spiritual environment. Through this man is a member of a spiritual world. Therein resides man's 'other self', which finds its expression in repeated Earth-lives. 4) The 'true ego' in a super-spiritual environment. In this world man finds himself as a spiritual being even though all experiences of the senses, of thinking, feeling and will, should fall into oblivion.

From the following allusion in the chapter 'Concerning Repeated Earth Lives . . .' it becomes clear that by 'other self' is meant the 'higher self': 'In the form of a picture and yet essentially real, as though wishing to reveal itself as an independent being, there emerges from the ebb and flow of the soul a second self which seems to be independent *and higher* with respect to that entity which one has hitherto called one's self: it appears as the inspirer of this self. As this latter self, man merges into a unity with this inspiring, *higher* self'. And further: 'In encountering this "other self", clairvoyant consciousness learns to say "I" to the *totality of life's destiny*, just as physical man says "I" to *his own* being. What one speaks of—using the oriental word—as "karma" grows together in this way with the "other self", with the "spiritual ego-being".'

9. GA 124, lecture of 19 December 1910.
10. Ibid.
11. GA 10, chapter 'Life and Death. The Greater Guardian of the Threshold'.
12. Ibid.
13. At the corresponding point in *Occult Science*, there stands the word 'soon'.
14. GA 10.
15. A clairvoyant can of course research even further into the past but on different paths, not through plunging directly into his own inner being but through reading in the Akashic Record, just as we can learn to know about our life on Earth before the age of three, not through our personal memories but from those who were adults at the time.
16. What is of significance here is the fact that the day of Adam and Eve (24 December) precedes Christmas, with the result that the thirteen Holy Nights can, as a whole, also be regarded as representing the path of human evolution from ancient Lemuria until the beginning of the Christian era, from the first outpouring of ego-substance into man until the appearance in the flesh of the cosmic Ego of the Christ. Rudolf Steiner refers to this as follows: 'Thus it is right to regard 6 January as the birthday of Christ, it is right to regard these thirteen Holy Nights as the time which represents the power of seership within human souls, when one perceives everything that man must accomplish throughout life in the incarnations from Adam and Eve until the Mystery of Golgotha' (GA 127, lecture of 26 December 1911).
17. That the Nathan Soul has a quite special ego has already been discussed in the pages of this book (see p. 33).

18. GA 149, lectures 28 December 1913–2 January 1914.

19. Ibid.

20. GA 148, lecture of 10 February 1914.

21. GA 152, lecture of 5 March 1914. See also Note 19 to Part II.

22. GA 146, lecture of 3 June 1913.

23. GA 142, lecture of 30 December 1912.

24. See GA 146, lecture of 5 June 1913.

25. GA 146, lecture of 3 June 1913.

26. GA 142, lecture of 30 December 1912.

27. Ibid. In another cycle Rudolf Steiner speaks as follows: 'And today we must say: we stand at the end of that age which was beginning in the time of the *Bhagavad Gita*' (GA 146, lecture of 5 June 1913)—that is, of the Kali-Yuga. Thus the Nathan Soul works on three occasions directly among people on Earth: 1) Five thousand years before the Birth of Christ, as Krishna; 2) in the events of Palestine; 3) beginning from the twentieth century (that is, from the end of the Kali-Yuga), as the light-filled sheath of the Risen Christ. In the latter case it is, indeed, not incarnated in a physical body but nonetheless abides in the spiritual sphere that is closest to the earthly world.

28. Words spoken at the laying of the Foundation Stone of the General Anthroposophical Society, 25 December 1923 in Dornach.

29. Compare with the first chapter in GA 15.

30. See GA 152, lecture of 7 March 1914.

31. GA 114, lecture of 26 September 1909.

32. GA 175, lecture of 20 February 1917.

33. GA 127, lecture of 26 December 1911.

34. Ibid.

35. Ibid.

36. We should at this point not be confused by the fact that the Nathan Soul also in a certain sense represents the impulse of love, which can be experienced especially strongly now in the outer world in the exoteric celebration of Christmas. This problem is, however, resolved in that the impulse of love which the Nathan Soul bears within itself has a more human-microcosmic character (and is hence so close to all human beings), while the impulse of wisdom has a more macrocosmic character in that it is connected with the *entire* wisdom of past evolution.

Rudolf Steiner says in this connection: '. . . in the case of the Nathan Jesus-child of the Luke Gospel we have to do with a physical body, etheric body and astral body which are ordered in such a way that they harmoniously represent man as the end-result of Saturn, Sun and Moon evolution' (GA 131, lecture of 12 October 1911). And in another cycle we find these words: 'Hence this [Nathan] Soul has all the love of which the human soul is capable' (GA 142, lecture of 1 January 1913). While at Epiphany, in contrast, we celebrate the birth on Earth of, on the one hand, Zarathustra—the representative of all *earthly* wisdom, and, on the other, of the Sun Spirit of Christ at the Baptism in the Jordan—the bearer of universal, cosmic love.

37. GA 13, chapter 'Present and Future Evolution of the World and of Humanity'.
38. See GA 236, the lecture of 4 June 1924.
39. GA 127, lecture of 21 December 1911.
40. GA 119, lecture of 29 March 1910.
41. GA 124, lecture of 6 December 1910.
42. Ibid.
43. During the thirteen Holy Nights the cosmic events of the circle of the zodiac are experienced not directly but through their reflection in the depths of the Earth. One could also say that at Christmas-tide the Earth with all its creatures is immersed in the *memory* of its summer experiences in the widths of space (in the starry macrocosm). For the pupil who strives to experience this time *consciously*, penetration into the starry world takes place *not* through a direct ascent into the macrocosm but *in the manner of a reflection* through a union with, or a 'reading' in, the Earth's memory. The passage through the zodiacal spheres is made in a backwards direction with respect to the visible movements of the Sun (from the Ram through to the Fishes), and corresponds to the direction of the movement of the point of the spring equinox (from the Fishes through to the Ram). On this path—if, of course, he traverses it consciously—the pupil can truly experience the Christ Being, who since the Mystery of Golgotha has been 'the representative of *all* macrocosmic forces on the Earth'.
44. GA 102, lecture of 27 January 1908.
45. GA 15.
46. More will be said about this in the chapter 'The Vidar-Mystery'.
47. See GA 102, the lecture of 27 January 1908.
48. Compare GA 130, the lecture of 9 January 1912, and the notes to the lecture of 28 November 1911, and GA 201, the lecture of 18 April 1920.

Part IV: From Epiphany to Easter

1. GA 123, lecture of 10 September 1910.
2. GA 123, lecture of 11 September 1910.
3. See GA 123, the lecture of 10 September 1910.
4. In connection with this first stage it is necessary to be aware of the following. According to Rudolf Steiner's lecture of 20 September 1912 (GA 139), it became possible for the Apostles to reach this stage only because they were overshone by the spiritual being of John the Baptist, who after his death became their group soul and enabled them to begin the ascent into the higher worlds. (Hence in the Gospel of St Mark, Chapter 6, the scenes of the feeding of the five thousand and the walking upon the waters follow immediately *after* the description of the martyrdom of John the Baptist.) And as this first stage is a prophetic indication of our fifth cultural epoch, in the course of which there opens up before people the possibility of con-

templating, in a quite natural way, the Etheric Christ in the supersensible world bordering upon the Earth (see the chapter entitled 'The Virtue of Faith and the Fifth post-Atlantean Epoch'), we may say: in our time, too, we need to have something which can help us *from the spiritual world* to attain this new contemplation of Christ, just as the spiritual being of John the Baptist helped the Apostles in their attainment of the first stage of the ascent into the higher worlds. More will be said about what can help humanity in this connection in the chapter entitled 'The Exoteric and Esoteric Working of the Etheric Bodies of the Great Initiates in the Twentieth Century'.

5. St Matthew, 17:1.
6. Ibid. verse 2.
7. St Mark, 9:6 [based on Emil Bock's translation].
8. There is no allusion to this third stage in the lecture-cycle *The Gospel of St Matthew*, although it is a natural consequence of the process of development reflected in the scenes from the Gospel that have already been considered.
9. GA 97, lecture of 2 December 1906.
10. Hence it was John who was able to describe with the greatest precision the process of the gradual union of Christ with the *physical body* of Jesus of Nazareth. Thus, for instance, only in the Gospel of St John do we find (12:28–31) a reference to the driving of the luciferic and ahrimanic forces out of the physical body which took place before this union, culminating in the words: 'Now is the hour which is decisive for the whole world. The prince of this world is to be cast out' (12:31) [following the Bock translation]. See further about this in the lecture of 5 July 1909 (GA 112).
11. GA 113, lecture of 31 August 1909.
12. One could also say that, for John, the Mystery of Pentecost began as he stood on the Hill of Golgotha and ended on the eve of Christ's Resurrection. Thus only in the Gospel written by him do we find not merely Christ's reiterated *promises* in the farewell discourses (Chapters 14, 15 and 16) regarding the sending of the Holy Spirit but also a direct indication of this event (20:22). There is, however, one further mystery that is connected with all that has been said, in that according to the laws of world-rulership the twelve Apostles who surrounded Christ Jesus on the Earth were in a certain sense the earthly reflection of the primordial twelvefoldness that surrounded the macrocosmic Being of Christ in the world of Buddhi or Providence. Rudolf Steiner has this to say regarding this connection of the Apostles with the primordial twelvefoldness: '... When the time was fulfilled, after the first third of the fourth post-Atlantean epoch had run its course, there came in place of the Moon influences the working of the Christ, surrounded as it was by the twelvefold working of the Bodhisattvas, to which relates—and which also really is—the surrounding of Christ by the twelve Apostles' (GA 227, lecture of 28 August 1923).

While, however, one could say that what worked at the previous stages of the Apostles' spiritual development was of a more unconscious nature, now with the ascent to this third stage it would have become a *fully conscious*

413

experience for them. They would now have experienced in full consciousness their connection with the sphere of Providence, with the cosmic sphere of the Holy Spirit, in order through this to become direct witnesses of the Mystery of Golgotha. That, however, did not happen. Of all the twelve Apostles, only John was able to reach this stage and hence to become the greatest representative of humanity on the Hill of Golgotha.

The individuality of John the Baptist also participated supersensibly in this 'standing beneath the Cross' (this individuality united with John at the moment of his initiation as Lazarus), now helping John to ascend to an exalted level of spiritual understanding. (See GA 238, Rudolf Steiner's *Last Address*, 28 September 1924 in Dornach, and especially the notes to the lecture by L. Noll and M. Kirchner-Bockholt in the German edition of 1924.) [Reference is made to Ludwig Noll's verbal explanation in Alfred Heidenreich's preface to the English edition of 1967.—Translator's note.]

13. GA 130, lecture of 21 September 1911.
14. Ibid.
15. GA 130, lecture of 4 November 1911.
16. GA 130, lecture of 18 November 1911.
17. Ibid.
18. GA 130, lecture of 4 November 1911.
19. According to an East European legend, the name 'Sophia' was also attributed to a Christian martyr who was put to death in the second century in Rome with her three daughters Faith, Love and Hope.
20. Rudolf Steiner speaks of this as follows: 'There is a difference between knowing what the ego must become [as is the case with Buddhism] and receiving into oneself the stream of the living power *which can then flow from this ego into the whole world, in the same way that the power which proceeded from Christ worked upon the astral, etheric and physical bodies of those around Him.*' And further: 'What Christ has given is not a teaching but above all a living power. He sacrificed His very Self. He came down to Earth not in order merely to flow into human astral bodies but into the ego, which is why this has the power inwardly to generate *the substance of love.* Christ brought to the Earth not a love that is full of wisdom but the substance, the living essence, of love. That is the main point.' (GA 114, 25 September 1909.) (Compare with the words from *Occult Science*, quoted on pp. 104–105 and the lecture of 2 October 1913, GA 148.)
21. GA 114, lecture of 25 September 1909.
22. Ibid.
23. GA 130, lecture of 3 December 1911.
24. GA 130, lecture of 18 November 1911.
25. Ibid. These words correspond in a remarkable way with the principal task which Michael places today before the two groups of souls which as Platonists and Aristotelians are to work together on Earth at the end of the twentieth century. Rudolf Steiner concludes his description of this task with the words: '... when at the end of the twentieth century there comes that

spiritual renewal *which leads what is merely intellectual into the spiritual*' (lecture of 18 July, 1924). From these words we may see a further aspect of how the Michael-impulse and the Christ-impulse unite in their rulership of humanity in the twentieth century: the Christ-impulse works from within outwards in man's astral body through the development of the power of faith, while the Michael-impulse, in its striving to spiritualize modern intellectual culture in order to prepare it for the new manifestation of the Christ, comes towards it from without inwards.

26. In the Russian language the words for 'faith' and 'confidence' derive from the same root.

27. GA 130, lecture of 2 December 1911.

28. In the lecture of 13 April 1922 in the Hague, GA 211, Rudolf Steiner speaks as follows about the power of faith: 'But if you could rise to the insight that the Earth acquired its meaning only through the fact that in the middle of earthly evolution there occurred with the Mystery of Golgotha a divine event which cannot be comprehended with earthly understanding, you would be giving rise to a quite special power of wisdom (and the power of wisdom is the same as that of faith), a special power of spirit-wisdom, a power of faith born of wisdom. For it is a sign of great strength in the soul when one can say: I believe, I know through faith what I could never believe and know through earthly means.'

29. GA 127, lecture of 14 June 1911.

30. GA 130, lecture of 2 December 1911.

31. GA 123, lecture of 10 September 1910.

32. Matthew 14:15.

33. GA 113, lecture of 31 August 1909.

34. From the standpoint of the astral world one could say that the twelvefoldness which belongs in Devachan to the good Gods at once separates in the lower worlds [the sphere of the Moon] into the realms of light and darkness, into the domains of Lucifer (7) and Ahriman (5).

35. GA 113, lecture of 31 August 1909.

36. GA 113, lecture of 30 August 1909.

37. The principle of sevenfoldness works also in the etheric body, but it has there a different (non-luciferic) character.

38. In the sphere of Devachan (the sphere of the Sun), in contrast to the astral world (the sphere of the Moon), the law of seven belongs not to Lucifer but to Christ. Hence Rudolf Steiner frequently characterizes the Sun-realm of the Christ as the domain of cosmic time (see, for example, the lecture of 4 June 1924, GA 236). While in higher spheres (higher Devachan or the world of Buddhi) Christ encompasses twelvefoldness, that is, the whole macrocosm that is connected with the Earth, with His Being.

39. GA 113, lecture of 30 August 1909.

40. Ibid.

41. Matthew 14:16.

42. GA 113, lecture of 30 August 1909.

43. Mark 6:37.
44. Ibid.
45. See GA 104, the lecture of 29 June 1908.
46. Mark 6:47–48.
47. Matthew 14:25–26.
48. Matthew 14:27.
49. Matthew 14:31. (In the Bock German translation these words are rendered to this effect: 'O how weak is your heart'.)
50. Mark 6:52. (Compare also the Gospel according to John, 12:40.) The Russian canonical translation has in both cases the word *okamenyélo* [petrified], which would seem to be a particularly exact translation. (Emil Bock uses the word *verhärtet* [hardened].) For the essential point here is that Ahriman, in taking possession of man, wants to make his heart, the source of life and, in future times, of higher knowledge, like a *stone*, that is, dead and incapable of spiritual development.
51. GA 175, lecture of 6 February 1917.
52. See GA 262, the 'Barr manuscripts', notes written by Rudolf Steiner for Edouard Schuré in 1907, Part 3.
53. See GA 178, the lecture of 18 November 1917.
54. Ibid.
54a Rudolf Steiner gave two different pieces of information in this connection, which, however, form a complete picture of the spiritual trials awaiting humanity in the near future when considered together. He spoke on the one hand about the ahrimanic being 'who incarnates only as far as the etheric realm' and whom the Western secret brotherhoods would like to set in the place of the Etheric Christ, who in our time has entered the spiritual world adjacent to the Earth (lecture of 18 November 1917, GA 178). And on the other hand he spoke several times in subsequent lectures about the future incarnation of Ahriman (i.e. of a purely ahrimanic being) in the physical body, which will take place at the beginning of the third millennium in the American West. (See regarding this the following lectures: 27 October and 4 November 1919, GA 193; and 1 and 15 November 1919, GA 191.) It follows from these two insights of the modern spirit-researcher that the former 'etheric' ahrimanic being will inspire the second, physically incarnated, being and will help him in every possible way in his endeavour to entice mankind towards an anti-Christian, wholly ahrimanic line of development. It is, moreover, not impossible that there will be a temporary incorporation of the first being in the second at the high point of the earthly activity of the latter, in order to intensify his occult power and his magical influence upon earthly human beings, 'so as—if possible—to lead astray even the elect' (Matthew 24:24). See further in: Sergei O. Prokofieff, *The Spiritual Origins of Eastern Europe and the Future Mysteries of the Holy Grail*, Temple Lodge 1993, and *Die geistigen Aufgaben Mittel- und Osteuropas*, Dornach 1993.
55. More will be said about the intentions and practices of these 'brotherhoods' in the final chapter of the book.

56. In the Revelation of St John, this danger of 'not recognizing' the Etheric Christ is referred to with the words that are directed to the Church which represents the fifth cultural epoch, the Church of Sardis: 'strive to awaken and to strengthen what is still alive in your soul [that is your inner forces which know the Spirit] ... give new life to all your memories of what you have received and heard from out of the worlds of the Spirit. Nurture them and change your ways. If you will not awaken to a higher consciousness, I shall come like a thief. And you will not know what hour I will come upon you' (3:2–3). Further on, St John speaks prophetically of that very small group of human beings who were already then able to behold the Christ in the etheric: 'you have a few names even in Sardis which have not defiled their garments. In a while [that is in their etheric bodies] they shall walk with me; for they are worthy.' (3:4)
57. GA 175, lecture of 6 February 1917.
58. Matthew 14:27.
59. Matthew 14:28, 29.
60. See Note 57.
61. Matthew 14:31 (see Note 49).
62. In 1911 the term 'Theosophy' was still being used in this context.
63. GA 127, lecture of 14 June 1911.
64. John 6:28–29. (Emil Bock, instead of the word *believe*, here uses a word equivalent to 'have confidence in', 'trust' [*vertraut*].)
65. Mark 6:48.
66. GA 130, lecture of 1 October 1911.
67. Mark 6:34.
68. Matthew 14:14.
69. See Note 75.
70. See the book, S.O. Prokofieff, *Rudolf Steiner and the Founding of the New Mysteries*, the chapter entitled, 'The Path of the Teacher of Humanity'.
71. John 6:28–29 (see Note 64).
72. See GA 93a, lecture of 4 November 1905.
73. John 6:27.
74. John 6:32. See also S.O. Prokofieff, *Rudolf Steiner and the Founding of the New Mysteries*, the chapter entitled 'The Path of the Teacher of Humanity'.
75. In the Gospels, faith plays an especially important role in all healings which concern the astral body. Thus Christ very often says in connection with an act of healing: 'The faith in your heart has healed you' (e.g. Mark 5:34, after Emil Bock's translation).
76. In both cases, Emil Bock uses instead of the word 'believes' words equivalent to 'has trust', 'has confidence'.
77. See Note 76.
78. Of particular importance in this conversation is also the fourfold reference to the 'raising up at the last day' (verses 39, 40, 44, 54) and the description of the communion with bread and wine that follows it (verses 53–56). It is only possible to touch briefly upon these profound mysteries at this point. In the

Apocalypse of St John we find a reference to the first and second death (Chapter 20) which precede the 'raising up at the last day'. According to Rudolf Steiner (GA 104, lecture of 30 June 1908), the first death corresponds to the falling away of the physical body and the second to that of the etheric body, after which man will live in his astral body, or 'body of faith' as an immortal being who has attained a certain stage in the transformation of the astral body in the Spirit Self. This will be possible only through a conscious receiving of the Christ-forces into the astral body as a process of fulfilling on Earth the 'will of the Father'. If, however, the first and second death are to be undergone in the right way, it is not merely a question of transforming the astral body—a deed *which depends upon man himself*—but to a certain extent also the etheric and physical bodies. Such a transformation of the two outer sheaths cannot as yet be achieved through human forces alone, and so another kind of help is needed on the part of Christ. If for the transformation of the astral body man needs to develop within himself the soul-power of faith, for the transformation of the etheric and physical bodies he is in need of something substantial, of what in the conversation in question is called the blood and flesh of Christ: 'He who eats my flesh and drinks my blood has eternal life, and I will raise him up at the last day' (John 6:54). In these words reference is made to the blood of Christ, which gives eternal life to the etheric body, and to the 'flesh of Christ', which leads to the 'raising' of the forces of the physical body. And so this conversation forms a certain parallel with the Last Supper. Here, however, the significance of the communion is revealed in the context of our fifth post-Atlantean epoch, which is particularly intended for the development of the power of faith in the astral body; while the Last Supper, which is impregnated principally with the powers of love and hope, relates more to the sixth and seventh cultural epochs.

79. GA 102, lecture of 4 June 1908.
80. It was they who called the First World War into being through the *darkened consciousness* of individual people who held leading posts at that time, and the Second through certain people becoming *possessed* by them; and they are now preparing a third, which would give them still wider opportunities for the fulfilling of their goals among mankind.
81. GA 130, lecture of 1 October 1911.
82. GA 240, lecture of 27 August 1924.
83. GA 240, lecture of 19 July 1924.
84. See GA 123, the lecture of 10 September 1910.
85. Luke 9:30–31 (after Emil Bock's translation).
86. Matthew 17:2.
87. Matthew 17:5 (after Emil Bock's translation).
88. Matthew 16:28.
89. GA 130, lecture of 2 December 1911.
90. GA 127, lecture of 14 June 1911. Hence the etheric body's constant yearning towards the Sun. See GA 224, the lecture of 7 May 1923.

91. Matthew 16:17.
92. Matthew 16:23 (after Emil Bock's translation).
93. Matthew 16:16.
94. Matthew 16:21.
95. Matthew 16:24 (after Emil Bock's translation).
96. Matthew 16:25–26.
97. Thus only in the Gospel of St John is there lacking the description of the Apostles sleeping in the garden of Gethsemane. For of all the Apostles John alone was able to stay awake and not succumb to a darkening of consciousness. (See GA 148, the lecture of 2 October 1913.)
98. Luke 22:45.
99. Mark 14:50.
100. Rudolf Steiner speaks as follows about the connection of Intuition (see the beginning of the chapter) with the principle of hope: 'For those who do not merely hold on to faith but ascend to Inspiration and to *Intuition*, there arises a spiritual world in which, for the initiate, the Mystery of Golgotha presents itself as the great *comfort* [that is to say hope] of world-existence'. (GA 211, lecture of 15 April 1922.)
101. GA 130, lecture of 2 December 1911.
102. Ibid.
103. Ibid.
104. Ibid.
105. GA 130, lecture of 21 September 1911.
106. Regarding this rulership over the past—as it is inscribed in the Akashic Chronicle—on the part of Christ, see GA 155, Lecture 3.
107. This process is really somewhat more complicated. For in our time—in so far as human karma is concerned—Christ takes upon Himself principally the karma of the Egypto–Chaldean epoch and brings it into equilibrium. According to the law of reflection, however, He thereby also penetrates the karma of the Lemurian epoch and, ultimately, the karma of Old Moon. Something similar takes place at the subsequent stages: in the sixth epoch the second epoch will be redeemed, and through this Christ embraces the karma of the Hyberborean epoch and penetrates the karma of Old Sun. And, finally, in the seventh epoch, the first epoch (the Ancient Indian) will be redeemed and, through it, to some extent also the Polarian epoch, and, ultimately, Old Saturn itself. It is clear from the words of Rudolf Steiner quoted below in the text that the union with the karma of individual human beings (in so far as this is connected with the world karma) is impossible without a spiritual penetration right back to the forces of *Old Saturn*. Hence the words 'Christ is becoming the Lord of Karma' also signify that He is entering upon a path that leads to the overcoming of those forces which originate at the beginning of our world, in the epoch of Old Saturn. (This should not, however, be understood in an absolute sense, in that for the *full* karmic redemption of our whole cosmos the three future incarnations of our Earth—Jupiter, Venus and Vulcan—will be necessary.)

108. GA 161, lecture of 10 January 1915.
109. GA 127, lecture of 14 June 1911.
110. GA 218, lecture of 19 November 1922.
111. If such a possibility, which will emerge within the period of the seventh cultural epoch (six to eight thousand years after the birth of Christ), seems to the reader of these lines to be thoroughly improbable, it should be emphasized that by this time the outer conditions of the Earth and of the human life upon it will have changed considerably more starkly than it would generally be imagined. We shall refer at this point to two facts, drawn from the communications of modern spiritual science, which are to become realities by this time.

1. By the seventh millennium women will have completely lost the capacity to bring children into the world as they do today. The continuation of the human race will then be made possible in a more spiritual way. (See the lectures of 7 and 8 October 1917, GA 177.)

2. In the seventh millennium the Moon will be significantly closer to the Earth and in the eighth millennium will fully unite with it, whereby all the outer circumstances of human life on Earth will also become quite different. (See the lecture of 13 May 1921, GA 204.)

112. As preparation for this great twofold sacrifice of his *physical body* prior to the events of Palestine, the following events in Zarathustra's individual development may be observed:

1. Five thousand years before the birth of Christ: Zarathustra founds the Ancient Persian culture out of the Sun-forces of his *ego*.

2. Three thousand years before the birth of Christ: Zarathustra sacrifices his *astral* body to Hermes, the founder of the ancient Egyptian culture.

3. Two thousand years before the birth of Christ: Zarathustra sacrifices his *etheric* body to Moses, the author of Genesis, the law-giver of mankind and the herald of the coming Christ.

113. See Note 110.
114. GA 130, lecture of 21 September 1911.
115. GA 155, lecture of 30 May 1912.
116. Ibid.
117. See the third lecture of GA 104, 20 June 1908.
118. Revelation 3:20–21 and 4:1–2.
119. Revelation 4:5.
120. Revelation 4:6–8.
121. Revelation 5.
122. Further details regarding the revelation of Christ in the seventh epoch from the world of Providence (Buddhi) were given in the chapters 'The Path of the Christ-impulse through the Sheaths' and 'The Virtue of Hope and the Seventh post-Atlantean Epoch'.
123. Revelation 3:21 (after Emil Bock's translation).
124. Revelation 4:1.
125. Ibid. The words 'like the sound of a trumpet' are an indication of the fact

that, to begin with, it is *inspirative* and not intuitive knowledge that is being spoken of here.

126. Revelation 4:1.
127. Revelation 4:2.
128. Ibid.
129. Revelation 4:9–11 and 5:14.
130. In 1912 the word 'theosophical' was used instead of 'anthroposophical'.
131. GA 155, lecture of 30 May 1912.
132. See GA 116, the lecture of 2 May 1910.
133. According to Rudolf Steiner, in former times man passed immediately after death through a contemplation of world justice, which appeared before him in two forms: as the Cherubim with the flaming sword, the representative of cosmic conscience (this image also refers to the arising of the impulses of conscience from the sphere of the First Hierarchy, that is, from the region of the fixed stars); and as Moses with the Decalogue (the image of hope in its pre-Christian form, still connected as it was with the necessity of fulfilling the law). From our time, however, an essential change takes place in the nature of this experience after death. In place of Moses there gradually appears the form of the Etheric Christ as the Lord of Karma (see the lectures of 21 September 1911 and 2 December 1911, GA 130), and at the same time as the representative of the cosmic forces of hope, which are now connected with the full freedom of man. For from now on Christ will direct the process of our karmic compensation in such a way that it will be for the greatest good of all mankind: 'To ensure that in future our karmic account may be balanced out—that is, when in the future, having found our way to Christ, it will be inserted into the cosmic order in such a way that the process of compensating for our karma may serve the greatest possible good of mankind for the rest of human evolution. This will be the concern of Him who from our time onwards will be the Lord of Karma, this will be the concern of Christ' (GA 130, lecture of 2 December 1911). And this will also be the beginning of the realization of the innermost hope of mankind.
134. The contemplation of the karmic consequences of one's deeds (see GA 131, the lecture of 14 October 1911) as the further metamorphosis of the voice of conscience within man, which is associated with the new appearance of Christ in the etheric, is not yet a direct vision of *karma itself* but only its reflection in the world of Imagination. A true knowledge of karma is possible only at the stage of *Intuition*. The forces of hope which are to be developed in the seventh epoch are directed towards this supreme future capacity of intuitive consciousness. In the present age such a development is attainable only for an individual who has attained the highest levels of initiation. Rudolf Steiner speaks of how a true picture of karma is attainable only through intuitive consciousness: 'Anyone who rises to Intuition penetrates through the physical world up to the spiritual realm of the Father. Anyone who has intuitive knowledge can work upon karma in a factual way. He begins quite consciously to limit his own karma . . . In so far as man

can work upon his karma, to that extent must he be possessed of Intuition, or he must have this as a great binding commandment from the great initiates [in the form of the Mosaic Law, for instance]' (GA 93a, lecture of 12 October 1905).

135. GA 130, lecture of 3 December 1911.
136. GA 116, lecture of 25 October 1909.
137. See the following lectures: GA 107, 22 March 1969; GA 113, 31 August 1909; GA 114, 21 September 1909; and GA 116, 25 October 1909.
138. GA 97, lecture of 2 December 1906.
139. See GA 104, the lecture of 30 June 1908.
140. See GA 103, the lecture of 22 May 1908.
141. The full completion will come only at the end of the *whole* of earthly evolution; on the other hand, in the seventh epoch there will be a preliminary stage as a foundation for the evolution of the *race of the good* within mankind.
142. In the (German) translation of Emil Bock the word 'trust' is used instead of 'faith', and in verse 12 it speaks of receiving the Christ-Ego. In verse 11, first 'faith' and then 'trust' serve to render the same word in the original Greek.
143. According to the laws of reflection there is in the farewell discourses an allusion also to the future conditions of the Earth—Jupiter, Venus and Vulcan—just as in the prologue of St John's Gospel there are references to the former conditions of Saturn, Sun, Moon and Earth (see GA 103, the lecture of 19 May 1908).
144. See GA 124, the lecture of 7 March 1911.
145. The virtues of faith, love and hope here referred to, despite being particularly connected with certain cultural epochs, can nevertheless be developed simultaneously by man. Thus not merely in the first but also in the second and third chapters of the farewell discourses we find references to all three virtues, even though on each occasion one is particularly singled out.
146. See S.O. Prokofieff, *Rudolf Steiner and the Founding of the New Mysteries*.
147. In the present work it is unfortunately impossible to examine these relationships in more detail, for to do so would lead too far from the main theme. Thus it is only possible briefly to consider this one particular aspect of the farewell discourses. Deeper study of this theme is left to the reader himself.
148. In the Bock translation it says, instead of 'Comforter', 'Helper', Bestower of spiritual 'courage'.
149. John 14:16–17, 26; 15:26; 16:7, 13.
150. Matthew 26:38, 41 (after Emil Bock's translation).
151. Luke 22:42.
152. See S.O. Prokofieff, *Rudolf Steiner and the Founding of the New Mysteries*, the chapter entitled 'The Foundation Stone Meditation'.
153. GA 150, lecture of 23 March 1913.
154. Matthew 28:20.
155. In considering Rudolf Steiner's various indications regarding the sources of

inspiration for Anthroposophy, it is possible to distinguish three in particular which relate to these three categories of Spirits of the Third Hierarchy. Thus the first source is connected with the sphere of the Angels, for it is especially the Angels who in our fifth post-Atlantean epoch bear the knowledge of the Christ to humanity (see GA 15, Chapter 3). Then follows the supersensible preparation of Anthroposophy in the sphere of the Archangels under the rulership of Michael (see GA 237, 238, 240). Finally, there are the inspirations flowing into spiritual science from the sphere of the Archai or Spirits of Personality, of which Rudolf Steiner speaks in the lectures of 28 and 31 December 1918 and 1 January 1919 (GA 187).

156. See GA 237, the lecture of 1 August 1924.

157. GA 131, lecture of 8 October 1911.

158. GA 26.

159. Regarding the particularly deep relationship of the First Hierarchy—Seraphim, Cherubim and Thrones—to the fashioning of human karma, see, for example, the lecture of 31 March 1924 (GA 239).

160. GA 214, lecture of 13 June 1906.

161. GA 94, lecture of 6 November 1906.

162. John 5:21–24.

163. In the Gospel of St Luke there sound from the Cross, in addition to the words 'Father, into Thy hands I commend my spirit!' (Luke 23:46), the words addressed to the people, 'Father, forgive them, for they know not what they do' (v.34) and the words to the robber, 'Truly, I say to you, today you will be with me in Paradise' (v.43). In these three utterances it is not difficult to sense the fundamental moods corresponding to the seventh, sixth and fifth cultural epochs. (Compare with the final lecture of GA 114.)

164. GA 114, lecture of 26 September 1909. In the Foundation Stone Meditation, the lines

> Where in the wielding
> World-Creator-Life
> Thine own I
> Comes to being
> Within the I of God.

correspond to the words from St Luke's Gospel 'Father, into Thy hands I commend my Spirit'.

165. GA 214, lecture of 30 July 1922. One could also say that the ascent from Epiphany to Easter through the virtues of faith, love and hope corresponds to the experience of the Trinity in its hierarchic aspect (through the mediation of the Third, Second and First Hierarchies), while with the Mystery of Golgotha the possibility of *directly* experiencing the Trinity, which abides *above* the world of the Hierarchies, is opened up to all mankind. (Compare with the chapter entitled 'The Significance of the Mystery of Golgotha for the World of the Gods'.)

1. See GA 103, the lecture of 31 May 1908.
2. GA 100, lecture of 20 November 1907.
3. John 1:32.
4. GA 100, lecture of 20 November 1907.
5. Compare with the description of the three heavenly deeds of the Nathan Soul and their reflection in the period of Advent in the first and fifth chapters of Part II.
6. See the chapter 'The Time of Advent and the Four Mystery Virtues of Antiquity'.
7. Leonardo da Vinci said: 'Great love is the daughter of great knowledge'. To this we may add: not only great love, but also great faith and great hope.
8. The original text has at this point the word 'Theosophy', a term that was at the time employed by Rudolf Steiner for referring to anthroposophically-orientated spiritual science.
9. GA 127, lecture of 14 June 1911.
10. See also GA 10, the lecture of 12 April 1909 (morning).
11. GA 180, lecture of 6 January 1918.
12. GA 148, lecture of 18 December 1913.
13. GA 15, Chapter 3.
14. A prophetic image of this future, free and conscious union of man with the world of the Hierarchies is given in the following words from the Gospel of St Matthew which conclude the scene of the temptation in the wilderness: 'Then the devil left Him, and behold, angels came and ministered to Him' (Matthew 4:11). (Compare with what is said on p.82.)
15. This indication regarding the connection of the virtues of faith, love and hope with the beings of the Third Hierarchy is not at variance with the fact that these virtues open the way to an experience of all three (that is to say, nine) Hierarchies (see Note 165 to Part IV). For through faith man comes into more intimate contact with the Angel being who works in his astral body. Through this means he is able to raise himself in Imagination to a knowledge of the ego in his astral body, which lives in the astral world amongst beings of the *Third* Hierarchy. Through love he comes in contact with the Archangel who works in his etheric body. This enables him to rise to a knowledge in Inspiration of the ego of his etheric body, which dwells in lower Devachan, amongst beings of the *Second* Hierarchy. And finally, through a development of the power of hope, one can draw near the Archai, whose activity extends to his physical body. This enables him to gain access to an intuitive experience of the ego of his physical body, abiding as it does on the plane of higher Devachan amongst beings of the *First* Hierarchy (see the lecture of 20 November 1907, GA 100). Thus one can say that the development of these virtues leads above all to an experience of the activity in human sheaths of beings of the Third Hierarchy, and *through them* to the contemplation of the Second and the First, for in man, as microcosm, the

Third Hierarchy works through the Angels, the Second Hierarchy through the Archangels and the First through the Archai. (See in connection with this theme also the following lectures: GA 214, 23 July 1922; GA 226, 18 May 1923; GA 227, 29 and 31 August 1923; GA 231, 14 November 1923 and GA 233, 31 December 1923. See also the articles of 18 and 25 January 1925 in GA 260.) To this should also be added that the forces of all three (nine) Hierarchies represent the impulses of the Father, the Son and the Spirit in the *macrocosm*, while the forces of the beings of the Third Hierarchy, the Archai, Archangels and Angels, the bearers of the evolved Spirit Man, Life Spirit and Spirit Self, are connected with the *reflection* of the macrocosmic Trinity in man's being, in the microcosm. (See the lecture of 20 February 1917, GA 175, and also the lecture of 25 March 1907, GA 96.)

16. GA 142, lecture of 1 January 1913.
17. Ibid.
18. GA 146, lecture of 3 June 1913.
19. One could also say that at Christmas the Nathan Soul was born on the Earth as the archetype of the aims of all the ancient Mysteries, as a being who was fully permeated with the consequences of the threefold 'manifestation' of Christ in the macrocosm. While at Epiphany, when the Nathan Soul 'received Christ into itself', it entered upon the path of the *new Mysteries*, which reached their culmination and fulfilment after three years at Easter when, on the Hill of Golgotha, the Nathan Soul was able to 'receive Christ into itself', right into the physical body. This sheds a certain light upon the significance of the encounter of Jesus of Nazareth with the old Mysteries in their three principal aspects (Jewish, pagan, and that of the Essenes) before He had attained this thirtieth year. Because of these encounters, He was able to become convinced that the old ideal of initiation, which He embodied within Himself as a result of His cosmic activity in the past, was no longer attainable on the Earth at the time of the events of Palestine. For in the Jewish Mysteries the voice of the Bath-Kol no longer reached to the sphere of the Sun—while in the pagan Mysteries demons worked to ever greater effect, and the Essenes were able to embrace only certain chosen souls and abandoned the rest of humanity to a still sadder fate. (See GA 148, lectures of 5 and 6 October 1913.)

Moreover, it should be observed that all these, and similar, experiences of Jesus of Nazareth were strengthened in a remarkable way through the circumstance that from his twelfth year onwards the ego of Zarathustra united with him. Because of this, Jesus of Nazareth was able, on the one hand, to receive the sublime achievements of the Sun Mysteries (encompassed within the ego of Zarathustra) and above all their experience of ascent into the sphere of the Sun, from below upwards. On the other hand—as we have seen—he himself bore in memory a heavenly reflection (a counter-image) of such an ascent, from above to below (that is, in the direction in which the Nathan Soul descended from the realm of the Sun to incarnation on Earth), thus preparing the way for the descent on Earth of the Sun-Spirit of the

Christ. Through such a *twofold* experience, the sense of the *impossibility* of approaching the Sun-sphere must have been experienced by Jesus of Nazareth with particular strength. For at that time, not even the ego of Zarathustra, the supreme Sun initiate, had the strength to accomplish such an ascent. This could, nevertheless, take place (because of the altogether exceptional nature of the Nathan Soul) at the moment when the ego of Zarathustra left him for a short while. This took place during his encounter with a certain pagan cult. He was led by the people who crowded round him to the altar and there 'fell down like one dead' (that is, the ego of Zarathustra left him for a time). Then, according to Rudolf Steiner, 'the enraptured soul of Jesus of Nazareth felt himself being carried away as though into spiritual realms, into the realm of *Sun-existence*. And now it heard words which seemed to sound from the *spheres of Sun-existence . . .*' (GA 148, lecture of 4 October 1913.) Then from the 'transformed voice of the Bath-Kol' it heard from out of the Sun-sphere itself what Rudolf Steiner went on to communicate to mankind as the words of the macrocosmic Our Father, words which reveal the reasons for the ending of the epoch of the old Mysteries and point to the need for the advent of a new impulse.

Thus Jesus of Nazareth had first to experience the fact that the once mighty voice of the Bath-Kol, which had still inspired the prophets of old, could no longer lead the human soul up to the sphere of the Sun (that is, the path from below upwards was no longer accessible). And when he was subsequently able in a quite remarkable way to ascend to that region, he heard there only the words of the macrocosmic Our Father, words which indicated that Christ could no longer be found on the Sun, for He had entered upon the path of His approach to the Earth. (See S.O. Prokofieff, *Rudolf Steiner and the Founding of the New Mysteries*, Chapter 3.) This meant that an event akin to the cosmic sacrifice of the Nathan Soul (from above downwards) had also become impossible. Such a *duality*—that is, the complete impossibility of a connection with Christ according to old forms—was what was to fill the soul of Jesus of Nazareth with the greatest sense of tragedy and was also to prepare him for the highest mission: that of receiving Christ into himself *on the Earth itself* in the name of the salvation of human evolution.

20. GA 233, lecture 21 April 1924.
21. See F.W. Zeylmans van Emmichoven, *The Foundation Stone*, Rudolf Steiner Press 1963, the chapter entitled 'The Pentagram and the Sun of Christ'.
22. See further about this in Note 166 to Part XII.
23. GA 142, lecture of 1 January 1913.
24. Ibid.
25. Hence, according to Rudolf Steiner's indications in the eighth lecture of GA 124, the Gospel of St Luke was written for the sixth epoch, and was inspired in particular through Paul and Luke by the Nathan Soul. The Nathan Soul, being pre-eminently of an etheric nature, will in the sixth epoch bring to manifestation in the sphere of the Sun the form of Christ in His macrocosmic etheric body.

26. See the chapter entitled 'The Three Supersensible Deeds of the Nathan Soul'.
27. GA 152, lecture of 1 June 1914.
28. This is not in contradiction with the fact that our fifth cultural epoch is mainly concerned with the development of the consciousness soul, the sixth with the Spirit Self and the seventh with the Life Spirit, for this has to do with a stream of development that concerns the whole of mankind. However, those who today embark upon a path of *spirit-pupilship* will even now be seeking the transition from the consciousness soul to the Spirit Self and, as they continue this development in their future incarnations, will in the sixth epoch seek the transition from the Spirit Self to the Life Spirit and in the seventh epoch from the Life Spirit to the first rudiments of the Spirit Man. (Regarding the character of this second stream of development, see, for example, the lecture of 15 June 1915, GA 159/60.)
29. As to the question of whether it is, in principle, *possible* to tread such a path *in our time*, an esoteric study of the life-path of Rudolf Steiner himself—such as it is given in the first part of the book *Rudolf Steiner and the Founding of the New Mysteries*—will provide an answer.
30. Rudolf Steiner refers to this already in a lecture on 16 October 1921 (GA 207) in the following words: 'Not merely gazing upon Christ but *being filled* with Christ—such will be the Christianity of which Anthroposophy must speak' (GA 207, lecture of 16 October 1921).
31. Concluding verse of the Foundation Stone Meditation (see p. 392). In accordance with what was said above, the words: '... that good may become ...' can be experienced as connected with the principle of *Hope*; the words '... what from our hearts we would found ...' with the principle of *Love*, and that which from our 'Heads' will be directed with single purpose, as an expression of *Faith*. However, this must not be understood in the ordinary but in an esoteric sense.
32. See GA 187, 22 December 1918.

Part VI: The Mystery of Easter

1. GA 243, lecture of 22 August 1924.
2. See GA 239, the lecture of 24 and 25 May 1924 and also S.O. Prokofieff, *Rudolf Steiner and the Founding of the New Mysteries*, the chapter entitled 'The Christmas Conference of 1923–24'.
3. See GA 227, the lectures of 29 and 31 August 1923 and also GA 110, the lectures of 14 and 15 April 1909.
4. See S.O. Prokofieff, *Rudolf Steiner and the Founding of the New Mysteries*, 'The Christmas Conference of 1923–34'.
5. See the 'Conclusion' and GA 219, the lecture of 31 December 1922.
6. GA 194, lecture of 22 November 1919.
7. GA 211, lecture of 2 April 1922.

8. GA 211, lecture of 13 April 1922.

9. Rudolf Steiner also speaks of this as follows: 'Thus he [man] must live in the presence of the Spiritual Sun, Christ, who has united His existence with Earth-existence, and receive from this Spiritual Sun into the soul, in a living way, what in the spiritual world corresponds to warmth and light.

'He [man] will feel himself permeated by "spiritual warmth" when he experiences the "Christ in me". And as he feels himself thus permeated he will say to himself: "This warmth leads you back to the divine origin whence you came." And in this feeling of deep inner warmth of soul, *the experience in and with Christ and the experience of a real and true humanity* unite in man. "Christ gives me my human existence", that will be the fundamental feeling which will well up in the soul and pervade it. And once this feeling is present, it is joined by another—man feels himself to be raised by Christ above ordinary earthly existence; he *feels himself united with the starry surroundings of the Earth and with all that can be recognized in these surroundings as spiritual and divine* [that is, as the divine and spiritual Hierarchies]. It is the same with the spiritual light . . . In the light which Christ brings to the human ego, the light of primordial times again appears . . . And in this spiritual light he [man] will feel the power that will lead him who perceives with an ever higher and wider consciousness to the world in which, as a free human being, he will find himself associating with the Gods who were connected with his origin.' (GA 26, 'Michael's Mission in the Cosmic Age of Human Freedom', 9 November 1924.)

10. See GA 148, the lecture of 2 October 1913.

11. Acts 1:3.

12. GA 152, lecture of 2 May 1913.

13. In the scene of the Baptism, the image of the descending dove is an indication of the Holy Spirit, while the *voice* from Heaven (Luke 3:22) points to the inspirative character of the whole scene. On the basis of the lecture of 27 August 1924 (GA 240), one can also say that the image of the dove is in this scene an indication of the Spirit Self of Christ by which He descends to Earth from the Sun.

14. See GA 131, the lecture of 10 October 1911, and GA 235, the lecture of 2 March 1924.

15. See GA 153, the lecture of 13 April 1914, and GA 124, the lecture of 19 December 1910.

16. See GA 238, the lecture of 28 September 1924, and also the two additional elucidations given by Rudolf Steiner which were published in the (German) edition of 1974 as reported by Dr Ludwig Noll and Dr M. Kirchner-Bockholt.

17. See GA 139, the lecture of 20 September 1912.

18. GA 114, lecture of 21 September 1909.

19. Rudolf Steiner speaks of this in these words: 'We see that, by its thirtieth year, the ego of Zarathustra had completed its task of developing to the highest degree all the qualities residing in the soul of the Nathan Jesus. It had, so to speak, concluded its mission on behalf of this soul; *everything which it had*

acquired in the course of previous incarnations had been transmitted to this soul and had become part of it, and now it could say: "My task is accomplished!" And then the ego of Zarathustra withdrew from the body of the Nathan Jesus.' (Lecture of 21 September 1909, GA 114.)

20. GA 112, lecture of 5 July 1909.

21. The fact that, according to spiritual science (see the lecture of 17 December 1913, GA 148), the Solomon Jesus-child was outwardly a child who matured very early does not contradict what has just been said, for we must always distinguish between outer and inner development. The fruits of the latter came to manifest themselves directly only *after* the scene of the conversation of Jesus in the temple of Jerusalem (Gospel of St Luke 2:41–47).

22. In connection with the general process of the incarnation of the ego into the sheaths, as occurs in the development of every child, the following needs to be added here. Every child comes into the world as the result of a physical birth. Then there follows around the seventh year the birth of the etheric body, at about the fourteenth year the birth of the astral body, and only during the twenty-first year does the ego finally incarnate into the sheaths that he has prepared previously, though to some extent still *from the spiritual world.* (At the time of the events of Palestine these stages always came two years earlier, that is, in the fifth, twelfth and nineteenth years. See the lecture of 21 September 1909.) From this we may see that in the first seven-year period man's ego is separated from the physical body by two 'unborn' sheaths (the etheric and the astral). After seven (five in olden times), when it still largely abides in the spiritual world, man's ego is separated from the physical and etheric bodies only by one 'unborn' sheath (the astral), that is, it is still unable to incarnate in them. And only from the fourteenth (twelfth) year, after the birth of the astral body, does the way become free for the ego to begin the process of its gradual incarnation into the sheaths through astral and etheric bodies to the physical. The ego which up till then worked on the sheaths more *from* without, from the spiritual world, begins, as it slowly incarnates now, to accomplish this work from the inside.

23. GA 114, lecture of 21 September 1909.

24. See GA 112, the lecture of 6 July 1909 and GA 130, lecture of 1 October 1911. Rudolf Steiner says of this: 'And if only we have the right way of regarding death, if only we have learnt through the death on Golgotha that outward death has no significance, that in the body of Jesus of Nazareth there lived the Christ with whom we can unite ourselves; if only we have recognized that, although on the Cross the image of death is represented to us, this is only an outward event, and that the life of Christ in the etheric body *before* death is the same as it is *after* death, that this death cannot therefore cause life any injury—only then have we grasped that we have before us here a death which does not extinguish life but which is itself life; and with this we have in the figure on the Cross a sign for all ages that death is truly the *bestower of life*' (GA 112, lecture of 6 July 1909). See also Rudolf Steiner's words quoted on p. 236.

25. GA 112, lecture of 5 July 1909.
26. See GA 130, the lecture of 1 October 1911.
27. For this reason there is, in the only work that has been preserved of ancient Gnostic literature (the *Pistis-Sophia*, which tells of the conversations of the Risen One with the disciples), reference to Elijah-John, and also a clear reference to the Mystery of the *two* Jesus children.
28. A similar process takes place later in the initiation of Christian Rosenkreutz in the thirteenth century (see GA 130, the lecture of 27 September 1911).
29. It is also for this reason that the individuality of Zarathustra will in the future (which, however, begins even in our time) be the teacher and helper in the process of the balancing out of karma, as was described at the end of the chapter entitled 'The Virtue of Hope and the Seventh post-Atlantean Epoch'.
30. This is a further similarity between the Master Jesus and Christian Rosenkreutz after his initiation in the thirteenth century. Thus Rudolf Steiner speaks in this sense of Christian Rosenkreutz in virtually the same words as he used regarding the Master Jesus: 'And Christian Rosenkreutz will come again and again [to Earth] in a great number of incarnations. But because of his particular personal nature he works *right up to modern times* also *in those short intervals of time* when he is not incarnated; indeed, he works spiritually upon human beings through his higher members in such a way that he has no need of a spatial connection with them.' (GA 130, lecture of 9 February 1912.)
31. GA 114, lecture of 21 September, 1909.
32. Ibid.
33. Ibid. If one tries to immerse oneself in the nature of the life-path of Rudolf Steiner (as in the first part of the book *Rudolf Steiner and the Founding of the New Mysteries*), one can clearly distinguish in the character of what he has unfolded in the various lectures and cycles on Christological themes a threefold source of the inspiration which can be traced back to three individualities, each of whom was present in a quite special way at the forty-day conversations with the Risen One. The first individuality is Lazarus-John who, because of the initiation which he had undergone and also as a result of the union with the entelechy of John the Baptist, was the one who was able to receive the teachings of the Risen One with a far greater degree of *consciousness* than the other physical participants in the forty-day conversations. In Rudolf Steiner's Christology one can feel the inspiration of this individuality especially in the description of the two principal paths of Christian initiation: in the description of the Christian-mystical path founded upon a meditative study of the John Gospel, which was the principal path of inner development in the epoch that precedes the arising of the Rosicrucian stream (the most important teacher of this path is the second individuality, who will be spoken of next); and in the description of Christian-Rosicrucian initiation, which is the only spiritual path that is suitable for man today.
The second individuality is Zarathustra, who, as we have seen, appears in the

being of the Master Jesus as the preserver of the entire wisdom of esoteric Christianity, which has its source in the forty-day conversations. We find the inspiration of this individuality in all Rudolf Steiner's principal Christological and Gospel cycles and also in individual lectures that are directly connected with the content of the conversations of the Risen One (see, for example, GA 211), for all these lectures and cycles are chiefly concerned with *knowledge* of the various aspects of the Christ Mystery. And finally, in the content of the Fifth Gospel and in the lectures on the preparatory stages of the Mystery of Golgotha we have an example of the direct inspiration of the Nathan Soul, which is expressed above all in the very character of the lectures devoted to this theme. For what is essential in them is not knowledge (as with the cycles on Christology and the Gospels) but a *narration* directed towards the human heart of the events in which the Nathan Soul participated to the full extent of its three and thirty years.

It is also surprising to sense the uniting of the various sources of inspiration in certain lectures and cycles by Rudolf Steiner. For example, in the lecture-cycle that is devoted to the Luke Gospel, we have a whole series of communications derived from the content of the Fifth Gospel, in particular all that concerns the heavenly and earthly destinies of the Nathan Soul. However, the cycle as a whole bears a more cognitive character. It is as though we are given a description of the history of the Nathan Soul through the inspiration of Zarathustra. We find the opposite situation in the lectures on the Fifth Gospel. There the whole approach, even when the subject matter concerns Zarathustra (see in particular the lecture of 3 October 1913, where a description is given of the Persian initiation which is also the ancient initiation of Zarathustra himself, and also the lectures of 5 and 6 October 1913, GA 148) is bathed in an altogether special atmosphere of sincerity and tenderness which flows from the inspiration of the Nathan Soul. (The reader who is familiar with the content of the book mentioned above, and with its third chapter in particular, may be referred at this point to a further source of inspiration which is associated with the Christological studies of Rudolf Steiner: that of the leading Bodhisattva of our time, the future Maitreya Buddha. Through his inspiration, Rudolf Steiner was able to appear as the great herald of the Etheric Christ in the twentieth century (see the lecture of 10 September 1910, GA 123).

34. GA 130, lecture of 5 May 1912.
35. GA 211, lecture of 15 April 1922. (Regarding the hierarchic beings connected with the Moon, see the lecture of 16 April 1909, GA 110.)
36. The following words of Rudolf Steiner from a lecture of 2 April 1922 (GA 211), give a particularly clear indication that by 'ancient Teachers of Wisdom' are meant in *this case* 'Gods', that is, hierarchic beings: 'This wisdom extended above all to what was imparted by the *Gods* to human beings regarding the sojourn of human souls in the divine spiritual world before their incarnation in earthly bodies. The Gods instructed people in what these souls experience before their descent through conception into an earthly

body . . . So that today we can look back at a divine-spiritual wisdom which people acquired here on Earth in the [previously described] circumstances *from the Gods themselves*—and this should be understood not in a figurative sense but just as it stands' (GA 211, lecture of 2 April 1922). And in another lecture we find these words: '. . . Those beings of the higher Hierarchies, who were the teachers of the first human beings, had never experienced in their worlds either birth or death' (GA 211, lecture of 13 April 1922). However, elsewhere in these same lectures Rudolf Steiner speaks of these ancient 'Teachers of Wisdom' in such a way that there arises a picture of those beings who formerly lived on Earth but who, after the departure of the Moon, 'migrated' to the Moon-sphere. Rudolf Steiner calls them the 'Moon Teachers of Wisdom' and describes in detail their role in world evolution in, for example, GA 240, the lecture of 28 January 1924: 'Such a similarity of characterization of two kinds of spiritual beings is not, however, accidental, for higher hierarchic beings ['Gods'] have worked in a particularly direct way through the Moon Teachers of Wisdom.'

37. GA 211, lecture of 15 April 1922.
38. Ibid.
39. Thus Rudolf Steiner says of this: 'Then it would have happened that people would have felt themselves to be dead in the etheric body and, on beholding the death of the physical body, they would have been forced to say: simultaneously with birth on Earth, my soul-nature begins to die; it participates in the death of the physical body. If the Mystery of Golgotha had not taken place, there would have come about the death of the soul, together with the death of the physical body of earthly man, at first in a less intensive sense but in later times spread over the whole Earth.' (GA 211.)
40. GA 148, lecture of 18 December 1913.
41. Ibid.
42. From this it becomes clear why the fifth stage of the Christian-Rosicrucian path of initiation corresponds to the stage in the Christian mystic path which bears the name of 'mystic death'.
43. GA 211, lecture of 15 April 1922.
44. GA 224, lecture of 13 April 1923.
45. GA 153, lecture of 10 April 1914 in Vienna.
46. In 1925 Rudolf Steiner writes: 'Man is the Ideal of the Gods, the aim of the Gods' ('What is revealed when one looks back into former lives between death and a new birth', 18 January 1925, GA 26).
47. It could also be said that what the Gods formerly experienced by opening themselves up to the light of the highest Divinity they could now behold on Earth.
48. Hence we may say: what the spiritual Hierarchies have hitherto experienced only through opening themselves up to the light of the most exalted divinity they have now been able to behold down on Earth. This also has a bearing upon the transition from the fourth rhythm of the Christmas Conference to the seventh, wherein is expressed the arising of a new connection between

the heights and depths of the world—between the sphere of the most exalted spirituality and humanity—as a result of the Mystery of Golgotha. (See the book, S.O. Prokofieff, *Rudolf Steiner and the Founding of the New Mysteries*, the chapter entitled 'The Christmas Conference of 1923/24'.)

49. Acts 1:3 (following the Bock translation).
50. GA 211, lecture of 15 April 1922.
51. GA 112, lecture of 6 July 1909.
52. Ibid.
53. See Note 59 (below).
54. GA 112, lecture of 6 July 1909.
55. Ibid.
56. Ibid.
57. GA 13, Chapter 'Man and the Evolution of the World' [essentially the translation of G. and M. Adams]. In a lecture of 1923 Rudolf Steiner supplements this as follows: 'And as He [Christ] passed through the Resurrection, He appeared—I would put it thus—to certain spiritual beings beyond the Earth as a star shining out from the Earth, a star which now radiated out to them from the Earth into the spiritual world. Spiritual beings mark the Mystery of Golgotha by saying: a star has begun to shine from the Earth into the spiritual realm.' (GA 223, lecture of 1 April 1923.)
58. GA 112, lecture of 6 July 1909.
59. In the final line of the macrocosmic Lord's Prayer we find the words 'Ye Fathers in the Heavens'. See also Rudolf Steiner's explanation of the words in the Gospel 'The Father sent the Son' (John 3:16–7, and the first Epistle of John 4:9) in the lecture of 18 December 1913 (GA 148).
60. GA 112, lecture of 6 July 1909.
61. John 16:28 (following the Bock translation).
62. John 12:32 and 13:36.
63. See GA 15, Chapter 3.
64. John 1:1.
65. See S.O. Prokofieff, *Rudolf Steiner and the Founding of the New Mysteries*, the chapter entitled 'The Christmas Conference 1923/24'.

Part VII: The Mystery of Ascension

1. GA 13, Chapter 'Knowledge of the Higher Worlds'. See also the description of the fifth stage of Christian-Rosicrucian initiation in the lecture of 29 June 1907 (GA 100).
2. See GA 224, the lecture of 7 May 1923.
3. Ibid.
4. Ibid.
4a Lecture of 5 July 1909 (GA 112). The next quotation is from the same source.
4b Lecture of 13 April 1908 (GA 102). The next quotation is from the same source.

5. Mark 16:19 (following the Bock translation).
6. GA 119, the evening lecture of 28 March 1910.
7. GA 119, the morning lecture of 28 March 1910.
8. GA 119, lecture of 26 March 1910.
9. GA 119, the evening lecture of 28 March 1910.
10. In other lectures Rudolf Steiner calls this world of Archetypes—that is, the world which lies *above* higher Devachan—the sphere of Buddhi or the world of Providence (see, for instance, the lecture of 25 October 1909, GA 116). For further details about the connection between the supersensible world closest to the Earth and the world of Providence, which arose through the deeds of Christ on the Earth, and also about the relationship of this new connection to the appearance of Christ in the etheric, see the chapter entitled 'The Foundation Stone Meditation' in the book by S.O. Prokofieff, *Rudolf Steiner and the Founding of the New Mysteries*.
11. GA 224, lecture of 7 May 1923. The quotations that follow are from the same source.
12. GA 215, lecture of 15 September 1922.
13. Ibid.
14. Ibid.
15. GA 215, lecture of 14 September 1922.
16. In the lecture of 28 August 1923, Rudolf Steiner speaks of how the Mystery of Golgotha had to be accomplished so that man '... might, through the teaching regarding the Mystery of Golgotha on Earth, receive the great strength needed to make the transition [after death] from the world of souls to the land of spirits, from the Moon-region to the Sun-region' (GA 227).
17. This can also be called Moon-karma, in contrast to the light-filled Sun-karma through which individual human karma is united with world-karma.

Part VIII: The Mystery of Pentecost

1. GA 148, lecture of 2 October 1913.
2. In a somewhat different connection Rudolf Steiner refers to this in the following words: 'Through the Ascension, the Christ-impulse, in so far as it was manifested in the outer sheaths, disappeared in the wider spiritual world; and it appeared again after ten days, working from the *hearts* of separate individuals, who were the first to understand it.' (GA 118, lecture of 15 May 1910.)
3. John 20:17 (following the Bock translation).
4. GA 148, lecture of 2 October 1913.
5. Ibid.
6. Ibid.
7. GA 148, lecture of 3 October 1913.
8. GA 13, Chapter 'Knowledge of Higher Worlds'.
9. In the lecture of 4 July 1909, Rudolf Steiner speaks with particular clarity

about this impossibility of preserving one's individual ego-consciousness in the old initiation: 'Let us once more consider this initiation, as we have pictured it in the last few days. What took place in such an initiation? In an initiation of this nature the etheric and astral bodies were withdrawn from the totality of physical, etheric, astral bodies and ego, while *the ego remained in the physical body*. It was for this reason that one would have been without self-consciousness for the duration of the three and a half days of the initiation. One's self-consciousness was infused into one from the higher spiritual worlds by the priest-initiate, who guided one in every aspect and placed his own ego at one's disposal.' (GA 112.)

10. GA 112, lecture of 7 July 1909.
11. In rescuing 'the form of man's physical body' in the Mystery of Golgotha, Christ also rescued the human ego, in so far as this principle belongs to all people on the Earth as beings who are passing through their 'human stage'. One could also say that in the Mystery of Golgotha Christ rescued the very substance of the human ego, which was in former times poured into man, through Yahveh, by the six Sun-Elohim, the totality of whose forces Christ bore once more into Earth-existence (see the lecture of 20 May 1908, GA 103). The principle of individual *ego-consciousness* can, however, be rescued only if the efforts of each individual human being are directed towards a *conscious* knowledge and union with the Christ-impulse as it has worked in the earthly sphere since the Mystery of Golgotha, and this is attainable only through an inner Whitsun, through an inner experience of the new Holy Spirit sent by Christ.
12. GA 102, lecture of 4 June 1908.
13. One could also say that this initiation is the initiation of Zarathustra himself, which he passed through in the epoch of Ancient Persia and then bequeathed to his followers.
14. We find an analogous stage in antiquity and in the Egyptian Mysteries, and also in the Mysteries of the ancient Hebrews (see John 1:47–50).
15. GA 148, lecture of 3 October 1913.
16. Ibid.
17. Ibid.
18. GA 224, lecture of 7 May 1923.
19. We should not be surprised if the Holy Spirit proceeding from Christ is characterized by Rudolf Steiner in some cases as the Spirit who brings people *knowledge* of the Mystery of Golgotha (see the lectures of 22 March 1909, GA 107; 31 August 1909, GA 113; 21 September 1909, GA 114; and of 7 May 1923, GA 224), and in other cases as the Spirit of Universal Love (see the lecture of 2 October 1913, GA 148). For the Holy Spirit who has since ancient times proceeded from Christ in the world of Providence and worked through the circle of Bodhisattvas is pre-eminently the Spirit of Christ-knowledge, who since the Mystery of Golgotha has united with the substance of cosmic love, borne by Christ into Earth-existence, so that the Spirit-impulse which descended upon the Apostles at Pentecost unites and

435

bears within itself both principles and can therefore be called the Spirit of 'wisdom permeated by love'. Rudolf Steiner puts it thus: 'First wisdom, then love, then *wisdom permeated by love.*' In the world of the Hierarchies this forms the foundation whereby the Spirits of Wisdom and the Spirits of Love that have, since ancient times, worked in so many different ways in the cosmos might in future be brought into harmonious interplay—one might even say, to a 'reconciliation'—through the free activity of human beings who are filled with the spirit of Whitsun (see GA 102, the lecture of 24 March 1908, and also the chapter entitled 'The Uniting of the World Impulses of Wisdom and Love in the Experience of Christ').

20. GA 26, Leading Thought No. 143.
21. GA 224, lecture of 7 May 1923.
22. See Rudolf Steiner's words quoted in Note 2.
23. In the lecture of 30 July 1922 (GA 214) we find a detailed description of the fact that Christ, who is an all-encompassing cosmic being and enters directly into man's inner nature, would have inevitably extinguished all trace of individual ego-consciousness if He had not sent the Holy Spirit, who has since Pentecost enabled Him to dwell in every human ego without extinguishing its consciousness.
24. GA 26, Leading Thought No. 1.
25. GA 100, lecture of 29 June 1907.
26. GA 260. From the Address given at the Christmas Conference on 25 December 1923.
27. In the Gospel the scene of the Holy Spirit's descent at Pentecost is described in the following words: 'And suddenly a sound came from heaven like the rush of a mighty wind, and it filled all the house where they were sitting' (Acts 2:2).
28. See Note 26.
29. GA 114, lecture of 20 September 1909.
30. GA 236, lecture of 4 June 1924. [In view of the length of this quotation the published English translation has been followed with only minor alterations.]
31. In the words of Rudolf Steiner quoted above, four principal elements can be distinguished which go to make up the experience that has been referred to:
    1. 'The divine *cosmic fire*, as man's essential being.'
    2. 'Feeling oneself within the world ether.'
    3. 'Experiencing the revelations of the spirit in the cosmic astral radiance.'
    4. 'The inner experience of the spirit-radiance which is man's high calling in the universe.'
    (With this latter experience is connected what is then described as 'the ascent of the *Spirit-Selfhood* of the universe'.)
    With deeper, meditative penetration of these four stages one can also feel their inner connection with the four parts of the Foundation Stone Meditation, and this enables us to approach—even though only tentatively— somewhat closer to its sources of inspiration.
32. GA 103, lecture of 31 May 1908.

33. See S.O. Prokofieff, *Rudolf Steiner and the Founding of the New Mysteries*, Chapters 2 and 3.

34. So as to avoid possible misunderstanding, it should be emphasized that the word 'Apostle' is used here not in the usual but in an *occult* sense. For the esoteric stage of 'Apostle' is reached by every individual who *in any particular historical epoch* has passed personally through the experience of Pentecost.

Part IX: Easter, Ascension and Whitsun

1. See, for example, GA 236, the lecture of 4 June 1924.
2. GA 148, lecture of 3 October 1913.
3. See GA 153, the lecture of 13 April 1914.
4. In the lecture of 11 October 1911, Rudolf Steiner says: 'His [Christ's] Resurrection is the *birth* of a new element in human nature; the *birth* of the imperishable body.' (GA 131.)
5. GA 112, lecture of 6 July 1909.
6. Ibid.
7. Ibid.
8. In the passage quoted above, Rudolf Steiner calls the *reflection* itself the Holy spirit, although it follows from certain other of his lectures that the Holy Spirit, that is, the 'Spirit-Selfhood of the universe' proceeding from beyond the stars, manifests itself and works only *in* and *through* its reflection in the earthly sphere. We can, nevertheless, relate these two concepts to one another in this particular case with complete justice, in so far as the aforesaid reflection has an *astral nature*, as has the 'Spirit-Selfhood of the universe' (the Spirit Self is the transformed astral body). In a similar way we find in several of Rudolf Steiner's lectures that the concepts of the Sophia and the Holy Spirit are related to one another. This also becomes understandable if one takes into account that in esoteric Christianity what is understood by 'the Sophia' is the purified and spiritualized *astral* body, while by 'the Holy Spirit' is meant the principle of the Spirit Self that permeates it. (Compare Rudolf Steiner's words on pp. 167 and 230 with the lectures of 2 December 1906 and 3 February 1907, GA 97.)
9. See Rudolf Steiner's words quoted in Note 4.
10. See further in the lecture of 7 May 1923 (GA 224) and Part VII, 'The Mystery of the Ascension'.
11. See GA 112, the lecture of 5 July 1909, and GA 104, the lecture of 30 June 1908.
11a Lecture of 24 April 1917 (GA 175).
12. See GA 114, the lecture of 26 September 1909, and also GA 15, Chapter 1.
13. One can also say that whenever a man has died the higher Spiritual Powers ensure that his etheric body is dissolved as soon as possible. For if this etheric body were not to undergo a rapid process of dissolution in those parts not yet penetrated by the Christ-impulse it would become exposed to the danger of

being seized by the forces of Lucifer and Ahriman and would then be condemned to the fate of which more will be said in the last part of this book. (See also the lectures of 20 November 1914, GA 158, and 28 December 1915, GA 165.)

13a To this it should be added that, in future, a knowledge of the Mysteries of the 'etheric ring' will serve as the foundation of a new *spiritual ecology*, which will alone be capable of really solving the problems associated with the etheric-physical state of our environment now standing before the whole of humanity.

14. Lecture of 1 October 1911 (GA 130).

15. See S.O. Prokofieff, *Rudolf Steiner and the Founding of the New Mysteries*, Chapters 3 and 5.

16. See Note 11 to Part VIII.

17. Regarding the relationship of the four members of man's being to the events of Easter, Ascension and Pentecost, see the words of Rudolf Steiner quoted on p. 226.

18. The following lines from the third part of the Foundation Stone Meditation also refer to this working of astral light within Earth-existence since the Mystery of Golgotha.

> Where the eternal aims of Gods
> World-Being's Light
> On thine own I
> Bestow
> For thy free Willing...

See further in S.O. Prokofieff, *Rudolf Steiner and the Founding of the New Mysteries*, the chapter entitled 'The Foundation Stone Meditation'.

19. GA 112, lecture of 6 July 1909.

19a Here the question arises: if the Holy Spirit can only work in the reflection of the Christ-light through the etheric bodies which—filled with the Christ-impulse—have entered into the 'etheric ring', *to whom* did these etheric bodies belong at the Turning Point of Time? In other words: whose etheric bodies were participating in the Mystery of Pentecost?

This was of course primarily the etheric body of Jesus of Nazareth (the Nathan Soul) himself as the bearer of the Christ during His three years on Earth. Of all etheric bodies which had ever existed on Earth, this one was *alone a fully Christianized etheric body*; and it was also the source of the reflected Christ light through which the Holy Spirit descended at Pentecost in fiery tongues of flame on the heads of the twelve Apostles (for the Christ light, when it is reflected by the etheric body, becomes spiritual fire, that is to say, it comes a stage nearer to earthly humanity). In other words: *the etheric body of the Nathan Soul reflected back the Christ-light at Pentecost and so made it possible for the Spirit to descend upon the Apostles.* If, moreover, we recall that the Nathan Soul at its incarnation had brought with it a quite special etheric body, which had preserved two of the higher kinds of ether in their original form, untouched by the Fall, the sound and life ethers (see the lecture of 21 September 1909, GA 114), it becomes more understandable why this unique etheric body could serve as the foundation for the first outpouring of the Holy Spirit at the event of Pentecost.

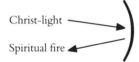

Christ-light

Spiritual fire

Etheric body of the Nathan Soul:
sound and *life ethers*
untouched by the Fall

In the Gospels two further instances can be found where a state of being filled with the Holy Spirit is described. These have to do with the two individualities who stood in full consciousness beneath the Cross at Golgotha: the Solomon Mary and the disciple whom the Lord loved, John, who as Lazarus was initiated by Christ Jesus Himself (see the lecture of 22 May 1908, GA 103). In both cases the connection with the Spirit arose through the fact that these two individuals had—albeit in different ways—been permeated by another individuality who at that time was already dwelling in the spiritual world. Through the soul of the Solomon Mary there worked the soul of the Luke Mary as a mediator between her and the cosmic sphere of the heavenly Sophia (see further in S.O. Prokofieff, *Eternal Individuality. Towards a Karmic Biography of Novalis*, Temple Lodge 1992, Chapter 12), and through John the Evangelist—after his initiation as Lazarus—the individuality of John the Baptist, who at that time was already in the spiritual world. As these two individualities who had died were so intimately connected with the Christ, their etheric bodies were also able to serve as mediators for the working of the Holy Spirit on the one hand in the Solomon Mary and on the other in John the Evangelist. The consequence of this was that Mary could lead the twelve Apostles in their receiving of the Holy Spirit (which is why she is sometimes portrayed in artistic representations of the Whitsun event at the centre of the circle of the Twelve) and John received the Holy Spirit from the Christ not after fifty days—as did the other Apostles—but on the day of the Resurrection itself. Because of this it is only in his Gospel that there is a reference to this special—personal—descent of the Spirit, for he alone was in a position to receive it in full consciousness (Chapter 20, verse 22). (See further regarding the two Marys in Rudolf Steiner: GA 15, Chapter 3; the lectures of 18, 19 and 20 September 1909, GA 114; and also in Emil Bock's *Kindheit und Jugend Jesu*, Stuttgart 1982. Concerning the connection between the two Johns, see the lecture of 28 September 1924, GA 238, and especially the verbal explanations with which Rudolf Steiner supplemented this lecture, published in the German edition of 1981 and in part in Alfred Heidenreich's preface to the English edition.) Finally, the etheric body of the Solomon Jesus, which for twelve years had been prepared by the individuality of Zarathustra and has already been spoken about in Chapter 2 (of Part VI), without doubt also participated in all these events.

20. See S.O. Prokofieff, *Rudolf Steiner and the Founding of the New Mysteries*, the chapter entitled 'The Foundation Stone Meditation'.
21. Ibid.
22. John 5:24.
23. See Note 20, and also GA 153, the lecture of 14 April 1914.
24. GA 130, lecture of 27 September 1911.
25. Ibid.
26. Ibid.
27. See S.O. Prokofieff, *Rudolf Steiner and the Founding of the New Mysteries*, the chapter entitled 'The Years of Apprenticeship' and 'The Great Sun-Period'.
28. In connection with this essential aspect of the earthly mission of Rudolf Steiner, the following observations should also be made. One of Rudolf Steiner's most important indications regarding the work of his pupils after his departure from the physical plane was that *under no circumstances was his work to be separated from his name*, an end to which, however, the efforts of the ahrimanic powers would be particularly devoted. (See in this connection the testimonies of Marie Steiner and Ita Wegman, quoted in Rudolf Grosse's book *The Christmas Foundation; Beginning of a New Cosmic Age*, Steiner Book Centre, Vancouver, 1984.) We can feel today how the activity of the ahrimanic powers in this direction is increasing. By the end of the century this tendency will have become even stronger. Then it will be the essential task of anthroposophists rightly to recognize the activities of the opposing forces in any given circumstances. Three points in particular will have to be considered:
   1. If in a certain place someone speaks of the etheric (that is, the supersensible) coming of Christ which begins in the twentieth century *without* mentioning the name of Rudolf Steiner as His *first* herald.
   2. If in a certain place someone adduces certain facts from the content of the Fifth Gospel *without* mentioning the name of Rudolf Steiner as the *first* to initiate the revelation of its Mysteries in the present time.
   3. If in a certain place someone spreads the teaching regarding reincarnation and karma *in their Christian form without* mentioning the name of Rudolf Steiner as the one who *first* brought this teaching in its Christian form to western man. (These three elements can be found, in a form intended for general circulation, in Rudolf Steiner's book *The Spiritual Guidance of Man and Humanity*.)
29. Rudolf Steiner speaks regarding the preserving of the etheric body of a highly developed individual, and especially of an initiate, on several occasions in connection with references to the law of 'spiritual economy' (see GA 109 and the lecture of 24 August 1906, GA 95).
30. After the Christmas Foundation Meeting, Rudolf Steiner gave the following imagination in response to the question as to his relationship to Christian Rosenkreutz: beside an altar there stand Christian Rosenkreutz and Rudolf Steiner. One is on the left in a light blue stole, the other on the right in a red stole. They stand next to one another (see *Mystery Streams in Europe and the New Mysteries*, by Bernard C.J. Lievegoed, Anthroposophic Press. 1982).

As regards the influence of the etheric body of Christian Rosenkreutz upon Rudolf Steiner, the following words—spoken by Rudolf Steiner in 1911— give some indication: 'Everything that is proclaimed as spiritual knowledge is strengthened by the etheric body of Christian Rosenkreutz, and *those who proclaim it are overshone by this etheric body*, which is able to work upon them while Christian Rosenkreutz is in incarnation but equally when he is not' (see Note 24). Moreover, one should take into account the quite unique spiritual constellation of the years 1910 and 1911, which correspond to the time when Rudolf Steiner began to speak of the Etheric Christ.

1. In the year 1910 Rudolf Steiner was forty-nine years old, he was entering the eighth seven-year period of his life, the epoch of the Life Spirit, the spiritualized *etheric* body.

2. On 12 January the first lecture about the New Advent was held in Stockholm.

3. The first Mystery Drama, *The Portal of Initiation*, which bears the subtitle 'A *Rosicrucian* Mystery', was written *through* Rudolf Steiner. There the new Advent of Christ receives its artistic formulation.

4. In the year 1911 the book *The Spiritual Guidance of Man and Humanity* (GA 15) appeared, through which this knowledge became accessible to wide circles of people for the first time. (Reference is also made here to the significance of the year 1250 and to the sources of the 'new esotericism' associated with the founding of the Rosicrucian stream.) In the same year numerous lectures followed in various European towns, and also the first tidings of the esoteric foundations of Rosicrucianism.

31. For further details regarding the significance of the Christmas Conference and its place in the life path of Rudolf Steiner, see S.O. Prokofieff, *Rudolf Steiner and the Founding of the New Mysteries*.

32. See S.O. Prokofieff, *Rudolf Steiner and the Founding of the New Mysteries*, Part 3: 'Anthroposophy—the Proclamation of World Pentecost'.

33. Ibid, 'The Christmas Conference of 1923/24'.

34. Hence in Eastern Europe the Whitsun Festival is also called the Festival of the Trinity.

35. The Foundation Stone Meditation, Appendix 6, Part IV, line 3.

36. See GA 121, the lecture of 11 June 1910.

37. See the chapter 'The Significance of the Mystery of Golgotha for the World of the Gods'.

38. See GA 121, the lecture of 11 June 1910.

39. See Rudolf Steiner's words quoted on pp. 236–7.

40. GA 26, the article entitled 'The Condition of the Human Soul before the Dawn of the Michael Age' (31 August 1924).

41. An ordinary person, one who has not entered upon the path of initiation, would simply not be able to endure such an influence in the present cycle of development. It would deprive him of all freedom and would bring about the total extinction of his ego-consciousness.

42. GA 148, lecture of 18 December 1913.

43. It is because of the working within man of the new Holy Spirit sent down by Christ that beings of the Third Hierarchy will, through His mediation, be able rightly to lead mankind through the fifth, sixth and seventh cultural epochs. Compare GA 15, Chapter 3.

44. Luke 2:14 (following the Bock translation).

45. Address at the Christmas Conference, 25 December 1923 (GA 260).

46. GA 26, lecture of 2 October 1913.

47. Rudolf Steiner speaks on several occasions in his lectures about the significant changes which came about as a result of the Mystery of Golgotha in the astral aura of the Earth (e.g. in the lecture of 25 March 1907, GA 96). While in the lecture of 1 April 1907 (ibid.) he speaks of the changes not merely in the astral but also in the etheric aura of the Earth.

48. GA 26, Leading Thought, No. 143.

49. Hence Rudolf Steiner, in the words quoted (see p. 191) from GA 112, the lecture of 5 July 1909, speaks of how as a result of the Mystery of Golgotha there began to flow into man's etheric bodies a new *wisdom*, which is at the same time *life*, that is, *a life-bearing wisdom*. But this cannot be wisdom of the ordinary human kind but only imaginative wisdom, for imaginations work in the etheric body as life-forces. Rudolf Steiner also speaks from a somewhat different point of view of the connection of the human etheric body with living wisdom in the lecture of 28 December 1911 (GA 134) and of its connection with cosmic imaginations which in it become life-forces in the lecture of 13 June 1915 (GA 159/160).

50. GA 233, lecture of 21 April 1924.

51. Now that it has ceased to be possible for him to darken the consciousness of human beings after death (see the words quoted from *Occult Science*, GA 30, on p. 204), Ahriman tries in our time to fulfil his purposes through shortening as much as he can the second half of man's life between death and a new birth (see the lecture of 24 April 1922, GA 211).

52. Rudolf Steiner employs this particular formulation at the Christmas Conference on the day of the laying of the Foundation Stone of the General Anthroposophical Society (25 December 1923). See further in S.O. Prokofieff, *Rudolf Steiner and the Founding of the New Mysteries*, 'The Foundation-Stone Meditation' together with the appended notes.

53. GA 112, lecture of 5 July 1909.

54. This living wisdom, or *vitae sophia*, which Christ introduced into human etheric bodies as a result of the event of the Ascension, has in an astonishing way been able to preserve man's etheric body from two extreme tendencies in his development after death: from the more luciferic tendency to dissolve in the widths of space (that is, complete de-individualization) and from the ahrimanic tendency to become chained to the sphere of the Earth, the so-called 'ahrimanic immortality' (see more about this in last part of the book). The etheric body is protected against the first tendency by the principle of wisdom, which strengthens its forces of individualization, and from the second by the principle of life, which prevents it from uniting after death

with the forces of earthly matter. Taken as a whole, this *vitae sophia*, the combination of the two principles, the union of the life and wisdom of the World Imaginations, leads the etheric body of an individual who has received the Christ-impulse into the 'etheric ring'.

55. GA 112, lecture of 5 July 1909.
56. See also GA 236, the lecture of 30 May 1924.
57. See Note 8.
58. Address at the Christmas Conference, 25 December 1923 (GA 260).
59. Ibid.
60. In *Theosophy* (GA 9), Rudolf Steiner also calls man's etheric body the body of the formative forces (footnote in the chapter entitled 'Body, Soul and Spirit').
61. Address at the Christmas Conference, 25 December 1923 (GA 260).
62. Something should briefly be added at this point regarding one further characteristic of the 'dodecahedral Stone of Love'. It was indicated in the present work that in the spiritual events which stand behind the Christian festivals of Easter, Ascension and Whitsun we are concerned with the rescuing of the *fourfold* human organism, as it appears on the Earth. According to Rudolf Steiner this relationship can be expressed as follows:

> Easter—rescuing of the physical body
> Ascension—rescuing of the etheric body
> Whitsun—rescuing of the astral body and ego.

But in so far as the 'dodecahedral Stone of Love' was (as we have seen) formed directly from the forces of Easter, Ascension and Pentecost, so in those forces from which it was formed—and which, therefore, can be comprehended by every anthroposophist who has laid it in the ground of his soul—do we have something which embraces, and leads to the spiritualization of, man in his *entirety*. These relationships can be expressed as follows:

> Physical body—World Love
> Etheric body—World Imaginations
> Astral body—World Thoughts
> Ego—'Spirit-Selfhood of the Universe'

This indication of a path to an understanding of the nature of the 'dodecahedral Stone of Love' can also serve as a supplement to what has been said on this theme by the present author in the concluding chapter of the book *Rudolf Steiner and the Founding of the New Mysteries*.

Part X: St John's-tide

1. Rudolf Steiner speaks of this as follows: 'The human soul endeavours in spring to follow the outbreathing of the Earth's Soul as it seeks union with

443

the cosmos. But the human soul is unable to attain this. Owing to the influence of the sense of freedom and ego-consciousness, it has become powerless with regard to the heavenly heights' (GA 226, lecture of 21 May 1923). In ancient times, however, such an ascent was still possible for those who had passed through initiation: 'Hence in ancient times there existed summer Mysteries, in which it was possible to perceive the secrets of the universe through the experience shared by the Soul of the Earth—which the soul of an initiate would follow into the widths of space—with the stars' (GA 224, lecture of 23 May 1923).

2. GA 223, lecture of 31 March 1923.

3. Also for the Earth itself, it only became possible to recall at Christmas-tide all that it had experienced in the macrocosm at St John's-tide because the Christ Being had united with it through the Mystery of Golgotha. By His presence within it in winter time, Christ awakens its awareness for life in cosmic memories.

4. GA 13. The words quoted are taken from the sixth (German) edition. In later editions of the book these words are omitted. (See also GA 96, the lecture of 6 June 1907.)

5. See GA 240, the lecture of 19 July 1924.

6. See GA 229, the lecture of 13 October 1923.

7. See GA 229, the lecture of 7 October 1923.

8. Luke 1:26–38.

9. In the figure of the Luke Jesus (the Nathan Soul) we have to do with a *human being* although in a certain sense also with a being of angelic or archangelic nature (see p. 33), as the following words of Rudolf Steiner show: 'This particular ego [the Nathan Soul] was endowed with something quite special; it had the particular quality of being untouched by all that a human ego had generally to assimilate on the Earth. It was, therefore, untouched by all luciferic and ahrimanic influences; it was altogether something which—if we were to compare it with other human egos—we could imagine to be a hollow sphere, something completely virginal with respect to all earthly experiences, a nothingness, a negative element over and against all these earthly experiences. Thus *the impression arose* that the Nathan Jesus-child ... did not possess a human ego at all, that he had only a physical body, an etheric body and an astral body ... which were so ordered that they harmoniously represented man as a sum-total of Saturn, Sun and Moon-evolution' (GA 131, lecture of 12 October 1911).

10. GA 120, lecture of 22 May 1910.

11. This is why it was that, at this time, according to spiritual science, the knowledge that Christ came to the Earth from the Sun finally became lost to humanity (see the address of 17 May 1923, GA 226). For in order to experience Christ as a Sun Being, one would need not merely imaginative but also *inspirative* knowledge.

12. GA 114, lecture of 16 September 1909.

13. Quoted from J.W. von Goethe, *Faust*, 'The Prologue in Heaven', by

Rudolf Steiner in the lecture of 11 June 1910, GA 121. (Translation by Anna Swanwick.)

14. See GA 114, the lecture of 15 September 1909.
15. GA 124, lecture of 6 December 1910.
16. John 1:32 (following the Bock translation).
17. John 1:36 (as above).
18. GA 214, lecture of 28 July 1922.
19. Hence one can say that Christ descends to Earth *directly*, from the Sun itself. For this reason, it was also not possible for Moses to perceive Christ *in the Moon-sphere* directly but only as a reflection, through the Moon Elohim Yahveh: 'And so Yahveh, or Jehovah, is none other than the reflection of Christ before He Himself appeared on the Earth ... Yahveh, or Jehovah, is Christ though seen not directly but as a light reflected [by the Moon].' (Lecture of 21 September 1909, GA 114.)
20. Luke 3:22. These words from the Gospel are quoted in accordance with Rudolf Steiner's lecture of 21 September 1909 (GA 114).
21. See GA 222, the lecture of 11 March 1923 and GA 224, the lecture of 6 April 1923.
22. GA 243, lecture of 22 August 1924.
23. GA 131, lecture of 11 October 1911.
24. GA 131, lecture of 10 October 1911.
25. Regarding the connection that exists between ancient and modern Saturn, see GA 110, the lecture of 17 April 1909.
26. See GA 110, the lectures of 14 and 15 April 1909, and also GA 233, the lecture of 4 January 1924.
27. Hence the Jesus of the Matthew Gospel, that is, the reincarnated Zarathustra, was born on the very day the great Sun-birth of Christ was to take place. For Zarathustra was the greatest earthly herald and teacher of the *inspired* wisdom of the Sun Mysteries.
28. GA 114, lecture of 15 September 1909. Herein also lies a definite polarity between the Gospel of St Luke and the Gospel of St John, with the other two Gospels forming a sort of transition. Compare with what is said about this polarity in the book by S.O. Prokofieff, *Rudolf Steiner and the Founding of the New Mysteries*, the chapter entitled 'The Path of the Teacher of Humanity'.
29. Regarding the significance of these three births in the ancient Mysteries, see the lecture of 20 April 1924 (GA 233a).
30. In the lecture of 12 August 1908 (GA 105), Rudolf Steiner defines Imagination as planetary consciousness, Inspiration as consciousness of the entire solar system, and Intuition as world, universal consciousness, that is, a consciousness which extends beyond the limits of the solar system and enters the worlds of the fixed stars.
31. GA 114, lecture of 15 September 1909.
32. GA 224, lecture of 23 May 1923.
33. Rudolf Steiner speaks elsewhere about this as follows: 'Mankind must reach

a certain *esoteric maturity* in order to be able not simply to think abstractly but to think concretely, in order again to be in a position to create festivals' (GA 223, lecture of 1 April 1923).

34. GA 224, lecture of 23 May 1923.
35. GA 13, Chapter 'Knowledge of Higher Worlds'.
36. Ibid., foreword to the 16th–20th (German) editions.
37. GA 223, lecture of 28 September, 1923.
38. GA 257, lecture of 13 February 1923.
39. GA 223, lecture of 1 April 1923.
40. GA 223, lecture of 8 April 1923.
41. The establishing of the Michaelmas festival followed fourteen years after the publicizing of the new path of initiation in *Occult Science*, (1909–1923), and twenty-one years after the time when the results of this initiation began to be revealed among the German section of the Theosophical Society (1902–23).
42. Here it may be recalled that the three Magi from the East learnt of the approach of the Turning Point of Time through *reading the starry script*.
43. In the esoteric tradition of medieval Rosicrucianism, the Stone of Wisdom was always revered as the 'imperishable body of the Risen One'. Rudolf Steiner says in this connection: 'Thus the alchemists always affirmed that man's physical body does, in truth, consist of the same substance as that of which the wholly transparent, crystal-clear Stone of Wisdom consists' (GA 131, lecture of 10 October 1911). See also Zeylmans van Emmichoven's book *The Foundation Stone*, Rudolf Steiner Press 1963, the chapter entitled 'From the Philosopher's Stone to the Stone of Love'.
44. GA 13, 'Knowledge of Higher Worlds'.
45. Compare with what is said in *Knowledge of the Higher Worlds: How is it Achieved?* (GA 10), the chapter entitled 'The Stages of Initiation'.
46. What is said here does not contradict the indication on p. 127 that, at the time, Christ also makes the reverse transition from time to space, from the law of seven to the law of twelve. For as Christ Himself comes from the spheres which lie *beyond* the realms of time and space, He has, since His union with Earth-existence, constantly striven towards the gradual spiritualization of these realms, bringing a spiritualized time to the realm of space, which is subjected to Ahriman, and a spiritualized space to the realm of time, which is subjected to Lucifer. Thus everywhere, whether in the outer world of nature or in the inner world of the human soul, where it is a matter of overcoming the forces of Ahriman, there is a transition from twelve to seven. And where, on the contrary, it is necessary to overcome the forces of Lucifer this arises through the transition from seven to twelve.
47. See the words of Rudolf Steiner quoted on p. 229.
48. GA 26, Leading Thought, No. 1.

1. GA 124, lecture of 19 December 1910.
2. See GA 114, the lecture of 19 September 1909.
3. See GA 202, the lecture of 23 December 1920.
4. GA 236, lecture of 4 June 1924.
5. Compare with what was said in the chapter, 'The Uniting of the World Impulses of Wisdom and Love in the Experience of Christ'.
6. GA 202, lecture of 23 December 1920.
7. Ibid.
8. *Wahrspruchworte*, GA 40.
9. GA 223, lecture of 31 March 1923.
10. Ibid.
11. GA 26, the article of 2 November 1924, entitled 'The Michael-Christ Experience of Man'.
12. Ibid.
13. Ibid.
14. GA 202, lecture of 24 December 1920.
15. In this sense, Rudolf Steiner's references to the connection existing between the Christ-impulse and the experience of spiritual warmth (love), and also between the Michael-impulse and the experience of spiritual light (wisdom), are pertinent. See the article 'Michael's Mission in the Cosmic Age of Human Freedom' in GA 26, and the lecture of 19 November 1922 (GA 218).
16. GA 202, lecture of 24 December 1920.
17. Ibid.
18. Ibid.
19. GA 202, lecture of 23 December 1920.
20. GA 202, lecture of 24 December 1920.
21. Ibid.
22. GA 202, lecture of 23 December 1920. What has been said here does not contradict the fact, about which Rudolf Steiner speaks in the cycle *The Search for the New Isis, the Divine Sophia* (GA 202, 25 December 1920), that on the *new path* the Shepherds come to inspirative, and the Magi to intuitive, knowledge. For the half of the year when we travel on the new path of the Shepherds is connected more with Christ, the Logos, the Word; this does, however, stand closer to spiritual listening, that is, to *inspirative* knowledge. The other half of the year, when we travel the path of the Magi, is connected rather with the Sophia, with the divine wisdom, with the *World Thoughts* of the Spirit, which is accessible more to imaginative knowledge.
23. Compare with Rudolf Steiner's words quoted on p. 280.
24. The following words of Rudolf Steiner speak of the inner connection or (as one could say) the spiritual succession between the festival of Whitsun and the festival of Michaelmas: 'Through the festival of Easter Christ Jesus graciously entered into the evolution of humanity in such a way that when

the riddle of death approached human beings with particular force He appeared as the bearer of immortality, as (one could say) the Archetype of man, immortal man, who passes through death and must find resurrection. This was understood even in ancient times... On Earth one saw death; in Christ Jesus one was to see resurrection. But Christ Jesus also allowed the Mystery of Pentecost to be fulfilled. He sent mankind the Spirit, the healing Spirit; and He indicated thereby that man must come to the Christ-experience out of himself. But this he can only do if he can go in a reverse direction—if he can first experience resurrection and then, once resurrection has been experienced, pass rightly through physical death, that is, enable the soul inwardly to resurrect. Between birth and death the soul is raised, through a full enlivening of its relationship to the Mystery of Golgotha, to a higher level of vitality in order that it may feel a spiritual resurrection within: I am passing, as one who is resurrected, through earthly death.' (GA 226, lecture of 21 May 1923.)

Compare this with Rudolf Steiner's words about the Michaelmas festival as quoted on p. 26 and with what is said on pp. 52.

25. Regarding the question as to what is meant by the words 'the Archangel Michael is the Son of *Soph-Ea*' (Sophia), the lecture of 10 January 1915 (GA 161) offers an indication: Rudolf Steiner speaks there of how, in the evolution of philosophy on Earth in the period from 800 BC until the present, the law of the Sun has held sway, and that this has been manifested through the activity of the Spirits of Wisdom (*Kyriotetes*)—they are especially connected with the Sophia-principle in our cosmos—and beings of the Hierarchy of the Archangels. Here, this activity occurs in the same form in which it took place on Old Sun, when the Spirits of Wisdom endowed the Archangels with the principle of the individual ego; or in other words, they became in a certain sense their *fathers* in so far as the arising of their ego-consciousness was concerned. (Regarding the special position occupied by the Archangel Michael among the Archangels since the age of Old Sun, see Part II, Note 24; as the Sun Archangel and the ruler of the heavenly Intelligence in the Earth-epoch, see the chapters on his autumn festival and his activity in connection with the Christ-impulse and the Nathan Soul.

26. See S.O. Prokofieff, *Rudolf Steiner and the Founding of the New Mysteries*, Chapter 6. What is said here does not contradict the indication in the next chapter as to the descending half of the year (autumn and the beginning of winter) being more connected with the working in the yearly cycle of the Father-forces. For what is pertinent to, and especially necessary for, our time is the penetration of the new Christ Spirit—whose revelation we encounter in modern Anthroposophy—directly into the practical activity of human beings on Earth, which is associated with the gradual transformation of the natural Father-sphere. The foundation for such a penetration is the autumnal festival of Michael that has now been established through the will of the spiritual world, the truly spiritual celebration of which will become possible only if the new Christ Spirit, enkindled in the human soul at Whitsun,

becomes so strong that He can penetrate into the second, descending, half of the yearly cycle until the end of September and enable us '... *to bring the spiritual into our deeds*, to rule our lives according to the spirit. For this is what it means to serve Michael: to establish our lives not out of purely material laws but to be aware that Michael—whose mission it is to overcome the lower, ahrimanic forces—must become the genius of the evolution of our civilization.' (GA 224, lecture of 23 May 1923. See also Rudolf Steiner's words about the Michael festival quoted on p. 265f.)

27. See GA 229, the lecture of 12 October 1923.
28. GA 202, lecture of 24 December 1920.
29. In the lecture of 1 December 1922 (GA 219), Rudolf Steiner speaks of how human thinking is connected more with the rhythm of the day, and human *feeling* with the rhythm of the year.
30. Quotations are from the lecture of 20 February 1917 (GA 175).
31. Ibid.
32. GA 236, lecture of 4 June 1924.
33. Ibid. In this same lecture Rudolf Steiner points out that this experience of the spiritual Kingdom of the Father, which lies immediately *behind* the physical world of the senses, develops in the cycle of the year with particular intensity during the period of autumn and winter and attains its culmination at Christmas, as is expressed in the dictum *Ex Deo nascimur.*
34. Not even Jesus of Nazareth (the Nathan Soul), with whom the cosmic Christ Being unites at the Baptism in the Jordan through the mediation of the Spirit-principle, is an exception in this respect: 'And John bore witness, "I saw the Spirit descend as a dove from heaven, and it remained on Him"' (John 1:32).
35. GA 214, lecture of 30 July 1922.
36. GA 118, lecture of 15 May 1910.
37. GA 153, lecture of 14 April 1914.
38. GA 214, lecture of 27 August 1922.
39. GA 132, lecture of 31 October 1911.
40. In another lecture Rudolf Steiner says: 'And the whole of past evolution until the age of Saturn and the whole of future evolution until Vulcan will be seen in such a way that the *light* to behold this [which is to say, the light of the Holy Spirit] will radiate from knowledge of the Mystery of Golgotha' (GA 207, lecture of 16 October 1921).
41. GA 161, lecture of 10 January 1915.
42. Ibid.
43. GA 214, lecture of 30 August 1922. In the same lecture Rudolf Steiner says that in that sphere of the fixed stars, where '... in the person of Christ there emerges a Guide who can *bring order* to the intricate events of this sphere', a man's karma is revealed to his spiritual vision.
44. All these three stages can be traced in Rudolf Steiner's life-path. First, his penetration of the Father-sphere through the clairvoyance that awakens within him in his seventh year. Then around 1899 there is his direct

encounter with Christ in the spiritual world (the sphere of the Son) and the subsequent union with Him, the consequence of which was that he experienced the spirit-impulse out of whose direct revelations Anthroposophy was founded as 'the wisdom of the Holy Spirit about man'. This impulse of the new Christ Spirit, in the course of three seven-year periods, brings into effect the earthly development of Anthroposophy (1902–24): revealing the secrets of the Spirit-sphere during the first of these seven-year periods (the establishment of the foundations of the anthroposophical view of the world); revealing the secrets of the Sun-sphere during the second seven-year period (Christology and Mystery-art); and the secrets of the Father-sphere during the third seven-year period (the penetration of anthroposophical impulses into various areas of human practical activity as the beginning of a gradual spiritualization of modern culture). Finally, we have the culmination of the entire twenty-one year development of Anthroposophy in the Christmas Conference of 1923 and in the all-embracing karmic investigations of 1924, which relate to the 'Mysteries of the sphere of Michael'; the latter Rudolf Steiner could only impart once he had attained his sixty-third year, whereby he became able to 'penetrate into the secrets of the universe through the Saturn wisdom' (GA 240, lecture of 20 July 1924). See further in S.O. Prokofieff, *Rudolf Steiner and the Founding of the New Mysteries*.

45. We may see from what has been said that when looked at in this way the year takes on a threefold aspect, as it was for the Ancient Indians and also in still more ancient times—although in a completely different way, for in those times the natural foundation of the year was still spiritually perceived (see GA 223, the lecture of 2 April 1923). While now, in the new world-epoch that began after the Mystery of Golgotha, the revelation of the primordial Trinity must be found again in the cycle of the year, though now not as working out of the foundation of nature but from the forces of the Christ Being who is connected with the Earth. Such an experience of the forces of the Trinity in the cycle of the year will become more and more widespread as the impulses of the Etheric Christ are manifested within man.

46. See Note 1 of the Foreword.

47. GA 130, lecture of 17 June 1912. In another lecture, Rudolf Steiner says: 'Its mission [he is referring to the mission of the spiritual-scientific movement] consists in this: to create conditions which will make it possible for Christ to be understood on the physical plane, in order that people may then behold Him' (GA 130, lecture of 21 September 1911). And elsewhere he says: 'But this is precisely the reason for the spread of the anthroposophical world-view, that man might prepare on the physical plane for being able either [while still dwelling] on *the physical plane or on higher planes* [after death] to perceive the Christ Event' (GA 131, lecture of 14 October 1911).

48. It is indeed so that, having once begun the exercises, one should continue them for a *whole* year and sometimes, even, for many years. The present concern is simply to bring into focus the relationship between the spiritual

forces working in the cycle of the year and the principal elements of the anthroposophical path of knowledge, that is, to consider the most suitable periods for passing through one stage or another. Moreover, all the facts that have been set forth above are, by nature, extremely complicated, which is why one can only speak of one particular *aspect* of the whole.

49. GA 214, lecture of 27 August 1922.
50. The spirit-pupil should, therefore, here attempt, in a microcosmic way, to bring about inwardly a spiritual process akin to what Rudolf Steiner has described as a macrocosmic process in the lecture of 14 April 1914 (GA 153).
51. GA 130, lecture of 2 December 1911.
52. With regard to the description of the working of the forces of Michael and the forces of the Sophia in the cycle of the year (at the beginning of this chapter and in the previous chapter), the following thoughts should be added. As the son of Sophia, Michael's task in the cycle of the year is, during the present epoch of his rulership, to bear the impulses of the Spirit into earthly, natural, existence (the sphere of the Father). Rudolf Steiner refers to this in the following words: 'Michael must permeate us as a mighty power who can see through the world of matter, who beholds the Spirit in matter, who beholds the Spirit in everything material.' (GA 194, lecture of 22 November 1919.) Hence in the cycle of the year Michael is the principal source of the impulses behind three of the nine stages, and they may best be passed through at the end of summer and in the autumn.
1) The study of Anthroposophy. 'Michael wishes man to become a free being who in his ideas and concepts gains insight into what comes towards him by way of revelation from the spiritual world' (GA 240, lecture of 19 July 1924). By 'revelation' is meant here what is imparted by modern spiritual science, for 'Anthroposophy would wish to be the message of this Mission of Michael' (GA 26, article of 10 October 1924).
2) The etheric contemplation of the elemental world. 'Michael's mission is to bring to human etheric bodies the forces through which shadowy thoughts may again be enlivened; then the souls and spirits of the super-sensible worlds will approach these enlivened thoughts' (GA 26). This comes about through the gradual 'entering of the power of Imagination into the general intellectual awareness of humanity' as a result of the working of the Michael-impulse (Ibid.).
3) The fulfilment of karma. 'Through the advent of Michael's rulership . . . through [his] penetrating into the domain of the Earth . . . Michael bestows the power which is to bring order to the karma of those who have gone with him. Thus we may ask: what unites the members of the Anthroposophical Society? They are united through the fact that they bring order to their karma!' (GA 237, lecture of 8 August 1924). And it is Michael who gives the will-forces for this, because 'Michael is the Spirit of Strength' (GA 194, lecture of 22 November 1919).
Thus Michael helps the soul three times in three different circumstances in the cycle of the year to find the path from the realm of the Father to the

451

realm of the Son or Christ. This is 'the path of Michael which has its continuation in the path of Christ' (GA 194, lecture of 23 November 1919). For Michael '... begins in our time to reveal the Christ anew' (GA 152, lecture of 2 May 1913). 'This,' says Rudolf Steiner, 'is indicated in the twofold nature of what we must go towards. In the first place, to recognize the supersensible in the surrounding sense-world, the world of man, animals and plants—that is the path of Michael [that is to say, the beginning of etheric clairvoyance]. And the continuation [of this path]: that in this world which we have recognized as supersensible we find the Christ [in our time principally in etheric form]' (GA 194, lecture of 23 November 1919). And finally, in the Sophia-impulse bestowed by Christ—'It is not the Christ that we lack ... the Sophia of Christ is what fails us' (GA 202, lecture of 24 December 1920)—we may find the forces for passing through all three levels of the Spirit-stage, for we need the Sophia of Christ, the new Isis, in order rightly to meditate, to behold the workings of karma and to strive towards the spiritualization of the Earth.

53. The *three-year* cycle here described also has a certain relationship to the *three years* when the Christ Being dwelt on the Earth in the sheaths of Jesus of Nazareth. However, a more detailed study of these relationships lies beyond the scope of the present work.

54. One could also say that the first cycle (the first year) leads to the spiritualizing of the human thinking, the second of the feeling and the third of the will.

55. GA 175, lecture of 13 March 1917.

56. Galatians 2:20.

57. Matthew 18:20.

58. GA 26, article of 9 November 1924.

59. See GA 153, lecture of 13 April 1914.

60. Modern materialism leads the soul after death to an ever greater solitude in the spiritual world (see GA 13), and the consequence of this is the predominance of antisocial over social tendencies in the earthly world.

61. See GA 186, the lecture of 12 December 1918.

62. GA 194, lecture of 23 November 1919.

63. See GA 112, the lecture of 24 June 1909.

64. Ibid.

65. GA 218, lecture of 18 November 1922. The threefold division of the yearly cycle outlined in the previous chapter has a direct connection with the theme of 'social threefoldness', although a fuller analysis of these relationships lies beyond the scope of this book.

66. To this it should be added that it is the task of Anthroposophy, as the modern expression of the Rosicrucian-impulse, to unite again what has until our time worked in a divided form as science, art and religion (see the address of 20 September 1913 at the laying of the Foundation Stone of the First Goetheanum, GA 245). Thus every anthroposophically formed festival must essentially consist of three elements (see GA 224, the lecture of 23 May 1923, and GA 257, the lecture of 20 January 1923):

1. The spiritual-scientific understanding of its nature.

2. Its artistic form.

3. The attainment of a real experience of communion with the spirit through communion with human beings who are striving towards the same higher purpose, that is, the true 'religion', *union* with the spiritual world, which Rudolf Steiner characterizes in the following words: '... that we feel as though a Being, who hovers over us and is present in a spiritually real sense, were gazing upon us from above and listening to us. The spiritual presence, the supersensible presence that arises because we are concerning ourselves with Anthroposophy, is something we must feel. Then each individual anthroposophical deed itself becomes a realization of the supersensible' (GA 257, lecture of 27 February 1923). And if in the festive periods of the year, when we make particular efforts to strengthen our 'anthroposophical deeds' through bringing them into harmony with the spiritual deeds of Christ in the Earth's surroundings, if in such spiritually replete periods of the year we are able to experience the reality of the formula of the new social communion, 'where two or three are gathered in my Name, there am I in the midst of them', the above-quoted words regarding the spiritually real Being who gazes upon us and listens to us in the course of our anthroposophical work acquire their full spiritual significance and their true actuality. Then there awakens in us a premonition of what it means to work in the world 'at the behest of Christ', to work for the forming of the spiritual foundations of the sixth cultural epoch, to prepare that which in the sense of anthroposophical community-building is the task of each individual anthroposophical group and the General Anthroposophical Society as a whole (see GA 159/160, the lecture of 15 June 1915).

67. What is said in this chapter regarding the new cultus that arises out of living spiritually with the cycle of the year and is more concerned with its significance for the social life of mankind. Its significance for the development of the individual will be considered in the final chapter. Both aspects in their inner nature form two sides of a single whole, corresponding to the two 'commandments' that Christ gave to mankind: 'Love your neighbour and love God' (Mark 12:28–31). The fulfilment of these two commandments as mankind is increasingly permeated by the Christ-impulse will, through *social* (festivals) and *cognitive* (the path of initiation) cultic acts, become ever more a religious rite, a kind of sacrificial cultic service. As a result of this, man will come more and more to succeed in learning to behave in social life with other human beings 'at the behest of Christ', while following in his individual spiritual development the path of the 'imitation of Christ' as this is now possible in modern Christian initiation.

68. In GA 15, *The Spiritual Guidance of the Individual and Humanity*, Rudolf Steiner expresses this thought in the following words: 'In future there will be chemists and physicists who will teach chemistry and physics not as they are taught today ... but will teach: "Matter is constructed according to how Christ has gradually ordained it to be!" The Christ will be found even in the

laws of chemistry and physics.' This will be the time when, according to another observation of Rudolf Steiner, the laboratory table will become an altar, and scientific endeavour a religious rite. Such a fully Christianized science will become a universal phenomenon in the sixth cultural epoch.

69. It is this 'being imbued with reality' that Christ imparts to our moral deeds, if we only seek a conscious connection with Him, for example on that path which was described in the previous chapter.

70. GA 175, lecture of 27 February 1917.

71. See GA 13.

72. Mark 13:31 and Luke 21:33.

73. See GA 104, the lectures of 29 and 30 June 1908.

Part XII: The Modern Mysteries of the Etheric Christ

1. See S.O. Prokofieff, *Rudolf Steiner and the Founding of the New Mysteries*, Part 3, 'The Michael Age and the New Grail Event'.

2. See the chapter 'The Fourth Deed of the Nathan Soul. The Transformation of Michael's Mission at the Time of the Mystery of Golgotha'.

3. See GA 152, the lecture of 2 May 1913.

4. Michael's becoming the 'Representative of Christ' in the Sun-sphere is also connected with the fact that, owing to his ascent to the rank of the Archai, he was able to acquire a quite particular relationship to the *Spirit Man of Christ* which Christ had left behind on the Sun in the course of His descent to the Earth (see the lecture of 27 August 1924, GA 240).

5. GA 243, lecture of 18 August 1924.

6. See the chapter 'From Michaelmas to Christmas (Michael and the Nathan Soul)'.

7. One is, of course, speaking only of *a certain part* of these responsibilities, that part which, in the first instance, is associated with the fact that until 1879 Michael worked in the cosmos from out of the Hierarchy of the *Archangels*. It is hardly necessary to mention that, in rising to a higher rank, he nevertheless retained many of his previous functions.

8. In the lecture of 6 February 1917 (GA 175) Rudolf Steiner singles out 1909 as the year when the new manifestation of Christ began.

9. GA 152, lecture of 18 May 1913.

10. GA 152, lecture of 20 May 1913.

11. See GA 137, the lectures of 11 and 12 June 1912.

12. See also GA 114, the lecture of 25 September 1909.

13. See GA 105, the lecture of 14 August 1908.

14. GA 106, lecture of 12 September 1908.

15. GA 121, lecture of 14 June 1910.

16. Ibid.

17. GA 222, lecture of 11 March 1923. There is one further aspect of the connection between the historical Buddha and the Archangel Wotan which

is of interest. The Roman historian Tacitus (who lived one century after the birth of Christ), in his survey of the religious views of the ancient Teutons, refers to Wotan by the name of Mercury, associating his name with the corresponding day of the week—Wednesday (*Germania*, IX). H.P. Blavatsky, too, refers in the third volume of *The Secret Doctrine* (Theosophical Publishing House, London 1990) to the ancient esoteric formula, 'Buddha-Mercury', which we may comprehend through the teachings of Dionysius the Aeropagite. The latter writer also refers in his works to how the Archangel-sphere has a correspondence with Mercury (see the morning lecture of 12 April 1909, GA 110).

18. See further in S.O. Prokofieff, *Rudolf Steiner and the Founding of the New Mysteries*, the chapter entitled 'The Path of the Teacher of Humanity'.

19. This does not mean that still higher Spirits, including those as high as the Hierarchy of the Spirits of Movement, are unable to work through a Bodhisattva (see the lecture of 13 April 1912, GA 110).

20. GA 13, the chapter entitled 'Man and the Evolution of the World'.

21. This is in contrast to the Spirits of Wisdom, who may be called the 'Bestowers of Life' in that on Old Sun they endowed man with his etheric body and were at the same time the guiding Spirits of the Archangels as they passed through their human stage.

22. GA 121, lecture of 14 June 1910.

23. Frey and Freya to a certain extent form an exception, in that, according to Rudolf Steiner, they belong to the Hierarchy of the Angels and at the same time represent the second generation of the 'Vanir'. They appear as 'children' of Niord (see the lecture of 17 June 1910, GA 121).

24. In the lecture-cycle devoted to the Gospel of St Luke we read: 'Such a Being [the Nirmanakaya of Buddha], who no longer descends into a physical body but still has an astral body, can unite with the astral body of another human being and work within it. This person can then become a figure of importance, for the forces which are now working within him are those of a being who has already completed his last incarnation on the Earth. Thus such an astral being unites with the astral nature of a certain individual on the Earth. A union of this kind can take place in the most complicated way. When the Buddha appeared to the Shepherds in the field in the form of the "angelic host", he was not in a physical body but in an *astral body* . . . And so we may see that the Nirmanakaya of the Buddha appeared to the Shepherds in the field in the form of the angelic host. Buddha shows forth in his Nirmanakaya and manifests himself in this way to the Shepherds.' (GA 114, lecture of 17 September 1909.)

25. Luke 2:13–14.

26. GA 114, lecture of 17 September 1909.

27. In the two quotations from Rudolf Steiner that follow, instead of the words in the Bock translation, 'a multitude of choirs of heavenly Angels', the words are in the one case from the Lutheran translation, 'the heavenly host', and in the other, 'in the form of the angelic hosts'.

28. Luke 2:8–14. [The translation given is basically that of the revised standard version, though it follows the Bock version used in the author's Russian text where there is any appreciable difference.—Translator's note.]
29. GA 114, lecture of 16 September 1909.
30. GA 114, lecture of 17 September 1909.
31. This process is really even more complicated. For the second impulse, through which the ego of John the Baptist was awakened, was the influence of the Nathan Soul during the visit of Mary to Elisabeth (see the lecture of 19 September 1909, GA 114).
32. GA 114, lecture of 20 September 1909. At another point in the same lecture Rudolf Steiner characterized this connection between the Nirmanakaya of Buddha and John the Baptist as follows: 'The Buddha, now in his Nirmanakaya, shed his radiance upon the Nathan Jesus-child and continued his preaching, now speaking through the lips of John the Baptist. What the lips of John the Baptist uttered was inspired by the Buddha ... He speaks—even when no longer in incarnation—when he inspires through the Nirmanakaya. We hear from the lips of John the Baptist what the Buddha has to say six centuries after his life in a physical body ... And what lived in the Sermon of Benares blossomed in the preaching of John the Baptist by the Jordan.'
33. Mark 1:2 [following the Bock translation; most English versions have 'messenger' or some equivalent.—Translator's note].
34. In Rudolf Steiner's commentaries—in his lecture-cycle GA 114—on the preaching of John the Baptist as a rebirth of the Benares Sermon of Buddha, one can clearly distinguish the elements that stem from the Nirmanakaya of Buddha from those proceeding from the Angel of the Gautama-Bodhisattva.
35. Rudolf Steiner elsewhere uses the words '*a leading Angel*' (GA 124, lecture of 2 February 1911).
36. The words about the Angel at the beginning of the Gospel of St Mark (1:2) appear in the Book of Exodus (23:20) and in the Book of the prophet Malachi (3:1), while only the words that follow (1:3) appear in the Book of the prophet Isaiah (40:3).
37. GA 124, lecture of 6 December 1910.
38. Luke 2:11.
39. GA 124, lecture of 6 December 1910.
40. Elsewhere Rudolf Steiner describes him as follows: '... the Angelos whose task was, as an Angel, to proclaim *what man is to become through taking up the Christ-impulse*, for an Angel must proclaim in advance what man will become at a later time' (GA 124, lecture of 12 December 1910).
41. GA 127, lecture of 25 February 1911.
42. John 1:6–8.
43. GA 124, lecture of 6 December 1910.
44. See Luke 2:11.
45. GA 114, lecture of 17 September 1909. Rudolf Steiner characterizes the new condition of the Nirmanakaya of Buddha after its union with the maternal astral sheath of the Nathan Jesus in the following way: 'From this

moment we have to do with a definite entity consisting of the Nirmanakaya, the spirit-body of Buddha [which is, as we have seen, of an astral nature] and of the maternal astral body which separated as an astral sheath from the Jesus-child in the twelfth year of his life' (GA 114, lecture of 18 September 1909).

46. GA 114, lecture of 17 September 1909.

47. At that time the separation of the etheric and astral sheaths took place not in the seventh and fourteenth years respectively, as is the case today, but somewhat earlier, approximately in the fifth and twelfth years (see the lecture of 21 September 1909, GA 114).

48. GA 114, lecture of 20 September 1909.

49. GA 114, lecture of 18 September 1909.

50. Ibid.

51. It should here be emphasized that, as the incarnation as Jesus of Nazareth was the Nathan Soul's *first* incarnation on Earth since ancient Lemurian times, this was not merely a considerable sacrifice on its account but also the most difficult of all possible trials. Hence it stood in need of a quite particular kind of help, which was best provided by that being who was equally familiar with the laws of both spiritual and physical worlds and who had in former times brought to mankind the teaching that the earthly world is Maya and that it must be overcome. Rudolf Steiner also speaks of the Nathan Soul's role in this respect: 'Thus we look with the Shepherds at the manger where he who is usually called Jesus of Nazareth was born; we look and there from the first we see a halo above the child and know that in this picture is expressed the power of the Bodhisattva who became the Buddha, the power which had hitherto streamed forth to human beings and now, working upon mankind from the spiritual heights, sheds its light upon the child in Bethlehem in such a way that *it was able to find its rightful place in the evolution of humanity.*' (GA 114, lecture of 26 September 1909.)

52. One could also say that through such a deed this being—in human terms—gave an example of what the Nirmanakaya of Buddha was later to 'repeat' in another realm.

53. We have something similar in the case of the spiritual individuality of Buddha. For he is able to unite the forces of the maternal *astral* sheath of the Nathan Jesus with his own being only because the body of the Nirmanakaya with which he is clothed in the spiritual worlds is none other than his own *astral body* which has to a certain extent been transformed into the Spirit Self (see p. 307).

54. Emil Bock, *The Three Years* (Floris Books, Edinburgh 1987) 'The Events of Holy Week' (translated by Alfred Heidenreich).

55. Ibid.

56. See further in S.O. Prokofieff, *Rudolf Steiner and the Founding of the New Mysteries*, the chapter entitled 'The Path of the Teacher of Humanity'.

57. GA 114, lecture of 21 September 1909.

58. What is meant here by the 'Fall' is the entry of the forces of Lucifer into human evolution in the Lemuriah epoch, which led to the intervention of

457

the forces of Ahriman in the epoch of Atlantis and, with these, the forces of death.

59. Christ does not conquer death in the Garden of Gethsemane but only provisionally wards off its power. The final victory takes place on Golgotha, *not* through the victory over *dying* but through the conscious passage *through* death and the subsequent *Resurrection*.

60. [In his Russian text, the author here follows the Luther translation and then adds the following note. Most extant English translations, including the Revised Standard Version employed in the English version of the present book (though, as here, adapted where this is demanded by the original Russian), bear at this point a closer relationship to Bock's translation than that of Luther.—Translator's note.] In his book *The Three Years* Emil Bock inserts in place of 'And when the struggle with death began' the words 'When He was in agony ...'

61. GA 150, lecture of 21 December 1913.

62. It needs to be emphasized here that the mission of Vidar with respect to mankind had at that time already passed far beyond the scope of a single human individual, even one as outstanding as the Gautama-Bodhisattva (Gautama Buddha). Here the description that follows characterizes only one of the aspects of the activity of this high Spirit. This would be a way of referring to the connection described above (p. 310) between Vidar and John the Baptist. For both of them—John the Baptist on Earth and Vidar in the spiritual worlds—embody at once the relationship of, and also the transition from, the old cosmos of the Father to the new cosmos of the Son, or, within the context of external history, from the pre-Christian to the Christian epoch. For John the Baptist, the last Old Testament prophet and the first to meet the Christ on Earth, recognizes Him and calls Him the Son of God (John 1:34), and Vidar is the only one of the pre-Christian or 'pagan' gods to survive the 'Twilight of the Gods' and thereby forms in the spiritual worlds the transition from the past to the future and appears there—as does John the Baptist on the Earth—as the great servant and proclaimer of the end of the old aeon and the beginning of the new.

63. GA 15, Chapter 3.

64. Regarding the particular connection of old atavistic clairvoyance with the development of the sentient soul and, hence, its rapid extinction in the epoch of the intellectual or mind soul, see for instance Rudolf Steiner's article of 15 February 1925 under the title of 'Gnosis and Anthroposophy' (GA 26).

65. GA 116, lecture of 25 October 1909. In the same lecture Rudolf Steiner also says that only a *part* of the task of developing the consciousness soul within mankind devolved upon Gautama Buddha. The other part rested with another Bodhisattva who was venerated among the ancient Greeks under the name of Apollo-Orpheus.

66. Ibid. The Bodhisattva was, therefore, able to develop the consciousness soul already in this epoch because at that time he was—uniquely, for his part—

incarnated in the physical body, whereas in all his previous incarnations he had been only partially connected with it.

67. It is in this sense that one should understand what Rudolf Steiner says about finding direct inspirations of Gautama Buddha in the works of such European thinkers as Schelling, Leibnitz, Soloviev and Goethe (GA 130, see the lecture of 18 September 1911).

68. See further regarding the new task of the Archangel Wotan in: Sergei O. Prokofieff, *Die geistigen Aufgaben Mittel- und Osteuropas*, Dornach 1993.

69. See GA 191, the lecture of 1 November 1919, and also GA 193, the lectures of 27 October 1919 and 4 November 1919.

70. It becomes apparent from Rudolf Steiner's later lectures that the expression 'signs of the time' is an occult term for the rulership of Michael in our time. (See, for example, the lecture of 17 February 1918, GA 174a, and also S.O. Prokofieff, *Rudolf Steiner and the Founding of the New Mysteries*, the chapter entitled 'The Christmas Conference of 1923–24'.)

71. GA 121, lecture of 17 June 1910.

72. In the lecture of 14 October in Karlsruhe, Rudolf Steiner says: 'In order to understand this event [the New Advent of Christ] in the full light of day, man must be prepared. It is for this purpose that the world-view of Anthroposophy is disseminated in our time so that man might be prepared on the physical plane or on higher planes [that is, after death].' (GA 131, lecture of 14 October 1911.)

73. This clairvoyance, according to Rudolf Steiner, can, as it approaches the Christ, at best call forth no more than 'an hallucination of Christ'. (See GA 191, the lecture of 1 November 1919.)

74. See Rudolf Steiner's words quoted on p. 175.

75. See Part V, the chapter entitled 'The Working of the Nathan Soul in the Old and the New Mysteries.'

76. See GA 149, the lecture of 30 December 1913.

77. GA 175, lecture of 6 February 1917.

78. GA 200 and GA 202. See the quotation from the latter cycle in the chapter 'The Cycle of the Year as a Path Leading to a New Experience of the Christ Being'.

79. GA 175, lecture of 6 February 1917.

80. Ibid.

81. In certain cases, however, a reverse order of events is possible: first the contemplation of the etheric form of Christ and then the beholding of the elemental world.

82. In the words of Rudolf Steiner quoted on p. 175, where he characterizes the relationship of the Nathan Soul to Christ *after* the Mystery of Golgotha, particular emphasis is placed upon its connection with Krishna, that is, upon its *Angel*-like nature, upon its kinship with the principle of the Spirit Self (see also the chapter entitled 'From Michaelmas to Christmas').

83. The fact that, from the time of the Mystery of Golgotha, the Nathan Soul continues to be connected in the spiritual world with the Being of Christ

emerges with full clarity not only from the words with which Rudolf Steiner characterizes the manifestation of Christ and the Nathan Soul to Paul at Damascus: 'Christ has taken Krishna [i.e. the Nathan Soul] as His own soul-sheath, through which He then proceeds to work...' (GA 142) but also from his description of the Damascus experience as it is reborn in our time, of which Theodora tells in the first Mystery Drama.

If we turn directly to her words, we find the following. First of all we see that her speech is divided into *two* parts (the pause between them is marked in the German text with a line of dashes). In the first part Theodora says:

> Before my spirit stands
> *a Form of shining light,*
> and from Him there come words...

And this Form goes on to speak the following words *in the first person*:

> You have been living in faith,
> you have had comfort in hope,
> now let your comfort be in vision;
> *receive new life through Me.*
> *I lived within the souls*
> who sought Me in themselves...

From all that Rudolf Steiner has said in general about the appearance of Christ and in particular about his proclamation through Theodora in the first Mystery Drama, it follows clearly that these words can be attributed only to *the Etheric Christ Himself*, whom Theodora experienced in her vision. This is further confirmed by the fact that Christ appears to her as a form, of which Rudolf Steiner speaks in the lecture of 9 November 1914 in Dornach (GA 158): 'This event of the appearance of Christ, which is what Theodora refers to, can come about only if the rulership of Michael is ever more extended... For this, he [Michael] needs his hosts, his warriors... Through this they [the souls of human beings who have after their death joined forces with his hosts] are especially able to summon the forces which will provide, in perfect purity, the *form* in which Christ is to appear, so that He does not appear in a false aspect, in accordance with subjective human imagining, but in His rightful *form*; for this must Michael fight his battle.'

The second part of Theodora's proclamation is of quite a different kind. Here she speaks of how from the *shining light* that surrounds the form of Christ a *human being* comes forth:

> A human being
> separates from the shining light;

and this human being, turning to Theodora, speaks:

> You shall proclaim to all
> who have the will to hear
> that you have seen

[here is meant the form of Christ from the first part of her speech]

what as experience will come to men,

and then to her is imparted *knowledge* of the events of Palestine and of Christ Himself, in that He is referred to and spoken of in *the third person*:

Christ lived once upon the earth
and from this life has come about ...
(Translation by Adam Bittleston)

Thus first of all there appears to Theodora '*a Form in shining light*' although she does not at first know what this form is (which is why the name of Christ is not mentioned in the first part of her speech). Then from 'the shining light' there 'separates a human being' who imparts to her *knowledge* of that form which stands before her, namely that it is the Christ who reveals Himself to her in this form. As to *who* this human being is, the following question and answer of Rudolf Steiner testify with the fullest clarity: 'What, then, was that *light-filled radiance* in which Christ appeared to Paul before Damascus? ... When Paul had his vision before Damascus, what appeared to him was the Christ. But the *light-filled radiance* in which Christ was arrayed *was Krishna*' (GA 142, lecture of 1 January 1913).

And so this *human being* who appears from the light-filled radiance (the shining light) is none other than the *Nathan Soul*, who even now accompanies the Etheric Christ and awakens within human beings (in this case in Theodora) 'the new Christ-consciousness' (of which more will be said in the chapter entitled 'The New Appearance of Christ in the Etheric Realm'). As for the human antecedents of the Nathan Soul, see the references to Rudolf Steiner's observations on this theme in Part II, Note 19, and the chapter 'From Michaelmas to Christmas. Michael and the Nathan Soul'.

84. GA 152, lecture of 2 May 1913.

85. From what Rudolf Steiner says in the lecture of 2 May 1913 (GA 152), it is fully evident that, in speaking of the repetition of the Mystery of Golgotha in the supersensible worlds in the nineteenth century, one is referring not to the extinction of the consciousness of Christ as such but only to the extinction of *that aspect* of it which after the historical Mystery of Golgotha remained connected with the angelic being: 'This spiritual death, which brought about the annihilation of the consciousness of that angelic being, is a repetition of the Mystery of Golgotha in the worlds which lie immediately above our own ...'

That this angelic being is the Nathan Soul is confirmed by the fact that in GA 152, the lecture of 7 March 1914—the only lecture in which the two themes of the Second Coming and the four sacrifices of the Nathan Soul are brought together—in the course of a description of the Second Coming, the expression 'Angel-like being' is used (see the quotation on p. 331), and that is the form of words with which (in many lectures of those years) Rudolf Steiner defines the being of the Nathan Soul (see Note 19 to Part II and Note 166).

Moreover, one needs to keep in mind that in the spiritual world after death, immediately after the separation of the etheric body, every human being arrays himself with the Spirit Self as an outer sheath, and later on with still higher spiritual members (see GA 168, lecture of 18 February 1916 and GA 208, lecture of 21 October 1921). In other words, he truly becomes an Angel-like or even an Angel being. Rudolf Steiner employs the latter expression in, for example, the lecture of 19 July 1924 (GA 240) where he speaks of how, in the supersensible School of Michael in the fifteenth to the eighteenth centuries, Michael was surrounded by 'those human souls ... who had gathered round him at that time as *servants of the Angeloi*'.

86. See GA 240, the lecture of 27 August 1924. In a certain sense it is also possible to say that, from this moment, that hitherto concealed Angel-nature which the Nathan Soul had possessed through union with the forces of Christ's Ego now becomes clearly manifested through union with the forces of His Spirit Self. (See further in Note 166.)

87. In this process something is repeated supersensibly that is akin to what took place in former times on Earth by way of preparation for the historical Mystery of Golgotha, when in the persons of Zarathustra and the Nathan Soul two streams bearing, respectively, the most *spiritualized* (mature) and the most celestially *pure* (innocent) fruits of human evolution were united in one physical body. While now, with the supersensible repetition of the Mystery of Golgotha and the new manifestation of Christ, His etheric sheath is similarly fashioned by Vidar from the most mature (those preserved in the 'etheric ring') and the most innocent etheric forces.

88. This enables us to understand not only that special connection which exists between Vidar and the 'etheric ring' around the Earth but above all the relationship to this 'ring' of the Christ Himself. This relationship comes to expression in the epoch of the Second Coming in that Christ will, to an increasing extent, become the great Leader of humanity in its ability to absorb the cosmic forces of the 'etheric ring', the spiritual sphere in which the Earth even today manifests its future *Sun nature* (see p. 237). In certain of the lectures which he devoted to the new appearance of Christ in the etheric, Rudolf Steiner calls this sphere by a name derived from the esoteric tradition of Ancient India. For example, in the lecture of 6 March 1910 in Stuttgart he says: 'And the first thing that human beings will see when Shamballa appears again will be Christ in His etheric form ... Christ will lead human beings to Shamballa ... If humanity realizes that it must not sink ever deeper into matter but rather change its course and understand that a new spiritual life must begin, then at first for a few, and thereafter during the next 2500 years for an ever greater number of people, the radiant land of Shamballa will open up, shining with *light*, filled with *life* and permeating our hearts with wisdom!'(GA 118, lecture of 6 March 1910. See also the lecture of 9 March 1910, GA 116.) The words light, life and wisdom mentioned in the above quotation also correspond fully with the characterization of the 'etheric ring' given on p. 246 ff. of the present work. (Compare also the two

references to the Second Coming in Emil Bock's translation of St Luke's Gospel, 17:24 and 21:27.)

89. GA 114, lecture of 26 September 1909. Compare with the first chapter of GA 150.

90. Rudolf Steiner speaks on several occasions in his lectures about the connection that exists between the faculty of memory and the development of imaginative vision. For example, in the lectures of 2 and 3 September 1921 (GA 78).

91. Rudolf Steiner says in this connection: 'The Christ-power must unite with what are the best forces of the child-nature in man. It cannot link itself to capacities that have been spoilt by man, capacities that stem from a being that is born of the intellect alone. Rather it connects itself with that best part in man which has been preserved in his child-nature from ancient times. This must be reinvigorated and must therefore fructify the rest ...' (GA 114, lecture of 26 September 1909.)

92. See GA 114, the lecture of 21 September 1909.

93. GA 152, lecture of 7 March 1914.

94. GA 165, lecture of 2 January 1916.

95. This etheric light, permeated as it is with the spiritual thoughts of human beings, then begins again to radiate outwards. For in contrast to the life- and sound-ethers, which have a centripetal tendency, that is, serve principally as a focus for receiving spiritual impulses from the macrocosm, the light-ether has a centrifugal tendency and hence is particularly suited to the bearing of spiritual thoughts out into the macrocosm (see Günther Wachsmuth, *Etheric Formative Forces in Cosmos, Earth and Man*, Anthroposophical Publishing Company 1932, Chapter 2), where these are imprinted in the astral light. (This is today the new, next stage in that evolutionary development to which Rudolf Steiner pointed in the lecture of 13 January 1924, GA 233.) From this 'transformed' astral light the Nathan Soul now fashions a new garment of light for the Etheric Christ (see p. 237).

96. See GA 233, the lecture of 13 January 1924. See also Note 97.

97. At this point it is necessary to touch briefly upon one question which may arise within the reader, namely, how to relate all that has just been said about the extinguishing of the astral light that is connected with the Nathan Soul (and which is subsequently transformed into the light-ether in the human life-body) with the description on p. 239 of how the experience of the Etheric Christ is made possible through man's being penetrated with the impulse of the Holy Spirit. The position here is as follows. If we consider the four ethers of which the human etheric body is composed, there are—according to spiritual science (see GA 114, the lecture of 21 September 1909, and GA 121, the lecture of 11 June 1910)—at the same time etheric reflections of the corresponding spheres of the macrocosm. Thus the life-ether is an etheric reflection of the sphere of the fixed stars (higher Devachan, the world of Intuition), and the sound-ether (or chemical ether) a reflection of the sphere of the moving stars (lower Devachan, the world of

Inspiration). Furthermore, *the light-ether is an etheric reflection of the elemental world (the astral plane, the world of Imagination.)* Only the warmth-ether does not have such a macrocosmic archetype, in that it works on the boundary between the etheric body and the physical body. But precisely for this reason it is the foundation for man's free development and experience of his individual ego. (See GA 233, the lecture of 31 December 1923.)

This brings a certain clarity to that particular connection which exists between the light-ether and the astral light. For it becomes evident that the former is an etheric reflection of the latter. And now we must address the following question: if the life-ether is the reflection of the sphere of higher Devachan, of what is the astral light that works 'behind it' and 'above it' a reflection? In order to find its 'archetype' in the macrocosm, we need to turn to a still higher region than higher Devachan, that is, to the world of Buddhi or Providence, to the sphere lying *beyond* the fixed stars *where the Holy Spirit works directly* (see p. 118). A reflection of this sphere, which is at the same time the true abode of the Akashic Chronicle, the cosmic memory of the world (in the lecture of 28 May 1907, GA 99, Rudolf Steiner says that it has its source in the realm *above* higher Devachan), is the astral light in the spiritual surroundings of the Earth. In other words: in the spiritual surroundings of the Earth the Holy Spirit works *through* and *in* the astral light (compare with what was said on p. 240). Thus we have a twofold process of 'reflection' connecting the sphere of the Holy Spirit (the world of Buddhi) with the astral light, and the astral light, in its turn, with the light-ether.

We also spoke above (see p. 327) of how the process of extinguishing the Christ-consciousness of the Nathan Soul is at the same time a process of extinguishing the astral light connected with it, in whose streams lives its consciousness. Now we are able to characterize this process with greater precision. If we turn to the higher aspect of the Christ, which we find in the sphere of Buddhi or the world of Providence, *there, as the content of Christ's consciousness, appears the Holy Spirit who proceeds from Him*; while in the immediate surroundings of the Earth he appears as the content of Christ's consciousness working *in* or *through the mediation of* the astral light. This astral light, which is to the highest degree permeated (one could even say 'saturated') by the Holy Spirit, is also the content of the consciousness of the Nathan Soul. Hence as a result of the extinction of the Christ-consciousness of the Nathan Soul and its 'resurrection' in the light-ether of the life-bodies of human beings (that is, through the altogether new relationship of the Holy Spirit-permeated astral light with the light-ether), it is now for the first time possible for the impulse of the Holy Spirit directly and 'naturally' to penetrate human etheric bodies. This latter circumstance sheds further light upon what was said in the chapter on 'The Exoteric and Esoteric Working of the Etheric Bodies of the Great Initiates in the Twentieth Century'. For a person who is overshone by an etheric body with such special qualities experiences in his etheric body to a still greater degree the influence of the Spirit-impulse, which thus penetrates it by means of the astral light *on the path traversed by the Nathan Soul* as it passes through the second Mystery of Golgotha.

98. See GA 165, the lecture of 2 January 1916.

99. Ibid.

100. Ibid.

101. Thus from the standpoint of the spiritual world, such an extension of this 'dark clairvoyance' of the Wolf amongst human beings will be like a darkening of the Spiritual Sun. A prophetic indication of this has already been given in the images of Norse mythology. And Rudolf Steiner, in his observations about them, has this to say: 'The expression for everything which is of the nature of a *darkening, falseness of vision* is some kind of animal—here in the North [that is, in Norse mythology] it is chiefly the Fenris Wolf ... This is the astral figure for falsehood and for any kind of untruthfulness that proceeds from an inner conviction. But wherever man approaches the outer world, Lucifer meets with Ahriman, so that any element of error which infiltrates into the realms of knowledge—*and this includes knowledge of the supersensible*—all illusion, all Maya, is the consequence of this propensity to falsehood. Thus in the Fenris Wolf we have a representation of the forms that enshrouded man because he does not see things in their true light. Wherever the outer light, the light of truth, is obscured in darkness, the ancient Northmen speak of a Wolf. And when the ancient Northman gave his impression of what he saw during an eclipse of the Sun ... he chose the image of a Wolf pursuing the Sun who, in overtaking it, causes an eclipse' (GA 121, lecture of 15 June 1910). This is a further reason why Vidar in his battle with the Wolf tears its jaws apart so that it cannot devour the Sun. (Compare with the description in *Occult Science*, of the demonic beings that inhabit the lower sphere of Kama-Loka, whose activity '... consists in the destruction of the [human] ego, if this nourishment is available to them.' To imaginative vision these beings appear in the form of a 'ferociously prowling wolf'.

102. In this inner struggle with the ahrimanic powers that work within man's etheric body, the forces of Michael also participate; for according to Rudolf Steiner the great imagination of Michael's battle with the dragon refers in our time primarily to man himself (see GA 223, the lecture of 27 September 1923), that is, in the sense of the above, to his etheric and physical bodies. Thus if we examine these inner processes in man with greater precision, we must say: both Michael and Vidar participate in them. It is only that the efforts of Vidar are directed more to the awakening of the new clairvoyance in human souls and to defending them from the danger of succumbing to false atavistic spiritual experience, while the task of Michael is more associated with the overcoming of the ahrimanic demons in man's etheric body and, through it, also in the physical body. (This will be spoken of later: see p. 349).

103. This is an important addition to the indication that the Fenris Wolf in our time tries to call forth among human beings an atavistic clairvoyance which

has its foundation not in the consciousness soul but in the sentient soul (see p. 319). For the unwarranted immersion of individual ego-consciousness into the sentient soul necessarily results in an intense darkening of the etheric body, and in the end this leads to illness of the physical body.

104. See GA 174a, the lecture of 17 February 1918.

105. In the lecture of 19 November 1922 (GA 218) Rudolf Steiner says: 'In our age Michael's task is to become ever more and more the being who serves the Christ.'

106. GA 152, lecture of 20 May 1913.

107. GA 152, lecture of 2 May 1913.

108. See the chapter 'The Fourth Deed of the Nathan Soul. The Transformation of Michael's Mission at the Time of the Mystery of Golgotha'.

109. See the lectures on this theme in GA 177.

110. GA 26, the article entitled 'The Experience of Michael in the Course of His Cosmic Mission' (October 1924).

111. At this point attention should be drawn to the quite special relationship between the aspirations of the Wolf and certain qualities of the opposing spirits that had been cast down by Michael around 1879 into the earthly sphere. The latter are often characterized by Rudolf Steiner as the spirits of *darkness* and as the inspirers of *falsehood and untruthfulness* (see GA 177, and GA 174a, the lecture of 17 February 1918). He says something of a similar kind about the Fenris Wolf (see the quotation in Note 101).

112. What has just been said is not at variance with what Rudolf Steiner says in the passage quoted in Note 6 to Part 1. For although, as a result of the development through which Michael has passed from the 1840s onwards, his impulses can now work directly within the world 'below', he does, in accordance with his inner nature, nevertheless remain connected with the Sun. Christ, on the other hand, occupies an altogether different position in the cosmos, in that since the Mystery of Golgotha He has been fully connected with the Earth.

113. These three lectures are contained, respectively, in GA 158, GA 174a and GA 174b.

114. In a number of lectures Rudolf Steiner speaks of how the forces that are being brought to mankind by the Etheric Christ will unfold gradually over a period of some 2500–3000 years.

115. GA 174a, lecture of 3 December 1914.

116. GA 174b, lecture of 14 February 1915.

117. GA 158, lecture of 9 November 1914.

118. Rudolf Steiner speaks of this as follows: 'We see that one part of Michael's activity is directed towards assisting in the [most rapid] dissolution of the highly cultivated etheric bodies of Western Europe, which have so fixed a form, and we [also] see how Michael makes use of Eastern European souls in this struggle. And we see Michael, surrounded by hosts of Eastern European souls, fighting with Western European etheric bodies and [we see] the impressions which souls are having after death' (lecture of 14 February 1915,

GA 174b). It should here be added that the certain inclination towards Lucifer that is quite natural to East European souls also facilitates the rapid dissolution of their etheric bodies after death and is perhaps made use of by Michael in his battle with ahrimanized etheric bodies (see the lecture of 3 August 1924, GA 237, where Rudolf Steiner speaks of how Michael receives help in this battle with the ahrimanic dragon from certain elemental luciferic beings).

119. In the lecture of 17 February 1918 (GA 174a), Rudolf Steiner refers to the fact that the spiritual forces which work within the etheric body of a person who has undergone sacrificial death on the field of battle are related to those forces which in other circumstances the spirit-pupil develops in the course of his meditative practice. In a number of lectures of the war years Rudolf Steiner also often speaks of the etheric bodies of people who have undergone sacrificial death in war that now abide in the spiritual world. The mighty spiritual forces of these etheric bodies which have, so to speak, been 'liberated' for a time from the conditions generally prevailing in the world can be employed equally for good or for evil purposes. In the first case, these etheric bodies can—through spiritualized, Christ-permeated human thoughts—find the path to the 'etheric ring' and thus strengthen its forces still further. Hence the most essential task of modern spiritual science is to devote all its forces to developing an understanding of these relationships and to creating opportunities whereby these etheric bodies may serve the good (see, for example, the lecture of 13 June 1915, GA 159/60), so that their spiritual forces cannot be made use of by those dark occult brotherhoods that are spoken of below. (All this acquires an even greater relevance in our own time, after the Second World War and after the most intense efforts have been made from a certain quarter to make use of the forces of the etheric bodies of the dead in a manner *contrary* to the true evolution of humanity.)

120. GA 152, lecture of 20 May 1913.

121. See lectures of 18, 19 and 25 November 1917 in GA 178.

122. The word 'western' is in the present instance merely an indication of the fact that the 'earthly rulership' of these societies issues for the most part from western countries, while their influence is diffused throughout the *whole* of the civilized world, albeit at a variety of levels.

123. GA 178, lecture of 18 November 1917 (compare with GA 144, the lecture of 4 February 1913).

124. Ibid. Elsewhere in the same lecture, Rudolf Steiner speaks of this as follows: '... These initiate-materialists cause souls to remain *connected with matter* even after death.' The consequence of this is that the influence of materialism amongst mankind is intensified. 'Through this,' says Rudolf Steiner, 'the materialism of our time becomes a sort of super-materialism' (GA 174, lecture of 20 January 1917). While in the next lecture he adds: 'Here on the Earth materialistic thoughts hold sway; while in the spiritual world, as their karma, there rule the materialistic consequences [of these thoughts], or rather, the *realization of what has been spiritually embodied in the dead*' (GA 174, lecture of 21 January 1917). And on 18 November 1917 (see GA 178) he

adds: '... these initiates of materialism ... cause the souls to remain with matter even after death'.

125. GA 174, lecture of 20 January 1917.
126. GA 178, lecture of 18 November 1917.
127. That is, in that sphere where during the fifteenth to the eighteenth centuries the sub-earthly ahrimanic school began its operations (see in this connection the lecture of 20 July 1924, GA 240) and from which (sphere) the many so-called 'unexplained' phenomena of our time, mistakenly ascribed to extra-terrestrial influences, proceed.
128. In the book *The Spiritual Guidance of Man and Humanity* (GA 15) Rudolf Steiner writes: 'But those [angelic] beings who remained behind at the time of the Egypto-Chaldean cultural epoch also interfere with our cultural inclinations; they are revealed in much that is thought and accomplished in the present and the immediate future. They are manifested in everything that gives our culture a materialistic stamp, and are frequently discernible precisely where there is evidence of a striving towards the spiritual.' See also the lecture of 20 January 1917 (GA 174).
129. These ahrimanic spirits of darkness, who also bear the nature of retarded angelic beings, are characterized by Rudolf Steiner in one of his lectures as follows: 'Of course, the highest point of materialism was attained in the forties [of the nineteenth century]. At that time, however, it transmitted its impulses to humanity in a more instinctive fashion. The ahrimanic hosts at that time still transmitted their impulses to human beings instinctively from the spiritual world. Only since the autumn of 1879 have these ahrimanic impulses become people's personal property, that is, forces of cognition and will. What was formerly common to all has thus been given over to people's personal lives. Thus we may say: since the year 1879, through the presence of these ahrimanic forces in the human realm, there has existed the personal ambition, the personal tendency, to explain the world materialistically' (GA 177, lecture of 14 October 1917).
130. In the book *The Spiritual Guidance of Man and Humanity* (GA 15), Rudolf Steiner writes: 'And the retarded nature of those beings [Angels], of whom it has been said that they work as forces of hindrance, derives from the fact that they have *not* placed themselves under Christ's guidance, with the result that they work on independently from Him.' They stand in opposition to those Angels who already then had received the Christ into themselves, and who '... in our fifth post-Atlantean epoch are the ones that bear Christ into our spiritual evolution ...' This means that in our time, Christ works among people in a certain sense *through the angelic Hierarchy*.
131. GA 174, lecture of 22 January 1917.
132. Ibid.
133. See GA 167, the lecture of 4 April 1916.
134. Hence Rudolf Steiner says in the lecture of 20 January 1917 (GA 174): 'The right attitude today is never to accept anything that is incomprehensible, such as is now offered in many occult societies.'

135 GA 174b, lecture of 14 February 1915.

136. It is hardly necessary to point out that the etheric body, which has become part of the 'etheric ring' and so also remains in the surroundings of the Earth, does not *in any way* hinder the right ascent of the soul after death into the higher spheres of the macrocosm. On the contrary, it enables man to attain, not only in life but also after death, to an experience of the Etheric Christ (see GA 131, the lecture of 14 October 1911).

137. GA 219, lecture of 3 December 1922.

138. It is not explained in the lecture in question what is meant by such 'rare cases', though from what has been said above one might suppose that what is under consideration here are, in the first instance, the members of the aforesaid brotherhoods who have attained the highest stages.

139. GA 219, lecture of 3 December 1922.

140. Even today, however, one can under certain conditions arrive at experiences which give one an indication of the real *possibility* of such a line of development. This can arise as a result of a meeting with one's own *double* (see the description of such an encounter in Rudolf Steiner's Mystery Drama), which is none other than the parts of the human etheric body that have been most fully condensed and objectivized by Ahriman. (See GA 147, the lecture of 30 August 1913), and also the lecture of 20 November 1914, GA 158, and the lecture of 28 December 1915, GA 165.

   In the present time such condensed parts of the etheric body cannot, *in the natural course of human evolution*, remain after death under the power of Ahriman (with certain exceptions), although this is what these occult brotherhoods are trying with particular stubbornness to achieve. (See GA 178, the lectures of 16, 18 and 19 November 1917.)

141. As a small-scale, but deeply prophetic, foretaste of the events that have been referred to, there was the fact that, as the etheric body of Bacon of Verulam passed through the gate of death, a whole host of 'demonic idols' was engendered, while from the spiritual forces of Amos Comenius there arose the 'spiritual milieu' which they could inhabit (see the lecture of 27 August 1924, GA 240).

142. GA 178, lecture of 18 November 1917. And just as with the development of the new clairvoyance around the Etheric Christ, individualities who in former times prepared for the physical manifestation of Christ on the Earth (Patriarchs, Prophets and others) will appear in the etheric vestment drawn from the substance of the 'etheric ring' (see the lecture of 25 January 1910, GA 118), so for the distorted atavistic clairvoyance that is inspired by the Fenris Wolf there will appear the ahrimanic spectre surrounded by a throng of 'human spectres' that have arisen in this way.

142a Lecture of 9 July, 1918 (GA 181).

143. This 'anti-ring' will then arise immediately below the surface of the Earth in its liquid and solid parts through a further 'earthification' of etheric bodies that have already become sufficiently hardened. Such a condition will come about through a kind of 'absorption' of the substance of these etheric bodies

into the indicated parts of the Earth, the consequences of which will be their final separation from that etheric cosmos whence they originally came and with which they must, according to their natural predisposition, ever remain connected.

144. GA 174a, lecture of 3 December 1914.

145. GA 174b, lecture of 14 February 1915.

146. Such a union with its Angel enables the soul after death not merely to find a direct connection with the Etheric Christ, who works now among mankind through the Hierarchy of the Angels (see Note 130), but also to reach as soon as possible the realm of the Archangels, into whose sphere its Angel leads the soul after death, so that it might from thence find the path beyond the confines of the earthly sphere. While if the soul remains, for the reasons referred to above, too long in the vicinity of the Earth and falls prey to the guidance of a retarded Angel, this being will then try to prevent its ascent to the realm of the rightly evolved Archangels and instead direct its path to the region of the Archai who have remained at the stage of the Archangels—and they would then permeate such a soul with forces that would arouse in it the strongest possible yearning toward ahrimanic immortality (see GA 174, the lecture of 22 January 1917).

147. GA 158, lecture of 9 November 1914.

148. In the lectures that have been cited, Rudolf Steiner indicates that an individual who has passed through his previous incarnation in Eastern Europe has a natural predisposition to a particularly intimate connection with his Guardian Angel. It should, however, be added (and Rudolf Steiner speaks of this in his other lectures) that *every* man who really dedicates himself to spiritual science is thereby *consciously* achieving as intimate a relationship to his Angel as an East European already has through his natural predispositions (see GA 182, the lecture of 9 October 1918, and in particular GA 237, the lectures of 3 and 8 August 1924). A similar relationship to his Angel is also acquired by a person who has undergone sacrificial death (for example, killed in the field of battle).

149. GA 158, lecture of 9 November 1914.

150. Ibid.

151. Luke 17:37. Emil Bock translates this even more closely to its original meaning (except that one word, placed here in brackets, is not absolutely correct): 'And they asked Him: Whither must we turn our gaze, Lord? And He answered: Become aware of (your) etheric body and you will see the eagles gathering.' Compare with the analogous words in the Gospel of St Matthew (24:38).

152. GA 223, lecture of 27 September 1923.

153. Ibid.

154. Ibid.

155. Ibid.

156. See S.O. Prokofieff, *Rudolf Steiner and the Founding of the New Mysteries*, the chapter entitled 'The Path of the Teacher of Humanity'.

157. See, for example, GA 131, the lecture of 14 October 1911 and GA 130, the lecture of 2 December 1911.
158. GA 237, lecture of 3 August 1924.
159. GA 237, lectures of 3 and 8 August 1924.
160. Hence one of the most significant Michael meditations given by Rudolf Steiner ends with the words: '... this day might become a reflection of your destiny-forming [literally, bringing into order] will' (quoted in the book by Emanuel Zeylmans, *Wilhelm Zeylmans van Emmichoven—ein Pionier der Anthroposophie*, Arlesheim 1979).
161. See Note 134 to Part IV.
162. Regarding the connection of especially the First Hierarchy with the forming and fulfilment of human karma, see, for example, the lecture of 31 March 1924 (GA 239).
163. The particular connection of Michael with the sphere of the Cherubim is founded primarily upon the relationship of the Hierarchy of the Archangels to that of the Cherubim, which originally came into being on Old Sun. See further regarding this in the evening lecture of 13 April 1909 (GA 110), and compare with the description of the Greater Guardian of the Threshold in the final chapter of *Knowledge of the Higher Worlds: How is it Achieved?* (GA 10).
164. Rudolf Steiner uses such a combination of the two names in the 'letter' of 2 November 1924 (GA 26).
165. As Rudolf Steiner has frequently described, the gradual development amongst mankind of the faculty of perceiving in imaginations the consequences of one's own actions (see for example GA 120, the lecture of 28 May 1910, and GA 131, of 14 October 1911) is directly connected with this appearance of Christ and Michael before man's birth and after his death, for these imaginative experiences will to a certain extent be the result of subconscious *memories* of these two encounters.
166. To what has been said here concerning the Nathan Soul, the following should be added. In the distant past before the Fall, the Nathan Soul was still fully in the general stream of human evolution. Subsequently, at the time of the temptation by Lucifer, it was held back in the higher world, where it became the guardian of the unfallen pristine forces of the etheric body of primordial humanity. Thus that 'earthly experience' through which the rest of mankind passed on the physical Earth was altogether outside the sphere where the Nathan Soul lived and worked. And so despite the fact that in the spiritual world at that time, because of its primal purity and its direct connection with the higher Hierarchies, it appeared as an *Angel*-like, even as an *Archangel*-like, being, nevertheless for it truly to attain the Angel stage was in the full sense of the word impossible. For the attainment of this stage necessarily presupposes passing through the earthly experience of mankind. In other words: the attainment of Angel-existence always has to be preceded by the *human stage*, the experience of the individual ego on Earth.
The Nathan Soul had to pass through this stage as well, although for this it

needed *only a single incarnation*; with the help of Buddha and Zarathustra, and especially through union with the macrocosmic Ego of Christ, this *single* incarnation was enough in order to make up for the lack of the earthly experience of the individual ego, and to embark upon the path of fulfilling the evolutionary goal of the entire Earth-aeon, of which it came to stand as the human archetype for all future ages. Thus one can say: directly after the Mystery of Golgotha, the Nathan Soul, in passing through its human stage, began to ascend to the sphere of the Angels; and a significant part of this ascent had been completed by the beginning of the twentieth century, by the time of the new appearance of Christ in the etheric realm.

167. One frequently finds Rudolf Steiner's allusions to the effect that Christ, after the Mystery of Golgotha, works in particular through the three categories of Spirits in the Third Hierarchy which represent the impulse of the Holy Spirit in our cosmos. Thus, for example, in his book *The Spiritual Guidance of Man and Humanity* (GA 15), Rudolf Steiner speaks of how in our time Christ works through the Angel-sphere as a whole, while in GA 152, the lecture of 2 May 1913, he refers especially to *one* Angel-like being (see Note 85). Then in the lecture of 20 February 1917 (GA 175), Rudolf Steiner speaks of the working of the Christ Being through the Hierarchy of the Archangels, and in the lecture of 24 December 1922 (GA 219), he refers to how Christ now takes the place of that Spiritual being who was worshipped in olden times as the Year God and who belongs to the Hierarchy of the Archai.

Thus with regard to what we have said about the angelic being of the Nathan Soul, about the archangelic being of Vidar and the Archai being of Michael, we should also bear in mind that Christ now works not only through them but also through *other beings* belonging to these stages of evolution, even though it is *these* three beings who, through their particularly deep connection with the sphere of Christ, occupy the position of supreme importance in all these events.

168. There is one further aspect, which embraces all three of these beings. The Nathan Soul in its third sacrifice, of which its present fifth sacrifice is the spiritual repetition, overcomes the Python serpent (see p. 322) which at that time fought as an *astral* being against the true path of evolution (see GA 149, the lecture of 30 December 1913). In Norse mythology this corresponds with the Midgard Serpent. In his turn, Vidar enters into battle with the Fenris Wolf, which is active as an *etheric* being. And, finally, Michael fights with the dragon, which since 1879, having been cast out of the higher worlds, dwells in the supersensible foundations of the *physical* world (see GA 215, the lecture of 15 October 1922 and GA 233, the lecture of 27 September 1923). In Norse mythology this corresponds to some extent to the figure of the monster Hel (see GA 121, the lecture of 15 June 1910).

169. In the same lecture Rudolf Steiner characterizes the Life Spirit of the Christ that passes from West to East as 'the etherized stream of the pre-Christian Christ', as 'the spiritual-etheric image', and as 'the cosmic image' (GA 240, lecture of 27 August 1924).

170. Ibid.

171. The new relationship between the Spirit Self and the Life Spirit of Christ which arose after their spiritual meeting in the year 869 can illumine, from an altogether new aspect, the fact that Vidar, who had since 1879 become the bearer of Christ's Life Spirit, also had to take upon himself the mission of being the guardian of the Nathan Soul (see the chapter entitled 'The Vidar Mystery'), who acquired at this time a particularly intimate relationship to Christ's Spirit Self.

172. This ascent of the spiritual thoughts of human beings into the macrocosm will come to fulfilment on the path paved by the Nathan Soul as a result of its fifth sacrifice, a path which leads from the etheric to the astral light (see Note 97).

173. GA 254, lecture of 19 October 1915.

174. GA 150, lecture of 21 December 1913.

175. See GA 130, the lecture of 1 October 1911.

176. These imaginations are awakened within man in the course of Vidar's conquest of the Fenris Wolf. They are founded upon the Christ-consciousness and lead to the development of the new clairvoyance 'illumined by reason and scientific thinking' which will work within man in opposition to the clairvoyant forces proceeding from the inspiration of the Wolf. One particular characteristic of these latter forces is that they will be diffused among mankind as though enshrouded in darkness and without being permeated by the *light of thought* of the new Christ-consciousness. In Norse mythology the image that refers to this is that of the Wolf devouring the Sun (see GA 165, lecture of 2 January 1916).

177. Vidar fashions the etheric form for Christ on the basis of his connections with Christ's Life Spirit, as described on p. 329.

178. The words in quotation marks are taken from GA 174a, the lecture of 3 December 1914.

179. Ibid.

180. See the chapter entitled 'The Quest for Isis-Sophia and the Quest for Christ'.

181. See the chapter entitled 'Michaelmas—the Festival of Enlightenment'.

182. GA 26, the article entitled 'The World Thoughts in the Working of Michael and in the Working of Ahriman', 16 November 1924.

183. GA 221, lecture of 2 February 1923. In this sense one can also say that Christ brought into the earthly world the spiritual essence of the 'threefold Sun' of which Rudolf Steiner speaks further as follows: 'At all times one has spoken within the confines of instinctive knowledge of the threefold Sun: of the Sun as the source of light, the source of life, and the source of love. This trinity is wholly contained within the Sun.' (GA 208, lecture of 29 October 1921. See also GA 211, the lecture of 24 April 1922.)

184. If we recall at this point how even for the medieval Rosicrucians *the process of dissolution* was always an indication of the working of divine love in the world (see the lecture of 28 September 1911, GA 130), it becomes clear how Michael fights for the rapid dissolution of ahrimanic etheric bodies in the

spiritual world nearest to the Earth (see p. 347). He fights with them through the help of the *forces of the love of Christ*, whose bearer he is in the present epoch.

185. In GA 240, the lecture of 12 August 1924, Rudolf Steiner says: 'Now the present rulership of Michael, which began only recently and will last for three or four centuries, signifies that the cosmic forces of the Sun pass fully over *into man's* physical and etheric bodies.' See also the lecture of 2 January 1916, GA 165.

186. GA 223, lecture of 31 March 1923.

187. During the 'Michaelic' half of the year Michael, going *before* Christ, also wages a particularly intense battle with the ahrimanized etheric bodies which make possible the formation of the 'etheric anti-ring' in the solid and liquid regions of the Earth. And during the other half of the year, in contrast, when Michael is following on *behind* Christ (see GA 223, the lecture of 31 March 1923), his efforts are more directed towards the further consolidation and strengthening of the 'etheric ring' around the Earth. In this task the Archangel Vidar is able to offer him considerable help.

188. In connection with these six lines from the fourth part of the Foundation Stone Meditation the following should be added. According to Zeylmans von Emmichoven, the first line relates to the Nathan Soul, while the last four lines are in a certain sense connected with the words,

> Light
> That gives warmth
> To simple Shepherds' Hearts,
> Light
> That enlightens
> The wise Heads of Kings

and can be related to the figures of Buddha and Zarathustra (see his book *The Foundation Stone*, the chapter entitled 'The Pentagram and the Sun of Christ'); this means that they can also be related to Vidar and Michael, who inspire these beings. (Vidar was in former times the Guardian Angel of the Gautama Bodhisattva, while Marduk-Michael was one of the most important inspirers of Zarathustra, especially at the time of his incarnation under the name of Zaratos in ancient Chaldea.) Hence in ancient times the forces of Vidar worked more through the stream of the Shepherds, and those of Michael through the stream of the Kings. Subsequently, as was already indicated in the chapter 'The New Path of the Shepherds and the New Path of the Kings', the inner direction of these two streams becomes altogether different as a result of the fulfilment on Earth of the Mystery of Golgotha. In the present epoch there is added the fact that, beginning with the new period of his rulership, Michael no longer strives to work through human heads, as was the case in ancient times, but wishes rather to enter directly into people's hearts (see GA 26, the article entitled 'At the Dawn of the Michael Age', 17 August 1924, and, in particular, GA 240, the lecture of 21 August

474

1924). He now assigns this working through human *heads* to his 'younger brother', the Archangel Vidar, whose task it is to awaken within modern man a right 'head-clairvoyance' (see the lecture of 27 March 1915, GA 161), that is, a clairvoyance 'illumined by reason and scientific thinking'. Thus in these six lines, with which Rudolf Steiner *concluded the Christmas Conference* on the evening of 1 January 1924, the very essence of the new Mysteries of the Etheric Christ and of the Spirits who serve Him appears before our eyes.

Conclusion: The Spiritual Experience of the Cycle of the Year Viewed as the Beginning of a Cosmic Cultus Appropriate to the Needs of Present-day Humanity

1. See S.O. Prokofieff, *Rudolf Steiner and the Founding of the New Mysteries*, the chapter entitled 'The Christmas Conference of 1923–24'.
2. GA 15, Chapter 3.
3. See S.O. Prokofieff, *Rudolf Steiner and the Founding of the New Mysteries*, RSP/AP 1986, the chapters entitled 'The Path of the Teacher of Humanity' and 'The Foundation Stone Meditation'.
4. Matthew 28:20 (after the Bock translation).
5. GA 130, lecture of 1 October 1911.
6. The following words of Rudolf Steiner from the first edition of the *Calendar of the Soul* (1912) are a further indication of the connection of this work with the etheric mystery of Christ: 'He [man] finds in his own being a reflection of the world archetype ... Thus the year becomes the *archetype* of human soul-activity and hence a fruitful source of *true self-knowledge*.' The new experience of Christ comes about now through the fact that the super-sensible stream from the *world of Archetypes* is arrested within man's being through the intensified activity therein of the Holy Spirit, and a capacity for etheric clairvoyance is awakened which also leads to a direct knowledge of one's own karma, that is, to 'true self-knowledge'. See further regarding this in S.O. Prokofieff, *Rudolf Steiner and the Founding of the New Mysteries*, Chapter 6.
7. See GA 130, the lecture of 1 October 1911.
8. GA 219, lecture of 29 December 1922.
9. See Rudolf Steiner's words from the lecture of 4 June 1924 (GA 236), quoted in the chapter 'The Experience of the Holy Spirit in the Present Time'.
10. By 'spiritual space' is here meant the principle of the primordial twelve-foldness that is revealed in the Buddhi-sphere (the world of Archetypes) and which forms 'the body of the Holy Spirit' in the macrocosm. See further regarding this in the chapter 'The Spiritual-Scientific Idea of God-Manhood and its Reflection ...' and also in the lecture of 31 August 1909, GA 113, and that of 25 October 1909, GA 116.
11. The first thing that man experiences at the stage of imaginative knowledge is the panorama of his past earthly life in which the temporal stream of events

475

becomes to some extent perceived spatially (see the lecture of 29 May 1924, GA 236).

12. This does not contradict the indication—referred to in Note 46 of Part X— that the transition from the twelve to the seven is connected more with the overcoming of Ahriman, and the transition from the seven to the twelve with the overcoming of Lucifer. For according to GA 145, the lecture of 28 March 1913, *one of the aspects* of the original Mystery of Golgotha and its supersensible repetition in our time is that through the original Mystery of Golgotha the foundation was laid whereby humanity might gradually overcome the forces of Ahriman in Earth-existence, and through its repetition overcome the forces of Lucifer in the course of the new ascent into the higher worlds.

13. GA 219, lecture of 31 December 1922. What has just been said is directly connected with the spiritual impulses which find their reflection in the architectural and sculptural conception of the First Goetheanum, which was constructed on the basis of the relationship between the principles of the twelve and the seven. (See further in S.O. Prokofieff, *Rudolf Steiner and the Founding of the New Mysteries*, the chapter entitled 'The Earthly and the Supersensible Goetheanum', and also Appendix 4 in the present work.)

14. In the same lecture Rudolf Steiner gives two mantric verses, which can help one to attain a purely inward *communion* with the spiritualized (Sun-like) flesh and the etherized blood of Christ. Moreover, the path which they indicate also has a direct relationship to the cycle of the year. For what man receives into himself by way of solid matter as an image of the fixed stars and then changes in his will, which has been warmed by spiritual understanding, into spirit through the transition in the yearly rhythm from the twelve to the seven, leads him to an inner experience of the spiritualized (Sun-like) flesh of Christ. And what man receives into himself by way of liquid substances as a reflection of the deeds of the moving stars and then changes in his feeling, which has been enlightened by spiritual understanding, again into spirit through the transition in the yearly rhythm from the seven to the twelve, leads him to an inner experience of the etherized blood of Christ. In the entire lecture-cycle GA 219, we have a description of *both transitions*, from space to time and from time to space, and these are in each case presented as proceeding from a consideration of the cycle of the year in its relationship to the inner activity of man's being (see the lectures of 17 and 29 December 1922).

To this we may also add that in the transition from the twelve to the seven man approaches more the secrets of life after death, that is, he embarks upon a path which leads him to an experience of the nature of *immortality*, while in the transition from the seven to the twelve he approaches, rather, the secrets of the soul's life before birth, thus embarking upon a path which leads to an experience of the condition of *what is unborn*. In the union of these two principles we confront, therefore, the highest mystery of all, which opens the gates to *eternity* itself (see GA 236, the lecture of 18 May 1924). Thus a true spiritual communion must necessarily consist of two parts: of an experience of immortality through the inner communion with the spiritualized (Sun-like) flesh of Christ and an experience of what is unborn through the inner communion with His etherized blood.

15. GA 219, lecture of 31 December 1922.
16. Ibid.

Notes to Appendix 2: *The Mystery Temple of the Year*

1. See the lecture of 21 May 1907 (GA 284/285), and also the quotations that follow.
2. GA 120.
3. See Part III, Chapter 2: 'From Christmas to Epiphany'.
4. GA 10.
5. Ibid.

Notes to Appendix 3: *Concerning a Representation of Vidar*

1. In one of the early anthroposophical lectures Rudolf Steiner speaks of how the left arm and the heart belong to those parts of the physical body which, in contrast, for example, to the right arm, bear the seeds of the new spiritual organs of the far future (see GA 93a, the lecture of 29 September 1905).
2. In the lecture of 23 November 1909 (GA 117), Rudolf Steiner speaks in the following way about the occult significance of human hair in ancient times: 'We should regard our hair as the residue of certain emanations whereby *the power of the Sun* entered into man in former times ... In order that man might progress from his old clairvoyant gifts to conjecturing and thinking about the outer world, it was necessary that he came ever less and less to appear as a being covered with hair. We should imagine that people of Atlantean and the first post-Atlantean ages were richly endowed with hair, a sign that they were still strongly permeated by *spiritual light*.'
3. See Rudolf Meyer, *Nordische Apokalypse*. We may conceive of the images of the side of the stone that we have been considering not merely in a spatial sense but also as a *process* extending through time. In the latter case we shall have not three heads of one animal or three separate animals but three successive assaults by the one and the same demonic being with gaping jaws, threatening to seize hold of, in turn, all three realms of the human organism (that is, respectively, man's thinking, feeling and will). It is natural that such a *time-process* can be depicted in the arts of painting or sculpture only in spatial form.
4. According to the Prose *Edda* (Part 1:52), Vidar, in his battle with the Wolf, sets his 'iron shoe' on its lower jaw, seizes its upper jaw with his

hand and tears the monster's throat in two. While according to the Poetic *Edda* (Völuspa, 54), Vidar thrusts his sword through its gaping jaws into its heart.

5. See Rudolf Meyer, *Nordische Apokalypse*.

6. In the *Edda* we read: '540 gates has Valhalla and from each of these there go forth 800 warriors at one and the same time to fight with the Wolf' ('Grimmismal' 20).

7. The triangle is a form in which the centrifugal law of the light ether is manifest. See G. Wachsmuth, *The Etheric Formative Forces in Cosmos, Earth and Man*, Anthroposophical Publishing Company 1932.

8. In Rosicrucian schools, in connection with the esoteric tradition of the Grail, the image of the lance was given to the pupils as an imagination of 'the spiritual ray of the Sun', 'the so-called holy lance of love', as a sign of the fructifying power of the Sun Spirit (lectures of 5 November and 15 December 1907, GA 98). In GA 99, the lecture of 6 June 1907, Rudolf Steiner employs in this connection the expression, 'spiritual ray of wisdom'.

9. 'Thund's waters roar and the fish of the giant wolf plays merrily in the flood' (*Edda*, 'Grimmismal' 18).

Appendix 4: When Should the Festivals be Celebrated in the Southern Hemisphere?

1. See G. Wachsmuth, *The Etheric Formative Forces in Cosmos, Earth and Man*.

2. GA 237, lecture of 1 August 1924.

3. GA 204, lecture of 13 May 1921.

4. GA 11.

5. GA 126.

6. Compare also GA 130, the lecture of 29 January 1912.

7. See Note 1.

8. These three later epochs represent for the post-Atlantean age a kind of repetition of the first three epochs (see GA 15). Thus in the third epoch (the Egypto-Chaldean) the thinking was developed, in the second (Ancient Persian) the feeling, and the first (Ancient Indian) the will, though in these earlier epochs thinking, feeling and will were wholly guided by the Gods from the spiritual world.

   In contrast to these, thinking, feeling and will are developed in the three later epochs (fifth, sixth and seventh) as independent human qualities; and the fourth epoch forms the transition between the two phases.

9. Lecture of 31 December 1922 (GA 219). The next quotation is from the same source.

10. GA 40.

11. Fred Poeppig, *Abenteuer meines Lebens*, Schaffhausen 1975.

Appendix 5: Some Words about the Icon 'The Council of the Holy Archangel Michael'

1. See the lecture of 1 April 1907 (GA 96).

List of Works by Rudolf Steiner referred to in the Present Book

The English title is given only in cases where a similar (though not always identical) volume to the original German edition from the collected works—the *Gesamtausgabe* (abbreviated as 'GA')—has been published in English translation. In many cases, lectures are available in typescript or in print as single lectures or compilations from the collected works. For information on these contact Rudolf Steiner House Library, 35 Park Road, London NW1 6XT, or similar anthroposophical libraries around the world.

Publishers:

AP:	Anthroposophic Press (New York)
APC:	Anthroposophical Publishing Company (London)
GAR:	Garber Communications, Inc. (New York). Imprint: Spiritual Science Library.
MER:	Mercury Press (Spring Valley, New York)
RSP:	Rudolf Steiner Press (London)

GA

9	*Theosophy* (RSP, 1989)
10	*Knowledge of the Higher Worlds* (RSP, 1989). *How to Know Higher Worlds* (AP, 1994)
11	*Cosmic Memory* (GAR, 1990)
13	*Occult Science* (RSP, 1962)
14	*The Four Mystery Plays* (RSP, 1983)
15	*The Spiritual Guidance of Humanity* (AP, 1992)
17	*The Threshold of the Spiritual World* (RSP, 1975)
26	*Anthroposophical Leading Thoughts* (RSP, 1985)
40	*Wahrspruchworte*
60	*Antworten der Geisteswissenschaft auf die großen Fragen des Daseins*
78	*Anthroposophie, ihre Erkenntniswurzeln und Lebensfrüchte*
93a	*Foundations of Esotericism* (RSP, 1983)
94	*Kosmogonie. Populärer Okkultismus. Das Johannes-Evangelium. Die Theosophie an Hand des Johannes-Evangeliums.* Some lectures appear in *An Esoteric Cosmology* (GAR, 1987)
95	*At the Gates of Spiritual Science* (RSP, 1970)

96	*Ursprungsimpulse der Geisteswissenschaft*
97	*Das christliche Mysterium*
98	*Natur-und Geistwesen—ihr Wirken in unserer sichtbaren Welt*
99	*Theosophy of the Rosicrucian* (RSP, 1981)
100	*Menschheitsentwickelung und Christus-Erkenntnis*
102	*The Influence of Spiritual Beings upon Man* (AP, 1961)
103	*The Gospel of St John* (AP, 1984)
104	*The Apocalypse of St John* (RSP, 1985)
105	*Universe, Earth and Man* (RSP, 1988)
106	*Egyptian Myths and Mysteries* (AP, 1971)
107	*Geisteswissenschaftliche Menschenkunde*
109/11	*Das Prinzip der spirituellen Ökonomie im Zusammenhang mit Wiederverkörperungsfragen.* Some lectures appear in *The Principle of Spiritual Economy* (AP, 1986)
110	*The Spiritual Hierarchies and their Reflection in the Physical World* (AP, 1983)
112	*The Gospel of St John and its Relation to the Other Gospels* (AP, 1982)
113	*The East in the Light of the West* (GAR, 1986)
114	*The Gospel of St Luke* (RSP, 1988)
116	*The Christ Impulse and the Development of Ego Consciousness* (AP, 1976)
117	*Die tieferen Geheimnisse des Menschheitswerdens im Lichte der Evangelien.* Some lectures appear in *Deeper Secrets of Human History in the Light of the Gospel of St Matthew* (RSP, 1985)
118	*Das Ereignis der Christus-Erscheinung in der ätherischen Welt.* Some lectures appear in *The Reappearance of Christ in the Etheric* (AP, 1983).
119	*Macrocosm and Microcosm* (RSP, 1985)
120	*Manifestations of Karma* (RSP, 1984)
121	*The Mission of the Individual Folk Souls in Relation to Teutonic Mythology* (RSP, 1977)
123	*The Gospel of St Matthew* (RSP, 1985)
124	*Background to the Gospel of St Mark* (RSP, 1985)
126	*Occult History* (RSP, 1982)
127	*Die Mission der neuen Geistoffenbarung. Das Christus-Ereignis als Mittelpunktsgeschehen der Erdenevolution*
128	*Occult Physiology* (RSP, 1983)
130	*Das esoterische Christentum und die geistige Führung der Menschheit.* Some lectures appear in *Esoteric Christianity and the Mission of Christian Rosenkreutz* (RSP, 1984)
131	*From Jesus to Christ* (RSP, 1991)
132	*The Inner Realities of Evolution* (RSP, 1953)
133	*Earthly and Cosmic Man* (GAR, 1986)
134	*The World of the Senses and the World of the Spirit* (Steiner Book Centre, N. Vancouver, 1979)
136	*The Spiritual Beings in the Heavenly Bodies and in the Kingdoms of Nature* (AP, 1992)

137	*Man in the Light of Occultism, Theosophy and Philosophy* (GAR, 1989)
138	*Initiation, Eternity and the Passing Moment* (AP, 1980)
139	*The Gospel of St Mark* (AP, 1986)
142	*The Bhagavad Gita and the Epistles of St Paul* (AP, 1971)
144	*The Mystery of the East and of Christianity* (RSP, 1972)
145	*The Effects of Spiritual Development* (RSP, 1978)
146	*The Occult Significance of the Bhagavad Gita* (AP, 1968)
147	*Secrets of the Threshold* (AP, 1987)
148	*Aus der Akasha-Forschung. Das Fünfte Evangelium.* Some lectures appear in *The Fifth Gospel* (RSP, 1985)
149	*Christ and the Spiritual World and the Search for the Holy Grail* (RSP, 1963)
150	*Die Welt des Geistes und ihr Hereinragen in das physische Dasein*
152	*Vorstufen zum Mysterium von Golgotha*
153	*The Inner Nature of Man and the Life Between Death and Rebirth* (APC, 1959)
155	*Christus und die menschliche Seele*
158	*Der Zusammenhang des Menschen mit der elementarischen Welt*
159/160	*Die Geheimnis des Todes. Wesen und Bedeutung Mitteleuropas und die europäischen Volksgeister*
161	*Wege der geistigen Erkenntnis und der Erneuerung künstlerischer Weltanschauung*
165	*Die geistige Vereinigung der Menschheit durch den Christus-Impuls.* Some lectures appear in *The Christmas Thought and the Mystery of the Ego* (MER, 1986)
167	*Gegenwärtiges und Vergangenes im Menschengeiste*
168	*Die Verbindung zwischen Lebenden und Toten*
174	*The Karma of Untruthfulness*, Vol. 2 (RSP, 1992)
174a	*Mitteleuropa zwischen Ost und West*
174b	*Die geistigen Hintergründe des Ersten Weltkrieges*
175	*Cosmic and Human Metamorphoses* (GAR, 1989), *Building Stones for an Understanding of the Mystery of Golgotha* (RSP, 1972)
177	*The Fall of the Spirits of Darkness* (RSP, 1993)
178	*Individuelle Geistwesen und ihr Wirken in der Seele des Menschen*
180	*Mysterienwahrheiten und Weihnachtsimpulse Alte Mythen und ihre Bedeutung.* Some lectures appear in *Ancient Myths and the New Isis Mystery* (AP, 1994)
182	*Der Tod als Lebenswandlung*
186	*Die soziale Grundforderung unserer Zeit*
187	*How Can Mankind Find the Christ Again* (AP, 1984)
191	*Soziales Verständnis aus geisteswissenschaftlicher Erkenntnis.* Some lectures appear in *The Influences of Lucifer and Ahriman* (AP, 1993)
193	*Der innere Aspekt des sozialen Rätsels. Luziferische Vergangenheit und ahrimanische Zukunft.* Some lectures appear in *The Inner Aspect of the Social Question* (RSP, 1974)

194	*Die Sendung Michaels.* Some lectures appear in *The Mission of the Archangel Michael* (AP, 1961)
200	*The New Spirituality and the Christ Experience of the Twentieth Century* (RSP, 1988)
201	*Man—Hieroglyph of the Universe* (RSP, 1972)
202	*Die Brücke zwischen der Weltgeistigkeit und dem Physischen des Menschen*
204	*Materialism and the Task of Anthroposophy* (AP, 1987)
207	*Cosmosophy,* Vol. 1 (AP, 1985)
208	*Anthroposophie als Kosmosophie—Zweiter Teil*
209	*Nordische und mitteleuropäische Geistimpulse. Das Fest der Erscheinung Christi.* Some lectures appear in *Self-Consciousness* (GAR, 1986)
211	*Das Sonnenmysterium und das Mysterium von Tod und Auferstehung*
214	*Das Geheimnis der Trinität.* Some lectures appear in *The Mystery of the Trinity* (AP, 1991)
215	*Philosophy, Cosmology and Religion* (AP, 1984)
216	*Supersensible Influences in the History of Mankind* (RSP, 1956)
217	*The Younger Generation* (AP, 1984)
218	*Geistige Zusammenhänge in der Gestaltung des menschlichen Organismus*
219	*Man and the World of Stars* (AP, 1982)
222	*The Driving Force of Spiritual Powers in World History* (Steiner Book Centre, Toronto, 1972)
223	*The Cycle of the Year as a Breathing-Process of the Earth* (AP, 1984). *Michaelmas and the Soul Forces of Man* (AP, 1982)
224	*Die menschliche Seele in ihren Zusammenhang mit göttlichgeistigen Individualitäten*
226	*Man's Being, his Destiny and World Evolution* (AP, 1966)
227	*The Evolution of Consciousness* (RSP, 1966)
229	*The Four Seasons and the Archangels* (RSP, 1984)
231	*Supersensible Man* (APC, 1961)
232	*Mystery Knowledge and Mystery Centres* (GAR, 1989)
233	*World History in the Light of Anthroposophy* (RSP, 1977)
233a	*Rosicrucianism and Modern Initiation* (RSP, 1982)
234	*Anthroposophy and the Inner Life* (RSP, 1992)
235	*Karmic Relationships* Vol. I (RSP, 1981)
236	*Karmic Relationships* Vol. II (RSP, 1974)
237	*Karmic Relationships* Vol. III (RSP, 1977)
238	*Karmic Relationships* Vol. IV (RSP, 1983), *The Last Address* (RSP, 1967)
239	*Karmic Relationships* Vol. V. (RSP, 1984), *Karmic Relationships* Vol. VII (RSP, 1973)
240	*Karmic Relationships* Vol. VI (RSP, 1989), *Karmic Relationships* Vol. VIII (RSP, 1975)
243	*True and False Paths in Spiritual Investigation* (RSP, 1985)
245	*Anweisungen für eine esoterische Schülung.* Extracts from this volume translated as *Guidance in Esoteric Training* (RSP, 1972)

254   *Occult Movements in the Nineteenth Century* (RSP, 1973)
257   *Awakening to Community* (AP, 1974)
260   *The Christmas Conference Proceedings* (AP, 1990)
262   *Correspondence and Documents* (1901–25) (RSP, 1988)